FORTEAN TIMES 1–15
YESTERDAY'S NEWS TOMORROW

Mr and Mrs Wildsmith of Pinner, Middlesex, look forlornly at their new car restyled by the impact of an 18-inch lump of ice from the sky in March 1974. See FT6:11.

FORTEAN TIMES 1–15
YESTERDAY'S NEWS TOMORROW

Edited for volume publication by
PAUL SIEVEKING

FORTEAN TOMES
LONDON 1992

This first edition is published in August 1992 for John Brown Publishing Ltd.

by Fortean Times, PO Box 2409, London NW5 4NP.

Fortean Times is now published every two months by John Brown Publishing Ltd, and distributed to the wholesale newstrade by UMD Ltd, for newsstand sale. It is also available by subscription -- inquiries to:
Fortean Times, 20 Paul Street, Frome, Somerset BA11 1DX, UK.
☎ 0373 451777.

British Library Cataloguing in Publication Data

**Fortean Times 1--15: Yesterday's News Tomorrow.
I. Sieveking, Paul
001.9**

ISBN 1-870870-26-3

1 3 5 7 9 10 8 6 4 2

Printed in Great Britain by

Bookcraft (Bath) Ltd, Midsomer Norton, Avon.

Cover illustration by Hunt Emerson for FT29, reproduced by permission of Bob Rickard.

PREFACE

This volume makes available once more the long-out-of-print first fifteen issues of Fortean Times. It began life as *The News* -- a contraction taken from Samuel Butler's *The News from Nowhere* -- and changed to *Fortean Times* with FT16. The transition was fairly seamless and out of habit and for simplicity we refer, retroactively, to these early issues as *Fortean Times*.

The story of our beginnings would be incomplete without acknowledging the quiet heroes who nurtured FT through its larval stage. I am glad for this opportunity to pay particular tribute to them, Forteans and well-wishers all.

Originally intended as a hobbyish newsletter for circulation among friends, my production values were restricted by very little income and few facilities: text bashed out on an uncooperative typewriter, headings in Letraset, pictures and graphics snipped from papers, and the pasted-up pages bundled off to a newfangled photocopy bureau who also collated and stapled. All pretensions to the promised regularity of schedule were abandoned early on; issues appeared whenever sufficient material accumulated and I had saved enough spare cash to print.

I knew of Charles Fort long before I read his books. Years of reading science-fiction had thrown-up the occasional mention of Fort and his weird ideas. John Campbell, the editor of *Astounding Science Fiction* (as *Analog* was then titled), for example, encouraged many of his writers to expand Fort's data and comments into imaginative stories. Later, when I went to Birmingham Art College (where I studied Product Design) I made contact with fellow sf fans, and tribute must go to Peter Weston, on whose *Speculation* I learned the art of putting together a fanzine.

At the same time, I used to clip the papers out of instinct, wildly and without much sense of purpose except a gut feeling that they 'might be important'. In 1968, shortly after leaving college, I attended a science-fiction convention, and on a stall run by Derek Stokes, I found copies of the Ace paperback editions of all four of Fort's books. I read them at one sitting and all my interests fell into place.

In 1969 I noticed an ad in the underground magazine *Oz*; it was for an American group called the International Fortean Organisation (INFO), founded in 1966 (after the demise of the old Fortean Society) by Paul and Ronald Willis. My inquiry was answered by artist--author David Coxhead, who, after a brief correspondence, handed over the agency to me. Such was the joy at finding in each other a kindred Fortean spirit, the Willises and I plunged into an intense trans-Atlantic correspondence.

At first I bombarded INFO with clippings from British papers, and it was disappointing that INFO's *Journal* was appearing less frequently and with hardly any of my material. Only later did I learn that Ronald Willis was seriously ill with a brain tumour, and after his death Paul fought a losing battle to keep up with things. It was Paul who inspired me to put out my own periodical, and sadly Ronald died before the *News* was born.

Especially high in my gratitude is Steve Moore, whom I first met at a London comic convention in the days when he used to work as a sub-editor for IPC's comics. We hit it off, both sharing a love of Chinese mysticism and other absurdities. Steve, together with Paul Screeton (then editor of *The Ley Hunter*), both urged on the first few uncertain issues. Steve would join me for a few days in Birmingham or Aldermaston, or wherever, and we'd stuff envelopes and hand-write a few hundred addresses before going to see Chinese sword-fighting films at three in the morning. Steve has been with FT every step of the way ever since; always unassuming, polite and erudite, and always ready to listen, comment, or pitch in.

Then came Ion Will. Ion is one of the world's great browsers, sampling everything in his path. He discovered us in Summer 1974, probably in Compendium or Dark They

Were and Golden Eyed, for both bookshops had the foresight to stock the fledgling *News* (thanks, there, to Derek Stokes and Nick Rochford, respectively). Over the years, and throughout his perpetual and random wanderings 'east of Suez' in a number of disguises -- including, incredibly, the abbot of a Sri Lankan monastery -- Ion has kept up a constant flow of valuable clippings, books, postcards and entertaining letters.

The next to put shoulder to FT's wheel was cartoonist Hunt Emerson. In late 1974, with seven issues behind me, I wanted to improve the graphics (there had to be something better than a stark Letrasetted heading). Destiny intervened in the form of the good people running Japetus Bookshop, one of my watering-holes in those days. Carol and Nick Moore introduced me to their friend Hunt Emerson, then working on his Large Cow Comix. I liked Hunt's style immediately; he was as much a disciple of George Herrigel (whose *Krazy Kat* I adored) and my favourite artists from *Mad* (Bill Elder and Wally Wood), as I was of Charles Fort. The inherent surrealism of Fortean phenomena appealed to Hunt and he agreed to draw a set of headings for our clipping summaries.

Carol went on to establish Knockabout Comics in London with Tony Bennett, and Hunt became daily more famous. He even took over my flat when I left Birmingham, but kept up his work for us through all our format experiments. The now-regular strip by Hunt is a feature I am particularly proud of; you'll see a prototype in FT11. In view of this long association with FT, it is doubly appropriate to use, on the cover of this volume, the painting Hunt made for FT29, since it depicts some of the wide range of phenomena with which we deal.

In those early days I also made contact with Janet and Colin Bord, whose friendship and encouragement has helped keep me and FT going. Janet wrote for *Flying Saucer Review* and Lionel Beer's *Spacelink*, while Colin, a club photographer by night, had first come to my attention with a Fortean article in *Gandalf's Garden*. After the publication of their well-received and influential books *Mysterious Britain* and *The Secret Country*, the Bords moved to Wales and began work on their now-successful picture libraries.

A few others remain to be mentioned. There is Phil Ledger, a peripatetic marine biologist who was our first enthusiastic fan; Ken Campbell, who incorporates a great deal of Forteana in his plays; John Michell, who has been a model of eclectic and open-minded scholarship; Richard Adams of AdCo, who has advised on layout and provided many graphics services over the years; Dick Gwynn, an indefatigable Aussie ex-forensic scientist with only a quarter lung left (current whereabouts unknown after a trek to Oz via the trans-Siberian railway) who oversaw our transition to proper typesetting and lithoprinting in the late 1970s; the stalwarts at Swiftprint (Stroud) who gave us a great service for so many years; Chris Squire, who helped us get our first subscription database organised; the Canadian Mr X, a Fortean purist; Mike Dash, a recent but increasingly invaluable recruit; and many correspondents, clipsters, donors, friends, advisors and well-wishers, too many to mention here, to whom I am personally indebted. I thank you all.

Finally, I must say a special thank you to my co-editor Paul Sieveking, who has corrected (by hand!) countless mistakes and slips of the typewriter to prepare these magazines for re-publication.

Here, then, in their simplicity and rough vigour, are the first issues of *Fortean Times*.

Bob Rickard
June 1992

FT

FORTEAN TIMES 1–15 (1973–1976)

CONTENTS

THE NEWS 1 – NOVEMBER 1973

2   *EDITORIAL* introducing the magazine and its philosophy.

3   *ÆRIAL CURIOSITIES* – kestrel attacks – massive moth swarm in Lincs – thirsty vampire bats – battle between eagle and fox.

3   *ANIMAL CURIOSITIES* – Austrian wolf – Iron Age swine – animal theatricals? – cows attack helicopter – goat and hippo friends escape – UK adder bites – vicious duck – wallabies in Kent.

4   *APPEARANCES* – deadly South American cobra hunted in Windsor Great Park.

4   *ARCHÆOLOGY* – Chinese discovery of America – image of Stone Age man overhauled.

4   *BODIES* – mutilated body found during bomb hoax – ten years dead in bed – body in burnt field – plus assorted discoveries.

5   *DEAD HERRINGS* – like their red cousins, these are stories that smell and lead nowhere, in this case – the coffin of rock musician Gram Parsons' kidnapped and burnt in desert – the Bulgarian cyclops.

5   *DEATHS & ATTACKS* – diver's lungs burst – boy dies from overeating – the crazed lodger – massacres of birds and kangaroos – 'death-duel' of two gamekeepers – 'unconnected' murders of four women in pairs of locations – novelist Ann Quin's mystery 'suicide'.

7   *DISAPPEARANCES* – toothless nude riddle – Christine Markham vanishes.

7   *ESP* – are cats telepathic? – twin fears for lost sister.

8   *FALLS* – two 1954 Birmingham-area frog falls, Sutton Park and Hopwas – thousands of toads fall on Brignoles, southern France.

9   *FIRES* – mystery car blaze death and other mystery fires in Birmingham – Charles 'fires follow me around' Sandell.

10   *FISH CURIOSITIES* – carp at Deptford – Arabic writing on side of fish – pollution inhibiting lobster shell growth – 18 whales beach in Mexico – shark killed on San Francisco street.

11   *GHOSTS* – coastguards see phantom on cliff – ghostly doings at the Malt Shovel, Cheadle Hulme; the (BBC) Langham, London – ghost girl in Kensington house.

12   *HEAVENS ABOVE* – investigation and debate continues about the Tunguska 'meteorite' – the coming of comet Kohoutek.

12   *HOAXES* – who wired-up the prize-winning dahlias? – sexton's ghost prank at graveside – another psychic 'discovers' Atlantis.

13   *HUMAN CURIOSITIES* – Britain's smallest woman, Joyce Carpenter, dies – the struggle to 'civilize' the wolf boy of Abruzzi, plus discussion of other recent feral children cases – Ines Fernandez, who hasn't slept in 30 years, and a man who slept too deeply – girl swallows fork – impaled man lives – naked 'Tarzan' caught in Tanzania.

15   *JINXES & CURSES* – rector ritually curses church thief – sikh threatens to behead vandals.

16   *LIGHTNING* – deaths in Lagos, Taunton and Birmingham - ranger Roy Sullivan struck for fifth time.

16   *MASS HYSTERIA* – collapse of 135 pupils at school in Esher – tens of thousands afflicted with runs in Portsmouth area – epidemic of ulcers in mouth and on extremities in West Country.

17   *OCCULT CRIMES* – Degas painting vanishes.

17 *PLANT CURIOSITIES* – rare orchids found in Leicestershire.

17 *POLTERGEISTS* – Middlesborough family flee home.

18 *RIPLEY OR NOT!* – 'Scum" on Seychelles banknotes – 225th anniversary of Academy of Liars – two holes-in-one.

18 *SCIENTIFIC CURIOSITIES* – volcano in Kuriles erupts – radar beam activates church organ – a strange sulphuric lakes on Kamchatka – new species of fly.

18 *UFOs* – the 1973 flap in Georgia.

18 *WITCHES* – news of the publication of some original testimony from the Salem trials of 1692.

THE NEWS 2 – JANUARY 1974

3 *APPEARANCES* – 250 fish in an old tank.

3 *ARCHÆOLOGY* – 2600-year-old skeleton with dagger at Oundle.

3 *DEATHS & BODIES* – parents of Philippa Coon, who vanished in India, reject Foreign Office claim to have identified her – assorted unidentified bodies, mysterious 'suicides' and 'accidental' deaths – entombed alive in Argentina.

4 *DISAPPEARANCES* – thousands of fish vanish from Smethwick pond – seance clue to Doris Symonds' disappearance – nuclea-protest ship missing off New Zealand.

5 *ESP & POWERS* – son's sixth sense saves family – Uri Geller's BBC TV debut.

6 *FIRES* – mysterious fire deaths in Chester, Birmingham, Dudley.

8 *GHOSTS & POLTERGEISTS* – hauntings of council properties in Chichester and Plumstead, the Royal Circus hotel in Edinburgh, Winchester's ancient Crown Court dungeons, and a Wolverhampton pub.

9 *HEALING & CURES* – infertile women flocking to Naples to sit on ancient temple stone – Australian aborigines 'sing' for contraception.

9 *HEAVENS ABOVE* – more on comet Kohoutek – the 'breathing' clouds of Venus – Russians claim to detect radio signals from space – Bolivian Indian ritual festival may be relic of ancient observation of nova – plasma detected near moon.

11 *MYSTERIOUS MOON. Nigel Watson* outlines the classic Fortean mystery of flashes of light seen near the moon, crossing the moon's disk, and even apparently on its surface.

12 *HUMAN CURIOSITIES* – sleepwalking boy wakes up on roof – Henri Rochatain, who can sleep soundly on a tightrope in high winds – Catman, the athletic nuisance terrorising a Buckinghamshire caravan site – girl revived from a 15-minute 'death' and old Rose discovered snoring after her coffin lid was screwed down – Johannesburg man carries severed arm to hospital – high static charges make Balham woman's life a misery.

13 *MONSTERS* – report on failure of a Japanese entrepreneur's expedition to Loch Ness – something (possibly a giant pike) lurks in the waters of Norton Mere near Dudley – a radio-controlled fake in a lake near Slough.

14 *PLANT CURIOSITIES* – alien seaweed threatens UK's south coast – giant vegetables at Shipston-on-Stour (the effect of the comet?).

15 *POSSESSION & CURSES* – a veritable horoscope – haunted atmosphere of Oakley Court at Bray, Berkshire, and the unusual frequency of deaths in the Thames alongside it – Rev. Dr Donald Omand claims vampire attacked him during an exorcism.

16 *RIPLEY OR NOT!* – name and number coincidences.

16 *SCIENTIFIC CURIOSITIES* – twins by different fathers – bacteria that thrive in alkali environments – search for the 114th element – Soviets map Earth from space – a renegade Italian professor's claim to have nurtured successfully a test-tube baby long before the British successes.

17 *SO WHAT ELSE IS NEW?* – Laotian peace treaty signing determined by astrologer – a glass pyramid proposal for county hall – reconstruction of Archimedes' solar weapon.

18 *UFOs* – at Llandrindod Wells, Wales, and at Barr Beacon, near Birmingham – mystery 'distress flares' in Channel – the 1974 USA flap continues.

18 *UNCLE CHAO'S GLEE CLUB* – more on lightning-prone Roy Sullivan – the fad for trivia – scientists discuss 'reality' at Disneyworld.

19 *REVIEWS* – *Black Holes* (Taylor) – *Lost Worlds* (Charroux).

THE NEWS 3 – MARCH 1974

2 *ÆRIAL CURIOSITIES* – game birds, and a dog, that turn the tables against their hunters – a chicken with swollen feet pops into a chiropodist's.

3 *ANIMAL CURIOSITIES* – claims that a chimp can read – a lost dog finds its way home over 1200 miles, plus other lost dogs rediscovered by chance – three bears rescue Goldilocks (really) – 968 pigs eat a plane.

4 *APPEARANCES* – phantom farmer sows and harvests wheatfield unseen – rare tropical fish found under Southend pier – wounded salmon found in trout-only fish-farm pond.

5 *ARCHÆOLOGY* – doubts about the Vinland Map (ostensibly a Viking map of New England coast) – a Roman prototype of Snoopy.

6 *DISAPPEARANCES* – Lucy Partington vanishes – Dmitrenko family lost in desert near Caspian Sea – phantom plane crashes in woods near Southend – Patricia Lincoln vanishes.

6 *ESP & POWERS* – more on Uri Geller and his 'effects' – his relationship with Andrija Puharich – his teleportation successes – his UFO encounters.

8 *FALLS* – a brief review of the falling-ice-chunk phenomenon – ice falls at Sevenoaks, Bracknell, Isleworth, Wombwell (featured on cover) – rain of soot over Kent, and frozen ducks over Arkansas – the date of the 1954 Sutton Park frog-fall pinpointed, and discussion of frog-falls by Izaak Walton and Cardan.

10 *FIRES* – series of odd fires at Heathrow and in Srinagar – blaze inquiry judge flees fire – Christine Warren and James Matson die in their blazing beds.

11 *GHOSTS & POLTERGEISTS* – hauntings at factories in Soham and Ilkeston – exorcisms requested for a British ship, the Muslim crew of a Malaysian ship, and a council house in Scunthorpe – violent polt plagues Winchester family – hauntings in Italian cemetery, old manor house in Sandford Orcas, a discount store in Colwyn Bay, a sports club in Bradford – a phantom pianist in Coventry – brother and sister reunited by ghost – author James Pope-Hennessy sensed the diminutive ghost of a man murdered on the stairs of his lodgings, then he too was similarly killed at the same location.

14 *HEAVENS ABOVE* – anxieties increase about Kohoutek's arrival – assorted bangs, thumps and flashes of light in the sky – meteorite flashes across Scotland – first reports of the Llandrillo 'meteorite' in the Berwyn hills, north Wales.

17 *IMAGES & ECHOES* – hoax 'alien' radio signals baffle Grimsby police – untraceable 'mayday' signal from Channel – Russians receive more 'ET' signals – image of numeral on egg.

18 *METEOROLOGY* – a road-like depression observed in cloud-layer – weather chaos over Britain.

19 *UFOs* – 'cigar' over Northamptonshire – phantom helicopters in Manchester region.

20 *THAT DAMNED PROCESSION AGAIN. Phil Grant* makes unsubstantiated claims

for the high correlation of Fortean phenomena with leys and a Cabbalistic number-letter-colour code. This article brought many letters from readers wanting to know more, but we never heard from Mr Grant again.

THE NEWS 4 – MAY 1974

2   *ÆRIAL CURIOSITIES* – chickens lay green and blue eggs – did a goose fly backwards?

3   *APPEARANCES* – a mysterious leopard-like predator (later named the 'Beast of Bungoma') terrorises Kenya – new egg found buried in a garden – some practical jokes – boys find gold ingots on cliff-top.

4   *BLASTS, QUAKES, LIGHTS* – subterranean rumblings, tremors and mystery explosions in south Wales.

5   *WHERE DO WE GO FROM HERE–THERE? Bob Rickard* muses on the state of Fortism, 42 years since the master faded into the positive-absolute.

7   *DISAPPEARANCES* – more on the family that vanished in the Russian desert – more on the missing trawler 'Gaul' – Tom Gatch, the missing trans-Atlantic balloonist – Jean Baxter, Porton Down scientist, vanishes.

8   *THE GLASTONBURY ZODIAC: Too Good to be True, Too Big to be Seen! Mary Caine* gives a guided tour of figures made up of landscape features, their origins and meaning.

14   *HUMAN CURIOSITIES* – the gazelle-boy of the Spanish Sahara – 12-year-old boy dies of old age – a man with four kidneys.

14   *ILLNESSES & ATTACKS* – assorted cases of mystery mutilations and slayings of domestic animals.

16   *MONSTERS & ABSMs* – expeditions: French to Siberia looking for wildmen; Japanese to Himalayas looking for yeti; Japanese plan new hunt for Nessie – silver lake-monster in Peru – Don Whillans claims yeti sighting.

17   *RIPLEY OR NOT!* – more curious name coincidences.

18   *SCIENTIFIC CURIOSITIES* – the Earth is pear-shaped – taxonomical rethink: arthropods are not a unified phylum but at least three different phyla who share similar physical charactistics – Bakker and Galton's rethink on the classification and descendants of dinosaurs.

19   *UFOs* – seen over Wearside, and filmed buzzing Concorde.

19   *UNCLE CHAO'S GLEE CLUB* – an open safety-pin up his nose – a link between phone repairs and gas cookers?

19   *REVIEWS* – *The Old Stones of Land's End* (Michell) – *New Lands* (Fort) – *The New Apocrypha* (Sladek).

THE NEWS 5 – JULY 1974

2   *DEATHS & BODIES* – a father still alive after a week unconscious in a fume-filled house in which his wife and daughter were suffocated – sudden deaths in Turkey, Blackpool and Enstone – bodies (some headless) by railway tracks – cases of multiple deaths mysteries.

4   *EGNARTS* – a red pulsating blob in Texas – a modern 'fairy' footprint – a runaway train.

5   *ESP & POWERS* – a prophecy of the Flixborough chemical plant explosion? – Geller blamed for bent IUD – premonition saves family from collapsing house – Ingo Swann's mental influence of temperature in metal.

6   *HEAVENS ABOVE* – lights seen on the moon by astronauts and others.
7   *HOAXES* – bogus maths lecture fools academics – bogus chemical formula is 'Martini' – Houdini fails to appear on 100th anniversary of his death.
7   *FOWL FUNNIES* – riddle of the blue rooster – egg inside another.
8   *MARK HALL'S FORTEANA USA* – the metal sphere found in Florida and others – powdered petrol? – more on missing balloonist Tom Gatch – UFO filmed by Skylab? – double and coloured eggs – a modern Houdini – search for giant squid.
10 *RUMBLINGS FROM ARTHUR'S TABLE. William Porter* reports on the strange events at Llandrillo in the Berwyn hills, Wales, which seemed to be an explosion, a tremor, a meteorite and a sky-quake simultaneously or coincidentally. A genuinely strange event with a wide range of witness descriptions.
14 *MARINE MYSTERIES* – curious biplane-like torpedo found at Holyhead – diver to investigate claim that bells of submerged Dunwich are still to be heard ringing – two mystery subs off Ireland – Formosan tanker lost in busy shipping lane.
15 *STRANGE RELATIONS* – spider omen – affectionate fishes – lizard follows soldier from Africa to Sicily.
15 *RIPLEY OR NOT!* – coincidences involving relatives, including the discovery of unknown or lost ones.
16 *THE INTERFACE AND THE PATHS OF DESTINY. Paul Screeton* on why the study of leys encourages interdisciplinary approaches and emphasises the obstacles inherent in narrow specialisation.
17 *SWARMS* – crickets and ants in Brazil – clouds of webs in Australia "blot out sky".
18 *REVIEWS* – *Strange Phenomena* (Corliss) – *Strange Artifacts* (Corliss) – *Secret Places of the Lion* (Williamson) – *Uri* (Puharich) – *Psychoanalysis and the Occult* (ed. Devereaux) – *Magic, Science and Religion* (Malinowski) – *Zen Buddhism and Psychoanalysis* (Fromm).
20 *DID YOU SEE...?*

THE NEWS 6 – SEPTEMBER 1974

2   *EDITORIAL* – Ken Campbell's play *The Great Caper* at the Royal Court, London – including a description of the prophetic *Book of Brighu*.
3   *ANIMAL CURIOSITIES* – a winged cat – albino bison – killer wolves in Spain – a puma in Ayrshire – Australia's 'Emmaville Panther' – animal attacks on humans.
4   *EGNARTS* – pale-skinned, fair-haired, blue-eyed Amazon tribe found – ERTS satellite apparantly photographs Ark-like formations on the slopes of Mt Ararat, plus Navarra's return from Ararat with bits of old wood he claims are remains of the Ark.
7   *FALLS* – detailed account of a fall of brick pieces in a schoolroom of an ashram in Pondicherry, Madras, in December 1921 – an aside on the Kahuna magic of Polynesia – showers of stones upon houses in Manchester, Croydon, and in Swallowfield (Berkshire) – molten blob hits screen of car in Saskatchewan – falls of chunks of ice in Brive (France), Shirley (Surrey), West Wickham (Kent), Pinner (Middlesex), Scunthorpe – fall of mystery animal in Sweden in 1708 – two falls of single large fishes – plummeting pelicans at Lake Waco (Texas).
12 *MARK HALL'S FORTEANA USA* – the dog-sized 'Beast of Arlington' (Washington) – assorted swarmings – UFOs over Connecticut, Missouri, Alberta and California – a waiting dog – assorted 'fireballs' – 'mass hysteria' illnesses in Florida and Ontario – more on missing balloonist Tom Gatch.
16 *FIRES* – questionable fire deaths of Maureen McGlynn, Purvis Mayweather, Elizabeth McPherson and Eldon Fronk in their comfy chairs – five stories of

odd blazes involving child victims.

17 *MARINE MYSTERIES* -- waterspouts on UK's south coast, including one coinciding with meteoric-type lights in the sky.

18 *NOTES ON LINCOLNSHIRE GHOST PHENOMENA 1. Nigel Watson* tells of disembodied shining eyes in a field, a phantom cyclist, and a domestic poltergeist.

19 *SCIENTIFIC CURIOSITES* -- the revival of bacteria after tens of thousands of years in Antactic ice -- similar revival of a frozen triton from Yakut permafrost -- unusual properties of water.

21 *SWARMS* -- plagues of money-spiders, ladybirds, crane-flies, houseflies, and caterpillars

22 *DID YOU SEE...?*

THE NEWS 7 - NOVEMBER 1974

2 *ESP* -- Uri Geller put to the test.

3 *FIRES* -- prisoners mysteriously burnt to death in their cells.

4 *FLOWS* -- flooded pub -- plate weeping blood -- non-stop flushing loo -- flowing water follows hospital boy.

5 *GHOSTS & POLTERGEISTS* -- haunted house, Thornton -- outdoor ghosts -- round-up of ghost reports -- some weirdos -- visions of the Blessed Virgin Mary, and others.

6 *SOME FORTEAN RAMBLINGS. Janet Bord* on leys, black dogs and a phantom cottage.

12 *MARK HALL'S FORTEANA USA* -- Bermuda Triangle -- aircraft in ice -- chamber beneath Mexican pyramid -- Minnesota runestone -- fossil dinosaur footprints in coal -- Arkansas stink -- swarms -- revue of cattle mutilation cases.

15 *LIGHTNING* -- ball lightning at Glencoe and north Wales.

17 *RIPLEY OR NOT!* -- loss of the yacht 'Morning Cloud', its curses and coincidences -- brief notes on other recent notable coincidences.

18 *THE EVOLUTION OF THE FORTEAN SOURCEBOOKS. William R Corliss* outlines the birth of his massive ongoing rescue programme for data on scientific anomalies.

20 *UFOs* -- more on phantom helicopters around Manchester, and others in Canada.

21 *LETTERS* -- unusual properties of water -- white Indians in Amazon jungle -- miracle petrol -- a Charles Fort index.

22 *REVIEWS* -- *The Romeo Error* (Watson) -- *Ghosts* (Bord) -- *Colony Earth* (Mooney) -- *Secret of the Ages* (Trench) -- *Supernature* (Watson) -- *The Dragon and the Disc* (Holiday) -- *Flying Saucer Vision* (Michell) -- *The Spear of Destiny* (Ravenscroft).

23 *DID YOU SEE...?*

THE NEWS 8 - FEBRUARY 1975

3 *BEHAVIOURAL CURIOSITIES* -- strange animal behaviour -- coincidences featuring animals -- rescues of humans by: giant turtle, shark, cow, and dogs.

5 *A MESSAGE FROM MAGONIA. Jerome Clark* on American mystery animals.

6 *METEOROLOGICAL CURIOSITIES* -- mock suns -- unusual darknesses and clouds -- whirlwinds in Wales.

8 *OCCULT CRIMES* -- locked room death riddle -- one-legged ghost -- 'Houdini gang' raid strongroom -- incense hater plagues church -- some odd thefts.

9 *PHANTOM SMELLS AND TASTES* -- mystery illnesses, viruses, collapsings and

'mass hysteria' -- cases: Rickmansworth, Warley, Gillespie (Illinois), Chicago, Birmingham, Willenhall, Hauppauge (NY), Pinxton, Warley, Halesowen, Newcastle-upon-Tyne, Wolverhampton, Hazelrigg, Blackburn, Portsmouth, Bournemouth, Workington, Selby, Filey, Los Angeles.

13 NOTES ON LINCOLNSHIRE PHENOMENA 2. *Nigel Watson* on Lincolnshire hauntings and mystery light-flashes.

15 SWARMS AND MIGRATIONS -- ants -- flying insects -- marine swarms -- rodent rampages -- toads -- porcupines in Devon.

18 SCIENTIFIC CURIOSITIES -- magnetic anomaly in Canada -- Cosmos 666 launched -- Laithwaite's gyroscopic 'anti-gravity device' demonstration and the hostile establishment reaction -- the Dean Device.

21 BOOK REVIEWS -- *A Revised Cosmology* (Taylor) -- *Quicksilver Heritage* (Screeton) -- *The Old Straight Track* (Watkins).

22 LETTERS -- 'hollow Earth' photos -- ghosts, leys and phantom cottage.

24 DID YOU SEE...?

THE NEWS 9 - APRIL 1975

2 EDITORIAL -- Obituary, Ronald J Willis -- announcement of Paul Devereux & Andy York's Charnwood Forest earth tremor project.

3 ANTIQUITIES -- Greek lead scroll -- ship and 40 dead mariners found in a mine, 1460 AD -- early man in Australia -- copper mines in Israel -- discoveries in museum basements.

5 DISAPPEARANCES -- Disappearing dogs, trout, farm animals and frogs -- vanishing children -- a proto-Stonehouse -- the Glen Miller story (cont) -- more missing persons -- Siamese balloonist vanishes -- an eerie location on a Yorkshire moor from which a wife seemed to have been "taken by fairies" and returned.

9 LIGHTS & FIREBALLS -- mystery coastal flares -- fireballs -- ghost lights & corpse candles.

12 PYRAMID SLOPE & NORTHERN LATITUDES. *Stuart W Greenwood* examines possible connections between the angle of the slope of various Egyptian pyramids and the latitudes of prehistoric monuments and sites in north-western Europe.

15 OUT OF PLACE -- baboons on the loose in the midlands and northern England -- bears and racoons in Hong Kong and England -- the Eastern panthers in NY -- more Home Counties 'Pumas' -- wallabies and kangaroos in UK and USA -- a Tasmanian Tigers at Bournemouth?, a Thing in Cheshire backwoods and some other mystery animals.

21 BOOK REVIEWS -- *Ice and Iron* (Tucker) -- *Ghosts - The Illustrated History* (Haining) -- *The Bermuda Triangle* (Berlitz) -- *The Bermuda Triangle Mystery - Solved* (Kusche) -- *Posted Missing* (Villiers) -- *Mystery of the Ancients* (Umland) -- *Strange Planet* (Corliss) -- *The Other Side* (Pike) -- *The Humanoids* (Bowen).

23 DID YOU SEE...?

THE NEWS 10 - JUNE 1975

2 EDITORIAL -- INFO convention -- Kaspar Hauser film -- Revised Edition of Fort.

3 GHOSTS & VISIONS -- factory ghosts -- foreign ghosts (Venezuela, S Africa) -- road ghosts -- animal ghosts.

5 IMAGES -- face in cottage floor, Spain -- ghost in photograph, Chingle Hall -- faces in photos -- Richard III appears in photo -- photo of ghost, Co. Wicklow.

11   *AMAZING MENAGERIE. Colin Bord* on monsters and mystery animals, and their possible connection with UFO sightings.

14   *UFOs AND LIGHTS* -- alien bodies in Ohio? -- fireballs in Thuringia, 1398, and in Sweden, 1910 -- UFO sightings: Sedgeley Beacon, Bournemouth, Pembroke, Hanging Houghton, Runcorn, Harbourne, Stockton, Plumstead, Brockenhurst, Japan.

18   *UNIDENTIFIEDS* -- the Barmouth sea-monster -- Indian Ocean sea-serpents -- an Alpine monster c.1660 -- Nessie sighted -- Malayan unidentified animal c.1939 -- a smelly Surrey 'thing'.

21   *LETTERS* --the madness of crowds -- Tasmanian wolf.

22   *BOOK REVIEWS* -- *Mysteries of Time and Space* (Steiger) -- *The Flying Cow* (Playfair) -- *There are Giants in the Earth* (Grumley) -- *Mysteries of the Earth* (Bergier) -- *Our Haunted Planet* (Keel) -- *A History of Magic, Witchcraft & Occultism* (Crow).

THE NEWS 11 - AUGUST 1975

3   *ALCHEMY AND ELIXIRS* -- mystery automobile fuels.

4   *SYNCHRONICITIES* -- lost things found (rings, cap) -- things found inside other things (money in fish, safety pin in pie, knitting needle in woman's back, sparrow in turnip) -- spate of coach crashes -- aftermath of Moorgate Underground disaster -- comments on the 'Prime Minister's Yacht is Missing', the Stonehouse vanishing, the Tania Hearst affair, and numerous other examples of the coincidence of an actual event following a fictional one.

5   *PORTRAIT OF A FAULT AREA (Part One). Paul Devereux & Andy York* examine the Leicestershire/Staffordshire fault area, its connection with UFOs, tremors and local mythology. The geographical lay of the land. The mythology of Llyr and his connection with the area. The meteorological landscape. The Ufological landscape. The seismological landscape.

11   *FORTEAN FUNNIES* cartoon strip by *Hunt Emerson*, words by *Bob Rickard*.

22   *UNIDENTIFIEDS* -- more on the Barmouth Monster -- Florida river monster -- Tanzanian sea-monster.

23   *LETTERS* -- ghost photographs -- aliens on ice.

24   *DID YOU SEE...?*

THE NEWS 12 - OCTOBER 1975

3   *GEOPHYSICAL CURIOSITIES* -- quake listing -- Midlothian polter-quakes -- underground fire -- erratic boulders -- smelly goo in Birmingham.

5   *METEOROLOGICAL CURIOSITIES* -- heat-wave -- hail-storms -- tornadoes -- storms -- deluge at Hampstead.

8   *PORTRAIT OF A FAULT AREA (Part two). Paul Devereux and Andy York* continue their examination of the Leicestershire/Staffordshire fault area. The seismic landscape. The supernatural landscape. The psychic landscape. The Oaks Hanging Stone. Shugborough.

21   *POLTERGHOSTS* -- poltergeist at Birkdale -- ghost at Woolton -- sexy ghosts (Greenwich, Wandsworth, Lewisham, Lewes, Worksop).

23   *SYNCHRONICITIES* -- accident groupings -- lucky escapes -- falling babies.

26   *BOOK REVIEWS* -- *The Unidentified* (Clark & Coleman) -- *Magic and the Millennium* (Wilson) -- *The Natural History of the Vampire* (Masters).

27   *DID YOU SEE...?*

THE NEWS 13 - DECEMBER 1975

2   INSECTS -- mass bee attack, Indiana -- African killer bees spread north from Brazil -- lack of bees in Kent.

3   UFOS AND LIGHTS -- round up of recent sightings -- UFOs at Reading/Basingstoke -- the abduction of Travis Walton.

6   ON THE SLOPE OF SILBURY HILL. Stuart W Greenwood on possible connections between Silbury Hill and the Egyptian pyramids.

7   FALLS -- showers of frogs in East Anglia -- Jerome Cardan's theory of frog-falls -- frog-falls, USA -- ice chunk falls at the feet of a meteorologist in Manchester -- ice falls at Cashel and Rouen -- weather conditions and TV interference.

10 HEAVENS ABOVE -- Russia's Venera probe sends data back from Venus -- TV interferance across Europe blamed on 'strange weather' -- Cosmos 777.

12 LEYS, UFOs & CHANCE. Robert Forrest challenges the assumption that UFO sightings and ley-lines are linked together by more than chance.

14 MYSTERY ATTACKS -- the mysterious death of Frederick Merry -- more deaths from unknown causes -- attacks by 'invisibles' -- amnesiac injuries and curious deaths -- simultaneous cardiac arrests -- phantom snipers.

19 BOOK REVIEWS -- Miracles of the Gods (von Daniken) -- Gods of Air and Darkness (Mooney) -- On the Shores of Endless Worlds (Tomas) -- The Link (Manning) -- The Magic of Findhorn (Hawken) -- Strange Powers (Wilson) -- The Hero with a Thousand Faces (Campbell) -- UFOs from Behind the Iron Curtain (Hobana & Weverbergh) -- Strange Universe (Corliss) -- Violent Universe (Calder) -- The Magic of Uri Geller (Randi).

22 DID YOU SEE...?

24 UNCLE CHAO'S GLEE CLUB -- strange tales of the trousers of the universe.

THE NEWS 14 - JANUARY 1976

3   THE 'SURREY PUMA' & FRIENDS: More Mystery Animals. Bob Rickard rounds up pumas and other mystery felines -- three-page listing of sightings -- the wild beast of Gevaudan, 1764 -- the Southampton 'Wolf', 1876 -- mystery animals in Asia Minor, 8th cent. AD.

9   LEYS AND THOSE WHATSITS. F W Holiday responds to Robert Forrest's challenge (NEWS 13) on leys, UFOs and chance.

11 THE EMPEROR'S NEW MONSTER. Bob Rickard discusses the Rines photos of something in Loch Ness.

18 NOTES ON GREENWICH PHENOMENA (Part One). Steve Moore examines the phenomena and topography of Greenwich with a view to interpretation by Chinese yin and yang theories. Greenwich phenomena -- the Shooters Hill 'cheetah' -- UFOs -- ghosts -- ice storm, 1925.

23 DID YOU SEE...?

THE NEWS 15 - APRIL 1976

2   EDITORIAL -- title change to Fortean Times announced.

3   GHOSTS AND VISIONS -- blob with red eyes, California -- visions of Jesus, Ohio -- vision of Blessed Virgin Mary, Bayside, NY -- BVM vision, Australia -- a Celtic werewolf.

6   THE MALTON MUTANT -- a curious pony foal with no ears and other odd features

including malformations of the legs and head, Yorkshire – plus other notes on strange horses.

9   *UNIDENTIFIEDS* – strange chimera in Indonesia – the lizard-like 'Goro monster', Italy – lizard, Australia – manimals sighted in Chile, Venezuela and Washington state – lake and river monsters in Ontario, Brazil and Loch Ness – more on the Barmouth monster – unidentifiable creatures in Tanzania and Mexico – the beginnings of saga of 'Morgawr', the Falmouth sea-serpent.

14   *THE GIZA-STONEHENGE CONNECTION. Stuart W Greenwood* suggests that an alignment from Stonehenge points toward the Great Pyramid at Giza.

17   *FALLS* – ice-block falls on Denver – toilet contents fall on Bridgewater – a silver notecase hits a housewife in Hull – falling sausages.

18   *NOTES ON GREENWICH PHENOMENA (Part Two). Steve Moore* continues his examination of Greenwich phenomena and a Chinese interpretation. Theoretical background: Fort's continuous universe; the Chinese universe; geographical connotations.

22   *REVIEWS AND NEWS* – mysterious woundings – Comet West – *The Tao of Physics* (Capra) – *Number and Time* (von Franz) – *The Eighth Tower* (Keel) – *The Invisible College* (Vallée) – *Mazes & Labyrinths of the World* (Bord) – *Strange Life* (Corliss) – *Strange Phenomena vol 2* (Corliss) – *Did Spacemen Colonise the Earth?* (Collyns) – *Hidden Worlds* (van der Veer & Moerman) – *In Search of Ancient Gods* (von Daniken) – *Secret of the Ages* (Trench) – *Passport to Magonia* (Vallée) – *Extraterrestrial Intervention* (Bergier/INFO) – *In Search of Lake Monsters* (Costello) – *Destiny Mars* (Saunders) – *The Devil's Triangle* (Winer) – *No Earthly Explanation* (Spencer).

27   *JOURNAL REVIEWS.*

THE SUBSCRIBERS TO THIS VOLUME

David Alexander, James Dean Allen, Alan Lance Andersen, Mark Anderson, Dr Gail-Nina Anderson, Jan Arter, K.C. Austin, Michael Avis, M.D. Baker, Paul Baker, John Ball, Mrs A.E. Barnes, Tony Barnes, Jeremy Beadle, C. Beales, Andrew Beaumont, K.A. Beer, Chester L.Behnke, M. Belderson, Anthony J. Bell, C.J. Berry, Gordon Black, Richard Blacklaw-Jones, Michael R. Blair, C.M. Bone, Janet and Colin Bord, Andrew Boulton, Jon R. Bowcott, Chistopher M Broadbent, Peter Brookesmith, P. Brough, Martin Brown, Donald A. Buchanan, D. Buckmaster, David J. Burns, Ros Calverley, Rachel Carthy, Miss R. Cashen, James Challis, Brian Chapman, D. Checkley, Virginia Chetwynd, Peter Christie, Adam C. Clark, David Clark, A.P. Clarke, Ronan Coghlan, R.F. Collins, Terry W. Colvin, Geoff Connelly, David T. Cooper, Bryan Cooper, R.G. Coppen, Les Cornwell, Andrew Corrigan, G. Coulson, Mat J. Coward, Kay Criddle, A.S. Crisp, S.P. Croucher, John A. Crow, Jim Darroch, Mike Dash, Bruce L. Davies, C. Dawson, C.P. Dean, Dr Michael K. Diamond, Stephen H. Dickens, Joseph M. DiGiacomo, Eugene Doherty, Dr Franziska Dokter, Mrs E.C. Donkin, Bruce Dunham, John Eastman, M. Eaton, Mark Ellis, A.S. Evans, Bob Everett, Harold J. Faretto, Harry Fearnham, George Featherston, Craig Fees, Michael A. Ferrier, John T. Fleming, Robert Fletcher, The Folklore Society, Susan M. Ford, Robert Friede, Jon Paul Fry, Richard Furlong, David Galea, Paul Gamer, R.J. Gandy, Alan R. Gardiner, Wojtek Gaworzewski, Dr T.J. Gaynard, D. Godbear, Vladimir Godic, Henry C. Goodrich, Marilyn D. Gray, A.J. Greenhalgh, Paul Green, James Griffin, David Grimbleby, Mark Hagan, Michael R. Haigh, Nick Hamil, Kim Möller Hansen, B.D. Harder, Cyril Harper, Clive Harper, M.K. Harris, J. Haslam, Miss I. Hayes, David Heppell, Jenny Hierons, John Holman, M.J. Holman, Gordon Hopkins, Dean Howard, David Hudson, David Hughes, Gareth Hughes, Ellen D. Hume, Chris Hylton, P.M. Imber, Paul Jackson, G. Jacobs, O. James, Ricky Jaworek, Karl P. Jeffery, Edward Jenkinson, Jason Trevor John, I.K. Johnson, Paul Johnson, P.O. Johnson, H.A. Jones, Gordon Keast, T.S. Keeble, John Keeble, B.H. King, Gary Kingham, Jake T. Kirkwood, Daniel Kleinman, W.A. Knight, Walter Krieger, J.G. Lane, Walter Langbein, Bob Langford, Martin Lasko, Glenn Law, Stephen Leadbetter, Peter Lee, P.W. Lewis, Peter Lewis, Cameron Lindo, David Lister, Nick Lowe, M. Luke, Alexis Lykiard, Mick Lyons, Ulrich Magin, Christopher Makepeace, Nick Maloret, Dr Eric J. Margolis, J. Marriott, Gary Marshall, L.F. Marshall, John E. Marsh, J.K. Marston, Marcus J. de Gaughy Matthews, Angela F. Matthews, Colin McKay, David McKinnon, Gordon McLellan, Jim McLennan, Rev David J. McNaughton, Miss P. Merriman, Barbara Millspaw, Robert Mitchell Jr, Allan Moffet, Edward Molloy, Anne C. Moody-Smith, Carole A. Moore, Mark L. Moravec, Val Morgan, Colin Morrison, D.N. Morris, Dale Neiburg, Larry Neill, Simon Nicholls, David Nicholls, David Norman, Terry Norman, P. O'Halloran, C. O'Neill, Michael Orson, Peter Overton, Floyd Palmer, G.A. Palmer, Dave Parker, R.H. Partridge, Mrs Robin Pascoe van der Raaij, Elaine Paul, Tom Perrott, Mrs J.L. Petrie, Sergio Pettinelli, Dr Hugh Pincott, Andy Pitchforth, Ian Pollard, A.R. Portsmouth, Dr Lawrence Potter, M. Potterton, Colin Potter, John Powell, Carolyn Pyla, Terry Pyle, Simon Queen, A. Quinn, J.L. Railton, L.R. Ramsey, F.W.G. Rau, H.D. Rees, Enrico Restani, Barry J. Reynolds, John Ries, Alasdair Robertson, Frank Roberts, Glen Robins, B. Rogers, Dr Serena Roney-Dougal, Sven Rosén, David Rossiter, Steve Roud, Grant Rowland, Craig A. Saunders, G. Savin, Robert J. Schadewald, Conrad Scott, Ronnie Scott, Stephen Scott, V.E. Shearman, Robin Shelley, Neil Shenton, Alan Shepherd, Michael T. Shoemaker, Dr Karl P.N. Shuker, Caryl Sibbett, Adrian Sill, Ian Simmons, Bruce A.S. Skeer, Mr and Mrs D. Skeet, Gordon Skinner, Jeff C. Smith, Norma Smith, Michael Spragey, John Sproull, P. Stallard, Paul R. Standing, Dr Gordon Stein, Mark W. Stephenson, Martin Sterne, David D. Stevens, Dr Hugh N. Stiles, J. Storey, Nicole A. Stranko, R.J. Stronach, Roland Sweet, Henry Tenhovaara, Lars Thomas, Bob Thompson, Paul Thornber, G.A. Thredder, Mark Tinkler, W.J. Toombs, Leonard Trievenor, Andreas Trottmann, Michael Truelove, Miss L. Veale, Leen Verhoeff, Wendell Wagner Jr, David Walley, G.E. Wallwork, Dr Michael Walsh, A. Ward, Geoffrey Wareing, Bruce Warring, S.P. Whatley, J. Whiskin, Julie Whitaker, Owen Whiteoak, Nigel Whitmore, Mark Whittam, J.C. Wiesen, Terry Wilkin, N. Williams, Ian P. Wilson, Paul Wilson, R.A. Wilson, Jason Winter, Gene Wolf, R. Wollaston, S.J. Wooders, Kevin Woodward, Miss J.H. Woolridge, Jeane Worthington, C.E. Wren, Z. Zogoid. **FT**

THE NEWS

no.1 a miscellany of fortean curiosities

ᏔᏂᎬ ᏁᎬᏫᏌ vol.1. no.1. Nov. 1973

is a non-profit-making bi-monthly miscellany of Fortean notes and news.   Edited and published by Robert JM Rickard: 31 Kingswood Road, Moseley, Birmingham B13 9AN.
* *
Single issues - 35p. 1 year subscription - £1.80. inc. post. Cheques and POs payable to RJM Rickard, please, not the NEWS.

Welcome to the News, Britains first Fortean magazine. The omens have been good, and the public has been prepared for a magazine like this - but the core of our readers will be researchers and others interested in extrapolating the ideas of Charles Fort.

Many people are under the impression, from reading the variety of fringefortean books currently flooding the market, that anomalous and enigmatic phenomena are rare, and even more rarely reported. We can draw no conclusions about incidence (though some work has been done on Fort's data to determine cycles of incidence) - but this magazine will be testimony to the papers being as full of the damned stuff now as they were when Fort ruined his eyes in the British Museum.

He was quite definite on this point: "... I never write about marvels. The wonderful, or the never-before-heard-of, I leave to whimsical or radical fellows. All the books by me are of quite ordinary occurrences...But it is not that I take numerous repetitions as a standard for admission. The fellow who found the pearl in the oyster stew - the old fiddle that turned out to be a Stradivarius - the ring lost in a lake, and then what should be found when a fish is caught - but these often repeated yarns are conventional yarns. And almost all liars are conventionalists....But when I come upon the unconventional repeating, in times and places far apart, I feel - even though I have no absolute standards to judge by - that I am outside the   field of ordinary liars." (Wild Talents. V.)

And that, for those of you who have asked, is the reason behind our quiet, unassuming, unsensational name - the contents are preposterous enough without blatant hysteria.

Cover: adapted from an old advertisement for Selfridges, by Bernard Partridge.

The News will function more or less like a 'news clipping agency', except that our clients are also our clippers - in that way we cover a wide field, especially in the local regional papers which should carry fresher stories. Besides contributing cuttings, we would like to ask our readers to take the opportunity to verify any local stories (we will even publish their findings gladly). But remember - we are not in the business of offering truths, only leads and clues for those of you who thrill to the chase, and even the armchair philosophers. Credit is given as a matter of course wherever possible - and all uncredited items are from the editor's own files. If you need to quote from our pages, no permission is needed, just an acknowledgement.

The whole business of the categories is arbitrary - some stories clearly belong in several categories simultaneously. In this matter, and in the general running of the mag. we will impose our opinions with reluctance, and where necessary ,briefly.

Lastly, we hope the response to this first issue will allow us to expand next issue to include, among other things, readers' letters and reviews of books that arrived too late for inclusion in this issue.

Skyward Ho!

change to bi~monthly publication

The editor sincerely regrets to announce a slight change in the schedule proposed for the NEWS. Because of many factors, not the least being the daily pressures of earning a living, the NEWS will be published bi-monthly and not monthly as planned and announced in our publicity. The price will remain £1.80. for a year's subscription; and single copies including those on public sale will cost 35p each. Those of you who have kindly paid the full amount under the impression that there were to be 12 issues per year, are asked to bear with us. The editor hope that you will agree that this was preferable to any compromise on the volume of Fortean content, or quality of printing - or editing (whatever that is!).

aerial curiosities

KESTREL MAKES TERROR ATTACK ON KIDS.

The village children were thrilled when a kestrel perched on a pavilion above their playground. But minutes later they scattered in terror as the young bird of prey swooped down on them. The bird, with razor sharp talons, attacked about a dozen screaming boys and girls in the playground at Haxby, near York. Frightened mothers also raced for safety as the kestrel 'buzzed' the playground for two hours.

As police arrived, garage manager Dennis Bellerby, 35, lured the bird to the ground using bacon as bait. Then he threw a coat over the kestrel and placed the bird in a cardboard box. Yesterday it was in captivity in York's RSPCA home for unwanted and stray dogs. Bill Stericker, who runs the dogs home, said yesterday:"The kestrel is a bit of a problem. It should be out in the wild, and eventually we will have to free it."

Sun. 7 Aug 73.

THE CROP EATERS.

A Massive invasion of diamond-bat moths from the continent is attacking crops in Lincolnshire.

Daily Mirror. 13 Aug 73.

VAMPIRES SHORT OF BLOOD.

Vampire bats at Houston zoological gardens USA, are getting thirsty. Because of the meat shortage their supply of beef blood (£1.20/gallon) has stopped. Curator Richard Quick said that the beef packer who supplied the bats' monthly blood ration had closed. They would have to wait for local hospitals to discard human blood.

Sunday Mirror. 8 Aug 73.
Credit: A Smith.

WAR IN THE AIR.

A fox, carried high in the air by a golden eagle in Austria, buried its teeth into the eagle's throat. Both crashed to their death.

Sunday Mirror. 3 June 73.

animal curiosities

HELLO - AND GOODBYE.

A gamekeeper at Murau, Austria, shot the first wolf to be seen in the country for 30 years.

Sunday Mirror. 2 Sept 73.

GINGER PIGLETS.

Striped ginger piglets have been bred by crossing a wild boar and Tamworth sows to give an Iron Age village project at Little Buster, near Petersfield, Hampshire, authentic Iron Age swine.

Reading Evening POST. 3 Aug 73.

ANIMAL THEATRICALS?

Our dog, Armstrong, is not exactly renowned for his bravery and will only put on a show when he is assured of an audience. But after my experience the other night, I wonder whether other animals act up just for the benefit of humans.

I looked out onto the lawn which is partially lit by a nearby street lamp. There I saw a large dog fox strolling slowly toward the fruit trees. Following closely, was our cat, Microbe, and behind in Indian file was Armstrong. All three were quite contentedly sniffing their way along apparantly without a care in the world.

I stepped on to the patio to get a closer look and all three animals saw me. It was only then that Armstrong, aware no doubt that he was not being a proper dog, suddenly turned and barked half-heartedly at the fox. The fox trotted off into the hedge and Microbe leaped into the air and ran into the house.
                    MARLENE DOVE.
                    Croham Valley Road,
                    South Croydon, Surrey.

Letters to the Editor.
Sunday Express. 2 Sept 73.

COWS HOLE A HELICOPTER.

A herd of cows took a fancy to a BEA helicopter in a field at Malden, Essex, when the pilot Captain Dick Hensen left the machine for a few minutes to make a telephone call.

When he returned he found most of the plane's paint licked off - and the perspex cockpit cover holed by a horn. The helicopter had to be taken out of service.

Sunday Express. 2 Sept 73.

HIPPO WHO GOT THE GOAT.

The Hippo was fed up with the zoo routine, so he and his pal the goat went for a walk one night. Startled Policemen in Las Vegas later found the goat and his 2 ton friend strolling down the highway out of town...and took them quietly home.

Daily Mirror 27 July 73.

SNAKE IN THE SAND BITES SEASIDE GIRL.

A holiday romp at the seaside landed little Gail Harwood in hospital last night - with a snake bite. Gail, 10, was bitten on her left leg by an adder while playing in the sand dunes at Winterton, Norfolk.

Last August Bank Holiday Monday, another holiday maker at Winterton spent two weeks in hospital after being bitten on the hand.

Daily Mirror. 28 Aug 73.

A DUCK WAS OUT FOR BOB.

While Bob Crowthall of The Broadway, Bourne-mouth, was sharing his sandwiches with ducks in a local park, one of them reared up and pecked a piece out of his nose. He said:"I was amazed those birds could be such little monsters."

Sunday Express. 2 Sept 73.

IT'S ENOUGH TO MAKE A POLICEMAN HOPPING MAD.

A big police hunt is on...for two wallabies on the run. The wallabies, smaller versions of the Kanga-roo, escaped from Heathfield Safari Park, Sussex. Now one of them has been spotted leaping over hedges near Hawkhurst in Kent.

Mr Julian Moore, 18, who works at the safari park owned by his father, Dr. Gerald Moore, explained that they are not really dangerous but have a ten-dency to kick. He said :"We have a devil of a job keeping them from vaulting the enclosures. We keep on building higher fences - but once a wallaby, even a small one, decides he's going, it's pretty hard to change his mind. The two missing animals are about 3ft. 6in. high and greyish-brown."

Sunday Mirror. 2 Sept 73.

appearances

KILLER SNAKE HUNTED BY PARK GUNMEN.

A 4ft. South American cobra, which has venom that can kill in 20 minutes, is still on the loose in Windsor Great Park. Visitors were warned to keep to paths as keepers with shot-guns searched for the killer snake. It was seen by four people in the Savill Ornamental Gardens yesterday before rearing up to display a four-inch 'hood' and sliding off into the undergrowth. It is still a mystery how it got there.

A Windsor police official said: "From the description and checks we have made with experts at Regents Park Zoo we are satisfied it is a South American Cobra."

Express & Star. 23 July 73.
Credit: A Smith. Steve Moore sent a cutting from Daily Mirror (same date) which only added that the cobra was brown and female.

archaeology

BRAVELY RISKING ANTAGONISING THE MAFIOSI IN THE Italian-American Civil Rights Association, who regard Columbus as their founding member, an archaeologist is pushing the theory that America was discovered by the Chinese 4000 years ago. He claims that ancient maps that he has translated had California labled as the 'Land of Gentlemen', and Britain down as 'Fair Maiden Country'.

Daily Mail. 14 July 73.
Credit: Steve Moore.

A BRIGHT NEW IMAGE FOR STONE-AGE MAN.

French archaeologists have begun the task of changing public opinion about the character of our remote ancestors - the 'apemen' of Stone Age times.

High on a hill near the village of Thonac (Dor-dogne), the French have built a new centre dev-oted to prehistoric culture, including cave drawings, statuettes and engravings collected or copied from every part of the world. In the grounds roam species of bison, deer and wild horse, which have changed little in thousands of years.

The centre, called Le Thot (now open to tourists was designed by Paris architect Denis Soulie, himself a keen archaeologist. He says: "The purpose of Le Thot is to present our remote ancestors in a more kindly light. The popular notion is that they were all ill-tempered sav-ages who went about snarling and attacking one-another on sight. But this could hardly have been so. We believe the evidence of the painted caves found in different parts of the world points to the fact that Dawn age man had a sensitive and even reverent side to his nature."

Sunday Express. 26 Aug 73.

bodies

STORE BODY RIDDLE.

Police found the mutilated body of a young man in a yard behind Boots store in Derby yesterday. The premises had been evacuated after a hoax call that a bomb was due to go off.

Daily Express. 1 Sept 73.

MAN DEAD 10 YEARS FOUND IN BED.

The fully clothed body of a skeleton was found in a bed at a terraced house in East London yesterday, by a man who went to insp-ect the roof after heavy rainfall. Murder Squad detectives were called but after a post-mortem last night it was discovered the man, later identified as William Blackhally, had died of natural causes nearly 10 years ago.

Neighbours thought that he had moved and left his wife. But yesterday, Geoffrey Wilson, 18, who had rented the downstairs flat in Lidding-road, West Ham, found his skeleton. Also in the house was Mrs. Violet Blackhally, who was given medical attention.

Daily Express. 22 Sept 73.

BODY FOUND IN BURNT OUT FIELD.

The charred body of missing Eastern Electricity foreman Stanley Albert Seymour was found yest-erday in a burnt-out cornfield in Brentwood, Essex, after an all night search. Police said 63-year-old Mr. Seymour of Charles St, Epping, died of a heart attack before his body was burnt.

Daily Express. 5 Sept 73.

'BODY IN SEA' SCOUT IS IGNORED.

Boy Scout Roger Sargant, 13, was ignored when he swam to a crowded beach yesterday and yelled that he had found a body. Roger tried for three minutes to explain that there was a dead man in the sea at Shoreham, Sussex.

Then he ran to a friend's house and phoned the police who later pulled out the body. Roger of Old Fort Rd, Shoreham, said later: "I don't think anyone believed me."

Daily Mirror, 27 Aug 73.

ITS NOT GETTY.

Police today said a clubbed, strangled, bullet-riddled and burned body found near Rome was not Paul Getty III, missing grandson of the oil tycoon.

Daily Express. 28 Aug 73.

DEAD MAN FROM MISSING FASTNET SLOOP.

A man whose body was picked up from the sea by the crew of a tanker and taken to Milford Haven, Pembrokeshire, on Wednesday, has been identified as one of the three members of the crew of a sloop missing while on her way from the Irish Republic to take part in the Fastnet race.

He was Mr Felix Desmond Morris, 28, of Morville, Co. Donegal, who was on board the Grannaile when she was reported missing. She has still not been found.

Times. 18 Aug 73.

dead herrings

Unfortunately the original reference has been lost, but the oblique reference to the smoking remains of a pop singer found in the desert had caught our eye. A few days later however the story below was disclosed and some of the mystery cleared. We publish stories in this section mainly as guides that show how a press appearance seems to imply a mystery by only presenting a few facts, and probably the more sensational ones at that. Nevertheless, as Forteans we cannot ignore the improbable on being faced with even blatant sensationalism, without a knowledge of the facts (and if we are really being honest, refraining from forming any opinions).

POP STAR BODY SNATCH CHARGE.

Police have arrested a rock music manager alleged to have taken part in the bizarre body-snatching and cremation of Gram Parsons, former lead singer with 'The Byrds'. They claimed that Philip Clarke Kaufman, 38, the dead singer's road manager, hi-jacked Parson's body from Los Angeles airport in an old black hearse last Thursday and drove it to the desert where it was set on fire.

Parsons, 27, a former singer with the Byrds and the 'Flying Burrito Brothers', died in a desert motel at Joshua Tree, near Los Angeles, a week ago, apparently from a heart attack. After an autopsy, his body was taken to the airport to be flown back to New Orleans.

Police claim that two men - one dressed in cow-boy clothes and with a patch marked 'Sin City' the name of Parsons recent hit song, on his vest - waylaid the car carrying the body, and drove off with it in the hearse.

Birmingham Evening Mail. 27 Sept 73.

ONE IN THE EYE FOR THE DISBELIEVERS.

Sofia: The complete skeleton of a cyclops - the one-eyed creature of Greek muthology - has been discovered by Bulgarian archaeologists, an official report from Sofia claims.

The discovery was made during excavations near Razlog in south-western Bulgaria. The skull, it is claimed, had only one eye socket which was placed directly over the nose and the skeleton measured 5ft 11in.

Sunday Express. 12 Aug 73.
Credit: A. Smith.

The News phoned the Bulgarian Embassy on the 17th. and was asked to try again later for the Press Secretary. The second time, we were told that more details were on their way from Bulgaria, and would be forwarded to us when they arrived. But the only thing that came through was the following cryptic and puzzling note dated 28 Aug 73:

" With reference to your telephone call, concerning the report in the 'Gardian' (sic) news-paper of a 'cyclops' being unearthed in Bulgaria we checked this matter with the authorities in Bulgaria. We have now received their reply and are informed that this report is untrue and was the mistake of one of the local correspondents."

If the report were true, then we can understand the Bulgarian's embarrassment at the hostility this discovery would inevitably release, and at the risk of appearing too credulous, deciding to issue a denial. On the other hand we find ourselves a trifle credulous and note our disap-pointment. INFO Journal 11. carries a few notes on the congenital condition of 'cyclopia'.

deaths & attacks

DIVING SUIT BAN AFTER DEATH RIDDLE.

Breathing equipment used by an American company's North Sea oil divers has been withdrawn for tests after a diver died. Fears that a temporary fault may have caused the death of Paul Havlena, 29, will be investigated, it was announced yesterday.

Havlena, an American, died when his lungs burst on a routine pipe-laying job 320 feet down. Two divers with him survived. An official of Taylor Diving said: "Havlena's death may have been caused by faulty equipment, human error, or both'.'

Daily Mirror. 1 Sept 73.

An earlier account in the Daily Mirror for 29 August 73, said that Havlena was returning, apparently normally, to a diving bell when his companions heard him cry out feebly: "Help me... help me." 'They got him into the bell, but he was dead. Later officials said that nothing appeared wrong with his gear.'

DEATH RIDDLE OF 15lb BOY.

Police and welfare officials were yesterday investigating the death of a four-year-old boy who weighed only 15½lb. Anormal weight at that age is between 36 and 44lb.

The boy, Max Piazzani, died in Basildon Hospital, Essex, on Saturday. He was admitted on Thursday after a fall at his home in Long Meadow Drive, Wickford. The investigation revealed that Max fractured his skull in an accident two years ago. An Essex County Council official said yesterday: "This incident could have led to an organic condition which in turn might have resulted in malnutrition."

Dr. Frederico Piazzani, Max's father said: "The boy ate like a horse, but there was something wrong inside which meant he could not digest his food. We did not know what his illness was, and the doctors did not tell us - if they knew. We have had four years of the most terrible anxiety with him. It could have been an accident in his infancy or he could have been born with this condition."

Sun. 7 Aug 73.

The editor's underlining.

THE CRAZED LODGER. Some of you may remember the case not long ago in which David McGreavy, a 21-year-old lodger in the house of Mrs. Elsie Ralph, savagely murdered her three children by wire, razor and pickaxe. Police said: "No investigating officer has ever had to witness such a scene of indescribable horror." The slaughter took place in April and was discovered by the children's parents, and a policeman later found the children's bodies impaled on the railings of a neighbours house, in Gillam Street, Worcester.

At the risk of being labled ghoulish, we note with a cautious amount of curiosity, the fol-incidental reference in the Daily Mirror, 31 July 73, by reporter Paul Connew:

'The house where the three children died had been linked with death before. A young couple who lived there moved after their baby suffocated in a cot. Just after World War II, a man who had been brought up in the house, moved to a new home a few streets away. There he went berserk - and killed his wife and children.'

POLICE HUNT BIRDS KILLER.

Detectives were yesterday hunting the killer of 13 prize pigeons worth £300 owned by fancier Fred Simpson, of Hobart Road, Cambridge, who said yesterday: "Whoever is responsible must be hopelessly twisted and insane."

Daily Express. 28 Aug 73.

DEATH RIDDLE OF GAMEKEEPERS.

Police were last night investigating reports of a shotgun duel between two gamekeepers which ended in death for both of them on the vast estate of Guiness brewery chairman, the Earl of Iveagh, in Eriswell, Suffolk. They were found at dusk on Saturday in a field near Rakenheath Farm. The men, John Messelis and Jack Brunning, both 53, had worked on the estate for many years.

They were near neighbours in the Victorian estate worker's cottages in Eriswell. Gossip was rife among families in the closely-knit hamlet last night. One estate employee said: "It has come as a terrible shock. There was no vendetta as far as we know." Both men were married and had children. Post mortems will be held today.

Daily Express, 6 Aug 73.

DUEL THEORY.

Police believe they have disproved a theory that two Eriswell, Suffolk, gamekeepers died in a duel on Saturday, because the fatal shots came from one gun.

Daily Express. 7 Aug 73.

MURDER IN PAIRS.

Two women - both aged thirty - were found murdered less than a mile apart yesterday. Pathologist's reports revealed they apparently died within hours of each other. But detectives said last night the murders were not linked - just a bizarre coincidence.

Nightshift worker Frederick O'Neil, 27, spotted Nancy Donaghue's body at 6.30am as he walked past the Wagon & Horses public house in Balsall Heath, Birmingham. She had been kicked and beaten about the face and neck in a 'violent struggle'. Ten minutes earlier, Mrs. June Rosser, who had been strangled, was discovered in Sandford Road, Moseley by Miss Joyce Downing, 49, who was calling her pet cat.

In Essex, a murder-scale hunt was launched after two other women were found battered to death. They were Mrs. Irish Thompson, wife of a city banker, and her widowed mother, 79-year-old Mrs Caroline Woodcock. Detective-Chief Superintendant Len White, head of Essex CID, who is leading the hunt at Coombe Rise, Shenfield, said: "It seems like a killing by someone who has gone berserk."

Daily Express. 12 Sept 73.

KANGEROOS KILLED.

Thirteen tame kangeroos were found slaughtered today in their enclosure at Sydney's Waratah Animal reserve. One appeared to have been shot and others battered or mauled to death. Park officials said they believed a big dog had been among the killers, as a large paw mark was found nearby.

Express & Star. 3 April 70.

DOG KILLED KANGAROOS.

The fifteen kangaroos believed to have been killed by gunmen in a Sydney park last week were in fact the victims of a large dog, Australian police said yesterday. The park is the home of Skippy, the famous TV kangaroo - but he was in a special compound when the dog attacked, and so was unhurt.

Daily Mirror. 6 April 70.
Credit: both above items - A Smith.

The materialisation of two extra carcases seems to have gone unnoticed in the hubbub, and we are amused by the notion of Mr. Smith of a search for a one-legged dog with a gun.

LAST-CHAPTER RIDDLE OF NOVELIST'S DEATH.

The mystery novelist Ann Quin's death could have come from one of her books. A man fishing at night on Brighton beach saw Miss Quin, 37, strip off and wade out to her death, an inquest was told last night.

Next day her body was found floating two miles out in the channel. But the Deputy Coroner at the Shoreham, Sussex, inquest, Mr. Mark Calvert Lee, said there was no way of knowing · whether she intended to commit suicide. He recorded an open verdict on Miss Quin, of Lewes Crescent, Brighton. She had written four books, and several TV plays. She was described at the inquest as excitable and tempramental, with a furious temper.

Daily Express. 14 Sept 73.

disappearances

RIDDLE OF THE TOOTHLESS NUDE.

A man's complete outfit of clothes and a full set of false teeth were found by police investigating cries in the night at the cemetary by St. Mary's Church, Felling, Co. Durham. But there was no sign of the owner. A senior officer said: "There are no reports of anyone looking suspiciously undressed."

Daily Mirror. 28 Aug 73.
Credit: Robert Forrest.

MYSTERY OF LITTLE GIRL LOST.

One of the most intensive hunts ever known in Britain is going on to trace a nine-year-old girl. Police say it is a murder investigation, but "so far there is no evidence of a killing. More than 24,000 people have been questioned in the search for red-haired Christine Markham. Helicopters, sub-aqua teams and dogs have been brought in - but there is not a single clue as to what happened to her.

A police officer heading the investigation at Scunthorpe, Lincs, told me:"A crank suggested she'd been picked up by a flying saucer. ·I know thats absurd, but the fact is this girl seems to have vanished into thin air. It's baffling."

She stayed out on the night of Monday, 12 May, and was last seen running down a street only a few yards from her home, at nearly ten past eleven. It had rained very heavily earlier in the evening. Det. Inspector Gordon Cairns said "There have been close discussions also with Norfolk CID who still have an 'open file' on the disappearance of 13-year-old April Fabb in 1969, though police do not think there is a connection." Police searched every house in the area of Christine's home in Robinson Road, Scunthorpe - without warrants. They looked in lofts and under floorboards, handed out 24,000 questionnaires and took 1,400 statements - but have been unable to discover any clues.

News of the World. 12 Aug 73. Condensed from a much larger feature by Graham Maclean.

esp

CAN CATS READ THE SECRETS OF YOUR MIND?

Cats are notoriously aloof. They appear to regard all human activity with disdain. But once a cat decides to throw in his lot with you he will often go to extraordinary lengths to prove it. Should you be insensitive enough to give your pet to somebody else the chances are that he will soon be back even if it means travelling miles across unfamiliar country. Of course, it might be your house rather than you that your cat is missing.

Cats are very much averse to moving and it often happens that when a family ups sticks and goes to a new address taking him with them,their cat finds it hard to believe they have been so foolish. He just has to go back to the old place and make sure it is deserted. But just how cats find their way back is a mystery, one in which scientists have shown surprisingly little interest.

Some research however has been carried out at the Institute of Parapsychology, in Durham, North Carolina, where scores of cat-journey stories have been collected and investigated. One story concerns a cat called Smokey, easily recognisable by a dark red tuft on his head, who leapt from the family car en route to a new home and two weeks later showed up at his old home. He stayed around for a few days and disappeared. Months later he turned up on the porch of the family's new home, looking very bedraggled. Parapsychologists reckon this is a clear example of a cat's ability to navigate by extra-sensory-perception, since Smokey had never seen the family's new home.

This may also have been what guided another cat called Whisky, last month. Whisky, who had been given away, pussyfooted 150 miles in 25 days from Cambridge to Bingley, Yorkshire, to get back where he started from. But even that was no world record. Lost or abandoned cats have been known to travel several times that distance, taking months over it, in an effort to resume their old way of life.

Whether they become more attatched to a particular family or a particular place has never been scientifically determined,but zoologists reckon that

on balance it is the _place_ that matters most to
the cat. An experiment carried out by two German
neuro-physiologists went a fair way to establishing that cats have a strong homing instinct, but
how it worked they could not say.

They took a group of household cats out to a
rural area they had never seen before and
released them one by one in a special maze
with 24 exits pointing in different directions.
Within an hour eight of the animals had located the exit pointing toward their home and
were soon happily on their way.

One experiment tried at the Institute of Para-
psychology involved two sealed containers, one
empty and one filled with food placed a few
yards away from a selection of hungry cats in
a bare room. The animals could not see the
food and all smells were eliminated both from
the containers which were identical, and from
the surroundings. Nevertheless the majority
went unerringly to the filled container. There
was absolutely nothing the researchers could
see to guide the animals in their choice. The
only possibility seemed to be that they were
using telepathy to pick up thought waves from
the researchers themselves.

Sunday Express. 16 Sept 73. By Robert Chapman.

A TWIN FEARS FOR HER LOST SISTER.

Housewife Mrs. Margaret Cassells and her twin
sister were very close to one another. Not only
did they look and talk alike but they often
thought and acted in a similar way. Then five
months ago, Mrs. Cassells' sister, 34-year-old
Mrs. Ann Law, vanished. Now Mrs. Cassells says
that she reluctantly believes her to be dead.

At her home in Beadling Gardens, Fenham, Newcastle-upon-Tyne, she said: "I knew the night
Ann disappeared that something was wrong, even
though I was at my own home. We always could
sense each other's feelings and thoughts. I have
lived in hope these past few months but now I
have to admit I think she might be dead.

"Just a month before Ann went missing, I decided
to prepare the hall for decorating. Later that
day I met my sister and she told me she had done
the same thing - at precisely the same time. It
was the same when we were youngsters. Ann went
to hospital with appendicitis and I suffered
from the same agony, although the doctor said
there was nothing wrong.

Mrs. Law who lived at Denton Square, Newcastle,
vanished a few days before her divorce became
absolute on April 2. She is believed to have taken
about £70 in cash and the clothes she was wearing.
Efforts by police and family to trace her have
failed. Mrs. Cassells and her husband travelled to
London to search for Mrs. Law and visited an Essex
public house about which she had once talked. But
there was no trace of her.

Mrs. Law's former husband, Gilbert, 37, a ship's
engineer, who was at home at the time of his wife's
disappearance, has now gone back to sea. A police

spokesman at Newcastle said: "We are keeping an
open mind about her disappearance and our inqui
ies are continuing."

Sunday Express. 16 Sept 73.

falls

THE DAY IT RAINED FROGS.

From Letter Page:

"I wonder if any readers recall the following
incident. I am not sure of the year, but I thin
it was either 1954 or 1955. It was in early Jun
and a Royal Navy display was held on the Meadow
Platt just inside the (Sutton) park.

I attended this display with my young son and
daughter. It was a Saturday and there were freq
uent heavy showers. When we had visited all the
exhibitions, we decided to have a quick look at
the fair, which at that time was permanently
situated between Meadow Platt and Windley Pool.

Whilst we were waiting there, we tried to shelt
from a shower under the trees which fringed the
patch, when we were bombarded by tiny frogs,
which seemed to come down with the rain. There
were literally thousands of them. They descende
on our umbrellas, on us and we were afraid to
walk for fear of treading on them. When we rela
it to anyone we receive incredulous disbelievin
looks.

I would like to know if there are any people wh
also witnessed this event (there were lots of
folk around us), and would appreciate it if the
would write either to your paper or to me, and
thus confirm our experience. Maybe there is a
naturalist among your readers who could explain
this phenomenon."
                        S. MOWDAY (Mrs.)
               Bodorgan, Conway Old Road,
               Capellilo, Penmaenmawr. Caerns.

The Sutton News. 3 Aug 73.
Credit: Cathy Purcell.

The News was very interested to receive this
data and wrote to Mrs. Mowday, asking her to le
us know if she should hear from others. On the
3rd Sept she kindly forwarded the following
from Mr. John W. Pitman:-

Whilst I cannot confirm the 'Rain of Frogs' in
1954 or 1955, I did have a similar experience i
1944.

As you know D Day was near and the public were
asked not to clutter up the roads and railways
during the summer. So my wife, Caroline, our 2
children and myself went by Midland Red bus fro
Yardley, Birmingham, to the small village of
Hopwas, along the Lichfield Road. When passing
Whittington Barracks (then occupied by the Americans), we were caught in a shower of rain,
which also contained many hundreds of frogs.

I can only surmise that they were caught up by
a current of air from the low lying fields by
the river at Tamworth, then deposited on the

relatively higher area at Whittington."
Letter dated 18 Aug 73.

The occurrence of two falls of frogs so geo-
graphically close to each other in the Midlands just north of Birmingham is worthy of
note, even if they are ten years apart. A
letter from Mr. Pitman brought out a few more
details:
"
1) The incident took place in August 1944, at
about 10.00 or 11.00 am.
2) Weather conditions, hot sun, blue sky with
several seperated masses of cumulus clouds,
showery.
3) Several flights of flying fortresses had
passed in the previous hour flying Eastward.
4) Location, on the A51 road between Tamworth
and Lichfield, exactly opposite the Whittington Barracks. This spot is 320 ft. above
mean sea level. As you will see on an Ordin-
ance map, there is a canal, lake, river or
reservoir within 1-2½ miles radius.
5) Prior to the heavy shower of rain the road
was completely clear. When the shower began,
shelter was taken under a tree. Whilst I cannot
say I actually saw frogs fall, the road and
path became covered with living frogs whereas
the dry area under the tree remained clear.
6) I guess the size of frogs was approximately
15mm overall. As it was a hot day, soon after
the rain stopped the well drained dried quickly,
leaving the gutters still flowing with water.
It was noticed that the frogs jumped from the
drier areas to the gutter or to any puddles
that were left. "

So far the editor has only been able to establish (subject to confirmation from Mrs.
Mowday) that the date of her incident is
likely to have been either the 12th or the
14th of June 1954. A search through the
weekly reports of the Birmingham Observatory
(primarily a weather recording institution)
failed to turn up any record of either Mrs
Mowday's or Mr. Pitman's event. But during
the search in the Birmingham Evening Mail for
June 1954 (here also there was no report) we
came across the following items for the same
period as Mrs. Mowday's fall - we can offer
no correlation other than their coincidence
in time:

* A black swan disappears from the estate of
Sir Winston Churchill at Westerham in Kent,
on June 1. On the 11th June a black swan
which turned up near Uden in Holland was
reported to be a completely different one.

* On the 8th June we find a report that 8000
racing pigeons vanished completely on their
way from Milford Haven in Wales to Northern
Ireland. Only 15 turned up at their destin-
ation totally exhausted, and six more in the
same condition were found at Swansea. We note
in passing that we have quite a few clippings
on the disappearance of large flocks of birds.

* The 14th June edition carried the note that
the police of Metz, France, were asking the
British police to help identify an 18-year-
old girl amnesia victim who was found exhausted on the road at Auten-le-Tiche and taken to
Micheville hospital. She was capable of speech
only in monosyllables and wrote a note:"Vincent Howard, Mimosa Gardens Avenue, London."
She indicated that the man was her father and
and an Army captain, and she had a brother who
was an airman. Her own address she gave as
54 Butcher St, London.

A foot-note to the report added that there
seemed to be only one Mimosa Street in the
London area, in Fulham, and no Vincent Howard
could be found there. Similarly, the reporter
could find no Butcher Street in London.

So here's another mystery for some enterprising researcher to unravel.

FREAK STORM SHOWERS VILLAGE WITH TOADS.

Toulon, Sept 23 - Tens of thousands of small
toads fell on the southern France village of
Brignoles in a freak storm today. They probably
had been sucked up into the clouds by recent
tornadoes - Agence France Presse.

Times. 24 Sept 73.
Credit: Steve Moore, Michael Balfour.

Those of you who are not familiar with the
phenomena of falls of objects from the sky, we
refer you to Fort's Book of the Damned in the
first place. The explanation that the objects
were 'sucked' up by some freak wind is a most
common one - but does not explain the extraordinary selection that goes on. Often the fish,
toads, worms, whatever are of the same size; or
in the same state, living or dead; or uniformly
of the same species (often completely foreign
to within thousands of miles - and if they did
stay up there, 'tens of thousands' of them, by
some means, how could they stay alive for that
time?).

On top of that is the similar phenomenon, as
pointed out by Fort, of the apports and precip-
itations of stones, buckshot, blood, water, oil,
or coals, etc. in connections with poltergeist
and other forms of haunting.

fires

CAR BLAZE DEATH RIDDLE.

A man died in a mystery car blaze on a busy
main road in Birmingham last night. The young
woman driver was dragged out by passers-by and
taken to hospital in Birmingham.

The car suddenly burst into flames on Coventry
Road, near the Sandy Lane traffic lights. Among
people who rushed to help was a West Indian
wearing a blue shirt who helped pull the woman
clear. Before he dissappeared without giving a
name, he told people in the crowd that he could
not get the man from the passenger seat because
the seat belt was still clipped in position.

Minutes later the two-year-old Austin 1300 was a charred wreck. As police investigations began, traffic was diverted in both directions.

Sunday Mercury. 19 Aug 73.

BLAZES PROBE.

Police continued enquiries today into unexplained fires which twice in four days damaged a garden shed behind a house in Armoury Road, Small Heath.

Birmingham Evening Mail. 13 Sept 73.

SICK MAN IN BLAZE HOUSE.

Birmingham firemen, called to a house in Severn Road, Hall Green, put out a number of fires in the premises. A man living at the house was taken out of the premises by neighbours. He was thought to be ill and was later taken to hospital.

Sunday Mercury. 16 Sept 73.

I'M NO FIREBUG - I DON'T EVEN SMOKE.

As detectives hunted a murderous firebug, a 33-year-old security guard complained: "The police are harassing me because fires follow me around" writes Charles Sandell. He explained that by coincidence he had been near the scene of "six or eight" of the firebugs blazes.

Mr. Anthony Evans, who has worked as a security guard for ten years, said that he had been questioned a number of times. Now he has telephoned Scotland Yard to protest about being harassed.

The arson rampage has terrorised the Forest Gate, Stratford and Canning Town areas of London, with 15 fires in the past two weeks. Two cars, two vans, a motor-boat on a trailer, a pillar box, a church, a school gymnasium and tuck shop were among the targets.

And the search turned into a murder hunt last Tuesday. Then three men died as the firebug threw petrol into the Tudor Hotel, Stratford, and set fire to it.

Mr. Evans, who lives with his wife and tree children in Garvary Road, Canning Town said: "Recently fires seem to happen wherever I go. They literally follow me around. The police seem to think I had something to do with starting them. It's ridiculous. I don't smoke. I don't carry matches. I think the police have got it in for me and are trying to frame me for the fires".

He told me that he first got close to one of the spate of blazes when he was driving home, and saw a church on fire in Upton Lane, Forest Gate. "I was about to call the fire brigade when I heard a fire engine coming. Then I was near the £1000 motor boat which went up in flames, though I didn't see this until it was all over.

"Three of the fires have broken out near my home. Its just coincidence that I happened to be around at the time. But I've had absolutely nothing to do with starting them." Mr. Evans added that

he had given up his job as a security guard with a local firm because of the fires. "If I'd been able to pass the educational requirements, I might have become a fireman. I like fire-fighting and did some part-time training with the auxiliary service at Whitechapel seven years ago."

A senior detective at Forest Gate police station denied that Mr. Evans had been harassed. He said "In such a grave situation, it is our duty to question anyone who may know something about the fires." Mr. Evans had been questioned two or three times, but so had other people.

News of the World. 2 Sept 73.

MYSTERY BLAST.

Crime scientists are investigating the cause of a mystery explosion and fire which destroyed the assembly hall of Rednock comprehensive school at Dursley, Gloucestershire.

Daily Mail. 27 Aug 73.

fish curiosities

CARP AT DEPTFORD.

A 5lb carp rescued from a tidal stretch on the Thames at Deptford Creek in London was revived and released at Greenwich Pier.

Times. 18 Aug 73.

THE WRITING ON THE FISH.

A branch of the National Westminster Bank is guarding a magic fish, which was bought in a Dar-Es-Salaam market eight years ago.

It is $5\frac{1}{2}$ inches long and has Arabic writing on a fin. When deciphered it reads: "Divine Universal truth. There none but God to be worshipped." (Sic).

An expert said the writing could not possibly have been put on the tail of the Butterfly fish by human efforts.

It was sent to London by the Moslem who bought it, and has since been exhibited around the world. The man now in charge of the fish is living in Perivale while trying to find a suitably splendid place to exhibit the thing.

London Evening News. 15 Aug 73.
Credit: Cathy Purcell.

DOOMWATCH FEAR FACES THE LOBSTER.

Lobsters, crabs and other shellfish may be off the world's menus in 2008. This Doomwatch warning to shellfish-lovers is given today by New Zealand atom scientist Dr. AW Fairhill.

He says in Nature, the scientific journal, that man is now burning oil and coal so quickly that the oceans are becoming overloaded with carbon-dioxide. The result: Shellfish may soon be unable to go on growing their shells - and become extinct by 2008.

Daily Mirror. 7 Sept 73.

WHALE OF A FATE.

Eighteen great whales committed collective suicide on a remote Mexico beach after their leader, wounded by a harpoon, made for land and the others followed him.

Sunday Times. 9 Sept 73.

KILLED: a jay walking shark was struck by a car as it slithered across a San Francisco street. The shark either entered the city's sewers at high tide, or fell off a truck en route to the fish market.

Daily Express. 11 Aug 73.

ghosts

DID HE SEE A GHOST?

Did an experienced coastguard and a policeman direct a lifeboat to rescue a ghost? And in broad dayilght too? The mystery of the vanishing man puzzles Derek Vine, 26, a coastguard at Eastdean, near Eastbourne, Sussex. Local men were called out to search beaches for a person reported trapped by the tide. The lifeboat was launched.

Derek, at the watch tower, spotted the man with his binoculars. "He was facing the cliff and edging around a jutting rock with the waves at his feet, " Derek said.

For confirmation, he handed the glasses to a policeman. But two coastguards lowered by ropes fonund no one. Nor did the lifeboat. The cliff is thought to be unclimbable. Derek is embarrassed. "An Excise man was lured to death by smugglers in the 18th century. Perhaps it was his ghost." he said.

Sunday Mirror. 5 Aug 73.
Credit: A. Smith.

WARNING OF A PUB GHOST.

Ex-landlord Tom Ward turned up again for an eerie midnight meeting in the cellar of his old pub. He slipped out of the shadows, pale and haggard, and gave a grim warning to the pub's new manager, Brian Withington, 31. Which shook Brian...for the old landlord had died two years before.

After his death, another landlord moved into the pub, The Malt Shovels in Cheadle Hulme, Cheshire. But he too died - in a motorway crash. Then Mr. Withington took over as manager. Yesterday he described his meeting with the ghostly Mr. Ward, who died aged 58.

He said; "I had gone to the cellar to turn off the beer when I saw a small grey-haired man standing beside one of the tanks. He was stooping, and his face was pale and drawn. His lips moved as though he were trying to say something, but incredibly, his words came from my own mouth: "Take care of yourself."

Mr. Withington was later visited by the dead man's son. 29-year-old Colin Ward, who said: "One theory is that my father's spirit is not at rest and reappeared to warn Mr. Withington to take care following the two deaths."

News of the World. 17 June 73.

A BOOT THAT WENT BUMP AT THE BEEB.

Something went bump in the night at the Beeb. It was a well-aimed left boot belonging to radio News reader James A. Gordon. He threw it at a ghost that appeared at his bedside in a room provided for night-shift news readers in The Langham, a BBC administration building.

Gordon fled clutching his trousers and right boot, and spent the rest of the night in his office across the road at Broadcasting House. None of his colleagues laughed when he told them about it - for two other news readers, Ray Moore and Peter Donaldson, admitted they have had the same experience. Moore says:"I have seen the figure twice, it is like a bright white light. It is a big thick-set man with his hands behind his back." Donaldson said;"I woke up to find a force trying to push me out of bed. The curtains were closed but there was a glowing light inside the room."

The Langham was once a hotel; parts of it are centuries old. The ghost is seen only on the third floor, where the overnight accommodation is. "The whole floor is very moody at night", said Ray Moore. "Two of the Commissionaires wont go near it after dark. Sometimes if you press the third floor lift button, it goes shooting up to the sixth. But only at night." Daily Mirror. 1 Aug 73.
Credit: BR Bates.

A GHOST WHO COMES TO DINNER.

When the dinner-party conversation dies at the Kensington Church Street house of Sue Griffiths, a model, it is because another guest has joined the party - a ghost she thinks she has in the house. Says Miss Griffiths, 21; "I've lived here for nine months and I've seen the ghost of a little girl dressed like Alice in Wonderland in a pinafore and petticoat. She's a very pleasant ghost and seems to like me, and a friend of mine, Maggie Mansfield, a model who used to live here too.

"During a meal we would often stop talking together and look at each other. If other people were there we wouldn't say anything, but if we were by ourselves, we would say 'She's here'. The other guests noticed nothing. At night she plays little tricks, like rotating the chandeliers or rattling a decoration of sea-shells. I have some toys and children's games in the house including my great grandmother's teddy-bear and some thimbles. I think she likes them. Most are in the spare room and while I'm there I get the strongest feelings of her presence."

Maggie Mansfield, 20, says:" When I was at a meal with Sue, I often felt that someone else was there. Not a creepy sensation. Just a pleasant awareness of someone else."

Sunday Express. 12 Aug 73.

`heavens above´

THE TUNGUSKA 'METEORITE'.

In a recent letter to the editor, Philip Ledger wrote:

'The Tunguska explosion of 1908 which destroyed forest over several hundred square kilometers of Siberian Taiga, has been attributed to many causes. Assumed at first to have been a meteorite, it soon became a lump of snow - an enormous block of ice - of iron - of rock - a comet (1) and, more recently, the explosive end of an unknown visitor from space (2). But now 'science' has at last given us a credible answer - it was a black hole from space (3). Yes, a hole weighing 10^{20} grams, and yet only millionths of a meter in diameter. Moreover, what goes in must come out, so the authors predict a smaller set of shock waves where the hole emerged from the earth'.

1) Zolotov, AV. (1967) Sov. Phys. Doklady, Vol.12. p108.
2) Von Daniken, E. (1969) Chariots of the Gods. p151.
3) Jackson, AA. & Ryan, MP. (1973) Nature. Sept. 14. Vol. 245. No.5420.

We also saw the following note in the Novosti Bulletin No. 14124. (1 Aug 73):

EXPEDITION CONTINUES STUDY OF 'TUNGUSKA METEORITE',

Expeditions of Tomsk University, the Astronomic and Geodetic Society and the Commission on Meteorites of the Siberian branch of the USSR Academy of Sciences, have started work near the settlement of Vanavara in the basin of the Podkamennaya Tunguska to continue studying the area that was hit by what has become known as the 'Tunguska Meteorite' on June 30, 1908.

Scientists have for a long time been trying to explain the fall of the 'meteorite' and its explosion, which had a force equal to that of several thermonuclear bombs. Many things still remain to be explained, but bit by bit expeditions which are continuing the work year by year are unravelling the mystery. It is believed now that it was not a meteorite but a small comet which disintegrated at a distance of several kilometers above the earth.

Scientists are studying a vast marsh south of the epicentre of the explosion where it is highly possible that fragments of the comet may be found.

A COMET FOR CHRISTMAS.

Scientists are thinking of sending an unmanned spacecraft to observe the new comet Kohoutek when it approaches the earth next Christmas. The comet is named after German astronomer Lubos Kohoutek of Hamburg who first spotted it as a smudge on a telescopic film more than 18 months ago. The comet is expected to be so bright when it arrives that it will be visible even in daylight when the sky is clear.

Astronomers reckon that it will be ten times brighter than any previously observed comet. Its tail they say could be up to 30 million miles long. Kohoutek is hurtling towards us at an estimated speed of 26 miles a second. The closest it will come to the earth (between December and January) will be 75 million miles; and it may be thousands of years before it reappears after a long looping journey through the solar system. In the hope of gaining close-up photographs and other scientific information reports Science Digest, American scientists are considering sending the spacecraft to rendezvous with the comet; perhaps even to run along with it for a while.

Sunday Express. 16 Sept 73.

hoaxes

SHOWPIECE RIDDLE OF WIRED-UP DAHLIAS.

Everything in the garden was lovely as the championship dahlia show reached its thrilling climax. First prize in the small cactus variety went to the breathtaking display by local Champion Cyril Gardiner. It was his third win in three years giving him the coveted trophy outright. Mr. Gardiner, of Birchwood Road, Bristol, left the West of England Dahlia Society Show at Plymouth with congratulations ringing in his ears.

Then a spectator accidentally brushed against one of the winning dahlias, and the head fell off revealing . . . a length of wire. Officials found that eleven more heads were supported by bits of wire stuck up their stems. Now the society has asked Mr. Gardiner to return all his trophies from this year's show. And it has asked the National Dahlia Society to ban him from all future contests.

A show spokesman said: "Anyone can turn dahlias into prize exhibits by putting wires up their stems. " He said wired dahlias had been found when the exhibits were cleared away after previous shows, but officials had been unable to trace the culprits.

Mr. Gardiner said last night: "I don't know anything about a wired dahlia at the show."

Daily Mirror. 31 Aug 73.

GHOST THAT KILLED.

Dusk was falling as the mourners gathered round the grave. As 67-year-old Boleslav Mierzkov was lowered in his coffin and the priest prayed, there was a sudden commotion.

In the dim light, a white figure seemed to rise from the grave, falter over the mourners and then vanish. Mierzkov's 62-year-old widow screamed and then dropped dead from fright. Police at Sosnowiek, Poland, however, refused to believe in ghosts, and started to search the cemetary. They soon found in the sexton's loft a life-sized doll dressed in a white sheet, together with 100 yards of nylon line.

The sexton told the police that Mierzkov's son-in-law, Wieslac Walczak, had paid him 2,000 zloty to work the trick at the funeral 'to teach his mother-in-law a lesson'. He was jailed for fifteen years.

Sunday Express. 16 Sept 73.

THE GREAT ATLANTIS SAGA - OR IS IT A HOAX?

The recent reports of the discovery of Atlantis by the Ancient Mediterranean Research Association (AMRA) has attracted widespread coverage and quite shameless hoots of derision from most quarters of the press, who nevertheless have pursued the story relentlessly. The News is able to offer the following condensed sequence of events from its files which (it is hoped) may place the story into some kind of perspective.

The news of the expedition broke on the 6 July, as the AMRA team headed by Mrs Maxine Asher leave New York en route to Cadiz. The Daily Mail of that date quotes Mrs Asher: "I simply know we will find it because I am psychic. O God, how strong the vibrations are these days." 42-year-old Mrs Asher, reportedly a teacher at Peppardine University, Los Angeles, hocked her family jewels for £30,000 to float the expedition. Most of the 70 members of her team are supposed to be psychic also, and have donated about £1000 each, and been promised 6 credits for the six week expedition.

Those readers who are aquainted with Fort's 'LO!', will know the great suspicion he cast on scientific discoveries which were found in the place predicted. Perhaps Mrs. Asher really did precognize the site of her Atlantis, or see it clairvoyantly; we would like to remain openminded about it in principle. However, the papers (eg. Daily Mail) announce, almost ten days later; 'Found - Lost City of Atlantis', on the 18 July. Evidence of roads and columns were said to have been found 'in the exact place described by the Greek philosopher Plato'. The expedition co-director, Dr. Julian Nava, Professor of History, California State University, says no more details would be given until underwater photos could be studied by the team.

Next comes a brief and emphatic UPI note in the Observer on the 22 July: That the Spanish police have stepped in and halted everything. The AMRA team are said to 'claim to have photographed the roads, columns and walls, 95 feet down and 14-16 miles out from the Spanish coast'. Oh yes. It also says that Atlantis vanished 14,000 years ago.

In the Daily Mail for July 30 is a feature by Jane Gaskell, who puts the cataclysm date at 11,000 years ago. She gives the interesting information

that Dr. Egerton Sykes, the 'tall, snow-haired, vigorous' 78-year-old British archaeologist, is in Cadiz 'now' to observe what transpires. The Spanish officials are being difficult because the diving-permits were 'incorrectly applied for' and insist anyway, that 'it is impossible for the team to have found anything new. It is well known the area here is full of Roman remains. Dr. Sykes is said to believe that what is being found is far older. "The water level here changed about 8000 years ago, and obviously before that, this large village or city was already here, or in a well-advanced state." But he goes on to caution: "All this need be nothing to do with Atlantis." There is also the additional information, via Mrs. Asher again, that the columns posess 'strange rubrics'.

The denouement comes from a (justifiably) cynical piece in Newsweek for 6 August. Mrs. Asher is described as a 'part-time mystic...who dabbled in parapsychic phenomena' and 'decided the search for the Lost Continent was her mission in life after a book on Atlantis tumbled from her bookshelf during a 1971 earthtremor.' Julian Nava is reported to have quit, two days into the expedition; and Pepparding University is revealed as a small Los Angeles liberal-arts college. Besides the 25 students at $2000 each, 'she enlisted (at $2800 apiece) two dozen mid-fortyish divorcees and widows anxious for a summer of cultural enrichment and adventure.' Well, they got it allright. When the highly skeptical Spanish Government stepped in - Mrs. Asher vanished.

In Cadiz, an expedition spokesman, John Sims, admitted to Newsweek reporter Scott Sullivan that the discovery was an 'illusion'. 'Her original story had been that, on July 18, 3 members of the team diving 14 miles off Cadiz, found signs of ancient streets and broken columns. At first Sims stuck to this story. But Olga Vallespin, a young archaeologist assigned by the Spanish Ministry of Education told Sullivan that she doubted the divers had made the alleged descent. A student then said she saw the press release two days before the alleged find was made.' And for those who are interested in such things, the name AMRA figures strongly in the 'sword & sorcery' fictions of the late Robert E Howard set in the antideluvian era of Atlantis and Valusia.

'As for the irrepressible Mrs, Asher, when tracked down by Newsweek in Dublin, she refused to discuss the students she had left behind in Spain. Mrs. Asher merely stated she was preparing to leave for the west coast of Ireland with a new group of 20 Irish students - to continue her search for Atlantis.' (Credit for most items: Steve Moore.)

No promises - but, keep watching this space.

human curiosities

BRITAIN'S SMALLEST WOMAN DIES.

Miss Joyce Carpenter, known as Britain's smallest woman, died at her home at Bromsgrove today. She had been very ill for some time, said her brother.

Miss Carpenter, who was 43, and who led a very active life, was only 29 inches in height. About two years ago she passed her driving test in a specially converted car. At Easter, she drove to Weston-super-mare and back to her home in Grafton Crescent on the Charford Estate in her Mini. Miss Carpenter used to drive to many parts of the country in her capacity as a member of the Small Peoples Association.

She had an interest in the arts and crafts, and was a leader of a Brownie Group. A funeral service is to take place at St. Andrew's Church Charford, at 11 am on Friday.

Birmingham Evening Mail. 7 Aug 73.

DOCTORS FIGHT FOR WOLFBOY.

Doctors are fighting a tough battle to bring a little boy back to civilisation after living most of his life among wild animals. The boy, aged about six, was found by a shepherd in a cave in the rugged Abruzzi mountains in Central Italy. He walked on all fours and bit anyone who came near him. And doctors at Milan hospital think he may have been suckled by wolves. Attempts to trace his mother failed, and two attempts to civilise him in foster-homes ended in disaster.

Sun. 15 Aug 73.

Shortly before, another wolfboy was discovered in Ceylon - or rather, a monkeyboy (see the Sunday Mirror. 24 June 73). Then both cases were discussed in an article by Peter Watson in the Sunday Times:

THE NEW 'WOLF CHILDREN'.

After an interval of twelve years, 1973 is turning out to be another year for a curious anthropological event - the discovery of 'wolf-children'. They are young children found living in the wild in remote areas, allegedly brought up, in some cases even suckled, by wild animals. Since 1344, when the first case was formally recorded, there have been 53 such children, allegedly reared by everything from wolves and bears to   leopards and panthers. The last case (a gazelle-child) was in 1961.

This year has already seen two. In June, a boy aged about 12 was found living with monkeys in the jungles of southern Sri Lanka (Ceylon). He was named Tissa after the village near where he was found. The boy cannot speak, but barks and yelps, crawls on all fours, and when at ease, reclines in a monkey-like posture. And last week Italian paediatricians and psychiatrists have debated whether Rocco (named after the rocky crag in the Abruzzi mountains where he was found) really was brought up by wolves. He too is speechless, grunts in a 'half-wolf, half-goat' way, and bites and claws at anyone who shows him affection.

Exotic as these children are, there is considerable doubt as to whether these 'animal' characteristics are really animal at all. Wolf children seem to be of three basic types. There are those who are mentally deficient and often physically handicapped as well. Usually, it seems, they have been abandoned by their parents when they find their child too much of a handful. These children spend little time in the wild - they would be incapable of surviving for very long. They walk on all fours, not because they are imitating animals they have lived with, but because their bones allow them to walk no other way. The same applies with their speech: they have small brains and so are capable of only monosyllabic grunts and growls.

There are also those suffering from a very ill-understood ailment, early childhood autism. Probably in these cases the parents just do not know what is wrong with their child and again it is abandoned. Severely autistic children in Britain will crawl around on all fours, grunt or growl, and even eat their food on the floor, animal-like. But in their case there is no known reason why they do this: they have the physical equipment to behave normally. But mentally retarded and autistic wolfchildren rarely change their habits once back in civilisation, and this suggests that their 'animal' qualities are something they were born with and not due to their experience in the wild.

Possibly most interesting are those who were abandoned, not because of something wrong with them, but because their parents for economic or emotional reasons of their own, simply cannot cope with children. In these cases it seems that the children really may live in close proximity to, if not actually with, wild animals and imitate their habits. Two Indian children, for example, discovered living near wolves some years ago, always slept curled over one another. Quite often such children develop superb physical skills. A Syrian gazelle-child discovered by a local prince on a hunting party, was said to be capable of running at 50 mph with the gazelles. He also had superb eyesight and very acute hearing.

These children, although they may not be able to talk when found, who may even lap milk from a plate like a dog, readily adapt to civilisation and do learn how to talk, eat and wear clothes, sometimes within months. Unfortunately, both Tissa and Rocco appear to be mentally retarded.

Stunday Times. 26 Aug 73.
Credit: Steve Moore.

THE OLD LADY WHO HASN'T SLEPT IN 30 YEARS.

For more than 30 years a little old lady in a Spanish village has gone without sleep. In that time she has never dozed for a second, nor gone to bed, but has still managed to stay healthy.

Now her husband's recent death and a growing nervous frustration had led an eminent surgeon to appeal to specialists in London and New York to help her.

The sad case of Señora Ines Fernandez, 57, started on a warm afternoon on July 8, 1943. She was standing at the door of her cottage in Sierra de Fuentes, near Caceras, south-west Spain, watching a religious procession. "I suddenly yawned and a searing pain went through my head, " she says, "And since then I have never slept. I have taken thousands of pills and medicines and consulted many doctors, but nothing has been of any use.

"There were long agonising nights sitting in my armchair next to the bed watching my husband sleep soundly. Now he's gone and I can't stand the terrifying lonliness of the night."

Señora Fernandez always changes into a white dressing gown at nights - but only to sit in the chair with her feet on a stool clutching a rosary. She used to embroider and read but now even that is gone because of her poor eyesight. "I just pray for the morning when daylight comes and I can do my work." She runs a nursery from her home and takes in 20 children a day.

In her 30 years without sleep she has been treated by Dr. Padlos Abril, a neuro-surgeon. He says: "I have never known a case like this. I now think an operation would be useful but it would have to be in England or America where such specialist clinics exist."

The Doctor describes her condition as chronic colesistites and total insomnia. He said the sleep section of the brain appears to be permanently impaired.

Robin Chapman, science correspondent, writes: A London doctor said that cases of this kind were extremely rare. The cause was probably of psychological origin rather than due to any physical illness. But it could be cured by a brain operation.

Sunday Express. 26 Aug 73.

RIP VAN JOE GOES ZZZZZ AND HIS WIFE CALLS 999.

Crane driver Joe Green's 40 winks in the sunshine turned into a nightmare yesterday - for his wife. After missing his lift to work, Joe, of Valley Road, Pudsey, Yorkshire, sat for a while on his garden wall. But he fell into a snooze and keeled over on to the lawn. And there he stayed.

When his wife Alice tried to rouse him he just slept on and on and on. Even the neighbours couldn't rouse him. So, thinking that Joe might have collapsed ill, Alice dialled 999. But the ambulancemen who dashed to the scene got a ticking off from Joseph for waking him up.

An ambulance spokesman said: "We received an emergency call to the house, but he was found only to be sleeping, and was rather annoyed because we disturbed his slumber. Said Joseph: "My wife often has trouble waking me even in the mornings. I could sleep even on a clothesline."

Daily Express. 8 June 73.

Senora Fernandez should have his troubles. We have no room here but with reference to Joe's statement about sleeping on a clothesline, we shall see in the next issue a story of a man who slept on a tightrope 82ft up.

A GIRL GULPS DOWN A FORK.

Waitress Pat Yearsley had a tickle in her throat. So she tried to scratch it with a dinner fork. Then, gulp ... she swallowed the eight inch fork. Pat, 20, who works at the Trefeddian Hotel, Aberdovey, Merioneth, said yesterday: "Everybody thought I was joking. Even the hospital doctors did not believe it at first. Then they took an X-ray and realised I was not having them on.

Then doctors operated on Pat, from Widnes, Lancs, to remove the fork, and she spent 11 days in the hospital. Now Pat has an eight inch scar across her stomach. But she was not allowed to keep the fork. She said: "The surgeon wanted it for his private museum. He said he was frightened I might swallow it again."

Sun. 24 Sept 73.

MAN IMPALED.

A man impaled through the throat when he fell from the balcony of his home in Pimlico, London, was 'satisfactory' in hospital last night.

Sun. 28 May 73.

NAKED TARZAN IS CAUGHT.

A real life Tarzan has been captured in an African game reserve. Rangers swooped at dawn on the naked man's tree lair in Tanzania's lion-infested Mikumi Reserve. They found him whimpering like an animal. He was unable to talk. This mysterious man who had defied several previous capture attempts, had apparently lived in harmony with the park's animals, living on berries and fruit. Now he is being kept in a cell while police try to identify him.

Daily Mirror. 7 Jan 1969. (?).
Credit: A Smith.

jinxes & curses

CHURCH CURSE WILL HOUND IVORY THIEF.

The Rev. Harold Cheales devised an unusual way of preventing valuable objects in his church from being stolen. He placed a curse on them.

The 62-year-old Rector placed the curse earlier this year from the pulpit of the Church of St. Laurence at Wyck Rissington (pop. 160) near Cheltenham, Glos, to render its victim accident prone and bring him nothing but bad luck. Only if the thief returns the object can the curse be lifted. Mr. Cheales said:" Thefts from churches have become very widespread lately, although it had not happened here before. However I decided to take precautions, and included a curse against anyone stealing from this church. Now someone has taken the ivory

carving depicting two angels taking the body
of Christ down from the Cross. It is about 10
in. high and 4 in. across. He would be well
advised to return it quickly.

"What makes it specially interesting is that it
must be one of the largest lumps of ivory in
the world. No animal alive today could yield
that much, and is thought to have come from the
tusk of a frozen mammoth. It was insured for a
nominal £50, however its true value may well
run into thousands of pounds." The rector
used a little known service for the first day of
of Lent called 'Commination' which contains
10 curses against wrongdoers and allows the
priest to add a few of his own.

Could the curse cause the death of its victim?
Mr. Cheales said :"It will not cause harm in
that sense. His death would undo the whole
point of the curse which is to give him a
chance to put things right. I have had much
experience lifting evil curses from people who
are the victims of witchcraft cults. I myself
would never be vindictive like that. But I
certainly believe these curses work". A Church
of England spokesman at Church House, Westminster, said: "It is very rare for the 'Commination' service to be used now. In fact we have
never heard of its happening before."

Sunday Express. 2 Sept 73.

SIKH SAYS: "I'LL BEHEAD THUGS."

Vandals who wrecked a Sikh temple in Glasgow for
the second time in two days received a dire warning yesterday. Mr. Pritan Singh, an ex-Indian
Army colonel, said: "I will be there every night,
and if these infidels return I will cut off
their heads. They will be dealt with in the
normal manner. Their headless bodies will drape
the trees surrounding the temple."

Daily Mirror. 11 Aug 73.

lightning

LIGHTNING KILLS 3.

Lagos, Friday. - Three evangelists were struck
dead by lightning during a service.

Daily Express. 22 Sept 73.

LIGHTNING BLAST KILLS GOLFER. (1).

A golfer was killed, and six others injured,
when lightning blasted a tree as they sheltered
from a storm yesterday. The dead man, Mr.
Michael Poole, 50, of Wellington Road, Taunton,
was playing at the local Vivary Park course.

His six companions were knocked unconscious by
the blast. They are recovering in hospital. One
of them, Mr. David Whiting, 25, said last night:
"We were standing under a tree laughing and
joking. The next thing I remember was a flash.
I came to lying on the ground paralysed. People
were lying all around me, including the dead
man. My mate Jim Hardie got up and pulled us
away and someone tried the kiss of life on the
chap who died."

Daily Express. 28 Aug 73.

GOLFER WHO WAS STRUCK BY LIGHTNING DIES. (2).

A golfer who was struck by lightning on a Birmingham golf course a fortnight ago has died in
hospital from his injuries. Robert Broadmore,
18-year-old assistant professional at Harborne
Golf Course, was struck as he was walking along
the fairway of the 12th hole. His home was in
Chase Grove, Erdington.

Sunday Mercury. 30 Sept 73.

Some however are luckier...

FAMOUS CONDUCTOR.

Park Ranger Roy C Sullivan of Virginia, has been
on the phone to the Guinness Book of Records.
They'd better make a fast revision, he said, as
he'd just been hit by lightning for the fifth
time. As the most lightning-struck person in
the world, Mr. Sullivan has a reputation to
keep up.

Daily Mail. 28 Aug 73.
Credit: Steve Moore.

'mass hysteria'

SCHOOL HIT BY MYSTERY BUG.

A mystery illness which hit a school's pupils
and staff yesterday is being investigated by
health officials.

Seven teachers and 135 children stayed away
from Hinchley Wood primary school at Esher,
Surrey, after being taken ill in the night.
Headmaster Bill Kinnock said last night: "The
illness is peculiar in that it seems to be
restricted to my school. No one at the Secondary School next door has been affected.

"It has nothing to do with school meals, which
come from the secondary school's canteen. And a
lot of the children taken ill do not stay for
lunch. The local Medical Officer sent his Inspector who will spend the weekend trying to find
the cause. He believes that it is a virus and I

hope it is one that lasts for only 24 hours."

Daily Mirror. 31 March 73.

TUMMY BUG HITS 10,000 A DAY IN NAVY CITY.

Doctors are baffled by a mysterious bug affecting up to 10,000 a day in Britain's biggest naval base.

It causes severe stomach pains, sickness, diarrhoea and headache. "The sum total of human discomfort it causes must be considerable," said a health official at Portsmouth.

So far scientists have made hundreds of tests with no result. They've attempted to grow the bug in laboratory samples and failed. "We've investigated every one of the saner theories put up by the public," the official said. "We have established it's not the water - and we're pretty certain it didn't come from abroad."

The plague has been raging since the start of the summer. Portsmouth City Health Dept believe that up to 5% of the population is affected at any one time. It is hoped that the outbreak will die away naturally. Sufferers are being advised not to handle food and to drink a lot of liquid - but not alcohol or fizzy drinks.

Shellfish imported from Japan were blamed for a similar outbreak which hit the Christchurch area of the South Coast last month.

Sunday Mirror. 12 Aug 73.

HOLIDAYMAKERS TOLD OF MYSTERY BUG.

BY Michael Jeffries.

An epidemic of gastro-enteritis - source unknown - is hitting parts of South East Hampshire on a serious scale. At Portsmouth, where 600 new cases are being reported each week, it is believed to have contributed to the deaths of four people.

Cases are occurring in areas around the city such as Gosport, Fareham and Havant. The disease has mystified local health authorities who have appealed to the Department of Health and the public to help find the cause. Holidaymakers and visitors to the city should be on the alert. The disease, which can be caused by food poisoning, produces symptoms of acute stomach pains, sore throat, diarrhoea and vomiting. Dr. Peter Roads, Portsmouth's Medical Officer of Health,said:"If people develop serious symptoms they should go directly to their doctor."

London Evening News. 31 Aug 73.

SCHOOLCHILDREN HIT BY A MYSTERY BUG.

A mystery bug is giving Britain's schoolchildren hand, foot and mouth disease, a health watchdog body reported yesterday. The disease causes painful ulcers around the mouth and on the hands and feet said the Public Health Laboratory Service. In a warning to all doctors, they said that the disease may be more widespread than the 107 cases so far confirmed.

The counties hardest hit are Norflok, Somerset and Gloucestershire. One primary school had 11 of its 200 pupils go down with the disease. The Service group also asked doctors to help track down another mystery bug which is hitting the Portsmouth area. They have called it the X Bug and it causes diarrhoea and vomiting. A party of women who went on a day trip to Portsmouth were all struck down by the X Bug nineteen days later.

Daily Mirror. 3 Sept 73.

occult crimes

Several times in his four books, Charles Fort brought himself up and said that (unfortunately) he had no time to develop an 'Occult Criminology'. The News has decided to give the idea room to develop and will be publishing anything 'suspicious'.

£250,000 PAINTING RIDDLE.

A painting worth nearly £250,000 has disappeared without trace. The picture, a Degas showing a group of women washing clothes, was aboard a Swissair flight from London to Zurich. But when agents went to collect the painting, which is about three feet square, it could not be found.

Hurried checks were made at the airline and with London. Scotland Yard's art squad was instantly alerted. Widespread inquiries by airport police failed to produce anyone who had seen it. A spokesman for the agents said last night:" As far as we can discover, it was loaded on the plane. It did go."

Sunday Mirror. 24 June 73.

INVISIBLE GIANT.

Thieves at Lutterworth made a slow getaway yesterday - in a 16 ton bright yellow mechanical digger they stole from a building site. But nobody saw them go.

Daily Express. 7 Feb 73.

plant curiosities

SECRET ORCHIDS.

Ten thousand wild orchids have been found growing wild in a disused iron-ore quarry near Melton Mowbray, Leicestershire. Naturalists are keeping the location a secret.

Daily Express. 19 Sept 73.

poltergeists

FAMILY FLEE FROM 'GHOST'.

A frightened family quit their council flat yesterday - because of ghosts. Steelworker Arthur Allan, his wife Jennifer, and their three children walked out of their Middlesborough, Teeside, flat. Mr. Allan, 26, claimed the place was gripped by a magnetic force which had sent him crashing through a glass door.

The Sun. 27 July 73.

ripley or not!

COUNTRY CASHES IN ON SCUM.

A hidden word is pushing up the price of 50 rupee banknotes in the Seychelles. A joker has written the word 'scum' into the design - making them collectors pieces.

Sun. 24 Sept 73.

UNCLE CHAO STRIKES AGAIN.

The Academy of Liars will celebrate its 225th anniversary next month in the tiny village of Moncrabeau, in south west France, where it was founded by an imaginative old monk. A grand competition is planned. All entrants will tell a story and villagers will judge which one is the most outrageous, and the winner will be crowned 'King of Liars'.

Daily Mail. 9 July 73.
Credit: Steve Moore.

FORE....AND PLONG!

Golfers Mrs. Vivienne Berry, 60, and Les Johns, 63, both holed in one on the same day at the same par-3 second hole at Bridport and West Dorset golf club.

Sunday Express. 26 Aug 73.

scientific curiosities

VOLCANO ERUPTS AFTER 160 YEAR REST.

Mysterious black dust which descended on a Japanese fishing boat near the Kurile Islands came from a volcano which erupted for the first time in 160 years, the meteorological agency reported in Tokio today. The magnetic black dust alarmed the fishermen when it fell from a dark cloud about 40 miles long and 3 miles wide.

The volcano, on the southern Kurile island of Kunashiri, between Japan and the Soviet Union, erupted on Friday night. Its last reported eruption was in 1812. The Soviet news agency Tass said yesterday that the volcano, named Tyatya, belched flames and showered surrounding areas with stones and ash, causing nearby settlements to be evacuated.

Express & Star. 16 July 73.
Credit: A Smith.

FANCY THAT.

The faithful at St. Augustine's were baffled by a phantom organist who played every day except the Sabbath. The 'ghost' was traced to a Royal Navy radar beam from nearby Yeovilton, Somerset. It was tuned in to the electric organ - but switched off every Sunday.

Daily Express. 5 Sept 73.

VOLCANIC ACID LAKE.

Soviet scientists have begun exploring a volcanic lake which is filled with a mixture of sulphuric, hydrofluoric and hydrochloric acids and not water. This is believed to be the strangest and most dangerous lake on the Kamchatka peninsula and it lies in the crater of the Maly Semyachik volcano. Its stony shores are 200 metres high and the lake can only be reached with the help of a rope.

There is absolutely no vegetation around the crater because of the suffocating gasses escaping from it. The scientists have to work in gas masks. They sail on the acid-filled lake in rubber boats which, however, soon become unfit for use.

The lake is 140 metres deep. Hot acid keeps com coming up from its bottom. The golden film collected from its surface becomes a piece of sulphur when wrung out and it instantly blazes up when taken near a fire.

Novosti Information Service Bulletin 14225. 29 Aug 73.

NEW SPECIES OF FLIES.

The 200 horseflies in the San Francisco office of Cornelius Philip are welcome visitors. Mr. Philip is a tabanidologist who has found 250 previously unknown species in a 50-year career. He says :"It's like stamp collecting. You try to find somebody who has one you want and do a trade."

Daily Express. 1 Sept 73.

ufos

IT'S UFO TIME again in the deep South and non-sceptics should make their way to Sandersville, Georgia, where our friends have been showing up with almost monotonous regularity. Some are red, some are green, some blue and gold. But none it seems actually wants to set foot on our planet. I don't blame them, although astronaut Pete Conrad says he's sure they are benign.

Daily Mail. 8 Sept 73.
Credit: Steve Moore.

TROOPS FLEE AS SAUCER DIVES.

Two American military policemen saw a 'flying-saucer' swoop down on their car in Savannah, Georgia - then it chased them as they fled back to base. The UFO had flashing lights and dived to tree-top level, said the patrolmen. Later police in nearby Manchester also said they saw it.

Daily Mirror. 10 Sept 73.

witches, etc.

NEW TALE OF THE SALEM WITCHES.

Witchcraft hysteria swept the Massachusetts seaport of Salem nearly 3 centuries ago. Now the witchtrial evidence, which sent 20 people to their death, is finally being published. An old English record of courtroom testimony details the fear that gripped the village in 1692, when teen-aged girls said they had been put under spells. Within a year, 19 people had been hanged and one crushed to death.

The formal charge against the accused witches was the practice of 'certain detestable arts called witchcraft and sorcery wickedly, maliciously and feloniously used, practised and exercised at and in the town of Salem.' Included in the trial records is Benjamin Hutchinson's statement that his wife was tortured by a witch.

"My wife was much afflicted after the last execution with violent pains in her heart and teeth and all parts of her body, she being in such excessive misery that she said she believed she had a spell cast upon her. Whereupon I went to Mary Walcott, one of our neighbours, to come and look to see if she could see anybody upon her; as soon as she came into the house she said that our two neighbours - Sarah Buckley and Mary Whitheridge - were upon my wife; and immediately my wife had ease and Mary Walcott was tormented."

Mary Walcott, aged 16 at the time, was one of the group of teenage girls who would scream, cry and go into convulsions, claiming they were being attacked by invisible witches. The girls later named the witches as friends and neighbours ranging in age from a child of 5 to a grandmother.

Express & Star. 14 July 73.
Credit: A Smith.

WITCHES KILLED MY CAT, SAYS POP STAR.

A pop star is threatening legal action against a witches' coven because his cat was killed in a sacrificial ritual. And last night the leader of the witches admitted: "We killed the cat - we thought it was a stray."

Animal-lover Long John Baldry lost his two year old tabby, Stupzi, over a week ago. Now he has discovered it was the victim of a weird Ceremony of the New Moon, in Highgate Woods, North London.

Said the 6ft. 7in. tall singer at his home in Muswell Hill, London, last night:" This lot needs locking up. If the police and animal organisations are not prepared to take legal action, I will prosecute them myself."

The witches claim that killing the cat was a necessary part of the ritual as a sign of homage to their deity. Said 33-year-old David Farrant, president of the British Occult Society:" Shedding blood is essential and it was dabbed on the forehead of the eight witches present. We have used many cats in the past and will do so in the future, no matter what the outcome of this incident. I know it sounds ridiculous, but I am also an animal lover at heart."

Daily Express. 7 Sept 73.

You're right Mr. Farrant, it does sound ridiculous. The corrolary of Fortean studies seems, inescapably, the formidable chronicles of human foolishness in all its wide variety - but we publish the stories for whatever we find in them - and it is our feeling that the children in the next story display the only sane attitude to it all:

UNLUCKY 13th FOR WITCHES.

A Friday the thirteenth duel between two witches featuring a ceremonial cat sacrifice was banished by the powers of the Police and RSPCA.

One witch was seen running away from Hampstead Heath pursued by hundreds of laughing children. The other witch didn't turn up.

Sunday Mirror. 15 April 73.

news

FAR-SIGHTED LECTURES.

Local authority-sponsored lectures on UFOs start today at Bournemouth where a council spokesman said: "There is tremendous interest in UFOs - it's time to take them seriously."

Daily Express. 17 Sept 73.

THAT'S THE SPIRIT.

A course on haunted houses and hiding holes is being organised at Pendrell Hall, near Wolverhampton, by the Staffordshire County Council college of adult education.

Daily Express. 19 Sept 73.

LETTERS

From next issue on, we hope to be carrying a letter column - so please write, at the very least, about any way that the News could be more helpful or interesting. We are eager to help in any way on private research, and will publish short notices from readers wanting specific aid or information, freely, as long as it is reasonably short and to the point. We will endeavour to do our best on readers queries though we claim no infallibility.

All letters to the editor will be considered for publication (or parts thereof) unless the author specifically states his wish against it.

THE NEWS

ᴛʜᴇ ɴᴇᴡs vol. 1. no. 2. JAN. 1974

THE NEWS is a non-profit-making bi-monthly miscellany of
Fortean news and notes. Edited and published by Robert JM
Rickard,(with an arrangement with INFO.) - 31 Kingswood
Road, Moseley, Birmingham B13 9AN. *@*@*@*@*@*@*@*@*@*@
Single issues - 35p. 6 issue sub. £1.80. or $4.50. POs &
Cheques payable to RJM Rickard, please, not the NEWS.

Yesterdays news tomorrow!

APPLAUSE...APPLAUSE...

NEWS 1 seems to have gone down well with you
all. Many thanks to all those who have written,
alas time does not permit a reply to each one.
We need more subscribers if we are to cover the
cost of a year's issues - simple economics - we
are not yet out of the woods. So if you know
any potential Fortean - beat him into subscription.

THE HAUNTED TYPEWRITER.

No prizes for those who spotted all the mistakes
and typoes in the last ish. which apart from our
pet gremlin in the machine, was the unfortunate
byproduct of our unholy impatience to see the
end result and sudden blackouts while typing.
We never did pay much attention to the 'Improve
your wordpower' page of the old Readers Digest
- but we're a dab-hand at lame excuses.

CATEGORIES ? ARTICLES ? OR FEATURES?

We have been keeping back a few notes on falls
of chunks of ice from the sky with the intention of making the category more substantial. It
will appear next ish. But this has caused us to
reflect on the feature Vs the notes as they
come in one by one. The former is something you
can get your teeth into; the latter is likely
to be more 'up to date'. But then since our
schedule has a built-in editorial and printing
delay of 4 - 8 weeks, does 'currency' really
matter? Please let us know what you think.

In this issue we print a short piece by Nigel
Watson on anomalous phenomena on the moon. For
those not familiar with such things, here is an
introduction. Hardened Forteans will be interested in the reply by the librarian of the Royal
Astronomical Society to Mr. Watson's inquiry
about one of Charles Fort's data sources. We
heartily welcome researches like this, and can
only exhort our readers to feverish curiosity
and to look into local events - we will give
their work a hearing.

Further to all this, we observe that coverage of
professional and learned journals is conspicuous by its absence from the NEWS so far. The
popular impression that the newspapers and scan-
dal-rags were Fort's major source is a complete

Cover by Lynne
Willey depicting
'The Ghost of
Christmas Presents.'

fallacy. Analysis of his sources shows that the
much greater majority were culled from 'respectable' periodicals. Well..our record on this has
been sadly lacking (not that we have any urge to
become 'respectable'— whatever that is!) and we
urge our readers to keep an eye on the journals
pertinent to their professions, or any they run
into in their work.

INFO.

It wasn't made clear, or stated in our colophon
last issue, but we are forging a strong working
relationship with the International Fortean
Organisation (INFO) who are the only and legit-
imate successors to the original (now defuct)
Fortean Society. The NEWS was primarily conceived
to supplement the excellent INFO Journal in reportage of local and current notes etc, and a deal
less formal. It is not aimed at INFO members but
Forteans everywhere - We'll see how things go,
since there is quite a lot of potential in the
air.

SPECIAL CHRISTMAS MESSAGE.

By superhuman effort we are bringing forward the
schedule on this issue - not because of any
sound and practical reason - but simply because
we wanted our cover - rendered for us by Lynne
Willey - to remain, to some degree, topical by
the time you receive it. Referring to the above
paragraph on being more particular about our
sources and data - we can only give here an
appropriate quote from the man himself:

'I say to myself: "You are a benign ghoul, digging up dead old legends and superstitions, trying to breathe life into them, well then, why
have you neglected Santa Claus?" But I'm particular in the matter of data, or alleged data.
I have come upon no record, or alleged record
of mysterious footprints in snow, on roofs of
houses, leading to chimneys, Christmas Eves.'
LO! XIII.

Skyward Ho! (But keep dodging the ice chunks).

NOTES
appearances

MYSTERY OF 250 FISH IN AN OLD TANK.

A few old bicycles and the odd waterlogged boot
were all the firemen expected to find in the
water tank they had been sent to empty in a town
centre. Instead they found something much more
lively - 250 plump roach and perch, happily
swimming about in the 40 ft. wide tank, a relic
of wartime fire precautions.

They couldn't leave them in a tank without water
- so the firemen scooped them into a dustbin.
Then leading Firemen Collin Caswell and Ken Major
went back after work to the dustbin in Albert St.
Redditch, Worcs and dragged it half a mile to a
pond, where they let the fish go. But how the
fish got into the tank was still a mystery last
night. Collin said: "All we can think is that
someone dropped in a couple of fish years ago and
they bred from them."

Daily Mirror. 30 Aug 1968.
Credit: A Smith.

It would appear that there is much tooing and
froing in the universe. Fort postulated some
teleportative force that responded to a need or
that made provisions for future needs. If this
is so then we observe that the sentience is of a
different order and akin to that of an idiot,
albeit a cosmic one. In some future issue we
shall open the file on the elusive pumas, wild
boars, exotic birds of Surrey, Sussex and Hampshire. In the meantime, see also our Disappearance
category.

archaeology

THE DAGGER MAN.

A man's skeleton, believed to be over 2600 years
old, has been found in a shallow grave at South-
wick, near Oundle, Northamptonshire. A dagger
was in his right hand. The legbones of a sheep
were also in the grave.

Sunday Times. 14 Oct 73.

Following the Cyclops sensation (see News 1.) we
were half expecting news of a Satyr.

deaths & bodies

DEATH RIDDLE OF LAST SNAP.

A new mystery has developed over nurse Philippa
Coon, said to have drowned herself in India.
Eight months after her reported death the Foreign
Office have sent her parents a photograph alleg-
ed to be of Philippa. But her mother, Mrs Olive
Coon, said yesterday: "There is no doubt in my
mind that the photograph is not of my daughter.
The bone structure of the face is different and
the body is of a different build."

Her husband Laurie added: "Effects alleged to be

our daughter's do not appear to be hers, and a
ring just wouldn't fit her fingers. We have told
officials that the photograph is not that of our
daughter but they appear to have ignored us."

Philippa's parents of Braemar Crescent, Leigh-on-
sea, Essex, were told of her death in February.
Suicide was only mentioned to them after Philipp-
a's body was cremated. Mr. Coon, chief tax acc-
ountant for a big firm, has called in a private
detective, and Mrs. Jean Leach, a medium.

News of the World. 30 Sept 73.

MYSTERY OVER BURIAL AT SEA.

A woman whose body was found off a crowded holiday beach was still unidentified last night, despite a big police investigation. Tests showed
that the woman died from natural causes and had
been enbalmed to be buried at sea. But the police
want to know how her coffin came open and which
ship 'buried' the body so close inshore. Fishermen found the woman, aged about 40, on Tuesday
6 miles off Seaford, near Newhaven, Sussex.

Daily Mirror. 5 July 73.

DEATH VERDICT.

Police yesterday announced that a tramp found
with serious head injuries in a churchyard off
Whitechapel Road, Stepney, London probably died
'accidentally'.

Daily Express. 1 Oct 73.

BODY IN CELLAR.

Police were yesterday trying to identify the body
of a young girl found in the cellar of an empty
house. Murder is not suspected.

Sunday People. 30 Sept 73.

WOMAN IN SEA

An unidentified woman was found dead in the sea
yesterday off Meadfoot Beach, Torquay.

Daily Express. 6 Oct 73.

RIDDLE OF THE BODY IN GIRL'S BED.

The widow of a man found dead in 16-year-old
Moira Cleland's bed, said: "I'm not satisfied
with the inquiries into his death." Three mysteries confront the police. 24-year-old chef Thomas Law died from an overdose of sleeping pills
belonging to the girl's mother. Yet, according to
his widow, Gladys, 23, he could not stand drugs
in any form. He would not even take aspirin.

Secondly; a bottle the pills were taken from had
just two fingerprints on it - both Mr. Law's. Yet
the girl's mother said the bottle had previously
been handled so much it should have had 'a load
of fingerprints on it'. The inquest was told by
a police sergeant that prints could have been
put on it after the death, though that was thought unlikely.

The third riddle is that the bottle was emptied
yet was found after Mr. Law's death in its usual
place in the mother's room.

Mrs Law said that she and her husband had a minor argument at the Devon Coast Country Club holiday camp near Paignton. He refused to come to bed and went back to the club. Later he left with Mrs Cleland and her daughter; they went back to the staff premises where they woke up Mrs Cleland's common law husband, Bernard Sime. Law went to sleep on their bedroom floor, and the couple went to a spare room. The inquest heard that Mr. Law woke up, dressed and went to Moira's room.

She says: "I didn't sleep with him. He just wanted to talk." She then went to the other room leaving him in hers. In the morning he was found dead. Mrs. Cleland said: "Honest to God we had nothing to do with Tommy's death. The sleeping tablets were mine, but I don't know how he got to take them. The police gave me a rough time." A police spokesman said: "We have turned this case over and over and we are still puzzled."

News of the World. 28 Oct 73.

SISTER' DEATH PLUNGE.

An airline stewardess and her sister yesterday plunged to their deaths from the seventh-floor window of their New York hotel room. Police said they were searching for the elder sister's boy-friend.

Sunday Mercury. 21 Oct 73.

BRIDEGROOM DIES AT HIS OWN STAG PARTY.

Senior Aircraftman Ian Woodward, a 6ft.3in., 23-year-old rugby player, died suddenly during a stag party at RAF Lyneham, Wilts.

Daily Express. 27 Oct 73.

WIFE FOUND DEAD IN BATH.

An inquest will be held on Mrs. Jenowefa Jabczynski, aged 51, who was found dead about 8.30 am. yesterday in the bath at her School Road home, Hall Green, Birmingham, by her husband. She went to have a bath around 12.30 am. When she was found, the taps were still running. A police spokesman said there did not appear to be any suspicious circumstances.

Sunday Mercury. 28 Oct 73.

Unless Mrs. Jabczynski had been lying in the bath with the taps running unnoticed for twenty hours , it is likely that she was found at 8.30 pm. and that it was a typographical error.

RIDDLE OF DEAD BOY.

A murder hunt started yesterday after a 9-year-old boy was found dead on waste ground. The body of Richard Sutherland, who had been missing from his home in Myreside St, Glasgow, was discovered near the spot where a toddler was found dead earlier this year. Richard's parents contacted the police when he vanished on Wednesday. In April, 3-year-old Gordon McEwan was found dead on the same waste ground.

Sun. 2 Nov 73.

MAN IN TOMB WAS ALIVE.

A doctor who was buried in a family mausoleum after being certified dead from a heart attack may have been entombed alive, police revealed yesterday at Mendoza, Argentina.

Three nights after Dr. Vincente Polimeni's funeral, a night watchman heard noises in the tomb. The coffin was found to have fallen on the floor damaged, and the doctor's body bore new bruises and scratches.

Daily Telegraph. 5 Jan 73.
Also in Daily Express of same date.

disappearances

DIVERS HUNT FOR THE FISH THAT GOT AWAY.

A crack squad of police frogmen have been called into action...to track down thousands of very slippery characters. Escapers that appear to have disappeared from a special 'top security' prison' - a 14ft. deep pool. The pool which belongs to a works angling club at Smethwick, Staffs, was stocked with thousands of roach, perch, bream and gudgeon three years ago. Members looked forward to some heavy work with rod and reel - but all they have caught were a few 'tiddlers'.

The club is the Guest, Keen & Nettlefold Sports & Recreation Club in Thimblemill Rd, Smethwick. Committee member Bill Blick, 40, said yesterday: "We can't understand where the fish have gone. So we asked the police to help." Mr. Blick of St Katherine's Rd, Smethwick added: "We expected to be pulling out fish weighing at least a pound But we are lucky if a sixteen-man fishing team weighs in with a catch of several ounces". Chief Inspector Kenneth Cocayne said, "Samples of pool-water have been sent to the public analyst." One of the frogmen added: "If there are any big fish in the pool we haven't seen them. The biggest are 3 in. long."

Contributor A Smith was unable to give the exact source for this interesting cutting, but thinks it might have been the Daily Mirror, sometime in 1969. See back to Appearances for the mysterious arrival of perches and roaches, in an inaccessible tank, not very far away from Smethwick. Can anybody help date this item?

SEANCE CLUE TO MISSING WOMAN.

Mrs Doris Symonds disappeared while shopping in Plymouth in 1963, leaving behind a 4-year-old son and all her posessions. Her husband was aquitted of her murder at Exeter Crown Court in February this year. And now a medium has told police that he spoke to her while in a trance, and she said that she had been strangled and dumped in a flooded quarry on the edge of Dartmoor. A police spokesman said: "We are taking what we consider relevant. There are certain aspects in the report which may interest us." From Daily Mail 12 Nov 73. Credit DJ McAllister.

MISSING YAUGHT.

David McAllister also sent us a note from Daily Mirror 8 Sept 73, which mentions that French authorities in Papeete, Tahiti, have denied that they have seized the New Zealand nuclear-protest yacht 'Spirit of Peace'. Its whereabouts, and whether the 3-man crew are still alive, were, at that time, still a mystery. Does anyone in the Great Out There know the follow-up to this one?

FLYING PIG VANISHES.

Farmer Ted Jewell yesterday lost an 11 stone pig while taking it in a lorry to an Eastleigh, Hants, slaughter-house. Said Ted; "A pig jumping over a 5ft. tailboard, then down 6ft. on to the road is almost as daft as a pig flying. But that's all that could have happened."

The People. 17 July 1966.
Credit: A Smith.

esp & powers

SON'S SIXTH SENSE SAVES FAMILY.

Housewife Margaret Woellner was busy preparing dinner in the kitchen of her new home when her 10-year-old son Joachim burst in. He stood terrified in the doorway as he said: "Mummy, get out of the kitchen quickly...Something terrible is going to happen."

Mrs Woellner only had to look at Joachim's ashen face to realise he wasn't joking. She scooped up her 3-year-old daughter Ulrike and dashed out of the house in Witzhelden, West Germany. Seconds later an explosion - caused by a faulty gas main connection - wrecked the three-bedroomed house.

Mrs Woellner then asked her son how he knew the accident was going to happen. Joachim replied: "I honestly don't know. I just had this strange idea that something was about to happen. It was as if there was a voice saying 'Go and fetch your mother and sister otherwise it will be too late'." His mother said later: "It was a marvel. I still don't understand it."

Professor Hans Bender, head of the para-psychology department at   Freiburg University, South Baden, explained the case differently. He said: "There are people who have a sixth sense. For years we here at the university have been investigating similar cases where people have known that something tragic was about to happen. Mostly such cases take the form of dreams and visions. In children, this so-called sixth sense is often pronounced."

Sunday Express. 2 April 72.

TELEKINESIS MAN GOES ON BENDER.

At the time of typing, the UK has been subjected to a mind-boggling flying visit by Uri Geller, a 26-year-old Israeli, who can demonstrate quite remarkable powers of telekinesis. He had flown in to appear on the BBC's Dimbleby Talk-in on the 23rd November. In the afternoon before the show, he gave a press preview of what he could do.

'Somebody offered a key and the donor held it while Uri stroked it with his forefinger...but the key remained straight. "I might not be able to do it - I'm nervous," he said calling for another key. But again he failed. Then suddenly the shaft of the third key began slowly to curl, and kept on curling. Next he demonstrated telepathy by accurately reproducing a drawing made by David Dimbleby, and unseen by anyone else. Uri also announced that he had undergone many tests at the Stanford Research Institute in California, and by astronaut-turned- psi researcher Edgar Mitchell. Two of the Stanford scientists were reported to have said that they could not claim Uri had any psychical powers but they had observed phenomena for which there was no scientific explanation. From Daily Express. 23 Nov 73.

The papers the next day were full of journalistic gasps. We missed the programme ourselves but heard many 'I see it, but I still don't believe it' reports. The TV show went off spectacularly enough with his mind-reading and fork-bending. Even to breaking a paperknife on Jimmy Young's Radio show. But something far more amazing and unexpected was happening. For while Uri was in London, a gold bracelet belonging to Maureen Cox began to buckle, 30 miles away in Godalming, Surrey. In Dunstable, Beds, Police constable John Cole's spoons and knives just curled up. A jeweller phoned the BBC to say that a canteen of cutlery had taken a turn for the worse. Then a watchmaker saying his tweezers had bent. Mrs Dora Portman of Harrow, Middlesex, said: "I was stirring the soup and suddenly the ladle started bending." When asked if he could straighten them all out he replied that he could if he tried, but best to leave them bent, beacuse seeing is believing. There were many other calls from listeners all over the country about the antics of their cutlery etc, as Uri appeared on the Radio show. This info. from Daily Mirror 24 Nov 73. Credit: Steve Moore.

All that was on the Saturday. Sure enough the reporters were after him in earnest for the

Sunday nationals. He gave a demonstration to the newshounds in his hotel room on Saturday night. First he did his mind-reading tricks. Then, as Jack Lewis of the Sunday Mirror (25 Nov 73) takes up the story: "Uri asked us to produce our keys. He chose one belonging to a woman reporter, and asked her to hold it, while he gently rubbed it with one finger. He also held his palm over it, and clenched his fist. When she opened her hand, the key had curved visibly. When he lay it on an upturned metal wastebasket, within seconds it had bent grotesquely. Throughout the experiment, I held my own RAC key in my hand. I glanced at it and was astonished when I saw it had become as bent as the other one." The report in the News of the World (same date) has a few more details. 'Uri was offered a steel comb. He tossed it on to the bed and carried on answering questions. Suddenly the teeth of the comb closed together and it began to bend. Another reporter fumbled for his cigarette lighter which had been functioning normally all morning. The metal casing was buckled. Uri apologised: "I don't know how it happens."'

Finally, Uri Geller was driven to the airport - with Bryan Silcock of the Sunday Times in the car with him. "He bent a very tough key to my office desk without even touching it. I tried to bend that key myself before leaving the office. I could not do it with my bare hands - Uri did it in seconds. It is the same key. It was lying flat in the palm of photographer Bryan Wharton's hand at the time. At the airport, Mrs Tessa Trapmore on the KLM desk, who had seen him on TV the night before, asked him to mend her watch. It was stopped at 11.10. He held it between the palms of his hands for a few seconds. The hands moved to nine o'clock. Geller then stroked a thick paper-knife until it started to bend. He gave it to Mrs Elna Burroughs, also of KLM, to hold and the knife continued to bend. Uri Geller finally boarded the plane to Paris leaving this initially highly sceptical science correspondent with his mind totally blown."

There are many questions raised by all this, of course. Was there a selection operating for items of jewellery or domestic ware, things of relative unimportance? Did the objects have to be metal? If Uri was projecting or catalysing a force that affected metallic objects at quite a radius all around him - then did any machines go haywire? What about the sophisticated gadgetry of TV and radio studios, and the airport computers? We see that dashing young scientist-about-TV studios Prof. John Taylor, who took part in Dimbleby's Talk-in, has said: "I would like to try to find out how. Some kind of explanation along conventional scientific lines might be possible. I would very much like to get in touch with people who had odd experiences during the TV programme as they might have similar but less developed powers." Now that's an interesting thought - that Uri was triggering latent TK abilities in others. In the News of the World report (above), Uri says "When I was 19, we moved to Israel, where I toured theatres. Even Golda Meir gave me a plug."

(Which no doubt bent.). But we can't help wondering about this - about Uri being called up in the future (God forbid) - being sent to the front to catalyse all the latent TKs - and putting a few kinks in tank gun-barrels; triggering a few bombs before the enemy fires them; shutting off jets in mid air - pray, one and all, it never happens.

The Uri Geller story is far from ended - at the time of going to press, more reports are coming in - so we'll save them for next issue.

"It's Uri the Israeli mind-bender"

No sooner was the (unoriginal) speculation above typed, than cartoons, like this one by Waite (Daily Mirror. 26 Nov 73) began appearing.

fires

DEATH BLAZE MYSTERY.

The cause of a fire in a Handsworth house, where a 64-year-old man died, remained a mystery after a Birmingham inquest. The City Coroner, Mr George Billington, recorded a verdict of 'Accidental Death' on Mr John Joseph McRory, a factory labourer, who was dragged from his blazing house at Victoria Terrace, Booth St, on April 8. A Fire Brigade officer who attended the fire said that he could see no definite cause of the blaze. There was an electric fire in the corner and a gas meter cupboard nearby had been severely damaged.

Birmingham Evening Mail. 20 April 73.

BLAZE VICTIM.

The soldier burned to death in a Chester camp during the weekend was identified by a dental surgeon yesterday as Lance Corporal William Hawkes, 25, of Woodbank, Tiverton, Worcester. An inquest on him was adjourned.

Daily Express. 18 Oct 73.

FOUND DEAD.

Mr. William McLeod, a pensioner in his 80s, was found dead in a fire-damaged room of his home in St. Silas Square, Nechells, Birmingham, yesterday.

Sunday Mercury. 21 Oct 73.

BURNED WOMAN'S RUN FOR HELP.

A 23-year-old woman ran 200 yards to a friend's house after suffering severe burns at her home in Coseley, Dudley, yesterday. Miss Diane Mold is believed to have suffered a blackout and fallen onto an open coal fire at her Childs Avenue home. She ripped off her burnt clothing, put on a coat and ran for help to a friend, Mrs Doreen Wright of Swann Rd, Coseley. Ambulancemen were called and Diane was taken first to Dudley Guest Hospital and later transferred to the Burns Unit at Birmingham Accident Hospital. A hospital spokesman said later that Diane had suffered 15% burns but was fairly comfortable.

Sunday Mercury. 27 Oct 73.

HOSPITAL GIRL IN FLAMES.

A girl student was seriously ill with back and chest burns today after being turned into a flaming torch in a Birmingham hospital ward. The girl, who is 18, ran from a ward where she is a patient to a bathroom with her nightdress on fire. A hospital spokesman said a nurse on duty heard her screams and found her in the bathroom with the taps running. Her bed in the ward was smouldering.

"The nurse wrapped her in blankets and put out the fire. First Aid was administered before she was taken to the Burns Unit." The girl apparently had some matches in the ward at All Saints Hospital. An enquiry has been started.

Birmingham Evening Mail. 26 Oct 73.

As Forteans we cannot hold firmly to any belief in coincidences, but must also consider, however unlikely, that two young girls catching fire and running so near each other in time and space, might very well have some more sinister aspect. See Lo! and Wild Talents for Fort's speculations on attacks by beings with a fiery hunger. In the meantime however, the editor has written to both hospitals involved (on the 27th), but has received no reply to date. One of the more puzzling aspects about spontaneous combustion cases (not that these are definitely) is that the victims, usually young girls with unhappy backgrounds seem not to notice their predicament until it is almost too late. They have been hypnotized, or by some means their sensibility has been reduced until they cannot fail to notice - then, suddenly they feel the pain dreadfully, and take much longer than normal to recover from the burns.

BREAK-IN MAN WAS TRAPPED BY BLAZE.

A man who broke into a factory was seen later trapped in the building by a severe fire, a jury at Birmingham Crown Court was told. Alan Brick-

nell, 24, of Argosy House, Castle Vale, pleaded guilty to burglary with intent to steal and was found guilty of arson, to which he had pleaded not guilty.

The prosecution alleged Bricknell broke into the premises of Brook Welding Company in Fazely St, and when he was unable to find the keys to the safe, he set fire to the premises. In the early hours of Sunday August 5th, two policemen in Masshouse saw smoke and flames coming from the factory. Sometime later, while firemen were fighting the blaze, a man was seen at the window of the first floor. He broke a pane of glass and shouted for help.

A ladder was put up to the window and the man, Bricknell, climbed down. He told the police that some other men had left him in the building. He also said: "We broke in to do the safe. I thought I was going to get roasted. I'm so glad you came." He was arrested for breaking into the building, and when searched, a cigarette lighter was found in his pocket. Mr. David Crigman, for the Crown, said the main seat of the fire was on the staircase below where Bricknell was trapped. There were also three other minor seats of fire, completely independent of the main seat. It was estimated the main fire had been burning for at least 40 minutes before firemen arrived.

Birmingham Evening Mail. 26 Oct 73.

The man could have been as foolish as suggested of course - but it could have been something else too. I am reminded of a case in Fort where a thief (I think) was pursued into a hardware store and 'just happened to pass under a scythe as it fell. The other 'apparently' unconnected fires in the building are interesting, though I dare say some ultra-rationalists could spoil our fun by attributing them to the would-be thief.

MYSTERY FIRE. NO SMOKE WITHOUT FIRE?

"Following an article by Lanning Roper deploring the destruction of trees by farmers burning stubble (Gardening. Sept 16), you published a photograph of a pile-up on the M1 which you described as 'one consequence of out-of-control stubble burning'.

I farm the field which caught fire, the smoke from which caused the accident on the motorway. I had bales of straw in the field, 150 of which were destroyed, and I had growing oats in an adjoining field. For these two reasons alone I would not have been burning stubble at that time. The police and the National Farmer's Union were most concerned about the fire, but were quite satisfied that I was in complete ignorance of its cause."

> Mrs. Nan C Lewin, Luton.
> (Letters to the Editor).

Sunday Times. 28 Oct 73.

ghosts & poltergeists

EVICTED...GHOST IN A COUNCIL HOUSE.

A spiritualist medium has 'evicted' a ghost from a council house. She was called in after tennants claimed they were living in terror. They were renting a 70-year-old house bought by Chichester City Council, Sussex, to reduce its housing list. The medium was called in by Mr. Jeremy Adams, Chichester's housing manager.

Mr Adams said: "The wife heard the ghost's footsteps on the stairs at night and rooms would suddenly go cold." The medium, Mrs Joan Stillwell, said: "I went to the empty house with Mr. Adams and at once sensed a presence. Then I saw it - the ghost of a small, old, gery-haired lady. She told me she did not like anyone being in her house. Then I told her what trouble she was causing people. At this she looked shocked and then she just drifted away through a wall." The ghost has not been seen since - and the house is now occupied by new tenants.

Sunday Mirror. 4 Nov 73.

FAMILY QUITS HAUNTED FLAT.

Things went more than bump in the night for Jeremiah O'Leary. He was sleeping peacefully. At about 2am he suddenly broke out in a cold sweat and felt icy breath on his face. Slowly he opened his eyes and saw the pale face of a white-haired old man with a goatee beard gazing down at him. Thinking it was a burglar, Jeremiah screamed out and leapt out of bed. But the old man, dressed all in white, disappeared - through the bedroom-wall. That was four months ago. Today Jeremiah O'Leary, his wife Christine, and two-year-old son Stephen are living with Christine's mother in Eltham, because they are afraid of going back to their haunted flat in Barnfield Gardens, Plumstead.

Said 21-year-old Christine: "This was not the first time we were visited by the ghost. Soon after we moved in 18 months ago, I was in the kitchen when I felt something cold brush the back of my legs. Some months later, the lights kept switching themselves on and off, and Stephen, who always slept like a log, began screaming every night. When I finally told my husband that the place was haunted, he laughed at me. But now he has seen it, he is convinced. I can't live here anymore. I'm a bag of nerves."

The O'Learys, who did not believe in ghosts before, now want Greenwich Council to find them a new flat. "We were quite prepared to stay there for a few years, and we bought new furniture and spent more than £100 redecorating the place. So its not as though we are doing this just to get another flat." said Christine.

Ghosts or no ghosts, Greenwich Council is prepared to help. "The O'Learys are on the transfer list, but are not high priority. As far as we are concerned, they are adequately housed," said a council spokesman. "However we are sending the Area Housing Manager to have a chat with the family. The object of the exorcise, sorry, I mean exercise, is not so much to transfer them, but to investigate whether there is any substance to their story." The Barnfield flat was built before the war, but the council spokesman was unable to say if it had ever been the scene of some horrible crime.

Kentish Independant. 4 Oct 73.
Credit: Steve Moore.

STRIKE FLOATS INTO THE HAUNTED HOTEL.

The ghostly lady in white who is apparantly walking the corridors of a hotel is about to cause a strike. Three night porters claim that they are terrified by the mystery apparition. To beat their haunted feeling, they are asking the management to let them work in pairs with all the lights on. Otherwise, they say - when the ghost walks, they will walk out.

The 'phantom' of Edinburgh's 150-year-old Royal Circus hotel is a tall beautiful woman. One porter who saw her, James Brand, 42, said: " She just vanished. I was petrified." Now the porters union, the General & Municipal Workers', wants the management to call in a ghost-hunter and, if necessary, a minister to exorcise the phantom.

Daily Mirror. 24 Oct 73.
Credit: Steve Moore.

GHOST HUNTER CALLED IN TO PREVENT STRIKE.

A ghost-hunter is being called in to settle a dispute between an hotel and three of its night porters. The porters say they have been scared by a ghostly white lady flitting through the corridors at the Royal Circus Hotel in Edinburgh. And they threatened to strike unless the management got a ghost-hunter to deal with the apparition.

Daily Mirror. 25 Oct 73.
Credit: Cathy Purcell, Steve Moore.

GUN POLICE TRY TO LAY A GHOST IN DUNGEONS.

Armed police guarding Winchester's ancient Crown Court, scene of the marathon London bombs trial, thought they were ready for anything ... until a ghost came on the scene. But last night disbelieving detectives were combing the old dungeons beneath the court building on the lookout for a strange figure who 'disappeared through a wall'. They were hoping to catch a glimpse of the ghost reported to be wearing a three-cornered hat, breeches and a cut-away frock coat. The police were called in in case the ghost in 300-year-old clothing turned out to be a present day intruder. But nothing was found.

The security ghost hunt began after a prisoner from nearby Winchester Jail on a working party at the castle rushed from one of the old dungeons which he was cleaning out. Trembling and shocked, the man stammered to his guard that he had clearly seen a figure 'disappear'. While he was sent off for medical treatment, security men acted. "Whatever he saw or thought he saw, the

man's terror was genuine enough," said a prison
officer. The identity of the frightened prisoner
who later returned to normal working party duty,
was being withheld.

Daily Express. 17 Oct 73.

The Daily Mail of the same date adds the following details. The dungeons are beneath the 13th
century Great Hall courthouse, which forms part
of Winchester Castle. "It is believed by some to
be the seat of the legendary King Arthur's court.
Sir Walter Raleigh was imprisoned there and
Hanging Judge Jeffreys held one of his bloody
assizes there in the 17th century after the
Monmouth rebellion." The ghost is said to have
disappeared through a 2ft thick wall and the
reluctant witness collapsed outside the cell.
(Credit: Steve Moore.)

A GHOST AT THE TURN OF A TAP.

The ghostly White Lady has abandoned her old haunt in the cellar at the Stag's Head. The old place (circa 1670s) at Penn Common, Wolverhampton,
will never be the same without her. For one thing
the customers will no longer have their beer cut
off without warning. She was always leaving them
short. "She must have had some mechanical knowledge," said the landlord Harry Urwin yesterday,
"She knew exactly how to do it. The beer would
stop suddenly and I would find the taps turned
off in the cellar. I would turn them on, and then
without any explanation, they would go off again.
Once this happened 22 times in a month. It must
have been the ghost because there is only one
entrance to the cellar and no one could get down
there without everyone in the pub knowing."

Turning off the taps was about the worst mischief
the White Lady ever did. The landlords daughter,
Christine, 18, spotted her once from the top of
the cellar steps. "I saw a woman in the form of a
grey cloud on a barrel. I was pretty frightned.
She moved across the cellar and disappeared." Now
the White Lady has disappeared once more, this
time, it seems, for good. For nothing has been
heard of her since builders came in to do some
alterations.

Daily Mail. 27 Dec 72.
Credit: Steve Moore.

healing & cures

WOMEN FLOCK TO THE FERTILE STONE.

Thousands of women are travelling from all parts
of Europe to sit on a stone - because they believe it makes them pregnant. The stone is part
of a temple built in 700 BC to a goddess of fertility and love in Paestum, near Naples. Reports
got round that women who sat astride the 3ft
carved stone, as if on horseback, had later experienced 'miracluous pregnancies'. Tourists, including some from Britain, began to join the
queue at the stone as the word spread.

Mrs. Nora Colasanti of Verona said: "I was married for 14 years and my husband and I desperately
wanted a child. But we had no success until I sat

astride the stone at Paestum. Two months later I
was pregnant." Camp-site manager Donato Stromillo,
who has seen his business rocket since the story
spread, said: "It's just a common stone, like
many others you find at Paestum. But women seem
to think it has special powers of fertilisation .
The women sit astride the stone for as long as
they like. You would be amazed how many have
come back later with a baby in their arms."

Sunday People. 28 Oct 73.
Credit: Mrs J Adams.

BIRTH OF THE BLUES.

Family planners who taught Aboriginal women in
South Australia a song giving advice on contraception have hit a snag - the women think all
they have to do to avoid pregnancy is to sing
the song.

Sunday Mirror. 21 Oct 73.

`heavens above´

KOHOUTEK.

The comet due at Christmas will begin to be seen
as a pale smudge in the eastern sky, but it is
hurtling through space at nearly 100,000 mph,
trailing a tail 30 million miles long. The best
naked eye viewing time will be after sunset and
following New Year's Day. The Skylab crew will
be the first men to observe a comet from outside
the earth's atmosphere, who will have their telescopes trained on it all the time and take thousands of pictures. They will try to obtain 3D
photographs with the aid of apparatus on earth.
No one alive today will see the comet again - its
next visit will be in 10,000 years time.
(Condensed from Sunday Express. 4 Nov 73).

At the end of November the comet will be visible
just above the south-eastern horizon, and just
before dawn from all over Britain. The comet was
discovered by Czech astronomer Lubos Kohoutek in
March this year at the Hamburg Observatory. It
is expected to miss earth by about 75 million
miles. It has a head half the size of the moon,
and its tail will   streak across one-sixth
of the night sky. Observatories around the world
will study where it came from and what it is
made of. A favourite theory is that the core of
ice, rock, gas, metal and dust came from near
the outermost planets Uranus and Neptune. Across
America,planetariums are planning special attractions. The Morehead Planetarium of North Carolina is taking advantage to show that the Star
of Bethlehem was not a comet. The QE2 departs
New York on Dec 9th for a three day amateur
astronomer cruise with lecturers and telescopes
on board. The London Planetarium is ignoring the
event.
(Condensed from Sunday Times. 11 Nov 73.)

The Russians will be observing 'Kogoutek' from
special observatories on the slopes of Tien Shan,
not far from Alma-Ata, the Kazakh capital.

Novosti Bulletin 14474. 19 Nov 73.

RIDDLE OF PLANET'S BREATHING CLOUDS.

Venus is becoming increasingly mysterious. So thickly clouded is the planet that astronomers have never been able to glimpse the surface. Now however, they have discovered that the whole atmosphere of the planet moves up and down, almost as if the planet were breathing. This strange discovery has been reported by a research team at the Jet Propulsion Laboratory, USA, using special infra-red equipment on Table Mountain.

The team say that the Venusian cloud pulses up and down over a distance of two thirds of a mile. But they do not know why. Dr Louise Young says: "We seem to be observing a fundamental feature of atmospheric dynamics that is not explained in terms of atmospheric current or circulation. An extremely large amount of energy must be available to cause the movement. It is difficult to see where it can come from on so slowly a revolving planet."

Sunday Express. 5 Aug 73.
Credit: DJ McAllister.

RADIO SIGNALS FROM SPACE.

Soviet scientists have recorded radio signals from space that they have never received before. These signals were recorded first in Gorky, on the Volga, and later in other cities, but it is too soon to say if they are natural or artificially-produced signals, and it is clear they are not from any artificial satellite. The signals come in pulses after definite lapses of time; they last for several minutes and are repeated several times a day.

The search for radio emissions from space has been conducted under the guidance of Vsevolod Troitsky since 1970. Observations over the entire hemisphere are conducted in the centimetre and decimetre wavebands. The search for signals is conducted simultaneously from four points lying far apart from one another.

More than 30 Soviet scientists are now searching in earnest for signals from extra-terrestrial civilisations. The pulses received will be studied for several years.

Novosti Bulletin. 14394. 17 Oct.73.

THE HEAVENLY HUNT FOR A 20,000-YEAR OSTRICH.

For thousands of years, a remote colony of Bolivian Indians have gathered once a year to dance and drink for days. Why? They have forgotten, they told archaeologist George Michanowsky. But astronomers of the Americam space programme now think that those celebrations may pin-point a cataclysm far out in space, 10,000 to 20,000 years ago.

The Indians, they believe, are commemorating the violent death of a star - a super H-bomb explosion that blazed up in the sky and for a few months would have been as bright as the moon. John Brandt, one of the NASA astronomers who did the detective work told me: "If this is right - and their is no obvious argument against it - it

would be the closest explosion to earth that we have identified."

The astronomers started the hunt when they found a giant wisp of gas, the so-called Gum Nebula, surrounding one of the mysterious pulsars that flash like a lighthouse many times a second. It was in the constellation Vela, in the southern sky, and it was very like the debris left when a star comes to a violent end, part of it exploding out into space, the rest collapsing into an unimaginably dense and tiny 'crushed' star - the pulsar.

The Vela space catastrophe should have been nearer, and more spectacular, than any of the four such explosions historically recorded, the astronomers argued. But there was no record of it until the astronomers called in the archaeologists and advertised for anything that could conceivably be a primitive record of an explosion in the sky. Their advertisement stirred the memory of Michanowsky. He had first recorded this unexplained Indian rite nearly 20 years before. And it had seemed to be associated with ancient carvings on a rock, of which he could make no sense.

For there were four small circles which fitted a rough cross of stars in the sky - and a larger circle, in the place where the bright star Canopus can be seen. There was a still larger circle nearby - at a point where nowadays we see no star at all, but very close to the mysterious Gum Nebular and its pulsar. Could this be a primitive record that once a very bright star had blazed up at this point? Nowadays this bit of sky looks very unremarkable. Yet it still has some special meaning for the Indians who call it the Gateway to Hell. According to another legend, one of their sacred symbols, the Heavenly Ostrich, was hunted across the sky by savage dogs and killed at this point. Michanowsky hopes, by radiocarbon dating the rock with the carving, to put a date within a few hundred years to this closest-ever explosion. The Hunt of the Heavenly Ostrich has become a quest for one of the strange experiences that primitive man recorded without comprehension.

Daily Mirror. 27 Oct 73. Article by A Macpherson.
Credit: Steve Moore.

PLASMA NEAR THE MOON.

Cosmic plasma was discovered on the lighted side of the moon when space near the moon was explored by Luna-19. Professor Mikhail Kolesnov of the Soviet Academy of Sciences' Institute of Radio Engineering and Electronics says that the maximum concentration of the matter was at an altitude of 10 kilometres from the lunar surface - but even at that attitude it is much less than on the earth, he says. The origin of plasma near planets is still unknown and scientists have different opinions about this. Many believe that plasma is affected greatly by solar wind, on which the concentration and distribution of space plasma around the earth depends.

Novosti Bulletin 14347. 3 Oct 73.

mysterious moon by nigel watson

With the advent of lunar exploration by men and vehicles, there has been greater scientific interest in our nearest celestial body than ever before - so it is interesting to find that since the 19th century, astronomers throughout the world have observed many strange manifestations which apparently seem to be emanating from the moon's surface.

One such observation was made during an eclipse of the moon, on September 7th, 1820. Many astronomers reported seeing the same thing; strange objects which were apparently moving in straight lines and evenly spaced, crossing the face of the moon slowly, and turning in what was described as military precision.

In 1837, a selenographer startled astronomers by producing a map with a 65-mile-long area with what looked like a white cross in the centre, located on the edge of the Mare Frigoris. This particular object was worked out to be 250 to 350 above the lunar surface.

One object that moved across the moon on 30th September, 1870, was reported in the London Times, and described as elliptical in shape with a kind of tail, crossing from one side of the moon to the other in half a minute. A similar event was reported in the American journal Popular Astronomy on 27th January 1912, in which a Dr. Harris described an intensely black object which he observed crossing the moon. With slight under-statement he said: "I think a very interesting and curious phenomenon happened last night."

In my own study of Lincolnshire UFO reports, I have found many such reports of elliptical objects seen crossing the moon - due to lunar illumination these objects are only seen when they are between the observer and the moon. A typical report from my files is the observation made on 19th November 1953 by a 31-year-old steelrigger whilst going home from the Appleby-Frodingham steelworks. He saw a huge elliptical object gliding across the moon from left to right - it was 1/6th the diameter of the moon and its length was seven times its width.

On the matter of observed objects on the moon itself, I came across a report that in 1871 an astronomer gave the Royal Astronomical Society a file of 1,600 observations he had made of light changes, moving objects, flashing lights and geometrical patterns inside Plato crater.

I contacted the RAS and their librarian, Dr. EW Maddison, kindly sent me the following reply: "The matter of 1,600 (it is sometimes given as 2,000) observations of flashing lights on the moon is a perennial one. It would seem from enquiries that I have made, that the statement has no foundation. I have found no reference in this Society's publications that members of this Society made these observations between 1869 to 1871; and there is no mention in the Catalogue of Lunar Events by B. Middlehurst et al, (NASA Technical Report R-277, 1968), which is pretty exhaustive as a chronological survey of the phenomena you are enquiring about.

I have been given to understand that the story originates in The Books of Charles Fort, an American publication which is not in this library and which I have not seen; and as so often happens, the story has been repeated uncritically ever since. The story is probably a garbled version of Brit's observations on the crater Pluto, and his reports to the British Association for the Advancement of Science in 1871 and 1872."

Coming up to the present day, in 1959, Lee Munsic of Denville, New Jersey took a picture of what appeared to be flying saucers marching towards the moon, although the US Air Force quickly identified them as 'static electricity'.

One explanation for the lights observed on the lunar surface by astronomers is that they are 'gas emissions' called Transient Lunar Phenomena (TLP). Indeed, Patrick Moore has done much to catalogue the TLPs.

We shall now mention yet another puzzling manifestation on the moon's surface. In November 1966, a US space probe sent Lunar Orbiter 11 on a survey mission to the moon. On 21st November, from a height of 30 miles above the lunar surface, its camera zoomed in on a small section of the Sea of Tranquility, relaying back to Earth pictures of what appeared to be six spike-like shadows.

Although most scientists have remained content with the theory that these structures are probably due to some natural occurrence, some think differently. Mr. William Blair, a Seattle anthropologist and member of the Boeing biotechnology department, has stated that the 'spires' form a geometric pattern, similar to columns built by man.

In reply to this theory, an expert on lunar topography said that by picking some at random (because there are so many of these rocks on the moon) you would, as in this particular case, eventually find a group that would conform to a pattern. Mr. Blair said that if this were the case, much more than half of the present known Aztec and Mayan architecture would still be sitting in tree-studded undergrowth.

So to re-cap: astronomers have seen what is probably natural geological activity, TLPs; satellites in orbit around the moon have recorded strange structures on its surface; and people have reported UFOs crossing the sky against the moon's illumination.

** * **

Nigel Watson is Chairman of the Scunthorpe UFO Research Society (SUFORS).

human curiosities

MARK SLEEPWALKS ON THE ROOF.

Schoolboy Mark Henderson yawned and woke up to
the biggest audience of his life yesterday. He
woke up to find himself perched 40ft up on the
roof of his home in Accrington Road, Burnley.
Dressed in his pyjamas and fast asleep, Mark, 14,
had climbed out of his attic bedroom through a
tiny window. Still asleep, we walked 10ft down
wet, slippery slates to the edge of the roof
above their backyard. Neighbours spotted him and
called the emergency services. He was rescued by
firemen and returned to bed, shaken but no worse
for his 'night out'.

Daily Mail. 18 Sept 73.
Credit: DJ McAllister.

WHY THE DOCTORS ARE UP IN THE AIR OVER HENRI.

Henri Rochatain was so tired that he slept on a
clothesline - probably the only man who has ever
done it. Now doctors are   trying to fathom out
how he managed to snooze without falling off. You
might think M. Rochatain is a nut - once he walked 4000 miles around France on a pair of stilts
- but his exploits fascinate doctors because they
push human endurance beyond limits previously
thought possible.

He has just come down from a tightrope, 82ft up
above a carpark in Saint Etienne, France. He lived for six months on the rope, fitted with a
covered toilet and a board bed - but these were
simply balanced along the line, there was nothing holding them there. "It is fantastic that he
managed to sleep at all," said Dr. Paul Monet,
whose team had Rochatain wired up with electrodes
to monitor reactions. "He slept well even in
thunderstorms and high winds. It is quite astonishing that he could rest, knowing that if he
turned over in the night he would plunge off the
rope."

He spent most days walking up and down, and oc-
casionaly doing stunts, like standing on his
head or pretending to fall off. His menu was
sparse - seaweed soup, biscuits and tea. A local
supermarket presented him with a fat fee for
using the tightrope attraction as an advertisement.

Daily Mail. 4 Oct 73. From article by W. Lowther.
Credit Steve Moore.

IT'S A DOG'S LIFE AS WILD CATMAN POUNCES.

The scatty antics of the phantom ginger catman
are making nights a misery for families on a
caravan site. The man has a mop of ginger hair,
and wears a black coat and plimsolls. After
lights out he bounds through the site banging on
the caravans and smashing windows. He even stamps along the roofs. His nasty acrobatics have
forced wives and children to huddle in fear in
one caravan while their husbands stand guard
outside.

The catman has been seen several times but he
has given his pursuers the slip by dodging into
the woods surrounding the site at Wyatts Covert,
Denham, Bucks. "He outruns everybody," said Mrs.
Jacqueline Davies, one of the caravan wives.
"He's obviously very athletic and moves like a
cat. You never hear him approach. He seems to
enjoy the chase. One night he leapt straight
over a six foot fence, then found a police-car
blocked his way. Even that didn't stop him. He
just jumped over the bonnet of the car and disappeared".

Mrs. Davies, a 25-year-old mother of three, said:
"We can't take much more of this. I've not had a
proper night's sleep in 3 weeks. We simply dare-
not go to bed with this man around. Things have
got so bad that I've had to send my son Daren to
live with my mother. We've done everything we
can - even rigging up temporary searchlights,
but this still hasn't stopped him. If something
isn't done soon we plan to go to Gerrards Cross
police station with our children and sit-in
there until this man is caught."

Mr Brian Knight, deputy housing manager for Eton
Rural Council, owners of the caravan site, said:
"We have given residents permission to cut down
undergrowth which has been providing cover for
the prowler." A police spokesman at Gerrards
Cross said: "We have sent men and dogs to the
site but so far we have not managed to catch the
prowler. He moves so quickly."

News of the World. 4 Nov 73.

... and with one bound he was free, eh!

PLAYTIME FOR A GIRL WHO 'DIED'.

Four-year-old Jacqueline Rumble was playing in a
Hull, Yorks, park yesterday, just 24 hours after
she 'died' for 15 minutes. Firemen revived her
with mouth-to-mouth resuscitation after a blaze
destroyed her home. Sunday Express. 21 Oct 73.

ROSE SNORES BACK TO LIFE IN HER COFFIN.

The mourners grieved for old Rose Hanover as she
was laid in her coffin. But two hours later old
Rose started to snore... and gave the undertaker
the fright of his life. He opened the coffin lid
and saw that 85-year-old Mrs. Hanover was alive
and breathing. He covered her with a blanket,
dialled 999 and she was taken to hospital. A
spokesman for the North Middlesex hospital said
that she was much improved but that she did not
know what had happened to her.

Daily Mirror. 16 April 73.

CRASH VICTIM TAKES HIS ARM TO HOSPITAL.

Nurses fainted in horror when motorcyclist George Bereza walked into hospital after a road
accident - carrying his left arm tucked under
his right arm. It had been torn off at the elbow
in a collision with a van. George, 19, hitch-
hiked to the hospital near Johannesburg, where
doctors tried to sew the forearm back, but had
to remove it again a few hours later.

George said later: "The nurses keeled over or
scattered when I walked into the hospital, ble-
eding all over the place. I had to walk by myself to casualty. When I got there I passed out."
Several drivers he stopped wouldn't take him: "I
assume they didn't want their cars messed up."

Daily Mirror. 24 Sept 73.
Credit: Steve Moore.

WATTS SHE GOT THAT SPARKS 'EM OFF?

"Please help me with an old problem I have on my
hands. It's just that I seem to have the knack
of switching off electrical gadgets without even
touching them! During my holidays, for example,
I tried to dry my hands in the hot air machine
in a ladies loo - only to find that it turned
itself off right away, though it worked for everyone else. I even took my rings and shoes off,
but it made no difference. Its the same story
with automatic ticket machines on the Undergro-
und. They always reject my ticket. I also have a
funny effect on transistor radios, which go static when I walk past. Can any of your readers
come up with an answer? My friends are calling
me 'spooky'.
          Mrs. R Heath. Bedford Hill, Balham,
                           London SW12."

Daily Mirror. 24 Oct 73. Letters to Codgers.
Credit: Robert Forrest, Anthony Smith.

monsters

ROUND ONE TO NESSIE.

After the long catalogue of disappointments in
this comedy of errors, the Japanese Loch Ness
Monster Search Party has packed up and retired.
Finances, originally described as 'unlimited',
finally dried up - but fear not, the intrepid
team from Tokyo will be back again next Spring,
with a remote-controlled submarine containing
photographic gear and computers.

Yoshio Kou, styled Chief Producer, famous (in
Japan) Chinese-born impressario, said: "Despite
what local people think, we have not wasted our
time. We have much data, and the crew we will
send over next year will know much about Loch
Ness. We know now what can be seen under the
surface of the water, and it is very little. But
our computers should do better than a submarine
with men aboard.

The expedition, which cost £250,000 and comprised
     15 submariners, scientists and zoologists,
were described (in the quaint genre-language of
the show-biz paper Variety,5 Sept 73) as in a
race with a team from the Boston Academy of Applied Science, and "the first to capture the
monster-lass on film for world television stands
to win lotsa coin."

One man who won't be sorry to see them go is
Frank Searle, who claims to have seen the monster
more than 20 times from his loch-side tent.
Robert Glenton, in an article (with pics) on the
Lady of the Loch (Sunday Express. 16 Sept 73.)
wonders if we can call Mr. Searle potty. "Well,
if arms and a face that glow as brown as shining
chestnut, eyes as clear as a summer sky, and
utter contentment are signs of lunacy, then the
sooner some of us are certified the better." In
one newspaper report (which we seem to have lost)
Mr. Searle was commenting somewhat sarcasticly,
that when the Japanese sub attempt failed, they
took to steaming up and down the Loch in a noisy
fishermans boat hired out of Drumnadrochit.

Apart from the dated pieces, most of the above is
drawn from the last news mention of the caper,
Daily Express. 8 Nov 73. Credit: Steve Moore.

AND NOW .... A MONSTER IN THE MIDLANDS.

Could this be a scoop for the NEWS?- if so then
praise be to Anthony Smith, NEWS reader extraordinary.

The first news of this rival to Nessie and Morag
comes from the Express & Star, 21 May 1973. Three
members of a Dudley Diving Club were disturbed
while carrying out a survey of the lake on the
Earl of Bradford's estate at Weston-under-Lizard
(of all splendid names). David Gale, the club
instructor, said that they were doing a survey
of all the lakes on the estate, with Pat Smith
and Chris Lander. They were in about 10 feet of
water near the centre of Norton Mere three-quarters of a mile long, when they saw the wake of
something large moving below the surface. "There
was a large disturbance of mud just ahead - so
big that Chris thought one of us had got in front.

We were all amazed to see such a large wake. It
certainly must have been made by something quite
big."

Mr Gale said the three of them made a search but
were unable to trace what had made the wake. He
said that it could have been a very large eel or
perhaps a big pike for Norton Mere has provided
the biggest pike caught on the estate.

nice one, Colin!

Turn to last page.......for the <u>full</u> story!!!

Some weeks later there is a bigger article in the Express & Star (5 June 73). The stately home was built in 1671 by Lady Wilbraham, and the parklands in the 1,500 acre estate were laid out by Capability Brown. Much joking from the sixth earl Lord Bradford: "Goodness knows what it is but it is a big one. No-one in the family has ever mentioned the monster being in the mere, but they say it is something like whatever is in Loch Ness". It should also prove a great rival to Lord Montagu's motor museum at Beaulieu.

A band of 20 divers meet early in the morning to search the mere. The main group from Dudley Diving Group, led by David Gale, and the Wulfruna Sub Aqa Club, led by Dave Crockett. They would divide and start from opposite ends, driving the whatever toward the side banks. The foothills of Tong were heavy with silence, and the occasional flash of a florescent diving hood breaking the surface - the waiting was terrible.

Suddenly, a scream rent the air. Miss Pat Smith sent wildfowl scattering with her cry - an eel had bitten her foot. The search was resumed, and a second team joined the first in swimming in ever decreasing circles. All manner of fish and even a small sunken forest was found - but alas no monster. The experienced evasion tactics of its northern cousin were in evidence, and very little else. We wonder if we've heard the last?

plant curiosities

GIANT SEAWEED INVADES THE SOUTH.

We are a little late with this one, but the headline is quite attractive. South coast resorts are being threatened by a plague of giant seaweed capable of growing an inch a day and up to 30 ft long. 'The weed, a relative of the legendary peril of the Sargasso Sea, forms huge mats which can squeeze out marine life, destroy oyster beds, and foul fishing lines and propellers.

'How it got to Britain is a mystery - the theories range from being brought on the bottom of a boat, or in a consignment of Japanese oysters grown in France.' Figure that one out! 'Marine botanist, Dr. Bill Farnham, leader of the volunteer group fighting the menace said: "The only way we can get rid of it is to pull it up by hand - and that's a long job." Portsmouth is the port worst hit. Dr Farnham found the weed clinging to the bottom of the Royal Yaught Brittania. "It's very bad. Worse than Bembridge, Isle of Wight, where it was found last month. We think its fertile period is during Spring and Summer. But it could be all the year round."'

Express & Star. 28 July 73.
Credit: Anthony Smith.

A RASH OF GIANT VEGETABLES.

60-year-old Eric Jenkins, of Shipston-on-Stour, who already holds the record for growing the world's largest dwarf bean (look this is meant to be serious - just take a peek at the note on trivia-collecting in Uncle Chao's column) has now notched himself another place in the record books by growing $370\frac{1}{4}$lb of potatoes from one seed. He uses the fertilizer on himself too. With impeccable logic he reckons that what is good for the spuds is good for him - and takes a couple of drops in water every day. If he finds himself rooted in his allotment one day he has only himself to blame - in the meantime his fingers are proverbially green. Eric is out for the record of 2000lb of potatoes from 6 seeds - he just failed (if you can call that failure) with 1548lb. From Sunday Mercury 14 Oct 73.

Next we have Ernie Jones and the biggest onion in the world - a swelling 5lb $15\frac{3}{4}$oz. Grown at his home in Llanfyllin, near Welshpool, Montgomeryshire, it beat the previous world record by two ounces. From Sunday Mirror 14 Oct 73.

And now a monster carrot, a foot long, nearly a

foot in circumference and weighing 3lb. All you SF buffs can breath easy, because this one isn't on the move - its in the garden of Arnold Dixon, at Trunch in Norfolk.

We hate to seem like alarmists, but we don't think Alex Finer's remarks in his article on Kohoutek (Sunday Times 11 Nov 73) are as smart as they sound. He says: "Unlike John Wyndham's classic science fiction fantasy, the comet's brightness is not expected to damage human eyes or to be followed by the appearance of Triffids." All the same - if we were you, we wouldn't go down the bottom of our garden until <u>well</u> after March next year.

possession & curses

IT WAS IN THE STARS.

'Expect a windfall this week' said Mrs Rosalyn Palmer's horoscope. But it wasn't quite what the 57-year-old district nurse expected. Within 3 days it came true - literally. She went to visit her sister Marjorie Palmer, who was born under the same sign, and who was in hospital after breaking her right leg at her home just hours after reading the same 'scope. Miss Rosalyn, of Bolton, Lancs, was caught by a gust of wind as she came down the hospital steps, and broke her own leg.

Daily Mail 28 May 73.
Credit: Steve Moore.

THE HOUSE OF HORROR.

Mrs Penelope Gallereault, 26, lived in a flat in the Victorian-Gothic country house of Oakley Court, on the banks of the river Thames at Bray, Berks. They were warned by friends before they moved in that the place was spooky and frequently used by Hammer Films as a location for Dracula or Frankenstein. And in those three years she and her husband and children suffered many tragedies. Her marriage has broken up and two of her four children are dead.

The horror began in the summer of 1972. "I started to see people walking in the grounds wearing hoods," she says. Then one morning she found a box on their doorstep - and inside, the body of one of her cats, with its neck broken. And in December her two-year-old son, William, died. Mrs Gallerneault was running hime a bath, when the phone went. When she returned he was floating in the water. "I realise that many people might try to blame me for being careless, but that is just not the case. In a rambling old house like that, there are so many precautions you have to take." Then early last month, her son Edward, who was just two, was left in his playpen in the grounds. Somehow he got out, toddled down to the river, fell in and drowned.

The other residents at Oakley Court remember two more deaths. A man fell from a pleasure steamer in 1971 and drowned in the same stretch of river as young Edward. And an old lady, whose body lay in her flat in the Court, was found in November 1972 after at least a week. Mrs Gallerneault said "The house has an aura of evil and I could never go back there. Horror films being made there seem like a joke. I'm sure evil has rubbed off on the place." The Rev. Sebastian Jones, Curate of St. Michaels Church, Bray, added: "Oakley Court is definitely 'spooky' and I would not want to stay there myself. Evil can generate evil, and the grounds would be an ideal place to practise Black Magic." The police, called in at every stage, are mystified too. A senior policeman said: "There have been some strange happenings at the house, which have never been explained. We made regular patrols after complaints about witches, and things seem to have quietned down now. We never discovered how Mrs Gallerneault's cats died or who killed them."

The above story is from the News of the World 30 Sept 73. All of us cynics and pessimists know the phenomena of 'Famous Last Words'. The world's a stage, it seems. 'Things' have their entrances and exits - and their cues. 'Things' that are said to have died down, take it into their heads (probably under their arms) to start up again. As the News of the World went to press, back at Oakley Court, Mr William Griffiths, 40, was sailing past and trying to fix his boat's windscreen. He fell in and drowned - in the same spot as the other two deaths. This addition from News of the World 7 Oct 73.

HUMAN VAMPIRE ATTACKED ME, SAYS PRIEST.

A Church of England priest who claims to exorcise evil spirits says that he has been attacked by a human vampire. The Rev. Donald Ormand alleges that the vampire is a 22-year-old man with a history of attacking people with his teeth or nails to get at their blood.

The 70-year-old priest pointed to his own marked lips and said: "It was the most terrifying experience of my life. One moment he was talking quite rationally. The next, he had leapt at me - his face diabolical. He scratched my lips and had to be overpowered. He openly admitted that he got an extacy from sucking blood. It might be only a coincidence - but it's curious that the man's mother came from Transylvania - the very place where Dracula is said to have lived."

Dr. Ormand, of Honiton, Devon, talked to the man after being approached by psychiatrists at a Scandinavian nursing home. "I had previously worked with them as an exorcist." Dr. Ormand said the man had attacked other patients in the home. "What is even more terrible is that his victims then betrayed signs of the same vampire tendancies. I exorcised him, the day after he attacked me, with salt and water, and with those prayers which are used by the Church in such ceremonies.

"The next day he could remember nothing of his vampire history and the doctors are so convinced that the evil has been exorcised that they wanted to release him. But I suggested they should try to get him to stay as a voluntary patient for another six months. I cannot rule out the chance of re-possession." Since flying back to Britain last weekend, Dr. Ormand has been in constant contact with the doctors. "It's curious that Dracula is another name for the Devil, but this was the first time I've come up against someone possessed by this vampire evil."

News of the World. 28 Oct 73.
Credit: Mrs J Adams. Anthony Smith.

ripley or not!

THE GAME OF THE NAME.

We remember (with affection) an incident quoted by Fort in which three people called Green, Berry and Hill, were hanged on Greenberry Hill. Well, we seem to have collected a few more of such 'coincidences'. Reader Robert Forrest sent us a note from the Daily Mirror 22 Oct 73 which says: ' The Queen's visit to Australia to open the Sydney Opera House saw a bonanza for "Coincidence Punters". A horse called Opera House won at 5-2 on Friday. On Saturday Queen Hawa won at 4-1, Melody Prince at 5-2, and Rule Britannia at 5-2.' On the same cutting is a note that Members of the Government's new regional water authorities now include a Mr Wells, Mr Pipe, Mr Gill and Sir Samuel Fisher.

To this bizarre pastime of thumbing through Government directories we can add our own not insignificant talents for scanning dead news-papers. The Daily Express 26 Oct 73 yields the information that the Somerset Police force now includes Constables Michael Fox, Christopher Woolf, John Doe (really) and Keith Rabbitts. And from the Express again, 15 Oct 73, one of the best specimens of roach ever caught at Farndon Harbour, Notts, was landed by an angler called Salmon.

scientific curiosities

TWINS BY DIFFERENT FATHERS.

An Austrian Supreme Court ruling has allowed that twins can have different fathers. Blood tests had shown that a man could not be the father of one twin - a girl - in a remarkable paternity case heard in Vienna. But the Court decided that it was technically possible for him to have fathered the other, a boy. In this case twins from separate ova could have separate fathers. This modern judgement of Solomon can be found in the Sunday People for 21 Oct 73.

OUT OF SPACE.

This is being typed (appropiately) as news is coming through of the discovery of bacteria that can thrive in alkalis, and so might exist in various forms on Jupiter. The Lovecraftian head above is from a note from the Daily Mirror 10 Aug 73, sent by DJ McAllister. It mentions that the two Nobel prizewinners Francis Crick and Leslie Orgel were 'today' publishing their theory on panspermia - that life on earth was seeded from elsewhere in space. They base their theory on two facts. First, that all living creatures on earth, including plants, have the element

molybdenum in their make-up. And secondly that the cells of all living creatures carry another element that decides the shape, size and other characteristics. Crick and Orgel 'doubt whether these two astonishing likenesses can be either accident or coincidence. "There may be as yet unsuspected features which might point to a special type of planet as the home of our ancestors".'

THE SEARCH FOR THE 114th ELEMENT IN NATURE.

Soviet scientists are embarking on a programme t locate the 114th element of the Mendeleyev table It has not yet been synthesized in any laborato but they say it should exist in nature. It is an analogue of lead, the most stable element in the system. The scientists think that it should be sought in the most unlikely places, eg. ancient lead glass, or at a great depth near volcanoes.

Novosti Bulletin 14325. 25 Sept 73.

SOVIET EARTH-MAPPING FROM SPACE.

Soviet scientists have produced the first geolog ical map, based on photographs taken by Soyuz 9. The scale of the map is one millionth and covers 8,000 sq. km. In a press interview, Prof. Sergei Strelnikov said that unlike the existing maps of the same area the new one shows some hitherto unknown regularities in the geological structure of the earth. For instance, the photos show for the first time that this planet has ring-shaped structures which formed in antiquity and which resemble lunar craters.

These formations, with diameters of up to 100 kilometres, have been destroyed to a considerabl extent and it is hard to discover them on earth. The scientist assumes they have much in common with similar lunar formations in terms of origin

Novosti Bulletin 14381. 12 Oct 73.

It seems that the map is confined to an area of Central Asia - but this should be of some int-erest to Ley Hunters and others, at least.

TEST TUBE BABY HUNT.

Following the death of Professor Daniele Petr-ucci, 51, in mid-October police and scientists in Italy are anxious to find out if his claims were true. Nine years ago he announced that he had perfected test-tube fertilization in artificial wombs under pressurized oxygen, and the subsequent embedding of the foetus into the real or host mother. Italy has strict laws aga-inst artificial insemination, and Petrucci ret-ired from public life to continue his experi-ents at his own expense.

In 1964, he came to a special conference on the use of oxygen pressure chambers in medicine, and was cut short in mid-speech by ridicule and told that his lecture was irrelevant to the theme. Bu before his death the professor shocked Italy by disclosing that he had created 27 babies successfully by this method. In referring to British experiments, he said, in a rare intervie "By the time their first one is born, my first one will be married." In his final years, the professor said he was concentrating on cancer research and techniques for exploring inside the human body. A top American gynaecologist who secretly interviewed him said later: "I've seen and heard some things which were quite fantastic!" From News of the World. 21 Oct 73.

`so what else is new?´

Like most of our categories this one is simply a very loose grouping of notes - here, dealing with the survival, re-invention or re-discovery of what is now popularly presented as an ancient technology - literally, applied knowledge.

PEACE BY THE STARS.

A Laos peace treaty was signed at 9.40 am. precisely yesterday - because an astrologer told Prime Minister Souvanna this gave the pact the best chance of success. The treaty signed by the Government and the Communist Pathet Lao ends 10 years of war. Diplomats from the US, China, North Vietnam and South Vietnam witnessed the ceremony which ended with a champagne toast.

Daily Mail. 15 Sept 73.

THE PHARAOH TOUCH.

The Sunday Times of 28 Oct. 73. carried a report by Ian Nairn on the winner of an architectural competition for Northamptonshire's proposed new county hall. The designers, Jeremy & Fenella Dixon with Edward Jones, will break even with a £7,000 prize for their 9 storey glass pyramid. "This is an imaginative idea which won't hurt the landscape. There are too few new shapes and new ideas in architecture." says Nairn - but all is not well.

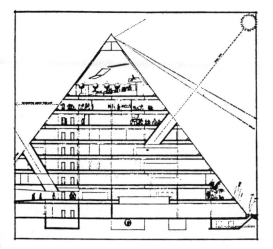

"The assessor's minority report is startling too: 'Incapable of satisfactory orientation...reminiscent of a Mausoleum and the Dead Pharaohs... totally unsuited to its environment.'" Tell that to Piazzi Smith, or the builders of Silbury and so many other 'celtic' pyramids.

"Wow! And double-wow," Nairn continues," when you realise that the two dissidents are the chairmen of the County Council and of the Council's General Services Committee. We have a Sydney Opera House situation on our hands."

ARCHIMEDES' SOLAR WEAPON IS TESTED.

Athens, Nov 6: Did Archimedes, the mathematician and inventor, use solar energy to destroy the Roman fleet besieging Syracuse between 215 BC & 212 BC? The story is challenged by many historians but a Greek engineer proved today that it could have been done.

Some 50 or 60 Greek sailors at Scaramanga naval base near Athens, today aimed large oblong mirrors to focus reflected sun rays on a small wooden boat moored 160 feet away. Smoke appeared within seconds and soon the boat was on fire.

Dr. Ioannis Sakkas had been puzzled about Archimedes' 'burning mirror' legend ever since reading about it in Anthemius's 'Remarkable Devices'. Anthemius of Tralles was one of the planners of the sixth-century church of St. Sophia in Constantinople. Earlier there had been vague references to the event in Polybius, Plutarch, and Lucian's 'Hippias'.

"Archimedes may have employed flat bronze mirrors the size of large shields, from the walls of the city to concentrate the solar energy and set the Roman galleys on fire," Dr Sakkas said. "The flat mirrors are, for this purpose, the most practical as they can be handled by men obeying commands.

"You can visualise the scene: the Roman ships would hold as they converged towards the 60 foot high walls of Syracuse within bowshot. The element of surprise was probably crucial, since the target had to be static. The defenders with their shield-like mirrors would focus the reflection of the sun on each galley and set it on fire within seconds."

In today's experiment, Dr Sakkas used between 50 and 60 mirrors of bronze-coated glass, each measuring 5ft by 3ft. They were held by a line of sailors along a narrow pier opposite the target. The doctor explained: "The reflective power would be about one-tenth less than the polished bronzes Archimedes would have employed, and the sun today was fairly weak. The heat generated today must have ranged between 280°C & 340°C."

The target was a 6ft navy rowing boat, one side covered by the outline of a galley made of tarred plywood. The board of slow-burning wood caught fire about two-minutes after the mirrors were beamed on it. This was the fourth successful experiment arranged by Dr Sakkas with the help of the Technical Chamber of Greece. Earlier trials on land involved the use of 50 mirrors which, at a distance of 130ft, set the target on fire within three seconds.

Times. 7 Nov 73.
Credit: Clive Million.

ufos

UFO IN RADNORSHIRE, WALES.

Reader Phil Ledger was listening to BBC Welsh regional radio news on the 18th Sept and caught a reference to a UFO sighting. He managed to track down the witness and wrote to him. He sent us the witness's reply dated 27 Sept 73.:

'Further to your letter concerning the UFO, I now give the following details. There were seven of us present at the time, we all saw it, and agree the following: Date: 17 Sept 73. Time; approximately 2030 hrs. Location; Lakeside, Llandrindod, Wells, Radnorshire. Weather; Clear and very bright.

The object was first seen when directly overhead and it travelled in a northerly direction. The sighting from directly over head to the horizon, was approximately 1 minute duration. All that was apparent was a light approximately twice as bright as the stars. The light itself was steady. It was not accompanied by other lights, eg. navigation lights. The course appeared to vary slightly either side of a straight line. The light was 'whitish', similar to the stars. There was no apparent sound, and there was no resultant trail. Military aircraft on manouvres are a frequent sight in this area, and we have all observed these, and civil aircraft in parts at night. The basic dis-similarity between what we saw on this occasion and those aircraft, convinced us that this was different.

> Yours etc. RT Long.
> 12 Llais-yr-Afon, Garth,
> Llangammarch Wells, Breconshire. '

RIDDLE OF GHOST SOS FLARES.

Mysterious distress flares being fired in the Channel are threatening to disrupt rescue services off the Kent coast. Coastguards, lifeboats and inshore rescue craft have wasted hours answering distress calls and found no one in need of help. Police are working on the theory that a gang of smugglers is deliberately drawing attention to one part of the coast while landing their illegal cargo or immigrants elsewhere. Dungeness lifeboat coxswain Tom Tart, 58, said yesterday: " On both times we were called out last month, visibility was perfect, but we found no trace of anyone in distress. The danger is that while we are chasing mystery flares, there will be a genuine disaster and we shall not be able to cope with it." A Department of Trade and Industry spokesman said: "There have been too many examples of people firing distress flares when they are not in real distress. But some of the recent calls cannot be explained that way. They are a mystery."

Over the years we have noticed many reports of mysterious activity on the south coast of England - and occasionally a UFO type of light drags a lifeboat out to sea. Could this be such?
> Sunday Mirror 14 Oct 73.

THE GREAT 1973 FLAP, USA, cont...

It seems that the USA is in the grip of another UFO flap - the papers over there being full of reports most days. What has trickled through the media over here has tended toward the hysterical and the supercilious. The list of 'official' sightings grows with the Governor of Ohio (Daily Mail, 19 Oct.); Air Force Chief of Staff, General George Brown, says US Forces in Vietnam were plagued with the things (Daily Mail, 25 Oct.); Senator Barry Goldwater (Daily Express, 8 Nov); and Georgia Governor Jimmy Carter (Daily Mail, 15 Sept), all this year; credit for above to Steve Moore and David McAllister.

Two 'abduction' incidents within 24 hours. Two Mississippi fishermen of Pascagoula River saw a strange object surrounded by blue haze. Creatures with crab-like hands grabbed them and dragged them into the craft. The aliens had pinkish-grey wrinkled skin, big eyes, pointed ears and noses, and no toes. The two were subjected to an examination and became weightless when touched by the creatures. (Sun. 16 Oct 73. Credit: Cathy Purcell.) (A fuller account appeared in the Guardian, but we have no date for it. Credit: Michael Start). The next day, 150 miles NWest, in Louisiana, at Slidell, a sheriffs deputy claimed his car was attacked by 'an orange-reddish object (no! not an orange raddish.) 'Our deputies spotted them, and so did a bunch of witnesses. One of the deputies was scared pretty bad,' said Deputy Sheriff Michael Moore. The object was about 15ft in diameter and glowing red. From the Sun. 17 Oct 73.

UFO AT BARR BEACON.

The following is a letter to the editor of the Sutton News - and Barr Beacon is a prominent Ley centre just north of Birmingham.

'About two or three years ago, I was leaving my friend's cottage, late one night, in company with her and her daughter, when this 'thing' like a brilliant orange kite arose from the trees, ascending and descending slowly twice. I was rendered rather hysterical and we returned to the cottage for a while. We were in the Blake Street area facing Barr Beacon, at about 11 pm. I am quite certain there was no aircraft around at the time and the night was eerily quiet. I am not a nervous person but that night I will not forget in a hurry.
> Margaret Carpenter.
> 69 Blackberry Lane, Four Oaks.'
Credit: Cathy Purcell.

Uncle Chao's glee club

We have a note drawn from the 'America' column of the Daily Mail (20 June 73. Credit: Steve Moore.) that a man received offers to appear as a celebrity in Las Vegas after lightning had struck him - and welded the zip on his trousers. We are reminded of our story (N1.p16.) of Ranger Roy Sullivan, who has been struck by lightning five times. In INFO 11 there are a few more details of his extraordinary story - including one bolt blowing his shoes off without undoing the laces. There just might be something in the concept of life being the 'Sport of the Gods'. We are attracted to the notion of a Cosmic Joke Department, despite its cynical overtones, and will give it room to develop.

LITTLE THINGS MEAN A LOT.

Many of our notes seem trivial - we suspect that we have very little idea of what makes something 'important', or even how relevancy can be assessed regarding the total picture, which, of course, we may never know. We can only go on collecting and hoping that somethings will click with someone, somewhere, sometime. Dermot Purgavie, demon reporter for the Daily Mail,wrote the following piece, (20 Oct 73):

A little respect if you please. You happen to be listening to one of the few people who know that if the progent of one pair of flies lived for a year, the earth would be covered by flies to a depth of 47 feet. I can't say too much more at the moment because I don't want to spoil my chances in America's National Trivia Tournament, in which 60 teams with a consuming madness for the insignificant will compete in San Francisco next month.

It is organised by Ron Myers of the California Trivia Society, an admirable man, erudite enough to share with me the knowledge that the smallest tube in the world has a bore of .00013 in. and is used for the artificial insemination of mosquitoes; and that the longest known palindrome is Saippuakauppias, which is Finnish for 'soap-seller'. I hope you will be appropriately proud when I've won, and over the cheering drift the strains of the National Anthem, which by the way was played 17 times in succession by a band on the platform of Rathenau railway station in Germany in 1909 while Edward VII was inside the rain struggling into his uniform." Credit: Steve Moore.

We rather like another of the notes sent to us by the puckish Steve Moore, from the Daily Mail 6 Jan 73. 'Presumably working on the theory that the further you get from things the more objective you become, scientists are to meet to discuss 'reality' at a convention hotel in Florida's Disneyworld.

REVIEWS

BLACK HOLES - THE END OF THE UNIVERSE? by John Taylor.   Souvenir. £2.50.

Steadily since the 18th century, Science has attracted more and more of the allegiances due to the Church. Well, Forteans can only give a knowing wink about all this, because very little has changed when it comes to handing out dogma. We see that Science has its devotees and fanatics; its high priests and rituals; its prophets and heretics. That pillar of materialism, physics, becomes more like metaphysics as particles are probed for their constituents. And of course Science has its own energetic eschatology - the Big Bang; Entropy; and now the added but equally inevitable doom of the Black Holes (stars so dense they collapse, inexorably dragging in the rest of the universe).

Here, for those who missed his Horizon TV programme, is it all again, with the dubious bonus of Prof. Taylor's thoughts on mysteries ingeneral For a scientist he is much given to sweeping generalisations on the mysteries, origins and evolution of man, though and universe. If only he'd been more careful - or stuck to the Holes he loves and knows.

The structure of his argument is that Science (man's supreme achievement) responds to a challenge - the unknown is a threat to man - the Black Hole is the ultimate unknown - and Science like Lochinvar, come riding to the rescue. "The only hope is to turn to science to get mankind out of the present chaos," he says, unassailed by nagging doubts. "In religion one has to be initiated with the faith and encouraged to make the leap of belief to accept the mysterious for what it is, as always mysterious. The scientist is trained in completely the opposite tradition, always to question how, always to penetrate the unknowable and make it clear," etc. Was that an Olympian guffaw I heard? Maybe I'm being difficult, but if it can be known, it is not unknowable - and how can I take seriously what he says about the Holes? By Clarke's Law alone it is going to be far more fantastic than we can imagine.

And what was that about Faith? Later Taylor declares that science "is an alternative method of defusing the mysterious to that of simply labelling it 'infinite' and kneeling before it." Does he really think it's as simple as that? The evidence in the book would make it appear so - ascribing the failure of the mighty civilisations of the past to their dependence on religion. On looking through his choices of emotive words we see that he has confused religion and faith with dogma and ritual; and knowledge with wisdom.

The quotes I've used contain the seeds of his own faith in science - faith that it is a true path to knowledge; faith that what are known as scientific laws and mathematical constants have some consistancy throughout time and space; and above all that some kind of value or positive virtue can be gained by steadfastly pursuing the rape of the 'infinite'. All of which can be summed up - that scientists' holiest task is to bang their heads against the brick wall of the 'unknowable'. The book does have a certain fascination - the discussions of the properties of Black Holes are quite interesting, but definitely 'popular science' stuff. I guess it'll do well enough.

LOST WORLDS - SCIENTIFIC SECRETS OF THE ANCIENTS by Robert Charroux.   Souvenir. £2.75.

In almost complete contrast, we have this book

by Charroux, the title of which seems to bear little relationship to its contents. A recent editorial in Flying Saucer Review pointed out the contribution to UFOlogy by the French, and in a way this is also true of fortean-related studies. Charroux himself is relatively unknown in England because of the lack of translations, but on the continent he has large followings, and even it appears, Robert Charroux clubs.

This book is another exposition in his quest to understand what he calls 'the mysterious unknown'. The first half contains the usual fortean mysteries (Bermuda triangle, Mary Celeste, the Nazca lines, Easter island & Mu, ancient transplant surgery, etc), but this time he gives us the results of a personal investigation, and admits to some unsubstantiated evidence in his writings before this. 'Mea culpa,' he cries, and rights his wrongs by seeing for himself. But this (now familiar) fare is only to be the hors d'oevres - the main course being a series of hypotheses, which are discussed to very little conclusion: that Love is more akin to a satanic than an Ideal state, affecting as it does our approach to morals, our judgement, our health, and our relationship to others; that eroticism has a rightful place in mysticism, in the worship of the Great Mother (the profoundest and oldest of religions from which none of us is free); the relationship between eroticism and creative imagination; the relationship between polywater, the philosophers' stone and Virgin Birth; and that the spacemen/Gods and many other visitors from elsewhere were Initiators in all senses of the word.

Next he devotes a heavy section to the idea that the foundation of Christianity was a conspiracy of gigantic proportions. The historical mystery of Jesus, is, as he phrases it, "examined from the most heretical viewpoints in a smell of fire and brimstone." Not, he is quick to stress, that this undermines the true spiritual values of the Church - only that doubts must be expressed about the orthodox version of the events in the life of Jesus, the authenticity of the Gospels, (over a hundred of the 'excluded' Gospels). Indeed, Charroux lays inspiration for the plot at the feet of the rather extremist and anti-establishment Essenes, and later perpetuated by various Popes. The book then ends in a succession of apparantly unconnected stories, as before including a discussion of fish-like alien visitors, and extra-terrestrial experiments , and whether the <u>dolphin</u> is not our ancestor.

The presentation, as a whole, is quite calm and reminiscent of the cool gallic style typical of the Pauwels & Bergier team. For Forteans who want more than a repetitious presentation of notes and stories, there is discussion and speculation but alas it is short and fragmented. Those working for the restoration of the mysteries of our ancient Isles will find interesting correlations abounding. Charroux (and the French Rosicrucians)are very much aware of our pre-Celtic heritage and the cult of the terrestrial currents.

One defect in this well illustrated edition is that many other illustrations referred to in the text (and they sound quite interesting ones too) seem to have been omitted in translation. Charroux seems to be working toward a magnum opus on the 'mysterious unknown' which I eagerly await - in fact anycontribution to the central body of speculative philosophy that Fortean and allied studies now needs to bind them into an effective and realistic force will be most welcome and timely. A nice one - but not a great one - worth it if you can afford it.

WASHED—UP!

THE "Loch Ness monster" is alive and well . . . and living in a lake near Slough.

She is the invention of 23-year-old Colin Gross, an electronics engineer, who loves making radio - controlled models. His "Nessie" is made of polystyrene.

The power for cruising on the lake comes from an engine and remote controls built into three washing-up liquid bottles.

Nessie revealed — with her inventor.

Sunday People. 21 Oct 73.

help

Paul Screeton, of 5 Egton Drive, Seaton Carew, Hartlepool, County Durham TS25 2A2, seeks personal accounts of witches, ghosts & elementals (fairies) in the counties of Northumberland & Durham. He is researching for books on these subjects.

THE EDITOR would like to hear from anybody who can help out with typing the copy for the NEWS, (access to an electric typer of some sort is fairly essential). We are also considering the idea of publishing, at the end of each volume, an analysis or reference index of notes - and we are looking for someone insane enough to take on the job of compilation. Please write if you'd like to discuss it or want more info.

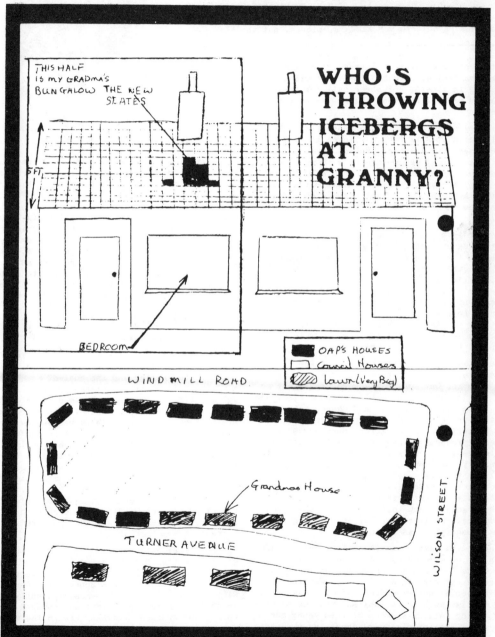

WHO'S THROWING ICEBERGS AT GRANNY?

ᚦᚻᛖ ᚱᛖᚹᛋ vol.1. no.3. MARCH 1974.

THE NEWS is a non-profit-making bi-monthly miscellany of
Fortean news and notes. Edited and published by Robert JM
Rickard, (with an arrangement with INFO.) - 31 Kingswood
Road, Moseley, Birmingham B13 9AN. *@*@*@*@*@*@*@*@*@*@
Single issues - 35p. 6 issue sub. £1.80. or $4.50. POs &
Cheques payable to RJM Rickard, please, not the NEWS.

We have collected so much material over the past
few months that we have had to be selective - no
bad thing in itself, but sheer hell for those of
us who do not believe that things can be categ-
orised.

We are begining to get the response that makes
it all worth it - letters, articles and heaps
of cuttings. For instance, Robert Forrest has
written asking if we could have a 'Rowdy Corner'
as most orthodox periodicals carry a 'Quiet Corner' for pithy potted philosophical witticisms.
We like the idea, but it got crowded out of this
issue - but send in contributions for future
gaps.

Our cover is by a T. Upton (aged 13), who wrote
a letter describing his Granny's house which was
hit by an ice chunk from the sky. We feature
this and other notes on the subject in our FALLS
section. Also in this issue is a piece by Nigel
Watson on Radio SOS 'Hoaxes' - and an outline of
the current research programme into the correlation of Leys and Fortean phenomena, from Phil
Grant and his intrepid band in the Bournemouth
area. We would like to hear more from local
groups of researchers of their work.

Financially, we are still not out of the wood.
We need more subscribers, as quick as we can
rope them in. Our sub. rates were worked out so
that they might remain stable for some time, and
that is despite Armageddon and Chaos, Acts of
Printers and the impending paper shortage. With
more subscribers we can afford more pages, and
better reproduction, and luxuries like airmail-
ing issues to our foreign friends. We are quite
a minority interest and growth to security is
likely to be slow - but each one of you can help.
If you have friends of a Fortean bent - or correspond with others interested in the pursuit
of the Unknown, then tell them about the NEWS,
or buy them an issue - or better still, give a
years subscription as a present.

Coming in the next issue is quite a scoop. Some
years ago we were entranced by an article by
Mary Caine on the Glastonbury Zodiac - she has
agreed to our reprinting a revised version, including aerial survey photos and diagrams. From
time to time we hope to publish articles on Leys
introducing various aspects of this young and
very vital area of discovery about our own past.
The Glastonbury Zodiac was the first of several

terrestrial zodiacs found landscaped into the
countryside of Britain, and form a central clue
to the use of the Leys in ancient pre-history.
HELP.

Richard Crowe has asked us to print his request
for any information on tracks or 'footprints' in
stone 'from the old Celtic countries' or anywhere in Western Europe. Anyone who knows of any
local curiosities of this nature are asked to
write to Richard, who is attempting to compile
a 'complete' list on the subject at: 5613 South
Keeler Avenue, Chicago, Illinois 60629. USA.

aerial curiosities
GAME GETS ITS OWN BACK.

We have a curious collection of notes from the
last months of 1973 concerning the reversal of
roles by the hunter and the hunted. For instance
a 73-year-old retired businessman Francis Wearne
out shooting pheasants on Dartmoor with a 79-year
old friend. A bird pops out of the hedges, and
Mr. Wearne fires, as the bird passes low overhead. The shot bounces off the bird and hits the
luckless hunter in the eye, which shortly became
bruised and swollen. He was admitted to Torbay
Hospital, Torquay for observation, but died
during the night. A police spokesman said: "It
appears that the pellet entered his eyelid and
touched the brain causing a fatal blood clot."
His widow commented: "It was a chance in a
million." (Daily Mirror. 23 Nov 73. Credit: R.
Forrest.)

The next incident was said to be a million-to-
one chance too. Bob Peace, of Scunthorpe, was
driving his lorry back to the firm's depot along
the A18 at Crowle. He was approaching Double
Rivers when 'he saw two swans apparently coming
in to land on the water. But one changed its
course and crashed straight through the windscreen of the lorry.' The swan was killed instantly, and Bob managed to keep control of the

vehicle as the dead bird landed almost in his lap. (Scunthorpe Evening Telegraph. 28 Dec 73. Credit: Nigel Watson). See our FALLS section for a tale of ducks plummeting out of the sky.

Yessir, someone or something Up There seems to be chucking things at people. Daily Mail 29 Nov 73 - Maryland Secretary of State Fred Wineland, was aiming at his second goose when the first one he'd shot fell on him from 100ft up. He was knocked out, cracked four ribs,and his dignity was badly bruised. Maryland also figures later.

From New England comes a report that hunters are suffering acute frustration because the grouse are committing suicide before they can be peppered with lead. For a week (says the note) tales of kamikaze birds were being told, flights through or into the sides of barns, walls and windows. Explanations have been ventured from being drunk on fermenting fruit or hallucinating on fungus, to the theory that they are responding to some unselfish stimulus to thin out over-populated flocks. (Daily Mail. 2 Nov 72. Credit: Steve Moore.) You notice how the most obvious theory is always overlooked? That out of some obstinate and cantankerous pique a plot may be hatching to turn the tables, to deprive the hunters of their explosive depravity. No? Well... we've always been a bit suspicious of the 'obvious' ourselves.

Perhaps pheasants were feeling particularly peeved at the end of November - leastways they had a few tales to tell wherever pheasants gather at the end of the day to tell their tales. Some, like Peter Cowtan, just come right out asking for it - striding around on a Berkshire moor with an ample, russet-coloured pheasant-like beard. Before the day was out somebody had shot half his beard clean off his face; miraculously he was unharmed. (Daily Express. 29 Nov 73). This seems far from the bizarre anomalies most think to be exclusively fortean. It may seem inconsequential, but it smacks to us of an outrageous justice, and after all, that is a <u>kind</u> of hidden universal force.

Some birds take a more practical way out - he who runs away lives to run away another day. James Twomey, a Nottingham chiropodist,was waiting for his next client, when in walked a cockerel with swollen feet. Said Mr Twomey: "My street door is always open in the daytime. Suddenly the cock came in, limped around, and look-at me with his head on one side. Its quite fantastic that of all the houses on the road it should seek refuge in a chiropodist's. Somebody had obviously tried to fatten it up...and the feet were swollen through having run a long way. (Daily Mail. 8 Dec 72. Credit: Steve Moore.)

From Westminster, Maryland, comes a tale of a dog shooting a hunter. Charles Brown, 69, was nearing the end of a day's shooting, when a companion put his gun down to pick up a bird. An excited dog, eager for more fun, jumped on the gun and Brown was hit in the lower right leg. (Daily Mail. 25 Oct 72.) We also have a note that

a dog in Brooklyn bit a policeman in the leg and immediately dropped dead. The dogs of Brooklyn are not noted for their sensitive palates. The policeman said: "It didn't bark or nothing. It just bit and died." (Daily Mail. 11 Nov 72. Credit for both items to Steve Moore.)

animal curiosities

A CHIMP THAT CAN READ.

Three days into the new year - and the Circus is in full tilt. The Daily Mirror (3 Jan 74. Credit: Robert Forrest.) carries an account of some experiments by Prof. Duane Rumbaugh, at Ape City, the primate research centre at Emory University, Atlanta, Georgia. Lana, a 2-year-old chimp, in a special cage with colour-coded push-button panels linked to a computer, can punch simple sentences to order food, watch TV, or listen to records. To our minds this achievement is in danger of being undervalued. Those of us afflicted with sticky nephews who can only grunt or scowl through a similar itinery, know that this is a significant step in some kind of direction.

Cathy Purcell sent us a note about a talking cat (Weekend. 5 Dec. but unidentified year, probably recent.) Mrs. Kamile Mutluturk of Konya, Turkey, was woken from her sleep, when her 5-year-old cat, Pala, jumped onto the bed, and whispered in her ear: "Mother, mother," She told her husband who naturally didn't believe her, until he heard for himself. Pala can say it's mistress's name (which is more than we can), the name of her daughter Alba, and the Turkish words for mother and father.

OF DOGS LOST...AND FOUND.

Barry, a huge Alsatian, was sold by his master (?), Armin da Broi, to a neighbour. On a visit to Bari in Southern Italy, the dog escaped. One year later Barry turned up on Armin's doorstep having travelled 1200 miles (at least) to find his changeable master in Solingen, West Germany. Armin has vowed they will not be parted again. (Ahhhh!) Sunday Mirror. 30 Dec 73).

Peter Rogerson sent us a note from the Daily Mail 3 Jan 74, that Santa, a huge St Bernard, had disappeared for four months, and was only recovered by his owners 'luckily' spotting a photo of the dog in the papers. I guess the odds on that would be quite large.

Before you put your handkerchiefs away, here is one more. Albert and Estelle Bondel from Belgium stopped in the Black Forest for a picnic, leaving their dog Rudi, a huge mongrel, asleep in the back of the car. When they had finished, they drove off. They didn't notice the dog was missing until they reached the Belgian border some hours later. In July 1973, almost 12 months later, they returned to the Black Forest in a half-hearted attempt to find him. For two hours they tried to find the spot they had picnicked. They were about to give up when they heard a barking. Yes..it was Rudi who came bounding up to them in happy joy. They learned from a local cafe proprietor that the dog had been seen frequently during the year, coming into the village in search of scraps, but always going back into the forest before nightfall. (Weekend. 5-11 Dec. 73. Credit: A Smith.)

GOLDILOCKS AND THE THREE BEARS.

Another Ahhhh! story... we're getting them over with before/we get all choked up and can't go on. This concerns the real-life adventures of a goldilocks, 5-year-old Goranka Cuculic, who got lost in a forest near her home village of Vranje in Yugoslavia. Parents and villagers with dogs and torches combed the forest. When woodcutters told of seeing bears in the vicinity, there was despair at ever seeing little Goranka alive... except for farmer Ivan Furian, who roamed deeper and deeper into the forest, armed only with a cudgel. A nice touch, that cudgel, the word gives this story an added storybook charm. Anyway, as in all goodfairy tales, Ivan found her, cold and hungry. Replete, she told of how she met the three bears. "One was big and fat, and the other two were quite small and as cuddly as they make them. I played in a meadow with the two small ones and shared my biscuits with them. The big one licked my face...its tongue tickled no end. At night I snuggled between the cubs and was beautifully warm. The next day I somehow lost my teddy bears. Then I found I was lost too. I spent another night in the cave, but it was cold and dismal and I was frightened. I was glad when Uncle Ivan found me and I hope I meet them again". (Daily Mirror. 3 Nov 1971. Credit: A Smith.)

968 PIGS ON A RAMPAGE EAT A PLANE.

Prompted by our note on the cows who licked the paint off a helicopter (NEWS 1. p3.), reader Robert Forrest was reminded of the following incident, which he duly sent to us.

Sam Cottle's hungry pigs went on a rampage, eating anything they could lay their snouts on... including the plane, an Auster, parked at the farm. They completely devoured the planes fabric. "This is a very unusual case...pigs eating an aeroplane," remarked the prosecuting council at Devizes Crown Court, Wiltshire. In the dock was Wilfred Grist, pigman on Craymarsh Farm, Seend, owned by Mr. Cottle.

Grist is accused of deliberately opening the Sty gate, and the Court heard that the pigs went on, tearing into $2\frac{1}{2}$ tons of hay, a straw rick, half a ton of cattle food, and 30 asbestos sheets. They uprooted 3 acres of pastureland, damaged four farm gates, and were 'running around berserk. Ten were killed as they fought among them-selves.'

We note our (almost) blasé acceptance of such behaviour - pigs is pigs, and eating is their thing. What is more curious is the odd behaviour of the people involved. Grist claimed that Cottle hit him, then Cottle and his brother put him in a car saying they were going to put him in a

slurry pit. Later, Cottle admitted, he changed his mind - they were going to put him in a giant animal-food mixer. Hmm. With food like that we would probably develop a hankering for aeroplane fabric ourselves. Anyway, the story is from the Daily Mirror 13 April 1972.

While we are on the subject of animals getting their own back, and eating on the attack, we have a little story of the San Francisco police chasing a zebra down a six-lane freeway at 45 mph. When stopped, it kicked in two doors, smashed a mudguard, climbed on the bonnet, chewed up the steering wheel and bit two handlers before being returned to the Marine World zoo. (Daily Mail. 27 Oct 1972. Credit: Steve Moore.)

appearances

THE PHANTOM FARMER SOWS ANOTHER GHOST CROP.

Madelon Dimont. Rome. The phantom farmer has struck again - and once more a 'ghost' crop of wheat is springing up. The crop is growing in a $2\frac{1}{2}$ acre field left fallow by a land-owner near Milan. No one has seen the phantom - but again and again he has planted wheat on uncultivated lands in North Italy. And each time the crop has ripened, the phantom has returned unheard and unseen, to reap the harvest. His acres of golden wheat have vanished overnight. Now, the angry land-owner has laid charges against 'unknown persons' for invasion of his land. And police have decided to leave the crop to ripen, and lie in wait for him. (Daily Mirror. 29 April 1968. Credit: Anthony Smith.)

Fort noted a few 'phantom crop' stories in his books. These stories bear some curious affinity with poltergeists and the falls of various things...the sudden appearance of something. This something being confined to a definite area and homogenous throughout. Consider the possibility of a fall of seeds, all of one kind, from some point more or less stationary above a field. Or that in response to a need elsewhere the seeds were caused to appear in unused ground, ripen and harvested by a mysterious process and sent to answer the call - or perhaps, to judge from our experience of having needy calls answered, the stuff was dumped down somewhere else, and the forteans of that place logged up one more curiosity. We have notes on falls of straw.

SOMETHING FISHY UNDER THE PIER.

Experts were puzzling over the appearance of a rare tropical fish...under Southend Pier. The $5\frac{1}{2}$lb. Plectropoma Oligacanthus, normally found only in the Pacific, was still twitching, say the three schoolboys who pulled it out of the water. One expert said: "Unless someone says they dumped such a fish in the sea nearby, it will remain a mystery." (Daily Mirror. 14 Aug. 73. Credit: Anthony Smith.)

SCAN YOUR LOCAL PAPERS, AND....

FISH MYSTERY.

From letters to the Editor, Sunday Express. 20 Jan 74:

Visiting a trout farm near the village of Valls on the German-Dutch border, I found the employees puzzling over a wounded salmon swimming among the baby trout. It had wounds on its back. It hadn't been there the day before and the farm had been guarded, as usual, during the night. The only theory we can think of, which fits our facts is that a large bird, possibly an Osprey, caught the salmon at sea, and lost its grip over land....more than 100 miles from the coast! Better theories will be welcomed.

William Fisher.
Grant St, Glasgow.

(Credit: DJ McAllister.)

archaeology

ANCIENT MAP WAS 'TOO GOOD'- IS IT A FORGERY?

We reprint here an article from the Sunday Times (3 Feb 74) - the map is from an introductory article in the same paper (27 Jan 74).

AFTER SO many years of mingled acclaim and doubt, what remains of the prestige of the Vinland map? Now that scientific tests have unmasked its supposedly medieval coastlines and portentous Latin captions as being entirely penned in modern ink, must the learned world now accept that someone tried to perpetrate on it the most elaborate and ingenious historical forgery of recent times?

At a private meeting of the Royal Geographical Society in London tomorrow, a gathering of scholars and experts, ranging in attitudes from the fairly loyal to the always-sceptical, will try to determine whether the costly piece of parchment now sheds any authentic light on early cartography and the claims of a Viking settlement of North America before Columbus.

Support for it was dwindling fast last week even at Yale University, one of whose benefactors reputedly spent £100,000 in acquiring the document on its behalf, triumphantly launching it on Columbus Day, 1965, only after it had been given several years of careful scrutiny. Yale's librarian, Mr Rutherford Rogers, says that the report of the ink-analysis from the laboratories who have re-examined it seemed "overwhelming evidence" that the Vinland map was a forgery.

The feeling among scholars on this side of the Atlantic was generally that the tests had simply confirmed long-held doubts about this intriguing maverick of cartography, which would have been the first-known Viking map, with the odd lump of "Vinland" stuck up in the top left-hand corner where Labrador or Newfoundland might be. "There appears to be hardly any loophole through which the Vinland map can regain credibility," comments Dr Helen Wallis, head of the map room at the British Museum.

The map has been questioned on many grounds over the years and the fact that Yale put an insurance value of $1.5 million on its head did nothing to cement its esteem with some. There should have been no school of Norse cartography at all, since the Vikings used an oral tradition of sailing directions, sun and star sights. Gerald Crone, formerly head of the Royal Geographical Society's map room, never found it credible. "Greenland was too good," he says—a phrase that may haunt the alleged forger as his biggest mistake—in the way it suggested that Vikings had rounded even the north coast of Greenland in open boats, centuries before their time.

As long ago as 1962 Dr Eva Taylor, Emeritus professor of geography at Birkbeck College, London, wrote a lengthy analysis of the map's false pretensions (to be published in the next issue of "Journal of Navigation"), concluding that the map had been cribbed from various source-books in American libraries.

But the forger, if there be one, was fiendishly plausible, as Holmes might put it, in the way he presented the package. To have kept cartographers, historians, geographers, and others, in a state of nagging doubt for 17 years is no mean feat. It was beautifully "laundered," in Watergate terminology.

The map apparently passed from an Italian bookseller in Barcelona to a now-defunct but respected Hampstead firm, Davis and Orioli. It was bound up with an undoubtedly authentic medieval manuscript called the "Tartar Relation." A second book, also authentic, called the "Speculum," which matched the script of the other perfectly, was found (by a coincidence that staggered some scholarly minds) by a Yale curator. Both hung perfectly together with the Vinland map.

George Painter, of the British Museum's department of printed books, is one of the few who still gives great credence to the way the three documents hang together, down to the very wormholes. He points out that a number of the captions on the Vinland map are taken verbatim from the Latin of the "Tartar Relation" which is itself unique and a definite historical discovery in its own right. For a forger to have kept dark about the "Tartar Relation" until he could present a bogus map with it argues a formidable patience.

No one can yet guess clearly what the motives of a forgery could be. The map was sold to Yale by Lawrence Witten, a Connecticut bookseller.

He bought it from Enzo Ferrajoli, a Barcelona agent in antique books, in Geneva in 1957. Mr Witten pointed out last week that he had no reason to suspect a forgery. He had dealt with Ferrajoli before. He only paid $3,500 for the map—a small amount of Ferrajoli had set up an elaborate forgery.

Mr Witten still does not think it is a forgery. He says that he has visited the Smithsonian Institute, the Washington museum, and given all details of his financial transactions to refute the "rumours" of passing off a fake as genuine.

He confirms that Ferrajoli did not give the previous owner's name. This is common practice, but scholars say they would very much like to know more about this provenance before dismissing Vinland as a truly dead but well-flown duck.

Roy Perrott

ROME'S IMPERIAL BEAGLE.

Snoopy, Charlie Brown's philosophical beagle, has just sprouted a distinguished and classical pedigree - according to the Vatican. The pensive pooch, says Professor Filippo Magi, director of the Vatican's Archeological Study and Research, first appeared 1600 years ago. A vast market of the first century after Christ has been discovered under the Papal Basilica of St Mary Major, one of Rome's most historic churches. And there, amid some crowd-scene grafiti, is traced a creature, which is pure copybook Snoopy. Some Rome newspapers are reported to be showing cartoons of Snoopy in his most comfortable, kennel-roof, prone position (tummy much in evidence), thinking: "Suspirium! Aetate progredi, heu!" (Translation: Sigh! The years roll on, alas!) Daily Mail. 22 Jan 1973. Credit: Steve Moore.

RUSSIAN MAMOTH BUGGED.

At a recent Academy of Sciences symposium on the mamoth, in Novosibirsk, scientists were able to examine the nearly complete skeleton and parts of the bowel of a mamoth reckoned to have lived 20,000 years ago on the Shandrin River. The remains of the animal were flown intact inside the 500 kilogram iceblock. Paleontologists then discovered larvae of an unknown species of botfly, which lived in and on the mamoth and died out with it. Novosti Bulletin 14677. 17 Jan 74.

PROFESSIONAL JOURNALS FOR DATA.

disappearances

Paul Screeton sent us this cartoon cutting with the question: 'Bermuda Triangle?'

RIDDLE OF MISSING STUDENT.

Lucy Partington, 21, on vacation from Exeter University, told a friend, Helen Render, of Culcross Place, Cheltenham, that she was just going outto post a letter, then catch the bus to nearby Gretton. That was at 10.15pm, and the busstop was less than 200 yards from the house. The bus never stopped at the stop because there was no one waiting there. Since then, the evening of 29 Dec 73 police have exhausted their enquiries. Thanks to Pete Rogerson who sent the above from Daily Mail. 31 Dec 73. A fairly long story of sorts appeared in the Sunday Express for 27 Jan 74. We learn that between leaving the house and the scheduled bus time was ten minutes, and whatever hapened happened then. The only lead the police have come up with, is that she was a recent convert to Catholicism and if she was alive somewhere or in retreat, she would not want to miss Mass, and so a watch on Masses 'throughout Britain' has been undertaken. But to judge from the silence in the media, the case is still far from solved.

FAMILY DISAPPEAR IN RUSSIAN DESERT.

Vladimir Dmitrenko, with his wife and two kids (only 18 months, and 9 years), was driving down to the Caspian Sea to take up a new job. At some point, he took a wrong turning, and drove on out into the desert for 175 miles before the car just stopped - no petrol. Vladimir decided to set out (off to the right), on foot. After a considerable time, his wife became worried, then desperate. She wrote a message for her husband in case he came back - then set off carrying the baby, to the mountains she could see off to the left. The boy went with her. Officials reconstructed all this from a diary the couple kept in the car.

'PLANE CRASH' MYSTERY.

Police searched Hockley Woods, near Southend, Essex thoroughly after a 'plane crash' report earlier today. A caller had reported hearing a crash followed by screams for help. Police reported no planes in the area missing. Express & Star. 3 Aug 73. Credit: Anthony Smith.

HUSBAND'S AIR HUNT.

After a report that his missing wife had been seen walking near their country home yesterday, antique dealer John Lincoln called in a friend with a helicopter, and they made an aerial search for the 37-year-old mother of five who vanished last Thursday. "We covered a large area but there was no sign of Patricia. She has suffered from depressions since an operation a year ago." Daily Express. 12 Nov 73.

TWO JETS MISSING.

RAF planes joined an air and sea search off Cape Town yesterday for two South African jets and their four crew members missing after an exercise. Daily Mirror. 26 Nov 73. Credit: A Smith.

esp & powers

URI GELLER.

Since our little piece on Geller in NEWS 2 his media exposure has been fantastic - with some organisations like the Society for Psychical Research, and the 'New Scientist' falling over themselves to test him, whilst the obstinately sceptical have their knives out for our mystic cutlery-twister. (And that is not an allusion to the threats on his life recently, which, looking at it callously, has neatly got him away from the test-hungry mobs.) Most of the arguments we have run across have confused two things in the desire to prove or disprove - that Telekinesis (TK) exists; and that Geller has it.

The first is what the NEWS is all about. We believe, if we believe anything at all, in the continuity of all phenomena, the totality and integrity of the organic universe. Fort, when he let it shine through, had a fondness for the idea of a 'Teleportative Force' (remember, he invented the word) that responded to universal need or will - it lifted frogs, blood and stones from one place and dumped it in others; it started fires and powered ghosts and UFOs - and often reacted to express a sentience - a life or living force. Men have run across it at various times giving aspects of names like Vril, Od, Orgone, Mana, Ley Power, etc. It certainly is about time the research-energy itself is coordinated. We see no reason to doubt the existance of TK or whatever - it seems a more efficient way of moving things around on the universal level. Indeed , by Occam's Razor, it simplifies and unifies many previously seperate and inexplicable events.

Does Geller have TK? Well - if he hasn't, some believe he has, and vice versa. Fortunately for us the universe is not run by the concensus of opinions; it goes on despite our beliefs. We have seen metallurgists come forward and say that on analysis, Gellerised items show no sign of work-hardening toward the fracture; that the break was more akin to a tensile than a flexing action. And in one case he would have had to apply 63lbs pressure on a stubby key with his thumb and finger - try it sometime! No wonder the magicians (how pathetic the modern usage of the word sounds.) are getting hot under their budgie-stuffed jackets - for it is clear he is using no tricks from their armory - from known science too, come to that. We have so much material that we will only cover the most pertinent and interesting. But the file is available to anyone who wants to follow each bend and twist in the saga.

TELEPORTATION.

Apart from the now familiar references to stopping escalators in Munich, and motor-yaughts in the Mediterranean, there have been inferences of more dramatic displays of TK. The News of the World (2 Dec 73) mentioned that Geller had TKed a camera-case from New York to Tel Aviv; and himself from NY to Brazil; and that he is going to try and return a camera-case from the Moon, left there by Ed Mitchell in 1969.

There were also stories of teleporting eggs: for instance, this story from author Felice Gordon: "Uri telephoned me from New York, he said that a black and orange papier-maché egg had just appeared in his living room. He felt it was mine and wanted to check. I said I had several decorative eggs but only one like that. I went into my bedroom where I keep it in a drawer. It wasn't there. If the one he has got is mine, I have no explanation of how it got there. He briefly visited my house in Kensington at my invitation - but he didn't go into my bedroom." (Sunday Express. 16 Dec 73.). In the documentary on Geller by an ITV team, it was mentioned that when Geller stayed at a friend's apartment in New York (we think), many witnesses saw a china egg follow them about from room to room, appearing near the ceiling and falling slowly to the floor. Dr Andrija Puharich, Geller's aegis at Stamford and author of a 100,000 word study of him due out in May this year, has said that Geller made his dog vanish into thin air (or to somewhere where the air might have been thinner), and reappear 60 yards away. In another experiment, he said, Geller brough a flowerbud to full bloom in 20 seconds. (Daily Express. 14 Jan 74).

If you can get hold of the latest Flying Saucer Review (Vol 19. No 5. Sept/Oct 73.), you will be rewarded by an excellent article on Geller and how Puharich found him, written before all the publicity. There is a fascinating reference to Out-of-the-body experiments, sending along a human transponder to learn about 'where' things go when he 'sends' them away. In Israel, Puharich put a Mexican silver 5 peso piece in Uri's hand and asked him to 'do' something with it, and bring it back deformed "..so that I would know something had happened to it outside the space in his hand. It takes about 600lbs of force to bend this kind of coin. Two hours later, Uri jumped up, ran to the telephone, and as he did so the 5 peso piece dropped from the ceiling, bounced off his shoulder and fell into my lap. It was bent to an angle of about 60 degrees."

GELLER AND UFO.

The rest of the reports contain few items of more than passing interest. Geller doing a Ted Serios and imprinting an image onto film in a camera with its lens cap still on (News of the World. 2 Dec 73.). The Daily Express gave half-pages to its reporter Don Coolican on 24, 25 & 26 Jan 74 for his 'expose' of Geller. He revealed the use by magicians of a liquid 'metal halide' that can force divisions on grain-boundaries in metals, making bending and breaking easier. But the Sunday Times (27 Jan 74) revealed that the substance is a cumulative poison that attacks the kidneys and is absorbed through the skin. "If Uri regularly bent spoons like this he would be 6ft underground by now." (Credit: Nigel Watson.)

In the Sunday Times,(2 Dec 73.), Puharich is reported to have said in an interview with the American magazine 'Psychic', that he and Geller drove into a desert and 'found' a UFO - 'a disc shaped metal object with a flashing blue light on top. Geller entered the UFO while Puharich filmed him, and filmed him emerging 10 minutes later. Unfortunately, Puharich explained, the record was lost, as the film cartridge dematerialised a few minutes later.' Bryan Silcock, who wrote the article, adds sarcasticly: "With friends like that, Geller has no need of detractors."

It might be amusing to note that Coolican later admitted publicly that after challenging Geller to disprove the things he had said about him, he was now back to being as puzzled as anyone else. We find that refreshing. In the Daily Express (28 Jan 74) is an account of what happened when Coolican took Geller back to a fully 'cleaned' hotel room. He frisked Geller; had him wash his hands free of any substances that might be there and then perform his key-bending in his shirt-sleeves, watched by two other reporters. After keys bent in the hands of the sceptics with Geller nowhere near them, they admitted their bafflement.

Dr Puharich rates Geller as the 'best find in 1000 years, and what we could learn from him could cause a whole new scientific revolution.' Perhaps so - but we muse on the fate of the bright hopes held out to such telekinetic powerhouses as Eusapia Palladino and DD Home, and beside whom some would say, Geller is but a psychic pstripling. If we are to get anywhere at all - we must find more Gellers; we must study, research and publish - or we may as well pack up now and go back to the oblivion of ignorance.

The scene...and results of Geller's camera experiment.   From the News of the World. 2 Dec 73.

falls

ICE FALLS.

The falls of masses of ice from the sky is only one of the many meteorological curiosities that occur from time to time. This particular issue seems to be particularly resplendant with examples of some of the others. As with any puzzling phenomena there are many theories, lots of guesses, and scientific doubletalk. Among the basic questions we should ask are, where in Heaven's name did it come from, and how did it get up there, and since some of these chunks have had calculated weights of up to half a ton plus, we must also ask how they managed to stay up there - that is, of course, unless they were teleported directly into the sky to fall?

The most common theory is that it is nothing more that a giant hailstone, or a conglomeration of the same. Investigation will show that the structure of such conglomerations, and the signs of ablation (partly melting and re-freezing) is quite distinctive and different from the blocks of homogenous ice that interest us. Giant hail is not uncommon - we have a note from the Express & Star of 23 March 1968: 'At least 20 people were killed and 150 injured when giant hailstones showered like bullets on a village on the River Ganges, near Monghyr, India, in the severest hailstorm in living memory, according to delayed reports. These said the hailstones, some weighing as much as 21lb, struck down those caught in the open; hundreds of mud and thatch houses were damaged and tiled roofs smashed. Many cattle were killed. Reuter.' (Credit: A Smith.)

For those interested in taking their interest further, we draw attention to an article on 'Ice. Falls' by Ronald J Willis, in Vol 1, No 3 of the INFO Journal. It includes a small reference list and a listing of 46 falls from 1802-1968. This list, by no means exhaustive, includes such monstrosities as the mass 'nearly 20 ft in circumference, and of proportionate thickness' that fell in August 1849 at Ord in Scotland. The problem of how they were sustained in the air is so boggling that it is not surprising to find suggestions that either they are ice meteorites, or that the darned stuff had formed and broken off the wings of overhead aircraft. It has been the-

orized that if an ice meteorite had pockets of gas within its structure and that these acted like breaking jets in steering and slowing the ice-mass, then it might survive the heat of entry into the earth's atmosphere with sufficient mass to cause what our notes have recorded. But it is quite clear from first-hand witnesses that the majority of these ice-chunks still have the pointed, sharp-edged and jagged irregularities that we normally associate with ice.

Let us quote from Willis: "If these ice masses are not meteorological products, then what are they? The common explanation today is that they fall from aircraft. However it is difficult to imagine how an ice-coating of more than several inches over the surface of the wings and control surfaces of an airplane could avoid bringing the plane down with it. Older de-icing equipment used an expandable rubber covering to break away any ice layer, and this layer could hardly be more than $\frac{1}{2}$ inch thich at any time. Modern commercial planes use an electrical heating system to melt ice as soon as it forms so there is nothing to fall. The Federal Aviation Agency informs the author that military planes usually do not have such de-icing equipment, but due to their speed and construction "the possibility of accumulating such an amount (10lbs) is extremely rare." In addition, in the modern cases, hardly any of them were correlated with any planes being in the vicinity. And the aircraft receives its final blow with the simple question: What about all the cases in the 19th century?'

Before we go on to some recent cases in our files we would like to add the quote from a letter Willis received from a Prof. Stewart, University of Virginia: "I have read of such ice falls and am rather mystified by them...I had read of the German who was killed by the 6ft mass of ice. No hailstone was ever that big. Perhaps there are ice meteorites that do not completely ablate away on the way down...this is a very mysterious thing...It can be put in the class with the small percentage of UFOs which cannot be explained away." Indeed, there are some correlations with UFO sightings, eg No 18 on the Willis list..in March 1887,'North Atlantic, Capt. Sweet reported two UFOs which fell into the sea and "immediately afterward lumps of ice fell."

ICE BOMB CRASHES THROUGH ROOF.

Pensioner Mrs Jane Williamson, 72, was bombed in her home yesterday by huge chunks of ice, more than a foot wide and six inches thick. One lump smashed through the tiles of Mrs Williamson's roof. A dozen more fell in her back garden, and one dented a car parked nearby. Mrs Williamson of Meadway, Sevenoaks, Kent, said: "I realised that even this summer, the weather couldn't be bad enough to do this. I got onto the police and they told me the ice probably fell from the wings of an aircraft."
(Daily Mirror. 19 Aug 68. Credit: A Smith.)

VAN 'BOMBED' BY ICE BLOCK FROM A PLANE.

The Mirror reporter who recorded this even seemed convinced it fell from a plane, though to be fair there is not much detail or evidence to judge either way: The 'ice bomb' fell from an aircraft flying over Bracknell, Berks, to crash through the roof of a van. The chunk was found in the driver's seat and more ice was scattered over the road. It was parked outside the home of Gerry Foulkes, in Calfridus Way, who said: "We heard a tremendous crash and thought there had been a road accident, or a plane had gone through the sound barrier. Then a neighbour came to tell us the van had been hit. My two children were playing outside shortly before. If the ice had fallen a few minutes earlier there might have been a terrible accident. A police spokesman at Bracknell, 15 miles from Heathrow Airport, said: "We are in touch with the airport about this. Until the facts are known, I can't say what action will be taken, but I think it would end up as a civil matter. An aircraft is not legally a vehicle and could not be prosecuted for having an insecure load, or anything like that." (Daily Mirror. 24 Feb 69. Credit: A Smith.)

This latter point brought to mind an article in the Times for 18 Nov 72 on 'Aircraft Damage' insurance policies. Technically, it advised, that although the damage was done by, say, the load impacting with the house, the load was not part of the plane at the time of impact, and that a successful claim does not necessarily follow. "There is, however, still plenty of worthwhile 'aircraft' cover. For instance, quite often, large blocks of ice fall from aircraft. They can cause serious damage to a house, and the chances are that one will not be able to discover from which aircraft a particular block of ice fell. In this case, the claim for cost of repairs can be made against one's own insurers, and they can try to make a recovery."

ICE CRASHES INTO HOUSE.

A huge lump of ice, big enough to kill, smashed into a house in Twickenham Road, Isleworth, Middlesex, yesterday. The family of four who live there were asleep when the block - thought to be from an aircraft - crashed through the conservatory roof. No one was hurt.
(Daily Mirror. 17 Aug 70. Credit: A Smith.)

"We've no fridge out here but we do get ice from aircraft wings delivered accidentally about once a month."
From The Times. 18 Nov 72.

ICE BOMB. 22 Sept. 73.

A ball of ice, believed to have fallen from a plane, crashed through the roof of a bungalow in Turner Avenue, Wombwell, near Barnsley, at the weekend. No one was hurt.
(Daily Express. 24 Sept 73. Credit: Phil Ledger.)
Phil Ledger followed this one up with a letter to the victims, and received the following reply from the thirteen-year-old grandson of the lady whose bungalow was hit:

"In reply to your letter. It was Saturday at 3 o'clock on the day of the Finningly Air Show. An hour after the impact three council workmen brought down a 6lb hunk of ice. Fragments of ice as big as a hand were scattered about 30ft around in the gardens of other houses. My Grandma is 76 next birthday. She has central heating in her home for about 18 months and it has never worked properly until this happened. Lately she has had constant hot water. No-one saw or heard the ice until it hit the roof, although it was a perfectly sunny day (It said in the papers it was raining at the time.) Barnsley is under the flight plan of the large planes from Europe when they start there desent over the Pennines and into Manchester. When the ice melted, there was not much water and it did not appear clean. My Grandma does not have a fridge, and is partly blind after slipping off the edge of a kerb. This is why she does not write. She is also a widow. She gave me your letter and I hope my reply is satisfactory.
T. Upton. (Age 13)."

Thanks very much, your reply is most helpful. We judge by your observation on the antics of your Grandma's central heating system, that you display commendable Fortean talents. The lad also sent with his reply, the diagram of the scene that we have used as this issue's cover, because we liked it a lot and it was relevant to this feature section.

'BLACK RAINS'

From the Daily Mail, 11 Jan 73, comes the story that Health Inspectors were trying to trace the source of a dense cloud of 'soot' which blanketed large areas of Kent, yesterday. The 'soot'

with grains the 'size of a large pinhead' covered parts of Dartford, Bexley and North Cray, and
was thought to have come from a factory, but
none in the area have admitted to causing the
pollution. (Credit: Steve Moore.)

From the Daily Mirror, 15 Jan 74, we learn that
office girls in Aldwych, London, found mysterious holes appearing in their tights, yesterday,
as a strange black rain fell. The cause was thought to be acid fumes given off by a boiler and
dissolved in the rain.

FALLS OF FROZEN DUCKS.

Frozen ducks came tumbling out of the sky above
Stuttgart, Arkansas. It was thought they had
been caught in a tornado, pitched into the sky,
'and like aircraft, got iced over'. The towns-
folk had them for dinner. This business of planes
and ice seems to be firmly written into the
human library of 'explanations'.(Credit for this
note from the Daily Express. 6 Dec 73 goes to
Paul Screeton. The same item appeared 2 days
later in the Daily Mail, Credit: Steve Moore.)
Neither tells us what we really want to know; ie
did they come down plucked and oven-ready? or
was it another case of the following: Three
deep-frozen seagulls found in the hold of a ship
carrying thousands of tons of herrings in ice
from Ullapool, Scotland to Norway, were thawed
out....and promptly flew away.(Daily Express.
24 Jan 74.)

THE FROG FALL OF '54.

Further correspondence with Mrs Sylvia Mowday,
has identified the time of the fall of frogs
she witnessed in Sutton Park, Birmingham, as
Saturday 12th June 1954. See NEWS 1. p8. for her
account. She also wrote to us something else of
interest. We quote:

'Whilst I was scanning the pages of 'The Compleat
Angler' by Izaak Walton, I came upon a reference
to 'raining of frogs' in Chapter VIII. There is
a conversation between Piscator and Venator about
frogs thus -
Ven:."But good Master, did you not say even now,
that some Frogs were venomous, and is it not
dangerous to touch them?"
Pisc: "Yes, but I will give you some rules or
Cautions concerning them. (I will miss out some
of it and continue.).. and the Land frogs are
some of them observed by him (Topsel), to breed
by laying eggs; and others to breed of the slime
and dust of the earth, and that in winter they
turn to slime again, and that the next summer
that very slime returns to be a living creature;
this is the opinion of Pliny; and Cardanus under-
takes to give a reason for the raining of Frogs;
but if it were in my power, it should rain none
but water frogs, for those I think are not venomous..." The reference is to the 19th book of
Cardanus, De Subtil, Ex. '

Always ready to bring a bit of culture to the
NEWS, we ventured to find out more and track
that 'reason' down. Hieronymous Cardanus, known
to the English as Jerome Cardan 'The Gambling

Scholar' after his work on games of Chance called
'Liber De Ludo Eleae', was in fact one Girolamo
Cardano, Italian, (1501 - 1557). And the work in
question,'De Subtilitate'.

The book was conceived in a dream - a master work
of 21 parts or books, which was completed in 8
months, and published in Nuremberg in 1550. He
was a brilliant and prolific writer. Someone
called Tiraboschi said of him: "A man of whom, if
we read only certain of his works, we should say
that he was the greatest fool that ever lived.
Who would think that he was one of the most profound geniuses that Italy had ever produced, and
that in medicine and maths he had made rare and
valuable discoveries." Sounds familiar. He was
despised by many orthodox scholars who were outraged by his apparent acceptance and belief in
dreams and superstitions, and thoroughly horrified that he dared to cast the horoscope of Christ.
Alas, our search for the literary remains of this
proto-Fort, turned up only one translation, and
only contained the first seven parts, which deal
specifically with scientific and physical notes.
So - the quest is still open. Can somebody out
there, with access to better facilities than ours,
discover exactly what Cardano said in his 19th
Book about rains of frogs? And please don't forget to let us know when you do.

fires

FIREBUG HUNT AFTER AIRPORT BLAZE.

After a wave of blazes at Heathrow Airport, the
police are hunting a probable fire-raiser, but
they are not quite sure. The lastest blaze was
in the long-distance terminal. Flames and a pall
of black smoke shot from the roof as travellers
and officials from many departments were rushed
to safety, and water poured through the roof on
to hundreds of passengers. Harvey Burrows, Deputy Chief Constable of the British Airports authority, said: "There is a possibility of a fire-
raiser on the airport - a man intent on damage.
There have been a series of fires since July. It
is all too much of a coincidence." From Daily
Mirror 27 Sept 73. Credit: DJ McAllister.

MYSTERY FIRES RIDDLE.

Srinagar, Kashmir. A Reuter's report in the
Express & Star, 19 May 1970, mentions some 538
houses in Kashmir destroyed in a series of fires
- 291 were gutted in three major incidents, two
'accidental' and one caused by a 'madman'. This
still leaves 247 conflagrations in mysterious
circumstances for the Cause-Unknown file. (Credit
Anthony Smith.)

BLAZE JUDGE FLEES BLAZE.

Mr Justice Cantley, who heads the Summerland fire
disaster inquiry on the Isle-of-Man, was among
200 people who had to be moved from a Douglas
hotel when fire broke out early yesterday.
Sunday Mirror. 25 Nov 73.

WOMAN DIES AFTER BED BLAZE.

We see a lot of this kind of story, where the
police or firemen can only 'suppose' a likely
cause for the blaze. We are interested in them
because there is 'reasonable cause for doubt'.
A conventional cause may well, in fact, be so -
the firemen are experts of a kind and generally
first-hand witnesses. While we recognise the
dangers of over-active imaginations, we also feel
in certain cases where evidence is lacking and
the circumstances are 'mysterious' (whatever that
may mean), there is the tendency to be conventional and deal only in 'safe' speculations. The
following story is from the Sunday Mercury. 25
Nov 73.

A young Birmingham housewife has died in the
burns Unit of Birmingham Accident Hospital after
she was found lying on a blazing bed by her neighbour. Christine Warren,21, had been in the
Unit since 16 Nov. after the fire in Ash Rd,
Saltley. She is believed to have knocked over a
parrafin stove in her bedroom, which set fire to
her clothing. Apart from certain questions we
have, we note that this event happened barely
three weeks after the double of similar fires
(see NEWS 2, p7.) to young women in the Birmingham area. The hospitals involved seem to have
ignored our request for more information.

Police were unable to give any statement about
the cause of a fire in a flat in Salford, in
which James Matson, 61, died in his blazing bed.
(Credit: Peter Rogerson.) In fact we may have to
drop the more suspect cases for lack of room -
the reports of cars, buses, homes found ablaze
and only a 'supposed' cause; like this one:

A 17th century farmhouse at Cannock was thought
to be set alight by a tramp or by children playing. The main staircase was destroyed and the
building, Newhall Farm, Cannock Road, Heath
Hayes, is unoccupied. (Sunday Mercury. 27 Jan 74).
We often have the feeling, that even if we did
have unlimited space and total news coverage and
access, the exercise might be one in futility.
In the meantime, however, we can only proceed to
record what we find, and find some small joy in
one lost sheep being found.

ghosts & poltergeists

WAITING FOR A GHOST.

A company boss and four of his workers sat-in
last night on the factory floor waiting for a
ghost. The vigil was arranged after night-work-
ers at Press Mouldings Ltd. in Soham, Cambs,
complained they had been scared by shadowy figures and mysterious voices.
(Daily Express. 24 Nov 73. Credit: Steve Moore.)
A further comment from the 'boss' involved, a
Mr Ronald Uden, was in the reportage of the
Scunthorpe Evening Telegraph (same date. Credit:
Nigel Watson.) "We didn't hear or see a thing.
The men seemed so convinced we may try again another night."

ITS...A GHOST.

The ghostly Lady in Grey walks a factory floor at
Ilkeston, Derbyshire. At least that's what women
workers at Denleen Separates say. They see her in
trailing gown, crossing the 100-year-old building
at eight in the morning. Managing Director Dennis
Whitworth said: "She's a friendly ghost and does
not worry anybody. I'd take her on if she asked
for a job."

Daily Mail. 23 Dec 72.
Credit: Steve Moore.

VICAR'S BID TO RID SHIP OF GHOST.

Sailors on a British ship docked in Hartlepool
called for assistance from the Vicar of St Osw-
alds, the Rev. Anthony Hodgson, when they discovered that a stowaway was on board - in spirit.
The seamen asked him to exorcise the unwelcome
passenger whom they firmly believed to be a ghost. The Rev. Hodgson spent about an hour on the
coaster Somersby Dyke at the Central Dock saying
prayers in various cabins on the ship. "They
said they had seen phenomena on board the ship
that they could not explain. The men were normal
intelligent sailors, and when I got down to the
ship they were obviously frightened of something
so I took their request seriously."
(Hartlepool Mail. 27 Oct 73. Credit: Paul Screeton.)

FRIGHTENED WOMAN ASKS FOR HELP.

Marie McFadden, 27, her husband Ben and son Benedict, waited for two years on a caravan site
before they got their council house in Avenue
Vivian, Scunthorpe. Now her dreams are shattered
and she has made a desperate appeal to the local
housing authority to accommodate the family elsewhere, and wants a Roman Catholic priest to exorcise the house. The shock from ghostly goings-
on was so dramatic, she claims, that it caused
the death of her other child, born prematurely
in March (1973).

18 months ago, she was sitting in her new livingroom in the early hours of the morning: "I saw
a face staring at me through the glass door of
my kitchen. I made a search inside and outside
but there was no-one to be seen." Then again in
February (1973) she saw the apparition in the
livingroom, of "a young boy with curly hair and
wearing a brown suit. It walked across the room
and straight through the window. I was trembling
all over." The following night Mrs McFadden
felt a 'strange presence' around her but saw
nothing. On other occasions there have been
knockings and bumps in the night - objects have
dropped from the mantlepiece without visible
cause - and once the plastic covering of the
settee she was sitting on depressed "as if someone was sitting on it." Her mother, who stayed
for a while was frequently disturbed by the
phenomena that happened over four months.

The McFadden's son, Benedict,4, is deaf and dumb
- "But when he was here, he woke up four times,
screaming, trembling pale-faced and would not
let go of my hand," says Marie. "If he could

only talk, I'm sure he would say there's something terrifying in this house." Her husband Ben, a steelworker on nightshift, sceptical about these happenings, "heard a knocking which seemed to come from the chimney-place." Seven families have left before the McFaddens, and neighbours appear frightened of the place. "I was told of a murder of a young boy many years ago further down the street and I am sure his ghost is haunting our house," said Mrs McFadden. Scunthorpe Star. 16 Nov 73. Credit: Nigel Watson.

A THREE GHOST FAMILY.

Ron Bowles, 42, saw a mirror and two brass plaques move several inches from their hooks on his livingroom wall. His son said he saw a ghostly figure. The milkman, Chris Smith, 26, swears he saw an armchair raise itself two feet from the floor. A friend of his wife's has been pelted with slippers, books and pillows. All this activity took place after the Bowles moved into their council house a year ago.

Ron, a railwayman, said; "I'd come home off night shift and find all the lights on. Yet my wife would assure me she switched them all off before going to bed." The cabinet at the bedside of Mrs Joyce Bowles seems to be the focal point. Her friend Mrs Briget White, who stays in the house when Ron is on nights, said: "I've seen the cabinet move four feet and rock from side to side." The first night she stayed, she began a little diary of events, and recorded: 'Cabinet creaks, and doors burst open. It moves forward 12in then sideways.' Then she was pelted with comics, a slipper, books and a nightdress case. As Mrs. Bowles woke up, the mattress began to rise under her and the two women struggled to push it back. When the disturbance ended, the cabinet moved back into place and they heard several knocks . "We now know that Our Friends give seven knocks when the show is over." On following nights the cabinet moved and pillows began flying.

One night: "My husband had gone to work early & and I saw the figure of a man in black by the livingroom table and thought it was him. I said: 'Why haven't you gone to work?' and the figure turned slowly. It had two gold buttons at the top of the cloak and a gold chain. I was paralysed and my eyes weren't focusing properly. I have also seen a nun-like figure in the house, & a woman in white. But each time I've been unable to move or speak.

Ron Bowles said: "I have not seen any apparitions but I have heard the noise of furniture being moved about. I woke one night and found a chair in a room had been moved. I could see an imprint on the seat as if someone were sitting there. It disappeared slowly. Perhaps it was a ghostly bottom?" The house has been exorcised twice already since the Bowles moved in, by the Rev. Ramsdale Whalley of Winchester. Mrs Bowles said: "It seems to have got worse since."
(News of the World. 2 Dec 73. Credit: Cathy Purcell.)

LONELY GHOST OF A VILLAGE CEMETERY.

Scores of people in the little village of Lariano, in Central Italy, say they have seen the figure of a woman in black struggling to get out of her tomb. Cemetery keeper Alberto Galente said: "Some people come from their homes after supper and stand outside the cemetery for hours - sometimes till dawn - hoping to see the ghost. The other night, when I passed on my bicycle just before midnight, there were about a thousand people looking through the railings." First to arrive for the nightly vigil is always Riccardo Candidi, whose wife lies in the only tomb in the cemetery, which was opened only last month, (the cemetery, that is, not the tomb). He believes she is lonely, and until her coffin is joined by others, her spirit will seek to escape. (Sunday Express. 23 Dec 73. Credit: DJ McAllister, Steve Moore.)

VISITORS FLEE THE COLONEL'S GHOSTS.

Colonel Francis Claridge has just taken a 14yr lease on an 11th-century manor house in the village of Sandford Orcas, near Sherborne, Dorset. "Scores of guests have been forced to flee," he says, with reference to the resident ghosts. "The place comes alive with them when visitors arrive" (Sunday Mirror. 23 Dec 73.)

NEW PLAY STARS A LOCAL GHOST.

The Lodenek Press, Padstow, have recently published 'A Cornish Quintet', a collection of five original plays with a distinct Cornish flavour, from the Cornish Drama Festival. But our interest centres on one of the five plays, 'The Happening at Botathen' by Donald R Rawe, for this is based on a strange incident which actually took place in the Launceston area just over three hundred ago. The Botathen ghost has been written of by many, Daniel Defoe and Charles Causley among them - of how the redoubtable Parson Ruddle, of St Mary Magdalene, Launceston, laid the troublesome Trebursye Ghost. His story is as reliably documented as anything of this nature can be, and we have knowledge that research is currently going on into the matter, indeed we may yet be publishing certain documents in our possession giving a contemporary account of the apparition. Remember, John Ruddle did exist, and wrote: "These things are true; I know them to be so, with as much certainty as eyes and ears can give me." (Cornish & Devon Post. 29 Dec 73. Credit: Nigel Watson.)

STRANGE GOINGS-ON IN THE STORE.

Members of Jeff's Discount Store in Abergele Rd, Colwyn Bay, claim there are strange goings-on among the kitchen-units and other goods. It all started when a large broom-cupboard in the balcony area upstairs suddenly crashed forward... and there was no-one near it. Mr Dave Mackie, the sales manager, saw a figure in evening-dress in the corner of an upstairs room. "He was tall,

WE NEED MORE SUBSCRIBERS .. .. ..

slim and middle-aged. He just stood there and, in a second or so, disappeared." A former employee, Roy Tebbitts, seeing a man go upstairs, went to see what the 'customer' wanted. There was no-one there - and on several occasions, footsteps have been heard with nobody to cause them.

One day Mr Mackie was standing near a packet of tile bath-trims hanging on a bracket on the wall - when he was astonished to see a tile detatch itself from the packet, move through the air horizontally, then drop to the floor. A woman customer, from Gronant, also saw the tile behave in this odd manor. Some members of Jeff's regard the spirit - if that's what it is - as a permanent feature of the place and call it 'George,' whom they regard as friendly. In the past despite the favourable position, the premises have often seemed to have a jinx on them. Even an estate agent once used the term - since many previous businesses on the site had not prospered as well as 'Jeff's'. A customer, who may or may not have been clairvoyant, once remarked to an assistant: "A heavy cloud has lifted since you have been here."

Jeff Gunning, the owner said: "We certainly feel that whatever it is, likes us. This has been a boom year for trade." Before the war, apparently someone had committed suicide on the premises, but that was a woman, and the figure seen was quite definitly a man. Mr Dryhurst Parry, now the manager of Jeff's new Tile Centre, was a definite disbeliever when Mr. Mackie recounted his adventure with the tile - and later, when in the cellar, he suddenly felt an unaccountable icy cold, and for no apparent reason a number of worktops 'fell' on him."That was an unnerving experience. There are more things in heaven and earth..." he mused. 'George' has gained another convert. (Bangor & North Wales Weekly News. 4 Jan 74. Credit: MR Mowday.)

CONCERT NIGHT FOR THE PHANTOM PIANIST.

Jean and Bill Duncan were sleeping peacefully, when weird strains of music made them sit up in bed, in their rented Victorian home, in Humber Avenue, Coventry. It was coming from downstairs and sounded like the strumming of an old-fashioned lute. When the couple investigated,they found the keyboard was not moving and the lid was shut. "At first we thought the cat might have got into the piano, but when we lifted the lid there was nothing inside," said Mr Duncan. In the last year alone,the piano-playing phantom has given about 100 impromptu concerts in their front room. "It sounds as though someone is plucking the strings, rather as a harp is played. It doesn't sound anything like modern music. As soon as we enter the room it stops. We weren't told anything about this before we moved in two years ago. But of course it may not have happened before." Other strange noises frequently give the couple a shaking at night - ghostly raspings and hammering on

the doors. And in the small general store next door, lights switch on and off inexplicably. (News of the World. 13 Jan 74.)

SNOOKER SPOOK RATTLES A CLUB.

The strange goings-on at the 300-year-old club-house of the West Bowling Golf Club, Bradford, Yorks, are unnerving the caretaker George Webster and his family - he is convinced 'something' is watching them and his two sons. Snooker balls have played themselves; A ghostly grey-suited man walked into the Ladies toilet and frightened the life out of a barmaid; footsteps echoed through the locker-room and out into the night, through a door found to be bolted from the inside; their bedroom doors have locked themselves; and a mysterious 'dead-rat' smell has been giving Mrs Webster sleepless nights.

Mr Webster said: "One night I distinctly heard snooker balls clicking about on the table. But when I went in they were all in the pockets!" Club member, David Cockcroft, added: "I went into the snooker room one night. As I was leaving I heard clicking and saw the balls moving about on the table. I was not frightened, but it was unusual and I cannot explain it away." Mrs Webster, who has been 'red-eyed with worry over the death-smell', said: "I have the feeling something is there all the time. My bedroom doors have locked themselves from the inside - and sometimes there is a horrible smell. I never go to bed without leaving a light on."
(Sunday Mirror. 13 Jan 74. Credit: Robert Forrest.

REUNITED - BY A GHOST.

A ghost,who haunted a house for six years,reunited a brother and sister, after 26 years apart, and has not returned since their reunion. Mrs Christine Adams of Imperial Road, Gillingham, Kent, said it was a bearded man in an 18th century cloak, who opened doors, turned lights on and off and threw things. A newspaper report of the ghost's activities was seen by her brother, John Simmons, who lives less than a mile away, and whom she had seen without recognising several times. (Sunday Mirror. 20 Jan 74.)

ANOTHER SHIP-BOARD GHOST.

A Muslim priest (sic) went aboard the Malaysian freighter 'Bunga Orchid'at Liverpool yesterday to exorcise the ghost of a woman which crewmen said they had seen.
(Daily Mirror. 24 Jan 74. Credit: DJ McAllister.)

OPENING THOSE GHOSTLY GATES.

The gates of a 17th century manor house near Stroud, Gloucestershire, will be left open tomorrow night to prevent a ghost from opening them. Legend says a blacksmith was hanged even though the owner, Judge Cox, offered a reprieve if he made the gates. Now every January 25 his ghost has allegedly returned and opened them.
(Daily Express. 24 Jan 74.)

BRING  TO YOUR FRIENDS!

GHOST IN AUTHOR'S HOUSE OF DEATH.

No doubt you remember reading of the murder of the author James Pope-Hennessy in the media recently. Well, it appears that the scene of the crime has a history of ghostly doings - in fact haunted by the ghost of a man knifed to death, as Mr Pope-Hennessy was, about 70 years ago, and the earlier murder took place on a staircase just yards from where he died bound and gagged.

Mrs Dorit Forte and family moved into the house in 1942, and six months later so did Pope-Hennessy, on the floor below, and suddenly things began to happen. Mrs Forte recalls: "My little boy, Henry, told me not to step on a certain couple of the stairs leading to the first floor, because there was a little man there who was always smiling and friendly. I didn't take too much notice until James (Pope-Hennessy) said the man was always there and even described him in detail. From then on I walked around the spot." Then a second presence made itself felt - roaming casually and clumsily around the upper floors of the house, once shattering a row of shelves nailed to the wall. "This was very upsetting for us all, including James. One sensed it was there. It seemed evil and sent a coldness through you." Mr Pope-Hennessy's curiosity made him investigate the history of the property, and what he found sent a chill through the tennants. Mrs Forte continues: "A man, an ostler who looked after horses for a nearby inn, had been stabbed to death on the staircase. The description fitted all that James and my son knew of the ghost which danced up and down on the stairs, except that he had <u>shrunk to about two feet</u> in size. As for the evil presence, it could have been the murderer making his getaway or entering the house. James told me the spirits were then exorcised and it was a relief for him. A Roman Catholic priest had done what was necessary." A friend of the family said: "James was extremely sensitive, almost psychic in a certain way. He spoke of the murder as if he had been there." (News of the World. 3 Feb 74. The Editor's underlining, of a most curious and interesting detail.)

`heavens above´

NOT SO PLEASED TO METEOR.

The coming of the comet has been accompanied by some pretty ironic turns. Dr. Alan Hunter, director of the Royal Observatory, has failed in his bid to get special permission from the Dept. of Trade & Industry to use his electrically driven tracking motors on his 26ft telescope on the days most favourably predicted to afford the best shots. Never mind, Alan, you'll get another chance in 75,000 years time - <u>if</u> we've solved the energy problem by then. (Story from Daily Mirror. 7 Jan 74.)

To judge from our general discomfort due to the social, political, financial and industrial unrest, we may feel that the supercilious portrayals of 'primitive peoples' gawping in weak-kneed terror at eclipses, and white men with lighters, is altogether too close to home. Some are beginning to suspect that perhaps they knew something we are painfully discovering for ourselves. The Daily Mail (3 Jan 74) has a note on two astrologers who have just completed a five year study of the effects of planetary movements on political situations. Peter Simester and Marion Flanagan say: "It was in June we heard about Kohoutek. By September the charts we were preparing for the long term still presented a stable overall picture. Then came a strange change in the stars. It was at that time we forsaw the Middle East crisis, and political upheaval in Greece." The effects of the comet, we are told, will be present until 1985 - and they feel 'convinced that Nixon will seize power very shortly by some form of coup d'etat. (Credit: Steve Moore and Pete Rogerson.)

As a matter of passing interest, being one of the few unexposed theories around, the begining of the present 'Jeff Hawke' strip in the Daily Express hinted that the comet might be some kind of alien trick - a cosmic trojan horse. And then Phil Ledger writes, asking if we had noticed the new arrival had coincided with the publication of Arthur Clarke's SF novel 'Rendezvous with Rama'?. Rama, for those not numbered among the cognocenti, is a vast, hollow, artificial asteroid approaching the solar system from far 'outside'.

''Scuse me guv'ner: Can you tell me where I can get a view of this 'ere comet?' A 'Punch' cartoon of June 1910, on the last return of Halley's comet

THE STING IN THE TAIL.

There was a lengthy comment on cometary technicalities in the Listener for 10 Jan 74 (and from
which our Punch cartoon is lifted) by Patrick
Moore. How Fort would have chuckled to learn
that Moore, who has done more to popularise astronomy than all the professionals put together,
is an amateur enthusiast. Moore mostly bewails
the comet's lack of cooperation, having provided
all the pyrotechnics of a damp banger on a cold
and rainy Bonfire night. "The comet really is on
the fringe of visibility. It can be seen in binoculars, if you know where to look for it - but
this is very different from the idea of a spectacular comet with a tail stretching across the
sky, as had been suggested only a few months ago.
The wrong prediction is not the fault of the astronomers. Comets are unreliable things, and it
is impossible to be certain how they will behave."
We find ourselves daring to smile - that Prince
among 'exact sciences' stooping to common or garden uncertainties. From across Olympian distances
we can hear Fort bellowing with laughter, as he
wrote: "Astronomers are led by a cloud of rubbish by day, and a pillar of bosh by night."

MYSTERY EXPLOSIONS, FIREBALLS & METEORITES.

Perhaps it's the comet - perhaps its not. These
are portentious times nevertheless . We have
lumped the following notes on bangs, thumps and
flashes together for no sounder reason than that
they seemed to belong in a similar bag.

OLDHAM: 21 Nov 73.

We blast off with a brief note, or rather a faint
report, from the Daily Mail, that an explosion at
Coppice, near Oldham, Lancs, was to be heard at
least a mile off, but no damage or cause could be
found. (Credit: DJ McAllister.)

KNIGHTSBRIDGE, LONDON: 11 Dec 73.

On the morning 11 Dec 73, there was a bang, and
a flash that lit the sky over Knightsbridge,
London, for a few seconds. Firemen were called
to Knightsbridge Green after several people had
witnessed the happening. The only clue was some
damage to a road surface in Old Brompton Road,
and it was not clear whether the damage had anything at all to do with the explosion. Police,
who are appealing to anyone with information to
come forward, described it as "one of the mysteries of London". Evening Standard 11 Dec 73.
Credit: John Brosnan.

WINDSOR: 22 Dec 73. A FIREBALL.

During the night of the 22 Dec. terrified residents of Windsor, Berks., rushed into the streets
or jammed the police switchboards with calls. A
huge fireball was seen in the sky over Windsor.
There was a loud explosion, and the fireball was
reported to have dropped into Windsor Great Park.
A police search of the park discovered nothing,
and a spokesman said: "It must have been a freak
storm, or thunderbolt." Reports appeared in
both the Sunday Mirror and News of the World,
on the 23 Dec 73.

BRIGHT LIGHTS, OR KOHOUTEK? 23 Dec. 73.

Nigel Watson sent us some reports from the Gainsborough News, on a series of sightings that
happened on the 23rd, the Sunday before Christmas. First, Mrs Edith Hart and her husband saw,
from their home in Park Springs Road, a bright
object like a four-pointed star moving slowly
in the sky in the direction of Middlefield School. This was about 3.24pm on the Sunday. 'A
spokesman for the Met. Office in Bawtry said the
description was something like the appearance of
a comet." (Gainsborough News, 28 Dec 73). In a
further report from the same paper (11 Jan 74),
Mrs Hart is quoted as saying that having since
seen Kohoutek, she knew the object she saw could
not have been the comet. The Gainsborough News
then got the opinion of the Appleton Laboratory,
(formerly the Space Research Station) that it
was a plane. Faced with the judgement of experts
(who hadn't seen the darned thing, and were given
only secondhand info) Mrs Hart's conviction begins to falter. It seems that she saw several
'things' that evening, the one above, and again
at 4.30 they went out to see Kohoutek,"and saw...
something that looked as if it had broken away
from Venus."

In the 4th Jan edition comes a corroboration. Mrs
Tacey was looking out of a window across to
Whites Wood from her home in Theaker Avenue. "I
was watching this bright light. It was just 3.15
and I thought 'why, its too early for a star! It
came from over the woods and went across to the
Baines Road area. I mentioned it to someone on
Monday and they said it must have been a plane.
But there was no sound and it was too bright."

Curiously, the same report also mentions a man
from Gainsborough who saw something at roughly
the same time as Mrs Hart and Mrs Tacey....but
while he was in Shelf, Yorks. Mr Blenkin was
walking along the main road in Shelf (between
Halifax and Bradford) with his daughter, when he
drew her attention to a lit-up Christmas tree.
"As I pointed, there was a break in the clouds
and this object was there. It was similar to an
illustration of Halley's Comet which appeared on
Patrick Moore's programme 'The Sky at Night' the
night before. It was like a bright incandescent
light with a tail on it. I looked at my watch,
and it was exactly 3.55. We were facing a south-
south-westerly direction. After a couple of minutes the cloud covered over and the object disappeared." Although he is not sure whether it
was Kohoutek he saw, he is quite definite that
it wasn't a plane or a star.

We could have put these reports in our UFO section but they seemed relevant to this collection.
The sightings were of something brighter than
aircraft, and with more movement than the comet (which
by all accounts wasn't very bright or visible.)
Perhaps it was another 'fireball' tracking over
the country - or perhaps the inhabitants of
Gainsborough were acted upon to see 'things' in
the sky by a conjunction of unknown forces.

LAKELAND SPACE SPECTACLE. 27 Dec. 73.   OVER/

Police have received scores of reports of what is believed to have been a spectacular meteorite seen over Cumberland and Westmorland. It was said to be green and white and lit up the countryside as it raced from east to west last night. A man at Appleby, Westmoreland, said the object lit up much of the town for about five seconds. Other reports came from the Scottish borders, the Penrith area, and the west Cumberland coast.
Scunthorpe Evening Telegraph. 28 Dec .73.
Credit: Nigel Watson. Phil Ledger sent an identical cutting from the Torbay Herald Express of the same date.
Well..that was how it was in the papers, and the extent of our own information - so we reprint the following from the New Scientist 24 Jan 74, and it may be that some of you could help Dr. Hindley in his quest for more information.

The evening of 27 December 1973 was mainly clear and moonless over northern England, Scotland and Ireland when, at 21.07 hours, an exceptionally brilliant fireball lit up the whole of northern Britain. Sightings have been reported from as far north as the Shetland Islands, as far south as Dublin, North Wales and Manchester, and over the whole breadth of the British Isles. Witnesses describe the object as having an intensely bright, deep green head about 1/4° across, set in a teardrop shaped coma, and trailing an orange-red tail containing a shower of red sparks.

The fireball began as a rapidly brightening meteor at a height of about 120 km, at a point latitude 57°·7 N, longitude 0°·2 W, out over the North Sea, moving downwards to the south west at a shallow angle of about 12°. It passed south of Aberdeen, almost directly over Dundee, Stirling and Glasgow and out over the Firth of Clyde and north Channel, to end just five miles in from the coast of Antrim only about 12 to 15 seconds after it had begun. The most notable things about the fireball were its intense brilliance and its colour. It was already brighter than the full Moon (magnitude −12·5) over Dundee and reached a peak brightness of about magnitude −18 (over 100 times brighter than the full Moon) over the Clyde. Here observers agree it was uncomfortable to look at directly and lit up the surrounding countryside brightly. Observers are remarkably concordant about the intense green colour of the fireball head.
The main fireball faded out at a height of 22 km, with a shower of two large, and several small, red fragments continuing down to 18 km—a very low end height. In the minutes that followed the disappearance of the fireball, strong sonic booms were

heard all over Scotland, Ireland and northern England, as far away as 300 km from the trajectory.
The smooth brightening and fading of the fireball with no major flares, coupled with the low end-height and the extensive sonic-boom reports, point strongly to a meteorite fall. An initial analysis suggests a fall area about eight miles by five miles (long axis pointing along the track), some five miles north east of Ballymena, County Antrim. Moreover, the smooth light-curve of the fireball and its intense green colour suggest that we may be dealing with an iron meteorite fall rather than a much commoner stoney meteorite.
Three groups of scientists are now canvassing the fall area, on the southern slopes of some of the Antrim mountains and the River Braid area. The region is sparsely populated and abounds with dark meteorite-like basalt boulders, but an intensive campaign over the coming months may yield some recoveries. Iron meteorite falls are extremely rare indeed, and so recovery of a sample would supply much valuable scientific data after exhaustive study.
The British Astronomical Association Meteor Section now has a nationwide network of reporters and observers to investigate events such as this, and the team were alerted across the country within hours of the fireball. We have interviewed several hundred people who saw the fireball, and who will continue to collect data over the next few months. Any New Scientist readers who witnessed the event are urged to contact us—write to Dr Keith Hindley, 44 The Turnways, Leeds LS6 3DU. We will continue to refine the preliminary track in the diagram until we get a definitive path. We can then compute a much more accurate impact area, using atmospheric wind velocities (which can carry falling meteorites considerably to one side) and perhaps narrow the region where we believe meteorites have fallen.
The irony is that we are also just initiating a system of all-sky fireball cameras at sites around Britain specifically to photograph bright meteorite-dropping fireballs such as this. On the date of this event, we had three stations making test-exposures in Edinburgh, Prestwick and Leeds, but, unfortunately, none was operating at the vital moment. Stations at Oxford, Stoke-on-Trent, Sheffield, Burton-in-Kendal and the Isle of Man will be functioning by the end of February, with more to follow in 1974. But statistics suggest that we may have to make hundreds, if not thousands, of exposures to catch an event of similar importance to that of 27 December.

Keith Hindley

MYSTERY EXPLOSION: 15 Jan. 74.

Back to Gainsborough, again, where, on Tuesday afternoon (15 Jan), something exploded loudly, somewhere. It was heard by people in Gainsborough and Misterton as they finished work at 5.00. Local RAF stations denied being responsible for any sonic booms, and the regional power station at West Burton could give no information on likely causes. The police were stumped too. The ubiquitous Met. Office at Bawtry could only say that there had been thunder about earlier that afternoon. 'The mystery persists'. ends the report. (Gainsborough News. 18 Jan 74. Credit: Nigel Watson.)

GIANT FIREBALL: 23 Jan. 74.

Not to be outdone, we have our own modest glory. Intrepid NEWShound Phil Ledger was on the loose. He wrote to us: "Here, behind the village in the BERWYN hills something had bumped in the night. You must have heard about the explosion/tremor/meteorite that rocked North Wales last Wednesday evening (23 Jan) and nearly tipped us into the sea, and reported on BBC radio news at 9.00 on Thursday. At the village of Llandrillo I found 4 mountain rescue people, two of whom had done a couple of searches in their landrover, but as they were now sure it wasn't an aircraft, they were rapidly losing interest. Apart from this there was an enormous crowd...of reporters, and photogaphers photographing reporters! So, not much I could do as I wasn't going to risk life and limb going into the hills by myself that day.

"So yesterday, Sunday 27 Jan, two other bounty hunters and I set off again in the hope of finding whatever there was to find up there. Set off very well in high spirits which decreased as the heather got thicker, the paths got scarcer, the snow got deeper and the mist came over....about 100 sq. miles covered in 2 foot of heather!! The thing would have to be as big as a bus to be found by a normal search. I had tried dangling my little pendulum over the O.S. map before we set out, but to no avail, it just wasn't interested. I think there might still be someone from Keele University out there. (He actually <u>wanted</u> 'it' to be a meteorite, the fool!) (What do you call a UFO when it has landed? A ULO?) It looks to me that the whole sordid business will now gradually fade away, recorded only in the annals of the NEWS."

The reports of this fiery monster didn't appear in the nationals until the 25th Jan. On the evening of Wednesday (23rd) the villagers of Llandrillo, Merionethshire, were considerably alarmed by a series of flashing 'green and blue' lights in the sky, followed by a huge explosion. The popular theory was that a meteorite had hit the side of Cader Bronwen in the Berwyn Hills. RAF photo-reconaissance planes made repeated sweeps over the mountain. Astronomer Dr. Ron Madison of Keele University said: "It is likely to weigh a ton, and it will be 4,000 million years old, and came through space from between Mars and Jupiter to hit the Earth. The crater

could be anything from 5ft to 50ft across....
unless it smashed into pieces on impact." This
must be the guy Phil mentioned. (Above info from
Daily Mail.) Amazing what you can tell about it
when you don't even know what it is yet.

The Daily Mirror reported that the 'thing' was
seen by hundreds as it swished over Central and
Northern Wales; that it exploded on impact; and
that seismographs at Edinburgh reported the
biggest earth tremours in England for five years.
The experts at Edinburgh said the thing could
only have been a meteorite. And meteorologist
Keith Hindley (rapidly becoming the superstar of
the craters) is quoted as saying: "Nothing will
be found in the Welsh Hills."

The Daily Express, however, takes a different
and altogether more stimulating tack (from the
Fortean point of view). The flash, they say,
could very well have been a meteorite or piece
of satellite junk, 'But the experts say that this
was completely unconnected with the tremor which
set the observatory graphs quivering in Eskdale
Muir, Dumfriesshire, and Edinburgh. The most
likely cause of the tremor: an underground rock-
slip. Result: A coincidence that produced a
mystery flash and bang that startled thousands.'
Gee - ain't science wonderful; a couple of
mystery events 'explained' by a doubly mysterious
(and more sinister) 'coincidence'. Fear not kids,
nothing fazes Dr. Hindley. "To have made that
noise and caused that tremor, a meteor would
have had to weigh 20 to 30 tons. And a meteor of
that size would have made a fireball so large
it would have lit up the whole country and woken
up half of Britain." Dr. Roy Lilwall of the
Institute of Geological Sciences, Edinburgh,says
"The brightness of the light in the sky was consistent with a small meteorite of a few pounds."
(Credit for these cuttings to Steve Moore.)

Well - if we accept the words of Hindley and
Lilwall, we are still left with the mysterious
coincidence of the two events. Oh well! We'll
just have to lump it with our other notes on
'coincident' bangs and flashes - but something
will have to be done about it sooner or later,
because a file full of 'coincidences' of a
similar nature begins to smell after a while.

In the meantime, we had another letter from Phil
Ledger (7 Feb) saying: "They're still talking
about it on the radio. On the evening in question
, there were three lots of lights ('fireballs')
between 8.30 and 10.00ish, and the latest appeared to coincide with the bang, but still nothing has been found on the ground." Phil also
sends us news of a most peculiar contraption
'thing' washed up on the beach near South Stack,
Holyhead. There is no apparent connection with
the various events in this section, and we will
be getting together a report on it for next ish.

We also hope to carry the results of investigation and gathering of eye-witness reports of the
Llandrillo hit next time.

images and echoes

MYSTERY RADIO SIGNALS.

We were pleased to receive the following write-up of
an earlier enquiry from Nigel Watson, who was
prompted by seeing our note on 'Ghost SOS Flares'
in NEWS 2, p18. * * * * * * * * *

During the August of 1971 many funny things appeared to be going on in the area of Grimsby,
Lincolnshire. These centred around a mad radio-
hoaxer whose activities were given quite a bit
of publicity. The first cutting I want to quote
from was in the Sunday Mirror of 31 Oct 71, entitled 'Joker who Squeaks'.

'The voice coming over the police radio definitely did not belong to the girl at headquarters.
It was high-pitched and squeaky, and said: "Take
me to your leader." And it came as the police
were being swamped with calls form people who
said they had seen an orange, cigar-shaped object in the sky. The message was the climax to
a whole medley of noises from screeches to warb-
les - which have been butting in on police messages in Grimsby. Police believe a joker is at
work. "He must have a knowledge of radio and our
frequencies," a spokesman said yesterday. GPO &
Home Office officials have been called in to
sort out the tangle.'

This is in contrast to the rather more critical
view published in Weekend (8/14 Dec 71.) titled
'Radio Hams.' 'They are a brilliant lot at
Grimsby HQ. A right bunch of little Maigrets in
fact. They were baffled when somebody got on
their patrolcar radio frequency and started
broadcasting weird noises. Then there were telephoned reports of a strange orange light in the
sky. Finally a sinister voice on the radio said:
"Take me to your leader." After much cogitation,
a police spokesman came up with: "We are beginning to think there is a joker at work." Personally, I'm begining to think that, if that's the
best the criminologists of Grimsby can do, someone should tell them about 'Z Cars'. They might
learn something about the blindingly obvious.'

I doubt if the police were at all pleased about
the whole affair - but being slightly curious
myself, I wrote to the GPO, to see if they could
shed any light on the matter, and this was the
reply from the North Eastern Telecommunication
Region, dated 29 Nov 71: 'In reply to your letter
dated 10th Nov. 71. concerning interference to
the private mobile radio of Grimsby Police, a
radio service can be, and at times is, affected
by interferance of many types from a variety of
sources. In the case of interference to Grimsby
Police, our investigation has proved the source
to be man-made and steps taken to suppress the
interference. Nothing is known in this case or
any other investigated in connexion with unidentified flying objects. Signed. MB Burrell for

Regional Director.' Although no definite date is given in either report, it is interesting to note that during August 71 many reports were published in the local press about a radio hoaxer transmitting several distress calls, upsetting local lifeboats.

Unfortunately I did not bother to keep most of these reports, except this cutting from either the Sun or Daily Mirror, dated 21 Aug 71: 'Police have stepped up their search for a hoaxer transmitting distress calls which seem to come from ships in the North Sea. Two lifeboats searched all night in thick fog off Lincolnshire after a coaster picked up a Mayday call claiming to be from a ship on fire. It was the third unexplained Mayday call in the Whitby area in two years.'

From what I can remember, I don't think anyone was caught by the Grimsby Police. Indeed, if the mysterious radio hoaxer had been caught, I doubt if they would have taken long to deal with this anti-social menace. That case brings us to the topic of 'frame of reference' - the police, GPO and Home Office were on the lookout for a hoaxer, a mad human agency who got a kick out of transmitting distress calls from the calm waters off the Lincolnshire coast, or who liked messing about with the patrolcar frequencies.

As Peter Rogerson recently wrote*: 'One of the most terrifying things that people can be confronted with is the random, disturbing event. Faced with one or many such events, there is a general tendancy among people to try to fit them into a convenient pattern. Any pattern, however irrational and capricious, is better than no pattern at all.'

This I think leads us to a paradox - we can be found guilty of labelling things 'Ufological' or 'Fortean' just because they sound mysterious; but on the other hand we can be found guilty of rationalisation in which we can even ignore the world of 'Magonia' - a serious crime indeed.

* * * *

Nigel Watson is Chairman of the Scunthorpe UFO Research Society.

*(Merseyside UFO Bulletin 6:2.
  Rogerson, Peter; "Interpretation of UFO Type
  Data in terms of Contemporary Panics.")

'TANKER BLAZE' HOAX SUSPECTED.

Well - it seems our hoaxer ham is still at it, as Nigel Watson sent this cutting through with his piece above, dated only 22 Jan 74:

Ships and planes resumed their search at first light today, after a Mayday call last night that a tanker with a dangerous cargo and a 35 man crew was about to blow up, and they were abandoning ship. A coastguard spokesman at St Margarets Bay, Kent, said: "It's begining to look rather strange. This could have been a hoax but we are still treating it as an urgent report. The position of the ship was rather vague so we will continue to search for some time yet. French coastal officials were saying much the same: 'It seems as if this is a hoax for no vessel can

disappear in a flash in such a congested area." They added later that the description of the vessel did not match anything in their register. (Scunthorpe Evening Telegraph.)

RADIO SIGNALS FROM OUTER SPACE.

At the second international symposium on extra-terrestrial civilisations held in October 73 at Baku, USSR, a Soviet project was revealed that had detected signals from outside the solar system. Since 1970 radio observatories in four separate places had been monitoring the entire celestial hemisphere on wavelengths in the centimetre and decimetre bands. The signals occur every few hours and last for a few minutes - the character of the impulses, their regular form and strict periodicity 'made it possible to assume that they were of artificial origin.' The monitoring equipment was designed to eliminate earth-based signals, and identify other sources within the solar system. There is also some speculation that the signals originate from an artificial satellite within the orbit of the earth. 'Now a lengthy period of observation, analysis, and finally the development of a theory about the phenomena' will follow before the speculations can be confirmed or otherwise refuted. More details can be found in Novosti Bulletin 14499. 23 Nov 73. (If anyone is interested The Novosti Agency, is a Soviet news service that sends out free bulletins from, 3 Rosary Gardens, London SW7 4NW.)

IMAGE ON AN EGG.

A hen in Arkansas has laid an egg with a '6' printed neatly on it at one end. 'All the experts are baffled,' says the smartalec reporter. 'I can't think why. I'ts quite obvious that 'Half a dozen.' wouldn't fit.' Ho Ho!
Daily Mail. 14 Dec 73. Credit: Steve Moore.

meteorology

A ROAD IN THE CLOUDS?

The following observation of a curious effect in the clouds was originally mentioned in The Ley Hunter last year. We managed to contact the lady who witnessed the phenomenon through Paul Screeton, editor of TLH, and we publish below her reply and description. She has requested to remain anonymous.

"It is some time since I saw the phenomenon...I think that it was on a morning flight from Edinburgh in mid-January; but whether this occured last year (1973), or in 1972 I am unable at this moment to say. I do this journey often. As I recollect, however, the weather was cloudy; the cloud lying well above the land, but we were flying a little above it so that this cloud cover was visible in detail. There was no break in it. I am afraid I cannot be accurate as to height.

"I was seated next to the window, on the left-hand-side of the plane as you face the engine. About half-an-hour before we touched down at London Heathrow I was surprised to see, on the

cloud below, an absolutely straight 'furrow',
about the width of a lane, or single-track road,
as though it had been cut with a 'digger' and
this was soft earth, for at either side the
cloud was 'rolled back'. This track ran in a SE
direction as far as the eye could see, nor did
it fade or change shape as I looked at it. We
soon passed out of sight of it, and I have never
seen such a thing again in all the flights I
have made in this country, or abroad. I wondered
if it could have followed the track of a Ley on
the ground below, but have never had this confirmed." The lady added a rough drawing, with
the post-script: "This furrow did not penetrate
the cloud cover, but lay on it smoothly."

WEATHER CHAOS OVER BRITAIN.

All the countries of the world have a climate,so
the saying goes, but only Britain has weather,
which got its name from the fact that you never
know for certain whether it will, or won't. Well,
over the last few months it certainly has, with
the worst rainfall, storms and winds on record
for many a year. Freak gales at the end of the
year killed three men and injured 140 others in
the Bradford and Leeds areas, with widespread
damage and injury reported from most of the
northern counties. (Sunday Mirror 28 Nov 73.
Credit: Robert Forrest.)

A freak whirlwind tore a path of destruction
through the Somerset town of Crewkerne, ripping
off roofs, breaking windows, and lifting garden
sheds, fences and a milk-float. Fortunately there
was only one casualty - a rooftile was flung
through his bedroom window hitting him on the
head - of the wind described as a 'terrifying
roar'. It struck at 5am during a thunderstorm.
(From the Manchester Evening News and Daily Mail.
7th and 8th respectively. Credit: Peter Rogerson).
The Daily Express of the 8th (these are all in
January 74 -sorry) says most of the damage was
caused in about 90 seconds. Then, the whirlwind
appeared to leapfrog , coming down in the quiet
town of Deanshanger, Northants, where it did
much the same sort of thing, including uprooting
elm trees. Then some 'hours later' it hit Camber
in Sussex. A London Weather Bureau spokesman said
"The whirlwinds are caused by a funnel-like
storm cloud which gets rid of its energy by uprooting trees and the like and then rises up
until an energy force is built up again, when it
comes down once more. Hence the leapfrogging
effect." Sounds tough on the trees,though such
hostilities are conceivable - our inbuilt suspicions, however, feel uncomfortable in the
presence of 'pat' explanations.

The Sunday Mercury (13 Jan 74) records a wind of
131mph for the previous day, at the Board of
Trade weather station on Great Dun Fell in the
Westmorland Pennines. In the continuous universe
, it seems to us that 'freak' this and thats
cannot be considered in isolation. All this
nasty weather is concurrent with the recent wave
of flashes, bangs and wallops currently puzzling
the various (seperate) interested parties. See
backward to 'Heavens Above'.

ufos

MORNING SIGHTINGS.

Three printers, on their seperate ways to work
at dawn this morning, spotted a yellow-white
cigar-shaped object in the sky over Higham
Ferrers, Northants. John Bartlett was driving
when he saw what he describes as: " a cigar-
shaped object travelling very high in the sky,
yellowish in colour and not leaving any vapour
trail." Dick Craddock, looking from Irthling-
borough, seemed to see it travelling towards
Higham Ferrers Church and then change direction
to head for Bedford. Glenn McDonald was waiting
for a bus on the A6 at Barton Seagrave as the
sun was coming up: "I saw a sort of straight
line sharp at one end but fuzzy at the other."
Sounds very much like the latter was a vapour-
trail, but that contradicts the first statement.
Everywhere we turn, contradictions and questions
abound - perhaps that's the nature of it all.

Northampton Evening Telegraph. 26 Nov 73.
Credit: BR Bates.

THE PHANTOM HELICOPTER RIDES IT OUT.

An odd sort of drama is being played out around
Manchester and regions of Derbyshire and Cheshire.
The Daily Mirror for 15 - 18 Jan 74 has carried
stories of the spook-chopper's exploits, which
include flying below the 500ft level at night,
without any civil markings, without clearance,
landing in fields and taking off again just as
the fuzz were about to nab him. Police from four
counties, including Special Branch,have been
involved, it was revealed, for over 6 months in
tracking down and mapping 'its' activities - and
to no avail. Bearing in mind the tales of the
early UFO/Airship scares, reports of the choppers'
bright, stabbing spotlight are quite interesting.
Curiously, red and green navigation lights were
also mentioned. 'The fact that it has not violated air space, even on inky nights, or caused
any danger to planes flying in and out of Manchester Ringway, brought this comment from a
controller: "Whoever he is, this pilot is no fool
- but he must have plenty of nerve. How he can
see baffles me." One theory is that the chopper
has an acomplice on the ground , somebody who
lights up a makeshift flare path. Maybe, too, he
refuels the chopper.' (DM 17th Jan)(Same date for
the following quote from a police spokesman:)

'We have a full sightings file on him for the
last six months. And more are coming in. He seems
to be up and about after midnight most of the
time and mainly about three in the morning. We
are literally lying in wait for him. But we can
only wait and watch. We have looked at places
where we thought it has landed. And even though
the investigations were made in daylight, we can't
find any trace of a touchdown - but it is easy
for us to be mistaken, easy to think it has landed when it has not. We only know it's medium-
size, with a single rotor on top and a tail rotor.
We feel it is coming from not too far away. It
uses so much fuel when it veers off straight

flight and starts hovering and changing direction that its range becomes limited.'

The landings appear to have been, just before
dawn on the 14th, near Goostrey, Cheshire; and
early on the morning of the 16th near the Arclid
traffic lights on the Sandbach-Congleton road,
Cheshire. In both cases the copter took off as
unmarked police saloons sped towards the spot.
If there was a ground based acomplice with the
aforementioned 'flare-paths' etc, these would
have been readily visible. It is also not clear
what kind of activities are involved, legal or
otherwise - both the IRA and sheep-rustling have
been mentioned, but the police are quick to
admit that there is no evidence of either. All
the cuttings involved were forwarded to us by
Robert Forrest, who has been scanning all the
media for further information without hearing
much - except: "One TV news item circa 21-22 Jan
to say it had been spotted again, but that was
all." It's our guess that we haven't heard the
last either.

THAT DAMNED PROCESSION AGAIN.
By PHIL GRANT.

Question: When is a ghost not a ghost; a UFO not
a UFO; and a puma not a puma?
Answer: When they all appear on a Ley line.

Well that's the riddle solved folks, now to the
meat of the problem. As a Fortean I was at once
attracted to the writings of Alfred Watkins -
the chap who rediscovered the 'ley' or straight
track system in the 1920s. He published a by now
famous, or should I say infamous, book, The Old
Straight Track (Garnstone Press) in which he
sketches the system of alignments through prehistoric and ancient sites. Both Fort and Watkins, although the latter may have not realised
it, were fighting against the same thing: so-
called scientific isolationism. With Watkins it
was the blinkered way the archaeologists and
anthropologists approached the massive ruin in
which we live, and that relates to some pretty
cute thinking way back. Both were struggling to
find a point, or points, of reference - a common
origin in fact - for all the bizarre and scientifically damned phenomena. Possibly with the Ley
system we have that very point - a key to the
enigmas of the world. Let us look further.

Taking an area 35 to 45 miles around my hometown
(Bournemouth) I first plotted the obvious leys -
some running through such key sites as Old Sarum,
Stonehenge, Maiden Castle and the Badbury Rings.
Grafting first the local UFO sightings since
1950; then the local ghosts, poltergeists and
spectres, I came to a dead stop. Over 90% of
both phenomena fall on the lines - With the UFOs
that could be plotted down to compass heading &
ground position the tie-in was truly amazing. If
the damned things did not appear bang over the
lines and siting points, they were going in the
same straight line as the ley underneath. Ghosts
and 'grounded' phenomena of this sort are much
easier to plot, and the ley/ghost tie-up can be
proven time and time again. ALL the local black
puma-type of mystery animal sightings plotted on

the same map, related to the leys. We have had
about 20 puma sightings since 1964 in the area
and they all fall on a ley line. This latter
phenomenon seems to have some relationship to the
'Black Shuck' dog ghosts, reported down in the
West Country for years.

The best way I have found to detect ley lines,
apart from map and fieldwork, is to dowse for
them. The same pattern of !water' lines appear
on every ley I have dowsed up to now, and judging
by the results got by friends doing the same
thing, we have a pattern too common to be pure
coincidence. The thing has been staring us right
in the face for centuries, and that's the truth.

The patterns we pick up using angle rods and
pendulums are best described in 'The Pattern of
The Past' (Abacus paperback) by Guy Underwood,
in the section on 'Track Lines'. Underground
water seems to be the main element of the leys -
the UFO and ghost having a possible origin in
the refraction principle of radiation or 'influence' being altered or 'bent' when in contact with
a surface or 'plane', the latter in this case
being the surface of the planet. Henri Mager, the
French dowser, did a lot of research on the
'bands' of radiation or force given out by underground streams. These bands take   on a very complex pattern of colour and wave elements from
the surface of the ground up. The fact that dowsers can pick up water from a plane at over two
thousand feet may be a clue to the UFO or aerial
phenomena. I believe we are dealing with subjective stimuli when the UFO, ghost and similar
'transient' phenomena are encountered. The fact
that the UFO often takes on a 'solid' space-age
form is no proof that it is purely restricted to
our modernday awareness of the external universe.

At the moment I am working with one or two others
on a code that relates to the etymology of the
ley place-names. So far we have uncovered some
amazing coincidences. Number-letter-sound-com-
pass direction relationships point to a once
common language that consisted of simple one-
syllable words - a functional 'vibratorary' tongue that was far more simple than our presentday
conceptualising, analogous, complex collection of
utterances. It appears that we are dealing with
a science that could utilise, activate or nurture
natural elements simply by making certain key
sounds-vibrations that set something in motion,
or completed a more complex nature-man set-up.
One of our little group is at this moment working out the frequencies of the local leys by
taking the cross-section (contour) of the ley
running over an important hill site or centre.
Sea-level to sea-level is the way to determine
the length, I believe. Of course this pre-sup-
poses a lot, but we are trying all the angles to
see just what comes up. The number-letter-colour
code, by the way, is the same one as used by the
Cabbalists.

I am collecting data for a book on the ley-UFO-
ghost tie-up and would appreciate any ideas,
comments or help from fellow NEWS-readers. Please
write to Phil Grant: 2A New Park Road, South-
bourne, Bournemouth, Hants, UK. and please enclose a SAE for the replies.

a miscellany of fortean curiosities

THE NEWS

CHARLES HOY FORT 1874 - 1932

'one measures a circle begining anywhere.'

THE NEWS

THE NEWS is a non-profit making bi-monthly miscellany of
Fortean news and notes; edited & published by Robert JM
Rickard: 31 Kingswood Road, Moseley, Birmingham B13 9AN;
affiliated to International Fortean Organisation (INFO).

SUBSCRIPTIONS:	AIRMAIL TRANSFER:	CONTRIBUTIONS & RIGHTS:
Per year -	Overseas subscrib-	Articles & Notes are
UK......£1.80.	ers can 'Airmail	welcome, and duly cred-
USA.....$4.50.	Transfer' direct	ited. All articles in
or Sterling	from their bank	THE NEWS are Copyright
equivalent in	to our account:	of the authors; and the
other Countries.	RJM Rickard No2.	views expressed are not
NB: Please make	A/c No: 0125008.	necessarily those of THE
out cheques, POs	Lloyds Bank, Priory	NEWS or the Editor. All
IMOs etc. to	Ringway, Birmingham	the Notes may be freely
RJM Rickard,	B4, England. Sort-	quoted, though we hope
not The News.	ing Code: 30-96-28.	for a credit in return.

HAPPY BIRTHDAY - CHARLIE!

The second annual convention of the International
Fortean Organisation also celebrates the Centenary of the birth of Charles Fort. It will be held
on the 9th,- 11th August this year in the Shoreham Americana Hotel in Washington DC. The registration fees for the Fortfest 74 are $10 for INFO
members and $16 for non-members. The events will
cover the range of Fortean interests and include
films, lectures and discussions - last year there
was a demonstration of Fort's ludicrous game of
Super-chequers played with armies of men on a
board with thousands of squares. Further details
may be had by writing to the INFO-USA address:
PO Box 367, Arlington, Va 22210, USA. We will be
bringing you news of the various events and
speakers, as they are known.

For our part we join the Celebration by initiating
a series of articles that will examine Forteanism
today - reports from the Front Line against the
Unknown. We hope too that they will be controversial and promote discussion and creative reaction. We must never become stagnant or complac-
ent - it will do us good to stand back and critically re-appraise our aims and methods. The
editor attempts to put the context of the discussion in an introductory article on p5. We will
welcome contributions to the great argument
from any quarter.

ALSO IN THIS ISSUE.

We present an illustrated article by Mary Caine
on the terrestrial Zodiac of Glastonbury. You
have probably heard of them from books like
Brinsley Le Poer Trench's 'Temple of the Stars'
(formerly 'Men among Mankind'.) published in
paperback by Fontana - but such books rarely
show any illustrations of the Zodiacs of Britain.
We thought it about time to remedy that... so
you will find one of the Mysteries of Britain on
p8. We also feature a short follow-up to the

Llandrillo incident by William Porter on p4. His
main article was too long to fit this packed
issue and will be presented in NEWS 5.

ADDENDA: NEWS 3.

1) p4 - 'Pigs on Rampage'- It has since come to
   our attention that this incident was also
   reported in INFO Journal 10. p16.
2) p11 - 'Man dies in Blazing Bed in Salford' the
   source of the story should have been noted as
   Manchester Evening News, 8 Jan 74.
3) p12 - 'Play stars Local Ghost'. The story was
   quoted directly from the clipping so the reference that "we may yet be publishing certain
   documents in our possession" refers not to us
   but the author (unnamed) of the article.
4) p6 - 'Family disappear in Russian Desert'. We
   somehow missed the ending of the story - so
   you will find it in this issue under 'Disappearances'.

CONFUSION DEPT.

The editor is going through a period of moving
to new employment (mainly looking for same) and
the domestic chaos that entails. So, pawn of
Destiny that he is, he humbly wishes to apologise in advance for any interruptions in the
schedule for the NEWS, that become unavoidable.

NOTES
aerial curiosities

FREAK CHICKENS LAY EASTER SURPRISE.

Two freak chickens are laying coloured eggs for
their owner Rita Freeland, a vetinary Nurse, of
Worple Road, Epsom, Surrey. The two share their
coop with six other hens whose eggs remain the
normal colour, while Blanche lays bright blue
ones, and Freckles's are green. This seems to
scotch the obvious idea of something in their

feed, and indeed, Rita seems to have checked that out. Both chickens hatched from eggs bought from a chicken-breeder. An agricultural eggspert said: "This is a very rare occurrence, although coloured eggs were quite common in the Middle Ages. It is caused by an unusual combination of genes." (Daily Mirror. 7 April 71. Credit: Anthony Smith.)

FLYING BACKWARDS TO CHRISTMAS...

A letter to the Daily Mirror,(18 Feb 71) from a Mr B Jupp of Brighton, Sussex: "Driving across the marshes towards Rye recently, I saw a wild goose flying backwards across the road and adjoining field. When I told my friends at work, they all laughed and said it was impossible. Is it; do you know?" Areasonable question. We don't know - do any of you? Anthony Smith, who sent us the note, says: "I remember seeing much the same thing when I was a very small child, but the memory is so hazy now that all the details are gone."

appearances

A SINISTER FORCE.

This is an excellent example of the inadequacies of our categories (which we will revise for the Index, onwards). However, for the present, take it as a story of something nasty turning up in the first place, despite its comings and goings since then. The story is from the San Francisco Examiner and Chronicle-Sunday Punch. 17 Feb 74. Credit: Loren Coleman.

By John Ryan
Chronicle Foreign Service

Nairobi

A STRANGE beast — believed by superstitious tribespeople to be a monster -- has been running amok in the Mayanja district of Kenya.

The beast has been described as a combination of lion, leopard and dog and has eluded all hunters. It has been devouring sheep, goats, calves and dogs in mud-hut villages over a large area. Other stories tell of a giant cheetah on the rampage.

Kenya Game Department officials have been called in to end the monster's reign of terror. Some villagers fear their children will be taken by the marauder, which has been active for three months. The last lion to be seen and killed in the district, 50 miles square, was over 20 years ago. Leopards are equally rare.

*   *   *

T HE BEAST has been described as "having the claws as well as the stubbornness of a lion, the teeth, neck and head of a tiger, the yellow and black spots of a leopard and a tracking smell of a dog."

One night, a team of game wardens tracked the animal, which was chasing a jackal. They shot and killed the jackal but the monster — believed by the people to be a bewitched animal bearing a charmed life — escaped unscathed.

Assistant Minister for Agriculture Joseph Khaoya, whose constituency is in the area, says that some families were so worried about their livestock that they had brought goats and sheep into their homes.

*   *   *

S OME Mayanja residents have suggested that the monster was set free from a cage by Asian's fleeing neighboring Uganda as the victims of a sweeping "Africanization" program by General Idi Amin. Others speak of legends related to visits of strange creatures to Mayanja long ago, signifying disasters or unusual happenings.

"The animal seems to be surrounded by a weird glow and it can disapear, it seems, at will." said the headman of one village. "We urged the government to kill this strange thing quickly and restore safety to our livestock and children. We fear it will attack children when its other prey is scarce."

*   *   *

D URING four years beginning in 1945, a fully grown bull elephant came down from a nearby mountain and ravaged the peasant farmers' crops.

"He was followed by a lion and a fierce buffaio," the headman said. "But there was nothing ghostly about them, and in the end we were able to kill all of those raiders. But the monster, rarely seen in the day, comes and goes in safety."

Game wardens plan to set camouflaged pit traps in the hope of catching the beast alive.

IN-EGGS-PLICABLE.

Ken Sainsbury is used to digging-up old bones buried by dogs in his garden in Aylesbury Road, Bierton, Bucks. But yesterday he dug up..an egg. "I can't figure out how it got there... there are no chickens near us." He said. The report mentions the egg being a 'new laid' one. (Daily Mirror. 4 Sept 68. Credit: A. Smith.

PUTTING IN THE BOOTS.

Worshippers at a church near Stockholm, on the way to morning service, found that someone had perched a tractor on top of the steeple. How it had been done is a mystery. Practical jokers in New York struck when a church advertised for a second-hand settee for its youth club. They broke into a furniture warehouse, took 42 settees, and jammed them into the church's main aisle. The operation must have taken several journ ies - yet nobody saw them arriving. A police official in Ecuador announced that two of his men had been robbed of their boots while they slept at a police post. He appealed for the return of the boots, and during the night, jokers blocked the entrance to his HQ with a pile of 3000 boots, which reached the ceiling - yet again nobody saw them dumped. (Weekend. 30 Oct 70. Credit: A Smith.) As Forteans we find such jokes by human or other agencies directly pertinant and funny into the bargain. However, as a general guide, this little collection is virtually useless to any Fortean research since there is no reference to the source or date of the original events.

BOYS FIND CLIFF-TOP GOLD INGOTS.

Nicholas Casley and Stephen Richards were chasing a rabbit when it darted into a hole on top of a 200ft cliff at Pentreath, Cornwall. They started to return along a path and saw a dull-yellow ingot on the ground. A search revealed seven others - and the next day when they returned with their fathers they found eight more. The ingots were about 1½ inches long and 'the thickness of a pencil' - together they weighed about 14oz. Dr. Andrew Seager, head of the geology department of Birkbeck College, London, who was staying at a cottage nearby, took them to his lab in London. "There is no doubt that it contained a large proportion of pure gold, although something had been added to make it harder." The police said that it may have been part of a robbery. or that 'a shipwrecked sailor could, at some time in the past, have lost his moneybelt while clambering to safety.' Further search was dangerous warned the police, because of repeated subsidence and

rockfalls - though the boys' fathers added they
had made sure there was no more lying about. It
seems a puzzle as to how tiny ingots of gold can
be found lying openly on the ground on top of a
cliff. Did someone throw them away, or drop them?
Exposure by subsidence or erosion, although
suggested, seems to us highly unlikely. Nor was
any mention made of finding of a moneybelt. Worthy
of note is that there was equally no mention
of any hallmarking by which ownership or the
minters could be traced. It was suggested then
that it was part of some smuggler's gold. Well -
however it got there, waiting for the first keen
eyed person to come along - a Coroner's inquest
was to be held to decide whether it constituted
trove or not. Sunday Express 18 Nov 73.

blasts, quakes, lights

Last issue we promised a report on the Llandrillb
incident (see N3, p16/17) - William Porter has
sent us the results of his investigation - but
unfortunately it is too long to fit into this
issue: so we will definitely have it in News 5.
In the meantime however, parts of Wales were
subjected to more subterranean tremors and William Porter also sent an account of this - which
we present here, shortly.

Upon browsing through Fort's 'New Lands' again we
were struck by the number of incidents therein
that concerned the simultaneous occurrence of
earthquakes, lights and mysterious explosions -
and indeed all the reactions of 'specialists'
had been met before and anticipated by Fort. Let
me quote from chapter XXIV:

"An explosion in the sky, and its vibrations
were communicated to the earth below, with all
the effects of any other kind of earthquakes.
Back in our earliest confusion of the data of a
century's first quarter, we had an awareness of
this combination and its conventional misinterpretation: that many concussions that have been
communicated from explosions in the sky have
been catalogued in the lists of subterranean
earthquakes......At times when we think favourably of this work of ours, we see in it a point-
ing-out of an evil of modern specialisation. A
seismologist studies earthquakes, and an astronomer studies meteors; neither studies earthquakes and meteors, and consequently each, ignorant of the data collected by the other, sees no
relation between the phenomena."

In that chapter Fort mentions the great event at
Reading on the 20th Nov 1887; an aerial explosion, meteoric lights and an earthquake. In his
chapter XXIX is an account of the 'Terrible Earthquake of Hereford' of 17 Dec 1896: a series of
9 concussions, and mysterious lights accompanied
it. It seems that this same combination of events
was no stranger to the area, since they happened
in Oct 1661; 6 Oct 1863; 30 Oct 1868; 2 Nov 1893;
and 25 Jan 1894.

Still on the Hereford Terror - Fort has this to
say, which is very pertinent to our present subject: "In an appendix to his book, 'The Hereford

Earthquake of 1896', Dr Charles Davidson says
that at the time of the quake (5.30am) there was
a luminous object in the sky, and that it 'traversed a large part of the disturbed area'. He
says that it was a meteor, and an extraordinary
meteor that lighted up the ground so that one
could have picked up a pin. With the data so far
considered almost anyone would think that of
course an object had exploded in the sky, shaking
the earth underneath. Dr Davidson does not say
this. He says the meteor only happened to   appear over a part of this earth where an earthquake
was occurring, 'by a strange co-incidence'." And,
friends, those damned co-incidences are still
occurring. Its time they were looked into.

- MORE WELSH RUMBLINGS - by William Porter.

Wales continues to quake under another series of
earth tremors and mysterious explosions. Two
earthquakes shook South Wales at 6.12pm and 8.20
pm on February 25th. Both earthquakes were of
greater magnitude than the reputed Llandrillo
incident on January 23rd.

The Western Mail reported on February 26th that
the tremors had caused damage in homes from
Bridgend to Abergavenny. Newport was worst hit,
but the tremors were also felt in Cardiff,
Cwmbran, Trelewis, Pontllanfraith, Abergavenny,
and Blackwood.

I was able to secure a first-hand report from
Mr. John G Williams, a solicitor in Abergavenny.
"On 25th February, my wife and I were sitting on
the couch in our lounge at about 8.10pm when we
were both looking down at a newspaper which listed the London plays and shows... Suddenly we felt
a terrific concussion as though a lorry had ran
into the side of the house, which could not
happen as it is back some 20 yards from the side
road. I saw the daffodils flutter in a vase on
the table and heard the china in the alcove above
rattle."

Reports came from Newport of cracked paving
stones and telephones put out of order. Gwent
police reported damage to the local houses; furniture had been overturned and pictures fell off
walls. At Pontypool many families rushed into
the street when the second tremor occurred at
about 8.20pm. Further east at Llangybi, the villagers said the second tremor was accompanied
by a rumbling. From Monmouthshire came reports
that both tremors were accompanied by explosions which were mistaken for sonic-booms. A
statement issued by the Institute of Geological
Science's Seismology Unit at Eskdalmuir in Dumfriesshire indicated that the second tremor
was considerably stronger than the first and
large enough to be detected on instruments throughout the world. It was the view of Dr. Patrick
Wilmore, head of the Institute, that these tremors and the Llandrillo incident could be linked.
He said: "What is typical of all earthquake belts
is that they go through periods of enhanced activity and then quieten down again."

....continued on p7.

1874 - 1932
CHARLES HOY FORT CENTENARY

Introducing a series of articles which will re-examine Forteanism, its data and its role in relation to Science, and related problems.

Where do we go from here-there?

by ROBERT RICKARD

As we celebrate the birth of Charles Fort, from whom we derive our name for collections of anomalous phenomena and a particular attitude towards them, I think it a fitting time to re-evaluate just what we mean by Forteanism. It is 42 years since he died - can we be said to be any wiser about the baffling complexity of the manifesting universe? - I think not. We have gathered more data to be sure - but Forteanism has come up with no coherent 'dynamic' or theory that can be explored scientifically, in that time, that is any advance on the total-universe organism proposed by Fort. It is not the part of Forteanism to suggest explanations or theories - but detatchment is hard to practice, so most Forteans have pet suspicions that are the beginings of theories. But this is a vast subject and one to which we shall return again in future issues. For now, let us look at our beginings.

Fort showed that Science, despite its vaunted impartiality, was not - the weakness was that its scientists were men first, and subject to human failings. As Dr. Hynek put it: "Science is not always what scientists do." (1) An elementary observation, you might think, but nevertheless, one which has deeply affected the evolution of western science. During the 1910s-1930s, Fort attacked what he called 'exclusionism' - an arrogant process of bigotry whereby phenomena which do not fit neatly into any known theory are either 'explained' away in a Procrustean manner, or deemed the province of cranks and charlatans and thus not 'worthy' of scientific examination. Both methods produced effective 'excommunication' from the orthodox body of Science. Are we mistaken in feeling that they sense a subtle threat to their neat and tidy view of the Universe? I generalise, of course. Forteanism, by contrast, is a mess of loose ends, and must seem like a horrid nightmare of Chaos. But somebody has to do the dirty washing; and this, Fort tells us, is a position more conducive to reflection on the sins of Pride and the lust for Knowledge.

Perhaps it is hard for some of us to appreciate the fanatical view of Science at the turn of the century - it was the 20th century's answer to Religion, and would save man from himself. Now, we know different, if not better - it is a tool like everything else, capable of being misused. But in those days, it was the supreme accomplishment of Man, himself the peak of a glorious evolution. Society too, has changed, is changing, shuddering, crumbling and reforming, adjusting to the momentous imbalances wrought by the escalation of western Science and Technology. Now, for example, we can no longer accept the popularised view of megalithic man as a hairy cave-dwelling dope - the evidence of their intelligence and sophisticated observational science is mounting up. John Michell writes of "the establishment of the modern European with his materialistic philosophy and science as the highest product of an evolutionary process..." as the "most ugly consequence of Darwinism, sociologically applied..." (2) Michell then goes on to quote Kathleen Raine: "Spokesmen of the new dominant culture speak of an 'advance' from 'ignorance' and magic to 'knowledge' and material science; yet in terms of philosophy, religion and the arts, the same event can only be seen in opposite terms as a decline from knowledge into ignorance." (3) This is exactly the spirit of Fort's feeling that 'specialisation' was an 'evil' of Science that perpetuated short-sightedness and reliance on Dogma.

Fort was labled by the papers of his day as 'The Arch-enemy of Science'- which is simply not true as even a casual acquaintance of his writings will show. He was the deadly enemy, though, of Dogma. He was above all true to the spirit of scientific inquiry - and I think he was both amused and saddened to see the malpractice with the body of Science. He held that, in an absolute sense, nothing could be proved absolutely - Man's knowledge of the local Universe was transitionary and phenomenological - it was a matter of approximating to the Truth. "I conceive of nothing in religion, science or philosophy that is more than the proper thing to wear for a while." Or as John W Campbell put it; that Science is the best educated Guess at any one time. Again, Fort said:"I cannot say that Truth is stranger than Fiction, because I have never had acquaintance with either." And from this context of opposite Absolutes we derive two fundamental tenets of phenomenological science - That all things are continuous with all other things - and the humility of the observer.

On the principle of Continuity rests the evaluation of what we are doing - or trying to do. Fort expressed the Fortean view of Continuity in the beautiful opening chapters of 'The Book of The Damned.' (4) The phenomenological world of our existence is an Intermediateness between Absolutes. Man, at least in his present form and confinement, cannot experience these absolutes (eg. absolute Hot or Cold) directly, but only in terms of approximating to them. Fort used the device of the hyphen to delineate these states. Local phenomena can only be interpreted locally, by purely arbitrary sets of references. If we could apply the word Absolute to anything, say a frog, says

Fort, then that frog would be God. Science is based on local definitions that 'exclude' the rest of the Universe from the thing 'defined'- in our terms this is nonsense because the 'included' is continuous with the 'excluded'. Or - it could only apply to a state of Absoluteness, where there is total 'inclusion' and nothing remains to be 'excluded'. This may seem abstruse - but it is the heart of Forteanism, nonetheless. In terms of the Local there can only be approximate definition. We can have Red and Yellow and the oranges in between approximate towards Red or Yellow; but red and yellow are not absolutes, but intermediary between Violet and Green, and so on. "In Continuity, it is impossible to distinguish phenomena at their merging-points, so we look for them at their extremes. Impossible to distinguish between animal and vegetable in some infusoria - but hipopotamus and violet. For all practical purposes they're distinguishable enough. No one but a Barnum or a Bailey would send one a bunch of hipopotami as a token of regard." Scientific method then, must be a gradual approximation to Truth, which in turn means that theories, or beliefs in theories must be temporary. It is the mistake that many scientists, pseudo-scientists, occultists and pseudo-occultists make when they believe the 'laws' of their belief to be consist nt throughout Time and Space, and indeed, any other dimension. Fort suggests that we substitute 'acceptance' for 'belief'; and make that temporary acceptance.

So where does this get us? The nature of Science has changed since Fort's tirades. One reason is that it has broadened the range of its 'definitions' to include a bit more of the 'excluded'. It is facing enigmas that would have been unthinkable even decades ago. Heisenberg's Princip of Uncertainty has become the hyphen between Physics and Metaphysics. Sociologically, things are changing too - with appreciation of the greater cycles of ecology in the ontological organism.

The early Forteans were a counter-point to the Exclusionism of Science - but if Science is becoming more Inclusive, what is left for us to do? Let us be clear that the collection of anomalous data is a task adopted by Forteans - it is not the whole, or the main purpose of Forteanism. "Our expression is that our whole existence is animation of the local by an ideal that is realizable only in the universal...That our whole 'existence' is a striving for a positive state... That there is only this one process, and that it does animate all expressions, in all fields of phenomena, of that which we think of as one inter continuous nexus...that our whole 'existence is an attempt by the relative to be the absolute, or by the local to be the universal...(In this book) my interest is in this attempt as manifested by modern science." (4) Science started out by attempting to give the local the attributes of the universal, and damning or excluding the evidence that conflicted with this purpose - Thus it was the perfect example for Fort's main thesis of Continuity . But it also served the useful purpose of counterbalancing Science - and that underestimated job is far from complete yet. If and when Science becomes all-inclusive,Forteanism will not be dead, but at long-last united with an old friend for which it has long cared, and we will march together in quest of the Truth.

"Well, you'll just have to find an antidote, won't you—you're not coming into tea like that"

The old Fortean Society, under the leadership of Tiffany Thayer, was composed of men subject to human failings - as are we. In the end its usefulness was buried under cult-reverence for Fort, and its vendetta against Science. Martin Gardner wrote: "It is true that no scientific theory is above doubt...But it is also true that scientific theories can be given high or low degrees of confirmation...When a Fortean seriously believes that all scientific theories are equally absurd, all the rich humour of the Society gives way to an ignorant sneer." (5) That sometimes happened too. Greater than Fort, greater even than his gifts to us of his humour and poetry (and Lord knows we haven't fully appreciated those yet), was his re-establishing the spirit of free inquiry away from being the sole right of Science. He delivered us from scientific superstition.

He also knew the dangers of Forteanism becoming institutionalised, and of the Fortean Society, which he said he would no more join "anymore than I'd be an Elk". He wrote: "The great trouble is that the majority of persons who are attracted are the ones we do not want; spiritualists, Fundamentalists, persons who are revolting against Science, not in the least because they are affronted by the myth-stuff of the sciences, but because scientists either oppose them or do not encourage them." (6) The manifesto of the International Fortean Organisation openly states that it owes no allegiance to the expressions of Fort, or anyother thinker or system of thought. And if we count ourselves Forteans, then so too must we. This is no betrayal, but an affirmation of Fort's own cherished ideal. He would not want us bound to anything that would hinder free inquiry, least of all a slavish addiction for his own works, about which he wrote:"I believe nothing of my own that I have ever written. I cannot accept that the products of minds are subject matter for beliefs."

This places us in the curious position of searching for something we know nothing about, hoping we can recognise it when we come across it. We know the quest is towards Truth, and the nearer we approach the Positive Absolute, that some call God, the less there is to distinguish between things. Forteans follow a noble tradition, that of the Greek Skeptics, the Mahayana Buddhism of Nagarjuna, the Ch'an and Zen schools of contemplation, and above all the metaphysical Tao. We accept the limitations of man's senses, and that if evolution is to have any meaning for us, it must be in terms of an ability to understand or facilitate (or a greater approximation to understanding and facilitating) the phenomenological universe. And this surely is also the aspiration of Science.

In the circle of Continuity it doesn't matter too much where you start - so we have started with ourselves. I hope the articles we present in future issue will examine some of these problems, as well as reflecting on the state of the 'art' - and above all I hope it will bring out some controversial points. One of the main purposes of Forteanism must be to promote thought and inquiry. Fort said: "I do not know how to find out anything new without being offensive ...I shall find out for myself: anybody who cares to may find out with me." Us too..Us too..

*   *   *   *

Notes:

1) 'The UFO Experience' by J Allen Hynek. Corgi paperback - 1974.
2) 'The Old Stones of Land's End' by John Michell Garnstone Press - 1974. Reviewed on p19.
3) Michell says the quote is from Kathleen Raine 's introduction to her book on Taylor the Platonist. That's all I know about it...but the quote is so apt, I had to use it.
4) Most of the unmarked quotes from Fort are from his 'The Book of the Damned' in the Ace edition, or the Abacus edition, both paperbacks, and essential reading for Forteans.
5) 'Fads and Fallacies in the Name of Science' by Martin Gardner; reprinted by Dover in 1950.
6) Damon Knight's excellent biography 'Charles Fort: Prophet of the Unexplained' currently only available in the Gollancz edition of 1970.

*   *   *   *

MORE WELSH RUMBLINGS / cont.

Another earth tremor shook parts of Wales, including Cwmbran, Newport, Pontypool and Abercarn, on the evening of March 8th. This tremor was less severe than the previously reported incidents, and no reports of damage were received. Scientists issued a statement saying South Wales is an area which has small tremors and it is possible that there will be additional quakes in the coming weeks. It is significant to note that South Wales is indeed on the northern end of the world's main earthquake belt, which has caused many of the recent earthquake disasters in the Middle East, but this does not account totally for the mysterious coincidental sequence of events on the mountain near Llandrillo on January 23. It could easily be,that whatever happened that night, was simply a catalyst and trigger for the subsequent tremors and earthquakes.

*   *   *   *

FIREBALL: CARDIFF 18 JULY 73.

Since our round-up of flashes and bangs in Wales in the last issue, it has come to our notice that a fireball was said to have exploded in Cathays Street, Cardiff,during the evening of July 18. A Met. Office spokesman was said to be puzzled since there had been no thunderstorms. From South Wales Echo, 19 July 73.

disappearances

FAMILY DISAPPEAR IN RUSSIAN DESERT:

Profoundest apologies for mislaying the end of the story in News 3, p6 - which should have ended thus:

But the rescuers were too late. Two miles from the car they found the mother and two children dead. In the other direction, they found the tracks petered out on hard ground and no sign has been found of Dmitrenko since, Sunday Express. 27 Jan 74.

MISSING: TRAWLER 'GAUL' .

On the 14th March there was a memorial service for the crew of the missing trawler 'Gaul' which vanished in the North Sea in early February. The Daily Express of 13 Feb 74 announced the growing fears for the 1100 ton trawler and her 36 man crew. (Credit: Mike Roberts.) Some relatives of crewmen stayed away from the service saying that there has been no sign of wreckage or reasonable explanation (despite extensive searches) for the disappearance, and they did not believe that their relatives among the crew were dead.

MISSING: ATLANTIC BALLOONIST.

Colonel Tom Gatch, left Harrisburg, Pennsylvania, on the 19th Feb in a helium-filled balloon, and headed for France across the Atlantic - and that's the last anyone saw of him. The Daily Express of 25 Feb 74, among other papers, announced the fears of him being lost. All American air and

....continued on p 14

To some of you, this article may not appear to be objective enough - and yet, if it inspires only one of us to set out to satisfy our own criteria for acceptance, to go and investigate, then we think it will have achieved its purpose. It has been revised by Mary Caine from its original appearance in Gandalf's Garden No4, 1969. The maps are based on Ordnance Survey sheets; and the aerial photos by Aerofilms Ltd, Borehamwood. Katherine Maltwood's original work is a book called 'A Guide to Glastonbury's Temple of the Stars' - James Clarke & Co., London, 1929 - and I believe a pamphlet from it is published by The Cokaygne Bookshop, 1 Jesus Terrace, Cambridge, for 75p + postage. My thanks to all those who helped get the various parts together.

The Glastonbury Zodiac:

TOO GOOD TO BE TRUE — TOO BIG TO BE SEEN!

by MARY CAINE

The source of Glastonbury's mystique - the bubbling fount of all its legends - the magnet which attracted so many saints, heroes, kings, pilgrims - is all the more mysterious for being invisible. This is the Zodiac, or Giants of Avalon, claimed by its discoverer, Katherine Maltwood, as at once the oldest and biggest of all Britain's antiquities. It's still largely unknown; ignored by archaeologists. Too Good to be True and Too Big to be Seen.

What! Twelve great signs of the Zodiac laid out in a huge circle from Glastonbury to Somerton, ten miles across? Impossible! Some of the signs measure five mile from tip to tail? Nonsense! Outlined by roads, paths and waterways, all done by Sumerians in search of metals about 2,800 BC? Crazy! Or by Atlantians in search of dry land and a change of clothing? Rubbish! Or by the Forces of Creation, stamping the earth with their own image? Insanity! Helped at nodal points by tumuli, lynchets and other prehistoric earthworks? Coincidence! Hinted at by innumerable place names? Pure Chance! Known to Homer and Hesiod, visited by Hercules, Odysseus, Jason, Perseus, Joseph of Arimathea? You must be joking!

Archaeologists will argue; historians will hiss; but why not try believing in the impossible for a change? The Red Queen in 'Alice' practised until she could believe in at least six impossible things before breakfast. It's exhilarating. Anyway it's a marvellous idea, and if it's not there, it ought to be. The Grey People will get you certified, but the map at least will be on your side, for these figures can plainly be seen on the 2½" Ordnance sheets. The roads which draw them are ancient, whatever they may say (and they will, believe me, they will) - for all were prehistoric paths leading to prehistoric camps and holy places in prehistoric times when people were more beautiful than they are now, and did crazy beautiful corporate things like Stonehenge and Silbury Hill and huge white Horses on hillsides. And the Lord must have loved them because they didn't lack bread and they got better weather than we do now.

Katherine Maltwood, like Schliemann who discovered Troy, must have been laughed at by all the very best universities. She died in 1961, but she won't lie down. Here, she said, is the Original Round Table, with Arthur, Guinevere and his chief knights still seated majestically round it as the twelve Zodiac figures. The Grail was said to be hidden in Glastonbury Tor's famous Chalice Well by Joseph of Arimathea.

Sir Percival, who found it, is Aquarius; here symbolised as an eagle or phoenix, enfolding Tor and town in great pinions like a guardian angel. The old monks knew this, carving an eagle on the Tor's tower for a clue. But why an eagle for the January Water Carrier? This Zodiac has only three human figures; Father, Mother and Son. Did the

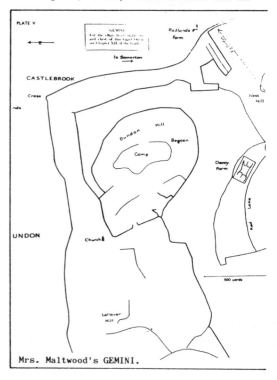

PLATE V

GEMINI

Redlands r. Farm

to Somerton

CASTLEBROOK

Cross

West Hill

Hill

Dundon

Beacon

Camp

Decoy Farm

UNDON

Church

500 yards

Lollover Hill

Mrs. Maltwood's GEMINI.

Waterman gate-crash later Zodiacs when its Trinity was forgotten? Crested eagle and phoenix in myth denote rebirth, and here the initiate in the solar Mysteries threaded the Tor's tunnel and maze to be 'reborn' with the spring son. Aquarian Ganymede takes off from Ida's summit on eagle's wings - already cupbearer to the gods, for Chalice Well and its Grail are in its beak. Winged Daedalus escapes the maze of earthly reincarnation. Perhaps the round-winged eagle is also Aquarius' Waterpot - the Celtic Cauldron of rebirth. The shape's the same.

Next to him lies Merlin - Capricorn, bearded goat of aged Saturn. Project his single straight horn across to Leo and you have the summer and winter signs of our Zodiac supporting the Royal Coat of Arms!

Here is the original White Hart, hunted by every prince of folk-lore; cooling his weary feet in Glastonbury's Hartlake - his heart still pounding from the chase at Hearty Moor. Ponters Ball, his horn, is a huge earthwork over half a mile long; once locally known as the Golden Coffin - though only the Zodiac can now remember why. Arthur of Avalon, the dying sun of Sagittarius, has one foot in this December grave. Older by far than the Arthur of history, he was Ausar (Osiris) and Arueris (Horus), sun-god of Egypt; Ahura, Asser, to the Chaldeans who put him in the sky as Sagittarius. The Pennard Hills modelling his horse echo his name - Arddur, and Breech Lane and Canter's Green occur - just where you'd ex-

pect! He is not a centaur, but looks like one, being dragged over his horse's neck by a great whale, a monster whose crocodile jaws and snake's head horribly mangle his arm - at Wallyer's Bridge. The name Plunging on the whale remembers the battle raging here between Light and Darkness, Good and Evil. Who wins? Well - a trophy of whale's jaws hangs on Glastonbury's Abbey Gate... Here in Brittania's Zodiac wheel is St. George of England, arms outflung in the patronal cross; Cornish St. Michael, complete with horse and dragon; even Scottish St. Andrew, who as dragon-quelling Indara of the Indo-Aryans, left diagonal crosses on pre-Christian stones all over Scotland. Andrew is a dragon-slayer in Syrian legend too - odd larks for a Galilean fisherman!

Scorpio, the death sign, is Mordred, gunning for Arthur with his claws. There are no Scales, as these only evolved from his claws in Roman times; but a dove here improves on Libra's peaceable, communicative air-sign. The Holy Spirit (Logos), it flies from dying Arthur's head, announcing to Virgo the new sun's Virgin Birth. The village on his head, Barton St. David, makes him the inspiration of Wales. Dove and David have a Welsh root in common - Dovydd, Divine Messenger. Here too, is Davey Jones in person, homing to his old love Mother Carey at Virgo. Gosling Street on his back makes him her favourite chicken. Silver Street, Hurtle Pool and Tootle Bridge here all proclaim the turtle dove hurtling down from Heaven to Mother Earth. Sad how the gods of the old faith become the devils of the new.

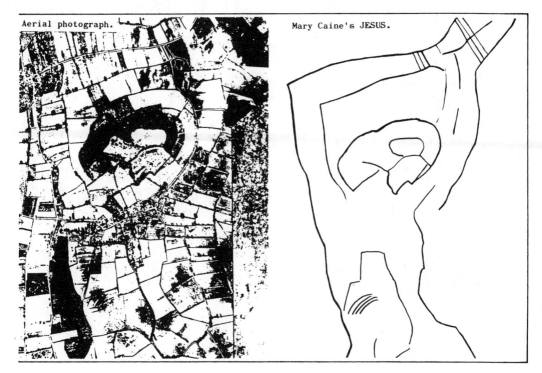

Aerial photograph.

Mary Caine's JESUS.

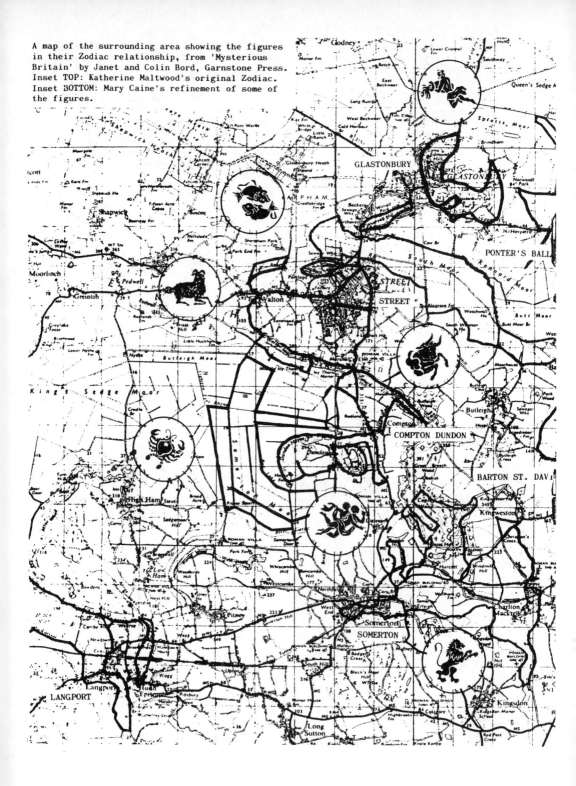

A map of the surrounding area showing the figures in their Zodiac relationship, from 'Mysterious Britain' by Janet and Colin Bord, Garnstone Press. Inset TOP: Katherine Maltwood's original Zodiac. Inset BOTTOM: Mary Caine's refinement of some of the figures.

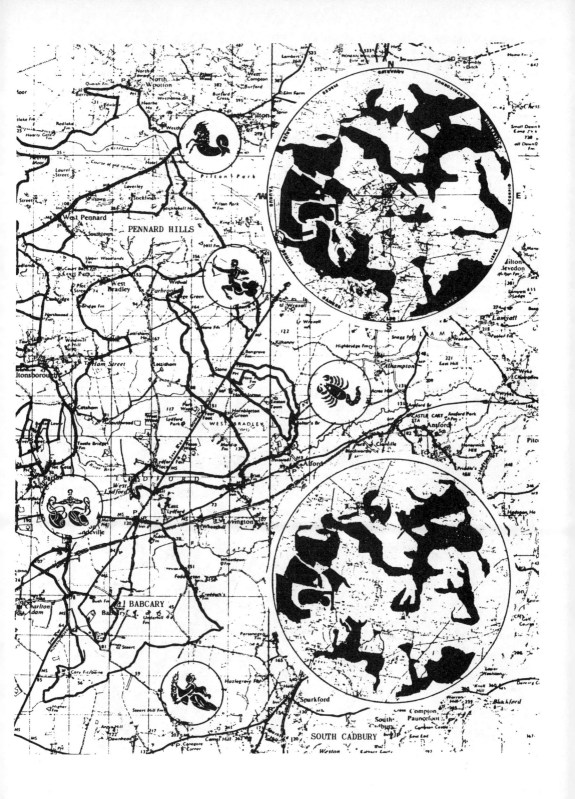

Drawn by the river Cary, complete with tall hat and broomstick (wheatsheaf), Britains first Witch has her baby at Babcary already on the way, shown in her pregnant bulge. Her breast has a tumulus-nipple, known as Wimble Toot. (Toot, tot, teat! Or so Tot as a suckling child and the sailor's bawdy tot of rum seem to show.) Her cauldron became the Holy Grail. Kore, Ceres, goddess of harvest - is at once Virgin, Mother and Black Witch - the three-phased Moon. As fickle Guinevere she abandons Arthur's winter sun for lusty Lancelot at Leo. The Earth Goddess prefers her sun-gods hot! Queen Camel village here reminds us of Camelot's Queen; Cadbury Castle, traditional Camelot, guards her still. Even the rigid Fosse Way makes an unaccustomed bow to kiss her hand.

Lying dangerously close to her is Leo; Lleu Llaw, the blazing summer sun-god from whom Lancelot derived. This lover was something of a father-figure, for Guinevere's father was Leo-degrance! One paw of this superb heraldic lion flattens Somerton, once Somerset's capital. Sumer-town? (Arthur, upside-down on the Zodiac Wheel, performs the first Somersault. His dream at the end Malory's Morte D'Arthur, where he hangs inverted on Fortune's Wheel, gnawed by wild beasts, secretly remembers our Sagittarian sacrifice.)

What, no crab at Cancer? Does the ship cradling a baby mark this watery maternal sign? (Argo Navis occupies this quarter of the sky.) Womb or crescent-moon of Isis and Mary, it holds Gemini, the sun's unborn son, ready to sail beneath the earth to his eastern rising. All heads turn west to adore him. Lohot was Arthur's son; here is Galehot (Galahad) in his Galley. The high (haut) sun brought low; the hot sun-set. He and Percival (who also sailed from mortal sight in the sun's, or Solomon's ship) are identical Heavenly Twins; they alone were found worthy of the Grail. Gemini's double shows up in aerial photographs; within the foetal outline appears a bearded youth, astonishingly Christ-like; a prefiguring that makes us wonder with William Blake "And did those in ancient times..?" Ox and ass protect him, for Asella (Ass) and Manger stars both occur in Cancer, and Taurus hovers above him. Only the bull's head and foot are shown. His horns are lynchets curved round Hatch Hill. Collard Hill is on his collar. (Someone has stuck a third horn on his head - the Hood obelisk!)

Place a star-map to scale on the Somerset circle - all the Zodiac stars fall on their earthly counterparts. The equinoctial stars Aldebaran (on Taurus' foot) and Antares (on Scorpio at Stone) were due east-west in 2,800 BC. Sumerian temples were so aligned. Arthur's finger stabbing the circle's centre, his eye and that of the Bull all lie on this line. The Archer, aiming at the Bull's eye, dates this Temple of the Stars! Chance? My foot, says Taurus.

Aerial photograph of Barton St. David, showing the outline of the DOVE, in Libra.

Aries, his head reverted at __Street__, is Gawain; the spring sun, rash, impulsive, promiscuous. He had to win his battles before mid-day, for then, sun-like, his strength began to wane. They still tan sheepskins on his Golden Fleece. One of the Fishes springs from his head. Charming to find Street famous for its shoes, for in Astrology, Pisces rules the feet. __Fisher's Hill__ leads to __Weary-All Hill__, the northern fish, the only sign recognisable from the Tor. On the back of this Celtic Salmon of Wisdom, Joseph of Arimathea planted his staff, the __Holy Thorn__, which has flowered at __Christmas__ and __Easter__ ever since. He chose this spot well. for Christianity's earliest symbol was the Fish.   Did he know what he was doing? Did he ever come at all? He may well have done if Cornish legend is true; it claims him as a wealthy Phoenician tin-trader, brother-in-law to St. Anne, who is claimed as a Cornish princess taken by Joseph to Palestine and married to his brother. As her daughter was the Virgin Mary, this made Joseph the great-uncle of Jesus. This ancient belief is echoed oddly enough in Coptic legend. Those feet it seems may well have trodden England's metal track from Cornwall through the Zodiac to the Mendip lead mines; and at Priddy in the Mendips they still say: "As sure as the Lord was at Priddy", while Looe island, Falmouth and other ports cherish sacred memories of his coming. Do we take these Celtic myths (or reject

them) too literally? __Is our Christ-like Gemini their origin?__ Esus, Hesus, was the third person of the Druidic Trinity long before Christianity; Taliessin in his coracle, Jason in his Argo, Odysseus the sailor, are but variants on the name of Jesus. Jesus in Welsh is Yesse - Essence of Man. Say 'Yes' and affirm your own divinity.

King Arviragus, the Arthur of the time, gave Joseph twelve hides of land around Glastonbury to maintain his mission. What were these but our twelve Hidden Figures? Old genealogies moreover give Joseph as ancestor of Arthur and his chief knights!

We have now come full circle back to Glastonbury, where we came in. Its Abbey, the greatest in England, was said to be built around Joseph's humble wattle church - the 'Secret of The Lord'. Some said this __round__ church was built by our Lord Himself, others that it wasn't built by human hands. Are these rumours dim memories of an earlier Secret still?

There is one more effigy - that of its guardian dog; its Cerberus - lying (all five miles of him) just south-west of the circle. He is Arthur's dog Cabal - 'The Mysteries'. The Somerset Wassail Song says of him: "The Girt Dog of Langport has burnt his long tail..." - a reference perhaps to the sacking of __Langport__ by the Danes. All in all a hot time for the dog, with Alfred burning his

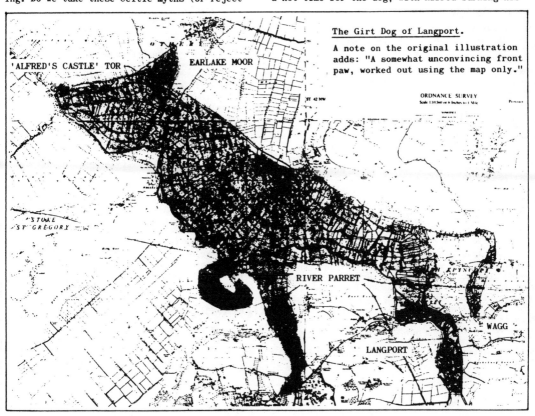

The Girt Dog of Langport.

A note on the original illustration adds: "A somewhat unconvincing front paw, worked out using the map only."

nose at the other end with his famous cakes. Alfred's Castle, a three-tiered mini-tor at Athelney, makes his nostril. Burnt barley cakes used to be thrown into the river Tone, his tongue. Was Alfred seeking admission to the Mysteries? Were his cakes a 'sop to Cerberus'? If so, he would take his vow of secrecy at Oath Hill, descend into Hades at Hellard and Hellyar, emerging with a sigh of relief at Paradise, east of the tail. He would sail up the river Parret (which draws the dog's underside from nose to back leg at Langport), much as Sumerian Gilgamesh did long before him when he travelled to the far west and "... sailed up the river Parutti to the place where the star-gods dwell..." in search of eternal life. You just can't miss this Dog, with his eye a double prehistoric circle on the aerial photographs, his head at Head Drove, his ear at Earlake Moor, and his tail at - wait for it - Wagg!

If Arthur beckons - if, that is, you need to find the meaning of life, your place and purpose in it - walk boldly past this Cerberus; his tail wags welcome to true-hearted pilgrims. Feast on the ancient wisdom of the Round Table; drink the Water of Life from Chalice Well; join the Quest for the illumination - the inspiration - of its Hidden Grail.

* * * * * * *

MISSING: ATLANTIC BALLOONIST / cont.

sea traffic in the Atlantic were alerted. The 'army in the Spanish Sahara' searched the coast of West Africa with 10 helicopters, since it was theorised that he may have come down anywhere between the Azores and that end of the Sahara. Gatch was equipped with nearly every survival aid including flares, mirrors, 10-day food supply, life jacket, and life raft with location transmitter, etc. But no sign of the balloons or the fibreglass gondola (which I think was florescent pink.) But no sign of anything. By 7th March-somepapers are telling of faded hopes. There is a note by Fort in New Lands which might be relevant here:"A balloon is lost near or over the sea If it should fall into the sea it would probably float and for a time be a considerable conspicuous object..." and he goes on to advise us to look for the mysterious appearance of luminous 'supposed-balloons' in other places at the time.

MISSING: GIRL SCIENTIST.

Police and friends were puzzling over why Jean Baxter, 29, a computer operator at Porton Down chemical defence establishment in Wiltshire, should drive to the coast at Swanage, Dorset, park her car on a hillside beauty-spot, then vanish. Five weeks later, after searches and investigation, there is still no clue...except a full bag of groceries was found on her back seat. Police say that she did not handle any classified material, and is seperated from her husband. Sunday Express 10 March 74.

human curiosities

GAZELLE-BOY IN AFRICA...STREAKS FREE.

French anthropologist Jean Claude Armen says he has seen a boy living in the wilds as a gazelle several times about 35 miles from Rio de Oro, the capital of Spanish Sahara. He appears to be in his late teens and is 'mothered' by a female gazelle. Mr Armen was reporting to the Life Institute in Geneva - the boy, he said, is long-haired, goes about naked, moving in leaps and bounds, though not as fast (or as graceful) as his companions.

"I have watched him approach gazelles and lick their foreheads in a sign of recognition," says Mr Armen, and he added that the boy is able to stand like a human (a curious way of putting it, but we can guess what he means), and has seen him dig for roots with his hands and feeding them to his four-footed friends. Dr Paul Roget, director of the Institute, said that this could be the most fascinating case ever of a human brought up by animals. (Daily Mirror. 1 Feb 71. Credit: Anthony Smith.)

12-YEAR-OLD BOY DIES OF OLD AGE.

Here is a story of Lovecraftian horror - but by all accounts is as real as a wart - the poor kid with the unlikely disease of Progeria, a malfunction of the pituitary gland which regulates the smooth functioning of many others in turn, had the unlikely name of Jomar Henregue Silva. Six months after he was born, in Vitoria, Brazil, he had all his teeth...but they were yellow and crooked. Before he was two-years-old his hair had turned white and began to fall out. He tried to lead a normal child's life but galloping senility left him with wasted limbs and creaking joints. At ten his skin was wrinkled and dry, and doctors confirmed that his blood vessels had hardened like those of an old man - then, his life was over before it had really begun. (Daily Mirror, 29 Jan 71. Credit: Anthony Smith.)

WOTALOT I GOT...

A man with four kidneys has amazed doctors at Farnborough, Hants. So strongly are we conditioned to be wary or fearful of deviations from 'normality'(whatever that is) that the need is to rationalise or to 'defuse'...we are assured that the lucky man is in good health, and that the kind doctors see no need to cut him open and rob him of his bounty.....for the present. The Sun, 4 Dec 73. Credit: Anthony Smith.

illnesses & attacks

What follows concerns the sadistic and largely fatal attack on pets and domestic animals that have at times broken out - something or things with a gory appetite that stalks through our hutches and coops. There have been invisible

---

SCAN YOUR LOCAL PAPERS, AND....

assailants and assassins; and while some of the locals in the area of Binbrook Farm, near Great Grimsby, were spontaneously burnt or flaming, something else was killing the chickens. Fort notes a vampiric attack on chickens on the 31st Dec 1904. And again later in January 1905: "Out of 250 fowls, Mr White says that he has only 24 left. They have all been killed in the same weird way. The skin around the neck, from the head to the breast, has been pulled off, and the wind-pipe drawn from its place and snapped. The fowl-house has been watched night and day, and when-ever examined, four or five birds would be found dead." And in nearby Market Rasen, on January 16th, 57 chickens were consumed in a fire, with no clue as to how it started. For the fuller picture of these grizzly killings that seemed to accompany a series of strange fires upon humans and fires during polergeist-type activities you will have to go to LO! chapter XIV (pages 120-123 in the Ace edition).

From our own files we have a note on 33 piglets killed when a fire swept through their sty at Croker House Farm, Gawsworth, near Macclesfield on 14 Jan 74. (from the Manchester Evening News of the same date. Credit: Peter Rogerson). No indication is given about the cause, or even if it was known. The day before, 24 pigs were killed by 'vandals' in the sty of Leslie Hewitt, in Thorpe Lane, Leeds. (Daily Mail. 14 Jan 74. Credit: Peter Rogerson.) But let's go back to the begining of our little pile of notes.

MYSTERY DEATH OF COW.

Nothing unusual, you might think, about cows being attacked - it must happen all the time. Sometimes, as in this case, the nature of the wounds gives rise to speculations beyond the usual and expected misadventures of country-life. Attacks were made on a herd of 55 Friesians on the Broomstair Farm, Hyde Road, Denton, of Mr. Stanley Phillips. His son gave this report:

"My wife brought the cows up and we found a newly calved heifer had a deep cut in her udder, which means her milk can't be used at the moment. Another heifer in calf had been very badly bashed on the back legs and it had a number of small cuts. My father went looking for a missing beast - another newly-calved heifer - and found it dead in the River Tame. It had four deep cuts on its back and down its leg and would have had to be destroyed."

The nature of the cuts caused him to add: "We don't know what has caused these things, but if it had been in Africa you would have said it was done by lion. Cows can outrun a man in a field, but someone may have used a dog to pen them, and then attacked them." (Manchester Evening News. 7 July 1969. Credit: Peter Rogerson.) See Ch. IX of Fort's Wild Talents for accounts of humans 'stabbed' by invisible attackers.

SADIST SLAYS 288 PETS.

A note in the Sunday Times for 3 Jan 70 announ-ces that the police have 'their first real clues' to a series of sadistic killings of pets in the Thorne district near Doncaster, which began in the previous October. The police had a dossier on 30 attacks in which a total of 288 animals have been killed - mainly rabbits, guinea pigs and chickens. Many belonged to young children, who were often the first to discover the atroc-ities.

The last of the raids mentioned - on rabbit hutches in the pit-village of Stainforth - "the killer slipped up for the first time, leaving a footprint in the snow. In addition, the hairs of an alsation dog were found on one of the hutches." My underlining - the lack of footprin-ts on snowy ground where there is one seems a curious detail. And the dog? Do maniacs take their dogs with them when they are bent on their massacres? They might if they were maniacs - but dogs would get excited, and no one heard anything at all. The police seem to think that it is a man: "The man has raided allotments and small private gardens every three or four days." Nice periodicity for a maniac - and yet the police failed to catch him; people failed to see or hear him, despite his regularity.

What remains is an unsolved mystery - a foot-print and some dog hairs - left, or carefully placed, like a signature, on the last act. But the people will remember: "Such brutality has been shown in the massacre of these animals that even hardened police officers have felt physic-ally sick." A ghastly thought comes to me - about possible poltergeist connections with all those young pet-owners. That a force that can lift tables, bend spoons, and bruise flesh could equ-ally cause serious damage if it got out of con-trol. And the line of a song ...'You always hurt the one you love...' We are not ghouls - we do not like to dwell on nastiness - but we cannot help feeling that tingle of curiosity when we sense the presence of the Unknown. Forces -uses-primal layers of mind. We continue:

KILLER CHIMP VINDICATED.

Anthony Smith sent us this note, but was unable to give any other indication than it was possibly from the Daily Mirror, and probably 1969. It con-cerns a court action brought by chimp-trainer Hans Vogelbein against Raymond Sawyer, the Super-intendant of three Greater London Council zoos for children. Vogelbein alleged that Sawyer spread a rumour that one of his chimps was resp-onsible for the death of forty rabbits, found mutilated at the Pet's Corner Zoo of Crystal Palace. Sawyer lost and was ordered to pay costs. Nothing is said about the killer that is still free. Maybe they didn't like to think about it?

PROFESSIONAL JOURNALS FOR DATA.

WELSH RABBIT KILLER.

Children were warned to bring their pets indoors at night as police were on the alert for yet another maniac pet-slayer, who has killed more than thirty pet rabbits in twelve raids on back-gardens in the mining village of Gilfach Goch in Glamorgan. The police say that he forces open locked hutches to strangle the rabbits, leaving their bodies on the ground. "Once he put a stray dog into a hutch to savage the rabbits. Another rabbit was found trussed up with wire. Eight rabbits kept by 8-year-old Rhydian Priday, of Coronation St, were found with their necks broken, carefully placed in a line down the garden path." Another signature? We note with interest the detail of the stray-dog - can we presume from the tone that when the hutch was checked in the morning a strange dog was found unacountbly where no dog could have been without a human accomplice? Perhaps the locks were in a condition to suggest that they were forced, the dog put in, and then replaced. Perhaps they were not tampered with at all, and the dog materialised in response to a desire for some rabbit. These are suppositions of course - but if we must stick to a human agency, then ponder on the curiosity of outbreaks of pet-killing among quiet mining villages not long after one another. Anyway, the story is from Daily Mirror. 11 Nov 70. Credit: Anthony Smith.

MOON THEORY OF WOLVERHAMPTON SLAYINGS.

On the night of 9 Feb 71 a rabbit's cage at the back of the Turley's house, 32 Oaks Crescent, Wolverhampton, was smashed apart and the little bunny inside was battered and torn to death. A guinea pig in a nearby cage was untouched. Police and forensic experts were called to the blood-spattered yard and the carcass was taken to a local vet for examination. Mr John Turley advanced the theory that the killer must be affected by the full moon which was   evident at the time. We also learn that the killer battered to death chickens and pigeons at two other addresses near-by. (Express & Star. 10 Feb 70.)

The Express & Star of the next day reported that there was a full-scale meeting of police, RSPCA, and animal experts to collect evidence and information to try and find any pattern. There was another killing the night before - a rabbit in in Cherry St, Wolverhampton, and two dogs were seen nearby. Last month in the Coalway Rd/Penn area, eight rabbits and guinea pigs were killed.

In the same paper on the 12th, the police say they suspect a fox which had probably been forced to forage in the centre of Wolverhampton by a 'disease' which 'has killed off a number of wild rabbits.' At the least they suspect two of the killings to be 'fox, stoat or dog'. Superinten-

dent Brian Morgan, in charge of the investigation said: "I am not saying that all the killings were committed by an animal, but our latest tests show this to be the case in the most recent killings."

In the grandest tradition of enquiry-stopping, sure enough, the next day someone reports a fox seen leaping over a fence on the corner of Paget and Compton Roads. It was "as big as a Labrador, and dark brown." Curiously that same phrase crops up in a number of the 'Surrey Puma' reports - whether that has any relevance we don't know. This witness said he saw the same 'fox' twice; a week before and three weeks before. The story was in the Express & Star of Feb 13th. In the same edition is a hammed-up story of a little girl, whose bunny has gone missing - has it become another victim of the horrid fiend? Time passes - yet if it has a head, it is raised again. 10th of Dec, 73, a rabbit is strangled in Bradmore, near Wolverhampton. In the next few days rabbits in Claverly Drive, Warstones, were torn apart. All this is in a note in the Express & Star of 13 Dec 73 - but the main story is about Mrs Harrington of Claverly Drive. A neighbour warned her to bring her rabbit in for the night. The night of the 12th - something came for her bunny, and finding it missing smashed the hut to pieces. "The dog heard nothing. I am sure it was more than a dog that did this." (All credit for the above cuttings to Anthony Smith.)

MANIAC KILLS FAMILY'S PETS.

As if all this wasn't bizarre enough. A brown envelope is pushed through the door of the Jolliffe family house in Priestly Road, Bournmouth. It contains a sheet of paper with the message 'TIMMY IS DEAD'. Timmy was the family's black terrier who had gone missing three days before. The first hint of trouble had come a few weeks before when they found a pet kitten beheaded in their front room one morning. Then Pinkie the duck, and Ozzie the gander went missing from their pen in the back garden. Their son found Ozzie a day later - or rather Ozzie's headless body was found back near the pen. Understandably the family are really frightened - and the police were called but have come to no conclusions. (Sunday Mirror. 28 Nov 71.)

monsters & absms
IN THE FOOTSTEPS OF THE YETI.

Madame Marie-Jeanne Koffmann, a French surgeon, has launched an expedition from Paris to the icy wastes of Siberia for an Abominable Snowman (ABSM). From an analysis of over 400 sightings (presumably from that area) she gives us this description: "Two short legs, covered with shaggy hair, and if he wasn't stooping he'd be nearly 6ft tall. He has long arms, a powerful body, and a small pointed head. His eyes are slanted and his nose is flat." Daily Mail, 14 May 73. (Credit: Steve Moore.) We wonder how she got on..

Daily Mirror, 17 Nov 73 - and an announcement that a Japanese team is going to set out in January to find the elusive Yeti. (We have a cutting from the Daily Mail, 11 Oct 72, that the leader of a Japanese expedition on Putha Hiunchuli in the Himalayas, reported seeing a yeti.) Anyway they set out and sure enough, back comes the word of photographs of 8"x 6" yeti-prints from an 'unnamed peak' in the Annapurna range. Daily Mirror and Guardian, 26 Jan 74. Credit: Steve Moore & Peter Rogerson.

Still smarting after their snub by Nessie, the 15 strong Japanese Loch Ness Monster team promise to return next year with a £30,000 robot computer (that's what it says here). Perhaps they are trying to revive the flagging sales from Toho studios, and we shall soon be enjoying on our screens 'Mothra and Nessie save the world from Ebirah, Terror of the Deeps!' Anyway - the robot was announced in News of the World. 11 Nov 73.

SILVER LAKE MONSTER IN PERU.

This story is verbatim from Independant Radio News, 22 March 74: "Villagers in mountains report a serpent-like monster rising from an icy lake on moon-lit nights, devouring sheep and terrifying villages. North Peruvians claim to have seen a fat silver shiny monster come out of Los Angeles Lake, 12,000 feet above sea-level, following a strong earth-tremor which caused landslides on a mountain near the lake. (Credit: Cathy Purcell.) Hmmm. Curious detail about the tremor!

BRITISH CLIMBER SEES YETI.

The Sunday Mirror of 24 Sept 72, says British mountaineer Don Whillans saw "a strange ape-like creature moving sideways on all fours," during his 1969 expedition in the Himalays. Well...we thought you might like to see a picture of Don himself. (From Sunday Times 30 May 71). Its no wonder the Yeti stay well clear.

ripley or not!

NAME GAMES CONTINUED.

Robert Forrest, who is something of a 'coincidence' freak, writes: "Would it be possible to appeal to NEWS-readers to send me tales of odd coincidences concerning numbers, names places, people - anything? It might be interesting to start correspondences like this - swapping coincidences for UFOs etc." (Anyone who wants to join the game can write to him at: 68 Chesham Rd, Bury, Lancs, BL9 6NA.) Meanwhile his current batch contains the following goodies. The cigar production manager at WD & HO Wills is a Mr Ronald Seagar. (Daily Mirror 9 Jan 74). A packet of rings lost on the London Underground by jewel designers Paul Ravn and Anne Buzzard, was found by Rose Crow, who works for the fashion house of Polly Peck. (Daily Mirror 15 Jan 74). This last reminded us of a cutting we..er..lost (blush), but Rob Forrest saw the item on TV news (1 Nov 73), that an escaped Eagle came down to rest for a while in Bird-in-the-Bush Road, which is to be found in Peckham, London.

The staff band of the Royal Army Ordnance Corps at Chilwell has a Major-General Key, a Lieut-Colonel Sharp, and its conductor is a Captain Beat. (Daily Express 12 Nov 73.) The leader of the Woodlands Ladies Choir, West Wickham, Kent is a Mrs. Trill and her accompanist is Mrs. Handy. (Sunday Express. 16 Dec 73.)

Peter Rogerson sent us a clipping from the Daily Mail.(14 Jan 73.) which mentions an article by Sarah Bunney, in Nature, on our present subject. In it she mentions; an international gynaecologist, Dr Zakarish Ovary; the producer of the BBC programme on acupuncture, Chuck Despins; among the attendees at a conference on population control was a Miss Mercedes Concepcion; Dr JM Looney who 'analysed the role blood played in mental disorder'; Dr WR Brain, author of a book on mind and matter; and Dr EG Boring, who compiled a history of introspection; wolf behaviorologist Dr MW Fox; Mr H Fish of the Essex River Authority; and among the botanists, AM Berrie (Glasgow), KD Gardiner (Dublin), BE Juniper (Oxford), RP Moss (Birmingham), and F Rose (London Kings College); GC Cheeseman of the Dairy Research Institute; JW Musty of the Ancient Monuments,Dept of Environment; PM Chalk, limestone expert from Wisconsin; and finally, DL Coffin, an air pollution expert.

23 years ago, a farmer in Austria found a baby boy on a lake, and named him, predictably, Moses. Three months later miles away near Stuttgart, in Germany, police found a child abandoned in a rowboat on a stream. They called the baby Moses not knowing at the time she was a girl. Now the two are to be married, having met by accident in a German youth hostel. (Titbits. 13/19 Dec 73. Credit: Cathy Purcell.)

scientific curiosities

CORE BLIMEY!

Dr D King-Hele and Dr GE Cook of the Royal Aircraft Establishment, Farnborough, have refined their knowledge of the earth's pear shape. Even ten years or more ago it was clear, as the RAE team put it, that "floating at sea-level at the North Pole, one would be about 40m farther from the equator than an equally undaunable explorer who bored down to sea-level at the South Pole." Now they have put together data from studying 27 satellites and find that the pear-shaped tendency is even greater, with the North Pole growing "a stem" some 44.7m high, relative to the South Pole (Nature, Vol 246, p86.) Relative to the mean spheroid, the stem is 18.9m high, and the South Pole depression is 25.8m deep. The only remaining question is: Where is the great Cosmic Tree on which the Earth grew.
New Scientist. 15 Nov 1973, (Credit: M. Roberts.) Come back Yggdrasil, Midgard needs you....

THROW AWAY YOUR ZOOLOGY TEXTBOOKS!

Once there were the Arthropoda: an extraordinary, successful phylum of 'joint-foot' invertebrates which included the Onychophora, the Trilobites; the Crustaceans such as crabs, lobsters and barnacles; the Myriopods, such as the millipedes; the Arachnids such as spiders and scorpions; and climactic in versatility and ubiquity, the Insects. They were varied, these creatures; indeed, there were more species of Arthropod than of all other kinds of animal put together. But they were so fundamentally similar, with their armour-plate and tough chitinous jaws; so obviously evolved from the more primative polychaete worms (such as the lugworm used as fisherman's bait), that no-one could doubt the essential oneness. They were nature's most supreme demonstration of adaptive radiation about a common theme.

All of which zoological folklore, restated in a thousand textbooks, is, according to Dr Sidnie M Manton of Queen Mary College, London, a load of rubbish. To be an arthropod is not to be a member of a particular genealogical dynasty: it is merely to have achieved a certain grade of organisation. In the same way, a bat is not a bird, simply because both can fly. Indeed, says Manton, 'arthropodism' has arisen at least three times...appearing now as three totally distinct phyla: the Uniramia, including Myriopods, Onchophora, and the five distinct groups of Hexapod (insect); the Crustacea; and the Chelicerata

(represented as Arachnids) which may or may not be closely allied with the extinct Trilobites.

Though corroborating her arguments with embryological data, Manton bases her thesis primarily on comparative morphology. One of the weaknesses of the traditional view of arthropod phylogeny - that all forms rose from the polychaetes via a common stock - is that it presupposed the existence of intermediate ancestral types. But there is no fossil evidence for such types, and there are no modern animals resembling those hypothetical types. Manton states not only that such types never existed, but that they could not have existed.

An ancestral type, besides generating future types, must itself be capable of survival; and the hypothetical common ancestor of today's arthropod types would have been functionally impossible. (from New Scientist. 8 Nov 73) Credit: M Roberts.

And then there is, of course, the hypothetical ancestor between modern man and his supposed Neanderthal (etc) forebears. Could 'man' have arisen twice; or more? See 'The Eternal Man' for some ideas on the successive regeneration of Man. Well, while we are on the subject of shudders and quakes within the theory of Evolution, here is an article that appeared in the Sunday Times for 17 March 74: 'A NEW THEORY OF EVOLUTION.'

DINOSAURS ARE (alive and well and living (among other places) in Britain. There is, however, no need to be alarmed by this warning just issued by two American scientists. They are not suggesting that there are tyrannosauri in Epping Forest. Their dinosaurs are to be seen every day in woods and fields — they are birds.

The astonishing claim that birds are dinosaurs is made by Robert T. Bakker of Harvard University, and Peter Galton of the University of Bridgeport, in Nature. The idea may mean little to the layman—but it cannot be ignored by fellow palaeontologists (fossil experts).

Bakker and Galton are proposing a drastic revision in the zoological classification of animals, something almost as controversial as altering scripture. Even those who disagree must take the theory seriously.

Conventional ideas about the evolution of dinosaurs took shape almost a century ago and have changed very little since. Briefly they amount to this: some 200 million years ago there was a large and flourishing group of reptiles called thecodontians (the name means that they had their teeth in sockets) from which five separate evolutionary branches emerged more or less at the same time. One became the birds of today; another gave rise to the modern crocodiles; the third consisted of the pterodactyls and their flying relations, all now extinct. The last two were the groups we now know collectively as dinosaurs (" terrible lizards "): the saurischians (" lizard hips "), and the ornithischians (" bird hips ").

According to this scheme of things the name dinosaurs has no strict zoological meaning. It is

a relic from the days when the remains were first discovered, before it was realised that there were two distinct groups of dino-

saurs which emerged quite independently.

Bakker and Galton have put forward a different theory. They suggest that only three branches emerged from the thecodontians 200 million years ago: the crocodiles, the pterodactyls and a single group of dinosaurs. The dinosaurs, they say, did not split into two until much later. The birds are supposed to have split off later still, as others have suggested recently.

According to Bakker and Galton it is, therefore, meaningful in evolutionary terms to group both kinds of dinosaurs and the birds into a new Class in the technical sense of the word—the Dinosauria. If so the vertebrates would not be divided, as they are at present, into fishes, amphibians, reptiles (including dinosaurs), birds and mammals, but into fishes, amphibians, reptiles, dinosaurs (including birds) and mammals. This, they claim, " reflects more faithfully the evolutionary steps."

The argument is highly technical, but a key point is the idea, which they did not originate, that the dinosaurs were warm blooded. This would be a major difference from the reptiles and there is evidence that dinosaurs may indeed have had warm blood. The microscopic structure of dinosaur bones, for example, is much closer to that of sheep or cows than of cold blooded modern reptiles. And in support of the later development of birds there is the fact that no remains of bird ancestors earlier than the 140 million years old archaeopteryx have ever been discovered, though this is very far from being conclusive as the previous 60 million years have left very few fossil remains of big land animals at all.

Palaeontologists acknowledge that Bakker and Galton have a case, but that is a very different matter from even beginning to consider the major reclassification they suggest.

"The proposals are based on three main arguments," commented Dr Alan Charig, Curator of Fossil Reptiles and Birds at the Natural History Museum in London. "First, that the two groups of dinosaurs have a common origin. Second, that they were warm-blooded. Third, that the birds evolved from dinosaurs. I am extremely doubtful about the first point, and it's so new that most palaeontologists have not even had a chance to consider it, let alone accept it. The second and third points may well be true, there are very convincing arguments on both sides, but they are still highly controversial. Palaeontologists are not going to start officially calling birds dinosaurs until they are virtually unanimous on these points and we're a very long way from that."

Bryan Silcock

ufos

DID YOU SEE...

the long (and funny) write-up of the Pascagoula Kidnap Case (mentioned in NEWS 2.p18), in The Rolling Stone, 17 Jan 74? Worth tracking down.

FLYING OBJECT OVER WEARSIDE.

Mrs Margaret Naylor, of Ewesley Road, Wearsode, Sunderland, described the object she saw for six minutes through a pair of binoculars as "a long black oblong, rounded more on top than underneath I saw a red light come round it, then green, yellow and orange, and it seemed as if it was going to go up in flames. Then the lights died down, and it became black again and buzzed around. It hovered over Barnes school and then disappeared. I have never seen anything like it in my life before." This was on 23rd Jan.

Earlier in the day when her son returned home at lunchtime from Thornhill School, he had said he had seen four UFOs together. Then on his way home again in the evening he saw another. "I didn't really believe him until he called me outside and showed me the one by Barnes School. Then Mrs Naylor adds a curious detail: "The object looked similar to a drawing in a book about cavemen. The likeness was really remarkable." The Sunderland Echo, 24 Jan 74. Credit: Paul Screeton. The more observant among you will note that this sighting is concurrent with the rumblings and lights at Llandrillo (see News 3) and about which we shall have a full report next ish.

CONCORDE IN UFO RIDDLE.

During the Concorde flight to gain information on the total eclipse of the sun in Africa last June, scientists managed to photograph a UFO. Enlargements of a 'luminous dot' that turned up unexpectedly, showed it to be 650ft across. After months of study, French government scientists have now officially listed it as a UFO. Daily Mirror, 1 Feb 74. Credit: Steve Moore.

Uncle Chao's glee club

COULDN'T BE CORNEA...

A routine X-ray has revealed why 7-year-old Roderick Allsop of Court Lane, Erdington, Birmingham has been troubled by watering eyes for the last five years - an open safety-pin was stuck up his nose. Whaaaaat?! Daily Mail, 1 Jan 73. Credit: Steve Moore.

THE UNIVERSAL CONTINUITY OF PHENOMENA.

"I had just finished a repair job down a manhole in the road when an old lady came up and tried to make me accept a 10p piece. 'Thanks ever so much,' she said. 'You are the only one who has put the gas right on my stove.' She wouldn't listen to my protests. How do you tell an old lady that repairing the telephone cables could hardly have helped her gas stove?"

A letter in Sunday Mirror. 20 Jan 74.

REVIEWS

'THE OLD STONES OF LAND'S END.' by John Michell, Garnstone Press, £4.25, 136p, 76 illos, IBSN: 0.85511.370.7.

Garnstone are building up a superb list of titles - and this one tops the lot so far. It gave me some pleasure to hold a book that does graphic honour to the work that went into it, and the message it contains. From the title page, and the splendid double-spread of poem and dedication to 'Charles, Prince of Wales, and Duke of Cornwall' it is clear that Michell is a traditionalist of rare quality.

There are three main sections: The Stones, The Crosses, and finally an essay on the nature of the Megalithic Science itself. Alas, we have too little room to discuss the many interesting aspects of the book - let me just say that apart from its value as a reference work on the Cornish stones (no mean thing in itself), it will stand as an eloquent vindication of Alfred Watkins's theories of the old tracks and their marker/artifacts, since it takes the well-defined area of Land's End and tests those theories out on its landmarks. To this extent we must regret the lack of participation or interest from the various learned professions, and offer thanks for the still small band of dedicated researchers who abide by the rules of true scholarship, scorning commercial hysteria.

The essay belies its simplicity - it is an excellent introduction to the whole vital and young inquiry, the re-discovery of our past - and manages to sumarise most of what is known about these stone reminders, with some speculations on the great traditions and purposes of our forefathers, things we have long since forgotten. Michell's plea, to try to come to a new understanding of the Earth as a living totality, will not fall on deaf ears among Forteans. We too are groping towards the idea and implications of universal continuity.

This cry is not aimed at the Jealous Professors, but to all those who are seriously interested in studying these ancient artifacts with the seriousness they deserve, and if necessary evolve to new methods of study and understanding. We heartily embrace the call to abandon the chauvinism of scientific specialisation, and its corollary of the myth of modern man's superiority as the crown of creation and evolution.

This disability, of only looking at things from one point of view and excluding the validity of others, is what Fort called an 'evil of modern specialisation' (see back to Blasts & Quakes). Here, Michell points out that these stones have been all things to all specialists - one of the main reasons we are only now getting round to finding out about one of the most exciting mysteries of this or any other century. For example: just how did the ancient articifers choose their sites to combine meaningful indications of astronomy, geometry, ritual symbology, a living folklore, political and topographical markers, and underground water, with one of holy significance. Or rather it was 'holy' because it was a node for these things - but how did they find such a place? Michell says: "In wondering how a modern surveyor would proceed in the matter, we are projecting our own methods onto the past, investigating the old science by reference to the modern."

Indeed, it can be said that we have solved all the easy things in Science with our vaunted analytical thought, and we are not doing so well with it on the harder problems. Perhaps it's time to turn to more inclusive forms of comprehension - a challenge our ancestors seem to have met and transcended. Give this book to your children (or any children) and help breed a new and hopefully more effective type of scientist.

'NEW LANDS.'
by Charles Fort, Sphere (paperback), 35pence, 206p, ISBN: 0.7221.3627.7.

We also welcome this reprint of Fort's second book - which deals with mainly astronomical, meteorological, seismological and other il-logical data, including the falls of various unsavory things from the sky.

Curiously, Sphere who own the 'Abacus' imprint under which they recently published 'The Book of the Damned', did not brings this out as its companion volume. From what I can gather contractural mix-ups has split their chances of making a set. Also, this edition of 'New Lands' has been re-set, eliminating some of the typographical errors of the Ace edition. Unless you have it already, you must buy it -since it concerns the substance and approach of THE NEWS.

'THE NEW APOCRYPHA'
by John Sladek, Hart-Davis MacGibbon, £3.25,376p, 20 illos, 10 tables, ISBN: 0.246.10715.4.

There are so few books that deal with the rich panorama of pseudo-sciences and crank cults, that a new one is an event of sorts. "The effort is made to distinguish between ideas which are off the beaten track and those which are simply off the rails." And with these criteria, Sladek sets downhill to give us a critical assessment of Atlantis; fossil astronauts; Velikovsky; UFOs; psychic research; health foods; Kennedy death theories; perpetual motion; Nazi occultism; the Great Pyramid; the Bacon codes; Ted Serios; the I Ching; Cycle theory, and many other loony past-times.

Sladek also says: "I try to describe them with a minimum of debunking. Although I must confess in advance my own bias against many occult and pseudo-scientific claims." Fair enough! But somewhere on the way his criteria becomes blurred, and his bias slips into a holier-than-thou mocking. I don't know which I find the most exasperating. I certainly think it very sad that after all his effort (and this volume represents a vast amount of reading) Sladek seems to prefer sarcasm and aphorism to compassionate discussion or any kind of constructive exploration, and I find this really lessens the value of this kind of stone-throwing.

However, the book is worth buying for its references and cross-indexing, and for the many areas where Sladek has brought Martin Gardner's excellent 'Fads and Fallacies in the Name of Science' up to date. Of some importance to us is that Charles Fort is one of the very few 'free thinkers' to emerge from both books unscathed - and both have some interesting comments to make on Forteanism (as Theory, and as it is practised), though this applies more to Gardner. Forming as they do, catalogues of human error and gullability, the moral is clear - uncritical acceptance of authority does nobody any service. And I found some worth in reading Sladek from this point - that his infuriating complacency lead me to examine the extent of my own credulity.

REMEMBER TO RENEW YOUR SUB SOON

As an indication of when to renew your subscription - we have put a number in the top right-hand corner of your address lable on the envelope. This is the number of issues you have left TO COME. We would appreciate renewals before your last one if possible, since it helps with the messy paperwork.

THE NEWS

a miscellany of fortean curiosities

RUMBLINGS FROM ARTHUR'S TABLE.
Llandrillo: 23 Jan 74 ... quake; meteor; what?

WILLIAM PORTER REVIEWS THE REPORTS - - - - - - - - - - - - p10

also in this issue ... runaway train.p5 ... lunar lights.p6 ... hoaxes.p7 ...
enigmatic sphere.p8 ... marine mysteries.p14 ... `coincidences`.p15 ...
Paul Screeton on Leys.p16 ... insect swarms.p17 ... reviews.p18.

The News

VOL.1. No.5.
July.
1974.

THE NEWS is a non-profit making bi-monthly miscellany of
Fortean news and notes; edited & published by Robert JM
Rickard: 31 Kingswood Road, Moseley, Birmingham B13 9AN;
affiliated to International Fortean Organisation (INFO).

SUBSCRIPTIONS:	AIRMAIL TRANSFER:	CONTRIBUTIONS & RIGHTS:
Per year -	Overseas subscrib-	Articles & Notes are
UK......£1.80.	ers can 'Airmail	welcome, and duly cred-
USA.....$4.50.	Transfer' direct	ited. All articles in
or Sterling	from their bank	THE NEWS are Copyright
equivalent in	to our account:	of the authors; and the
other Countries.	RJM Rickard No2.	views expressed are not
NB: Please make	A/c No: 0125008.	necessarily those of THE
out cheques, POs	Lloyds Bank, Priory	NEWS or the Editor. All
IMOs etc. to	Ringway, Birmingham	the Notes may be freely
RJM Rickard,	B4, England. Sort-	quoted, though we hope
not The News.	ing Code: 30-96-28.	for a credit in return.

FORTFEST 74.

The major event in the celebrations of the Fort
Centenary is to be held at the Shoreham Americana
Hotel, Washington DC, from Aug 9th (Fort's actual
birth Date) to Aug 11. Registration for INFO
members is $10.00 and $16.00 for non-members.

The planned events so far include talks by: Ralph
Blum, 'What we learned from the Fall of '73';
Stuart Greenwood, 'An Aerospace Engineer considers
the Unexplained.'; Tim Dinsdale on   Lake and
Sea Monsters; Aaron Sussman with personal recoll-
ection of Fort; William Corliss on the origin of
his Fortean Sourcebooks (see REVIEWS, this issue);
Sam Moskowitz on early influences on Fort's
writings; Allen Greenfield, 'Zen, Mysticism and
Forteanism'; ARG Owen of the New Horizons Research
Foundation; Paul Willis, 'Gods by the Bushel - The
Ancient Astronaut Syndrome.'; and a host of
others on a myriad interesting subjects. For more
information contact INFO/FORTFEST, PO Box 367,
Arlington, Virginia 22210, USA.

'A MAJOR FORTEAN DRAMA'.

Quite independant of the celebration comes news
of a production of the 'first major Fortean
drama' - 'The Great Caper' by Ken Campbell at
the Royal Court Theatre sometime in October. This
is a bit later than the Birthday celebrations and
we shall bring you more detailed news next issue.
Ken Campbell is himself a keen Fortean, and the
idea is being discussed of having a short programme of readings from Fort's various writings
at the same venue. More details as they become
known.

MARK A HALL.

We welcome Mark Hall to our ranks with the first
of his collections of current American Forteana.
He used to publish a now discontinued Fortean
Newsletter called 'From My Files' (FMF) and has
agreed to continue his collections as a column
in THE NEWS, for which we sincerely thank him
and look forward to with great interest. NB. If

you see the initials FMF arising in references,
then you will know we will be quoting from one
of Mark's issues.

INDEX TO THE NEWS, & CHANGE IN TIMETABLE.

We thought you'd like to know the Index to the
NEWS is going ahead, and hopefully, will be
ready with No 1 of Vol. 2.   Strictly speaking
Volume 1 should end with No 6, the September
issue. But we would like to keep to the year per
volume schedule - so here's what we will do. For
volume 1 only we will have seven issues, ie. including the November issue. This means that Vol.2
can coincide with the new year. But we will delay
the publication dates by one month from No.8. so
that we can time things with April (Fools Day),
August (Forts Birth month), and Dec. (with a
Christmas issue). This will also help avoid certain production difficulties a the printers. Got
that? Vol.2 will kick off with No.8. in Feb. 75.

The Index will be free to subscribers - but also
available to non-subscribers at a price we shall
fix later. It will be indexed under the Type-of-
Event; Place-of-Event; Time-of-Event; & NEWSref.

deaths & bodies

We have piles of bodies to clear from our files.
We are searching for patterns - something that
makes sense out of non-sense. And occasionally
our forays for data take us where we would not
normally think of going. Here are some of our
wanderings: down by the sea shore, along the
railway tracks, and even the privacy of someone's
home:

DEATH AT HOME.

A young father was still alive after lying for
a week in a house, thought to be filled with
fumes, and in which his wife and baby girl died.
Doom stalked the Lightfoot house in Westwood

Terrace, York. A Home Office pathologist said that the wife and baby were 'almost certainly' killed by carbon-monoxide fumes, thought to have come from a recently fitted central-heating unit. Coroner's Officer PC Gillies said: "It could have been a fault in the installation, or it could have been something like a bird's nest." The alarm was given by a workmate who told the police of Alan Lightfoot's absence...neighbours thought they had gone away. No indication of whether any bird's nest or flue blockage was ever found. What is perhaps more curious, is that the wife had complained of a 'mystery illness' which caused stomach pains, dizziness and sickness. The baby and the husband also caught 'it' - Alan Lightfoot eventually took three weeks off work to recover from what the doctors had diagnosed as flu. We learn that relatives now believe that the fault (if there ever was one) in the heating system was slowly poisoning them. From the Daily Mail, 7 & 8 Jan 74. Credit: P Rogerson.

SUDDEN DEATH.

Turkish villager Dempr Cevik won a £6 bet by eating a whole barbecued lamb. Ten minutes later he dropped dead. London Evening News 9 Jan 74. Credit : Steve Moore.

Mrs Dorothy Smith, 61, caught a bus from Lytham to Blackpool in the afternoon of Wednesday 2 Jan. Her movements for the next 12 hours remain a mystery. She was found unconscious in an open yard behind Blackpool Promenade in the early hours of the 3rd Jan. She was suffering from exposure; had some bruises on her legs; and died later in Blackpool's Victoria Hospital. Police were puzzled by the absence of any evidence of an attack - her handbag containing money was nearby. She never regained consciousness and so could give no clue as to where she had been, or what happened. From Manchester Evening News 3,4 & 7 Jan 74. Credit: Peter Rogerson.

Farmer John F Barratt, 46, of Manor Farm, Enstone near Chipping Norton, was found dead in his car in a field off a minor road from Enstone to Lidstone. Police said foul play was not involved. Birmingham Evening Mail 12 Feb 74.

THE LAST TRAIN.

The decapitated body of a young man was found by BR staff by the track near East Didsbury station near Manchester. He was believed to have been hit by a train. Manchester Evening News, 11 Jan 74. Four days later the body of a 67-year-old man is found on the rails at Star Lane Bridge, Macclesfield. There is no information whether he jumped, or was run over. Manchester Evening News 16 Jan 74. And the Daily Express (24 Jan 74) tells that a verdict of suicide was ruled on the curious death of Alan Beale, of Great Brickhill, Bucks. His neatly folded tie; and shoes placed by the line, where his decapitated body was found.

The body of an unidentified man was found on a railway line at Crumpsall, Manchester, early on 17 March. (Sunday Express 17 March 74). Indeed Manchester seems to be plagued with bodies near lines - see below and the following section. In the Manchester Evening Mail (26 April 74) we read that the jury deliberating on the death of Mrs Mary E Smith, 69, whose mutilated body was found on the Bury electric line near Woodlands Road station, were unable to decide whether she had committed suicide or not. They returned an open verdict. She was said to have undergone psychiatric treatment following the death of her husband three years ago - but there was little reason to believe that her depression had returned. Credit for all above to Peter Rogerson.

DEATH COMES IN TWOS AND THREES.

The bodies of a mother and her 6-year-old daughter were found in Epping Forest on the 15th Dec 73. In the Sunday Express (16 Dec) they are named as Mrs Sheena Mulhearn and Rachel, who vanished from their Harlow, Essex, home on the 10th Dec. The Daily Express for 17 Dec says that the police are not naming them until a relative from the North-west identifies them. There is said to be no signs of any violence in their deaths - nor is any more information known or available.

Death stalked Barton Road, Stretford, Lancs, on the 8th Jan 74, when two women, quite independently, collapsed and died while walking there within five hours of each other. Mrs Maud Richardson,69, and Mrs Hannah Bradbury,76, were both said to have died of natural causes. Urmston & Stretford Journal 16 Jan 74. Credit: Peter Rogerson.

Two youths were killed when they were hit by a deisel passenger train at Upton, near Birkenhead on the 2nd Jan. On the same day, the body of a 55-year-old woman was found on a railway line, near her home at Hest Bank, Morecombe. A police statement says that foul play was not suspected, which leads us to assume she was not hit by any train. Both items from Manchester Evening News, 3 Jan 74. The Daily Express (6 Feb 74) has a story: Nurse Margaret Forde, 17, was in hospital recovering from stab-wounds, which she received just before mid-night on the 4th - and unknown to her 13 hours later her boyfriend is found dead on the lines at Hale station, Cheshire. He is believed to have died from an overdose of drugs. A suggestive tale that - so make of it what you will.

On 22nd Jan the young parents of twin girls found them both dead in their bed, in the same room the parents shared with them, at a guest house in Hill Lane, Southampton. It is thought they might have suffocated. Daily Express. 23 Jan 74. The Scunthorpe Evening Telegraph of 18 Feb 74, reports the police are investigating the death of a newly-married elderly couple at North Hykeham, Lincoln, but they said they were satisfied that no third party was involved. (Credit: Nigel Watson.) Police were also called in when neighbours could get no answer from the house where two elderly sisters lived. They are called 'eccentric' for not wishing to see anyone.."even the gas and electricity inspectors; relatives were also turned away from the door." But then there is silence and no familiar repelling of visitors. The police broke in and found both sisters dead. One was found in bed upstairs and believed to have died 'a week ago', surviving the other who lay dead on the living-room floor for five weeks. Daily Mail, 5 & 6 Feb 74.

A 'beautiful girl' and a man were both killed by an express train at Poriton, near Bridgewater, Somerset. The only clue was that she had made a vow that she would not live beyond 22. "Police were convinced it was not a lover's pact. A spokesman said: 'They were not lovers, and we shall probably never know why they died. She was not long married - and had met the man, Sherman Wilson, when they were both receiving treatment for emotional problems. Daily Mail, 28 Jan 74). (Credit for most of above to Peter Rogerson).

A five-year-old boy was found shot dead in a car at Cheddar, Somerset, on the 4th Feb. He was named as Andrew Young from Berrow, Somerset. A Man was found nearby dying from shotgun wounds. He was taken to Bristol Royal Infirmary, where police were said to be treating the case as murder. The next day a similar event occurs - we Forteans who are striving for some understanding of the colossal forces that influence our lives, can only shake our heads, our wonder renewed. These forces don't owe us a living at all. We learn that a four-year-old boy is found dead beside an unconscious man in a parked car in Epping Forest (a favoured venue for mysteries, it seems). The man was taken to St Margaret's Hospital, Epping, Essex Manchester Evening News 5 Feb 74. Credit: Peter Rogerson.

The bodies of two women were washed ashore a few yards apart at Lossiemouth, Morayshire on the 23rd Feb. Perhaps there was some doubt because the man who found them said: "It looked as if the tide had gone out and left them exposed on the sand." The police were called, and it is said to be a mystery because there has been no identification of the bodies, or any evidence that they were connected in some way. From the Daily Mail, 25 Feb 74. Credit: P Rogerson.

A passing car knocked down 6-year-old Norbert Burke playing near his home in Limerick, Irish Repubic,on 27 April and began a bizarre triple tragedy. The 44-year-old father of the boy was brought to a nearby hospital where he died of a suspected heart attack. The driver of the car, farmer Gerrard Leonard, 45, also collapsed when he saw the boy, was rushed to the same hospital, where he died of the same suspected complaint.

Police discovered a woman dead with stab wounds when they called at her flat (again on the 27th April) to break the news of her husband's death. The lorry driver, Ron Griffiths of Birch Grove, Ruyton of the Eleven Towns, near Shrewsbury, was found dead in his new Ford Escort five miles away near Burlton. Police say no one else was involved. Nor do they give any information as to whether the two deaths were connected in any other way.

Daily Express 28 April 74. (Same for the Triple Tragedy above..sorry.) Credit to Peter Rogerson again, who seems to have a nose for odd deaths.

WASHED UP.

The body of a woman with her ankles tied together was found in the sea off Newhaven, the day before the report appeared in the Daily Express, 5 July 73. The naked body of a middle-aged man was recovered from Bramley Moor dock, Liverpool, by the police, 26 Aug. His clothes, or a pile of clothes assumed to be his, was found neatly stacked - a detail that puts us in mind of the disappearance reported in News 1, p7. This one is from Daily Express, 27 Aug 73. Credit: A Smith. The body of a well-tanned woman, about 40, was floating in the sea near Brighton's Palace Pier on the 11th Nov. Detectives were puzzled because all her underclothes were missing. Daily Express 12 Nov 73.

The Daily Mirror, 22 Dec 73, reports the collapse and death of a young sailor after surfacing from a normal depth in a submarine escape-training tank, in Gosport, Hants. Police recovered the body of a man from the river Weaver about half a mile from the town centre of Northwich on 28 Jan 74 - from the Manchester Evening News of that date. (Credit: P Rogerson.)

On the 6th Feb, the police at Wakefield recovered the body of an old man from a local canal. Daily Mail 7 Feb 74. The Sunday Mirror (17 March 74) describes how three farmworkers found the body of a man floating in the Bristol Channel at Lilstock, near Bridgewater, Somerset. Despite a nationwide inquiry, police have not managed to identify him.

Police are still trying to identify a middle-aged woman found in the Manchester Canal near the docks in the last week of March. They give a description (which we will dispence with here) and say she had been in the water between 4 & 8 weeks. Another mystery body found in the river Methly near Leeds was buried on March 26 in plot G10-5, on a hillside cemetary at Leeds. Police think he might have been a vagrant, but he was clean-shaven, wearing an expensive pair of shoes, and had a spectacle case bearing the name of a local optician...but even this clue drew a blank. He was found sometime near the begining of March and nothing new is known about him. Sunday Express 12 May 74. Credit for both above - who else but Peter Rogerson?

egnarts

Egnarts is (or are) 'Strange' backwards - and we use it, for want of anything more suitable, to designate a report that does not fit into any ready-made category, and if we chopped it about to fit one, there would be little left worth the telling.

THE RETURN OF THE BLOB.

From the Daily Mail (30 May 73) we learn that a red pulsating membrane found in a Dallas garden has been tantalising scientists. When a bit is cut off, it regenerates itself, and has increased its size 16 times in a week. That was some time ago, and we haven't heard of any investigation reports - though we have heard of a few other 'yeast'- like growths in the States, some even connected with reported UFO activity. See a review of 'Blob' cases in INFO Journal 10 pp29-30 (with photo of cute furry Blob). Credit for this one: S Moore.

FAIRY FOOTPRINT.

"I do not believe in fairies. I do not believe in ghosts. But for once I feel that the supernatural has set a trap for me. In a way I hope that it has: then I can stop worrying about something that seems to have no real explanation.

My pilgrims walk took me across land that at one time felt the shuffling feet of those struggling from the Isle of Ely to the revered acres of Little Walsingham. A thirty yard stretch of bare sandy soil had, by the searing winds, been given all the consistency of concrete. About 10ft wide, this patch was as smooth as a motorway, and except for one weird feature, as barren. In the centre, perfectly formed and dried hard, was the print of a bare foot.

Nowhere else on this dried ground could I find any other mark. Not a single explanatory indentation. The stretch of ground was too wide for anybody, especially with such a small foot, to have jumped across it, using only one foot to mark the soil when it was soft, in one gigantic leap."

From a nature column by Austin Hatton in Sunday Telegraph 28 April 74.

A GHOST TRAIN RATTLES LONDON.

At 6.34 on the morning of Friday, 29 March, a train pulled out of Caterham, Surrey. It had no passengers and no driver. For nine miles it headed for central London on what would be in about half an hour one of the busiest commuter lines, at speeds of up to 40mph. Urgent calls to signal boxes halted or diverted on-coming trains, as the runaway hurtled through seven stations before it was directed into a buffered siding at Norwood Junction.

The train had been readied for its commuter duty, complete with a pre-run test - then the driver and the guard went for a quick cup of tea. None of the four main drive motors had been switched on - and nearly all of the nine miles is on a downward gradient (in fact it was 1-in-90 just outside the station where the train was parked). But neither of these facts account for the train starting - somehow both the airbrake and the 'Dead Man's Handle' had been circumvented or otherwise rendered ineffective. Curiously, both driver and guard were due for retirement within the week.

A report in the press, a week later, said that no public inquiry will be held - and even the results of the private investigation by British Rail may not be published. All-in-all a queer event which seems innocent enough. Lord knows we have enough weird stuff on our hands without suspecting poltergeist hanky-panky - but at the back of our mind are stories of quite a few things which seem to have started up 'on their own', especially a particularly hefty lift which had no power to it, which we must tell about some time. Our sources for the train drama: London Evening News, 29 March; Daily Mirror & Daily Express, 30 March; and Daily Mail for 30 March & 5 April. Credit for most items to Steve Moore.

Diagram from Daily Express.

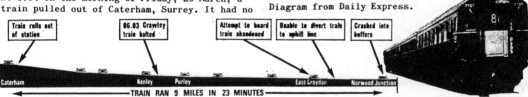

TRAIN RAN 9 MILES IN 23 MINUTES

esp & powers

PROPHETIC - OR INEVITABLE?

On the 1st June this year, the NYPRO plant at Flixborough, Lincs exploded causing considerable loss of life and damage to property. Concern over the safety of the huge cyclohexane tanks used in the manufacture of Nylon was too late. Nigel Watson sent us the following piece from the Scunthorpe Star (7 June 74).

'Macabre and strangely twisted, like the blackened hulk which is all that is left of Nypro - out of the past a prophecy of Saturday's holocaust.

"So you can see that Nypro,
Sometime during June,
Could well be blown to pieces
And be the First Plant on the Moon."

It was written in 1966 and appeared in Nypro's Dutch Newsheet. It is one of 25 verses by Fred Saxby, a shift superintendant at Nypro. He went to Holland in 1966 for training with 24 other men when the plant was first built at Flixborough. It is called 'The Ballard of Big N' and composed to the tune of the 'Lincolnshire Poacher'.

"We're all from Nypro
In famous Lincolnshire.
This is our song to all of you,
So hear it with good cheer."

Eight years ago when the plant first came into operation, it was a popular song. Even the verse about the blowing up in June was treated as a joke. Today nobody is laughing.'

* @ * @ * @ * @ * @ * @ * @ * @ * @ * @
The best stories often appear in your local news papers - so keep your eyes peeled and send your finds to us - NB.note: Date, Source & your Name.

SLEIGHT OF GLAND.

Its old hat now, but Uri Geller was forced to
flee Britain after threats on his life. (See most
papers around 4 Feb 74)..After going back to Israel, we have a note on a remarkable result of
one of Geller's performances in Sweden. It seems
that an unnamed Swedish couple were watching Uri
on a TV show two months before. The woman went to
her doctor who confirmed she was pregnant. They
were puzzled because they had had many trouble-
free years using IUD contraception. The doctor
discovered their copper-coil was so bent out of
shape it would have been useless as a contracep-
tive. The reluctant parents-to-be reckoned the
bending happened as a result of watching Geller
do his tricks with spoons, etc., and are said to
be consulting lawers to see whether she has any
claim against Geller. An Immaculate Disception,
mebbe...? Sunday Mirror 17 March 74. Credit: R
Forrest.(See REVIEWS for the Geller biography.)

DOUBLE HUNCH.

Something roused Mrs Noreen Croasdale from her
sleep - and she rushed her husband and four children into the street. Seconds later their house
in Wesley St, Accrington, Lancs, collapsed, destroying all their belongings. "I dont know why I
woke. Call it a sixth sense. I heard a creaking
noise which scared me and I woke my husband. We
went out and saw a big hole and cracks in a wall.
So we dashed back and got the children. We had
been in the street only seconds when the house
collapsed." Daily Mirror, Daily Mail 8 Jan 74.
Credit: P Rogerson, DJ McAllister. Photo from
Daily Mirror.

Mr. Croasdale and his three boys outside their home.

It is possible to rationalise such cases in terms
of subliminal awareness, and that the timing was
just 'luck'. We have less confidence and doubt
whether we understand either of those expressions.
Yet Mrs Doris Ingle of Blackpool could not have
sensed anything 'subliminally' when her son Clive
,18, was late for supper. She had a 'hunch' that
he was still at the bank where he worked and yet
something worried her. She called the police who
called the Branch manager. Mrs Ingle made the
unlikely suggestion of checking the vault - where
they found Clive and Stephen Goodall, 17. Both
had been trapped in the vault for seven hours -
they had gone in at the end of the day to fetch
something, and the door was closed on them, and
they were not missed as the bank was closed up.
Daily Express 14 Feb 74.

PSYCHIC HEAT.

From the SUN (30 May 74) we learn that Dr Gertrude
Schmeidler, head of psychology at New York's City
College, told of her conversion to belief in powers of psychic healing, to a conference on psychic research. She told of experiments with New
York psychic Ingo Swann who was asked to make a
metal object hot by mind power. Systematic changes in temperature were recorded in the laboratory
as 'occurring at the will of Swann'. "Occasionally
the metal's temperature fluctuated by as much as
one degree Farenheit in 45 seconds." said the
Doctor. Swann was at least 25ft from the set-up.
"Perhaps in the same manner, a healer can induce
changes in a person's body."

`heavens above´

MOON FLASHES ASTRONAUTS.

It appears that the Apollo 17 moon voyage at Chr-
itmas 1972 encountered a classic Fortean datum
only minutes after entering lunar orbit. Jack
Schmitt reported excitedly to Houston Control
that he had seen a flash near a crater on the
moon's surface. Space officials (a particularly
riduculous phrase) said the sighting - "The first
time any such active event has been seen on the
moon " - could be significant, but they had no
immediate explanation. They speculated on meteorite impact or volcanic activity - then it seems
in the excitement of the landing that followed,
this little 'mystery' was soon forgotten. We wonder if any of our readers in the States know of
this further. Our thanks to Nigel Watson who rescued this note from oblivion via the Scunthorpe
Evening Telegraph 11 Dec 72.

MORE LUNATIC LIGHTS.

From a letter to the Birmingham Evening Mail, 15
March 74:

"On Saturday, March 2, while travelling from Northfield to Hurley, Warwickshire, my husband and I
noticed a 'star' near the moon. The moon was just
over half and when you completed the circle this
'star' was just outside. We watched this 'star'
all the way to Whitacre, Coleshill, where we stopped at traffic lights. The star was still there
but when you completed the circle, it now appear-

ed _inside_ the moon. We went a few yards and it just disappeared. Could you please enlighten me if there is a 'star' that close to the moon - or was it a satellite. MRS S Walden; Hurley."

How would Fort have answered that? He certainly would have been delighted at the notion of a star this side of the moon. The paper goes on to quote comment by the Edgbaston Observatory: "If, as it appears, it moved in relation to the moon then it must be nearer the earth, and this would indicate it was a satellite." The good old BEM adds 'Unfortunately they could not say _which_ satellite it may have been.'

We follow this with a little gem from _Sweden 1869_ which we don't think appears anywhere in Fort. "Natural phenomenon. Yesterday evening at 9 o'-clock a strange natural phenomenon was seen. On both sides of the moon, a new moon, two giant balls were observed and from these balls came white beams of light, directed toward the horizon. The phenomenon lasted for a quarter of an hour." Many thanks to Anders Liljegren for this one, from: Norrkopings Tidningar, October 1869.

A NEW MOON.

Data sent back from the ultra-violet cameras on Mariner 10 zooming by Mercury, are said to reveal the existence of a moon in orbit around that planet. Dr A Lyle Broadfoot of Arizona's Kitt Peak observatory, has enshrined this achievement by naming the discovery 'Charley' after a dog he once had as a child. There's not much we can add to that except that the news comes on April Fool's Day. Daily Mirror, London Evening News 1 April 74. Credit both items: Steve Moore.

hoaxes

YOU CAN FOOL SOME OF THE PEOPLE...

Mark Hall sent us two amusing stories on hoaxes perpetrated in the name of science and advertising. The first, from the HOUSTON (Texas) CHRONICLE 8 May 74, (10/3), concerns a lecture on 'Mathematical Game Theory as Applied to Physical Education ' by 'Dr. Myron L Fox' said to be an authority on the application of maths to human behaviour. His lecture was pure nonsense - meaningless double-talk - but it fooled the 55 educators, school administrators, psychiatrists, psychologists and social workers listening. After the lecture and a 30 minute question period, the listeners were asked to fill out anonymous questionaires to evaluate the performance. 42 agreed that 1) 'Dr Fox' used enough example to clarify the material; 2) the material was well organised; and 3) the lecture stimulated their thinking. 14 registered a minor criticism - that 'Dr Fox' dwelled upon the obvious; and some expressed interest in learning more about the subject.

Not one guessed it was a hoax, and that 'Dr Fox' was an actor hired by three medical educators to prove a point, though one did say the lecture was "too intellectual a presentation." The hypothesis of Dr DH Naftulin, FA Donnelly (both of University of Southern California Medical School) and John E Ware Jr (of Southern Illinois University School

of Medicine) was that: "Given a sufficiently impressive lecture paradigm, an experienced group of educators participating in a new learning situation can feel satisfied that they have learned , despite irrelevant, conflicting and meaningless content conveyed by the lecturer." Their purpose, they say, was to demonstrate the importance of the personality factor in teaching. We can't really say that we have learnt anything new in this.

The second story concerns the scientific-looking formula used by the Parker Pen people in a photo which shows someone with a silly habit of noting formulas on the menu in a restaurant - but a good deal more intellectual one-upmanship than picking your nose while you wait to be served. 'We get letter from scientists and chemists who say they can't figure out the formula. Or that it is meaningless." said Gary Moss of the J Walter Thompson ad agency who thought the idea up. In fact it's simple when you know its for a martini: Three and a half shots of gin, plus half a shot of vermouth over four parts of water (taken down to freezing and cubed), then plus three revolutions (stirs) and...voila. The ad ran in Newsweek and Time. "We did get one critical letter...someone asked 'Who ever heard of a martini without an olive?'" From the MILWAUKEE (Wisconsin) JOURNAL 27 May 74.

HOUDINI GETS AWAY AGAIN.

Legend has promised that on the 100th anniversary of his birth, the executors of Harry Houdini's estate will open a box and reveal the secrets of his most mystifying escapes. According to a note in the DAILY MAIL 23 April 74 (Credit: Steve Moore), that date is now past; no lawyer has come forward; and authorities say there is no box.

fowl funnies

THE RIDDLE OF THE BLUE ROOSTER.

Amongst other papers, the Daily Mirror of 2 Jan 74, announced to the world that Charlie the Cockerel, owned by Alan Piper, landlord of the Wild Man Inn, Sproughton, Suffolk, had turned a livid

Continued on page 9.

FORTEARCHIVE

A myriad of conflicting reports has filled North American newspapers in mid-April about a metal sphere, reportedly found on the estate of the Antoine Betz family near Jacksonville, Florida. The object has been compared to the 'Giant Gyros' found in Australia - and it has also been dismissed as only a ball bearing such as is used as a check-valve in piping at chemical plants. One aspect of the story that is rarely mentioned is the following: "Mrs Betz said her family occasionally hears organ music of late, although there is no organ in the sprawling home. Doors bang without reason, she says, since the sphere showed up." SENTINEL STAR (Orlando, Florida.) 12 April 74. And according to other reports: "...it did strange things, such as rolling around the edges of a table by itself without falling off, and making their dog whimper." ST LOUIS (Missouri) POST DISPATCH 16 April 74 (p14A). Other sources include: SENTINEL STAR (Orlando, Florida) 15 April (p3B), and 16 April (p13A); WINNIPEG FREE PRESS 13 April (p13); MIAMI HERALD 13, 15 & 16 April; CHICAGO TRIBUNE 15 April; CHICAGO DAILY NEWS 16 April; HOUSTON CHRONICLE 14 & 15 April; SAN FRANCISCO CHRONICLE 15 April; SAN FRANCISCO EXAMINER 15 & 17 April.

"A nice, pleasant brain-teaser." is the way Dr J Allen Hynek characterized the mysterious metal sphere when he finally got a look at it. Before he did, publicity about the object prompted many explanations. Anonymous telephone callers suggested: 1) it was a 'giant gyro' such as objects said to be found in Australia after UFO sightings; 2) it was a tide and current transcriber that is floated on a buoy at sea. The US Navy examined the sphere and concluded it was probably "a giant bearing used as a check-valve in the piping systems of chemical plants." At Taos, New Mexico, a sculptor got his measure of attention by claiming the sphere was one he lost while driving through Jacksonville in 1971. He would not divulge the exact origin of the several spheres he said he got for his own use from a friend - but he said they were designed as part of an industrial valve.

Dr James Harder, who ran down to Pascagoula, Miss., last year to look into the UFO activity there, took an interest in the sphere long enough to get quoted in the press, as follows: "Harder said previous sightings of metal spheres were reported in the New England states and off Mississippi 'but not one could we get our hands on.'"

AP Wirephoto. Wayne Betz, 12, and the mystery sphere.

The Jacksonville sphere was eventually examined by many hands. The US Navy described the object as 8 inches in diameter; hollow; empty; high-grade stainless steel to a thickness of half an inch; & with a weight of 21.34 lbs. The UFO panel of scientists for a weekly paper studied the ball at a gathering in New Orleans, Louisiana. There Hynek, Harder and others concluded that it 1) possesses magnetic poles; 2) contains smaller spheres inside; and 3) is almost perfectly ballanced. The last word came from a spokesman for the US Geological Survey, Frank Forrester, who snickered at the activity of the newspaper panel and said the Survey would be "very receptive to analysing fragments" of the mystery ball. Amid all this action, another Jacksonville resident reached into the back of her garage and produced a similar but slightly smaller metal sphere that had lain there for fifteen years. A spokesman for the local St Regis papermill said they recognised that ball as part of a valve used 15 years ago in pipes moving corrosive liquid. Sources include: NEW ORLEANS TIMES-PICAYUNE 23 April; ATLANTA CONSTITUTION 16 April; MIAMI HERALD 18 April; & NATIONAL ENQUIRER 26 May 74.

"Gas from Water - Really?" by Jack Smith, Los Angeles Times Service. Reporter Don Dwiggins recalls his personal experience with a man who claimed and demonstrated that his secret formula, when added to water, would run an automobile. MILWAUKEE JOURNAL 22 March 74. (Green Sheet pages 1,3.)

* * *

The sister of missing balloonist Thomas Gatch returned to Rochester, Minnesota, after spending a month at Gatch's home in Virginia. She said: 'We have had a number of calls from persons claiming psychic powers who envision my brother on islands.' ROCHESTER (Minn.) POST BULLETIN 28 Mar 74 (p18.) Psychic Mrs Marcia Kuhn says she began getting 'receptions' of Gatch on March 8, and that he is dying on the island of Guadeloupe. SAN FRANCISCO CHRONICLE 29 March 74 (p12) and ARKANSAS GAZETTE 30 March 74 (p7B).

On 30 March a police helicopter searched for a balloon sighted east of Guadelopue. The search centred on the island of Petite Terre. US Vice Consul Thomas Randall at Fort de France, Martinique, confirmed that a balloon had been seen off Guadelope. ST. LOUIS (Missouri) POST DISPATCH 31 March 74 (p5C).

* * *

Dr Edwin Krupp, Curator at the Griffith Observatory, writes about 'Chariots of the Gods?' and its spin-offs: "If the books and the film are convincing, it is because they filter and distort the evidence to conform to a single notion. A more likely possibility is that ancient men were more clever than we moderns are normally willing to believe." LOS ANGELES TIMES 10 Feb 74 .

* * *

Photos from the second Skylab mission show a 'cylindrically shaped foreign object' in orbit below the Skylab spacecraft. AVIATION WEEK 7 Jan 74 (p1). UFOs over: Kona, Hawaii on 1 Feb, HONOLULU STAR BULLETIN 2 Feb 74 (pA12) -- Piatra Neamt, Roumania, MIAMI HERALD 16 Feb 74 (p9A) -- Rochester, Minnesota on 19 Feb, ROCHESTER POST BULLETIN 20 Feb 74 (p1).

* * *

Mrs Donald Shoup of Hickory Corners, Michigan, has a chicken that lays double eggs - one inside the other. Six eggs have been found thus far, each weighing about six ounces and containing inside a complete normal egg of about two ounces. ATLANTA (Georgia) CONSTITUTION 9 April 74 (p10A).

Again we read of hens that lay eggs coloured blue green, pink and gold. Mrs William Warnke of Burlington, Kentucky, wisely points out that her chickens are Araucanian fowl developed in Chile and introduced into the USA about 1928. HOUSTON CHRONICLE 14 April 74 (p1). Earlier this year the HOUSTON CHRONICLE (17 Jan) reported coloured eggs from Araucanian fowls in Riverton, Utah.

* * *

A 26-year-old Bridgeport, Connecticut man, Francisco Rodriquez, escaped from police custody on 21 Feb 74 for the 21st time in two years. The State of Connecticut has spent an estimated $100,000 trying to hold him, including $2,000 for a special cell. MILWAUKEE JOURNAL 22 February 74 (Part 1, p7.)

* * *

Frederick Aldrich, a marine biologist at St Johns Memorial University, Newfoundland, has ambitious plans to search at sea for a live giant squid in the next two years. He has studied strandings of the giant creatures for many years and points out that every thirty years there have been numerous strandings of these squid off the Newfoundland coast. He thinks an unexplained cold current that comes in cycles may be responsible. LOS ANGELES TIMES 5 May 74.

* * *

(We would like to thank Loren Coleman, who also sent us cuttings of the Jacksonville Sphere. Ed.)
■■■■■■■■■■■■■■■■■■■■■■■■■■
blue overnight. Two vets were said to be baffled, and as if that weren't enough, Mr Piper said that if Charlie was still blue in a couple of days, he'd "..take it up with experts." Our thanks to Loren Coleman and Mark Hall for notes showing this item had got as far as the Press-Scimitar (Memphis, Tenn) 2 Jan - and Houston Chronicle 3 Jan, respectively.

We wrote to several of the local papers to keep tabs on developments, and eventually got stats of clippings from the morgue of the East Anglian Daily Times. (Credit: EADT Librarian Mrs SM Yates) From what we can reconstruct the first account appeared on 29 Dec 73. Mr Piper discovered the change in Charlie the day before. "It just changed overnight to a really stupid colour. It is a brilliant bright blue. It hasn't been sprayed. It is blue under the wings, everywhere. Piper, who also breeds budgerigars, added: "I know you can colour-feed canaries to make them turn red, but that takes weeks. The cockerel turned blue overnight." A vet. in Ipswich said: "I can't see how one is going to get it to consume a dye that would change only its feathers without changing the other tissues. I can't see any dye doing this anyway."

A curious development occurs on the 8th Jan when Mr Piper discovers his profitable attraction missing - there it was, gone. The police were informed but there were no clues to culprit or motive. It was just as though it had upped and vanished. In a cutting from 15 Jan we learn that later someone phoned saying they were holding the bird -and two days later phoned again, saying it was back in its pen - and so it was.

By now Mr Piper is sick of accusations that he had sprayed the bird to attract business, that he resolved to clear the mystery. Charlie, he discovered, is a North Island Blue; a type introduced from America between 1939 - 1945. Mr Pussell Brown got five chicken eggs from a farmer in Suffolk, and Alan Piper's hens hatched them for him. He said: "By all accounts this farmer also has a blue cockerel, so my bird must be a throwback from his." There are photos - but these tell no more than a man holding a cockerel since they are in black and white. We wrote to Mr Piper with some unanswered questions - but no reply to date. It is our feeling that the throwback theory may explain why, but not how, and on that, nothing more is heard of any experts.

Continued on page 13.

William Porter assesses here the news coverage of the 'Thing' that happened at Llandrillo on Jan 23 and a few items of related information. This article was supposed to appear in the last issue but got delayed for a couple of reasons. Mr Porter also reported on the subsequent seismological phenomena in North Wales - see NEWS 4. Cover Note: the illustration used here is only a speculation of what may lie under the Berwyn heather and not any representation of the 'real' thing. It comes from an old encyclopedia we found and undoubtedly will be using again.

RUMBLINGS FROM ARTHUR'S TABLE.

by WILLIAM PORTER

Charles Fort would have been the first to acknowledge and detect the essentially contradictory, elusive and anomalous character of the incident reported initially as a meteoric strike, at the Cadair Bronwen mountain range near Llandrillo in North Wales on the evening of January 23rd 1974.

The national media coverage was frustratingly vague, but speculation was rife. Within two hours of the strike, radio stations reported a blue-green streak that crossed the sky and crashed with a very loud explosion that was heard for miles. It was added that a police search party of six men was sent out, but to no avail.

Several hours on, and news reports postulated that it could have been the re-entry of a Russian rocket section. ITN TV news contributed that a green light was seen traversing in an easterly direction, but at a time subsequent to the reported explosion. It was announced that the Institute of Geological Sciences, Eskdale Muir, Dumfriesshire, reported seismological records of unusually large magnitude. 'News at Ten' showed a detailed map of the Berwyn Hills and speculated that the incident was really an earth tremor. Coast guards were reported to have seen an object in the night sky going in an easterly direction.

By midday of 24th January I allowed myself two points of speculation - that no object would be found in the Berwyn Hills; and that the site will prove to be of prehistoric and/or mystical significance.

While the national newspapers did not cover the story until Friday 25th January , the Liverpool Daily Post reported the incident on the 24th. Testimonies were gathered from local witnesses - the tremor was felt as far away as Hoylake in Cheshire, but there were no reports of injuries or damage. A Llangollen man said it was a vibration that shook his house and knocked a cup and saucer from an armchair. Another said it was more of an earth tremor than an explosion. Local police had received reports from about 8.30pm on.

On Friday morning, the story appeared in the nationals - Daily Mail, Daily Express and Daily Mirror (see NEWS 3), while a short but intelligent piece appeared in The Times. It stated one witness had seen a fire on the mountainside, and a few amateur astronomers from the Isle of Man to Cheshire had tracked what they thought to be a meteor. The Global Seismology Unit of the Institute of Geological Science in Edinburgh, represented by Dr Roy Lilwall, said an earth tremor occurred at 8.38pm and was of magnitude 3.5 to 4. Dr Lilwall had been told that a meteorite had come down sometime after the tremor. He said he was certain that the meteorite had not caused the tremor. To have caused the kind of shaking recorded at Edinburgh, the falling rock would have had to weigh several hundred tons.

However, the best reportage of the Llandrillo incident came from the provincial dailies. On 25th January, the Liverpool Daily Post related that scientists were arguing whether it was a meteorite or an earth tremor that shook most of North Wales. It added that reports of lights in the sky also came from a wide area, although many sightings happened after the tremor itself. Police and Coastguards now believe that many people, especially in the Isle of Man, actually saw an RAF photo-flash night bombing exercise. The Liverpool Daily Post interviewed astronomer Dr Ron Maddison of Keele University who was convinced that a meteorite was responsible. He said: "I've never heard of that part of Wales being prone to any kind of earth tremors, and I don't think there is any other way of explaining the lights that people have seen."

Good coverage too was forthcoming from the Western Mail (25 Jan.) which announced that the scientists had called off a search for a meteorite near Llandrillo because they believed the explosion was caused by an earthquake or severe earth tremor. Drs Maddison and Aneurin Evans are also interviewed after their unsuccessful search. Reports Maddison received did not conclusively prove his initial meteorite theory, or the location of the strike, but on 24th January he had received two more independent sightings of fireballs or bright shooting stars in the Llandrillo area the night of the strike, which tied with previous sightings to strengthen his belief that the explosion was centered on the mountain. Dr Maddison once again returned to scour the whole range by helicopter, but nothing was found. Consequently, the notion of a large impact by a falling object has been dismissed. He added: "Instead we have settled on a more probable seismic ground disturbance."

Another feature in the Western Mail explored the hypothesis of a meteorite strike: if it was a meteorite it would be the largest in Britain; would have travelled at 100,000mph when it entered the earth's atmosphere and would have burned off 50% of its original weight. When it was spotted as a 'glowing ball' over Anglesey shortly before impact it would still have been travelling at thousands of miles per hour. Peter Jones, the science correspondent noted that unless it exploded while still 20 to 30 miles above the Berwyn mountains, or shattered on impact against rock, it is now probably lying under four or five feet of earth. Dr Robert Hutchinson of the Natural History Museum said it could have been $2\frac{1}{2}$' to 5' in diameter and composed of stony material called Olivine with small amounts of iron, nickel, chrome and cobalt. He added that the meteorite was unlikely to have come from Kohoutek's Comet and in fact was not convinced that a meteorite had actually landed at Llandrillo.

The Sunderland Echo, Jan 24, carried an article that described a UFO sighting ⟨ see NEWS 4. p19⟩ which concurred with the events at Llandrillo, however UFO author Raymond Drake doubted any significant connection. On the 26th Jan. the Liverpool Daily Post gave a third day of coverage when it suggested the 'tremor' was caused by a movement along a rock formation fault. Dr. Maddison was interviewed about his final conclusions and said: "We would have expected to find a large scar if a meteorite had fallen, but there was no trace."

Collectively the series of articles, from all the various sources, were as contradictory and basically inconsistent as any that I have so far gathered for analysis. One is confronted with a veritable maze of explanations and glib hypotheses wrapped and neatly packaged for the credulous. A further twist to the story came less than a week later from the Daily Mirror Science correspondent Arthur Smith ⟨ 28 Jan 74⟩: "Last Wednesday's fireball was comparatively small by fireball standards and probably disintegrated after travelling across East Anglia and Mid-Cheshire. It, in fact, had nothing to do with the 'bang' and lights seen in mid-Wales."

The 'meteoric strike' interpretation was subtlely reinforced when Dr Ron Maddison spoke on BBC Radio 4 (9.30pm on 21st Feb.) on the meteorite that was brighter than the moon and was tracked by a space satellite on the restricted list. The path of the 100-ton meteorite, travelling at 22,000 mph, took it to within 36 miles above Salt Lake City and Calgary in Canada on 10th August 1972. Infrared detection showed that energy loss was at a maximum 58Km from the ground, but if it had struck the Earth, its kinetic energy would have been sufficient to blast a crater 200 meters in diameter. A full report was published in NATURE 21 February 74. ⟨ Cuttings from the media following this publication were sent to us by Steve Moore and Loren Coleman. - Ed.⟩

The physical bias was to be expected from the scientific fraternity - but on the same day the Nature report appeared, a curious letter was published in the Daily Mirror; Mr WA Gray of Shirehampton, Bristol, wrote: "I have seen two fireballs :one in 1971, the second in 1972, both in the same place. You see, I was only 100 yards from them and felt the impact. All I saw was a collection of electricity whirling around in a ball. On impact it exploded and the electricity went to earth. I missed taking a photograph as I had just closed my camera. And that is all there is to it!"

I urge all free-thinking readers to seriously consider Mr Gray's innocent but potentially more significant description. I must confess to a particular affection for this kind of report, (much of my specific research is centered on wave-band para-electrical distribution at megalithic sites), but solid objective evidence is another matter; one must maintain a sound critical faculty and not allow oneself to become lost in a morass of subjective fantasy. However the application of heretical notions to the problematic incidents at Llandrillo are by no means close to producing an immediate or convenient solution, which if it was forthcoming would strike a much needed blow against all moribund pan-materialistic scientific philosophies.

Of the first hand witnesses from whom I was able to gather reliable testimonies; the Rev. GW Jones vicar of Llandrillo related: "I heard a long rumble which was frightening enough but although I live in a large house with many movable objects in it, not one of them moved that night. A scientist, Dr Maddison, believes it was an earth tremor and the appearance of blue lights was purely coincidental. I am inclined to believe him. In fact I was not worried after the rumble passed and everything was found to be safe that I thought nothing more about it. That is my testimony."

Douglas Hardman of Abergele, Noth Wales, made some interesting comments: "Talking to friends and neighbours, all are agreed that the explosion was felt as a shock wave rather than heard." And that "..certain papers killed the story with the official police conclusion that it was an earthquake and that the general attitude seems to be an anxiety to bury the story."

Heretical the 'powers phenomena' interpretation may be, but just as heretical was the 'meteorite' concept before 1800. In fact it is sobering to think that Parisian scientists in the 18th Century were highly amused when the Juillac Town Council reported to the Academy a fall of stones which had no less than 300 witnesses. Consider the ignorant and over-cynical reaction of the famous physicist Bertholou to the notion that stones can fall from the sky. He wrote, sardonically: "How sad is it to find a town council sanctioning fairy tales. Those who believe in these myths have our sympathy...an obvious falsity, a physically impossible event."

In Britain only 22 meteorites have been known to have fallen since 1623, two of which were in Wales; the last of these two being at Beddgelert in September 1949, when a 28oz. lump crashed through the roof of the Prince of Wales hotel. Northern Ireland had a fall in April 1969 and the heaviest British fall was at Barwell, Leicestershire, on 24th December 1965. It is incredible to consider that over 20,000,000 meteors enter the atmosphere daily, at a speed of 45 miles per second. Despite this, no death has been recorded, attributable to a meteorite strike.

Bob Halliday (Observatory Director for the Liverpool Astronomical Society) while discussing the Llandrillo affair, said: "Over the past few weeks we have had meteorites much more brilliant and active than anything in the last five years. It is very strange, as they do not fall into the normally predictable pattern of meteorite showers. It is possible that if one was big enough, and travelling slow enough, it could have survived entry into the atmosphere and come down. To produce a tremor of this scale it would have to be of tremendous size. Personally I would have thought it unlikely, but nevertheless it is possible."

The normal predictable pattern of meteorite showers to which Bob Halliday refers, occurs between January 1-4 (known as the Quadrantids, which reach their maximum on Jan 3). The Lyrids, which are very swift meteors, occur annually on April 19 - 22. Uncharacteristically for such phenomena, the recent meteoric activity (of which Llandrillo may be a part) falls between the known Quadrantids and the Lyrids, forming yet another inconsistent element in the enigma.

Meteorites, fireballs and UFOs seem to possess certain characteristics that are interrelated, and having gathered as many available details on the Llandrillo affair, it was but an obvious step to ascertain if any of the facts correlated with those collected by Ufologists. The results proved positive, and while correlations are on an objective basis, the interpretation of their possible

significance must unfortunately be seen subjectively. Five points emerged which I would like to present for the reader's consideration:

1) Reports indicate that lights were seen over the duration of several hours in the Cadair Bronwen area, and not just at the time of, or prior to, the reputed explosion or tremor. The aerial 'fireballs' were described as blueish-green, and while this is a characteristic colour of meteorites, it is also the most frequently reported colour in UFO sightings. UFO literature often contains a mention of Cyan (a blend of blue and green); and John Keel theorises that: "when the objects begin to move into our spatial and time co-ordinates, they gear down from the higher frequencies passing progressively from ultra-violet to bluish-green." I want to stipluate at this point that I am not promoting an argument for the physicality of UFOs, but that the phenomenon that is undoubtedly witnessed, does manifest Cyan as a common colour feature in the majority of cases.

2) The Llandrillo event took place on the night of the 23rd and early hours of the 24th of January - and it is somewhat weird to note that precisely these days of the month occur time and again in the events and lives of the personalities associated with UFOlogy. George Adamski, one of the first reputed UFO contactees, died on the 23rd; Kenneth Arnold, who started the modern awareness when he saw a "chain of saucer-like things at least 5 miles long" made his sighting on 24th June 1947; Arthur Bryant, another reputed contactee, died of a brain tumor on the 24th, and author Frank Edwards died only a few hours before Bryant. Richard Church, Frank Scully (both UFO researchers) and Willy Ley (a pioneer rocket authority) all died at this significant part of the month which recurs in the multitude of Ufo studies, and is included here in relation to the Llandrillo event, for even if it is a coincidence it is not one that should go unnoticed. ⚡ It will interest some of you that Dr Edward Condon, the distinguished researcher of UFOs, has recently died on the 25 March 74, aged 72. Not a hit with the recurring date of 23/4, but close enough to be interesting. An obituary appears in the MUFOB Bulletin (Vol 6, No 4.), and thanks to David J McAllister who spotted the announcement in the Daily Mail 28 March 74. ⚡

3) UFO activity and prehistoric sites are known to relate by virtue of some as-yet-undiscovered principle. The site of the Llandrillo event is also a complex of prehistoric constructions; Cadair Bronwen, a cairn 300 feet in circumference; Cadair Berwyn (Moel Sych) 180 feet around; a megalithic stone circle, Moel Ty Uchaf, which has 41 set stones; and on the opposite side of the valley, an ancient fort, the remains of which extend 225 x 265 feet with a 3ft bank or scarp. The vicar of Llandrillo kindly supplied details of the key sites in the area. An association between prehistoric sites and meteorites was discovered a few years ago by Mr Smithett of the British Society of Dowsers, when he ascertained that certain stones in megalithic constructions had originated from space. It was found that

some stones gave a count of 16, both on rods and pendulums - which suggests an extraterrestrial origin, because meteorites have also been found to give a count of 16. It is known that one of the stones in the Rollright circle is definitely meteoric. At the present time I have no data to indicate that such a test has been performed at Cadair Bronwem and the neighbouring sites.

4) The centre of the Llandrillo activity was focussed on the 2,572 feet high Cadair Bronwen (Ordnance Survey ref: SJ 077 347) which is recorded on many maps as Bwrdd Arthur (Arthur's Table). This is one of the 230 known Arthurian sites in Britain.

5) The final significant factor is that Arthur's Table, the calculated site of the Llandrillo explosion, is on a defined system of alignments, each intersecting at highly relevant angles when considered in relation to the Earth's obliquity of the Ecliptic. Arthur's Table is on five alignments with 47° between two lines; and one is connected to another by 47°. One of the first two runs to near-by Moel Ty Uchaf stone circle, and then onto the Gaer, or fort. The constructions forming these alignments have a direct relationship to the obliquity of the Ecliptic, for the lines intersect at angles of $23\frac{1}{2}^{\circ}$ and its multiples - 47, $70\frac{1}{2}$ and 94. How this sophisticated piece of knowledge was known to the ancients is beyond our present understanding, but it is embodied across Arthur's Table for all to see.

As unorthodox as these methods of investigation and research maybe, what does seem to be revealed is that on five counts the Llandrillo/Arthur's Table event (at that time and place), does not seem to be either arbitrary, nor unrelated to the enigmatic history and peculiar characteristics of similar occurrances. Further research may reveal other undetected and unsuspected patterns which, however open-mindedly they are viewed, continue to transcend and elude ordinary logic and intellectually based reasoning.

Whatever the relative merits or demerits of new or unorthodox investigative methods that are at present called heretical, the Llandrillo phenomena present the perfect opportunity for rational and unbiased research, avoiding the opposing dangers of superstitious credulity and rigid materialism - the former the blind spot of traditional occultism and the latter the Achilles heel of modern physical science.

The whole Llandrillo enigma remains a classical Fortean mystery indeed, but one that is probably more of a mystery than we had initially realised.

*   *   *   *   *   *   *   *

Some further information on Welsh earthquakes came our way by one of those 'happy accidents' that the library goblins cook up for us now and then. In the course of following up some other research we had Charles Davison's 'History of British Earthquakes' (Cambridge Universtity Press 1924) with several chapters on the quakes of north and south Wales. A couple of items were of particular interest. Firstly, William Porter

mentions above the meteorite of Beddgelert - well it seems that there was also an earthquake there, 45 years earlier, on 21 Oct 1904. Since both meteorites and quakes are not that common in the relatively small area of Wales this may be worthy of some note.

Secondly, from elsewhere, we had learnt that the Dee valley (which cuts through the Berwyn hills from Llandrillo to Corwen) lies on a known line called the Great Bala fault. And from Davison we learn that a quake occurred on 1 July 1903 at 1.16am, in an area 7 miles long and $2\frac{1}{2}$ wide from near Bala to near Llandrillo (its centre was about $\frac{1}{2}$ a mile NW of Llanderfel). For reference freaks the original report was in Geological Magazine, Vol 1 p539, 1904. On the strength of what has come to light one way or another, we can only endorse Porter's last sentence. The incident at Llandrillo, 23rd Jan this year, seems not to be the result of 'coincidence' of tremor & meteorite - and if it is part of a pattern, then this is too vast for us to determine within the conventionalities of modern science. As at Beddgelert, we have earthquakes and meteorites (or some mechanism that synchronises a display of aerial lights with the tremor) associated with a particular place. See Fort's 'New Lands' for many coincidences of aerial concussions & lights, quakes, and falls of stones. Indeed, if some of the listed earthquakes may not have been 'proper' quakes, then some meteorites deserve a closer look. For instance, the 'Barwell Meteorite' is numbered among the Included ... but we have come upon a datum that arouses our suspicions - that a village postman reported stones falling around him. We will attempt to discover more.

A brief but very informative survey of the megalithic artifacts in the vicinity of the Llandrillo incident, including a first hand account by its author is in THE LEY HUNTER No 53, March 74.; 'The Explosion and Earthquakes of January 23,1974.' by ACM Jones.

■■■■■■■■■■■■■■■■■■■■■■■■■■■■■■■■■■■■■■■

FOWL FUNNIES / cont...

WHICH CAME FIRST - THE EGG OR THE EGG?

Mrs Isabella Lees sat down to lunch and found something that has put her off eggs for a long time. Inside a normal egg she had boiled was an-another, smaller but perfectly formed. It is speckled brown and looks like a small bird's egg. Mrs Lees, of Northlands Rd, Winterton, showed it to Mr Bernard Walker, Curator of Natural History at Scunthorpe Museum, who said: "I've never known

it happen before." Scunthorpe Star. 22 March 74. Credit: N Watson. The moral is implied of the wisdom of subscribing to THE NEWS, beacuse our readers will be able to turn to Mark Hall's column (a few pages on) to learn of a hen regularly producing doubles. We certainly seem to be having a spate of en-egg-mas in this and the previous issue.

marine mysteries

MYSTERY OBJECT WASHED-UP ON BEACH.

Philip Ledger has been following the developments
surrounding the discovery of a mysterious 'plane-
like' object washed ashore near the South Stack
cliffs, near Holyhead,   Anglesey, on the night
of 4 Feb 74. It was described as being 9ft long,
with a wingspan of 5ft, with a black aluminium
body and the remnants of an aerial, and pretty
heavy. It bore obvious traces of being carried in
and out on the tide for a few days - obvious, that
is, to the police spokesman.

The RAF and the Aberporth Range Establishment
(which as far as mortals can tell, belongs to the
Army) have both said it is 'not one of theirs'.
A description of the device was sent to the Navy's
underwater research base at Portsmouth, but there
has been no sign of recognition in the subsequent
press. A Bomb Disposal Squad from Liverpool came
and pronounced it quite safe - nevertheless, the
Holyhead coastguards were reported to "have been
instructed not to comment" (North Wales Chronicle
7 Feb 74). Official speculation ran the gamut of
the obvious, including "it could have been towed
behind a ship, and the 'wings' could have regulated its depth."

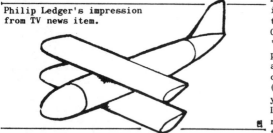

Philip Ledger's impression
from TV news item.

A filmed news item, on the local TV network, showed the device to thousands. Philip Ledger noted
that the 'wings' had a very definite aerofoil
section - and, sad to say, the end 'tail' had
been detatched by souvenir hunters. A coastguard
added that: "Several plugholes and discs on the
outside point to the fact that it is full of instruments." As far as we know, it is still there
- having been left until someone comes along to
identify it. (Credit: Philip Ledger. Other source
Liverpool Daily Post, 5 Feb 74.)

THE DOOM THAT CAME TO DUNWICH.

Diver Stuart Bacon is trying to solve the mystery
of the bell often heard clanging in the town of
Dunwich, which now lies under the sea off the
Suffolk coast. Fishermen and villagers nearby
say they often hear the bell in stormy weather.
Mr Bacon has a theory that the tidal flow causes
the bell, supposed to be in one of the old churches, to ring. He is chairman of a diving club
which is helping to chart the major buildings in
the submerged city - but the extremely poor visibility makes the work slow and difficult. Sunday
Express, 21 April 74. Credit: P Rogerson, Steve
Moore & R Cotton.

We seem to remember a documentary on vanished
English villages (BBC2, not long ago) and one of
the more memorable sights was the erosion of Dunwich, which began its slide into the sea in 1328.
All that remains of this once thriving Anglian
seaport is the cemetary and a few church walls
high on the cliffs above the town. But even here
the steady slip has worked its way through - the
face of the new cliff being gruesomely studded
with skulls and bones, recently exposed, staring
blankly as they await a new and watery burial.

MYSTERY SUBMARINE ALERT : IRISH COAST.

After the phantom helicopter (next issue will
carry a map of the sightings) we should be prepared for a phantom sub. At 4am on 30 March, the
Master of the 'Rathmines' radioed to coastguards
on the Irish coast at Limerick, that one of his
crew had just spotted the 'black superstructure
of a submarine' - and it disappeared when a
searchlight was switched on. (Credit: Nigel Watson, R Cotton & P Rogerson, for cuttings from the
Sunday Express 31 March 74). The Royal Navy dis-
owned the errant 'sub', and when the local police
were put on the alert, the inference was of arms
smuggling to the IRA - a convenient 'get-out'
also used in the phantom copter episode.

The hypothesis is also given that a 'foreign' sub
might have strayed off-course and came up to get
its bearings (or whatever). But it was also pointed out to be well within Irish territorial waters.
Credence could be given to this theory, since
'foreign' covers a multitude of origins, even
psychic ones. However, we need not look deliberately for exotic mysteries when perfectly mundane
ones abound. The Sunday Express, a week later,
(7 April) carried the story of a ship lost where
you would normally think it impossible. The 'Ken
Lung', a Formosan bulk-carrier held together by
rust, put out of Bordeaux bound for Hamburg - and
then got lost. The sea was calm, the weather was
clear, and the lookouts had been keeping their
eyes peeled (a curious expression) for any sign
of land or ship for two whole days - but nothing.
When the first ship came along, the Chinese skipper asked politely where he was. He was in the
middle of the English Channel - possibly the
busiest stretch of water in the world, where
normally a navigational error can lead to disaster, and where in the past 13 years, 107 lives,
and £40 million shipping has been lost. He was
put in touch with the St Margarets Bay, Kent,
coastguards who asked him to steam in a circle,
and then directed him on his way after identifying him. Now British marine experts are said to
be puzzled as to how a ship of 10,000 tons could
be lost for so long in a busy shipping lane on a
perfect day. It is not clear what navigational
equipment was on board and the experts are even
questioning the qualifications of the Captain.
Whenever a mystery arises, Lo! another mystery
of minor but explanainable sorts pops-up; and
then ipso fatso the first is rendered amenable to
the soft magic of logic. But if you look closely
you can detect the joins.

Daily Express 24 April 74 - A police alert on the
coast of Co. Cork, Ireland, after a mystery sub
was sighted - the second in a month.

strange relations

We have noted in the past some evidences of apparent hostility by a number of species toward
man. And before you shake your head and wonder
just why we should be disliked so grievously, let
us tell you of a few curious cases of infatuation
where few would suspect even friendship. Indeed
we were first alerted to the possibilities by the
following letter to the Daily Mirror (30 Oct 73.
(Credit: Robert Forrest) :-

DOGGED BY A PAIR OF SPIDERS.

"Two large black spiders cross my dining room
floor in the evenings. They move from opposite
corners. This has happened now in my past three
house moves, in three counties and miles from
each other. Furthermore it is always in the
dining room! I heard that spiders were supposed
to bring luck. I'm happy if I have my health.
Has anyone else experienced this unusual sight
in more than one move?

> Mrs. I Biden. St Marys Ave, Teddington,
> Middlesex."

We guess our datum might be that living things
not normally associated with concept of 'pet-
owning' should develop some form of reciprocal
relationship. Again from the Daily Mirror (27
Nov 73. Credit: Anthony Smith.) another letter:

GOLDFISH AND CHIPS (ALMOST).

"This is something I would not have believed if
I had not witnessed it myself. This speckled
goldfish about 6 inches long and about 5 years
old belongs to a friend of mine. His name is
'Jambo' - and when he is called by name he pops
out of the lily leaves and kisses your fingers.
But the other day he nearly had his chips, when
he jumped right out of the pond on to the path.
Fortunately for him my wife's friend returned him
to the pond. It made him very giddy but he was
alright again in a few days. Is this unusual, or
can he hear his name being spoken?

> WJ Earnshaw.   Clarence Road,
>   Leighton Buzzard, Beds."

Goldfish, we agree on second thoughts to be pets
of a normal sort, but leaping out of ponds when
called does not strike us as being respectable -
we can only call it 'Guppy Love'. In Mark Hall's
FROM MY FILES (No5. March 74) he notes two incidents - Oscar, a Siamese Fighting Fish kept at St.
Gregory's College, Shawnee, Okla., shows demons-
trable signs of recognising and liking freshwoman
Karol Kluge (Houston Chronicle. 5 March 74. p1-7)
- and also that Jo Welber of Smith Lake, near
Cullman, Alabama, has trained a school of Carp to
feed from a baby-bottle and leap from the water
for a reward of minnows. (Minneapolis Star. 10
Sept 73). If all this seems absurd, we have to
admit we print some preposterous stories - and
they don't come any more preposterous than the
story about:

THE SCOTSMAN, THE LIZARD AND THE TANK.

During World War 2, William Collison served in
the Argyll and Sutherland Highlanders in the
Western Desert - and it was there that he met and
formed a strong attatchment to Joey, a little
green lizard. Joey would follow Jock (William's
nickname) everywhere. Jock used to leave a saucer
of water for him - and Joey insisted on catching
his own food. At night Joey would creep into
Jock's tent and sleep on his shoulder. And once,
when on parade with 2000 other troops, Joey managed to single out Jock, climb up his leg and hide
in his haversack. Joey would come slithering
whenever Jock called - and the happy couple could
often be seen out together on Jock's motorbike.

This story has something of   interest (or
rather of more direct interest) to Forteans. As
in the best love stories, the inevitable posting
came - Jock was packed off to Italy after a sad
farewell. A few weeks after Jock got to his new
barracks in Sicily, Joey turned up. Just how he
got there was, and always will be, impossible to
discover. Flying and walking rule themselves out.
Did he stow away? Well, how would he know which
ship, etc? Did he swim? Is that possible? Perhaps
he teleported? - we know from our studies that
the appearance and disappearance of a wide variety
of species-members can lead to the supposition of
teleportation. Could the transference (if such
it was) have affected Joey's normal lightning
reflexes? Well, he was certainly sluggish enough
not to notice the massive tank that rumbled toward him, one day not long after his arrival in
Sicily. Too bad, really - it cured him of ever
feeling sluggish again, but Joey wasn't together
enough to appreciate it.

Jock now lives at Wheatland Close, Liverpool, and
still remembers the day he buried his little
green comrade. "He was the best pet I ever had.
And I've had dogs, cats and horses." (Weekend.
28 Nov - 4 Dec 73. Credit: Anthony Smith.)

ripley or not!

COINCIDENCE, FATE - OR WHAT?

Following the publication of the 'Roots of Coincidence' last year, the Sunday Times printed an article by Arthur Koestler on the patterns we often
read into chance events. It ended with a request
for readers to send in their stories. That was
25 Nov 73 - and recently (5 May 74) the Sunday
Times feature Koestler's follow-up using the
material sent-in - well several stories out of
the reported 'several thousand' at least. We often
wonder what happens to the material generated by
these big-name blow-outs. There were several
examples of a kind of story Koestler called
'Crossed Lines'... we find we have a few on our
files and they may as well be told here.

Passers-by ignored the old tramp sitting on the
wall outside the railway station at Kingston,
Surrey. Ron Hallard would have passed too, but
he looked up and saw - his long lost dad, who had
suffered a nervous breakdown during the blitz and
disappeared in 1958 without a word to anybody.
Even the Salvation Army had given him up for dead
News of the World, 17 March 74.

Continued on page 17.

THE INTERFACE
& THE PATHS OF DESTINY.
by Paul Screeton.

Once upon a time mankind did not pigeon-hole each branch of science - or rather the area it understood. In days long gone by man did not seek to departmentalize the factors of his existence. All formed one fundamental, coherent cosmology sustaining a stable society.

The critical question is inevitable: how did the equilibrium shift? Perhaps it was part of a great cycle of time? Whatever it was, we are now left groping in the ruined haunted house, awaiting illumination, but doing precious little to bring it about.

What is an unhappy reality is that astrology became a debased astronomy (c'mon, own up about Kohoutek!); alchemy which charged the soul became mundane chemistry (thalidomide, and terminal valium freaks); numerology was divorced from gematria and emigrated to academic tedium.

Charles Fort had his filing system and his categories, but like the late Alfred Watkins who discovered the Ley system, he did not take the negative, soft option of feebly specialising and concentrating on one miniscule aspect of our totality. Fort saw the vast panorama of the borderline bewilderment nudging us daily, yet ignored by official science.

Alfred Watkins had the fortune to rediscover the simple yet devastatingly valid fact that Britain - and all countries - are criss-crossed by a network of alignments linking sacred sites. He chose to present these as trackways, though subsequent generations have largely speculated that the lines are, in fact, the paths of a subtle current, whose nature is as mercurial as its archetypal guardian deity, Hermes. Indications are that Alfred Watkins, a psychic who suppressed his gift, had more than an inkling of the importance of the discovery he made in 1921.

The academic fraternity, predictably, was hostile to Watkins. Likewise today, the ivory-tower brigade are uncomfortable in the presence of disturbing evidence of a prehistoric civilisation equally advanced as today's and with an alien technology.

Verification of the Ley system is a simple matter. Using a six-inch Ordnance Survey map of any part of Britain, draw circles around all prehistoric sites and pre-Reformation churches; then using a ruler draw lines where four or more sites align exactly. You will find a great many alignments, beyond the bounds of mathematical probability, on any map - also, patterns and focal points with three or more lines passing through one spot.

I embraced the Ley philosophy like a long lost friend - as many do - but have rationalized my assessment of the lines' nature by the simple rule of experience. I now know by a biophysical reaction when a Ley's energy is active. It will take time, but I suspect that positive evidence can be produced to reveal that much 'interface' activity (ghosts, UFOs, elementals, etc) is directly linked to the Ley system.

But to be fair, not only the archeological professionals are blameworthy. It is disarming that while we might be regarded as a lunatic fringe, there is within our ranks a sloppy, woolly, ill-informed, uncritical element whose activities and writings, enthusiastic though they may be, do nothing but bring the subject into disrepute and ridicule.

The blinkered approach of archaeologists, who see sites in isolation, is so sadly pathetic that it is unworthy of incisive comment. Where the salaried pundits are out of step is the reality of today's Aquarian antiquarians' new-found 'live archaeology'. The sites are not ages-dead, but generate, as they did thousands of years ago, a spiritual sensitivity which transcends time - and linking them are the Leys, the power grid, the web of eternity, the enchanted everlasting lines of destiny.

*   *   *

Paul Screeton is Editor of the excellent LEY HUNTER, a duplicated magazine of articles and notes related to and exploring the triplet of Ley facets; the 'energy' and its technology, the spiritual and philosophic implications, and the rediscovery of the system by fieldwork and other research. See the advertisement elsewhere in this issue. Paul Screeton is also the author of an illustrated compendium of tales, folklore and folkwisdom from the north east of England. Called 'Quicksilver Heritage', it is due out this Autumn.

"Actually, it's a damn disgrace; it should have been let years ago."

by WILLIAMS

Stephen Malenda was urged by friends to go fishing to forget the recent disappearance of his 6-year-old boy in January. He settled down at a lagoon just 200 yards from his home in Mentor, Ohio, and cast his line...and reeled in his son's body. Daily Mirror, 16 March 74. Credit: R Forrest "Is this a million-to-one chance? 1 received two Christmas cards, one from a son in Britain, and one from a son in Los Angeles. There are both exacly the same." Letter from Mrs Freda Hurst in Daily Express 14 Dec 73.

Veronica Mullens and Anthony Pitt were married at Dowlais, Glamorgan. There names were recorded next to each other on the Merthyr Tydfil birth register 22 years ago. Sunday Mirror 3 March 74.

But perhaps the most remarkable tale is that of young Roger Lausier. When he was 4-years-old he strayed away from his mother, along the beach at Salem, Massachusetts. He paddled and got caught by a powerful undercurrent, and would have drowned but for a woman who brought him ashore and revived him. The rescuer, Alice Blaise, refused all rewards, and left wishing the infant luck. Nine years later, Roger was a strong swimmer and was tracking a shoal of bluefish when he heard a woman scream: "My husband is drowning! My husband is drowning!" Roger saw a heavily built man had fallen from his powerboat and was floundering helplessly. Roger paddled his inflated raft over in time to clutch the drowning man's hand - then the man's bulk and the weight of wet clothing threatened to collapse the frail support. Roger managed to keep the man's head up, but the stiff currents were pulling them further out to sea. Shortly another boat got to them, and they went safely ashore. In the hospital the woman kissed the boy: "I'm Alice Blaise, and I can't thank you enough for saving my Bob." Roger had no idea who Mrs Blaise was until the story came out during a presentation to him by the Massachusetts Humane Society. He had saved the husband of the woman who had saved him on the same beach nine years previously. Sunday Express, 21 April 74. Credit: P Rogerson & Richard E Cotton.

DOUBLE TROUBLE.

Two motorists who drove through thick fog with their heads out of their windows - cracked their skulls together. They are recovering in a Northern Italian hospital. Daily Mirror 20 Nov 73. Credit: Steve Moore. Another curious story comes from the Sun 23 April 74. Two cars smashed into each other head-on in the village of Outwick, Hants, and both drivers ran off in different directions. Both cars had been stolen.

Identical twins Frank and Jack Clatworthy were lying side-by-side in hospital after crashing in quite separate accidents on the same road. Frank was driving home to Washford, Somerset, from a party when his car overturned. An hour later, Jack, who knew nothing of his brother's misfortune, crashed on the same road returning from the same party. For other stories of enigmatic synchronicities concerning locations and events see back to 'Deaths in 2s and 3s.'

Another set of identical twins got their big break similarly on the same day and within minutes

of each other. Wendy Styles of Brading, Isle of Wight, broke her leg while vaulting in the school gym. While she was waiting for a doctor to arrive, her sister Denise was carried out having just broken hers. Daily Mirror 22 Dec 73. Individually these stories are ignored, or casually accepted as 'just one of those things' that happen all the time, and to everybody. What kind of forces, we ask, can move implacably, powerfully, by turns gentle and savage, through the events of our daily lives. It's the scale of it all that boggles We have a hypothesis that we only notice universal mechanisms when they go wrong - not that we have any idea of how to measure 'right' or 'wrong' in this context - and we suspect this will be a major battleground against the 'Unknown' in years to come. We at least will be working towards our understanding of such things. We mentioned earlier Koestler's books on Coincidences - its a step, but only just since statistics is no substitute for understanding. Indeed they handle only parts of the problem, and we harbour doubts that they can effectively come to grips with mechanisms that effect patterns not only on the macrocosmic scale but down to the minutest details of daily life that we tend to think of as uncoordinated and meaningless. It is likely to call for new methods of understanding, and our old chauvinisms could prove to be of little or limited value.

swarms

IT'S NOT CRICKET.

A massive invasion of swarms of crickets brought panic to two towns in Brazil. In Altinho, about 150 miles from Recife, families abandoned their homes and businesses have collapsed. Reporters who visited the town said: "One woman has gone mad. People march in religious processions, do penance, make votary promises and believe it is a punishment of God, the end of the world." A priest cabled yesterday from the other town, Cachoeirinha. He said the situation was intolerable there - and that millions of crickets were still arriving. Daily Mirror. 25 Oct 71. Credit: Anthony Smith.

ANTS ON RAMPAGE.

A column of killer ants a mile long and half a mile wide marched on the Brazilian town of Goiania and devoured several people - including the Chief of police. 60 firemen with flamethrowers took 16 hours to drive the ants back into the jungle. Sunday People. 9 Dec 73. Credit: Cathy Purcell.

GHOST SPIDERS IN THE SKY.

Millions of spiders floated across the sky in parts of South-Eastern Australia on strands of webbing. Huge areas are covered with the thick snow-like webs - and whole clouds of webs, some thousands of feet high, often blot out the sky. Daily Express. 27 May 74. Credit: HJ Wilkinson. From the same paper and date we learn that at the same time there are 'freak' storms along the East coast of Australia - may or may not be any connection, but those web-clouds couldn't have stayed up if they started to collect water.

REVIEWS

'STRANGE PHENOMENA' - ISBN: 0.9600712.1.0., 277p.
'STRANGE ARTIFACTS' - ISBN: 0.9600712.2.9., 262p.
Both looseleaf in a ring-binder format - and each
$6.95 from the compiler, William R Corliss,
POBox 107, Glen Arm, Maryland 21057. USA.

These two volumes are the first two in a new
series of sourcebooks on unusual phenomena and
Fortean enigmas generally. The result of many
years planning and reasearch, it goes without
saying that these and the promised additional
volumes belong in the library of every Fortean,
researcher and scientific historian.

Corliss has devised a flexible classification and
retrieval system that (thank the Lord) doesn't
straightjacket the phenomena and is not too
cumbersome if you know what you want info on. The
reference material itself consists of extracts
and (some) summaries of original papers and observations from scientific journals, going back
to the middle 19th century, and few of the sources
are less than 50 years old. Thus by collecting
the original statements and consequently often
the hardest to track down, he has done the whole
field of Fortean and allied interests a very
great service. Briefly, each volume is divided
into generic categories, as follows:

'PHENOMENA' (Vol-G1.)	'ARTIFACTS' (Vol-M1.)
Electromagnetic ph'ma.	Anthropological evidence
Falling Material.	on Physical & Social
Luminous phenomena.	characteristics, etc.
Crustal Movements.	Geological Artifacts,
Sound phenomena.	inc. Fossilised footprints
Weather phenomena.	Graphic Artifacts.
	Legends, Myths & Concepts,
(To come in Vol-G2.)	of Gods & Giants.
Electromagnetic (cont).	Manufactured Artifacts.
Falling material (cont).	Structural Artifacts in
Gravitation & Temporal	canals, Standing Stones,
anomalies.	Forts, Mounds, Pyramids,
Incendiary phenomena.	and Mines.
Magnetic & Electrical	
phenomena.	(To come in Vol-M2.)
Odors.	
Crustal movements (cont).	Anthropological (cont.)
Volcanic phenomena.	Graphic (cont).
Weather phenomena (cont).	Legends, Myths, Concepts
	of Dwarfs, Elementals,
	& Origin of Man.
	Manufatured (cont.)
	Structural (cont) inc.
	Obelisks & Walls.

All of the data is cross-referenced (where relevant) with Place-of-Event, Time-of-Event, and
Quote source Indexes. Corliss deserves our heart-
felt thanks for this invaluable and indeed essential reference work - a labour of love exceedingly well done.

*   *   *

'THE MAN IN THE SHROUD' - Peter M Rinaldi.
Futura pb. 40 pence. 125pp. ISBN: 0.8600.7010.7.

Rinaldi is a priest, and one of the few who have
been allowed over some time, to study the curious
Shroud of Turin, on which the image of the dead

Christ is reputedly imprinted. That the fragile
cloth bears the image of a wounded man fitting
the (often contradictory) details of the Christ
legend is attested to by the copious photos. This
'book' however is pretty thin and set in large
type - an annotated paper with illos and a useful
bibliography. But you can overlook that if you're
interested in the subject.

*   *   *

'THE SECRET PLACES OF THE LION'- George Hunt
Williamson. Futura pb. 40 pence. 230pp.
ISBN: 0.8600.7011.5.

This was one of the first influences on your editor's developing Fortean bent back in 58/59. It
was also one of the first to extrapolate the now
familiar themes of ancient astronauts and hidden
knowledge. But Williamson's story mainly concerns
a small group of 'teachers' (or Initiators, as
Charroux would say) who reincarnate in different
combinations at various times to guide Man's
bumbling steps, and mostly concentrates on their
exploits in 18th/19th Dynasty Egypt (the time of
Amunhotep, Tutankhamun, Akhnaton, and he would
have us believe, David & Solomon) preparing the
ground for the greater Initiator, Christ.

Like James Churchward (of the 'MU' books) Williamson claims secret knowledge was given him (in
this case by a hidden Brotherhood in the Andes)
which enables him to reveal the 'true' implications of key events and people in our past. And
there, in a gloriously lurid red and yellow blurb-
splash are such 'key' questions as: Is there a
secret temple under the Sphinx; and an ancient
spaceship under the Gt. Pyramid? Where is the
Holy Grail? Was Melchizedek also Shem? Did Atlantis & Lemuria ever exist? Who were the Hyskos?

Most of us (who haven't degrees in Aramaic, etc)
have no practical way of judging the validity of
such correlative studies of the (alien) origin of
Man - but much of this, I venture, seems like
conjecture substantiated by dubious and uncheck-
able references, made plausible by the obsssesive
confidence the man has in his thesis. The nuts
who think the 'alien gods' concept is TRUE because
they 'read it in a book' will see here more 'in-
controvertable' proof that what they have always
known and told themselves REALLY IS true. I don't
mean to be patronising, but I find these books
on probable pasts enormously entertaining - that
is if you don't take them too obsessively and
can wade through huge slabs of turgid prose. But
seriously - there are some really exciting ideas
here (it would be interesting to check out his
re-chronology of the Moses/Solomon period of
Egyptian history with that of Velikovsky in his
'Ages in Chaos', eg.) and we welcome every effort
to explore them. On this point the paperback carries a flyleaf appeal for funds to support Dr.
Williamson in the latest leg of his 'expedition
to Europe' investigating pre-Columbian landings
on the Americas, and Atlantean UFOs. We, as they
say, await developments .

*   *   *

'URI' - Andrija Puharich. WH Allen. £2.95. 285pp.
ISBN: 0.491.01960.2.

If Williamson's book (above) seems like fiction
dressed up as fact,   Puharich's biography and
study of Uri Geller and his powers gives the
impression of being the exact reverse. This book
is genuinely incredible. The accounts of telepathy, clairvoyance, psychokinesis and mystical
experiences, are by any standards remarkable, but
they pale and become quite ordinary when the
eons-old computer-linked alien intelligences in
their vast planetoid spaceships, hovering in the
furthest reaches of the galaxy, turn up. If you
take away the trappings of science-fiction imagery, Geller's seems like a classic case of possession. These beings speak through him, and any
cassette-recorder lying about; trances and visions
; a sense of 'things ordained by higher (or stronger) powers', and things moving 'by themselves.'

Indeed, these intelligences, which rejoice in
names like Hoova, Spectra and 'The Nine', reveal
that they have 'programmed' Geller's life, right
down to the crazy poltergeist pranks - and soon
it seems that a small circle of friends , including Puharich himself, come under their control.
Puharich seems to believe this implicitly. One of
the overall characteristics of Geller's proxy
talents seems to be some sort of influence over
what others see. Whether this is deliberate or
unconscious or working to an 'outside' direction
is secondary to the fact that different people
swear they have seen different things going on -
and sadly the possibility of an illusion-generat-
ing power (direct psychokinetic adjustment of
brain nurones?) is not considered in this book.
However, it does keep cropping up - in, for example, the almost constant UFO activity in the
vicinity of Geller's group, which no-one else
is able to see 'unless the Computers allow it! The
variety of the UFO (or rather were UFO) forms,
including an archetypal guardian 'White Hawk'
elemental - all evidence (of a sort) for the
psychological origins of UFOs. The awesome power
of the illusion-projection ability almost defies
thought - any amount of seemingly real evidence
could be manufactured. It all smacks of plots and
paranoia - John Keel country.

As the story unfolds of how Puharich came to
study Geller, and of their (at times) stormy friendship, the wonders come thick and fast - why
should Computers half a galaxy away interfere
with life on Earth to produce someone like Geller
receptive to their control, and then lark about
bending spoons, vanishing all the tape and cine
cassettes with valuable evidence on them, making
a watch appear on a wrist, etc etc? Geller says:
"I think somebody is playing games with us. Perhaps they are a civilisation of clowns. Or maybe
one of their clowns escaped and he is playing
games with us."

In the true tradition of cosmic jesting, the sinister is mixed in with the laughs. Puharich and
others experience peculiar 'time-jumps' and Geller
appears to suffer from periodic selective amnesia.
It could all be the result of seperate but co-or-
dinated illusions again. In one episode Geller

and Puharich got whisked away to the spaceship
and back (subjectively many hours) all while an
ashtray was frozen in its flight. No not TK this
time - Uri had thrown it at Puharich during an
argument. And then there is the matter of the
teleporting of Puharich's dog to some hundreds
of yards outside the house where seconds before
it was minding its own business. And as if this
wasn't enough, political intrigue gets dragged in
via the Israeli secret service who become concerned about the activities of Puharich and (we are
told) the little tricks the aliens are playing
on their efforts to bug and shadow Geller's
group.

Here too is the illuminating story of the campaigns to discredit Geller and Puharich and the
carefully calm film of the Stamford Research
Institute experiments (of which there is a transcript here) which show Geller, quite clearly,
mentally manipulating rows of matches and deflect
the needle in a shielded magnetometer. Reference
is made in the book to Geller bending a machined
ring with a force of 150lbs while they were constantly scanned by an 'acoustic' holograph device.
This showed up the bones of the hand holding the
ring - but as the ring began its deformation the
ring was affected, and the distorted
TV record was thought to be 'unsuitable' as evidence.

All in all, it is a surprising story to hear from
a 'respected' scientist - and Puharich readily admits his 'conversion' from scientific objectivity
to a mystical certainty that the lives of himself
and the small group are closely directed by 'The
Nine'. He is also eager to stress that though he
uses words like 'computers', 'mind control', 'programmed lives', 'UFOs', and is himself painfully
puzzled by the contradictory and sometimes trivial
phenomena, what is happening is beyond his (and
our) terms of reference, and so it is our normal
reaction to rationalise events in terms of our
preconceptions and conditioning. But this should
not deter us from believing that something extraordinary was going on, and that this small band
of psychically sensitive people (at once familiar
with psionic research and science-fiction) were
(willing or otherwise) the catalysts.

Indeed, this book seems quite different from the
'normal' run out to convert you to the expected
heresies - there is no close reasoning; facile or
dazzling explanations. It comes across as the
testimony of an honest and disillusioned scientist trying to come to grips with his experience
of the really Unknown.

                    *   *   *

Also received were:

'PSYCHOANALYSIS & THE OCCULT' - George Devereaux
editor. Condor/Souvenir Press. £3.00. pb £1.50.
432pp. ISBN: 0.285.64738.5. being collected
papers by Freud, Eisenbud, Fodor, Gillespie and
other psychoanalysts on the occurrence of telepathy, precognition, etc during analysis, dreams,
and everyday situations. Index and Bibliography.

'MAGIC, SCIENCE & RELIGION' - Essays by Bronislaw
Malinowski. Condor/Souvenir Press. £2.50. pb £125

274pp. ISBN: 0.285.64739.3. Malinowski, a disciple of Sir James 'Golden Bough' Fraser, collects here his essays on the parallels in 'primitive' archetypal thought patterns in science, magic and religion.

'ZEN BUDDHISM & PSYCHOANALYSIS' papers by Erich Fromm, DT Suzuki & R De Martino. Condor/Souvenir Press. £2.50. pb £1.25. 180pp. ISBN:0.285.64740.7 An excellent set of lectures by Suzuki on the relevance of Zen to the Western world. All three of the above books throw some light on the possible development of Fortean methodology. We note obvious points of contact between the Fortean view of the Universe, Zen and indeed the subconscious processes of mind (even Cosmic Mind). We would like to see this whole area explored more and invite comment from our readers.

did you see.....?

Hopefully we extend our coverage to mentions of articles etc. likely to be of interest to you all from the journals and other mags. If you come across anything you think might be of interest to other Forteans then please let us know. Just note the titles of the piece and publication, the author, date and pages if possible and drop us a post card. These days it is physically impossible to cover all the publications that interest you personally, so you might be glad to catch something here that you might have missed. So do someone else a favour - and make the effort. You know it makes sense.

'Velikovsky: AAAS forum for a mild collision.' Robert Gillette. SCIENCE Vol.183 pp1059-1062. 15 March 74.

'Leys and Energy.' MW Pearson. THE LEY HUNTER No 53 pp 5-6. March 74.

'Orientation of Homing Pigeons altered by a change in the direction of an Applied Magnetic Field' C Walcott & RP Green. SCIENCE Vol.184 pp180-182. 12 April 74.

'New Evidence for the Antiquity of Man in North America deduced from Aspartic Acid Racemization.' JL Bada, RA Schroeder & GF Carter. SCIENCE Vol.184 pp791-793. 17 May 74.

'UFO Reports from AIAA Members.' PA Sturrock. ASTRONAUTICS & AERONAUTICS May 74. pp60-64.

'Major Flap in US' Eileen Buckle. pp2-5. 'Abduction at Bebedouro' HB Alexio. pp6-14. 'Landing at Columbia, Missouri'. Ted Phillips. pp18-25. FLYING SAUCER REVIEW Vol.19 No6. Nov/Dec 73.

'Abominable Swampman of Florida's Everglades' W& E Hartley. MEN July 74 pp16-18,78,79.

'Extended Glow preceding Reappearance of Saturn during a Lunar Occultation'. G Reed, FJ Howell & TA Clark. NATURE Vol.247. 15 Feb 74. pp447-448.

'Seafloor Spread Theory & Odyssey of Green Turtle! A Carr & PJ Coleman. NATURE Vol.249 10 May 74. pp128-130.

'Northampton's Prize Pyramid' DESIGN No301 Jan 74. pp56-61. (Mentioned in NEWS 2 p17.)

'Danikenitis - Interview with Von Daniken.' Roy Stemman. PREDICTION Vol. 40 No6. pp18-20. June 74

'Are Psychoenergetic Pictures Possible?'. William A Tiller. NEW SCIENTIST Vol. 62. 25 April 74. pp 160-163.

'Psychic Uri Geller'. TG Beckley & H Salkin. SAGA July 74. pp28-30,54, 56, 58.

'Yin Yang Hypothesis of Growth Control'. Dr B Hogan & Dr R Shields. NEW SCIENTIST Vol.62. 9 May 74. pp323-325.

'The Brain's other Half'. Prof Robert Ornstein. NEW SCIENTIST Vol.62 6 June 74. pp606-608.

'Verdict on the Vinland Map'. Elia Campbell. GEOGRAPHICAL MAGAZINE Vol. XLVI No7. April 74. pp 307-312. (Good illustrations of the map.)

Compilation Credits: Mark Hall, Philip Ledger.

ADS

THE NEWS is available from the following specialist book services who keep wide-ranging stocks of Fortean, Occult, UFO and general books, including science fiction, etc. A ± denotes a mail-order service with lists available by request.

NEW DIMENSIONS (±). PO Box 323, Arlington, Va 22210, USA.

DARK THEY WERE AND GOLDEN EYED (±). 10 Berwick St, London W1V3RG.

JAPETUS. 201 Corporation St, Birmingham B4 6SE.

LIONEL BEER (±). 15 Freshwater Court, Crawford St, London W1H 1HS.

Please mention THE NEWS when you follow up any adverts as this not only promotes goodwill but allows the various parties involved to judge the value of their efforts. Thanks.

UFO LECTURE.

Nigel Watson writes that Norman Oliver will be giving a talk to the Scunthorpe UFO Research Society (SUFORS) on 'British Contact Claims' on Monday 7th October. Anyone interested further is invited to write to Nigel Watson at 1 Angerstein Road, Scunthorpe, Lincs, DN17 2LZ.

REMEMBER TO RENEW YOUR SUB SOON

As an indication of when to renew your subscription - we have put a number in the top right-hand corner of your address label on the envelope. This is the number of issues you have left TO COME. We would appreciate renewals before your last one if possible, since it helps with the messy paperwork.

THE NEWS

a miscellany of fortean curiosities

BUMPER `FALL´ ISSUE ~ falls of :
bricks, p7.. stones, p9.. ice, p10.. animals, p15

WATERSPOUTS IN THE ENGLISH CHANNEL.... p17

also --- winged cat, 3 --- Noah's Ark, 5 --- flaming kids & settee suttees, 16 ---
Nigel Watson on Lincs ghosts, 18 --- swarms, 21 --- the Book of Bhrigu, 23.

Vol.1. No.6.
September,
1974.

THE NEWS is a non-profit making bi-monthly miscellany of
Fortean news and notes; edited & published by Robert JM
Rickard: 31 Kingswood Road, Moseley, Birmingham B13 9AN;
affiliated to International Fortean Organisation (INFO).

SUBSCRIPTIONS:	AIRMAIL TRANSFER:	CONTRIBUTIONS & RIGHTS:
Per year: £2.10.	Overseas subscrib-	Articles & Notes are
Overseas & USA	ers can 'Airmail	welcome, and duly cred-
$6.00 or equiv-	Transfer' direct	ited. All articles in
alent; plus 10%	from their bank	THE NEWS are Copyright
if paying by	to our account:	of the authors; and the
cheque (to cover	RJM Rickard No2.	views expressed are not
bank-charges).	A/c No: 0125008.	necessarily those of THE
NB: Cheques etc.	Lloyds Bank, Priory	NEWS or the Editor. All
payable to: RJM	Ringway, Birmingham	the Notes may be freely
RICKARD,please.	B4, England. Sort-	quoted, though we hope
	ing Code: 30-96-28.	for a credit in return.

A GREAT FORTEAN CAPER.

As you will see from the attendant notes, Ken
Campbell's play, 'The Great Caper' opens at the
Royal Court Theatre, early October. Ken is one of
us - a Fortean, that is - and his love and fascination with the Fortean mysteries shines through.
It concerns the adventures of a hardened Fortean
and his companion, who decide,(rightly or wrongly,
it doesn't matter), that the bewildered young
man they find immobilised by shock in the street
is "at this moment carrying, or preparing, a sp-
erm of mind-blowing significance"; and convinced
that wonderful phenomena will attend its moment
of fertilization, set out to find the perfect
girl for him. Most of the Fortean stuff is brought into their constant chattering and asides:
curious meteors; plagues of fleas; Adamski's UFOs
and UFO kidnappings; a Lost Tribe of Israel; the
Tarot; a descendant of the Benjamin Bathurst who
"Walked around the Horses"; aerial sounds and
strange clouds. Phew! Lord knows what the uninit-
iated will make of that lot. Sensibly, it's not
laboured into heavy suet, but moves at a pace
through some good jokes to its lusty conclusion.
Some might take offence at some of the language -
but that is an accepted norm these days. No deep
philosophical discussions here - just an honest-
to-Fort ribald ~~romp~~ romp through the BOOK OF THE
DAMNED.

Only later - much thought comes on our susceptibility to control from 'Outside', on the ease with
which super-beings from other times or places
could manipulate the 'coincidences' of our daily
lives to suit the ends of their alien morality.

Cont/ p23.

ROYAL COURT THEATRE

Sloane Square, London SW1. Phone: 01-730 1745.

*   *   *

Warren Mitchell in THE GREAT CAPER; a visionary
drama in 2 acts, by Ken Campbell. Directed by
Nicholas Wright; Designed by Bob Ringwood. With:
Katie Allan, Judith Blake, Ken Campbell, Simon
Coady, Eddie Davies, Aharon Ipalé, Lisa Harrow,
    Mark Jones, Richard O'Callaghan.

*   *   *

Previews from 2nd October - 100 best seats @ £1.20
Previews from 2nd October - 100 best seats @ £1.20

INCREASES IN SUBSCRIPTION RATES

1) From this issue on, including renewals, the
UK rate will be increased to £2.10, the US rate to
$6.00 - all other countries to the equivalent of
the US rate. We're sure you appreciate that recent
world-wide events have pushed up costs all round,
and that this increase was inevitable.

2) We regret further having to ask all overseas
subscribers who pay by cheque to add 10% to cover
the commission taken by the banks who clear the
cheque during the payment transaction. In several
cases we have finally received only just over
half of what you intended us to receive. You
might investigate the 'Airmail Transfer' system
from your bank direct to ours (details up top on

our colophon) - but don't forget to let us know
its coming through.

3) All renewals received to date will be honoured
- and if any of you kind-hearted souls want to
make up the difference to the new rate, this will
be most gratefully accepted. But all renewals
must from now on be at the new rate. That's life

4) From this issue we adopt a different system of
keeping track of subscriptions. The number printed
in the top right-hand corner of your address
lable, is the issue number with which your sub.
expires. To those of you who throw away your envelopes, or have done so by the time you read
our reminder, renew anyway and keep well ahead.

animal curiosities

A CAT THAT'S BATS.

One of the more bizarre sections of John Keel's STRANGE CREATURES FROM TIME AND SPACE, is his chapter 4 on 'Flying Felines', in which he gives accounts of five 'winged' cats, all in the USA. We were recently sent a note from Weekend, 23-29 Jan 74, which tells the story of Thomas Bessie, a regionally famous winged cat in Yorkshire. It was born in a Leeds workhouse in 1900, and vanished from there after gaining some fame. The workhouse official, William Markham, eventually tracked it down in a fairground peepshow, and after some years it died of poisoning and was duly stuffed. When Markham died, the curiosity passed to his granddaughter, Mrs Amy Clague, who has since displayed Thomas Bessie in the various pubs she and her husband have run in Selby, Yorks, including her present one, The Hole in the Wall.

In this case the cat's 'wings' are said to be malformations of its rib structure - though Keel's items are afflicted with variables from twin lumps of thick matted fur to boneless but gristly furry flaps each nine inches long. The only mention of such sports being able to fly is in what seems to us a rather suspect report by Jean Revers of Ontario, (Keel) who saw a winged cat 'sailing' after a neighbour's cat: "It screamed like hell. And it tried to get away by making gliding jumps of fifty or sixty feet - wings extended - after a good running start. It could stay a foot or so above the ground." It was later exhumed (Revers had shot and buried it) and it was found to be "just an ordinary cat" with "growths of thick matted fur". (Credit: Anthony Smith.)

HUNTS FOR VARIOUS CREATURES.

Moby Buffalo? - Fish and Game officials are mounting a hunt, paid for by the Izaak Walton League of America, for a rare albino bison. Records show that 11 others have either failed to survive the Alaska winter, or fallen prey to poachers. Champaign News Gazette (Urbana, Illinois) 31 Oct 73. Credit: Loren Coleman.

The Beast of Bungoma Dies. - The monster that terrorized the Bungoma district 300 miles west of Nairobi, Kenya, killing hundreds of farm animals, was finally trapped and shot by a massive hunt by forestry Rangers. We suspect this to be one of those inquiry-stoppers, that crop up to allay the fears of the superstitious peasants, and expect that we shall shortly hear of continued depredations. This story by the way seems to be an attempt to ease the fears by villagers of a supernatural beast, a mixture of "lion, leopard and dog" which in turn makes it a probable continuation of the 'Sinister Force' reported from Kenya earlier (see NEWS 4 p3). The Rangers, in this case, said it was nothing more than a "huge and ferocious leopard." Daily Mirror 24 April 74. Credit: Steve Moore.

Campaign against Killer Wolves. - Two children were killed and another badly injured within two weeks after wolf attacks in the Orense province of Spain. Massive hunts with dogs and poisoned bait have been planned. San Francisco Chronicle 12 July 74. Credit: Loren Coleman. A note in the Sunday Mirror 14 July, mentions only one wolf. See item in Mark Hall's column for a wave of uncharacteristic coyote attacks in New Mexico.

Lion running Amok. - Nothing unusual, you might think, in a lion killing animals in South Africa, and yet those who live there say this is not lion country and they are unable to discover where it has come from. Wolf van der Merwe told reporters: "Being a big game hunter I recognised the tracks of a lion in soft mud. I could not believe my eyes, but when I saw the half-eaten carcases of two of my heifers, I had no further doubts." A police search was carried out, but apparently failed to turn up anything. Los Angeles Times 7 April 74. Credit: Mark Hall.

MYSTERY ANIMALS IN UK.

The Mystery Animal phenomenon (MA) has a long and chequered history in the UK, from the Black Dog ghosts of old to the modern 'Surrey Puma' through the 'wolf' hunts of 1904/5 chronicled by Fort in LO! In this issue Nigel Watson covers some info. about the Black Dogs, and coming shortly we have an article from Janet Bord relating a very curious Black Dog ghost story. Please see the current INFO 13 for a review of MA phenomena in the southern counties from 1962 - 1973 by your present editor. Often, when the press note the arrival of an MA, the Zoos are checked for escaped animals - so perhaps we ought to carry notes of escapes, though we are dubious about its value, since the escape that tallies with an MA is very rare indeed, and there is no accounting for private and illegal importings of associated critters - but we'll see what comes up.

PUMA HUNT...IN SCOTLAND.

A 40lb American Puma is believed to be roaming Ayrshire. Sharpshooters and police are standing by for the next sighting. No information is given about the 'several' previous sightings, and there have been no reports (that have come to our notice) of any killing of livestock - always an odd feature. Pumas are big eaters, and as in the 'Surrey' cases, killing of various domestic and wild animals for food seems to be unusually low - that is unless it's something else, or even non-corporeal. The only clue to its origin is that a 'mystery caller' to the RSPCA asked to have the teeth of his puma pulled, but failed to reveal his identity. Its thought he (presuming he was in Scotland) turned the damned thing loose.

Conversely, in the matter of killed evidence, is the case of the 'Emmaville Panther', Australia's answer to the 'Surrey Puma'. We don't think this has seen daylight before, so we duly note the report of a hunt for same by 50 crack riflemen after killing "hundreds of sheep" and even worse, "scaring tourists away." Sunday Express 2 March 69. Credit: Peter Rogerson.

THE GAME WAR HOTS UP.

In NEWS 3 we gave you the latest (and some of them were quite late) dispatches in the hostilities between bird and man , and though things have not yet reached Hitchcock proportions, they are definitely getting more blatant in the wing and beak department, not to mention their unsophisticated but effective software.

We have just dug out a batch while making a feeble and useless attempt to sort out our files - and we come across one note of flocks of magpies dive-bombing MPs as they leave the Australian Houses of Parliament, Canberra. One MP is reported to have had his ear sliced; another was pecked on the head; and a third was said to have been knocked down before fleeing to a nearby temple. A suggestion has been made to issue safety hats, and they'd be well advised to take that up. Birmingham Evening Mail 27 Oct 67. Another attack by magpies who managed to pin down a workman, teachers and children in a school in Adelaide, South Australia, is recorded in Daily Mirror for 19 Aug 71. Credit: Anthony Smith. It hardly makes it any more believable to learn that this feat took only two of the birds, and yet the siege was maintained until police came and shot them.

Magpies again figure in the story of an attack on a 3-year-old girl, in Ettymore Close, Sedgeley, Staffs, as she played with other children. The bird, thought to have been a pet at one time, swooped, scratching her arm and leg. It flew away when the other children started screaming. Birmingham Evening Mail 4 Aug 71. But no one knew where a vulture, perched in a tree near Taunton, Somerset, came from. Not even the Zoos owned up to this one. It sat in that tree glaring balefully for 42 hours at the house of Mrs Roger Sleap. Perhaps it knew something she didn't - we presume it went after this for there is no further news. Daily Mirror 3 Sept 69. Credit:A Smith

Perhaps the vulture was an advance scout for the bird Demolition Corps getting ahead of the action for we have no casualties as yet. But in 1971 we have a couple of attacks. At Dover, Kent, a motorcyclist and his girl passenger were attacked by a seagull in the market square. The girl was taken to hospital for treatment after being pecked on the cheek. Daily Mirror 1 June 71. Credit: Anthony Smith. Then we hear of a "huge black crow with evil, staring eyes" that has terrorised the Yorkshire town of Dodworth, near Barnsley. It perches on a garage roof and swoops to attack, frightening children from two schools; attacking a 17-year-old girl, and a 12-year-old who beat it off with a chain; bitten a woman's fingers, and sent a man fleeing over a wall. Mrs Agnes Audin, whose daughter had to be treated for shock after a flutter, said: "It's a really huge crow with a wicked looking beak and evil, staring eyes. It dive-bombs anyone who goes past." Her daughter said: "It tried to land on my head. I tried to fight it off with my handbag, but it attacked me again and again as I ran off. I was absolutely terrified. At first people regarded the tales as a joke, but now no one will go near the lane." Police were said to be "looking into the matter", and the only help an RSPCA man could give was for someone to entice it into a shed and lock the door since killing birds is prohibited. Sunday Express 21 Nov 71. Again, we have heard nothing more of what happened next.

Nearer to the present time is a cutting from Mark Hall, about a male redwing blackbird that haunts the second tee of the Maquoketa County Club golf course in Iowa. He waits for humans to tee up, then dives out of the sun. "He's a pretty smart bird. He'll just sit there on the telephone line, and as soon as you turn your back, Boom! he's gotcha - right in the middle of the back." said club manager Ken Simmons. Des Moines (Iowa) Register 15 June 74. Credit: Mark Hall. And lastly, for now, we have the boldest attack yet. A flock of crows, no doubt fed up with these ironbirds that chew up their brothers around airports, set about a three-seater plane still in flight, damaging its engine and forcing it to make an emergency landing. The plane came down at Maiquetia airport, Venezuela, with the birds still in pursuit. The plane's three occupants emerged shaken but unhurt. Saf Francisco Chronicle 18 July 74. · Credit: Loren Coleman.

Next issue we shall have a selection of stories about the more friendly engagements, mainly on the part of animals, not birds, who seem to have gone out of their way to rescue people and nice things like that.

egnarts

WHITE INDIAN TRIBE IN AMAZON JUNGLE.

If this story received any coverage in the UK press, it failed to come to our attention one way or another. A tribe of fair-haired, pale-skinned, blue-eyed Indians have been contacted and named after the Ipixuna river which runs through their 'territory' to meet the Xingu, itself a tributary of the mighty 'ocean-river' Amazon. From Brazil's National Indian Foundation (FUNAI) came an announcement that this portentious discovery was made by Raimundo Alives in December last year, and despite his detailed report with colour photos, FUNAI had not released the news because of their own scepticism. They dispatched an expedition under Helio Rocha, Commissioner of Amazon Affairs (a nice name for someone responsible for contact with new tribes: "Helio there, new tribes! We bring you Civilisation.), and a professional anthropologist to check out Alives's story. Alive had met only eight of the tribe, swimming in the Ipixuna, and though they spoke a completely strange language, it was established that there were about a hundred more back in the jungle. They appear to have very primitive customs; do not wear clothes; and have few ornaments. Meanwhile FUNAI have assigned more staff to study the new tribe, and prefer silence until they have some conclusions.

"The phenomena may be explained by the presence of whitemen in remote times, who might have stayed there and mixed with the Indian population," said Rocha. But Alives preferred another theory: "Despite the colour difference, they may belong to the Acurini group, which holds to common customs and lives in the same area. One of the white women we met was carrying her child in a roughly woven cotton sling - rudimentary cotton weaving is a technique peculiar to the Acurinis." Sources: San Francisco Chronicle, 2 Feb & 3 June 74; Milwaukee (Wisconsin) Journal, 1 June 74; Los Angeles Times, 2 June 74; Rochester (Minn.) Post-Bulletin, 10 July 74; Minneapolis (Minn.) Star, 19 July 74. Credit: Loren Cloeman, Mark Hall.

It won't be long, we feel, before we get claims identifying them as a 'Lost Tribe of Israel', or as degenerate survivors of the chauffers and mechanics of the Hot Rods of the Gods; St. Brendan/Quetzalcoatl's returning colonizers blown off course. But FUNAI have weathered such mysteries before, it seems - in 1973, a group of their workers found a tribe using pots and pans stamped "Made in the People's Republic of China." !!!

* * *

don't ignore it.
SEND IT IN TO THE NEWS.
but please remember . . .
to note: the SOURCE;
the DATE; &
your name (for the credit).

'ARK'-EOLOGY IN A TURKISH BIZARRE.

The Silly Season they call it - the Press whoops with joy and descends en masse on some unsuspecting madness. The morning of 23 Feb - the sussuration of eyebrows going up at the breakfast-table - crazy Yanks out hunting the Ark - but there it was.

The Daily Mail told of Senator Frank Moss telling the Senate Space Committee (of which he is Chairman) that the Earth Resources Technology Satellite (ERTS) had photographed, from 450 miles out, some foreign matter, 14,000 ft up the NE side of Mt. Ararat near the Turkish/Russian border. "It's about the right size and shape to be the Ark," he said, leaving us wondering how he can be so sure

about such things. Further identification would be forthcoming, he added, when photos from Skylab 3 were eventually processed - though in the coverage during the following weeks, not a mention is given to the Skylab 'proof'. The Daily Mail does not mention Dr. Montgomery. (1) In the Daily Express virtually identical statements are made but credited to Dr John Montgomery, a divinity professor, who, it is said, will lead an expedition to recover pieces of Noah's bad parking. No mention of Senator Moss. (2). If Dr Montgomery looks like making a fool of himself, at least he will be a qualified fool, since he is given a pedigree - no less than 7 degrees and 14 books are cited as evidence that if he's taking it seriously there must be something in it.

The US coverage was wider and deeper. A month later, Henry Morris, of Creation Research Institute, California, announced his intention to race for the Ark; the first expedition, he says, since one led by RE Crawford and Fernand Navarra in 1969, in which some ancient timbers were found preserved in a glacier. (3). And the Turkish Government steps in, proclaiming that from now on they will ban, for security reasons, tourist visits to the Ararat area. Since Morris claimed to already have his permit, the odds are going up for Dr Montgomery. (4).

After more weeks of silence, there is a flurry of activity. Much has been going on behind the scenes. According to an article by Russel Chandler, six more groups have declared their intentions, scrabbling to get permits. He interviewed Eryl Cummings, "grand old man of arkeology", who talked of 31 assaults on Ararat since 1961, seven of which included himself, and two, Dr Montgomery. (5). And there had at least been one in 1960, when an American team returned bearing only conflicting interpretations of a boat-shaped depression that some less romantic (or disillusioned) searcher attributed solely to fortuitous landslides. And Fort even recorded that upon 25 April 1892, Archdeacon Nouri climbed Ararat in the hope that he would find something. Fort comments that he did indeed find something. Exactly what, is not detailed, so you will have to look up 'English Mechanic, 56-184'. (6).

The most vociferous of the eight groups out to vindicate the Old Testament, is one led by Tom Crotser. His envoys in Turkey were said to be arranging their fifth trip. On one of the previous trips, he said, they found pieces of 'gopher wood' which were carbon-dated to "4 or 5 thousand years old. Man, there's 70,00 tons of gopherwood up there." (7). He then plans to turn a mere triumph into an ultimate demolition job on the credibility of modern science, by trekking 400 miles away to Mt Nimrud, where he will discover the Tower of Babel. (8). "The greatest discovery of the age will prove beyond a shadow of a doubt that the Bible is totally true." (9). The devoutly Moslem Turks are not amused to a man. They stress in early July: "We have not given permission yet to any group, and we do not intend to do so." - So there! (10).

Quite apart from questions of if and when there ever was an Ark, in the Biblical form or not; and irrespective of conclusive and conflicting evidence for the Biblical Flood, either local or universal (in 2000BC, as Dr Albright maintains (5)); and despite any identification of what the Bible calls 'gopher-wood', and the acknowledged vagaries of the carbon-dating techinique, etc; and (most damning of all) ignoring the more ancient and equally (if not more) valid Islamic tradition, recorded in the Koran and derived from Babylonian and Sumerian accounts, that the Ark came to rest on a smaller mountain, Judi Dag, in the 'far north ' of their world...despite all these and other considerations, implicit and dogmatic faith in Noah's Ark, the Tower of Babel and other such notions, continue to spring eternal in the hearts of fanatics. Cecil B DeMille has much to answer for.

Are they cranks? and who are we to be so superior? If they did come up with something it would create a most interesting situation - but all they have proved so far is that some of them have some pieces of old wood. And yet! - Navarra recovered some items in a 1955 trip - several worked planks of oak and an L-shaped beam, beneath a glacier where he claims the Ark rests. They were dated by UCLA as 1250 years old. Wood from his 1969 search was put at between 1500 and 1600 years - not old enough to tally with the Ark-myth, but old enough to be planted by some ancient jokers with a weird sense of humour and foresight. But there are doubts on these datings. Labs in Madrid, Paris and Bordeaux thought the

samples had been contaminated with Carbon-14 in the analysis, and put them nearer "5000 years", certainly "of great antiquity".(5). If not bits of Ark - then what? But there, for the moment, the mystery resides - the Press having gone on to matters of immediate concern, and the Turks effectively dampening our Arkeologist's ardour.

We think Fort should have the last, and probably the most sensible, word: "I accept that anybody who is convinced that there are still relics upon Mt Ararat, has only to climb Mt Ararat, and he must find something that can be said to be part of Noah's Ark, petrified perhaps. The meaning that I read in the whole subject is that, in this Dark Age we are living in, not even such rudimentary matters as the shape of this earth have ever been investigated, except now and then to support somebody's theory." (6).

1) Daily Mail, 23 Feb 74. Credit: Steve Moore.
2) Daily Express, 23 Feb 74. Credit: S Moore.
3) St Louis (Missouri) Post-Dispatch, 31 March 74. 18A. Credit: Mark Hall.
4) San Francisco Chronicle, 23 April 74. Credit: Loren Coleman.
5) Atlanta Journal & Constitution, 9 June 74, 18B. Credit: Mark Hall.
6) New Lands - Charles Fort. Ch.VI. (1923).
7) San Francisco Examiner, 29 June 74. Credit: Loren Coleman.
8) Winnipeg (Man.) Free Press, 3 July 74. Credit: Mark Hall.
9) Atlanta Journal & Constitution, 18 July 74, 7B. Credit: Mark Hall.
10) Windsor (Ontario) Star, 6 July 74. Cr: M Hall.

© 1985 Fernando Krahn

falls

FALL OF BRICK-PIECES : MADRAS 1921.

We have some pleasure in bringing you the following item, which by most accounts of stones observed falling in restricted places (eg. from the ceiling of a room) or from undetected origins (see the cases which follow this one) is remarkable because unlike them it is highly suggestive of the mechanism of teleportation - that is, we learn a little bit more than is hidden and glossed over in the vague and dismissive term 'poltergeist'.

The main credit should go to Stefan Mucha who sent us this transcript of a question-and-answer session , the answers being given by a character called 'The Mother' who is a leading disciple of the late Sri Aurobindo. It concerns a well witnessed fall of pieces of brick in the buildings of the Ashram, in Pondicherry, Madras - an event which is said to have occurred "sometime in the middle of December, 1921." And the transcript is from the 'Bulletin of Sri Aurobindo International Centre of Education' for February 1974.

Stefan pointed out that Fort mentions a similar case: "Madras Mail, March 5, 1888 - pieces of brick that, in the presence of many investigators were falling in a schoolroom, in Pondicherry." (LO! Ch IV.) Either Fort made an uncharacteristic error of some magnitude, or we have two quite seperate events which repeat their main details. We have no means of checking on this at the present and would be grateful if any of you could throw any light on this interesting case.

--   --   --   --

YOU HAD SAID YOU WOULD TELL US THE STORY OF THE STONES.

That is quite another domain. That's not the domain of death; it is a domain of the material vital, that which controls the physical - the material vital. There was a time when we were living in the 'Guest House' (1). Sri Aurobindo lived on the first floor, in the room right at the end which is now the meditation-room of the 'Boarding'. I believe there are two rooms side by side, one used to be a bathroom but is now an ordinary room, and a room next to it which was mine - the bathroom and another room. Sri Aurobindo was on one side.

How many of us were there in that house?..Amrita was there {turning to disciple}, weren't you, Amrita? Do you remember that day? {Laughter}. We had a cook called Vatel. This cook was rather bad tempered and didn't like being reproved about his work. Moreover he was in contact with some Musulmans who had it seems, magical powers - they had a book of magic and the ability to practise magic. One day, this cook had done something very bad and had been scolded (I don't know if any of you knew Datta, it was Datta who had scolded him) and he was furious. He had threatened us, saying: "You will see, you will be compelled to leave this house." We had taken no notice of it.

Two or three days later, I think, someone came and told me that stones had fallen in the court-yard - a few stones, three or four: bits of brick. We wondered who was throwing stones from the next house. We did exactly what we forbid children to do: we went round on the walls and roofs to see if we could find someone or the stones or something, we found nothing.

That happened, I believe, between four and five in the afternoon. As the day declined, the number of stones increased. The next day, there were still more. They started striking the door of the kitchen specially and one of them struck Datta's arm as she was going into the courtyard. The number increased very much. The interest was growing. And as the interest grew, it produced a kind of effect of multiplication! And the stones began falling in several directions at the same time, in places where there were neither doors nor windows. There was a staircase, but it had no opening in those days: there was only a small bull's-eye. And the stones were falling in the staircase this way { vertical gesture}; if they had come through the bull's-eye, they would have come like this {slantwise movement}, but they were falling straight down. So, I think, they all began to become truly interested.

I must tell you that this Vatel had informed us that he was ill and for the last two days (since the stones had started falling) he hadn't come. But he had left his under-cook, a young boy of about thirteen or fourteen, quite fat, somewhat lifeless, a little quiet, and perhaps a little stupid. And we noticed that when this boy moved around, wherever he went the stones increased. The young men who were there (Amrita was among them) shut the boy up in a room, with all the doors and windows closed. They started making experiments {shouting}: "Close all the doors, close all the windows." And there was the boy sitting there inside and the stones began falling, with all the doors and windows closed! And more and more fell, and finally the boy was wounded in the leg. Then they started feeling the thing was going too far.

I was with Sri Aurobindo: quietly we were working , meditating together. The boys cast a furtive glance to see what was going on and began warning us, for it was perhaps time to tell us that the thing was taking pretty serious proportions. I understood immediately what the matter was.

I must tell you that we had made an attempt earlier to exhaust all possibilities of an ordinary, physical explanation. We had called in the police, informed them that there was somebody throwing stones at us, and they wanted very much to come and see what was happening. So a policeman - who was a fine good fellow - immediately told us: "Oh! You have Vatel as your cook! Yes, yes, we know what it is!" He had a loaded pistol and stood waiting in the courtyard - not a stone! I was on the terrace with Sri Aurobindo; I said to Sri Aurobindo: "That's a bit too bad. We call the police and just then the stones stop falling! But that is very annoying, in this way he will think we haven't told the truth, for no stones are falling." Instantaneously the stones began falling again { laughter}.

You should note that the stones were falling quite a way off from the terrace and not one of them came anywhere near us. So the policeman said: "It's not worthwhile my staying here. I know what it is. It is Vatel who has done this against you. I am going." It was after this that we made the experiment of shutting up the boy and the stones began to fall in the closed room, and I was informed the boy was wounded. Then I said: "All right, send the boy out of the house immediately. Send him to another house, anywhere, and let him be looked after, but don't keep him here, and then, that's all. Keep quiet and don't be afraid." I was in the room with Sri Aurobindo and I thought: "We'll see what it is." I went into meditation and gave a little call. I said: "Let us see who is throwing stones at us now? You must come and tell us who is throwing stones." I saw three little entities of the vital, those small entities which have no strength and just enough consciousness confined to one action - it is nothing at all; but these entities are at the service of people practising magic. When people practise magic they order them to come and they are compelled to obey.(2) There are signs, there are words. So they came. They were frightened, they were terribly frightened! I said: "But why do you fling stones like that? What does it mean, this bad joke?" They replied: "We are compelled, we are compelled...{laughter}It is not our fault. We have been ordered to do it; it is not our fault."

I really felt so much like laughing, but still I kept a serious face and told them: "Well, you must stop this, you understand!" Then they told me: "Don't you want to keep us? We shall do all that you ask." "Ah!" I thought. "Let us see. This is perhaps going to be interesting." I said to them: "But what can you do ?" "We know how to throw stones." {laughter}. "That doesn't interest me at all; I don't want to throw stones at anyone...But could you perchance bring me flowers? Can you bring me some roses?" Then they looked at each other in great dismay and answered: "No. We are not made for that. We don't know how to do it." I said: "I don't need you , go away, and take care specially never to come back for otherwise it will be disastrous!" They ran away and never came back.

There was one thing I had noticed: it was only at the level of the roof that the stones were seen, from the roof downwards we saw the stones just till the roof; above it there were no stones. That meant it was like an automatic formation. In the air nothing could be seen - they materialised in the atmosphere of the house and fell.

And to complete the movement, the next morning (all of that happened in the evening), the next morning I came down to pay a visit to the kitchen - there were pillars in the kitchen - and upon one of the pillars I found some signs with numbers as though made with a bit of charcoal, very roughly drawn, and also words in Tamil. Then I rubbed out everything carefully, and made an invocation, and so it was finished - the comedy came to an end.

However not quite. Vatel's daughter was 'ayah' in the house, the maid-servant. She came early in the afternoon in a state of intense fright saying "My father is in the hospital, he is dying. This morning something happened to him; suddenly he felt very ill and he is dying. He has been taken to the hospital, I am terribly frightened." I knew what it was. I went to Sri Aurobindo and said to him: "You know, Vatel is in the hospital, he is dying." He looked at me and smiled: "Oh! Just for a few stones!" {laughter} That very evening Vatel was cured. But he never started anything again.

HOW COULD THE STONES BE SEEN?

That's what is remarkable. There are beings that have the power of dematerialising and rematerialising objects (3). These were quite ordinary pieces of bricks, but these pieces materialised only in the field where the magic acted. The magic was practised for this house, specially for its courtyard, and the action of the vital forces worked only there. That was why when I sent the boy away and he went to another house, not a single stone hit him any more. The magical formation was made specially for this house, and the stones materialised in the courtyard. And as it was something specially directed against Datta, she was hit on her arm.

There was yet something else...Ah, yes! We came to know later which magician Vatel had gone to. He had gone to a magician who, it seems, is very well known here and had said he wanted definitely to make us leave that house - I don't know why. He was furious and so he asked the magician to make stones fall there. The magician told him: "But that's the house Sri Aurobindo lives in!" He said: "Yes." "Ah, no! I'm not going to meddle in this business; you manage it, I'm not going to be involved." Then Vatel insisted very much; he even promised him a greater reward, a little more money. The magician said: "Well, look here; we're going to make a rule: in a circle of twenty-five metres around Sri Aurobindo," (I think he said twenty or twenty-five metres) "the stones will not fall. Always there will have to be twenty-five metres between the stones and Sri Aurobindo." And he arranged his order of magic in this way. And that was why never did a single stone come anywhere near us, never. They fell at the other end of the courtyard.

They know how to do that, it is written in their books. These are words and ceremonies having a certain power. Naturally those who do that must have a vital force. A vital force is necessary - a little mental force also, not much, even very little - but quite a strong vital power and knowing how to control these little entities, govern them. And these people rule them just through fear, for they have the power to dissolve them, so these entities fear this very much. But upon all these formations, all these entities, it is enough to put simply one drop of   the true pure light, the pure white light - the true pure light which is the supreme light of construction - you put one drop upon them; they dissolve as though there had been nothing at all there. And yet this is not a force of destruction; it is a force of construction, but it is so alien to their nature that they disappear. It is this they feared, for I had called them by showing this white light, I had told them: "Look, there is this! Come!" But their offer was touching: "Oh! We shall do everything you want." "Good, what can you do?" - "Throw stones!" {laughter}

* * * * *

NOTES:

1) A note in the transcription indicated that Sri Aurobindo lived in the 'Guest House', 41 Rue Francois Martin (presumably in Pondicherry) between 1913 and Sept. 1922.

2) As the story and description of Vatel's psychic varmints unfolds, it struck us that there was a great degree of parity with the systems of magic used by the Polynesian Kahuna magicians, particularly from the neglected works of Max Freedom Long. Many Kahunas had (or inherited) "usually about three" spirit minions, which, being of a lower order of consciousness and particularly subject to strong hypnotic suggestion, could be 'charged up' with mana ("vital force") and sent to pester the chosen victims. Long records instances of such unihipili spirits manifesting as 'poltergeists' in each of his books, perhaps the most useful for general outline of the whole system of Kahuna magic being SECRET SCIENCE BEHIND MIRACLES published in 1948 originally by Long's 'Huna Research Association'. We in no way wish to come out 'for' or 'against' the existence of an occult technology - that is prejudging the issue to some extent, either way. We see our task as stimulating the questions, not as supplying any answers. We, for example, note the increase in activity around the boy-cook, but he did not seem essential. The motives were plainly there for the rogue, Vatel - but the boy was not implicated in his vendetta. If the boy was a catalyst for the action, would the 'magic' have worked if he were not there? Those 'spirits'bring a vast 'fall' of questions, too.

3) We hesitate to suggest that this parallel can be meaningfully prosecuted, but the Huna system of magic was in fact quite systematically codified and symbols enabled simplified formulae to be written down for 'transformations'. A wavy line was the symbol for the lowest form of 'vital force' or mana; a double wavy line was the energy of the 'middle self'; and a triple wavy line was the energy of the 'High self'. Long postulated a series of 'voltage transformations' in which the three forms could be raised or lowered into forms for a particular use. The 'High Self' was the part of a being credited with the power to do the actual transforming. In apporting an object or healing a broken bone, for example, the 'High Self' would amplify the low and middle 'voltages' using the power to dematerialise (increase its rate of 'vibration'?), transport, and then re-materialise the form using the coherent form of the 'shadowy body' as some kind of mould or pattern. Please see virtually the whole of Max Freedom Long's output for details and discussion

of 'vital forces', apport mechanisms and psychic fauna.

In fact, if any publishers are listening: since we should be becoming more conscious of the need to re-cycle rubbish, a new edition of SECRET SCIENCE BEHIND MIRACLES or SECRET SCIENCE AT WORK would be a darn sight more nourishing than many other quite tasteless literary roughages.

* * * *

'NIGHT PROWLER' STONES CITY FAMILY HOME.

Let's come a bit nearer to the present, where we have a few curious incidents. The Manchester Evening News for 6 May 69 carries a story that a 'mystery bombardier' has kept up a barrage of bricks, stones and milk bottles on the back of the Parr family's semi-detached council house. They had moved in just fourteen months previously to these hazardous hails, which start up at midnight. There is much 'angle' on the story about the family's shattered nerves and windows.

A few weeks later, the story hits the nationals: we take our notes from the Daily Mirror, 29 May. Ah! The police have moved into the drama {giggle} Constant searches and stake-outs have revealed nothing - It, 'The Night Prowler' as they call it, just doesn't perform when the bobbies are about. The Parrs, of Blandford Drive, New Moston, Manchester, are even more tense, not having slept decently , often waiting up to 2 or 3 in the morning before daring to go to bed, since the rumpus began. Some nights, it is reported, the 'Prowler' struck as many as three times, and many windows have been broken during the period. The police state, rather blandly: "We have had reports of malicious damage at this address and we are looking into the matter." The last anyone heard was the sound of the police 'looking'. Yet we ask ourselves how, on a small housing estate where these events over a considerable period of time could hardly be kept quiet (in all senses), did no neighbours ever see anything, or anyone, acting suspiciously? Perhaps it's not an anyone or anything we ought to be looking for. It may have no connection at all, but we note that the Parrs have two sons aged 10 and 12, and recall the role of pubescence as a catalyst in poltergeist cases. (Credit for both clippings to Peter Rogerson.)

NIGHT RAIDER HITS HOME WITH STONES.

Much the same kind of mystery, but now we have the frightened family of Roger Ansell, of The Street, Swallowfield, Berkshire, whose life has been made a misery by the unknown 'Night Raider' for the previous nine weeks. Despite close watches over that period they still cannot understand it all. No one around them bears them any grudges; nobody has seen anything suspicious, even in the midst of the attacks. Three children again.

Its time to use our little device for constructive asides - A police officer is reported as saying: "We know the side from where the stones are being fired. Now its just a matter of catching the man!" {chortle and choke} Well no prizes for guessing that even knowing 'the man's' hiding place hasn't helped them catch anyone. And, what was about 'fired'?? We have looked closely and have found no reports of a man, or something that may be masquerading as a man, lugging a giant catapult from Croyden to Swallowfield. Report from Sunday Express 28 April 74. Credit: RE Cotton and Steve Moore.

CATAPULT MAN' SCARES FAMILY.

This time its the Muir family of Allen Rd, Croyden: the date, from 23 Oct 73 for at least a week: the source, London Evening Standard 20 Oct 1973: the credit, John Brosnan.

I don't know if this picture will come out clearly but it shows James Muir looking through one of his smashed windows, holding one of the large stones, one of more than 150 that have broken 40 panes of glass over the period of activity. Again a family is described 'at wits end' with no idea why anybody should wage such a vendetta of vandalism against them. Muir has even given up his work driving lorries to comfort and somewhat ineffectively guard his family and home.

The police were called and despite an intensive hunt with tracker dogs, during which stones still shattered windows at the Muir home, they found nothing...not even a clue. The police theory was that there was a man hiding somewhere on the housing estate, lobbing these massive stones, probably with a "giant catapult" {guffaw}. If the agency was a man, they must have thought, he would have to be pretty near the house to hurl things of some weight - but he wasn't - thus by superlative police investigation and deduction they establish that there must be a man with a giant catapult somewhere on the estate. A spokesman said: "We have investigated this pretty thoroughly, and still have no clue. We have talked to residents in the area but they have seen nothing". See Fort's BOOK OF THE DAMNED Ch.13, and Ch.22 and elsewhere in WILD TALENTS for many cases of stones that have fallen or been thrown from undetectable sources.

Muir has three young children, but no information on their ages is given. We wrote to Muir but have not received a reply to date. We wrote to the local police to discover if they had 'aprehended' anyone yet - but received in return a terse mind-your-own-business note from Scotland Yard. We were pleased to have succeeded in getting some kind of reply at least.

* * *

IS SHOOTING FISH IN A BARREL, SPORT FOR GODS?

In the erratically chronicled history of objects falling (or being thrown?) from the sky, accounts of deaths from such causes are conspicuous by their absence. As William Porter commented in the last issue: "It is incredible to consider that over 20,000,000 meteors enter the atmosphere daily, at a speed of 45mpsecond. Despite this, no death has been recorded, attributable to a meteorite strike." (N5 p12.) That's twenty million daily; and all those people below. It might correspond in scale to the random movement of particles, where some thermodynamic processes like the transference or flow of heat 'depend ' on 'chance' collisions...and the action of chance throwing up a situation in which the number of collisions was near to zero. (No doubt I shall be hearing from some outraged physicists shortly).

But conversely, the number of reports which recount 'near-misses' by things falling from the sky are quite prominent. This is to be expected, but in turn underlines the fundamental question that, given situations with high proportions of 'near-misses', why are the number of 'hits' so startlingly low? Is an unknown factor operating on the random processes of chance to eliminate or prohibit certain configurations? We may never know the answer to this - and we certainly won't if we don't ask questions. But meanwhile we can continue to collect clues to the solution.

CAR ATTACKED BY SKY CULPRIT.

A story has come our way of a youth in Yorkton, Saskatchewan, who was driving, about a mile south of the town, when a molten substance fell out of the sky and onto his car, burning a hole through the the grill and melting into the windshield. The ground around the car was also struck, setting fire to the grass. The Royal Canadian Mounted Police confirmed the boy's story and identified the substance as 'meteorite'. Decatur (Illinois) Herald 9 June 74 - this incident happening on the friday 7th. Credit: Loren Coleman.

GIANT HAILSTONE INJURES GIRL.

Daily Mirror 20 Aug 71: that a hailstone as big as a grapefruit fell on the head of an 18-year-old girl, near Brive, France, seriously injuring her. Other hailstones, weighing up to 3lbs, crashed through the roofs of houses. A rare story.

Daily Mirror 24 Jan 72: that a 4ft-square block of ice crashed to the ground in Shirley, Surrey, on the 23rd, narrowly missing a house. It was believed to have 'fallen from an aircraft.' It is conceivable that ice falls from aircraft (see NEWS 3 p8 for a brief discussion) - but chunks of solid ice 4 foot square takes a lot of believing. Credit to Anthony Smith for both above.

Daily Express 10 Jan 73: a 10lb block of solid ice fell out of the sky and shattered Walter Bowden's front porch. Walter was at his home in West Wickham, Kent, with flu, when he heard an 'almighty crash'. "I rushed downstairs to find the place littered with broken ice and tiles. It's a miracle no one was hurt. If this block of ice had fallen on the house proper, it might have come right through." He collected some and preserved it in his fridge. Walter says he heard the sound of aircraft at the time, which is not surprising as his house is near where planes make the final turn to come into London Airport; in fact about 700 of them a day, according to an official of the Airport Authority. Walter's plans to pin the legal blame on a aircraft was nipped in the bud, since it was impossible to prove which one was responsible, or indeed if it had fallen from a plane at all. Our thought is that if ice does fall from aircraft, and 700 a day fly over that area, then why hasn't it happened more frequently there?

Above: Mr. and Mrs. Wildsmith examine their newly acquired car damaged by the falling ice. Mrs. Wildsmith is standing where she was washing the car when the ice landed. Below: a fragment of the 18 inch cube of ice that hit the car.

MYSTERY ICE MISSES WOMAN BY INCHES. (Photo, left).

Mrs N Wildsmith of 664 Rayners Lane, Pinner, Middlesex, was cleaning her car at 5.10pm, 25 March, when a 'cube' of ice, 18 inches square, crashed into it. At the same time roof tiles were smashed at 31 Marsh Rd, nearby. Eye-witness Mrs Doris Fox who lives next door to Mrs Wildsmith, said she was working in her garden when she saw "a huge white ball which looked as though it were making straight for me." She said she ducked as it went over, making a noise like a firework rocket - then heard the loud crash as it hit the car. "I thought it was a bomb, it was such a crack." Her husband, Albert, was also in the garden: "I thought their fridge had exploded through a window when I first looked up and saw all the ice over the car and path. Mrs Wildsmith was damn lucky - she was just a foot or two away from being killed." A bucket-full of shattered yellowy-brown ice was collected and stored in a deepfreeze to aid any future analysis. Over in Marsh Road, Miss Elsie Urquhart said she heard a loud bang and rushed out to find a neighbour looking at the ice, smashed tiles and plastic guttering. She too collected samples.

There is no record of any analysis being made, in fact the Civil Aviation Authority seemed to be aware of some futility, saying: "Analysis would not help trace where the ice came from, as most airlines now use the same liquids in sanitary and waste equipment." Normally its the wings icing up that gets blamed - this is the first suggestion we have come across, of aerial effluent. But the waste tanks are normally emptied on the ground - unless there was some seepage. If so, surely such a copious leak would render the offending craft readily identifiable? Again the CA Authority seemed reluctant to take things further, falling back on the same arguments as put to Walter Bowden (in the previous story), offering only a list of landing times, saying: "All the liability rests with the operator of the plane."

The spokesman added that only two cases had been recorded of ice falling from aircraft that winter - both near Gatwick Airport and without injury or damage. At a guess from a map of the northwest London area we would venture that the iceblock came down from the north-northwest. The nearest major airport is London-Heathrow, nearly south-southwest, so it is possible for something to have come off a plane on a turn to approach, and as it came into lower warmer air. But it does seem to us that this ice block had a peculiarly flat and low trajectory to come over quite a few rows of houses at rooftop level. And the extent of the damage to the car (see photo) suggests a pretty smallish impact from something falling from the sky, whatever the trajectory. There is enough fresh data here for any enterprising reader to do an analysis of the event. We'd like to see that , and will help in any way if anyone should take it on. The details are from the Harrow Observer for 29 March 74. Credit: Carl Grove.

Cont/ p14.

'ARLINGTON BEAST' TERRIFIES WASHINGTON SUBURB.

An unidentifiable animal was reportedly responsible for the deaths of many small domestic animals during June, in northern Virginia, just across the Potomac river from Washington DC. the
depredations of the 'Arlington Beast' occurred
in the vicinity of a wooded hollow along Four
Mile Run, a tributary of the Potomac. Newspaper
accounts reflect the uncertain descriptions given
by observers - they said at various times that it
was a large animal, about 3 feet long with a hair
less tail 7 or 8 inches long; that it was as big
as a dog, with a stubby hairy tail; and that it
was thin, hairless, resembling a medium-sized dog
with no tail, and big teeth. It was active only
at night, but was readily recognizable, however,
by its whining, screeching, and shrieking sounds.
It was also reported to emit a high-pitched whine
or cackle or a 'shrieking laugh' after doing in
some small animal. The game warden for Arlington
County reported that two dogs and five cats were
attacked. Also, on 15 June the animal invaded a
rabbit hutch and killed 16 rabbits. Another person reported three rabbits killed and the hide
stripped from one. A peculiar feature of these
attacks is that none of the animals were killed
for food. One 15lb tomcat was attacked and died
7 days later - an autopsy revealed the attacker
was not rabid. At one point the 'Beast' was
caught in a small cage-trap, but it broke loose.
A second larger trap snared only a hungry German
shepherd, not the 'Beast'. The animal's screeching was not heard during the third week in June,
about the time it was actively hunted by local
officials with guns and dogs. On June 28, two
police detectives filed a report that said they
were unable to find any cats or dogs that were
attacked by any animal. (Perhaps they should have
interviewed some humans!) The headlines of the
Washington Post read, 'ARLINGTON MYSTERY CREATURE
NEVER WAS ', and officialdom had dispatched another mystery. Identifications of the animal,
meanwhile, continued, ranging from 'wolverine' to
'kangaroo' (!), with bob-cat being the most popular. But these activities are unusual for any
known animal, and the identity of the 'Beast'
remains a mystery (except, of course, to the
Arlington police and the Washington Post. Sources
Houston (Texas) Chronicle 21 June 74. Washington
(DC) Star-News 21 & 22 June 74. Northern Virginia
Sun (Arlington, Va.) 22 June 74. Washinton (DC)
Post 22 June & 2 July 74.

The inevitable happened. Almost a month after the
depredations of the 'Beast' ceased, an exotic
animal was captured three miles from the site of
the mystery. Arlington police, who had formerly
denied the existence of any mystery beast, said:
"We do not relate the animal to the unidentified
animal reported several weeks ago in south Arl-

ington." This time they were probably right. Civet cats do not scream - they growl and cluck
under stress. And so this male civet, the mark of
a collar indicating he had been somebody's pet,
dozed peacefully in a cage at the National Zoo
after being chased by policemen for one hour on
11 July. Once more the 'Beast' remains a mystery.
Washington (DC) Star-News 12 July 74. Washington
(DC) Post 12 July 74.

SWARMS.

An infestation of Norway rats was reported in
Carpentersville, Illinois, in early April. Chicago
Daily News 3 April 74, and Los Angeles Times 4
April 74. -- Locusts were reported swarming for
two weeks near Old Fort, North Carolina. Houston
(Texas) Chronicle 14 May 74. -- Fire ants report-
ed on the march from eastern regions of Texas,
toward the Rio Grande in June. Houston (Texas)
Chronicle 14 June 74. -- Field mice (Microtus
californicus) invaded San Jose, California, in
June, the worst outbreak there in eight years.
San Francisco Chronicle 21 June 74. -- Forest
Tent caterpillars were five inches deep in one
woman's yard, as they swarmed near Alonsa, Manitoba, in June, in massive conglomerations several
miles across. Atlanta (Georgia) Constitution 21
June 74. Los Angeles Times 21 June 74. Winnepeg
Free Press 26 June 74.

UFOs OVER :-

Griswold, Connecticut, for a period of six months
Norwich (Ct) Bulletin 7 April 74. -- Fairmont,
Minnesota, on 9 April. Sentinel (Fairmont, Mn)
10 April 74.

UFOs identified: Flashing lights from an aerial
billboard caused UFO reports near St. Louis. St.
Louis (Missouri) Post-Dispatch 26 April (p1C.) &
6 March (p1B). -- Sixty silver iodide flares
dropped by professional rainmakers generated reports around Drumheller, Alberta. Winnipeg Free
Press 24 May 74 (p15.)

UFOs hunted: Fifteen magnetometers intended as
UFO detectors are said to be in the homes of
scientists and engineers scattered around San
Diego county, California. Research psychologist
JF Herr, spokesman for a group of 35 people, also
said other sensing devices will be used in their
study. San Francisco Examiner 22 March 74 (p28.)

A DOG THAT WAITS.

By mid-April a shy dog, marked like a collie but
smaller, had spent five weeks sitting daily by a
busy intersection in Conyers, Georgia. A nearby
service station owner fed the dog but could not
make friends with the animal. The dog seemed to
be waiting for the owner who had probably left it
there. It chased tan-coloured automobiles for a

short distance and then returned to wait at the intersection. Atlanta (Georgia) Constitution 4 April (8A) & 18 April (25A).

OVERHEADS.

Shortly after 9.00pm on 14 June, a Washington newspaperman watched a ball of fire move slowly and silently overhead,from his Kensington, Maryland, home. Later he heard a meteor had passed by but a spokesman for NICAP did not think it was a meteor. For them the matter was still 'under investigation." Washington (DC) Star-News 17 June (pB1) & 19 June 74 (pB1). -- Explosions and a spectacular flash of light were reported seen and heard on 1 July from parts of Utah, Arizona, Nevada, and California. The airport tower at Santa Barbara, Calif., placed the light south and east of that city. Houston (Texas) Chronicle 2 July 74 (1-14). -- Something meteor-like passed over Florida the night of 8 July, and may have landed (watered?) in Lake Okeechobee. Paul Harvey News 9 July 74.

'MASS HYSTERIA'.

If you believe in 'mass hysteria' you can dismiss the plight of the tykes at the Bay Harbor Elementary School in Florida. On 13 May, 39 of them suffered nausea, vomiting and fainting. Eight of those went into hospital and the rest went home. One doctor called this a case of 'mass hyperventilation', while another said the children's symptoms indicated exposure to a toxic gas. Repeated checks of water, air and air-conditioning ducts revealed nothing.

The trouble began when one girl in the cafeteria became ill. She went to the school clinic. Another class then entered the cafeteria and the problem began en-masse when several of them became sick. One eleven-year-old boy felt fine until, as he helped other students into cars on their way home, he felt stomach pains and immediately fainted. His mother took him home where he passed out again and then went to hospital. He had trouble sleeping that night, and the next day he still had the pains in his stomach. The classes were not in the cafeteria to eat, but only for a music lesson. Their teacher said that two weeks earlier she had felt faint there herself. Miami (Florida) Herald 14 & 15 May 74.

Previously on 27 April, a similar incident occurred in Thornhill, Ontario. 28 girl hockey-players aged 13 to 14 were taken to hospitals suffering from dizziness and nausea. Police and fire officials professed to be baffled. Gas checks were again negative, but the dressing-room was found to be stuffy. "It could have been a lack of oxygen," said a police sergeant. Toronto (Ontario) Star 29 April 74. -- This must be the season for these problems, because on 28 June, a secondary school in Tabora, Tanzania, was closed due to an outbreak of 'laughing disease'. 47 girls, crying and laughing were all hospitalised. Minneapolis (Minn.) Star 29 June 74. -- When 9 women in Concepcion, Argentina, showed symptoms of 'mass hysteria', their neighbours thought they knew why, according to the Buenos Aires newspaper La Razon.

They tried to lynch a local mystic, Fu Man Chu, but he was given police protection. Atlanta (Georgia) Journal & Constitution 30 June 74.

GATCH, THE BALLOONIST.

The last accepted sighting of the gondola and balloons of the missing Tom Gatch is the report of the freighter 'Ore Meridian', made on 21 Feb 74. (see NEWS 4, p7. and NEWS 5, p9.) On 27 Feb Spanish news agencies Cifra and Europa Press, reported that thousands of people saw Gatch's balloon about 8am. over the Oratava Valley on the island of Tenerife. Only one balloon was seen, (not the cluster of eight reported on the 21st.) and was described as both blue, and rose-coloured, heading south-southwest at 3000 to 9000 feet.

Colonel Gatch climbs into the gondola of his balloon

These reports could not be supported, and later explanations included 'weather balloon', 'optical illusion', and 'a freak dust storm'. (1,2.) Nothing more has been printed about the air search made on 30 March in the vicinity of Guadeloupe island, but friends of the Gatch family searched for two days in that same area as advised by a Virginia psychic and found nothing. (3) The reward offered by the family has brought no results, but the family still hope Gatch may be found. And American ships participating in a weather study have been asked to watch for the floating gondola or balloons in the south Atlantic. (4). One coast-guard veteran sees the path and landfall of the floating balloon system this way. The balloon cluster would be off Puerto Rico during July; off Florida late in the summer; then travelling northward, crossing the north Atlantic, finally bearing down on the British Isles and possibly an Irish beach. (5). Sources: 1) Denver

(Colorado) Post 28 Feb 74. 2) Los Angeles Times 28 Feb 74. 3) Washington (DC) Star-News 1 July 74. 4) Rochester (Minn.) Post-Bulletin 15 July 74. 5) Washington (DC) Star-News 2 July 74.

GREAT 'INDIAN BATHTUB' MYSTERY.

Forest rangers and archaeologists have puzzled for years over the origin and meaning of depressions in rock, found in remote areas of Tulare County, California. The rock depressions, usually three feet across and 3½ to 4 feet deep, are situated in small groups at thirty different places near mountain peaks. All sites show signs of past Amerindian habitation, but present-day Amerinds can't give a clue as to how the holes were used. Speculation has included the idea that they were tubs for fermenting some unidentified plant, and the possibility of communal baths. Hence the rangers call this the 'Great Indian Bathtub Mystery'. Los Angeles Times 20 June 74.

HARD STUFF.

The UFO panel of the National Enquirer is puzzled by a piece of metal with a specific gravity of 14.9, denser than carbide and second only to diamond in hardness. The dense metal came from two Sewdish carpenters who say they found it after a UFO encounter near Stockholm in 1958. The National Enquirer 9 June 74 (p4.). Curiously enough, an engineering researcher at UCLA, Prof. Rointan F Bunshah, has just announced the development of "the second hardest material in the world, after diamonds." He calls it titanium carbide. Milwaukee (Wisconsin) Journal 19 April 74

COYOTE ATTACKS WORRY TOWN.

On the outskirts of Los Alamos (New Mexico) two girls were attacked by a coyote as they slept in sleeping-bags in their front yard. The father of one of the girls, James R Conn, said: "I can name incident after incident of people and animals attacked by coyotes here lately. People are run into their houses." Conn said the attack on the girls ceased when a neighbor heard their screams and came to investigate. "The neighbor said the coyote backed off when it saw him. But it just walked out into the middle of the street and calmly stood there, just watching to see what would happen."

Police say they see coyotes on city streets in early morning hours. "They'll come right up to the car, just like a pet dog. They aren't afraid of people at all, " said police Sgt. JR Keane. George Adamson of the State Fish & Game Department said that in 34 years with the agency he had never heard of a coyote attacking a human before. He theorized the behavior might be attributed to lack of food, the encroachment of humans into their former habitation, and predator control laws that restrict methods of killing coyotes "I can't figure out what's happening, " he says. Milwaukee (Wisconsin) Journal 4/9, 14 April 74.

■■■■■■■■■■■■■■■■■■■■■■■■■■■■■■■■

REMEMBER TO RENEW <u>YOUR SUB</u> SOON

See notes on page 2, for the new rates...Thanks.

ICE SMASHES HOUSE ROOF.

A piece of ice the size of a rugby ball burst through the roof of 77 Buckingham St, Scunthorpe, Lincs, while the occupants were downstrairs watching TV. Miss Doris Coult said they heard "two big bangs - and I thought it was a thunderbolt." Clarence Coult and his friend Frank Walker rushed upstairs and found a lump of ice, over a foot long, on the floor of Mr Walker's bedroom. It had broken through the roof and the ceiling. "We wondered if it came from an aeroplane - it was just ice. There was no metal or stone in it. We put it in the bath and it all melted away. It might seem funny now, but at the time it was quite frightening." The police were called, and though it's plain there is little they can do in such cases, this lot didn't help matter by pointing out that all the evidence had gone down the plug-hole.

Mr. Frank Walker inspects the damage to his ceiling.

Nigel Watson, who sent us this story, points out that the address in virtually in the town centre, and if any planes had thus strayed from accepted flightpaths then somebody ought to be responsible. But again, no clear evidence to like the matter to aircraft once and for all - except of course that it came down from up there. As Fort wrote in BOOK OF THE DAMNED : " Of all the meteorites in museums, very few were seen to fall. It is considered sufficient ground for admission if specimens can't be accounted for in any other way than that they fell from the sky - as if in the haze of uncertainty that surrounds all things, or that is the essence of everything, or in the merging away of everything into everything else, there could be anything that could be accounted for in only one way." The story is from the Scunthorpe Evening Telegraph 12 Aug 74; and the incident was on 10 Aug. (Please see NEWS 3 for further accounts of ice-falls.)

* * *

FALL OF MYSTERY ANIMAL.

We have accumulated a few notes on animals of
various sorts falling out of the sky, and we'll
include them here and make a bumper 'fall' issue.
Anders Liljegren, an active UFO researcher in
Sweden, sent us the following translation of a
record of a very curious event. "Bishop Rhyzelius
of Linköping, Sweden, wrote in 'Brontologia Theo-
ligico-historica', 1721, about a thunderstorm in
August 1708, when a strange animal fell from the
sky into a street of Norrköping. A number of eye-
witnesses described the animal as "like a beaver"
with a "big lower jaw", "small eye", a "short
backbone" and "brownish in colour". Everyone
thought it was a troll (old Scandinavian mythic(?)
creature) coming down from the sky." Source:
Norrköpings Tidningar 4 Aug 69. A certain ambig-
in the letter leads us to think that is <u>1869</u> and
not 1969; but we'll check on this.

FLYING FISHES.

River bailiffs have been told a fishy tale about
a mystery angler who made off with a 10lb salmon.
He was seen by late-night fishermen Bill Treen &
Bernard Bodmin, by the harbour at Poole, Dorset,
when a fish hit the man's head and fell into his
lap. They suppose the fish leapt from the harbour
- but it is questionable how they could determine
that, let alone its species in the darkness. Not
that we could tell any more than that. We only
consider it in the light of the many stories we
have (see Fort and previous issues) on fishes
that fall from the skies singly or in vast quantity, or they simply 'appear' where they were not
before. Above story from Sun 18 July 73. Credit:
Anthony Smith.

A TURNIP FOR THE BOOKS.

Recently we received the following letter from
Peter Roberts, a friend and Fortean: "I thought
of something Fortean the other day. My life has
been, so I always thought, singularly uneventful-
no midnight mutilations or manifestations of horses, nor even a spot of black rain. However, I
suddenly remembered the Falling Fish Incident
which may be quasi-Fortean in nature. One morning
in the summer of 1961 or 62 I noticed an object
lying in the garden. It looked like a turnip and I
didn't bother to investigate (though a fallen
turnip should have aroused curiosity). About two
hours later, my aunt went out with some washing,
came back, and said would I throw the dead fish
on the lawn in the dustbin. Still no activity on
my part. An hour later, about noon, I was reminded of the job with menaces, so I went out with a
shovel, prodded the fish, stirring it into unexpected life. A two gallon bucket was filled with
water and I stuck the fish in it, where it promptly started to splash around actively. Since it
was too big for the bucket I transferred it to
an old washing tub. One fin was off, otherwise it
was intact and unscarred.

"Now we do have a small ornamental fishpond and
the logical explanation offered by my grandmother
was that it had jumped out. Since the pond contained only small goldfish and the occasional newt

this was unlikely. (It wasn't deep and we did
stocktaking when we cleaned it out every few
years or so.) Not being an expert on fish, I
couldn't identify it, though it looked like a
straightforward freshwater kind. The nearest
river must be the Avon, about two miles away.
Explanation? Umm...seagull? I didn't know fish
could survive that long - especially in sunlight
on a mown lawn. We kept it till evening when we
took it to a nearby brook (about 200 yards) and
chucked it in. The brook is shallow and pretty
polluted, though it did harbour sticklebacks. It
certainly couldn't have produced a fish that size
(and it wasn't in flood or anything). A fish that
jumped over eight houses and a main road would
be a marvel in its own right, anyway. So it goes!"

The loss of the fin puts us in mind of the 'wounded' salmon that was discovered where no salmon
was the night before, (see NEWS 3 p5) where the
'dropped by a bird' theory is also ventured (and
it seems half-heartedly). Did it come from the
sky in the first place? Does anyone know of an
authoritative observation of a bird carrying a
fish far inland and then dropping it? Since this
theory, like the aeroplanes for falling ice, and
the whirlwinds for falls of frogs and periwinkles,
is trotted out every time we discover a fish in
an unlikely place, we would like to know its orthodox pedigree.

THE DAY IT RAINED PELICANS.

This time we have witnesses who saw the doomed
creatures plunge out of the sky. The giant white
pelicans were migrating inland from their winter-
on the Gulf Coast, and flying over Texas at the
time, on 13 April. "They looked like whitecaps
falling from the sky," said Leo Lyons, who saw
90 of the majestic birds dashed onto the waters
of Lake Waco. 33 other pelicans fell at Cranfills
Gap that same day. Those that fell at Lake Waco
could not be retrieved until the next day because
of storms there. Boaters on the lake found some
of them swimming around aimlessly, and 12 of them
had broken wings. The birds that fell at Cranfills
Gap showed no sign of being battered, though Waco
Game Warden Butch Young said: "They were apparently soaring at great heights, and of course, when
they hit the ground it was instantaneous death."

Scientists theorised that the birds may have been
caught in a tornado (a twister had been in the
Lake area that day, though there is no information about their respective times), or that a loud
noise, like a roll of thunder, had upset their
equilibrium (again, the report adds that thunderstorms 'roamed' the area). The question we would
like to ask is that if this was the case, why is
there no mention of any other birds falling in
the same areas? Is this the same selective force
that seems to operate on the frogs and fishes,
precipitating showers of things of the same
species or size or age ; that keeps seperate
ponds in the Super Sargosso sea floating above
us? And again,if those theories were so,why does
it not happen more often wherever there are birds
and thunderstorms? (See Fort's various books for
accounts of birds dropping out of clear skies,

sometimes dazed, sometimes dead to a man bird(?). The above story was from the Detroit (Michigan) News 26 April 74. Credit: Mark Hall.

Mind your heads - and windows - that's all we can say, while we wait for a corelating genius to come along . There is no guarantee that these things - the falls and flows and apporting of things - will make any sense, no matter how many cases we collect. We feel that all we can see are trees - we need to step back to see the wood - only which direction is back? Where can we find a more complete way of looking - one that is not subjected to the fragmentation caused by our perceptual chauvinism rooted in linear 'time'. Answers on a postcard, please, to the Editor.....

fires

SMOKING CHAIRS CAN DAMAGE YOUR HEALTH.

It seems that the only method those impious 'library angels' are acquainted with is an erratic one: nothing for long stretches of time, then several items bunched together. In the past couple of months we have been sent four notes on combustions in, by or on armchairs - three of them involve deaths.

The first is from the Daily Mirror, 14 June 71, which describes the fate of a pair of £80 armchairs, bought by Maureen McGlynn of Botley Road, Oxford. One started to split slowly and noticeably though no one was sitting in it. Days later, smoke began to pour out of it and the green vinyl began to melt - and the other one was begining to show signs of damage. The more obvious ideas of the foam-padding combusting, or some odd focussing effect of sunlight through a window, do not appear to be the actual causes - and the scientists to whom such obviousness would occur confessed to remaining baffled - or rather, more baffled than when they set out -after four months of tests. A Consumer Group in Oxford took on the case, and they too could discover no faulty materials or workmanship - even experiments focussing sunlight failed to ignite the chair. Mrs McGlynn now keeps them well out of sunlight and away from her living room , just in case. Credit: A Smith. Also in Daily Mail of same date, Credit: Steve Moore.

San Francisco Examiner, 7 Feb 74 - that 'elderly' Purvis Mayweather, was found dead in his chair in front of a stove at 814 Henry St, Oakland, California; the upper half of his body was severely burned. Police assume that the stove flared up igniting his clothing. Credit: Loren Coleman. We are prompted to comment on the freakiness of such a supposed flare, to shoot out to the furthest part of the body away, and to remain there long enough to light his clothes. And why was the fire contained on his upper half? And why did he make no apparent move to escape or put it out? It's as though he were hypnotised into paralysis or otherwise oblivious to the pain and the flames, as we have observed before in similar cases.

Daily Mirror, 28 March 74 - that Mrs Elizabeth McPherson, 35, was found dead in a blazing armchair in her council flat at Nant Peris, Blacon,

Cheshire. Police were unable to discover any cause for the fire. Credit: DJ McAllister. We wrote to the Chester Coroner's office but have so far failed to receive any reply.

San Francisco Chronicle, 26 April 74 - that Eldon R Fronk (a name to conjure with), 80, was found dead on his blazing living room sofa, by his wife Elsie, in their home on 1807 33rd St, San Francisco. Elsie said he had been smoking just before she left him to go to the basement garage, where she was when she smelt something burning, and returned to find him engulfed in flames. Credit: Loren Coleman. In the presence of mystery, a commonplace is grasped upon. It is conceivable that there have been cases where careless smokers have set themselves alight - but usually some evidence can be found. In nearly all our cases the various experts including the verdicts of Coroners and Inquests there are assumptions where there is a lack of evidence - and where our victims were non-smokers, parafin stoves, or candles or matches are rather dubiously supposed and duly blamed. Our only interest is in possibilities: that there is reason to believe that there are cases where people have spontaneously combusted and that these cases go largely unrecognised because of conventional suppositions. But whether the data, or alleged data, presented here are in fact such cases must depend on further research and your own inclinations.

*   *   *

HOT'N'TOTS.

Daily Express, 21 Sept 70 - that baby Simon Simeon, 6 weeks, was said to be comfortable after being burned in his blazing pram at the Simeon home in Arme Avenue, Poole, the previous night. Police are claiming that, in the absence of any clue to the cause of the fire whatever, that this must have been a deliberate act. They don't say by who or even how. The kid's mother Brenda, 24, indicated that the baby was "in the room" (no statement about which one), and so, if they don't suspect the mother, they feel that someone entered the house. But again, there appears to be no evidence, not to mention a motive, for any breaking-in.

London Evening News, 9 March 74 - three young children (Cosmo, 4yrs; Deborah, 2 yrs; Nicole, 11 mths.) died in a mysterious fire in their home in Savage Gardens, East Ham, London; the baby in her cot, one kid half under the bed and the other near a window. It is believed they suffocated, but the cause of the fire, which was confined to the bed and was out by the time police arrived, eluded a thorough investigation by both Fire Prevention officers and Forensic experts. Credit: Nigel Watson.

Birmingham Evening Mail, 16 April 74 - Mr Tarsen Kainth saw smoke and heard screams from nextdoor in Unett Street, Smethwick, Staffs, and he dashed in to find a blazing pram in a corner of the living-room, and in it was 7-month-old Parvinder Kaur. "The room was filled with smoke. I covered my face and threw a bucket of water into the pram to put out the burning," he said. The baby's sisters, aged 2 and 3 years, were in the room and carried to safety. Their father was at a Sikh temple at the time, and the mother had only just left the house to see a neighbour, leaving the kids alone for a few minutes. Fire experts could come up with nothing, and could only suggest that the kids could have been playing with matches. Doctors were still fighting to save the life of the baby girl at the Burns Unit of the Birmingham Accident Hospital, two days after the 'accident', which happened on the 14th April.

Birmingham Evening Mail, 22 April 74 - a week after the previous story, the same Burns Unit is tending to Mark Bradbury, aged 7, who was seriously ill after sleeping through a fire, which was confined to his bed, burning through two mattresses and severely damaging his legs and feet. When he eventually woke, his screams attracted neighbours, in Grimley Terrace, Selly Oak, Birmingham, and his parents,who were sleeping downstairs, and four other children,were taken to safety. No specific cause was found and identified, but there is some supposition about a lighted candle toppling over.

Even as I finished typing the above, another story appears in the Birmingham Evening Mail, for 26 Aug 74. A six-month-old girl, Lisa Tipton, one of five children of the Tiptons, died in a fire in a downstairs living-room at their home in Tennyson Road, Highfields, Stafford. Firemen were called by neighbours who saw smoke coming from the house - the fire being confined to that one room was brought under control in 10 minutes. Mrs Tipton, who was in the house at the time, and apparently noticed nothing, was taken to hospital and treated for shock. Gas and electricity engineers checked appliances, and a police official said there were no suspicious circumstances indicated. No cause was identified for the fire, but a theory is forwarded: "A cushion is thought to have fallen onto an electric fire, caught fire and, in turn, set fire to the settee, on which the child was sleeping."

marine mysteries

WATERSPOUTS ON THE SOUTH COAST.

Waterspouts are pretty rare phenomena around the coast of the British Isles, and yet several popped up near the Isle of Wight (IoW) on the 18th August this year. The Master of the Hull-registered ship 'City of Athens', Mr Charles Hanson, radioed to coastguards in the Isle of Wight that he had just spotted a spout that could endanger small craft. It was heading towards land about 6 miles off St Catherine's Point, IoW. "It was about a hundred yards from us and looked like a solid column of water about 20 ft high; and there was a disturbance in the water around it like a hovercraft would make". The coastguard at Bembridge, IoW, said: "I've seen only one before. We

put out a warning because they can be very dangerous. They're like a smaller version of a tornado - once they form they move very quickly."

Later that day the Meteorological Office confirmed that several had been sighted along the coast from IoW to Peacehaven, Sussex. They added: "They are formed when there is a very low level cumulonimbus - the black stormcloud. They are started off by a column of cloud reaching down to the level of the sea - but they are comparitively rare outside the tropics." (1). Another report numbered four spouts - and indeed, there had been thundery rain lashing the south of England for most of that day (2). Cryptic notes in both reports commented on the highest tides for 100 years on the coast.

A UFO SPECTACULAR, INCLUDING A WATERSPOUT.

The only other spout-note we have (and our records are far from complete in this) was about a very dramatic affair in 1967. Lobster fisherman Bertram Stride was suddenly confronted by a 400ft giant as he checked his pots, two miles off Highcliffe, Hants, early on the morning of 18 July. It was travelling at about 10mph and heading for the Isle of Wight. "I looked up, and there it was - a vast curtain of water about half a mile away, as high as Salisbury Cathedral."

As in the recent case of the Llandrillo pseudo-meteorite, this curious event seemed to coincide with a breathtaking display of aerial lights, so much so that again, as in the Llandrillo affair, the two events were treated together in the press. At about the same period as Mr Stride confronted his spout (which must have sprung up quite fast if he hadn't noticed it before) almost overhead, airline pilots said, they saw "clusters of objects streaming trails of lights", and observers in Kent saw a "bright ball of fire" heading toward France.

Brussels radio reported that UFOs with green lights in front and trailing bright sparks were seen over Charleroi. The US Airforce admitted that brilliantly lit objects were seen at 3 bases in West Germany; Ramstein, Spangdahlem and Sembach; and that they looked like they had flames coming out of them. Hundreds of eye-witnesses all over Switzerland described the objects variously as round, cylindrical and cigar-shaped, and "apparitions of light", crossing over the country at high speed leaving a red luminous trail several miles long; the entire circus lasting a mere 50 seconds.(3).

The observatories were goaded into trotting out the same old explanation - except Geneva, who had a new one on us - that the last rays of the descending moon crossed electrically charged clouds. And the waterspout by implication, is nothing but an overworked coincidence. We, at least would

Cont/ p19

Nigel Watson begins a series of three articles on his researches among the ghosts of his home county. Besides being Chairman of the Scunthorpe UFO Research Society (SUFORS) Nigel maintains an active interest in all aspects of Fortean phenomena and has put in much time 'on location'.

NOTES ON LINCOLNSHIRE GHOST PHENOMENA -- --1

by NIGEL WATSON.

In the October of 1972, myself and three other members of SUFORS were able to arrange to visit Mrs Ethel Rudkin at her home in Toynton All Saints near Spilsby. We spent a very interesting evening as she related to us several interesting tales and stories (and even revealed to us that there had been a plan afoot to launch a UFO in our midst).

Her 'Lincolnshire Folklore', although first published in 1936 in a limited edition of 400 copies, still shows its worth by its re-publication in 1973 (1). It followed in the wake of Gutch and Peacock's 'County Folklore, Vol.V.', 1908, on Lincolnshire folklore. However instead of taking her sources of information from already published works, as did the previous authors, Mrs Rudkin talked to and interviewed the people themselves, obtaining their stories and beliefs first hand.

Unfortunately, most of the old beliefs and practices are now almost dead. They began steadily to die out at the turn of the century, with villages turning into industrial towns, better communications, and people having a whole new outlook on life. The new folklore is now the world-wide one of flying saucers replacing the Black Dogs (2).

In a county like Lincolnshire, many apparitions and ghosts have been reported. The place is littered with them. Can so many reports be subjective? During my inquiries I received two interesting letters from Mr Sidney Benton of Horncastle, both of which are reproduced in full below.

GREAT, SHINING EYES.

"It was during the winter months of 1922 or 1923, when I was employed at a small local dairy. My job was to fetch up the cows from the fields, help to milk them and then deliver it to local people.

Part of my deliveries took me to one of the oldest parts of town. I usually took a short cut by going past an old Iron Foundry, over a small bridge with a water-wheel near it, then by the back of the Vicarage and past the old churchyard. On this particular evening I had made my deliveries and had just climbed over the small wooden palings on my way back to the dairy, when all at once, right in the centre of the path, appeared two great bright shining eyes.

I called out thinking the dog from the dairy had followed me, but got no answer. I climbed back over the fence and stood there almost petrified with fear. I don't know how long I stood there

but suddenly the eyes were just blotted out. I must have been braver then than I am now, for I took my courage in both hands and got back over the fence and walked back over the spot where the eyes had been.

My employer and his wife and niece, noting that looked white and frightened, asked the reason. They informed me that the dog had not left the dairy. After this experience, I was always sent on this particular part of my deliveries in daylight. On mentioning my experience to an old lady neighbour, she said that the spot was reputed to be haunted, as some people had been drowned when the ice gave way on the moat of what used to be an old castle there. A workmate friend tells me that he had seen the same thing some years earlier. I asked him for further information on these eyes and his second letter was as follows:

"It was such a long time ago, but all I can remember of that night are the eyes appearing quite suddenly, only a few yards in front of me, at about two or three feet from the ground. I do remember that everything was still and quiet and that after what seemed quite a few minutes the eyes were just blotted out. I have always been convinced that this was something very strange and the attitude of my employers at the time strengthened my belief. They did not wish to talk about it, and would never let me go that way at night afterwards; and also someone would accompany me when I had to take the pony to the field at nights."

PHANTOM CYCLIST.

"Some five or six years later, I had another strange experience. I was then employed as a baker's roundsman and made deliveries with a horse and tilted cart. On this particular occasion I had finished my deliveries at West Ashby - Far Thorpe and was on my way home. As usual, both the horse and I were pretty tired out after a long day, and I just let the horse jog along at its own steady pace.

It would be about 7.30pm to 8pm when we were approaching West Ashby village and near the old park gates. Suddenly something startled my horse which reared up and set off at a gallop, nearly pulling me out of the cart as I hung on to the reins.

I glanced to the left and saw a man on a cycle, who had an old dinner-bag over his shoulder, and he seemed to be trying to pass on the wrong side of the road. After getting my horse under control again, I looked back to see if the man was alright but to my great surprise there was no one there. I mentioned this to several people at the time, but no one could offer any explanation, nor could think of any worker who might be cycling along there at that time. I do remember that it was a rather hazy moon-lit night."

FAMILY HAPPENINGS.

"My grandfather (that is, my mother's father) who was a postman in the Spilsby area, was a great believer in telepathy. My mother used to tell my brother and sisters and I some very strange things that happened to her when she was about fifteen years of age. Her mother was very ill and in bed for two years before she died - and every night would have a small kelly lamp by her bedside. Sometime after her death, when my mother was only fifteen, she was taking her five-year-old sister and her brother up to bed. On reaching the top of the staircase, the kelly lamp suddenly came alight. The next day she had a message from the Lake district to say that her father who was holidaying there, had been taken seriously ill.

On several occasions on going up to bed, my mother has found ornaments taken off the dressing-table and put on the bed,. just like her mother used to do when dusting the bedrooms. At this time they were living at Spilsby, and my mother said she got so frightened that her father finally had to move house. All these people concerned have now passed on, but I can assure you that my mother was a very truthful and straightforward person and not the least likely to give way to idle fancies."

Well, I'd like to thank Mr Benton for letting me use the information he supplied me. Certainly, these instances seem most puzzling to us of the 20th century. Obviously, the incidents which Mr Benton related occured almost half a century ago, nonetheless   I regard them as interesting and
     worthy of inclusion in this present work.

1) 'Lincolnshire Folklore' by Ethel Rudkin. Reprinted by EP Publishing Ltd. (1973). £2.50. 112pp 7 illos. ISBN: 0.85409.992.1.

2) Accounts of Black Dogs are not, unfortunately, included in her 'Lincolnshire Folklore', but later covered in her article 'The Black Dog' Folklore Vol.49, 1938.

■■■■■■■■■■■■■■■■■■■■■■■■■■■■■■■■■
MARINE MYSTERIES/ Cont.
like to know why so many coincidences happen - in this case, what relationship is there between aerial lights and quakes or spouts? We have, alas, not had time to investigate whether our little spouts of the 18th August were in synchronisation with anything else; but no real hurry there; if there is, it'll come out in time as our data builds up. Meanwhile perhaps someone could track down the national and saucer-mag coverage of that 1967 circus, since we have only a London evening paper source.

1) Daily Mail, 19 Aug 74.   2) Daily Mirror, 19 · Aug 74.   3) London Evening News, 18 July 67. The credit for all items to Steve Moore.

scientific curiosities

THE SLEEPERS AWAKE!

Again, a ripple or movement in a dream-state of orderliness-disorderliness, throwing up a pattern , and then it is gone. The ripple of things coming together - the pattern of repeated discovery. When it's time for bacteriologists to find things , they do. In March this year, Dr Toshio Miwa,of Gifu University, announced to the Japan Bacteriological Society   that scientists at Japan's

Showa Base on Antarctica had discovered, in earth samples,   bacteria believed to have continued living for "tens of thousands" of years. These microbes, which have survived as viable spores, are of the 10- to 15-type anaerobes capable of causing gas gangrene in humans, and were originally cultured, Dr Miwa believes, in the intestines of whatever animals at that time. Denver (Colorado) Post, 10 March 74.

Hot foot, as it were, on this news, we learn of an announcement by Dr Roy E Cameron of the Darwin Research Institute, California, via the National Science Foundation, who, with NASA, were sponsoring methods of detecting micro-organisms for the Viking Mars-landing mission in 1976. He talked of two discoveries of deep-frozen live bacteria, unlike anything previously discovered, in drilling samples from strata 10,000 to one million years old, again in the Antarctica Cameron and a team of scientists on the international 'Dry Valley' drilling project at Ross Island, McMurdo, found the bacteria in core-samples of volcanic rock containing pockets of ice, at 420, 750, 1070 and 1400 feet, and each find was different, both from the bugs at the other levels and those at the surface. The scientists were startled to discover them moving as soon as they were put under a microscope, and Cameron reckons that the heat from the drilling could have jolted them into life. But there their exhibitionism ended apparently because they refused to reproduce - as indeed any self-respecting thing would when there were voyeurs about.

Not so reserved, however, were the lusty little fellers found in marine sedimentary rock at Taylor Valley, about 60 miles away, who couldn't wait to get down to starting all over agin. "They formed unusual doughnut-shaped colonies that grew, or flowed in toward the centre as the colony expanded. After a while the colony had the shape of an inactive volcano," said Cameron. The reaction of some bacteriologists was reported as 'sceptical', as they recalled how they had been stung once before, over reports, 10 years ago, of a critter that hibernated for 180 million to 230 million years in some ancient salt crystals...reports that were later discredited. Scources: Rochester (Minn.) Post-Bulletin 30 April 74. Winnipeg (Manitoba) Free-Press 3 May 74. Credit: Mark Hall.

RIGHT-ON TRITON.

In mid-73, the Novosti Agency released news of a male Triton (Hynobius Keyserling) that was thawed back to life from a 90-year stretch in a block of ice recovered from 11 meters down in permafrost in North Yakutia. A follow-up report from the Ukranian Institute of Geochemistry & Mineral Physics to a Leningrad conference said that the triton, whose age was determined by radio-carbon analysis, lived for a further 6 months, and even produced healthy offspring. It was previously believed, the report said, that amphibia such as frogs, tritons and tadpoles, could not remain viable after being frozen in a state of anabiosis for more than 20 years. Sources: Des Moines (Iowa) Register 5 June 74. Credit: Mark Hall. And the Novosti Bulletin No.15103,5 June 74.

ON VARIOUS UNORTHODOX PROPERTIES OF WATER.

One can hardly think of a challenge to Science emerging from the everyday use of a substance we all take for granted and think ourselves quite familiar with. The substance presenting some scientists with a problem that goes beyond their cozy cubbyholed approach, is that of our common or garden water - and we are turning out to know less about it than we originally thought. Our correspondent, Phil Ledger, kicked off our train of thought with the following note:

"Fringe scientific and folk literature has records of water with 'special properties', attributable to no gross chemical differences from normal water. (1). If any properties of the water are 'real' in the sense of being detectable by currently accepted scientific means, then they are very subtle and/or basic, and hence by implication, it is difficult from a traditional viewpoint to see how they could act directly upon a complex living organism. A possible clue to the nature of such differences (if not their mode of action) comes from New Scientist. (2). Water extracted from both healthy and tumorous human tissue, was investigated by the physical witchcraft of 'nuclear magnetic resonance'. It was found that in the hydrogen nucleus, of four basic parameters measured, one was consistently different between the two water samples . Cause and effect (ie. water causes tumor, or tumor influences water) were not surmised upon."

The sort of 'odd properties' that sprang to our minds were widely different: for example the observation that at 'miracle' or Holy centres, like Lourdes, or the Ganges at Rishikesh, whether or not you credit some paranormal healing, the fact exists that thousands of sufferers of contageous diseases bath in the same water as others of a weak and suseptable condition, and yet the incidence of transmission of disease is quite significantly low. The other extreme is the thesis held by Dan Butcher and others, of the symbolic nature of water in experiences of paranormal phenomena. (3). As far as we know there has been no detailed examination of possible correlations on this subject.

The problems facing scientists of 'the traditional viewpoint' (as Phil put it) were more poignantly delineated in an earlier piece in New Scientist (4) which explained the work of Prof. FA Brown into the 'biological clocks' of various organisms. He took random samples of dried beans; weighed them before and after a four hour soaking in water; and correlated the data on 8000 samples, to judge the rates of absorption of water. There was an immediate, unexpected yet clear correlation with the quarter phases of the moon, the peak up-takes of water occurring at these times. A staff writer on NS was moved to encapsulate the dilemma: "It seems quite inconceivable that any type of internal 'biological clock' so far envisaged could possibly continue to tick away in anything so biochemically inert as a dry bean seed." And yet it does - or water activates it - or water, somehow and mysteriously, is its transformer or amplifier. But Brown doesn't stop there - he believes that before long, a quarter lunar rythmn will be found in plants and animals widely.

In the field of Physical Chemistry, there appears to have been some sporadic interest at various times in what a commentator calls: "The alleged possibility of producing mysterious changes in the physical properties of water by the application of relatively weak magnetic fields." (5). Following this statement there is an account of an experiment of pushing water through a weak field and the subsequent claims that this altered the pH of the water; its surface tension and dielectric properties - and then a classic and meticulous "null experiment" that proved that nothing happened. Reminds me of a dictum of Dr Jack Cohen's: "For every expert, there's an equal and opposite expert."

But now as we move on, the matter gets more interesting for us Forteans. I quote from the writer in NATURE: "It seems that for a considerable time boiler engineers in many parts of the world have been passing feed-water through quite mild magnetic fields and obtaining a sensational reduction in the adhesion of scale. Some accounts claim that the passage of feed-water through the field of a small bar-magnet will actually lead to removal of scale already deposited. When I took this to a wise and experienced physical chemist, his reaction was that this was nothing to some of the almost magical practices resorted to by boiler engineers. For instance, had I heard of the use of glass globes filled with helium and a little mercury (a Tonisator) tethered in the water supply, and said to be almost as effective as the magnetic system?" (5).

It's begining to sound more improbable - ah! but more exciting. Alchemy in the waterworks - we expect to hear soon of a lucky-pixie charm in a reactor core. The vigorously proselytizing editorials of John W Campbell (editor of Analog SF) in the sixties who took every opportunity he could to point out that while physicists argued whether dowsing existed or not, down-to-earth water departments and farmers the world over used dowsers in their daily routine work, and to practical advantage most of the time. This he said showed the relative values to be placed upon Science and Technology - the latter making practical use of phenomena without any necessity of understanding the hows or whys. But again, we seem to be talking of a curious property of water - read the literature for discussions on fields and emanations from dowser and water, and resonances between the two.

But back to the NATURE article where we find that some Russian work claims other results of the weak-field magnetic processing of water: optical absorption altered up to 30%, and recovery to a normal condition varying length of treatment and strength of field. What next? - well, the question that if this is going on in neat water, what about consequent effects on water within an organism? It seems there are some known reactions to magnetic fields but these are so weak, elusive,(and poorly documented). Mice show no ill effects from a few hours at 150,000 oersted, and men have been exposed to 20,000 oersted for at least a quarter of an hour without screaming to be let out. Work is mentioned onthe magnetic susceptibility of (good ole) Drosophila, photo-bacteria, and mud snails, etc but controversy rages over inconclusive results. Does bird, or mud snail for that matter, navigation work insidiously through some way of monitoring changes in its bodily water, which in turn responds to geomagnetic and lunar fluctuations? (What was the question again?). Well scientists continue to vacillate; fields continue to fluctuate; and the boiler engineers continue to extemporate. There isn't much else to be said.

1) 'Mysterious Unknown.' - R. Charroux. Corgi.1973 'Supernature' - L Watson. Doubleday. 1973.
2) New Scientist, V62, No.669. 13 June 74. p902.
3) 'Water Symbolism in UFO encounters' - D Butcher Surrey Investigation Group on Aerial Phenomena. 1971.
4) New Scientist, 18 April 74. p111.
5) Nature, V248, April 26, 1974. p729. News and Views.

swarms

We'll have a few more notes on swarms of insects - we even have some on mice and frog plagues, but these will have to keep until next time. Please see Mark Hall's column (this issue) for other swarmings including a huge deluge of caterpillars in Manitoba.

13 Oct 67 - Thurnby Lodge housing estate, Leicester, invaded by "millions" of harmless money-spiders. Houses and cars covered with webs and number estimated at 2 million per acre. "It was eerie...like something from Outer Space," said a resident. Daily Mirror, 14 Oct 67.

16 Aug 71 - Great Yarmouth, Norfolk. Swarms of ladybirds invading the beaches, forcing holiday-makers to quit during the brightest weather for months. Observers said: "The sky was grey with millions of them." Roads were carpeted with bodies and swimming pools soon collected layers. A change in the wind is said to have cleared them away, but no comment on where they came from or where they went, until suddenly people were confronted by 'millions'. Express & Star, 17 Aug 71. Credit for above two: Anthony Smith.

28 Sept 73 - swarms of crane-flies roaming the West Country. No note on numbers, but sufficient to "worry" pest-control officers. Daily Express.

31 Jan 74 - Newlyn, Cornwall. Mild weather is believed to have brought the plague of flies currently pestering the village. They are thought to have hatched out from seaweed in the harbour. "Millions" are blackening the seawall and many houses. Daily Telegraph.

A CATERPILLAR CRAWLED IN BERKELEY SQUARE.
The following three items are from successive weeks in the Sunday Times - we print the initial report (by David Blundy) in full because it contains much interesting incidental information.

BERKELEY SQUARE, London, where a nightingale is traditionally supposed to sing has recently been alive to the sinister rustling sound of 100,000 caterpillars. The plague of caterpillars, or "pestilence of caterpillars" as Westminster City Council calls it, began two weeks ago. Thousands of the small furry creatures dropped 40ft from the square's plane trees.

Some dropped on to passers-by. Others fell on to the statue of the topless Greek lady with a pitcher standing at the southern end of the square, the gift, according to the plinth, of Henry, 3rd Marquis of Lansdowne.

The caterpillars made straight for the statue and formed a thick carpet over her pitcher, face and the more intimate parts of her torso. Other caterpillars disported on the grass, climbed on to the ornate pagoda in the centre of the square, and sat on the benches.

The reason for this sudden descent on Berkeley Square is still a mystery. Why not St James's Park or Clapham Common where there are more trees to defoliate? "They may have been attracted to Berkeley Square by the street lights," said Robert Humphreys, the head keeper of London Zoo's insect house. "But who knows? Who can tell?"

One man who wishes the caterpillars had chosen some other trees to plague is Berkeley Square's chief gardner and caretaker, Raymond Osborne, who has been waging a one-man battle against the insects. So far, he is losing.

"I go round and clear them off the seats," he says. "An hour later, hundreds of the little buggers are back again performing on the benches. I always have a good look before I sit down now, but some of the visitors just plonk down on the benches. A few minutes later, they start scratching and fidgeting around."

Mr Osborne says some people, including his assistant John, are allergic to caterpillars. "John has been in a bad way. If they touch him, he get a red rash all over his body. It lasts for a day."

The caterpillars, a common British species which change eventually into Lackty moths, are, according to Mr Humphrys, completely harmless. Unless, of course, you are allergic to them.

He says the Lackey is particular about the places it plagues. It likes the southern parts of England and dislikes the industrial North. It breeds in the south of Ireland but never appears in Northern Ireland. Last year, it caused a pestilence in Hertford, Ware and Bury.

The Lackey, about half an inch long, comes in tasteful hues of brown and achre and has four stylish tufts of white bristles on its back. Its only claim to fame in the insect world is that it builds little communal tents in the branches of trees where is breeds and prospers.

But Westminster City Council's infestation department is not concerned with the Lackey's pleasant life-style. "Our department has been working on the problem of how to exterminate this pest," the council's information officer said, yesterday. The problem is that liquid sprays are like water off a Lackey's back. DDT would be effective but could also damage residents of Berkeley Square and passers-by.

Other more extreme methods have been used in the past to deal with caterpillar plagues. When Brown Tailed moth caterpillars, said to be as big as a man's finger, terrorised the village of Telscombe, near Brighton in 1953, the local council brought out flame-throwers to exterminate them.

Westminster City Council says that it still has a few tricks up its sleeve. "We are working on a few techniques which should be brought into effect next week," said the information officer. "Our infestation officers are confident."

But Mr. Osborne, the gardener, who knows the Lackey only too well, says nature will take its course. "They're not so lively today. They're lying very still. I think they're about to turn into moths. The point is—the more you mess around with them, the longer they take."

2. CREEPING TO SCHOOL.

I WAS much interested in David Blundy's article on the current caterpillar plague in Berkeley Square (News, last week) but amazed at the implication that the phenomenon is something new.

Twenty years ago I used to trot unwillingly to my primary school near Park Lane, and term-time was made tolerable in summer only by the wonderful caterpillar invasion. From the moment I noticed the articulated armies on the march, my work began.

Starting at the East entrance of Berkeley Square and radiating zeal, I'd approach every unsuspecting person who happened to have taken a seat and inform them in portentous tones that they were being crawled on by thousands of furry feet. Ladies got up particularly smartly. Gentlemen tended to check first before leaping to their feet, but would then humbly ask me to brush them down with my beret.

My public-spirited duties ensured that I missed at least the first half-hour of morning and afternoon school every day, and on top of that came the gratifying bonuses I received—the sixpences pressed into my unflinching palm by palpitating elderly women and the bruising pinches administered by grateful galvanised businessmen.

The autumnal defection of the caterpillars was a yearly catastrophe to which I never adjusted. Warning people about wet paint just wasn't the same. — (Mrs) Alida Baxter, London W1.

3. WRONG PLAGUE.

THE CATERPILLARS which have recently appeared in Berkeley Square are not those of the Lackey moth, as reported by David Blundy (News, July 14), but those of the Vapourer moth.

The Lackey caterpillars are hairy but do not have the tufts of hair resembling horns possessed by Vapourers. The characteristic appearance of the Vapourer caterpillars is clearly visible in your photographs.

I saw only Vapourer caterpillars in Berkeley Square a week ago. Incidentally Richard South, in his "The Moths of the British Isles," first published in 1907, describes the Vapourer as "quite a Cockney insect, and is found in almost every part of the Metropolis where there are a few trees."—**Denys L. Coomber,** London N20.

Kelvin Brodie

Plagued with caterpillars, the marquis's shapely statue

1) Sunday Times, 14 July 74. 2) Sunday Times, 21 July 74; Letter to Editor. 3) Sunday Times, 28 July 74; Letters to Editor. Credit: Steve Moore, Leslie Shepard.

*   *   *

did you see....?

'Astronomical Alignment of the Big Horn Medicine Wheel: Cairns of an Unexplained Amerindian Rock Pattern appear to have been Aligned to the Summer Solstice.' John A Eddy. SCIENCE Vol.184 pp1035 ff. 7 June 74. (A 25 metre diameter ring of small stones in the Big Horn range, Wyoming, with a central cairn and spokes. Other cairns give the alignments. Snow is common in summer and it's inaccessible in winter solstice time. Local Indians did not know of its purpose or who built it. Dating by artifacts found there suggest a date of 1700 AD. Quite recent for such a structure.)

EXORCISM - a Tatler Special, Spring 74. 32 pages of chilling True Exorcist tales. Much of interest

'The Return of Superstition.' editorial by Frank B Salisbury. BIOSCIENCE Vol.24 No4 p201. April 74.

'Bill Roll isn't scared of Ghosts.' NR Kleinfield WALL STREET JOURNAL pp1,12. 7 Jan 74. (About the director of the Psychical Research Foundation.)

'Alaska's Snowman lives.' Leo Hannan. ALASKA magazine May 74.

'Geller Performs for Physicists.' Jack Sarfatt. SCIENCE NEWS Vol.106 p46. 20 July 74.

'Uri through the Lens-Cap.' Yale Joel. p75,77,135. 'The Making of a Psychic.' Charles Reynolds. p73, 74,76, 136-138,174. Both from POPULAR PHOTOGRAPHY June 74.

The link between UFOs and Bigfoot'. P Gutilla & BA Slate. SAGA magazine Aug 74 pp16-18,54,56-58, 60.

'Midwinter Sunrise at Newgrange'. J Patrick. NATURE Vol.249 pp517-519. 7 June 74.

'Do Black Holes really Explode.' PCW Davies & JG Taylor. NATURE Vol.250 pp37-38. 5 July 74.

'Correlation of Long Delayed Radio Echoes and the Moon's Orbit' George Sassoon. SPACEFLIGHT Vol.16 pp258-264. July 74. (Is Earth being probed from Outer Space, etc?)

'Von Daniken's Express.' Mike Bygrave. CLUB INTERNATIONAL Vol.3 No7. pp4,6. July 74. (The lowdown on the 'Gold of the Gods' Caper. Is it a hoax?)

'Mathematical Games' SCIENTIFIC AMERICAN pp116-121. June 74. Martin 'Fads and Fallacies In the Name of Science' Gardner applies his cool and erudite mind to extrapolations of pyramid numerology.)

'The New Frontier.' Alfred Douglas. PREDICTION magazine pp16-18. Aug 74. (Report on a conference on fringe medicine; doctors & psychics battling it out.)

'Beyond Human Understanding.' Jillie Collins. WOMAN'S OWN 22 June 74, pp30-32. (Yes, folks! They finally made it to the NEWS. A collection of 'true' psychic happenings involving people's pets - and some weird ones at that, happenings that is. Next issue: 'Why does Biffo wear red braces?' from the BEANO.)

'Mystery of Lost Atlantis.' Richard Tate. FATE & FORTUNE No4. pp44-48. (Some interesting illos.)

THE LEY HUNTER No56/57 June/July (now bi-monthly) 'An unobtrusive Divining Rod' Sid Birchby. pp10,11 'UFOs in NE England', some reports. p12.

'Chaos or Cosmos?' Dr Arthur Peacocke. NEW SCIENTIST Vol.63 No910, pp386-389. 15 Aug 74. (Half time score in the match between Science and Religion, with God and Chance as bat and ball.)

'The Place of Astronomy in the Ancient World.' PHILOSOPHICAL TRANSACTIONS (of the Royal Society, London) Series A, Vol.276. pp1-276. (A mass of papers on ancient astronomy. Includes Thom on European monuments; a re-evaluation of the megalithic yard; Hawkins on British, Egyptian & Peruvian alignments, (evidence for non-alignments in Nazca figures.)

'Electricity as Free as Moonrock was Free.' Arthur Hill. HOUSTON (Texas) Chronicle 17 April 74, 5/p3. In these energy-conscious days its nice to see a re-evaluation of the ideas of those whom orthodox science has been ready to junk as 'crackpot inventors'. Here, Loomis's 'Static Electric Motor' is given a whirl by West Virginia University; and the title refers cryptically to the economics of Loomis's method of 'concentrating electricity out of the air' - its there all right, but its going to cost you to get at it. Nows the time to dig out that old Keely Motor Co. stock your dad left you - if he didn't burn it, or put it to practical use in the john.)

'Scientist leaves Mind open to Psychic Mysteries! Terry Kliewer. DALLAS (Texas) MORNING NEWS, 37A, 17 March 74. (Interview with Sir John Eccles. Asked about scientists reducing 'self-awareness' to the discharge between brain cells, he "snorts: "Some philosophers want nice, neat philosophies with no loose ends. This is the ultimate illusion. The way to wisdom is to realise how much we don't know."

FLYING SAUCER REVIEW, Vol20. No1. July 74. Many interesting items including: 'Time Correlations between Geomagnetic Disturbances and Eye-witness Accounts of UFOs' by C Poher; 'Birthplaces of Prominent People in relation to BAVIC' by JC Dufour; & 'UFOs in Folklore' by Janet Bord.

INFO JOURNAL No.13. - Vol.IV, No.1. May 74. 'If You go down to the Woods Today' by RJM Rickard on a decade of mystery animal reports in southern England; 'Extraterrestials and the Tropical Zones BY Stuart Greenwood; 'Adgy?' by X, on Tunguska Event theories; 'The Stanford "Appors" Rediscovered' by Loren Coleman; 'Historical Miscellanies' by Ron Dobbins; and other items. Not to be missed.

'Healers - or Hoaxers.' Mark Frankland on the Philipino psycic-surgeons. OBSERVER COLOUR MAGAZINE, 25 August 74.

CAVEAT EMPTOR - May/June 74, No13. A UFO orientated American bi-monthly with some Fortean interests. Contributers include: Jerome Eden, Richard Shaver and Brinsley Le Poer Trench. 75¢ each or $4.00 for 6 issues to Nexus Enterprises, Box 688, Coatesville, Pa 19320, USA.

'Prepare to Avoid thy Doom.' a report by Ian Pollock, on the Psychic Research Centre, May Lectures at which whoever is who in the psychic research world tells of the strange things they've found. TIME OUT, June 21-27, 74; pp 12, 13 & 15.

'And yet it moves.' - Dr Colin West on the amazing (simple, effective & unexploited) Fluidyne chemical engine. NEW SCIENTIST 19 Aug 74, p530/1.

Compilation Credits: Mark Hall, Steve Moore, and Phil Ledger.

BOOKS RECEIVED: 'Reflexive Water - The basic concerns of Mankind' - philosophy discussions edited by Fons Elders; Souvenir Press. 'Flying Saucer Vision' - a welcome Abacus paper edition of John Michell's trail-blazing classic. Due to shortage of room we will have to review these books later, probably next issue.

■■■■■■■■■■■■■■■■■■■■■■■■■■■■■■■■

GREAT FORTEAN CAPER/ Cont.

Are we fished for? Are we really property? The only moral in this seems to be the Kafkaesque one that speculations on the end-goal are useless - the journeying is all the reality there is. In fact the last words of the play, said while our two main heroes are laughing in the rain (of an edible lichen), are: "There's a whole new caper coming."

THE BOOK OF BHRIGU - AN ENIGMA.

A key scene in the play concerns a prophecy in an ancient Hindu text called the 'Book of Bhrigu' that the main protagonists will meet in a certain place and a certain time. Like me, you will probably never have heard of this oracle - and be otherwise inclined to place it on the same shelf as the Necronomicon (of the mad Arab, Abdul Al' Hazred). Ken assured me it did exist, and gave me an obscure pamphlet which tells how an American Hindu monk, styled Kriyananda, was brought to meet this literary incarnation of the ancient rishi, Bhrigu. (1).

The 'Bhrgu Samhita' as it is more properly known, is tied into bundles of loose pages - and all over India there are pandits or interpreters who have a few bundles of Bhrigu in their care. No one seems to know how many bundles there are, but some are undoubtedly fakes. The pages, said to contain details of "millions of lives" are indexed by horoscope, drawn up for the precise time of consultation, which is a pretty neat idea. Even details of past are given, and the story is related of a woman told by Bhrigu that in a previous life she lived in 'Patel-Desh' (a footnote explains that this term appears often in old Sanskrit and is generally taken to mean 'America'), in the town of Washinton (this name being spelled phonetically in Sanskrit characters). My first reaction was to wonder what are ancient Sanskrit books doing with references to America, for Heaven's sake. The original Bhrgu Samhita is said to be hidden in Tibet - the existing 'volumes' being copied meticulously by hand. Kriyananda managed to get one page dated to about 150 years old at the Archeological Dept. of India's National Archives. Though that does not prove much about the antiquity of the textural tradition, either way.

There is an immediately apparant distinction to Nostradamus's cryptic quatrains - 'Bhrigu' is said to contain quite specific prophecies, up to two pages long, detailing names, birth-places, the precise reason for the consultation and very often a precise answer. And all this across an unknown number of centuries. Its reputed infallibility gives rise to some fascinating ledgends:

"I learned of one man who was told in a portion of the Bhrigu Samhita in Banaras that five years later he would die. He lived in dread of that day. After fives years had passed, he was still very much alive. He had lost all faith in Bhrigu. Much later, he happened upon a portion of the Samhita elsewhere. On impulse he decided to ask Bhrigu why the Banaras prediction had failed. A reading was found for him. Therein he was told that at the time his previous reading was copied, a line had accidentally been left off the top of a letter. As a result the meaning was changed completely. What Bhrigu originally intended was that after five years this person would lose all his property." (1)

And indeed, that was said to have been what actually happened.

A copy of part of the page referring to Kriyananda's consultation, from the Bhrgu Samhita, showing the horoscope, and his name (circled) in Sanskrit characters.

The original Bhrgu seems to have been a mythical characterer in the Rig Veda; and a Bhrgu is mentioned as one of 28 'Yogacaryas' (founders of the mainstream of yoga philosophies) in the Siva-Maha-purana. The Purana Index (2) lists no less than 9 Bhrgus. It seems certain that a group or cult

of priests (following the eponymous Bhrgu), and worshippers of the fire-god Agni, later evolved into a real family. One researcher Kriyananda met said the Samhita was not written by Bhrigu but by succeeding groups of highly trained pandits, the basis of an accurate astrological science formulated by the original Bhrgu. I searched both the Purana and Vedic Indexes but no mention could I find of the Samhita; perhaps it is later. Perhaps it doesn't exist. Or perhaps it is a victim of scientific banishment. This would make a nice project for someone. We remain critical, but realise its value, if it proves to exist and check on satisfactorily. If anyone picks this up - please keep in touch.

1) 'The Book of Bhrigu.' by Kriyananda.
   Hansa Publications, San Francisco. 1967.

2) 'The Purana Index' (Vol II.) VRR Dikshitar.
   University of Madras. 1952.

ADS

NEXT NEWS will include: William Corliss on the genesis of the Sourcebook Project; Janet Bord on Leys, Black Dogs and a phantom cottage; more spontaneous combustions (?); a whole heap (a spook?) of ghosts; and a couple of ball-lightning things. What more could you want? What? - a possession or two? Well, OK - but it scares the life out of me typing that kind of weird stuff. Wait! What's that? Good god...the doorhandle is moving

a miscellany of fortean curiosities

ᏩᏂᎬ ᏁᎬᎳᏕ

GHOSTS AND POLTERGEISTS, p5.

also ---- fire deaths in cells, **3** ---- flows of water and blood, **4** ----
Janet Bord on leys, 'black dogs', and a phantom cottage, **6** ----
visions, **11** ---- USA cattle mutilations, **13** ---- ball lightnings, **15** ----
the 'Morning Cloud' incident, **17** ---- phantom helicopter revisited, **20** ----
William Corliss on the Sourcebook genesis, **18**.

35p : $1·00.

THE NEWS

Vol.1. No.7.
November.
1974.

THE NEWS is a non-profit making bi-monthly miscellany of
Fortean news and notes; edited & published by Robert JM
Rickard: 31 Kingswood Road, Moseley, Birmingham B13 9AN;
affiliated to International Fortean Organisation (INFO).

SUBSCRIPTIONS:
Per year: £2.10.
Overseas & USA
$6.00 or equiv-
alent; plus 10%
if paying by
cheque (to cover
bank-charges).
NB: Cheques etc.
payable to: RJM
RICKARD, please.

AIRMAIL TRANSFER:
Overseas subscrib-
ers can 'Airmail
Transfer' direct
from their bank
to our account:
RJM Rickard No2.
A/c No: 0125008.
Lloyds Bank, Priory
Ringway, Birmingham
B4, England. Sort-
ing Code: 30-96-28.

CONTRIBUTIONS & RIGHTS:
Articles & Notes are
welcome, and duly cred-
ited. All articles in
THE NEWS are Copyright
of the authors; and the
views expressed are not
necessarily those of THE
NEWS or the Editor. All
the Notes may be freely
quoted, though we hope
for a credit in return.

ERRATA AND ADDENDA.

'Riply or not!' NEWS 5, p17. The story about the
Clatworthy brothers, who had accidents on the same
stretch of road, should have had the following
sources and credits: Times, 5 Jan 74 (R Forrest).
Daily Mirror, 5 Jan 74 (Steve Moore). Daily Mail,
same date, (Roger Randle).

'Puma hunt in Scotland.' NEWS 6, p3. The story
was from the Sunday Mirror, 23 June 74. Credit:
Robert Forrest. Peter Rogerson later sent us a
note from the Sunday Express a week earlier (16
June 74) which reported a myesterious animal "like
a mountain lion" being seen by drivers of two
cars near Beith, North Ayrshire. A lorrydriver
said it crossed the road into a field in front
of him at about 7am, bounding and not running.
"Its body was 2½ to 3½ft from the ground, had
heavy legs, fairly large paws, and a long curled
up tail." One of the drivers saw it at midnight
sitting in the road, and was forced to stop, his
headlights full on it, for five minutes. Then, as
it still refused to budge, the taxi and passengers
were forced to drive round it. "In doing so my
car brushed against it and it growled." We shall
be carrying an article by Jerry Clark on a mystery
animal, and a few more notes on UK sightings.

'Falls of Animals' NEWS 6, p15. The fall of a
curious "beaver-like" animal into a street in
Norrkoping in August 1708, was noted from a story
in a 1969 newspaper, not 1869, as I had thought.

esp

GELLER: PUT TO THE TEST.

To the accompanyment of noisy press fanfares (1),
Nature printed the long awaited paper by Drs Targ
and Puthoff on their experiments with Uri Geller
(2). Contrary to popular belief, spoon-bending
was not on the itinery; the tests being confined
to target-guessing , and Geller was only one of
several percipients tested. As expected, the
paper turns out to be thoroughly anticlimatic,
and its loose methodology has been severely criticised.

In an editorial justification (that is a wonder
in itself) Nature alludes to these technical
shortcomings, but believed them outweighed by the
fact that the paper comes from two initiated
members of their own secret-society (the orthodox
body of Science) and is backed (without reservat-
ion) by their institution, the Stanford Research
Institute (SRI). And besides, they add, their
readers expect them to run the odd "High-risk"
paper. The more I think about that, the less
sense it makes.

Most of the interesting action has been over at
the New Scientist, where Dr Joseph Hanlon led a
special investigation of Geller (after he backed
out of their agreed testing)(3). His approach,
in the long (16 page) report was that before we
can speak of a "Geller Effect", we must prove,
unequivocally, that the results were not, indeed
could not be, achieved through 'normal' physical
processes. Some will view this as   harsh, but
I believe it to be a practical approach, and necessary as a foundation for an 'unbiased' understanding of whatever is going on. Geller has
claimed that scientists are among the easiest to
fool. Dr Hanlon tells why: "Traditionally, scientists are not concerned with fraud - after all,
atoms and molecules do not play tricks on the
experimenters. So scientists do not expect
fraud, and it is not surprising, with their
orthodox background, that they approach the
paranormal virtually oblivious to this possibility. Perhaps it is we, not they(presumably
the Geller experimenters - Ed.), who are proposing a new philosophy of scientific research
by saying that fraud must be eliminated first!"4

As Forteans, we are not, strictly speaking, out
to change science or its ground-rules for accepting data, since this would be proselytizing

when we question certainty, and belief in opinions. It cannot yet be ruled out that paranormal effects vary in proportion to the degree of belief (by the principals, witnesses, etc) - and if even this relationship could be proved demonstrably, the question of the physics of the processes involved becomes doubly damnable. Nevertheless as an island of clarity, and as an admirable summing up of the Geller repertoire, we could do far worse than recommend Dr Hanlon's investigation.

We tend to be easily and readily impressed and convinced by data which makes science out to be a plodding short-sighted fool, forgetting that this too is to take sides in a propaganda war. Mind you, some scientists don't need any help in that direction. It was revealed that the spoons bent in Geller's British TV debut last year (see NEWS 2, p5.), during which Prof. John Taylor pronounced science baffled, had been left unattended in Geller's changing-room before the show (5).

The confusion over just what the SRI tests involved was generated partly by the contemporary announcement that Nature was to publish a paper that would vindicate Geller's psychokinetic powers (6). This seems a gross anticipation of the work of Profs. John Hasted and David Bohm (Birkbeck College, London) to which it referred, in which Geller amongst others were tested over 8 months. Prof. Hasted claims that these tests were more sophisticated than spoonbending - eg. Geller moved a Geiger-counter needle by producing "energy bursts of electrical origin." 'Steeth! Why aren't we hooking him into the National Grid? The papers made great play that Arthur Koestler and Arthur C. Clarke were witnesses to some tests, and were later trapped into uttering epithets, like "Impressive!"

The Hasted & Bohm paper will be slightly more exciting to me (if and when it appears)and if Nature print it,I'll be only slightly less convinced that for all its pussyfooting condescension it isn't just a hotbed of prejudices, (see their anti-amateur investigators, anti-Ley Hunting editorial,7). But It's my guess you ain't seen nut'n yet! - the in-fighting has just begun. The verification of psychokinesis (if and when) will have a far more immediate and fundamental impact on science - in physics, right where it hurts. Its debut in the journals is bound to be more traumatic, and there is a glint of knives being loosened in their sheaths. We could be entering a profoundly important stage in the development of scientific knowledge and from the turmoil will emerge new sciences and many old ones reassessed.

We had hoped to present a more detailed comment and coverage but this is all we have room for, it remaining necessary only to note references to Geller's return to active service (the bending kind) (8). Further developments will be covered next ish.

Sources: (1) News of the World; The Observer both 13 Oct 74. Some papers later printed a more cautious reassessment, eg. Daily Mail, 14 Oct 74. (2) "Information Transmission Under Conditions of Sensory Screening." by Drs. R Targ & H Puthoff. Nature Vol 251, 18 Oct 74, pp602/607. (3) "Uri Geller and Science." by Dr. J Hanlon. New Scientist 17 Oct 74, pp170/185. (4) "Uri Geller and Science." by Dr. J Hanlon. New Scientist 31 Oct 74, p314. This issue also contains very interesting letters in response to above item 3. (5) Sunday Mirror, 20 Oct 74. (6) News of the World, 13 Oct 74. The Observer, 20 Oct 74. (7) "Science Beyond the Fringe." Nature Vol 248, 12 April 74. See also a denunciation of same by a scientist: Correspondence, Nature Vol 249, 28 June 74; and a cool riposte by John Michell: Correspondence, Nature Vol 250, 23 Aug 74. (8) Daily Mirror; The Sun; and others, 30 Oct 74 Credits for many above items: S Moore & P Ledger.

fires

DEATH CELLS.
A confined space - something flares up, and there is no escape. The question is: What caused the fire? At Warrington (Lancs.) Police station, on Tuesday 15 Jan, firemen in breathing gear fought their way into a cell. William D Pindard, 26, facing charges of "unlawfully imprisoning and wounding" was rushed to hospital unconscious, but was dead on arrival. The fire was in his bedding according to the Manchester Evening News, 16 Jan 74. Credit: Peter Rogerson. There was to be an Inquest but no news has reached us. We have written to the South Lancashire Coroner for more information - though it looks as if it could turn out to be a fire caused deliberately yet desperately to 'get out' one way or another.

The following month there occurred a remarkably similar case. On 1st March, Patricia Cummins, 20, was rushed out of her cell in Holloway Prison, London, but died on the way to hospital. The incident received minimal attention in the papers on the 2nd March - partly because it was too early to say anything, and partly because there was a probability of wider issues being involved. We take our details mainly from an article written by Crispin Aubrey in 'Time Out', 3 May 74, which is largely a report on the Inquest, at which the facts first became public information. He kindly gave us permission to quote and use the photo. (See over)

"According to prison officers on duty that evening, Patricia was fed and sedated ((200mg of the depressant Largactyl)) at 7.25pm. It was soon after this that the woman in the cell opposite, the only inmate to give evidence, said that she heard Patricia shouting out that she was burning. "I rang the bell in my cell. When nobody answered the bell, I started shouting. Somebody answered back from the main observation unit, which is some way away. I was also banging on the door with a shoe." But it wasn't until 7.50 - 25 mins later - that a warder raised the alarm when she saw smoke coming out of the cell. None of the warders said they heard any other prisoners making noises. One officer said that when she went into the cell, "It seemed that the light had gone out, but in fact, it was covered with thick black soot.""

Aubrey goes on to raise other questions about treatment and social implications...but for our immediate subject we note the technicalities of the fire which was confined to a polyurethane mattress. A warder was said to have given Patricia a cigarette, lighting it for her before locking her in the cell - and during a court demonstration it was shown that polyurethane could be set alight well enough by a naked flame but that a cigarette tended simply to melt the stuff, combusting it with great difficulty. This may or may not have been the actual cause of the blaze - it is likely we will never know for sure. If you look at the photo, you will note the air-vent in the back wall near the floor. The only other source of through draught was the door-gaps and spy-hole - yet the soot-marks clearly indicate poor or ineffective ventilation. The flames may have shot up with such force they ignored the weak through draught - or the vent was func-

tionally inadequate. Other questions we have concern the apparent speed with which the blaze flared up (a factor common to most spontaneous combustions of people, though not of materials); and to what extent did her shouting mean that she herself was burning, or her mattress - again we will never know. Both Patricia Cummings and William Pindard were said to have died through inhaling fumes, and this is consonant with what we know of combusting plastics - but no mention is made in either case of whether these two unfortunates were burned in any way.

We mention these cases because we are interested in possible cases of spontaneous combustion of people - and here there is reasonable cause for doubt. But we stress that this is because of a lack of evidence one way or the other, and jump to no conclusions. Whether you conclude that a drugged girl dropped her cigarette, or a clumsy attempt was made to translate her to the Positive Absolute, is up to you. As Fort said somewhere: "I offer the data. Suit yourself." Credit: Crispin Aubrey and Steve Moore.

The cell in which Patricia Cummings (inset) died last February. On the floor her uneaten 'supper'

LONDON NEWS SERVICE

flows

Just as we have 'falls' of things, so we have 'flows'. We have a tentative hypothesis - that the teleportive force can transport liquids to points in the air (where it begins to drop) and points on the surface of things (from which it then appears to flow) - but we don't expect you to take that too seriously until it seems like the only remaining explanation. But lets see how you get on with the...

MYSTERY OF THE FLOODED PUB.
Landlord of the Peaks Hotel, Gorsey, Ashton-under-Lyne, Lancs, Harry Marsland, watched as water flowed from light-fittings behind his bar for seven minutes - then stopped as suddenly as it began. Plumbers were called, but left baffled, without finding any conceivable cause. The landlord later seemed quite nonchalant about the affair: "As long as it doesn't come out of the beer pumps I'm not too worried." Daily Mirror, 15 Jan 74. Credit: R Forrest, DJ McAllister.

Or how about...

THE PLATE THAT BLEEDS.
Pescara, Italy. A plate bearing the likenesses
of Pope John XXIII and President John F Kennedy
is miraculously "weeping blood" claims the wife
of a policeman, Pia-Luciana Sparvieri. The drops
of blood began oozing from the plate after New
Years Day. San Francisco Chronicle, 15 Jan 74.
Credit: Loren Coleman. And from the sublime to
the ridiculous...

THE NONSTOP LOO OF LEEK STREET.
Dolores Goodyear and family have been flushed
out of their home in Leek St, Leeds. Ever since
the family moved into their council maisonette
3 years ago, the toilet has driven them clean
round the bend by repeatedly flushing itself and
flooding their home. The family have been re-
housed while workmen attempt to solve the riddle.
Sentient malice is hinted at in hushed tones:
"For no reason at all it would start flushing,
and not know when to stop. It has ruined carpets,
lifted tiles and made the house very damp. It's
been a nightmare." All the obvious causes seem
to have been explored and so the plumbers will
resort to their more drastic arts...If thy
throne offends thee, pluck it out. (I said
drastic, not dramatic, you dope.) Daily Mirror,
1 June 74. It crosses our mind about the possibility of a connexion with poltergeistery,
and end with such a suggestive note. See Fort's
books for others.

BOY IN 'EVIL SPIRITS' MYSTERY.
Since 9-year-old Eugenio Rossi has been in hospital in Nuoro, Sardinia, water has started to
flow through the floor of whichever ward he is
moved to, and that is five to date. Patient have
had to be evacuated from each ward as the mysterious water seeped through the floor, and a
hospital official confirmed that this only happened in wards where the boy was being treated
for a liver complaint. Plumbers were unable to
find any faults at all in the hospital water
system. The boy is reported to be in a private
room awaiting a visit from the hospital chaplain
who will conduct an exorcism. Meanwhile, nurses
mop the floor several times a day.   The Sun,
30 Nov 72. Credit: Mike Roberts.

ghosts & poltergeists

THE NEW HAUNTED HOUSES.

It is generally believed that only ancient mansions and castles get haunted — but we note that
the number of hauntings involving new and council
owned houses or flats is on the increase. It may
be something to do with the particular site,
though this is not always the case.

A councillor will stay the night in a house in
Windsor Ave, Thornton, near Blackpool, claimed
by a frightened family to be haunted by a ghostly figure that had whipped the sheets from their
son's bed, proving to be the last straw in 3
years of fear for the Ross family. Daily Mail,
7 Dec 1971. Credit for both above: P Rogerson.

Six families in council flats at Tedbury Close,
Southdene, Kirkby, Lancs, have asked for new
homes. A Liverpool housing dept. spokesman said:
"These people are terrified and we can't ignore
their requests." One woman reported seeing the
figure of a boy about 10 "holding an arm in the
air as though clasping someone's hand." A neighbour said: "I have heard moans and childs laughter but not seen anything." Another resident said
her cat began to howl, then: "I saw the figures
of two small children by the fireplace, and an
adult by the door. Since then we have one or
other of these figures quite frequently, and
heard strange noises every night." Daily Mail,
20 August 71. Credit: Peter Rogerson.

A mother wants a new council house 7 weeks after
moving in to her present one in Cooper Avenue,
Walthamstow, London. Her 4-year-old son has been
terrified by a "white lady" who speaks to him
sharply, telling him to leave the room. Nor will
their dog go into the box-room used as their
son's bedroom. A council official has recommended the family to "redecorate the room." Daily
Mirror, 17 Nov 1969. Cr: Peter Rogerson.

Tom Appleford's council flat in Gosling Way,
Lambeth, London, is the haunt of a 6ft ghost
who has appeared several times, frightening
Tom's children. But most of the trouble has come
from 4 years of cutlery-stealing, carpets being
pulled up and other mischief. The council responded to Tom's request to be moved by sending
an exorcist...and now they wait to see if he
has been successful. Daily Mirror, 17 Aug 74.

Doncaster council refused to rehouse six families
after doing so for one recently in a spate of
claimed hauntings. Elsewhere, a family fled
their council flat in Nothfleet, Kent, after a
visit from a headless woman with noisy accompanyment. They were given another place by the
Kent authority. Daily Mail, 13 May 1969.

A Birmingham family were offered a new council
house after convincing the City's housing department that their present one was haunted. Two
exorcisms by local clergymen and £600 worth of
medium's services had failed to end their two
years of torment by a poltergeist. One medium
described a hooded and toe-less monk; and another
was thrown violently downstairs and had to be
taken to hospital for treatment. The wife said:
"It's nerve-racking living here. I have to keep my
purse and pills on me. If I don't, the poltergeist
hides them!" The husband added: "He loves to have
fun with my underwear. He throws them downstairs,
and if I don't pick them up he creates chaos in the
kitchen. Once I had a bath and asked my wife to
get my pants, but she couldn't find them. The next
morning I was astonished to see them hanging on
a branch at the top of a tree at the back of the
house." No names or location is given in the
report except that the house in "near the site of
an old monastery." Birmingham Times, 20 Sept 74.
Credit: David Driscoll.

Ghosts cont. p8/

SOME FORTEAN RAMBLINGS

Janet Bord

Occasionally, I have random thoughts which have to do with forteana and strange happenings in general. My thinking on these doesn't get too far usually, so I will entrust some of them to paper in the hope that perhaps someone else will be able to make use of them.

One thought that keeps returning to me, is, I feel, rather more important than many seem to realise. That is, the question of precision in Ley-hunting. Despite the growing interest in the subject, little has been written authoritatively on ley-hunting and plotting. I can only think of Watkins' OLD STRAIGHT TRACK and John Michell's VIEW OVER ATLANTIS, plus a few articles in THE LEY HUNTER and a soon-to-be-published book by that journal's editor, Paul Screeton, called QUICKSILVER HERITAGE. Newcomers to the field read some of this material, grab their 1" OS maps and begin finding leys all over the place. But how closely have they studied the 'rules of the game'? In many cases, not at all. Eager to discover leys, they disregard some of the basic criteria with unbelievable results (eg. hundreds of leys on one 1" map). The main point is that leys are lines linking ancient sites, and each point on a ley must be an ancient site of some kind - mound, stone, circle, religious building of some antiquity, moat, etc - not just a village, or a name incorporating 'ley' in some form. Also, sites must be accurately joined - no moving the ruler slightly so that the ley works. This problem is greatly accentuated when joining sites on seperate maps. To be accurate, compass bearings must be taken.

This introduces another point - how wide is a ley? No one knows. It could be only a few inches, or it could be thousands of yards. If the former, then it would be impossible to plot on a small-scale map such as the 1". Each symbol on these maps covers a lot of ground, and the pencil line drawn to join the sites is itself many yards wide on the ground. There is also no knowing which part of the site the ley passes through. But if a ley is very wide, the accuracy of plotting is not so important. In this case, though, more sites can be aligned by allowing a wide margin, but then with less precision there is no certainty that all are leys. If leys are wide, does an ancient site stand exactly in the middle, or to one side? The art of dowsing seems to hold many possibilities for the ley-hunter. The problems I have just outlined could probably be solved by a sensitive use of the divining rod or pendulum. (1).

It seems that we really know very little about leys, despite intuition, theory and pure guesswork, all of which have been frequently employed. All we really know is that ancient sites seem to align. Do these lines mark areas where a current of some kind runs through the earth, all the time or at certain times? Or do they mark points where power can be drawn down from the heavens   (the tall stones - with church spires copying them? - being instrumental in the drawing down?), to be stored in the stones, in the earth, or in the mounds? Were religious buildings constructed on these lines in order to benefit from the power received, as well as helping in the exchange of power? Are religious festivals long-distant remnants of ceremonials performed at the important periods of power reception or transmission?

How can we find out more about leys and their significance? It is surely not enough to plot them on a map. Perhaps, having verified as far as possible the existence of a ley, both on the map and in the field, a valuable exercise would be to investigate the activity, past and present, on the ley; local customs being particularly relevant. However, few of these are practised today, and old books on local history and folklore may well record some extinct ones. It would also be a good idea to get to know a ley, spending time on it, exploring its different moods and currents at different seasons and times of day. It helps if you are psychic - you might see something interesting. Find out if there are any records of ghosts along the ley, or of UFOs having been seen above it. It is possible there are connexions. (2).

Mentioning ghosts and UFOs leads me to another 'great British mystery' in which I take special interest, being an animal-lover. Mysterious dog-like creatures seem to have appeared throughout Britain for centuries and are still doing so, though they are now called 'the Surrey puma', even when they appear in Hampshire or Hertfordshire. (3). Folklore contains many references to these beasts - they were most often black, with large fiery eyes, and the size of a calf. Here are some examples.

The black dog is best known as Black Shuck, though that is his name only in East Anglia. (Shuck comes from scucca, Anglo-Saxon for demon.) He is particularly feared in Norfolk, where to see him is to die. In Essex however, he is friendlier, even protecting travellers on lonely roads.

The black dog is also recorded in the Channel Islands. On Guernsey near St Peter Port, he was called Tchi-co, and his howls presaged a death. On Jersey, the appearance of Le Tchan de Bouole (Dog of Bouley) warned of an approaching

Cardinal Croecentius and the Black Dog. (from Janet Bord's "GHOSTS".) Radio Times Hulton Library.

storm.

Devon was a popular haunt of the black dog, and they were often to be seen around the lanes, gates and bridges of that county. Conan Doyle's Hound of the Baskervilles was based on the legend of the Black Dog of Dartmoor; and one patrols a beat from Copplestone Cross to Downe St Mary. There is also a hamlet called Black Dog in the same neighbourhood.

In Wales he is the Dog of Darkness, the Gwyllgi. "This is a frightful apparition of a mastiff, with baleful breath and blazing red eyes, which shine like fire in the night." They were mainly confined to sea-coast parishes (as was Black Shuck) and were not pleasant to see, though they were not, in Wales, considered to be a death omen.

Other parts of the country also have their legends of the black dog, and he goes under different aliases: Mauthe Doog in the Isle of Man; the Barguest in Yorkshire; the Trash-hound in Lancashire; and the Pooka in Ireland. He is not even confined to Britain - I recently saw an old engraving depicting a Cardinal Croecentius in his study being faced by a large, fierce dog with glowing eyes, surely our old friend the black dog. ((see illustration - Ed.)). As yet I do not know the history behind this picture. And what about the Hans Anderson fairy-tale of a soldier seeking treasure underground, which is guarded by three huge dogs - one with eyes as big as

saucers, one with eyes as big as a millwheel, and the third with eyes as big as the Round Tower of Copenhagen. Did Anderson base these descriptions on stories he had heard about the black dog?

My descriptions of the Black Dog have all been in the past tense, and I have suggested that the 'Surrey Puma' is the modern equivalent. However, I have on file a letter written to me recently by a lady who saw a Black Dog herself when she was a girl during the Second World War, so maybe he is still around. The details she gives agree with many in the old legends, and so the letter is worth quoting.

"The cottage where we lived is still in existence, in Bredon, Worcestershire. My encounter took place one late afternoon in summer, when I had been sent to bed, but was far from sleepy. I was sitting at the end of the big brass bedstead, playing with the ornamental knobs, and looking out of the window, when I was aware of a scratching noise, and an enormous black dog had walked from the direction of the fireplace to my left. It passed round the end of the bed, between me and the window, round the other corner of the bed, towards the door. As the dog passed between me and the window, it swung its head round to stare at me - it had very large, very red eyes, which glowed from inside as if lit up, and as it looked at me I was quite terrified, and very much aware of the creature's breath, which was warm and strong as a gust of wind. The animal must have been very tall, as I was sitting on the old-fashioned bedstead, which was quite high and our eyes were level. Funnily enough, by the time it reached the door, it had vanished. I assure you that I was wide awake at the time, and sat for quite some long while wondering about what I had seen, and to be truthful, too scared to get into bed, under the covers and go to sleep. I clearly remember my mother and our host, sitting in the garden in the late sun, talking, and hearing the ringing of the bell on the weekly fried-fish van from Birmingham, as it went through the village! I am sure I was not dreaming, and have never forgotten the experience, remembering to the last detail how I felt, what the dog looked like, etc. "

I have no idea what these manifestations signify, if anything. They do not seem to be the same as straightforward ghosts, which in most cases have some link with a once-living person or once-existing place. Perhaps, as has been suggested elsewhere, they are a tenuous link with other planes of existence. If so, I have no wish to see further into their environment!

Finally, a mystery from Dartmoor, which I recently read about in WITCHCRAFT AND FOLKLORE OF DARTMOOR by Ruth E St Leger-Gordon (EP Publishing, 1973). Near Haytor, on Dartmoor's eastern edge, is a wood bounded by a lane. A newcomer to the district walked along the lane one evening and admired a cottage seen through the trees. When she later remarked on this to the owner of the wood, he was rather surprised because there is no cottage there. When she went back to look, no cottage was to be seen. Shortly afterwards, the cottage was seen again, this time by someone recently come to live in a new bungalow opposite the wood. She knew nothing of the earlier sighting. Later, an Ordnance Surveyor visiting the area looked down from a high vantage point and saw a cottage he had missed before. There was smoke coming from the chimneys and clothes blowing on the line. He walked down to the area but could find no trace of the cottage. He asked a lady who was out with her dog, and she too said that she had seen the cottage, but had been unable to locate it again. The author of the Dartmoor book, having all the details, ascertained that in all cases the same cottage was seen on the same spot. A careful search of the site produced no sign of old foundations, so the witnesses were probably not seeing the ghost of a former cottage.

Were they looking through into another existence, similar to ours but normally seperate from it? This suggestion causes me to recall certain parts of Robert A Monroe's book JOURNEYS OUT OF THE BODY where he recounts experiences of another existence, very similar to ours, during astral projection. It may seem extremely far-fetched to suggest that the space we live in is also occupied by others, living in similar sur-

roundings to ours but not normally visible to us. But the older I grow, the less I am certain of - especially relating to the wider meaning of life.

=+=   =+=   =+=   =+=   =+=

NOTES -- by the Editor.

1) For a good introduction to the use of dowsing, particularly in connection with the investigation of sites of antiquity, and the energy fields of ghosts, see TC Lethbridge's GHOST AND DIVINING ROD (Routledge & Kegan Paul), which also includes much interesting material on the haunts of the Scottish lake-monsters. But the fundamental research work into the application of dowsing theory and practice is continuing: see for example THE LEY HUNTER 34, Aug 72 for the results of several experiments in 'Ley Dowsing' by RG Wood, which is in turn an extension of Underwood's theories of geodetic-lines and emanations from blind-springs, as set out in his PATTERNS OF THE PAST.

2) This is the area of prime interest for Forteans in the Ley phenomena. Evidence is slowly building up that there is indeed a correspondence between types of Fortean phenomena and proximity to Leys. We hope to be presenting an exploratory article on this subject in future. THE NEWS feels that this connexion deserves our continuing interest.

3) By one of those 'coincidences' that seem to be happening more frequently within the sphere of my interests, my own summary of 'Surrey Puma' cases between 1962 and 1973 was published in the current INFO Journal (No 13). This also contains some speculation on the phenomenon in relation to UFOs, Astral Projection, ghosts and Leys. More cases have cropped up in the meantime (see last issue for reports of 'puma' in Scotland) and we shall be publishing them in due course.

GHOSTS / cont:

The Owen family have now got a new council flat after waiting two months. Their former residence, a 20-year-old terraced house in Godre'r Parc, Tregarth, near Bangor, north Wales, was said by them to be haunted by a ghost 6ft tall in modern clothes, who frightened their six children. An exorcism by Rev. Aelwyn Roberts of Llandegai, failed to end the trouble. Sunday Mirror 8 Sept 74.

A COUPLE OF OUTDOOR TYPES.

In August 1965, the Worcestershire village of Pershore was gripped by a week of ghost-hunting. We have no date other than that, but our source is The People. One Sunday, 3 little boys moonlight fishing were startled by something and ran in panic all the way home, where they said they had seen a ghost. Mr Paddy Weaver, a postman, said: "I was with two friends down by the river when I saw something. At the time we saw the thing, some small boys went dashing across the field. I don't know exactly what I saw except that it was a white square thing. On the Monday night about 20 people gathered by the river claimed they saw a "gleaming 6ft spectre float 3ft above the ground across the field to a cemetery." On Tuesday 50 fearless hunters said that when the spectre appeared they formed a ring around, then it vanished. On Wednesday the numbers were up to 100. Two women with umbrellas chased something that quite wisely vanished. (It wasn't me, I swear it.) On Thursday, 150 people rushed across the field to some trees but there was nothing there. (Good Lord!) On Friday it was 200 waiting till midnight for something to happen, and it didn't. And that seems to be the end of that.

Two workers at the paper-mill at Greenfield, near Oldham, claimed they were startled by a ghost on a landing jetty in the mill waters. One said he had never been so frightened in his life. "The ghost was more than 6ft tall, with hands at his side, about 75ft from us - but we could see it clearly. It was all white. We stood staring at this ghost for three minutes just after dawn had broken. Then I shouted 'Oh!' and it vanished into thin air." The other man said: "It made me go cold. We sneaked closer but it vanished when Les shouted at it." A young electrician was drowned at the spot many years previously. Manchester Evening News, 17 July 1967. Credit for both above to Peter Rogerson.

MORE GHOSTS

A successful exorcism at 54 Chester Rd, Buckley, where the Massey family and their five children were pestered by incidents over the 11 months previously. Several ghosts were seen upstairs, including an old man, and a man with a horse, and then a group of seven ghosts in quick succession at the foot of the stairs. Manchester Evening News, 26 Nov 1968. Credit: P Rogerson.

**   **   **

82-year-old Sarah Mayor reports a noisy ghost in her 100-year-old house in Lancaster Road, Hindley, near Wigan. After midnight it knocks on all the doors and ends with a loud tatoo on the front door at 2.30am punctually. Evening News & Chronicle, 28 Oct 1969. Cr: P Rogerson.

**   **   **

John Stonehouse, (then) Minister of Post & Telecomunications, denies moving out of his London flat in Kennington one month after moving in, because of ghosts. His son has said he "heard things", and two previous tennants testify to seeing "grey figures" and poltergeist activity. Sunday Express, 9 Nov 1969. Cr: P Rogerson.

**   **   **

Shimmering ghosts in old army uniforms of black buttoned tunics and cylindrical hats appeared in Imphal Barracks, Yorkshire, used by teenage privates. They were seen by at least three boys and one had to be taken to the sickbay to sleep after a duty officer was called. Daily Mail, 12 Nov 1969. Credit: Peter Rogerson.

**   **   **

Ghostly cavaliers and dark shapes have frightened staff working late at the Hippo Club, Nottingham. Some have felt "prickly hands" touch them. Daily Mail, 5 July 1971.

**   **   **

Caretaker and cleaners at Burnley Wood Primary School, Burnley, have been terrified by sounds of a baby moaning, and a ghostly kid who skips and sings down the corridors. Daily Mail, 10 Sept 1971. Cr above two: P Rogerson.

**   **   **

The ghost of a monk has been seen in the Classic Cinema, Lenton Abbey, Nottingham. Daily Mail, 27 April 1973. Cr: Steve Moore.

**   **   **

Cleaners at Warwick Castle refuse to go into the tower where Faulke Greville, the first Lord Brooke, was murdered by his servant in 1628, and took 2 weeks to die. Mrs Joan Ryan was polishing a floor when she heard loud scratching noises appear to come from a portrait of Greville. Birmingham Evening Mail, 20 June 73.

**   **   **

The dairies at Wellington, Somerset, have become such a place of mysterious groanings and footsteps at night, that the milkmen are being allowed later deliveries. Daily Mail, 9 Feb 74. Credit: Steve Moore.

**   **   **

Hotel developers wanted to pull down the 22 bedroomed Audrey Court Hotel, Lower Warberry Road, Torquay, Devon, but the Deptartment of the Environment have slapped a preservation order on it. Legend says that Edward VII bought the 114-year-old hotel for his assignations with Lilly Langtrey in 1901, whose ghost now haunts the corridors knocking on doors. Sunday Mirror, 21 July 1974.

**   **   **

The shadowy ghost of a longhaired red-coated man has taken up new lodgings in the pub-disco in Westgate Road, Newcastle-upon-Tyne, after the 103-year-old theatre next door shut down and later converted to X films. It is reported to have walked through a barman locking up late at night. News of the World, 21 July 74.

**   **   **

The Rector of Haworth has prevented the former Curate exorcising a ghost, reputed to be Emily Brontë, haunting the Toby Jug Restaurant in Haworth, Yorks, every year on 19 December, the anniversary of Emily's death. Hmmm...didn't Dennis Weatley write a novel called "The Haunting of Toby Jug"? Daily Telegraph, 2 Oct 74. Credit: David Driscoll.

**   **   **

Because of the generosity of a number of readers who have turned over their collections of Forteana to THE NEWS, we have a considerable backlog of material on ghosts (to name but one category). Many of these data go back to the middle 60s, and will appear in subsequent NEWSs.

SOME WEIRDOS.

Some of our data is not new, but we print it because we don't think it has been recorded elsewhere. Frinstance, this letter to the Manchester Evening News of 24 Oct 1968:

"I was interested to read in Saturday's issue the report headlined 'The Ghost Music Goes Round and Around..' for I too heard the same ghost more than two years ago.

(The report stated that the thin piping tunes that float down from the floor above come from — an empty office! And the two girls who work in Peter St. wonder if they have located the phantom flautist of the old Gaiety Theatre which used to stand on the site.)

I used to work in a shop thereand I and the Manageress frequently heard what we thought was an employee of the office above practicing on a clarinet or flute. We too heard the player practice only scales or snatches of tunes. In fact we used to joke that for all his practicing he didn't seem to be getting any better. He always played after 5pm when the offices closed. Thats why we presumed he was staying behind after work. We were generally the last to leave the building at 6pm. During the whole of this period we had no idea that there was no-one in the office! I do remember the plaque in the main entrance commemorating the old Gaiety Theatre, so I'd like to confirm the statements of the two girls mentioned in the report as being perfectly true." (Miss JA Jackson, Beverley Ave, Davyhulme, Urmston.) Credit: Peter Rogerson.

A hospital chaplain has been asked to exorcise a ward where ghostly footsteps are heard at night. Two senior nurses and a houseman of Guy's Hospital, London, told of an incident involving a woman who was dying in Addison Ward, about midnight. Along the corridor came the sound of heavy footsteps. "Students playing a prank," thought the houseman. But the sounds came through the door, down the centre of the ward — and stopped near the bed of the dying woman. Patient already awake heard the steps, and so did others who were awakened by the noise — but no-one saw anything. After a few minutes, the steps resumed as though with heavy and squeaking boots, going back the way they came. And in those minutes in between, the woman patient died. Daily Mail, 16 Jan 1969. Cr: P Rogerson.

Steve Moore sent us a note from the Daily Mirror 8 Aug 74, announcing a radio confrontation on the subject of ESP. One of the participants was Arthur Ellison, a professor of electrical engineering at City University, London, and member of the SPR, who recounts his introduction into the world of paranormal phenomena when he woke one night to see a hole in his ceiling. And through that hole there peered a face, looking at him intently. This reminded us of a note sent by Peter Rogerson, earlier, from the Daily Mail, 18 Jan 1968, in which a woman university lecturer told of her mother's fear of "strange noises in the night" at her terrace cottage in Lydgate, Lepton, near Huddersfield. She went to stay with her mother over Christmas "to find out if she was suffering from some delusion", and slept during the day to stay awake at night. At 3am one night her mother called her and pointed to the ceiling. "I saw a small circular light through a break in the ceiling, but I could not find any explanation for it. When I switched on the bedroom light, the other light stayed on for a few seconds then went out." Then she called the police to check the security and they confirmed that nobody had walked in the loft. A few minutes after they left the noises were heard again — running out of the house, the lecturer saw "a man through some curtains" though it is not clear whether this was in her mother's house. On the 14th Jan her mother was found dead in the gas-filled kitchen. The inquest was adjourned for further evidence.

From Hongkong came news of a giant exorcism involving 70 Buddhist priests to clear a new government building of "troublesome ghosts". It was built on the site of a Japanese public execution ground. One woman employee said: "The ghosts make all kinds of noises, screaming and giggling especially when a pretty girl is around. I personally believe they are sex-starved." The ritual was ordered by Traffic Commissioner Brian Wilson after complaints from his staff. San Francisco Chronicle, 9 Feb 74. Cr: L Coleman.

Cleaners working on jumbo jets at London's Heathrow Airport have refused to work alone at night in case they are attacked by a spook that holds them down by the throat and arms. Lal Parmar, foreman of a group of industrial cleaners, admitted to being very frightened when he met it in the rest room on the jet piers. "It all started when we opened the doors one day and there was a strange smell. It went away but came back later. I sat in a chair for a brief rest and was horrified when I could not get up again. My eyes shut and I could not open them. It was as if someone was holding me down by my shoulders for about four or five minutes." The British Airport Authority has launched an inquiry. Express & Star, 23 Oct 74. Credit: Frank Adey.

"When my sons were small and sleeping in our back room, they were woken up by a dwarf-like figure with a huge face. He pulled their hair, ran around and made a getaway through the window. He never woke them both up. It was one boy one night and the other the next. They were never hurt and said the dwarf wanted to play and got annoyed if they wanted to sleep." (Mrs MT; Swansea.) Letter to The Sun, 7 March 72. Credit: Nigel Watson. Some day, we fear, we shall have to account with the phenomena of kiddies' 'invisible' friends!!?!

Lastly, a tale of a helpful ghost. Or so we are told by Les Gibbons, a boilerman at the Royal Marine Barracks, Lympstone, Devon, who said:"I went to the boilerhouse about 4am. It was a clear windless night. By the far wall, about 60ft away, was a pile of wood shavings. Suddenly the pile rose about 2ft in the air and came towards me, dropping at my feet. Simultaneously two wires connected to the boiler sprang out of their sockets. I reconnected the wires and looked for an explanation but found nothing. The astonishing thing is that the boiler has worked perfectly ever since." Daily Mirror, 17 Jan 1968 . Credit: Peter Rogerson.

VISIONS.

Where in this continuous universe do ghosts merge away into visions, sacred or profane? Can we think that a vision contains some comunicable spiritual symbolism, as against a ghost which seems to be some mindless and automatic reflex between man and the universe? We begin this little section with the tale of Mowbreck Hall, Wesham, near Kirkham, rebuilt in 1730 on the foundations of the old hall built in the 1100s. By any standards, the events were 'normal' haunted house stuff, but they got troublesome enough for the proprietor, Ellis Kit, to call in an exorcist. What interests us is the reference to an incident in 1584, when the hall had a private chapel for Roman Catholics, who were forbidden to worship in Protestant churches. The son of the hall-owner of the time was betrayed and executed for Jesuit sympathies. His father was confronted at midnight by the spectre of the son's gory head above the altar, which said in Latin from bloodstained lips: "Your sadness will turn to joy." The father fainted and died shortly after. Manchester Evening News, 10 Jan 1968.

Two young children were in hospital being treated for shock. Their mother Martha McLeish was still shaking as she recounted the incident that decided her on moving from her council flat at 35 Northern Drive, Collyhurst, Manchester, and that caused her to take the children to Booth Hall Hospital at 2 in the morning. Two and a half years earlier, Mrs Mabel Potter, a widow, was murdered in the flat; a man was accused and then cleared, leaving the killer still unfound. Mrs McLeish says she has seen the ghost of Mrs Potter twice during 1972, each time being woken from sleep by a sensed presence. "Last Sunday (12 Nov) night when I was about to put Rhoda and Jackie to bed they came running to me, hysterical, screaming at the top of their voices: 'There's something in our room.' I could not get much out of them. My little girl said: 'She was on the cross.' Every night since they have refused to go into their bedroom and I have stayed up all night with them on the living-room settee." That was reported in the Daily Mail, 17 Nov 1972, and the same paper the next day added some detail of the elder girl's story: Rhoda, 5, said: "She had long hair like mummy's. She was on a cross. There was a big band playing. I was very frightened. The bogey woman said to me, 'You must wait for me in this room.' I said, 'Get out of the room.' She touched me and I ran for my mummy. I don't want to go back there again." Her 3-year-old brother added: "She touched my mouth and I was very frightened. I don't want to see her again." Altogether a curious case. Both above items are to Peter Rogerson's credit.

The villagers at Cafala Diana say that the Mad-

onna has appeared to at least 30 people in the tiny village in Palermo area of Sicily, and every afternoon for a week has appeared at the window of a ruined castle. The local priest has refused to go with the villagers to see the 'apparitions.' Daily Mirror, 2 June 1967. Credit: A Smith.

Church authorities are trying to calm excited villagers in Castelnau de Guers (pop. 800.) tucked away 20 miles inland from the Mediterranean coast in the apparently not-so-God-forsaken corner of southern France. The bishop of Montpellier has urged all Catholics in the region to act with "reserve and great prudence." The stir started when the local Abbé Caucanas and about 30 of his parishioners swear they saw the face of Christ appear clearly on a napkin covering the ciborium (a vessel for the eucharistic bread) on the altar of the Saint-Sulpice Church, and last for about 15 minutes. Father François Caucanas, greatly embarrassed by the uproar, said "I had just knelt before the altar. As I rose I saw, on the fine white napkin covering the ciborium, the face of Our Lord. His right eye was closed, the left open. The nose was bruised and swollen and the face bore an expression of pain." He shouted to the congregation and they all surged forward. Some say they saw tears on the cheeks, and another, a crown of thorns. Then the image disappeared when the priest lifted the napkin to take up the ciborium at the moment of Holy Communion. In all this cosmic seriousness, we warm to Gerard Lorquet, the sacristan, who attributes the vision to the fact that Caucanas still says the Mass in Latin. "This is a sign," he says, "A warning to others and an act of Gods gratitude for the abbé for not allowing electric guitars in the church." Milwaukee (Wisconsin) Journal, 20 April 74. Credit: Mark Hall. Over a month later the effects of that evening Mass on the Good Friday were still being felt. The small village is reported to be wishing they had kept their mouths shut. A huge invasion of the curious has caused chaos in their quiet lives; stones are hacked from the church walls; the font is constantly emptied of water, and pews are being chipped. "Soon they will be coming to cut up my trousers for relics," said Caucanas, whose curt remarks are in sharp contrast to his exuberent attitude just after the event. Scunthorpe Evening Telegraph, 29 May 74. Credit: Nigel Watson. Ah yes! They have a nice line in nice lines down in good ole Castelnau de Guers.

MARK
HALL'S

THE FABULOUS "BERMUDA TRIANGLE"

The foremost fable of our time is certainly the
ill-defined "Bermuda Triangle." This has been
alleged by a string of writers to be a zone in
the northwestern Atlantic where ships and planes
disappear without trace. In fact, no area of
recognisable shape can be found by plotting the
alleged vanishings. They simply string out along
the Florida coast and onward along the
islands from there to South America. They may
only be the toll to be paid in disaster in an
area of heavy air and sea traffic. Still, no less
than four new books on this subject have appeared
this year in the USA (1) and a fifth, simply
about disappearances at sea (2), has also been
published. For those persons who keep up with
these claims of oddities and disappearances,
here are the latest relevant items.

**A 51ft cabin cruiser was found on 24 Dec 73,
north of Nassau, Bahamas, with 8 persons missing
and presumed lost at sea. (3)
**A light plane that disappeared 21 July 1963
was found in March 1974 off New Port Richey,
Florida, in the Gulf of Mexico. (4)
**The 54ft yacht 'Saba Bank' left Nassau 10 Mar
74 with four men aboard and vanished. (5)
**Yacht 'Surefire', reported missing during a
race in the Gulf, docked at Coral harbor, Florida
on 6 May 74. The captain refused to say where he
had been. (6)
**'Niagara', a 200 ton freighter, disappeared
24 May 74 in the Caribbean. In July, fishermen
found 12 of her crewmen dead on a raft off Nic-
aragua. (7)
**US Navy divers searched a wreck off Wachaprege,
Virginia, in August 74, with hopes that it was
the 'Cyclops' that disappeared in March 1918. The
wreck was found to contain a cargo of scrap-iron
– the 'Cyclops' carried manganese ore. (9)
**The US Coast Guard disclosed at hearings in
Washington that drug smugglers are hijacking
yachts and other boats at sea. Vessels missing
along both seacoasts and in the Gulf and Caribbean areas are included. Only a few cases can be
conclusively documented, but 34 boats are specifically suspected of this fate. The 202 people
carried by those boats are still missing and
presumed murdered. (10)

Sources: (1) The Devil's Triangle by Richard
Winer; The Bermuda Triangle by Charles Berlitz;
Devil's Triangle by David Graham; No Earthly
Explanation by John W Spencer. (2) Posted
Missing by Alan Villiers. (3) Milwaukee (Wis-
consin) Sentinel, 25 & 26 Dec 73. (4) St Louis
(Missouri) Post-Dispatch, 24 March 74. (5)
Miami (Florida) Herald, 26 April 74. (6) Miami
Herald, 7 May 74. (7) Washington (DC) Star-News
22 July 74. (8) Milwaukee (Wisconsin) Journal,

26 July 74. (9) Minneapolis (Minn) Star, 27
July 74; Washington Star-News, 3 Aug 74. (10)
Des Moines (Iowa) Register, 28 Aug 74; Tampa
(Florida) Tribune, 29 Aug 74.

***   ***   ***   ***   ***

AIRCRAFT IN ICE.

Reminiscent of the ships seen on ice in 1851
(discussed by Rupert T Gould in Oddities), a
Finnish vessel bound for London reported sighting a twin-engined aircraft in an iceberg in
Notre Dame Bay, Newfoundland. This report was
made on 6 July to a lighthouse keeper by the
officers of the bulk carrier 'Burney'. Canadian
armed forces personnel followed up this lone
report of a Dakota-type airplane but said their
records did not show any plane to account for
it. They did not find such an iceberg, but did
observe a rapid thaw in progress. At mid-July
the sought-after berg was thought to have melted
away. Windsor (Ontario) Star, 16 July 74; and
Chicago Tribune, 22 July 74.

***   ***   ***   ***   ***

CHAMBER BENEATH A MEXICAN PYRAMID.

Numerous archeological discoveries have been in
the news. Now that North American tools and such
are permitted to date prior to 10,000 BC, such
finds are frequently made; the latest being in
Pennsylvania and Baja California. But a surprising announcement comes from the Mexican National
Institute of Anthropology and History about a
find made two years ago. A tunnel was found 16ft
underground beneath the 170ft-high Pyramid of
the Sun, 30 miles north of Mexico City. This
tunnel is a cave with walls smoothed with dark
clay, and runs east to west for 328 feet directl
to a point beneath the centre of the pyramid.
There three pathways open up in the shape of a
three-leaf clover. The discovery was made when
rain uncovered the opening. Bones and pottery
(dated 300AD) have been found in the cave.
Mexican archeologists have long maintained their
pyramids were only temples, not tombs, and are
calling this cave a "ritual chamber." Houston
(Texas) Chronicle, 25 July 74; St Louis (Mo)
Post-Dispatch, 8 Sept 74.

***   ***   ***   ***   ***

THE MINNESOTA RUNESTONE.

A British film director, Brian Branston, has
made a BBC documentary that labels as a hoax
Minnesota's foremost Viking artifact, the Kensington Runestone. The story of this stone is
too lengthy to tell here, but it bears a runic
inscription with a date of 1362. It came to
light in 1898, and all the original principals
in the early controversy are now dead. Mr Bran-

ston's documentary cannot be broadcast in the USA, so we here will not see it – but from what we read of him, he is a man who cannot tackle a mystery without finding a solution, perhaps even if it is the wrong one. Sadly there are no longer any local scholars who argue the authenticity of the stone, either for or against. And so it is ripe for exploitation by any travelling showman, and the solutions to this 'hoax' have shifted endlessly without solid foundation. Each new solution claims to find the culprits, but the stone remains, outlasting its detractors and awaiting our understanding. St Paul (Minn.) Dispatch, 6 Aug 74; Lake Region Press (Alexandria, Minn.), 9 Aug 74.

***   ***   ***   ***   ***

GIANT STEPS.

Coal miners in Utah are constantly threatened by dinosaurs stepping on them. The danger comes from fossilized footprints of giant reptiles that once walked atop swamps now turned to coal. As the miners tunnel through the coal, 3-toed tracks up to 4½ft long drop from the ceilings.

The largest of these tracks are the only known evidence of a two-legged dinosaur that was twice as large as Tyrannosaurus Rex. Milwaukee (Wisconsin) Journal, 1 Aug 74.

***   ***   ***   ***   ***

ARKANSAS STINKS.

Two years ago the people of Crooked Creek, in Boone County, Arkansas, noticed the fumes for the first time. The smell was so bad they fought for breath. Fumes seemingly from nowhere in subsequent months caused rashes on faces, necks and arms, swelling of glands, dizziness, watery eyes and other problems. Persons for a mile around the small community in the Ozark Mountains have been affected. No businesses or other possible sources for the noxious fumes have been found. The latest complaints in late August brought in state and federal agencies that are even now investigating. Miami (Florida) Herald, 2 Sept 74.

***   ***   ***   ***   ***

SWARMS.

Small brown moths of unknown type and origin swarmed in Cleveland, Ohio, and its suburbs on the morning of 15 July. Cleveland Plain Dealer, 16 July 74. — Rats "suddenly appeared" in great numbers in northeastern Hamilton, Ontario, say residents. Windsor (Ontario) Star, 26 July 74 — Field mice swarmed in the San Joaquin Valley, California, in one of the worst outbreaks in 20 years. San Francisco Examiner, 2 Aug 74. — A 3 month plague of mice on the southeast coast of Maui Island in Hawaii was stopped by providing poisoned oats for the rodents. Atlanta Journal & Constitution, 22 Sept 74.

***   ***   ***   ***   ***

CULTS, CATTLE, COPTERS, AND CURIOUS LIGHTS.

We dislike taking space to discuss the clandestine activities of criminals, but for the past year the activities of cattle rustlers using helicopters have become bound up with stories of mysterious lights, UFOs, strange animals, and cases of livestock mutilation. The rustling has been going on in several Midwestern states. Even the newsmagazine NEWSWEEK got into the act, reporting this story with such cryptic lines as: "A few residents reported sighting strange creatures resembling bears and gorillas, and at least one farmer claims that a shiny UFO landed in a field where a slaughtered animal was later found." (1) We hope to sort out some of the mystery for you now.

Helicopters are not new to cattle rustling. They were used five years ago in Texas (2) and are now linked with recent rustling. Press notoriety for these helicoptering bandits began in April 1973. Through the next 18 months, the areas of rustling and helicopter sightings shifted rapidly through the states of Iowa, Missouri, Illinois, Arkansas, Kansas, Nebraska, Iowa again, South Dakota, and Minnesota. While all these incidents need not be the work of just one group of men, the timing of them indicates they could be. So far two aircraft have definitely been determined to be in use. Two slow, low-flying aircraft were once seen on radar from Kansas City, Mo., (3) and in a bizarre daylight incident (related below) one helicopter and a small plane were seen. Tedious detail and complete references will be avoided in the following brief discussion.

Stories of mutilated cattle and horses began in Kansas in October of 1973. Most often cattle were found with sex organs and ears removed, and the carcasses were remarkably bloodless. Such finds continued later in Nebraska and South Dakota into October of 1974.

Diseases and predatory animals may have killed some of the cattle, but there was no doubt that

many had been deliberately slain. Rustling did
continue, but attentions became focussed on the
more frequent finds of mutilations and on the
lights seen at night where carcases would later
be found. Farmers began patrolling at night, but
these incidents were spread out over many large
counties.

The most bizarre occurrence had to be the experience of a 20-year-old farmer at his farm near
Honey Creek, Iowa, north of Council Bluffs, on
15 July 74. While cultivating corn with his
tractor, he saw two aircraft, a white helicopter
and a black twin-engined plane, come swooping
down over him. A man leaned from the helicopter
and began firing with a handgun - the shots
striking the ground near the tractor. The farmer
took cover and watched the aircraft buzz the
farm, then fly off. They bore no markings, and
investigating authorities could not learn anything about the craft. (4)   (For what it may
mean: the body of a Council Bluffs man was found
near North Topeka, Kansas, on 12 Sept 74. He had
bled to death from six puncture wounds.
"The cause of the wounds has not been determined,
officials said.") (5).

Almost all of the lights reported could well have
been produced by small aircraft. The shiny UFO
mentioned by NEWSWEEK appeared only in a pseudo-
factual article in a cheap tabloid. Shiny UFOs
have been reported recently, but at some distance
from the sites of animal mutilation. A farmer
near Langenburg, Saskatchewan, reported seing
five "stainless steel objects" hovering for 15
minutes over his property in early September.
They left depressions in grass that measured 11
feet across. (6). A few days later, on 11 Sept.
five children in Chisago City, Minnesota, say
they watched a descending saucer-shaped object
that hovered and then descended out of sight.
They described bulges on top and bottom with
white and green lights. (7).

To add to all these wonders, a 'wolf girl' was
declared to be running through the brush and
woods near Delphos, Kansas. In July 1974, a child
about 10 or 12 years old, dressed in red tattered
clothing, was sought unsuccessfully by sheriffs
after several reports. (8). I suggest this child
may have been one of a band of European gypsies
who were passing conspicuously through Kansas
that summer. (9).

The strange creatures mentioned above appear to
be two incidents that are not connected with
rustling, lights, or UFOs. On 26 August 74 a
"brown bear" was reported seen at Oakland, Nebraska. Later that same week, a resident ofSioux
City, Iowa, 50 miles north of Oakland, made a
detailed complaint about a "thing" resembling a
gorilla, that appeared in his backyard. This
animals was two-legged and hairy. (10). The
simple fact is that such reports of hairy creatures are not in the least unusual for all parts
of North America. Others for the same time
period came from Carol Stream, Illinois (11),
and near Dahlonega, Georgia (12).

Shading shows areas of helicopter, rustler,
and mutilation activities.

Back on the track of the cattle mutilations: in
July 1974, a university professor and a Nebraska
county sheriff both announced their conclusions
that members of a cult were responsible for the
mutilations then in progress. (13) A more specific suggestion has been made that a satanic
cult developed within American prisions may have
spread to these active rustlers. A more practical
use for blood and sex-organs of cattle has also
been suggested. A belief among cowboys is that
they can attract the wilder range cattle. (14)
While no conclusive proof exists, the facts so
far are consistent with the idea of a cult active among cattle rustlers.

At this writing, the mutilations continue in the
western counties of South Dakota. (Now the problem has moved away, Nebraska authorities are
referring to the "rumors of mutilations.") Ten
feet from a mutilated animal at Chester, South
Dakota, three pairs of holes were found in the
ground, four inches deep in a triangular configuration. This is the first report of such
traces, and I suspect the rustlers have been
reading the newspaper accounts that link them
with UFOs. Unfortunately the account of these
holes does not say whether they appear to have
been punched or dug in the earth. (15) On 4 Oct
a calf died on the Metzger farm, near Hills,
Minnesota. Disease and predators were blamed by
a vetinarian for the death and damages. The

owner and a local newspaper editor considered all the circumstances and were dubious. Emil Metzger expressed the sentiments of many Midwestern farmers: "Never before have I seen anything like this." (16).

Sources: (1) Newsweek, 30 Sept 74. (2) Des Moines (Iowa) Register, 22 April 73. (3) Herald-Whig (Quincey, Illinois) 30 Aug 73. (4) Des Moines Register, 17 July 74. (5) Des Moines Register, 13 Sept 74. (6) Windsor (Ontario) Star, 11 Sept 74. (7) Chisago County (Minnesota) Press, 18 Sept 74. (8) Kansas City (Mo) Times, 29 July 74. (9) St Louis (Mo) Post-Dispatch, 23 May 74. (10) Sioux City (Iowa) Journal, 31 Aug 74. (11) Chicago (Illinois) Tribune, 30 Aug 74. (12) Atlanta (Georgia) Constitution, 23 Sept 74. (13) Windsor Star, 15 July 74. (14) Miami (Florida) Herald, 9 Sept 74. (15) Waseca (Minn.) Journal, 9 Oct 74. (16) Hills (Minn) Crescent, 10 Oct 74.

FORTNOTES.

Water mysteriously seeped through the floor of a home in Coral Gables, Florida, for 9 weeks. Hydrologists finally realised that an artesian well had erupted beneath the house. Atlanta Constitution, 16 Aug 74. — Another lonesome traveller: a mixed collie dog, named Twinkles, walked from Inez, Kentucky, to Orient, Ohio. She covered 200 miles in 80 days to find her way home, Milwaukee Journal, 4 Sept 74. — A wrought iron chair resting on a porch in Peek's Crossroads, Alabama, has become an overnight sensation. Neighbors driving past say the chair moves by itself, and thousands have come to see the 'Haunted Chair' for themselves. The answer may be that the vertical bars of the chairback and horizontal lines on the house create an optical illusion. Houston (Texas) Chronicle, 3 Oct 74.

■■■■■■■■■■■■■■■■■■■■■■■■■■■■■■■

lightning

BALL LIGHTNING - GLENCOE, ARGYLSHIRE.

A spectacular manifestation of ball-lightning was witnessed by two climbers, though the opinion of one of them has now changed a little - he was struck by it in a literal way. John Graham, at 64 a veteran climber, and on the way to the summit of Bidean-nam-Bfan (3766ft) with his friend 61-year-old Jimmy Alexander, said the weather was fine when they set off but as they neared the top of this   highest peak in Argyllshire, a thunderstorm broke overhead and gave him his worst moments in 4o years of climbing.

Mr Graham has no memory of the actual event but his friend vividly recalls what happened: "I was about a yard behind John. I saw this thing, about the size of an orange and the same colour, only very bright as if it were lit from the inside. It seemed to be darting up the ridge towards us like a bouncing rubber ball. Then there was a blinding flash and a cracking noise and John went down with a bump. The next thing I knew I was on my knees - I though I had been

driven into the ground." Mr Alexander then rushed down the mountain, now in a mist, after a party of women climbers he had seen earlier.

One of them, Mrs Ann Murray, takes up the story: "It was the worst lightning I have seen in Scotland. You can imagine this desolate scene with lowering clouds - obviously something was going to happen. We started heading down the ridge. Then this call came from above, and we started up again." When the women arrived, Mr Graham had revived a little. There was another blinding flash nearby and they decided to take him down the hill. The slope is quite treacherous at the best of times and it took an hour to descend supporting Mr Graham, and another four hours to reach the Glencoe Youth Hostel where the two men stayed. They were unable to contact the local doctor because the phone was now out of order, and so the two friends, one thunderstruck, set out by car the next day for the Southern General Hospital in Glasgow. Mr Graham's injuries were mild considering the hazard he had experienced - a small purple spot on his bald head, with a fiery ring round it, and what appeared to be a blister on his heel, which turned out to be a wound cooked to an inch deep.

As far as we can check, the incident happened on the 15 August - and was reported in the Sunday Express 18 Aug 74. Credit: Steve Moore.

BALL-LIGHTNING?-NORTH WALES.

Report by Phil Ledger:
Monday, June 17, 4.20am. At Blaen-y-Wern above Trefriw in the Conway valley, Gwynedd, during a night of extremely heavy rain (severity stressed by everyone) another bang and flash occurred. The Owen family first heard a schhh...noise (above the pounding of the rain) - 5 seconds (estimated) later a ball of light was seen travelling slowly across the field of view from the window (direction, West $\pm$ 60°. Size: difficult to estimate, ie. small object nearby, or large object far off? but appeared to be 6" diameter). 10 seconds later there was an enormous bang, neard for miles around, which shook windows 3$\frac{1}{2}$ miles away and broke a lightbulb 3 miles in the opposite direction. Investigation the following day revealed that 150 yards away, the base of a small tree set in a dry stone wall had been shattered, splitting the tree apart. Rocks from the wall were split and thrown up to 100 yards around. (Map ref: SH 774 654.) There was no visible stony material not attributable to the wall, and the wood and soil were not charred.

Comments and anomalies: 1) If the ball of light caused the explosion, then from the slow travel of the ball and the lack of charring, it appears to be a case of ball-lightning (but this is only a label since we know very little about how they are formed and what they are.) If so, the severity of the blast is interesting. A recent series of letters to Nature (Vol 232 p187, July 1971; Vol 226 p252, April 1970 - both give further refs.) carried several anecdotal cases, only one of which ended in a large explosion. In that case too, the material shattered was wood, a large pier-pile, and again (by inference from

Photo (by Phil Ledger) of the blasted tree and standing stone, about 150 yards from the caravan in which the Owens were living while their house was being built, and from which they saw the passage of the ball of light. ((I hope that after processing you can make out some of the detail - Ed.))

***   ***   ***

subsequent letters) there was no charring.
2) If ball and bang are not directly related, then we are deeper into the realms of a Fortean mystery (see The News No4 p4).   3)Ley lines, I leave to others -- but 8ft from the tree is a 4½ft standing stone (not marked on the 2½" OS map either as a stone or as lying on a boundary). Also, within 200 yards,is a well supplied by water that lower in the valley is used by a commercial Spa; and a sulphur mine -- altogether an interesting place.   4) On a more personal level. the Owen family themselves feel part of the affair. Within a 12 hour period they experienced a potentially fatal accident when their car rolled off into a quarry after the handbrake failed; a particularly successful and interesting psychic time-travel experiment -- and then, to round it off...the fireball!

To a wandering fireball, a most attractive place to go to earth...but why? My thanks to Mr & Mrs Owen for their information needed to compile this report.
                ***   ***   ***

Lightning, or what was thought to be lightning, struck the stove of a mobile home in Geneva, New York. Mrs Dominick Massa said that on Friday, 21 June, she had left a roast on the stove and left the room. Minutes later, "The whole kitchen lit up," and she heard a thundering and searing noise. Firemen were called but found only damage to one burner, a hole in the broiler pan, and the roast cooked to a turn. No information is given of any weather conditions, or how the 'bolt'(?) got in. Obviously no damage was done to the roof. Story from the Winnipeg Free Press, 22 June 74. Credit: Mark Hall.
                ***   ***   ***

"Near my home a herd of cows regularly sheltered under a certain tree when it rained. However, one evening they chose a different tree. Later, there was a terrible thunderstorm and their usual tree was struck by lightning! Animal instinct, or just weather sense?" (Mrs B Lawrence. Waterloo Road, Smethwick.) Letter to Daily Mirror, 25 Sept 74.

EDITORIAL NOTES:

1) Due to the pressure of my commitments I have not been able to answer many letters or confirm subscriptions to both NEWS and INFO. Thanks to the many who've sent clippings (they shall appear in due course); and replies will also be sent in due course. If you feel you have missed issues of both mags you feel you should have received, then please let me know. Back issues still available.

2) At the end of our first year I am attempting to assess our merits and failings. Don't be too surprised if the next issue should have a different format. Costs are still going up, so economy is essential. Also coming up early next year will be drastic changes in the Editors personal circumstances and the far-reaching effects may disrupt the flow of NEWSs for a little while.

3) Because work on the administration and other routine aspects of the mag is increasing,the strain on the Editor's time is increasing. I would like to hear from anyone who can help with the compiling of general notes from current periodicals, new books, etc ideally without having to mooch suspiciously about newstands all day.

4) NEXT ISSUE: will be the first of Vol 2, and should be out early Feb on the new schedule, containing: Nigel Watson on Lincolnshire ghosts pt2; a curious animal account from Jerome Clark; latest poop on UFOs; some odd meteorology; odd behaviour of animals; and a psychic who out Gellers Geller. And the INDEX to Vol 1, of course.

ripley or not!

THE PRIME MINISTER'S YACHT IS MISSING!

On the morning of Wednesday, September 4, Britain woke to learn that the yacht 'Morning Cloud' belonging to ex-Prime Minister Edward Heath, had sunk, and two of the crew had lost their lives, late on Monday night, the 2nd Sept. What interests our (at times) ghoulish sense of the bizarre is the reporting of a few details sunk in the backwaters of the big news story.

But first, a few facts -- At 8.20am Sunday 1st Sept.'Morning Cloud' sailed out of Burnham-on-Crouch, Essex, where it had been competing in a week of racing. It was skippered by Donald Blewitt (the Joke God's hand is sure and cruel) and a crew of six. They headed across the mouth of the Thames and the weather grew rough, but nothing that these experienced sailors were not used to and couldn't handle. By 11pm on Monday they were in the Channel , and well out from the South Coast - the weather had become a Force 9 gale. A huge freak wave knocked two men overboard - one was pulled back by his safety-line, but the other's line sheared and he was lost to sight. The yacht turned about to search and was hit by a second freak wave - just as Christopher Chadd was coming up a companionway, and he too was swept away. This doubled the Tory leader's tragedy because Chadd was his god-son. The sloop was now foundering and the skipper gave the order to abandon ship - the remaining crew took to the liferaft. They were spotted 8 hours later on Tuesday morning where they and wreckage had drifted onto Brighton beach. They were utterly exhausted and had collapsed from their exposure.

The so-called freak waves are interesting. At the inquest, held in early October, Mr K Adlard Coles, described as 'Britain's leading expert on heavy weather sailing', put forward a theory based on two weeks of examination of the problem with Laurence Draper, a scientist of the Institute of Oceanography, who also gave evidence. They believe the yacht was in tidally slack waters of at least 10 fathoms. Within 5 hours, a gale of force-9 could produce waves of 26ft - and a 1% chance of waves of 30ft or more - entirely wind-generated. The two experts believe that 1% happened - helped along by the synchronisation of the peaks of two seperate wave-trains - indeed they said that the sailing belief that every seventh and eleventh wave were the highest in a train, was not unfounded. Mr Coles is planning to write this up as an appendix to his widely-accepted manual 'Heavy Weather Sailing'. (1)

Apart from our suspicions that the South Coast Channel is as mysterious in its way as the haunted triangularity off Bermuda (Past issues of The News and INFO Journal have recorded mystery sounds, missing ships, and waterspouts in the Channel), and the theoretical proof of the freak waves, it seems that 'Morning Cloud' (rather, that should be plural because there were two previous 'Morning Cloud's) was feted with bad luck - whatever that is.

'Morning Cloud I' was sold to a Jersey businessman in 1970 and renamed 'Nuage du Matin'. She was smashed to pieces in her moorings at Gorey Harbour, in a gale, at roughly the same time as 'Morning Cloud III' went down somewhere off Shoreham. MC No 2 did win a place in the '71 Admiral's Cup, but after it was sold and renamed 'Opposition' was a consistent embarassment to its owners. The doomed MC 3 got off to a bad start seconds after it was launched in 1973 - the wife of a crewmember fell into the slipway and was knocked unconscious. (2) It might be said that the sea-worthiness of these boats was never in question - they were all built to the design of specialists and sailed by experienced men.

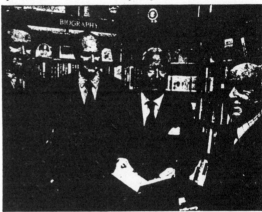

Now we come to the most remarkable and macabre twist to the plot - five days before the yaucht went down Mr Heath posed a picture (**ABOVE**) as advance publicity for a thriller by John Dyson called 'The Prime Minister's Boat is Missing' -- a novel in which "A blinding squall envelops a number of racing yachts in the English Channel ; when it clears, the boat with the Prime Minister aboard has vanished..." The publishers were said to be 'shocked and dismayed to hear of this strange and sad coincidence. " All the way to the bank, no doubt. (3) Well, Mr Koestler, here's another for your next book!!!

1) Observer, 13 Oct 74.
2) Most papers of the 4th Sept. 74. contained the story - but our facts are mainly compiled from
3) The Bookseller 7 Sept 74 - the photo of Mr Heath holding the culprit also from the Bookseller but the 14 Sept issue. Credit: Colin Bord.

• • •   • • •   • • •

Some other notable synchronicities in the last few months are 1) the discovery of breast-cancer in the wives of both the President and Vice-President of the USA; 2) On their way to the State opening of Parliament, the carriage carrying Princess Anne and Mark Phillips stopped in the Mall near the spot where the attempt was made to kidnap Anne. A horse had become lame. Geller was performing on the radio at the same time (??) . Daily Mirror, 29 Oct, and 1 Nov 74.

THE EVOLUTION OF THE FORTEAN SOURCEBOOKS

William R Corliss

Hopefully, most readers of THE NEWS are already familiar with STRANGE PHENOMENA and the other Fortean sourcebooks I have published recently. I term these sourcebooks 'Fortean' because in many ways they are extensions of Fort's work. They differ from Fort's books in that the original sources are usually reprinted completely, and are categorized and indexed. Thus, although they lack Fort's humor and philosophy, the sourcebooks should be better research tools.

The Fortean sourcebooks espouse no cause: there are no attempts to prove the existence of UFOs, ancient astronauts, the Biblical Deluge, sea monsters, or anything else. One might think this would make the sourcebooks dull reading, but I believe the contrary is true. The original accounts of atmospheric phenomena, geological conundrums, and the discoveries of inexplicable artifacts of ancient man are intrinsically exciting because the eye-witnesses were often astounded or at least highly intrigued by what they saw.

The Making of a Fortean.

For all these comparisons with Fort's efforts, it is rather ironical that my own Fortean proclivities (and therefore the sourcebooks themselves) did not begin with Charles Fort. Rather, the American geologist George McCready Price was the initial stimulus. One day in 1951, while browsing through a table of second-hand books in Berkeley, California, I came upon his EVOLUTIONARY GEOLOGY AND THE NEW CATASTROPHISM. This was my first encounter with 'outlaw science'; that is systematic investigations that are ignored or rejected out of hand by organized science of the moment. Price had collected many facts that he claimed undermined conventional geology and supported catastrophic hypotheses, such as the Biblical Deluge. Price and his small following worked contrary to the geological and biological philosophies set in motion by Lyell and Darwin.

Once my mind was adjusted to the heresy of it all, I quickly discovered the Crehore atom, the Drayson theory, and finally, in 1953, on a bookshelf at the University of Colorado library, the works of Charles Fort. It was all rather fortuitous. One has to be in the right place at the right time, because theories contrary to the prevailing dogma rarely hit the mainstream of literature. It has always been this way -- it is human nature -- and it does not annoy me nearly as much as it does most Forteans. I believe that inertia and skepticism play important roles in science. Furthermore, it has been my experience that Forteans have sacred cows too.

The foregoing aside has a purpose, for it betrays the fact that the sourcebooks have a different genesis from most Fortean literature.

To continue with the account of my discovery of the Fortean world, which I suspect is similar in emotional impact to that experienced by initiates in Rosicrucianism, Atlantism, etc; I will testify that my first contacts with Fort were identical in psychic content to my first heady encounters with idealised Baconian science. It took but a short while for me to realise that honest science and honest Forteanism are one and the same.

Should not the true Fortean, who dogmatically warns Science that its dogmas will be replaced ultimately, also admit that even Forteanism may be but an ephemeral vision? Perhaps Forteanism's "suspended judgement" is a poor way to approach the real world. Dedication and conviction of individuals may play important roles in the way things work. To illustrate: Tennyson had the wounded Arthur say: "More things are wrought by prayer than this world dreams of."

Such were my thoughts as I began to accumulate books and papers on the borderland of science during the 1960s. It was a Fortean collection in many respects, but it should be obvious by now that I cannot subscribe to the Fortean approach as the final solution. My collecting made a fine avocation, but I was led to the conclusion that something 'different' had to be done if any of the enigmas being regurgitated ad nauseum in the literature were ever to be understood. Almost everything, particularly the books in my collection, advocated one hypothesis or another. Many were the syntheses of carefully collected data. Each author saw the universe through his own particular set of glasses. It all made good reading, but it was not getting us anywhere fast.

Setting Some Goals.

Over and above all the isms and dogmas are the data -- the supreme arbiters, the facts that do not fit the prevailing theories. The data is there all right. If there is one thing Fort did not get across well, it was an appreciation of the true extent of the anomalous data, the great bulk of which still ticks away like a time-bomb amidst dusty library shelves. Fortean data may represent only 0.001% of all non-fictional literature, but summed over the centuries this is still a great deal. My experience has been that Fort merely skimmed off some of the cream and not all of that either. Not only is the foreign literature largely untapped, but little has been done with the last 50 years of anomalies, excepting for extensive files of newspaper clippings dealing mainly with UFOs and monsters. Truly revolutionary data that Fort never imagined may come from radio astronomy, the cell nucleus, and the offices of psychologists.

By 1972 I had decided that three things must be done if Fort's work was not to be in vain (I'm sure he didn't care if it was in vain or not):

    1) The scope of the Fortean approach had to be broadened to include all areas of Know-Iedge, in particular the life sciences.
    2)The scientific community must be brought in, for only scientists are likely to come up with more answers than questions.
    3) The older Fortean data had to be rescued quickly and organized into useful form, for it was suffering attrition in the libraries. In addition, the post-Fort data (the last 50 years) had to be collected. (Due to the exponential growth of the literature, the last 50 years of Fortean data may far exceed all previous data, even though it is of lower concentration).

Items 2 and 3 deserve some elaboration. One of my contentions is that Forteans by themselves may stimulate but cannot by themselves carry through scientific revolutions. Even individuals such as Velikovsky, von Daniken, and Wilhelm Reich have barely perturbed Science. I do not want to imply that these three gentlemen, just mentioned, are Forteans. Indeed their advocacy makes them distinctly anti-Forteans. I merely wish to point out that even existing hypotheses backed by some data will make little impression. Such challenges from without may even be counter-productive.

The third item in the list was stimulated by my observations in several large library systems. All data, particularly those from the Nineteenth Century and earlier, are sinking rapidly out of sight. Not that the data are being destroyed outright, as were the writings in the library of Alexandria and the temples of pre-Columbian America. They are just becoming unavailable. Libraries are increasingly expensive to operate, and the older books and journals are too expensive to place in modern information retrieval systems. In some libraries, books more than 10 years old are sold or stored somewhere where they are not available to the casual researcher. Soon, I am afraid, the only readily available data will be those that conventional wisdom has deemed worthy of indexing, cataloging and computerizing. Is this not as effective as fire?

The Sourcebook Idea.
....
    With the objectives presented above, and the constraint that anything I did had to be financially self-sufficient, I could have done several useful things with the material at hand and in the large libraries within 75 miles of my office. Fortean data could have been collected and manipulated to create one or more of the following:

    1) A comprehensive Fortean encyclopedia.
    2) A series of books written in a philo-sophical, stream-of-consciousness style, taking up where Fort left off.

    3) A large annotated bibliography.
    4) Regurgitations of the data in popular books.
    5) A Fortean handbook, organized by category rather than alphabetically, as in the ency-clopedia approach.
    6) Sourcebooks that reproduced, organized and indexed the essential Fortean literature.

I immediately eliminated possibilities 2 and 4 on the basis that they would be unlikely to in-fluence the scientific community. The annotated bibliography held promise but was discarded be-cause it would not provide researchers with raw material but only with annotations based on my personal predjudices. The encyclopedia idea was especially intriguing for I have worked on McGraw-Hill's Encyclopedia of Science and Tech-nology for many years. But who would provide the authoritative articles -- on mistpouffers, say? In addition, a comprehensive encyclopedia would entail many volumes and would present a risky investment for a publisher. The handbook was dis-carded for identical reasons. (I believe that some day a handbook and/or encyclopedia of Fort-eana will be economically viable.) This process of elimination left me with the sourcebook app-roach.

It was a good choice. It was financially acceptable because I could start with a limited field, such as geophysics, and, with the ring-binder and categorized format, take a modest bite of that field. With some modicum of market succ-ess, additional volumes could be published and combined category-by-category with preceding material. Since most sourcebook material came from scientifically reputable sources, scientists could not object strenuously no matter how ano-malous the data. (As it turned out, both Nature and Science recommended STRANGE PHENOMENA highly) Perhaps most important of all, the sourcebook approach rescues and preserves those tidbits that Fort considered forever "damned".

The relatively favorable reception of STR-ANGE PHENOMENA across the entire spectrum from serious science to the occult suggests that Fort-ean data may not be damned forever. I hope that the sourcebooks will be a common denominator. In any event, the sourcebooks are fun to research and produce. And if I read Fort correctly, he enjoyed his researches too. In fact, I am coming to believe that if you take Fort, the sourcebooks or even organized science too seriously, their real import may vanish into thin air like the UFO and Loch Ness monster.

    ***   ***   ***   ***

We heard from Bill Corliss not long ago with the news that in the STRANGE PHENOMENA series volume G2 and G3 are available now (if not shortly); volume M2 of the STRANGE ARTIFACTS series, like-wise. The first volume in series E (Geology) is well under way, and two other series (Astronomy, 'A', and Biology, 'B') are slightly more than twinkles in his eye. For more information on this valuable reference-work (worth its weight in oil) that no one in any field of reasearch can afford to do without, write to William Corliss's The Sourcebook Project, PO Box 107, Glen Arm. Mary-land 21057, USA.

ufos

THE PHANTOM HELICOPTER: Jan 1974.

In NEWS 3 (p19) we gave a summary of sightings of a 'phantom helicopter' in the region just south of Manchester. In the course of correspondence with David Rees of the Union of Northern Observers it became possible to give slightly more detailed information. Contributions gleaned from other sources build into the following picture:

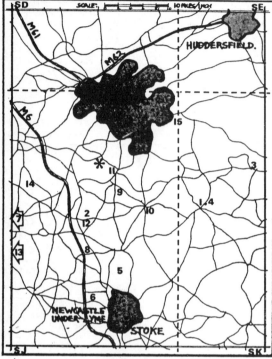

1) 26 Oct 1973 – Buxton, Derbys – Manchester
Evening News, 27 Oct 73.

2) 14 Jan 1974 – Goostrey, Cheshire.)
3) – Hope Valley, Derbys.)
Daily Mirror, 15 jan 74.

4) 15 Jan 1974 – Buxton.)
5) – Mow Cop.)
6) – Audley, Staffs.)
7) – Kelsall, Cheshire.)
8) 16 Jan 1974 – Arclid, Cheshire.)
Daily Mirror, 16 Jan 74.

9) 17 Jan 1974 – Alderley Edge.)
10) – Macclesfield.)
11) – Wilmslow.)
12) – Goostrey.)
Manchester Evening News, 18 Jan 74.

13) 18 Jan 1974 – A51, Duddon, Cheshire)
Manchester Evening News, 19 Jan 74.

14) 21 Jan 1974 – Comerbach, Cheshire.)
15) – Hyde, Cheshire.)
Radio News, 21 Jan 74.

*) Manchester Airport.
Sources: Many thanks to Mr DL Rees of MAPIT and UNO for his assistance and information. Nigel Watson, clippings. Robert Forrest, clippings. John Harney, article on 'Phantom Helicopter' in Merseyside UFO Bulletin, Vol 6. No 4.

CANADIAN PHANTOM COPTERS.

The Res Bureaux Bulletin (No 1. pp 10/11) carried some reports of "Tail-less helicopters" seen in Canada, interestingly before and after the Manchester group of sightings above.

"There were two reports of a UFO in early January (1974) near Snow Road Station, Ontario. One witness, whose account was filed with the Meteor Centre, described it as looking like the bottom portion of a hovercraft with two rotors on the top. And the other witness I located feels convinced it was a helicopter travelling away from her as she couldn't see the tail of it...Both witnesses stated that the craft was moving eastward."

Later in early March, a series of sightings of a weird aerial artifact occurred near the Lake Boshkung area. (Lindsay Post, 14, 20, 27 March, and 24 April.) "They were said to have four wings with an overall wingspan of 20 feet, dark in color, and with lights that appear to change color."

"They were monstrous planes, black in color, and shaped like a pollywog," according to Mrs Lunham. (She) said that they were noiseless with one exception when one of them appeared to have some difficulty taking off and gave a "thump-thump" noise. It is her belief (and that of the witnesses in the para above) that they are not from outer space but some experimental craft being tested by the US and Canadian military, and in her concern she has written to the Minister of National Defence without receiving a response. An effort to photograph the lights was made by Peter Courtney of the Minden Progress, but the lights were too dull and moved too fast for any good photographs. One description of the UFO was that: 'It looked like a helicopter with the tail off.' Markings of a landing behind the Lunham residence made several weeks earlier were examined; and though they were fairly old they were made up of a V-shaped marking with two pad-like markings at right angles to it."

Two further sightings were made by a Jerry Gavreau, to the south of Lindsay. "The first...was made when he noticed what he had first taken to be helicopters were 'tail-less' while watching them through binoculars; and the second...was made near Orono when a cigar-shaped object passed before him at low level. (Lindsay Post, 20 March)".

LETTERS

From: <u>Frank Adey</u>.

"Unusual Properties of Water"
I read the piece on 'Unusual Properties of Water'
in NEWS 6 coincidentally with the following item
which I quote from <u>Mensa Journal</u> (International)
No 180:

"ANY OLD ION. Nashville Mensa Newsletter is
appealing for information on how to build a
simple negative-ion generator suitable for
a 2000 cubic foot bedroom. Negative ions
are found near waterfalls or the sea, or
when it's sunny, or in the open country.
They are probably the active constituent of
the old remedy, fresh air. They have been
shown to relieve depression, and the easy
way to get a dose of them is to stand close
to a violently running tap for a few minutes. This is also effective with some
people's hay fever."

If all this is true, it's the damndest remedy I
have heard of in some time. I have visions of
American hay-fever sufferers with their noses
shoved under taps. It raises some interesting
points: are people who live near waterfalls less
prone to depression than expected from the
national average? Do people living on the coast
suffer less from hay fever? And how do the negative ions bring about these effects?

"White Indians in Amazon Jungle"
Another piece from NEWS 6. Actually, white Ama-
zonian Indians are mentioned in 'Exploration
Fawcett' by Col. PH Fawcett, first published in
the 1920s (1924, judging by the dedication.) I
quote firstly from Ch. 8, where a Frenchman describes them thus:

"'There are white Indians on the Acre,'
this Frenchman told me. 'My brother went up
the Tahaumanu on a launch, and one day, well
up river, was told that white Indians were
near. He didn't believe it and scoffed at
the men who told him, but nevertheless
went out in a canoe and found unmistakable
signs of Indians. The next thing he knew,
he and his men were being attacked by big,
well-built handsome savages, pure white,
with red hair and blue eyes. They fought
like devils too, and when my brother shot
one of them dead the others rallied to recover the body, and got away with it. People say these white Indians don't exist,
and when it's proved they do, that they are
half-breed mixtures of Spanish and Indian.
That's what people say who never saw them,
but those who have seen them think differently!'"

Now, the Acre river, mentioned above, is about
2,000 miles away from the Xingu area (at least on
my map). This may mean that white Indians are
more widely spread than Sr Rocha imagines. Actually, the tribe he has 'discovered' is almost
certainly the one mentioned in Ch 10. of the
same book:

"There was talk of white Indians again.
'I know a man here who has met one,' said the
British Consul. 'They are very savage, and have
the reputation of coming out only at night.
They're known as "Bats" for that reason.'
'Where do they live?' I asked.
'Oh, somewhere up in the region of the lost
Martirios goldmines, north or north-west of
Diamartino. Nobody knows quite where they are.
Matto Grosso is mostly unknown country.'"
The above conversation is recorded as having
taken place (as far as I can gather) in Corumba,
which is a few hundred miles to the southwest of
the Xingu region.

'Exploration Fawcett.' is in fact a goldmine of
Fortean data, as Fawcett collected every piece of
local folklore he came across; lost cities, surviving prehistoric monsters, poltergeists, all
make hearsay appearances in the course of the
book. One of the most interesting legends concerns a plant whose juice softens rock or metal
so that it can be worked by hand before it re-
hardens. (Ch. 7.) Fawcett was told that this was
how the old South American architects fitted
giant stone blocks together so snugly in their
buildings. He relates how he spoke to a local
inhabitant about the little hollows in certain
rocks in which kingfisher-like birds lived. Fawcett remarked that the birds were lucky to find
such holes to nest in, and noted that the holes
were rarely seen away from the bird's habitats.
His informant, who had lived in the area for 25
years, told him that the birds made the holes
themselves by rubbing a certain leaf against the
rockface until it went soft, and then pecking it
away. Fawcett considered it a tall story, but
remarks that he heard confirmation from various
other people. Maybe this if true (which is
bloody unlikely, but you never know) could explain the Great 'Indian Bathtub' Mystery? (Again
in NEWS 6.)

    ***   ***   ***

From: <u>CA Worth</u>.

"Miracle Petrol"
I found "Gas From Water, Really?" (Mark Hall's
Forteana, NEWS 5, p9.) interesting and hope I
will engender a similar response with my recall
of a feature that appeared in the Sunday Express
between the Wars.

During WW1 an American tried to interest Authority in his substance which when added to water
gave the same performance as petrol. Everybody
gave him the elbow but he did eventually persuade
the Admiralty to make a test. He was driven to
Portsmouth in a staff car which stopped on the
quay and had its tank drained. A bucket was slung
into the harbour and filled with water - salt -
to which was added the 'substance', and the mix
was poured into the tank. The car started and
was driven with results agreed to be better than
those obtained from 'official' petrol. The Yank
thought he had it made, but was soon disillusioned because the Naval brass could not eliminate the thought that they had been conned — and

the whole project was abandoned. He caught a ship for home and a few days out, disappeared with nobody able to decide if it was suicide or murder.

(Mr Worth contacted the Sunday Express in an attempt to fill in some details, and was inform- ed that the files that far back were no longer generally available, and a fee would be charged if a search were to be undertaken. So there the story must remain until someone with the inclin- ation has a few days to lose in the British Museum.)

From: MX (legally adopted name.)

"A Charles Fort Index."

I wouldn't mind finding out how many of your readers would be interested in obtaining original editions of Fort, and my index for his collected works. The Fortean Society edition was the one published by Holt; and it did have its own index and a very cruddy one at that, hopelessly incom- plete. I spent four months putting my index to- gether, typed it up for Dover Books who then decided to reprint the old index ((in a reprint of the Holt edition due out sometime before the end of this year – Ed.)). To celebrate, I went out and purchased original editions of each of Fort's books for less than $20•00 each, and I have an extra copy of 'New Lands' of which only 1,000 were printed. I have considered circulat- ing a list of out-of-print books among several reputable dealers and could add to the list if desired. But it would help to ask for an initial deposit for anyone wanting these editions."

Anyone interested in taking up MX's kind offer can contact him at: Box 1598, Kingston, Ontario, K7L 5C8, Canada; or via his London forwarding address: BM-RESOLOGIST, London WC1V 6XX.

***** *** *****

don't ignore it, SEND IT IN TO THE NEWS. and please remember... to note: the SOURCE; the DATE; & your name (for the credit).

REVIEWS

New hardbacks:-

THE ROMEO ERROR by Lyall Watson. Hodder & Stough- ton; £3.25; pp254. Romeo's error was to think Juliet dead when she wasn't – and from that you can guess that Dr Watson is this time expoun- ding on what we today know about the states of Life and Death, which are crucial to today's transplant technology. The latter chapters deal with more controversial theories such as 'Life after death', astral bodies and the existence of bio-plasma and/or ectoplasm, psychic-surgery, and so on. Bound to be another winner for the Doctor who is on to a 'good thing'. He must feel so too, because his 'Supernature' has just been printed in paperback.

GHOSTS by Janet Bord. David & Charles; £1.95; pp80; illos; ISBN 0.7153.6632.7. Although this has been written as an introduction to ghost hunting and psychic phenomena in general in a series of children's books, it is nevertheless, very matter-of-fact in its approach and would stand as a good general guide to any adult wish- ing to know where to start in the spook business. Also contains some new material, eg. the ghost-dog story mentioned in her article (p6, this issue.)

COLONY EARTH : EXTRATERRESTRIAL LIFE AND OUR ORI- GINS? by Richard Mooney. Souvenir Press; £2.60; pp251; ISBN 0.285.62145.9. Goes over much the same ground and evidences as any other Anci- ent Astronaut type of book you have doubtless read....except that this one is considerably less hysterical and takes time out to discuss its ev- idence instead of beating your gray-matter into a loss of critical sensitivity by sheer speed of 'fact' presentation. Mooney also sticks closely to his theme, giving it time and room to develop in the length of the book , being more concerned with the origins of man and life on Earth than with proving that gods were visiting aliens. In- teresting discussions of evidences for ancient atomic warfare.

SECRET OF THE AGES by Brinsley Le Poer Trench. Souvenir Press; £2.60; pp192; illos; ISBN 0.285.62153.X. In these days of ecology-con- sciousness, the term 'Spaceship Earth' is much touted (coined, I think, by Bucky Fuller.) Here the term is taken literally, as BLPT's thesis is that the Earth is hollow, inhabited still and littered with the machines of Old Atlantis, and occasionally used for the projected domination of the world by the forces of the Anti-Christ, Sat- anaku. Everything is here from the Green Children that appeared in Suffolk, to Shaver's Deros (der- anged robots.) I dont know how sincere BLPT is in this but he does himself or the theories of a 'Hollow Earth' no justice at all, when he writes in the sensational style of serials in the Sunday papers, peppered with italicised sentences like: "There may be an active fifth column already here among us."; "The puma, it should be emphasised, is indigenous to this planet."; and "Why is there so much dust in the farthermost northern areas of the Arctic?" and "If no rivers are flowing from the inside of the earth to the outside, then why are all icebergs composed of fresh water?". And I must confess a degree of bogglement at: "The centre of the earth would have to be made of solid material for it eventually to be proved hollow!" Perhaps the most curious evidence is a set of photographs taken by a NASA ESSA-7 satellite which show a black area some hundreds of miles across at the North Pole and that BLPT says is a hole. "Here then, are two of the most thrilling photographs ever taken. They are dynamite." I'd like to know what the NASA analysts said about them - the one photo out of one and a half million that showed the pole without its usual cloud cover. As a Fortean I think many other explanations can be admitted for some of the data herein - but I really don't know what to make of the hole at the pole photo. The 'secret' of the title refers to definite proof of the existence of the Hollow Earth as "..the most closely guarded international secret.." and the true (according to BLPT) origin of the UFOs. Why I ask myself, if this secret has been 'closely guarded' by human and demonic powers, has it been possible for BLPT to write and publish it? They figure it'll be ignored as just another crank book. Perhaps. I showed the book to some friends at a recent SF convention in B'ham, and when the howls of derision died down, heads were still pondering over that photo. Is it real? Was it retouched, etc? Until we know, our laughs are a little hollow too.

**   ***   **

The following books see their first UK paper printing:-

SUPERNATURE by Dr Lyall Watson. Coronet; 50p.
THE DRAGON AND THE DISC by FW Holiday. Futura; 50p; pp247; ISBN 0.8600.7056.5; illos.
FLYING SAUCER VISION by John Michell. Abacus; 60p pp170; ISBN 0.349.12319.5; illos.
THE SPEAR OF DESTINY by Trevor Ravenscroft. Corgi 60p; pp361; ISBN 0.552.09609.1.

All of these are thoroughly recommendable and destined to become required reading in their genres. ** 'Supernature' (if you haven't read it already) is an up-to-date compendium of hard and pseudo- scientific theories and discoveries assessed from the point of view of a biologist. .. Michell's 'Flying Saucer Vision' has long been regarded with great affection by those who knew of it, as perhaps the key departure from the prevailing trend of UFO books at the time (1967). Taking off from Jung's impression that UFO phenomena reflected a stirring portent of changes in the 'collective psyche', Michell re-examines the archetypes predominant in modern mythology and aspirations: flight; communication with 'other' intelligences (gods, aliens, demons & angels; fairies; etc); the dragon and its connexion with Leys and the fluxes of 'terrestrial magnetism'. There is also much sensible interpretation of Fort's data here, including Kaspar Hauser. ** Holiday's book takes up the theme briefly explored by Michell, indeed a worthy successor to FSV. Holiday's main effort depends on his personal

involvement investigating the monster legends of the Scottish and Irish lakes - then he discovers the connexion with Leys and UFOs in the symbology of ancient religion. Greatly readable too. ** Rarely have I been so absorbed by any book as during my reading of 'Spear of Destiny'. It may be a matter of personal taste but Ravenscroft's erudition and impressive insight had me spellbound. This tour-de-force of Germanic mysticism recounts the tale of the Spear of Longinus (that pierced the side of Christ) and its possession by all the critical leaders in the history of Europe who regarded it as a talisman of great power for Good as well as Evil. The legend of the Spear was bound up with Occult initiation groups throughout the centuries and became the foundation upon which Hitler based his power when he seized it from the Vienna Hofburg museum. This book tells how the Nazi theories of the 'Aryan Christ', and the 'Supermen', and their use of the Jews as their stepping-stone to power, and many other curious aspects of their movement emerged from the medieval Grail legends (eg. Wagner's opera 'Parsifal'), a wide-ranging occult knowledge (the Thule Group was a contemporary offshoot of the Golden Dawn, and Hitler, himself a considerable student of Teutonic occultism, was duly selected as their 'messiah' and initiated.); beliefs in reincarnation, the use of sex and drugs (Hitler's key-trip was on mescalin) in their rituals; the influence of the works Schopenhauer, Neitzsche, Houston Stewart Chamberlain, Madame Blavatsky etc. None of this is put across as sensationalist journalism, but with scholarly precision that makes it the more impressive. We have had myriads of theories about the origins of the two World Wars, but here for the first time is a credible analysis in terms of the perverted use of 'magic', a quite deliberate attempt by a few personalities to undermine what they called the corrupting, life-hating, impotent Christian Church, and restore to the German peoples the mystic way of the warrior. But along the line, Hitler took off on his dreams of world domination, and like the characters he believed himself to be reincarnations of, he revelled in the destruction of all that men held dear.   **   ***   **

A second paperback printing for:-

GODS & SPACEMEN IN THE ANCIENT WEST by W Raymond Drake. Sphere; 45p; pp240.
BOOK OF THE DAMNED by Charles Fort. Abacus; 75p; pp320. Nice to know the first run sold out.

did you see.....?

'Evolution of the Moon's Orbit and the Origin of Life'. DL Turcotte, et al. Nature Vol 251, Sept 13, 1974. (Evidence for an approach of the moon to the earth -- 3000 million yrs BC) -- and its possible indications in the evolution of life.)

'Comets: modifiers of human historic trends.' by MA Smollin. Horoscope Nov 74, pp20/23.

'Is all Witchcraft really Witchcraft?' by Christina Larner. A critical look at faddish revivals. New Society, 10 Oct 74.

The Ley Hunter 58/59, Aug/Sept. 'Abbots Bromley Sword Dancers' by John Radford. 'How Straight is The Old Straight Track?' by Peter Mabey, who has won the use of a computer-terminal in the Honey-well Dial-a-Computer competition, to carry out an analysis of the Ley-theory in Somerset and Dorset. 'Ancient Metrology' by RDY Perrett. 'Dual Nature of English Measuring Systems.' by Capt. M Stopani-Thompson. Both above are interesting discussions on the origins and derivations of old English metrology, especially as applied to the proportional systems indicated by the layout of megalithic monuments. Plus a Tyneside UFO. TLH is now bimonthly from: Paul Screeton, 5 Egton Drive, Seaton Carew, Hartlepool, Cleveland, TS25 2AT - £1.50 for 1 year.

Fate & Fortune No 6. 'Divining the Unknown', Martin Hillman on dowsing. 'Werewolves' by Chris J Smith. 'Stonehenge' by Eileen Buckle. 'Photographs of Thought' by Lynn Picknett, with some startlingly powerful photos of Ted Serios strutting his stuff. 'The Haunted Dreamer', a rundown on the works of HP Lovecraft by Angela M Errigo.

'In Signs' by Jeffrey Bernard. New Statesman 30 August 74....a send-up of astrology.

'Acupuncture Revisited' by Prof. P Wall (Head of Cerebral Functions Unit, Univ. College, London.) Also: Astronomers from Hale Observatory (USA) have discovered a previously unknown satellite of Jupiter, thus bringing the total to 13. This latest one is 20th magnitude and may possibly be a minor planet trapped by Jupiter. And some astronomers have now proposed that one of the larger moons, Io, may be covered with common salt. New Scientist 3 Oct 74,

'Cropmarks near the Sutton Courtnay Saxon Site' D Benson & D Miles. Antiquity Vol XLVIII No 191 Sept 74. (See also 'The Whippingham Ground Effects' by Leonard Cramp. Flying Saucer Review Vol 14 No 3, May/June 1968.

History Vol 59 No 196, June 74 - contains reviews of important ref. books: 'Witchcraft in the Middle Ages' by Jeffrey B Russell. (London: Cornell UP, 1972, 394pp, £5.95.). 'Witch Hunting in South-western Germany 1562-1684: The Social and Intellectual Foundations' by HC Erik Midelfort. (Stanford UP/ Oxford UP. 1972, 300pp, £5.75.).

'Generalisations' by Prof. Guy Ourisson. His view of why and how Science has developed the art of specialisation. New Scientist, 17 Oct 74, pp190/2.

'Colonisation at Lagrangea.' - Graham Chedd on Gerard O'Neill's proposals for artificial planet-oids moored in free-space or the Lagrange points in a Moon orbit. NEW SCIENTIST, 24 Oct 74. Curiously, the same issue carried a letter discussing the same Lagrange points in connection with Lunan's 'Long Delayed Echo' theories, from Lunan himself; and a letter on 'Dowsing'.

FATE & FORTUNE No7 : 'Flying Saucers' by Charles Bowen. And FATE & FORTUNE No8 contains an article on 'Poltergeists' by Dr ARG Owen.

LANTERN : The magazine put out by the Borderline Science Investigation Group (BSIG). BSIG was formed to look into folklore, UFO, ghost & fairy incidents, indeed anything unusual in the counties of Suffolk and Norfolk, and LANTERN has carried much interesting stuff, including notes on the phantom bells of Dunwich, Leys and the 'Green Children of Woolpit' (also quoted by Le Poer Trench in his new book 'Secret of the Ages' - see reviews.) They are still a small but active group (with much the same problems as THE NEWS) and well deserve your support. Contact: I Bunn. 3 Dunwich Way, Oulton Broad, Lowestoft, Suffolk. The mag seems to be quarterly at 12p an issue, so send along 50p or more if you wish; it is all in a good cause.

Compilation Credits: P Ledger &. Nigel Watson.

ADS

Note: Having pleaded in the last issue for some publisher to reissue the works of Max Freedom Long , it was of course inevitable that I be taken to task for my ignorance; herewith corrected. USA cloth editions of Long's books are available from COMPENDIUM (see above) from £2.75; and also in stock at NEW DIMENSIONS in the States.

THE ANCIENT ASTRONAUT SOCIETY.

The AAS was formed late last year as a non-profit society to promote scientific, literary and educational studies of the 'Ancient Astronaut' concept. "The Society's goals are to seek evidence to determine whether intelligent life existed on Earth before recorded history, and to determine whether Earth was ever visited by extraterrestrial beings." There is to be an official Journal, a newsletter called "Ancient Skies" (bi-monthly), lectures, studygroups, and probably most important, organised expeditions. An active Fortean, Richard T Crowe, is in the pilot-seat of the newsletter. Already they have held their first World conference, in Arlington, USA. A general membership, including the newsletter, can be had for $6.00. More details from: The Ancient Astronaut Society. 600 Talcott Road, Park Ridge, Illinois 60068. USA.

a miscellany of fortean curiosities

MYSTERY GROUP-ILLNESSES
and PHANTOM SMELLS.. 9

MOCK SUNS ... 6

also .... rescues by animals, **4** ....

Jerome Clark on a mystery beast, **5** .... strange clouds, **7** ...

Welsh whirlwinds; occult crimes, **8** ....

Nigel Watson on Lincs phenomena, **13** ... swarms, **15** ...

¨anti – gravity¨ devices, **18** .... and more.

35p:$1·00

8

ᏆᎻᎬ ᏁᎬᏔᏚ

THE NEWS is a non-profit making bi-monthly miscellany of
Fortean news and notes; edited & published by Robert JM
Rickard: 31 Kingswood Road, Moseley, Birmingham B13 9AN;
affiliated to International Fortean Organisation (INFO).

SUBSCRIPTIONS:	AIRMAIL TRANSFER:	CONTRIBUTIONS & RIGHTS:
Per year: £2.10. Overseas & USA $6.00 or equiv- alent; plus 10% if paying by cheque (to cover bank-charges). NB: Cheques etc. payable to: RJM RICKARD, please.	Overseas subscrib- ers can 'Airmail Transfer' direct from their bank to our account: RJM Rickard No2. A/c No: 0125008. Lloyds Bank, Priory Ringway, Birmingham B4, England. Sort- ing Code: 30-96-28.	Articles & Notes are welcome, and duly cred- ited. All articles in THE NEWS are Copyright of the authors; and the views expressed are not necessarily those of THE NEWS or the Editor. All the Notes may be freely quoted, though we hope for a credit in return.

Volume 2 No1 (8). Feb 75.

1) Well, we made it , you and us! The start of
our second volume/year. Buts let's have no illusions - we are not yet out of the woods, costs
spiralling rapidly while our sub-list grows so
slowly -- so do all you can - a personal recommendation goes a long way. In March the postal
costs will about double, and more paper and labor
increases are due - the only way to beat it is to
have more subscribers.

2) From this issue on, you will notice a new in-
gredient. Our Christmas present to you all is
a set of about 30 headings illustrated by the incomparable Hunt Emerson, to whom our thanks. The
rest will appear as the data dictates.

3) Also from this ish we experiment with envelope
substitutes. Its a crazy sign of the times that
a plastic bag and a couple of sticky lables work
out about half the cost of a paper envelope. So
please let us know if the bags cause any problems

4) We had hoped to mail the Index with this ish
but the damned thing is turning out to be bigger
than we thought. Its ⅔s done - and will definitely
come out with the next issue.

5) That sharp old lady, Ariadne, writing in the
NEW SCIENTIST (14 Nov 74) cried to the Gods for
someone to found an 'oldspaper' that would provide the endings to the stories that started off
well on the front pages, and then nothing more is
heard -- like, she says: "..that Japanese nuclear

ship which we left, idle upon the ocean, its reactor unaccountably stuffed with socks." ((Anyone
with any info on this please, please let us know))
But why stop at endings? Sometimes people wonder
just what THE NEWS is about (us too), and the
expression that comes to mind is that we present
stories of beginings, middles and ends - but who
knows which is what? It would be impossible to
claim that we are recording in any completeness or
truth. But some of you have strange inclinations,
and our notes are to be read as clues, by which,
if you're so inclined, you may pick up a trail of
sorts. Nevertheless we do our mortal best at recording what comes our way, and our pretence at
indexing the uncategorizable (?) is in Reality
only an approximation to usefulness. We mirror
the vapourings and vagaries of existance; we ming-
le with skeletons in closets; we run after things
best ignored, prying into dustbins and lifting
carpets to see what's new; we sing happily in the
red rain, or to the gentle patter of frogs on our
umberella; but perhaps most damning of all is the
reading of old newspapers spread on a wet kitchen
floor. Not for nothing is our motto: "Yesterday's
news Tomorrow!" Madam, look no further!

NEXT ISSUE: Well John Stonehouse and the Vanishing Circus eventually turned up, but we have some
notes on people who didn't; more Mystery and
Escaped Animal stories; Antiquities; and some
outbrakes of Fireballs or whatever they were.

BEHAVIOURAL CURIOSITIES

As man grapples with the task of unravelling animal speech, it has often occurred to us to wonder just what the animals make of all this? Do some attempts to communicate come across as mad ravings, for example, or impossible but vivid exhortations to go away and make one's self pregnant? We have a few assorted notes under the unexpected nuisances of animal sounds -- eg: recordings of wolf-howls being played by scientists to lure wolves out of the Shoshone National Forest, Wyoming, for census and study. It seems their population has dwindled through trapping, poisoning etc to about 20 - which is not much wolf in an awful lot of forest. (New York Times, 10 April 74. Credit: Mark Hall.)

And when five sugarcane toads escaped from a biology teacher's house in Darwin, Australia - samples of the toads' mating calls were broadcast to all radios as part of a public warning, because these 8" long critters can squirt a poison capable of killing dogs, cats and pigs. (Though the sensibleness of this escapes us, as not many dogs, cats and pigs listen to radios these days - at least not with the rising cost of long-life (joke) batteries, today. Anyway, these toads are described as walking vacuum-cleaners, displaying much civic responsibility in hopping about eating "cigarette-buts, ping-pong balls and other roadside debris." And if you haven't seen many ping-pong balls littering the streets of Darwin, pause to reflect on the efficacy of these toads. (San Francisco Examiner & Chronicle, 14 July 74. Credit: Loren Coleman.)

Now just imagine if all the sugarcane toads in the Darwin area converged on the radios booming out their favourite music - hmmmm! And Darwin was flattened recently by a 'hurricane', was it not?. There's a lesson to be learnt there somewhere. And here too! We read of Mr Noel McCabe having a peaceful evening at home in Kingston St, Derby. What could be more harmless, we ask, than to have the family gathered round the record player listening to Frankie Laine singing "The Cry of the Wild Goose"? Ahhh! You guessed! A window explodes inwards as a Canada goose crashes into their bedroom. And as though that's not enough, one came down outside a hospital at Aston near Derby, and another hit the pavement in the Chaddesden suburb of Derby. Inspector Farrow of the RSPCA said: "It's either an unbelievable coincidence, or Frankie Laine's record must have had a very weird effect on Canada geese. I have never known anything like it." (Thanks to Paul Screeton for this honey from the Yorkshire Post, 19 Nov 74.)

But we do know of things like it. For instance - A couple sleeping in their 7th floor apartment in Vienna, were woken up one night by the crashing of glass in their living room and rushed in to find a dazed and injured black swan. The most logical reason proposed seems to be based on the idea that it did not see the window in the dark - but surely that little dark patch is regularly spaced with others in a larger lighter monolithic and more visible bulk of building? Anyway there is no evidence that anyone below was conducting a well known pas-des-deux. (Sunday Express, 4 Aug 74.) But we don't think it wise to tempt the Cosmic Jokers too much, and have forsworn our blood-curdling renditions of "See you later Alligator " in the bath, and "Nellie the Elephant" in the broom cupboard under the stairs.

There is always the sneaky suspicion that some animals are having a great joke at our expense. Consider the blackbird that has become the bane of the Stationmaster at Berne-Stoeckacker, Switzerland. They have converted to hand signals to send off trains because the crafty devil had got the guard's whistle off to a tee. (Sun, 21 Sept 74. Credit: AF Ashcroft.) And we rather like the story of the black labrador that set up a dismal howling beside a pond on Bournemouth's Turbary Common. It was led away several times but kept returning -- and so local police fearing the worst called in the firebrigade, and the faithful devoted 4-footed friend watched with great interest as they set about draining 20,000 gallons in a search for a body. When they got to the bottom, they found instead the usual and traditional still life of old bedsprings, prams, boots and car doors draped in ooze. They looked around for the dog, but found nothing there either. In a face-saving statement police and firemen declared that at least the pond was now less of a hazard to children. (Bournemouth Evening Echo, 17 April 74. Credit: S Mucha.) And one more pond to swell the thousands that vanish from the English landscape every year.

Havoc was also created by 25 cows in the Italian ski-resort of Cortina d'Ampezzo. The local municipal brass band passing the end of their field in splendour and full cry was too much for these culture-starved creatures -- they burst through the fence, and butted the shiny instruments to the ground, licking them affectionately and gazing at them in adoration. A note in the report said that it took an hour to drag them away. (Weekend, 31 Jan/6 Feb 73. Credit: A Smith.)

The normally peaceful air of Preston Down Road, Paignton, Devon,was rent by a high pitched buzzing which was likened to a badly punished power saw - so residents call in police, and police set to tracking down the noise -- they found a pair of hedgehogs locked in passionate embrace, and serenading each other. (Daily Mirror, 22 Aug 74.)

"Be gentle with me, Harry!"

This brings to mind the mystery of the presence of porcupines in Devon, more on which you'll find in our "Swarms & Migrations" section.

Not all of these silly stories turn out happily, and a fine example of the thin line between farce and tragedy was the fate of Albert, a 45-year-old farmer, whose 'Accidental Death' was the verdict of an inquest in Colombo, Sri Lanka. He had a favourite bull -treated it like a pet. One night he got home drunk, tied the bull to a tree, and began to sing his heart out to it. The bull either loved it or hated it, for he broke away and made his point by dancing a fandango - all over Albert, for whom it was all over too. (Daily Mirror, 24 Aug 74. Cr: Steve Moore.)

RESCUES BY ANIMALS.

One of the few occasions where we have received notes on an incident from more than one person was on the rescue, last summer, of a woman by a turtle, in the Philippines. Mrs Candelaria Villanueva, 52, was on board the 'Aloha' when it caught fire and sank 600 miles south of Manila. She said she had been floating for more than 12 hours (with a life-jacket) when a giant sea turtle "with a head as big as that of a dog."(1) appeared beneath her. She was spotted on 4 June, having been in the water 48 hours, by a Philippine navy vessel, 'Kalantia', who thought she was clinging to an oildrum. "Someone threw her a life ring. The moment she transferred her hold to the ring, the drum sank. We did not realise it was a giant turtle until we started hauling up the woman, for the turtle was beneath her apparently propping her up. It even circled the area twice before disappearing into the depths of the

sea, as if to reassure itself that its former rider was in good hands."(2) One report added a detail not mentioned by others. Mrs Villanueva said that another , tiny turtle climbed on her back. "The small turtle bit me gently every time I felt drowsy. Maybe it wanted to prevent me from submerging my head in the water and drowning."(1) Compiled from: 1) News of the World, 28 July 74. 2) Knoxville (Tennessee) News-Sentinel, 24 June 74. Cr: David Dunthorn. Others) Minneapolis (Minn) Star, 26 June 74. Cr: Mark Hall. Daily Mirror, 24 June 74. Cr: R Forrest, DJ McAllister, S Moore.

Recently, we were struck by an odd story told by Max Freedom Long (Case 37, in his 'RECOVERING THE ANCIENT MAGIC.') Polynesians, he said, believed the souls of babies who died in birth transmigrated to inhabit some animals. In this case, a fisherman whose boat had sunk in rough seas, called out to his 'Shark-son' to aid him. A shark did come, and not only kept him floating but towed him back to shore.

Whether you believe that or not is up to you, but curious things like this do happen whether we can explain them or not. For instance, in Weekend, 6-12 Feb 74, you will find a first-hand account by a man who found himself waistdeep in quicksand on his uncle's farm on Darling Downs, South Queensland, Australia, and no one to help him. Soon the cows from the surrounding fields gathered round the pool, curious about his antics. Then an old brindle cow cautiously came down to drink, and eyeing him all the time, made very slowly toward him. He made a grab which startled her, but she returned and offered her horns to him. As she lifted her head and stepped carefully backwards, he felt his feet squelching out of their trap. She towed him to firm ground and then trundled off to join her mates. (Apologies for losing note of who to credit on this.)

Dog rescues are fairly numerous. An Alsatian saving an 8-year-old girl from a near fatal attack by a 700lb boar, can be read in the Sunday Express 10 March 74. And a collection of similar stories appeared in Weekend for 27 Feb/5 Mar 74. Credit: Anthony Smith.

And as we go to press, word comes of a blind and elderly lady who mistook the edge of the harbour wall at Torquay, Devon, for the edge of the pavement and fell in. Without much hesitation, Ruby, her two-year-old Labrador guide-dog, whom she had had only two months, jumped in after her - and pushed her gently toward the harbour steps, keeping her afloat until human recuers hauled her to safety. The Sun, 21 Jan 75.

LATE NEWS / LATE NEWS / LATE NEWS / LATE NEWS

INFO JOURNAL 14 -- Contains: 'Bang!' a 6½ page compilation of 'Mystery Explosions', rumblings and 'meteors' between 1969 and 1974; many from our own pages. 'The Maps and the Galaxies',by Charles Hapgood. 'About Monsters and Such' by FW Holiday. "Phantom Butchers", more on the mid-West cattle mutilations. "Phantom Islands". 'Anomalous Electrical Phenomena' 'The Ethio-

pean Discoveries' by Stuart Greenwood. 'Falls'. 'Mountain of Death', about the mysterious Black Mountain in Australia. "The Great Florida Mystery" of lights and strange goings-on in the swamp. 'The Delphos Wolf-girl' ((alluded to by Mark Hall, back in NEWS 7/p14)) -- A batch is on the way by seamail to UK subscribers who will receive them in due course - Ed.

A MESSAGE FROM MAGONIA

by JEROME CLARK

Late in March 1971 I was employed as associate editor of Fate magazine (1) in Highland Park, Illinois. One day, while perusing a pile of clippings readers had sent us over the past week, I came upon some fascinating articles about a series of creature sightings in central Oklahoma in February. Mary Fuller, Fate's editor, gave me permission to phone the witnesses and to write up their stories for the magazine. (The piece eventually appeared in the September 1971 issue as "'Manimals' Make Tracks in Oklahoma.")

The original sightings, the ones the papers had published, were of the by-now familiar NAWPS (North American Woodpersons), ie. quasi-anthropoids on the order of Bigfoot. The more I talked with the people involved, the more I heard about other kinds of encounters with even stranger animals. Someone who had had an experience would tell me: "My friend so-and-so saw something, too, one time." By the time I'd tracked all this down, I had amassed quite a collection of reports.

The weirdest one of all came from Mrs. Lawrence Laub of Calumet, Oklahoma, who said that early one evening in 1951 she stepped out of her farmhouse to check on the cattle, walked to the top of a hill between the farmhouse and the pasture and glanced down to see something that "looked like a cross between a wolf and a deer."

The creature's head and body superficially resembled a deer's. The thing stood on four thin deer-like legs, with huge pads for feet, and had long hair slightly lighter in colour than a German shepherd dog's. It was larger than a dog or a wolf and had small pointed ears and a bushy tail.

After watching it for about 30 seconds (its head was turned away from her), Mrs Laub tossed a stick toward the animal, attracting its attention. It stood watching her, apparently unafraid.

Unnerved, Mrs Laub beat a retreat, all the while glancing over her shoulder at the animal, which continued to study her. Her husband had seen the same or similar creature two years previously, and in the meantime neighbours had reported coming upon strange tracks in their fields.

I had never heard of anything answering this creature's description and consequently I was more than slightly interested. I asked Loren Coleman and John Keel, America's foremost authorities on these questions, if they were acquainted with beasts of this kind, and both said no. Keel suggested it might be a "one-of-a-kind transmogrification."

Some time later, as I was visiting my parents in Canby, Minnesota, my father, a veteran outdoorsman, told me of a weird animal he had encountered that spring. His story astounded me (I had not mentioned Mrs Laub's experience to him and the Fate article had not yet appeared) and I had him draw up a statement. It follows:

'About 1.00pm on March 27, 1971, HH Christensen of Canby, Minnesota, and I were driving north on the county highway, 8½ miles northwest of Canby where the highway crosses the Florida Creek. About halfway up the hill Howard, who was driving, slammed on the brakes and exclaimed: "What the devil is that?" Approximately 50 to 60 yards to the west of the highway in a 'pocket' on the hillside stood an animal that at first glance appeared to be a small deer. It was standing broadside to us, facing north, and in the open (no brush or weeds to obscure our view). The sun was shining brightly and visibility was perfect. The animal was about the size of a three- or four-month-old whitetail deer, of about 50 or 60 pounds weight, I would guess. Its head was unusually small, as were the ears; it was covered with short hair, red-brown in colour, similar to the summer coat of the whitetailed deer. Its tail appeared to hang below the level of the 'knees' on the rear legs, and was black, and appeared to be similar to that of a horse. It certainly was not like any deer either of us had ever seen before.

'After observing it for a couple of minutes, during which time the animal did not move, or even turn its head to look at us, I suggested making it run so that we could observe if it moved like a deer. I climbed out of the car and stood on the near shoulder of the road, and the animal completely ignored me. I yelled and waved my arms - still no response from the animal.

I then informed Howard that I would make it run, whereupon I took my rifle from the car (we were on a varmint-hunting trip), and fired a shot about 30 feet to the rear of the animal; it raised its head and looked at me, then resumed its original stance. I fired again, this time aiming at a point within two feet of its hind feet, and the bullet threw dirt on its legs. This time the animal responded by slowly turning away (to the west) and walking very sedately over to a brush patch about 30 feet away, where it calmly lay down and proceeded to ignore us. With Howard laughing at me because I could not frighten the animal, I put my rifle away and we drove on.

'Howard and I have hunted deer and have observed thousands of them in the wild of this area. If this animal had been 'just' a deer, Howard would not have stopped or questioned what he was seeing; in fact he probably would not even have commented on seeing a deer, as they are so commonplace in this area. And for my part, I certainly would not have even considered getting out of the car to 'scare' it.

'Whitetail deer fawns are born about the middle of April in this latitude and are spotted for the first three or four months of their lives. By the end of March last year's fawns weigh over a hundred pounds and like the adult deer still have their dark grey winter coat of hair.

The following day I drove by this place to see if I could see our strange animal again, but did not see it. However, I saw three mature deer and two last-year fawns, which crossed the road in front of me within a quarter-mile of the place where the sighting had been made. These deer were all dark-grey with their winter coat, and the two fawns were of normal size.

(sgd) DR Clark.
HH Christensen has read this statement and concurs with it.'

The strangest part of all this, of course, is that it occurred the same week that I uncovered Mrs Laub's 20-year-old experience. The Laub's report, and my father's, are the only ones I know of involving this bizarre creature which exhibits no fear of human beings or their weapons.

Recently, while we were discussing the incident, I asked Dad why he had not pursued the creature on foot in order to get a better look at it. His behaviour seemed quite out of character, for Dad is intelligent and highly curious about the world around him.

"I don't know," he said, clearly puzzled. "I've often wondered about that."

But that said, the question remains: could all this be a coincidence? Or is that stretching the concept of coincidence much too far?

Or was the creature's later appearance some kind of message to me, or maybe the Phenomenon's idea of a joke? I certainly wish I knew.

::*:*   *:*:*:*:*   *:*:*:*

1) The American Fate, not the magazine known to us on this side of the Atlantic.   -- Ed.

MOCK SUNS.

Mock suns, or Parhelia, are not particularly unusual or unknown, but are nonetheless a striking phenomenon when they do occur. Our interest is also on two other grounds: that a faulty or partial observation, or description may in fact indicate something else, a fireball/ ball lightning, or UFO for instance, so it is useful to know where and when mock suns were observable -- and that, as Fort showed with earthquakes and meteor/aerial lights, there may be hitherto un-noted correlations abounding in such natural phenomena. Mock moons, Parselena, occur too, and the incident described on NEWS 5 p6., an observation made in Sweden in 1869, would seem to be a good example. Our cover illustration of a classic Parhelion is taken from a wonderful (literally) late 19th century encyclopedia called THE WORLD OF WONDERS (Cassell Petter & Galpin; no date in book), containing many items not in Fort's works, or elsewhere for that matter. So in future issues, not only will we be using it as a source of our wonderful engravings on the cover, but we shall be telling many of its data to record them in a modern reference structure.

But for now, we have two observations of mock suns. The first is an aside reference in a report on the solar eclipse of mid-June 74, and the events around Walpole, a town at the southern tip of Western Australia, the only place in the world to experience a totality of eclipse at that time. Or would have been had not dense clouds settled over the hill with the observatory on it, while all around was clear. The light fell to the intensity of a moonlit night in less than a second, the temperature dropping from 73 to 53 degrees. Cows turned for home; birds fell silent and the night insects started up. It lasted four minutes.

And before this event, by an hour, a false sun appeared in the sky. Surely a sign of the coming practical joke on the astronomers who had planned for the eclipse for 10 feverish months. Details from the Los Angeles (California) Times, 21 June 1974. Credit: Mark Hall.

The second sighting happened a few months after the above, and is reported in a letter to the Daily Mirror, 17 Sept 74. (Credit: Steve Moore.)
"Did anybody else notice the 'sun dog' or mock sun, the other evening? There seemed to be two suns in the sky. My husband and I knew then that we were in for some rough weather. An old chap told us this weather sign some years ago. He also used to say that when you see shadows in the water, there will be rain or an easterly wind within twentyfour hours. He has been proved right so many times.
　　Mrs K Mortley. Wylie Rd, Hoo, Kent. "

DARKNESSES AND CLOUDS.

Speaking of clouds 'lurking' almost malevolantly and unexpectedly: We have a note of schoolchildren asking their parish council to investigate their suspicions that clouds hung over their village of Breaston, Derbyshire, while the sun shone brilliantly a couple of miles away. Something was stealing their sunshine. The councillors in turn became worried. "It has become particularly noticeable recently," said one, Mr Reg Gill. The only theory they could come up with, as to why there seemed to be so much cloud over Breaston compared with its surroundings, is that a huge power station a few miles away was creating the clouds artificially to drift to the town where they stay overhead, blocking out the sun. A Central Electricity Generating Board spokesman said vapour from the cooling towers does cause a cloud, but strong sunshine soon dispels it. Daily Express 19 March 1973.

Fort had many notes on unusual darknesses at noon or any other time of day when a darkness is most unexpected. No eclipses or fogs to blame -- normal weather conditions -- then, suddenly, a darkness. Loren Coleman sent us a note from the 'Paul Harvey News', American Broadcasting Corporation, or rather an item from the bulletins read out on 3 April 74 -- so we don't know the actual date of the incident.

"The Kemps of Peoria, Illinois, were driving in their car a while back on a sunshiny Sunday... When just past Morton, Illinois,on their way to Carlock... Suddenly their car was enveloped in darkness. Mr and Mrs Kamp and their two sons... did not have time to get frightened before it was light again. Thinking they might have passed through a dark cloud, they searched the sky and the horizon, but there were no clouds of any kind... The Kamps have no theory as to what caused the mid-day darkness but they are convinced it was supernatural."

This was read out with a preamble about people seeing Flying Saucers and not daring to tell. We are the last to complain about connexions being made between things... we believe there are cases of 'darknesses' in the UFO experiences -- or rather something acting to suppress information in the visible light spectrum, or even if you want to consider it, depressing the reception in the eye, perhaps acting on the nervous material, even brain, etc etc But we wonder if the newscasters knew this, or did they lump it in with UFOs alongside all other outbreaks of crank?

In November, a group of Michigan farmers paid out £25,000 to a professional rainmaker, Dr Irving P Krick, to strut his stuff. As they stood waiting expectantly, Michael Reinbold, a farmer 150 miles away, became aware of a little black cloud "descending on him from a virtually clear sky." Seconds later he was drenched as five inches of rain came down in two hours on his 800 acres just north of Detroit, during which hail the size of golf balls bounced off everything in sight. "I've never seen anything like it," he said, "This little black cloud just came straight at us." Now he is sueing Dr Krick, a former chief of the US Army Air Force weather forecasting office, for over £15,000 worth of ruined crops. "It's all his fault. You shouldn't mess around with the environment unless you know what consequences your messing will cause." Dr Krick argues that his cloud seeding operation had nothing to do with the events that took place on Reinbold's farm (150 miles distant). If we admit a connexion between the two - we are in a mystery; and if we don't, well we're still stuck with the mystery of the little black cloud. Damned if you do - and damned if you don't. Nothing is said about whether the rainmaker's efforts brought any rain over his client's farms - but no mention is made of them sueing him. Story from the 'America' column in the Daily Mail, 21 November 1974. Credit: Steve Moore.

WHIRLWINDS IN WALES.

If we are to display, as we occasionally do, a
more than casual interest in things that fall
from the sky, then in all sensibility and good
practice, we should balance the other side of the
hyphen, and keep an eye on what goes up, or gets
up, or is pulled or pushed up. Janet Bord sent
us news of a series of notes and letters in the
Mid-Wales County Times & Express on whirlwinds
in the Welshpool area of Montgomeryshire.

The initial incident occurred when children of the
Mochdre Primary School, near Newtown, were having
their lunch-break. They watched in amazement as
a pile of hay was lifted from a nearby field, and
carried in the air for nearly ten minutes before
breaking up and falling slowly into the fields
around the school. The Headmistress, Mrs Marjorie
Edwards, said: "I've never seen anything so fantastic in my life. The children were completely
flabberghasted. The hay was lifted up as high as
the highest little white cloud and drifted for
six to seven minutes." This was on the 4th July.

Some questions occur to us, mainly about the
wind conditions at the time -- if it was windy
(and we admit it does not say whether it was or
not) then how can hay rise up, and drift back to
roughly the same spot when the 'whirlwind' breaks
up. If it was not windy -- did some force pull
on the lump of hay, which soon broke up at a
height, and, the force, having less grasp on single
straws, allows them to fall back...The witnesses
can only suppose a whirlwind to explain the lifting. Far-fetched? could be, but anymore than
whirlwinds in Wales in the first place? We shall
have to find out more.

Another whirlwind was later reported to have
happened on the same day, on the farm of Mr W.
Summerfield at Llidiart, Moelygarth, Welshpool.
Or rather, a 'similar occurrence' was reported
from there. And on the 7th, another 'whirlwind'
scattered another Welshpool man's harvest over
a wide area...smallholder Jack Thomas, of Lime-
kilns, Belan, had just finished turning his hay
by hand when it was "scooped up and carried high
into the air" where it remained for several
minutes before breaking up and falling into the
surrounding fields and gardens. Reference is
made to other incidents in "recent weeks" on
"very hot days, which result in sudden movements
of air of this kind." It may be that there are
whirlwinds, and things that look like whirlwinds,
especially to those who have never seen a whirlwind before -- more information needs to be had
before more than that can be said.

In fact the only mention of rising hay being
twisted as it went up was in the recollection of
a reader in response to the stories above. Mr D
Edryn Morris, Ashfields, Rhos Common, Llandrinio,
remembered back to mid-July 1941, when he was at
Golengoed Farm, Llanwnog, with his late brother,
and they saw a "gigantic whirlwind whip a mass of
hay more than 200 feet in the air" and deposit it
on a neighbour's field. The air had changed, he
said, from sun, heat and dryness to sudden cool-
ness, breeze and humidity -- and the whirlwind
twisted the hay until it was "gathered into a
huge conical 'cock' of hay."

(ontinued on p20.

occult crimes

What a pleasure it is for me to use Hunt's witty
illo for this category. Fort said: "I have
collected notes upon 'mysterious robberies' wondering whether a teleportative power has ever
been used criminally... If a medium could transport seashells from the sea to his cabinet, he
could abstract funds from a bank to his pocket...
There may be criminal adepts who are not known
as mediums." (LO! Ch.4.) Here below are a few
'sealed room' type situations, and odd 'burglaries'.

LOCKED ROOM DEATH RIDDLE.
Batchelor, Anton Przewozny, a 59-year-old farm-
hand, was found beaten to death in his room on a
farm at d'Avrainville, Northern France. The shot-

gun used as the bludgeon was back in its proper
place, and the door was locked from the inside.
There was soft soil below the 17ft high window,
which was also bolted, but no footprints. Other
workers heard his cries for help and banged on
the locked door. When his cries stopped, they
called the police. Inside the room they found
another curious detail -- Anton did not smoke,
yet they found an ashtray full of cigarette ends.
Daily Mirror, 18 August 1966. Credit: A Smith.

A ONE-LEGGED GHOST.
Police answered a burglar-alarm call from the
home of Mr Kenneth Broadhead in Ashill, near
Thetford, Norfolk, and they found the house
supernaturally secure, with nothing stolen. But

what did make their hair stand on end was the single row of footprints - all made by the same foot - across the floor of a room ending up against a solid brick wall. Then the ghost apparently dematerialised through a door and set off a burglar-alarm. A senior police officer mentioned the tradition of a one-legged Jesuit priest ghost at the house, but added: "Why set off an alarm when you can just melt through a door?" No other details were available. Daily Mirror, 13 Feb 74 -- the incident happening the day before. Credit: Steve Moore, BR Bates & Michael Roberts.

'HOUDINI GANG' RAID STRONGROOM.
£143,000 disappeared from a strongroom at New York's Kennedy Airport on 12 April 1967, and an FBI spokesman confessed their bafflement. Somehow, whoever pulled this off, got pas: armed guards, a double-locked steel door, into the strongroom and out again, without being seen and without leaving a mark or clue anywhere. The money was part of a delivery from the Indo-China bank of Laos and had arrived on an Air France Jetliner. The theft, if that is what it was, was discovered when an armoured truck came to take the money to a Manhattan bank. The matter was said to be under investigation, and we don't know if it was 'solved' or not. Daily Mirror, 13 April 1967. Credit: Anthony Smith.

INCENSE HATER PLAGUES CHURCH.
A mystery 'incense hater' is thought by the vicar of a church in Bognor Regis, Sussex, to creep in seconds before a service and hide the censer. And after the services it would turn up again. So the Rev.Sinclair Snow hit upon a plan -- he stopped using incense in his services. We don't know if this fits as an 'Occult crime' but its manic and trivial enough. Sunday Express, 6 Jan 74.

SOME ODD THEFTS.
In March 1974, police were said to be worried by a spate of buglaries in the villages and towns around Guildford, Surrey. During the events, the faces and guts of the redident grandfather clocks were stolen, or otherwise disappeared. To the date of the report 20 homes had so far been left with disemboweled grandfathers. This may be of no consequence whatever, but the impression is given that the gang operating the area, if that is the culprit, is deliberately chosing houses with these familiar horological instruments of our childhood, which when we come to think of it is not only an odd criterion upon which to burgle, but information, the obtaining of which, could make one quite conspicuous. The police theory is that an antique 'ringing' racket is behind the burglaries. They could be right. Daily Express, 16 March 74.

A note in the Weekly News for 28 Sept 74 says that police were "stumped" by a theft in Rose Drive, Chesham, Bucks. Much expensive equipment and other items preferred by thieves with more orthodox tastes, were left untouched. What was missing though, was the lounge door. The paper adds: "It was a perfectly ordinary door." A door with wanderlust may be many things - but not, one would have thought, ordinary.

Toward the end of January 1973 the press spotlight fell on the curious practice of 'Glossolalia' after three members of a fringe sect were found in Yarmouth, exhausted and entranced from three days solid chanting. In the subsequent weeks, more cases, and the bizarre behaviour of 'crazed' 'speaking in tongues' freaks, came to light, causing more than an interested ripple.

But that is not our concern right now. Our eye was caught at the time by a casual reference in a write-up of the Glossolalia fad, by Peter Watson in The Sunday Times, 4 Feb 73. Talking about "socially shared psychopathology" cases, he said: "Some of these have concerned literally masses of people, like the wave of slow poisonings that went on throughout Europe in the 17th century (when 100 people had to be burned or hanged before the epidemic died out)." If any of you more historically oriented people could help identify this "wave" we should be most glad.

As Fort showed clearly, cases of mass illness of unidentified causes are still a frequent happening, though the fashion in names has drifted from 'Mass Hysteria' to 'Socially Shared Psychopathology'. But from the phenomenological point of view they are still very real, and never much fun for the victims. One or many are suddenly afflicted -- experts are said to be tracking a 'mystery bug' or 'smell' down -- there is often a recurrence -- experts pronounce themselves baffled -- parents complain, victims groan -- then perhaps the greatest mystery of all, the whole case drifts out of sight as smoothly as it called in the first place.

RICKMANSWORTH, HERTS.
A mystery sickness struck swimmers in a popular lake, and brought on a painful rash. Scientists from the Medical Research Council said there was no cause for alarm, hanging the blame on a microscopic parasite of snails "which may be responsible." But this was not confirmed, and if it was a parasite, surely its sudden nonmalevolence should have been equally á cause for wonder? Daily Mirror, 10 July 1970. Cr: Anthony Smith.

WARLEY, WORCS.
17 women workers collapsed and were taken to hospital from the Old Hill works of BSR Ltd. Experts who examined several theories ended up baffled -- oppressive heat, lack of ventilation, a 'mystery virus', and leakages of gas or other fumes were all checked for and discounted.

This is a doubly damned incident, because the previous Friday (4th), 25 women collapsed over a two hour period at the nearby Waterfall Lame premises of the same firm. Birmingham Evening Mail, 9 July 74. The next day, the Daily Mirror carried an interview with one of the victims, who complained of a strange ether-like smell sweeping through the factory. "I felt a burning sensation in my chest. My tongue felt all furry. I was dizzy and sick. All around me people were passing out." Factory inspectors, County Health officials and chemists poked around for a second day and still came up with nothing.

GILLESPIE, ILLINOIS.
84 people, most of them teenagers, were attacked by nausea, headaches and dizziness during a feature film in a movie-theatre on 28th December. Dr Lee Johnson, a trauma surgeon at St Francis hospital in nearby Litchfield, where 76 of the victims were taken, said that he didn't rule out the possibility of 'mass hysteria' -- whatever he means by that. Sheriff Richard Zarr feels differently: "It wasn't any kind of follow-the-leader type of thing. Seven or eight people were lying on the sidewalk in front of the show. These people were actually passed out. We were reviving them with oxygen." Those inside, he added, suddenly and without explanation began to feel ill during the film; they left the theatre and many began to collapse onto the sidewalk. The film showing was "Paper Moon", and whether or not you feel this explains things, one must feel that 'mass hysteria' as a form of critical protest would hardly be in keeping with the subject. Authorities were said to be investigating the ventilating system for 'foreign substances' etc -- but no sign of anything that would relieve the dicomfiture of the management, who would have been suffering alongside the wretches outside their establishment. Champaign-Urbana (Illinois) Courrier, 30 Dec 1973. Cr: Loren Coleman.

CHICAGO, ILLINOIS.
Not long after the above incident, we find 54 people, mostly children, collapsing during a Walt Disney double feature at the Riviera Theatre.

They were vomiting and complaining of headaches and dizziness. Police were said to have identified the cause -- carbon monoxide leaking into the theatre. Perhaps we are being perverse, but we have seen (and you will too by the end of this section) many of these mystery illness cases, so that an immediate positive identification sticks out like a sore thumb -- we reserve our option to take it or leave it. San Francisco Examiner, 20 February 74. Credit: Loren Coleman.

BIRMINGHAM. KINGSTANDING,
"More than 20" guests at a wedding party were taken to hospital after "collapsing like flies and being sick all over the place." The reception had been at the Drake's Drum, with many of the guests praising the chicken meal provided. Then they returned to the bride's mother's house in Kingstanding, where they started to collapse. Both victims and venue received visits from officials of the Medical Officer's department, in a bid to find out how the business began. A curious detail comes to light: the first girl to collapse turned out to have appendicitis. Then the bride's grandmother, who was thought to have succumbed to the excitements and the heat in the house. Then the rest. Ah yes! The Medical Officers have come up with something -- The Drake's Drum was the site of a similar incident about 12 months previously, and they will look into that too. Prompted by this hint of a periodicity, we wrote to the proprietor of the pub, but we never received any reply. Par for the course. Birmingham Evening Mail, 18 July 72.

WILLENHALL, BIRMINGHAM.
The Moore family, with four kids, were all taken semi-conscious to Walsall General hospital, where a doctor declared the 'illness' to be caused by a lack of oxygen or carbon monoxide poisoning. Almost a Pavlovian response, we feel -- people faint, and nothing much can be found wrong with them, (a lightbulb springs into illumination overhead) and, its "Lack of oxygen, or carbon monoxide poisoning." Gas Board officials duly investigated, and, you get the gist by now, found nothing wrong in the house in which they collapsed.

Later, on 15 Dec., there was a repeat performance -- Keith Moore dropped to the kitchen floor. Then daughter Siobhan had convulsions and frothed at the mouth. Nothing is said about the other children except that they are recovering. Mrs Angela Moore managed to stagger to neighbours to call for help again. Nothing much is said either about what the police, health officials or the Gas Board, who investigated the first incident and found nothing suspicious. Sunday Mercury, 16 December 1973.

HAUPPAUGE, NEW YORK.
A 'mystery illness' killed two young sisters, and caused their father, mother and their five other children to move out of thier Long Island home. A next-door neighbour also moved out with his wife and child. Health officials, despite working the whole weekend on the case, failed to

link the two deaths to the use of Chlordane, a termite killer, on the two properties. "The fumes are still there and killing little birds. They just flop out of the air," said Mrs Frances Impastato, the dead girls' aunt. But we, while not claiming in any way to be wiser, but knowing as we do of 'mystery illness or attacks' on birds who then drop out of the sky, would prefer to say that 'something' was acting on these birds, rather than identifying the villainous fumes. A later report -- Commissioner of Health for Suffolk County said autopsies on the two girls have not shown any findings of the pesticide Chlordane, so far. Houston (Texas) Chronicle, 15 July 74. Miami (Florida) Herald, 16 July 74. Credit for both: Mark Hall.

Speaking of fumes, and the repeated searches for fumes in these cases, brings us onto our notes on smells and phantom smells, which as we have seen merge away with phantom illnesses.

PINXTON, DERBYSHIRE.
'Mysterious fumes' have driven a couple from their council house. The County Council have so far spent more than £1000 in various bids to identify the cause of the fumes which give Herbert Slater and his wife "burning sensations" in their throats every time they enter into their home in Church Street. The Council is trying to rehouse them. The Sun, 19 August 74.

CHICAGO, ILLINOIS.
We have a note on 15,000 people being evacuated from their homes in Chicago, many of them needing treatment for sore throats and eye trouble, after what is described as a "Five-mile long cloud of Acid fumes" hung over the city following a storage leak. It is possible that this is indeed the actual cause -- but we include the item because of its similarities in other respects to "Mystery Smell" cases. It is equally possible that the leaking storage tank was a convenient get-out for a mystery of colossal proportions -- 15,000 people is a lot of voters. Perhaps someone could look into this for us?. Note is from Sunday Mercury, 28 April 74.

WARLEY, BIRMINGHAM.
You could be forgiven for thinking by now that Birmingham must be the smelliest place on this Earth. The West Midlands Gas Board investigated complaints from 20 people, protesting about the smell of gas in the West Smethwick area of Warley. The Fire Brigade was also called to a similar complaint from a block of flats at Royal Oak, off Windmill Lane. Investigations of both incidents revealed no leaks, despite the smell. Express & Star, April 3, 1970. Cr: Anthony Smith.

HALESOWEN, STAFFS.
Yes, another town near Birmingham. This time health officials were investigating complaints from residents of the Quinton area who noticed a "sulphurous smell" between 3 and 4 am. David Isaacs, of 1 Oak Tree Crescent, said: "The smell brought tears to my eyes and I felt like vomiting." The officials describe it as a "cloud of gas" though of course, phenomenologically speaking, there was no evidence to suggest it was such, since all through our notes there have been suggestions of a "hysterical" (in the literal sense) and subjective aspect to these reactions. Anyway, despite police and health official attention, the cause and nature of the elusive 'cloud' avoided them completely. Birmingham Evening Mail, 4 October 1972.

NEWCASTLE-UPON-TYNE & WOLVERHAMPTON.
I heard the story on the radio -- that 63 nursery school kids were taken to hospital after supposedly eating seeds from a laburnum tree in the playground. I had doubts. 63 is a big bunch of kids to be all copying each other -- and surely the trees presence would have posed a similar problem in previous years, enough to have had it removed. If this was the first seed-eating mania it would in itself be a curiosity. The paper the next day carried the story , but surprise surprise. Also a note that Wolverhampton Corp. was having branches removed from a laburnum tree in an infants school playground after 21 kids had taken ill through eating berries from the tree. Same tree, same type of victims, similar sites, same day -- Hmmmm. Birmingham Post, 21 July 72.

HAZELRIGG, NORTHUMBERLAND.
150 children, aged between 9 and 14 spent the weekend in hospital after a mass collapse at the Hazelrigg carnival site. Police and hospital scientists took away samples of ice cream and other foods for testing. Also a piece of turf after it was suggested that this might be the result of a spraying of the area with insecticide over 24 hours earlier. No results of the testings was ever printed in the national papers that I monitored subsequently. Daily Mirror, 10 July 72.

Now we are into a whole sub-category -- mystery illnesses in schools, and at risk of great trauma to myself I reach back into my files, or more accurately, down the back of the draw, where it fell over three years ago -- a note on a saga from 1965. Its a good excuse to fish it out, finally.

BLACKBURN, LANCS., & PORTSMOUTH, HANTS.
St Hilda's Church of England Secondary Modern School is the scene -- 90 girls, the victims. They were taken to Park Lee Isolation hospital after complaining (on the 7th) of dizziness, pains in the chest, and some of their number losing consciousness. Blackburn Medical Officer, Dr John Ardley steps in to conduct tests.

On the 11th, St Hilda's reopens -- and within minutes 63 girls collapse and are taken to the same hospital. Dr John Moss, Consultant Paediatrician to the Blackburn Group of Hospitals, said: "This is not a new outbreak but a continuation of the same one. I believe this is a type of encephalitis of virus origin. This virus causes inflammation of the central nervous system. I do not think it is going to spread from one sufferer to another. There is no evidence of where it originated. The patients tend to be well for periods of hours and then ill again and it is difficult to say how many are completely well." In other words a mystery illness. He added that nearly all the girls affected in the second incident were ill in the previous attack, but were not as seriously affected as those in the second attack for the first time -- if you follow?

At the same time as the second wave hit St Hilda's we learn (in the same report) that much the same sort of thing happened at St Luke's C of E Modern School, Portsmouth, where 70 girls were taken ill the previous week, and then again (11th) when 30 were "seized with giddiness and sickness". Both items from Birmingham Evening Mail, but 8 & 12 October 1965, recpectively.

The next day (12th) there were 118 girls absent from St Luke's, Portsmouth. A member of staff said there had been one or two recurrences. And at St Hilda's, Blackburn, only one more girl had collapsed. Experts in both investigations seem to have become less vociferous about their lack of progress in identifying the causes. Birmingham Evening Mail, 13 October 1965. See also NEWS 1/17 for other 'mystery illnesses' in Portsmonth.

BOURNEMOUTH, HANTS, & A CASE IN SUSSEX.
A 'mystery bug' shut down one of Britain's top private girl's schools for a fortnight. 15 girls were laid low by a 'feverish illness', and the medical officer of Wentworth Milton Mount School decided to take no chances until the 'bug' was identified, and various tests were in progress. Dr Barry Windsor said that until the results of these were known, he could not say if it was the same illness that caused a boy's death at Lancing College, Sussex, and a few others to be sent home. Daily Express, 3 October 1973.

WORKINGTON, CUMBERLAND.
Worried parents have threatened to keep their children away from Harrington infants school, after a foul and elusive smell has caused much illness among the 126 kids. No figures are given but they were said to have suffered with headaches and sickness. Heating systems, drains etc checked, experts prod and poke and test -- result: bafflement. The Sun, 22 February 73.

SELBY, YORKSHIRE, AND OTHERS IN THE AREA.
For the eighth consecutive year, pupils of Cliffe School, near Selby, have been hit by severe stomach pains and sickness, this time 77 were claimed. The headmaster, Mr Edward Wright, said: "I have seen children collapse in the school porch with violent pains. It strikes very quickly and always at this time of the year. The first outbreak was eight years ago and most of the children were affected. It lasted about six weeks and children were away from school between two and four days. But we have had the same problem every year since. Now children are off for only a day and I think we are becomming immune."

Because the illness is so short lived, he continued, it is often not reported, and so he found it difficult to persuade authorities to investigate. He started making inquiries himself and found

the Hemmingborough and Riccall primary schools 1½ miles away had also been affected. The headmaster at Riccall said: "It's happened every year for the four years I have been here, and my family have also had it. About 12 pupils have had the symptoms in the last few weeks."

Mr Wright took the matter to the new district community physician (after recent local government reorganisation), a Dr Wilson MacIntosh, who said: "It is difficult to theorise on possible causes. General hygiene, the water and this type of thing, will have to be checked - but it is doubtful whether this is responsible. Often there is no simple answer to something like this." Mr Wright tends towards thinking the crop-spraying in the area might be a contributing factor, but the National Farmer's Union have hotly denied responsibility, claiming only to use sprays listed by the Ministry of Agriculture as harmless to humans. Ahh! but there have been mistakes in the past, you cry! So why is the 'mystery illness' confined to so few country schools in the area.....or town schools and factories, for that matter? We still don't know the full extent of ecological effects and repercussions from the widespread use of hundreds of types of chemicals on the land. This is only one direction that occurs to us for investigation, but before we go onto another, we'd better add that the above story was from the Daily Express, 26 May 74. Credit: Peter Rogerson.

FILEY, YORKSHIRE.
Apart from being in the same county and happening at roughly the same time, there could be no connexion at all between this and the previous case. Kitt Waggitt and his wife have lived in their council house for 20 years, but the smell only started in earnest about two years ago making people giddy and breathless, and bringing tears to their eyes. In those two years Kitt and the Council have tried "everything" they could think of, digging up drains, rebuilding flues and fireplaces, checking the foundations, etc. "I have spent £150 installing extractor fans, air vents, and a special air-purifying machine."..but all to no effect. Even a £20 reward to a bright chemist, failed. All adding up to a big zilch, as Kojak would say. In desperation, Kitt turns to the outside chance thousands before him, and no doubt thousands more after him,will turn to when Science has failed to rid them of their daily discomfort -- an exorcism. (Gasp!) Yes, sooner or later we come up against these remnants (or are they foretastes?) of a psychic technology.

You cannot have failed to note the phantom smell aspect of the mystery illness cases having a distant cousin in the smells sometimes associated with hauntings or psychic activity of sorts -- there may or may not be such a connexion. We have no note subsequent to the above (Sunday Express, 7 April 74. Cr: Peter Rogerson.) as to any success in the operation -- though a brief note in The Sun, 23 April 74, merely said the Waggitts had had advice from all over the world on how to quell their smell.

Continued on p14.

NOTES ON
LINCOLNSHIRE
PHENOMENA : 2.

by NIGEL WATSON

To begin with, it must be pointed out that this article is in no-way at all complete. My intention has been to record several 'cases' that might in a general sense be classified as 'hauntings' and are in the main previously unpublished in the literature; the main exception being the haunting of the Rectory at Epworth.

The reports are restricted to the South Humberside and Lincolnshire regions recorded on Ordnance Survey sheet 112 in the 1:50000 First Series. Map references are given with the notes.

As I have said, this compilation is merely to bridge a gap in the available literature. The giant mass of excluded material on Lincs and S Humberside (1) can be found in the following: Lincolnshire Life; Lincolnshire Folklore by Ethel Rudkin; County Folklore Volume V by Mrs Gutch and Mabel Peacock; Journal of Paraphysics; and, of course, The News; etc.

Eventually I should like to compile a complete (well, as complete as possible) catalogue of this material, to give a comprehensive view of the whole of Lincolnshire (and S Humberside.)

LAUGHTON CHURCH   Map Ref: SK 849 974.

"Eerie footsteps on a circular stone stairway in the ancient tower of a country church have startled workmen and set villagers tongues wagging. The strange events have happened in a church popular with Canadian and US visitors for the quality of brass rubbings obtained from a family tomb. They led to one of the workmen repairing the tower declining for a few days to be alone in the church.

"Work began some weeks ago on repairs estimated to cost about £2,000 to All Saints Church at Laughton, about eight miles from Scunthorpe. The church tower, part of which is said to date from the Eleventh Century, needed cracks filling and its external surface touching up. Earlier, an elderberry tree had been discovered growing out of the tower after an adjacent tree had been felled. Some time after the work began, the two men on the job started hearing mysterious footsteps on the tower stairway. Not just one or two, but a whole series of footsteps.

"One of the men, Jeffrey Curtis, 18, heard the footsteps on two occasions. "It was as if somebody was coming up the tower but there was nobody there," he said. "I was a bit shaken at

first, and did not want to be alone in the church for a few days after." His stepfather, Mr Kenneth Curtis, of 64 Butterwick Rd, Messingham, also heard the footsteps on different occasions. Indeed, at one time he called out, thinking they had been made by some electricians working in the church. But they had left earlier and there was nobody there.

"Mr Curtis does not believe in ghosts yet says he cannot offer an explanation for the happenings. One man who does is Mr Roy Chappel, of Aspen Garth, Laughton. Some 25 years ago he was in the church one night as chairs were being changed for a whist drive. Hearing what he believed was somebody in the church, he called out that he had got the last of the chairs. But there was no reply, and on investigation, nobody in the church. Startled at first, he has since reasoned that the noises he heard were an echo. He has never heard of a Laughton ghost. Opinions about the strange noises are likely to continue to differ, and it is hardly likely they will ever be resolved."

This account has been edited from the Scunthorpe Evening Telegraph, 15 April 1974. I heard about these happenings the day before they were published in the local paper, from a relative of one of the men. He claimed that one of them had been in the tower on his own when he felt a hand tap him on the shoulder, and looking round he found that there was nobody else at all in the church tower.

EPWORTH RECTORY.

Most standard works on psychical research carry reports of the famous ghost of 'Old Jeffrey' who haunted the Wesley family during the winter of 1715-16.

The main activities of the manifestation were carried out in the large room at the very top of the Old Rectory, which has been known as 'Old Jeffrey's Chamber' ever since. John Wesley wrote up all the information he could find, publishing it in the Arminian Magazine of 1784.

A helpful little booklet is: "Epworth - The Home of the Wesleys." by W Le Cato Edwards.

I visited the Rectory in April 74 - an interesting place to look around, even if it has been practically rebuilt. I never met Old Jeffrey either!

IRONSTONE COTTAGE.   Map Ref: SE 892 108.

This building is attached to the Scunthorpe Borough Museum & Art Gallery, Oswald Road, Scunthorpe. It is reputed to be haunted, but no firm information is known.

CEMETERY ROAD (SCUNTHORPE). Map Ref: SE 898 097.

Cemetery Road is where a young man is alleged to have seen a weird phenomenon. He cycled up East Common Road, turning left into Cemetery Road, where he saw a vertical white cylindrical light cross the road from left to right. He did not go to work the next day because the event had disturbed him so much.

MESSINGHAM.

In 1971, I was, for a short time, in contact with Alan Beasty, who then lived in Scunthorpe. In a letter dated 25 November 1971, he reported an incident of some interest, which I quote:

"A friend of mine, Mr Cliff Todd of Wendover Estate, Messingham, encountered an unfamiliar event on Monday morning (2am). He told me that he was in bed, but awake, when his bedroom was bathed in a flash of intense white light, lasting for about 2 to 3 seconds. This was followed by a repeat performance at about 2.30am; this time the light lasted for roughly 4 to 5 seconds. Since I cannot get a satisfactory account of the weather situation at that particular time of day, I cannot rule out lightning. Mr Todd stated that the light was so intense and profound that daylight did not or would not compare in magnitude of illumination."

In the letter he added that the light was not associated with any sound or noise. In a further letter dated 9 December 71 he gave more information:

"Regarding C Todd's incident: His bedroom curtains were drawn; the curtains are of thick material and are lined. So the strength of the light would have had to have been sufficient to penetrate and illuminate to the unusual degree previously stated. The date (of the incident) was 22 November 1971."

* = * = * = * = * = * = * = * = * = * = * = *

Note:
1) Before local government reorganisation came into being on 1st April 1974, South Humberside was a part of Lincolnshire.   -- NW.

SMELLS..........cont:

As an example, we'll just use the following (which fell out of a folder we were moving). It is from a piece in the Daily Mail, 26 Nov 73, about Canon Henry Cooper's appointment as diocesan adviser on exorcism to the Bishop of London. He refers to an exorcism of a staff flat "at a famous London landmark" which he had promised not to identify. In the bedroom was a pervading and loathsome smell of decay which no amount of cleaning could remove, and some other manifestations of hauntings. After exorcism, he claimed, the smell, whisperings, etc disappeared forever.

LOS ANGELES, CALIFORNIA.
Fire officials were said to be puzzled over unidentified noxious fumes that filled two floors of a downtown clothing store on 3 Sept 74, sending 28 people to hospital. Eight were overcome and found unconscious - others complained they were dizzy and nauseous -- and three firemen without their masks were also affected. None were in a serious condition and were released within hours. "We don't know what kind of gas it was or where it came from," said a Fire Department spokesman. St Paul (Minnesota) Dispatch, 4 Sept 74. Credit: Mark Hall. Our datum is a collapsing or overcoming of people, and a subsequent investigation based on the assumption of 'fumes' or 'mystery bugs'. As JC Pearce points out, Nature may abhor a vacuum, but Man abhors an empty category as much if not more.

Our thought is, that whatever the mystery smell/ illness phenomenon is, its evidences are widely scattered in the different branches of human experience. Perhaps this is our task - the beginnings of cross-indexing the flora and fauna of phenomenology - as Fort correlated the annals of earthquakes and meteors, previously kept apart by specialists, to discover or open up a new path of inquiry. Smells, fainting fits and ghosts. What do we mean by 'auto-suggestion'; 'Mass Hysteria'; 'psychosomatic' ? We wont know unless we try to puzzle these things onto their next stage.

Daily Mirror, 2 Sept 74. In pure gothic hysteria Colonel Ethelwald Vella, assistant professor of pathology of the Royal Army Medical College, has warned us what to expect if Britain goes ahead with the Channel tunnel project -- swarms of rabies infested bats. Hah! He should see our 'Surrey Puma' file, and the notes of Fort-only-knows-whats that regularly stomp and flap in this glorified safari park of ours. And then there are the swarms and migrations of things...

ANTS:

Westfield Estate, Farnborough, Hants. (Puma country.) Residents complained to their local council that they were being invaded by inch-long ants, coloured red and black. Mrs Coralie Quaintance said: "You can hear them hissing. Its spine-chilling. They climb straight up the walls of the house and get in anywhere." Mr Richard Arthur, of Snowdon Close said he had seen ants marching in columns 50 yards long, and heard the sound of their feet as they tramped by. Mrs Christine Gill remembered: "Looking across the garden fence and seeing a dark patch. When I looked closer I realised what it was - a seething black mass of these giant ants." The council has advised the residents to sit it out, after identifying the little fellers as Formica Rufa, a rare pest-eating wood ant: "People expect us to go around killing everything they regard as creepy-crawlies, and we won't. As a basic principle, if an insect is useful we won't kill it, unless it becomes a terrible nuisance." In Germany these ants are protected by law, and Italians are encouraged to breed them (it says here). The British Museum commented: "The people on the estate should be grateful they have such fascinating creatures living so near." Daily Express and Daily Mail for 30 Sept 74. Cr: Steve Moore.

Millions of flying white ants have forced police to quit their station at Darlinghurst, Sydney, Australia. London Evening News, 11 Nov 74. Credit: Steve Moore.

A plague of crazy ants has over-run the island of Mahe in the Seychelles, and has so worried the islanders that they are to be given £30,000 over the next two and a half years to be spent on keeping the terror within bounds. The Anoplolepis longipes is small, red and doesn't bite or sting -- but they swarm, and keep on swarming. They are attracted by moisture, and so head in droves for wet areas. "They collect in large numbers, running up and down trees and all over people. Livestock suffers. Chickens just sit there and mope. Other insects clear out of an area when the ants move in," said Tecwin Jones, deputy director of the Centre for Overseas Pest Research. They run up and down trouser-legs in droves, cluster round the eyes and ears -- some animals and small children have reported to have simply died of shock when they were over-run. It is thought that the ant, not a native of the island, was brought by ship from elsewhere only a few years previously. It is difficult to wipe out because they can lay their eggs in leaves as well as anthills, and they have grown so fast they now dominate four different isolated areas of the small island. Sunday Times, 3 November 74.

WINGED THINGS.

The council of Cizre, Turkey, is paying £8 a lb. to any citizen during a plague of flies there. Sunday People, 10 November 74.

In 1967, most likely in the summer months, a swarm of crickets invaded the village of Stretham in Cambridgeshire. Sixty, live and chirping, were caught in one house alone. Ely council were said to be fighting back with insecticides. Alas, we have no complete date for this - perhaps someone could check with Ely council for us. Credit: Steve Moore.

Recently, Redding, in Northern California, also suffered a swarms of crickets. The police admitted that, despite many calls from houses in outlying districts, the chirping critters were crawling in through every available crack and aperture & there was nothing they could do - they were under attack too. An increase in the cricket population happens about once in every ten years, according to State Department of Fish & Game entomologist Ron Hawthorne, who also advised getting rid of the things quickly should they enter a house, because when they run out of normal food they start on clothes, curtains and other houshold fibres. San Francisco Chronicle, 25 July 74. Credit: Loren Coleman.

From our book of the moment, THE WORLD OF WONDERS mentioned more fully elsewhere this ish, comes a tale of striking plagues of flies, or rather, gnats, from way back. Fort, you may remember, decided to begin his searches for data at the year 1800, and so vast stretches of the past remain untapped of Fortean phenomena. Anyway, this item is quoted on p62 of WONDERS from a pamphlet inscribed "Printed for BB, London, in 1622 " No title is given but the pamphlet is said to be in the British Museum, King's collection.

"In the twelfth year of the reign of Richard II, a battle was fought between gnats at Shene, now called Richmond: their multitudes were so great, that the air was darkened with them. It was computed that two thirds of them were killed and the remaining third suddenly vanished."

We make the date of the event out to be 1389.

MARINE SWARMS.

Hundreds of giant freshwater mussels have been found in a lake at Loscoe, Derbyshire. This seems to have been a remarkable enough event to have been worth declaring by local specialists. Sunday Mirror, 1 July 73.

Thousands of 'Sea Mice' have been washed ashore on the south coast around Southsea, Hants. The mice - 5" long sea worms with grey fur-like backs (and said by one report to give off "flashing lights") - are harmless and rarely seen. Daily Express & The Sun, 19 Feb 74.

'Millions' of giant spiny crabs are invading the coastal waters off Bognor Regis, Worthing and Shoreham, some of them more than a foot across, ripping nets and blocking up lobster pots. Many fishermen are up in arms, complaining that their livelyhoods have been severely jeopardised. Mr Albie Ide, Bognor's 80-year-old fisheries officer, said: "These crabs have made net fishing impossible. I picked 500 of the blighters out of two nets yesterday. They are covered with sharp spines like razors and they can cut a net to ribbons in a few minutes. With nets costing £30 a time we just can't go on fishing with them." Mr Edmund Venables, curator of Bognor museum, said "We have had many invasions of spider crabs but nothing like the present one." Various theories have been suggested: that they are attracted by the huge outfall sewer completed two years ago; or the large amount of their favourite seaweed in the area. We have no further reports of any developments in this struggle. Sunday Express, 14 July 74. Credit: Steve Moore.

You may remember a note back in NEWS 2/14 about the explosive growth of the Sargasso-type sea-weed around Portsmouth. Well it seems it's still on the plant equivalent of a rampage -- and many "scientists" (it doesn't say who or from where) are urging the government to make control of the menace a national problem, and they want them to sponsor a £10,000, 3-year study on ways of stopping the weed. Daily Mail, 16 Dec 74.

RODENT RAMPAGES.

Thousands of tiny field-mice invaded 250 acres of sugar beet on ten seperate Worcestershire and Shropshire farms. In what the Ministry of Agriculture said to be calling "the year of the mouse", hoardes of 'brainy' rodents are outwitting the farmers. After extensive damage on ear-lier forays, the Ministry's only recommendation was that the farms use a special 'Cambridge Roller', which flattens out the telltale lumps on the ground after seed sowing. "We know of instances where 500 freshly planted seeds have disappeared overnight," said Dr Andrew Dunning, head of reseasch at Brooms Barn Research Farm, Bury St Edmunds. "Really its something of a mystery. The mice appear to be able to find the seeds by looking at the state of the surface of the field." Hence the advice to roll flat. But still the seeds vanished. Much puzzlement of experts. Mr George Field, a joint tennant of Sutton House Farm, near Tenbury Wells, Worcs, said even after redrilling and laying poison in land-tiles, the mice came back. "This has been astonishing. It will cost us nearly £2,000," he said. A heretical thought comes to us -- no mention of people seeing mice, only that mice are blamed when seeds disappear. We have notes on mysterious patches of crops that spring up where no one (to anyone's knowledge) has sowed any seeds - as though there has been a teleporting of seed to that patch from elsewhere. So we are always on the lookout for the vanishings of seeds. When seeds vanish, its natural, in their frame of reference, for farmers to blame mice - but whether in this case the mice were there or not can only be discovered by further work by someone. Sunday Mercury, 26 May 74.

A datum which weights our problem of putting the above in this section or 'Disappearances' or 'Falls'-- is a note in the Daily Mirror, 11 March 74, that a plague of mice has caused a shortage of mousetraps in Evesham, Worcestershire.

Thousands of field-mice and rats, this time in the fields around Villers-sous-Bereid, Verdun, France, where they polished off 500 acres of grain and other crops between them. The Mayor has declared the community a distance zone at the request of the regional authorities. One theory is that the lack of anti-rat campaigns in recent years and the killing of so many foxes (natural enemy of rodents) for fear of rabies, has allowed them to multiply heavily. Sacramento (California) Bee, 1 August 74. Credit: Loren Coleman.

Nor has Australia been free. Mice were over-running Kalgoorlie, a mining town in Western Australia, said to be driven out of the plains by bush fires. They are running amok in beds and baths and a resident is said to have found one in his beer. That for an Ozzy is the last straw. The town was pleaing for shipments of traps. The Sun, 30 Dec 74.

At Cairo airport, police fought a pitched battle with 45,000 desert rats, which had moved into seven airliners and eaten everything indide them. Sunday People, 10 November 74. The 'Year of the Mouse', indeed!

TOADS.

Last March, if you had chanced down Pix Farm Lane, Hemel Hempstead in Hertfordshire, you would have heard sounds of excitement, hoarse croaking, the honking of horns, and the odd squelch. "Thousands of toads, from literally miles around, were making

. . . a lucky toad escapes by inches to love another night

their way back to a lake at Bourne End. "We
don't really know where they all come from, but
toads always return to their birthplace to mate,"
said Miss Priscilla Oates, who organised a 15-
strong toad-crossing patrol. "But we think some
of them come for miles, and many have to cross
the lane. We scoop them up and carry them across
the road in a bucket, and put them safe and
sound on the other side." From the wording it
seems at least that they worked every night from
March to May the previous year, though nothing
is said about previous events. We shall watch
for a recurrence this year. Daily Mirror, 27
March 74. Daily Express, 29 March 74. And photo
from Sunday Mirror, 31 March 74.

DEVONIAN PORCUPINES.

Here is an example of our dilemmas of category.
Porcupines are discovered, breeding in Devon --
now do we stick this under 'Appearances', 'Animal
Curiosities', or what? To get it in this issue
we have lumped it under 'Swarms'. After all, a
population of 30 (estimated) where none should
be in the first place is an explosion of sorts.
And if the animal is turning up where it is least
expected...well that's a migration, of sorts, too.
Dammit, why do I feel I have to justify this
whole business of categories? Is there still a

subversive streak of orderliness in me that has
resisted punishment by editorial trials? As an
aberration it has its uses, but we are constantly
feeling that soon it should be left behind on
our travels. Now I admit to something else - a
fit of sloth which I intend to enjoy to the full,
refraining from précis-ing (?) the following
write-up by Rosemarie Wittman on the prickly
problems of the porcupines in Devon, from the
Sunday Times, 22 July 73:

New English wildlife

AN EXOTIC and new hazard for
tourists, growing trees and anyone taking a casual nature walk
down in the woods has appeared
near Okehampton in leafy Devon.
The name of the hazard is *hystrix
cristata*, less formally known as
the crested porcupine. Two porcupines escaped from a local
wild-life park, the Pine Valley
Zoo, about three years ago,. successfully survived the winter and
began to breed.

Although the species is from
India they are very adaptable
and are found in conditions ranging from arid desert to temperate
climate. Down in Devon they are
adapting to a British way of life
and loving it. They live on
tubers, roots and fruit (they
adore bluebell bulbs) and hide
in the undergrowth. New plantations of trees are ideal as the
undergrowth is thick and pro-
vides good cover.

Unfortunately porcupines have
some rather nasty un-British
habits. They strip the bark from
young conifers, thereby killing
them. The Forestry Commission
is therefore rather anxious to
catch them before they breed
further and decimate their
plantations. But *hystrix cristata*
is not that easy to catch. An
anti-social, shy animal, he can
get very prickly indeed when
pursued. Fully grown he weighs
about 60lb and is more than two
feet long.

That makes him the largest
terrestrial rodent in Europe—but
outside Devon he is actually only
found much further south, in
Spain, Italy, Greece and Turkey.
The Indian variety, alas, is not
the most attractive of porcupines.
He has a hairy nose, and none of
the poodle-like glamour of the
furry North American type,
which also climbs trees. He is
also notoriously short-tempered,
even by porcupine standards.

If discovered he will not curl
comfortably up into a ball, like
his British cousin, the hedgehog.
He will look you straight in the
eye, and then just as the enemy
is disarmed and perhaps takes
a step closer, he will turn round,
go sharply into reverse gear and
prong you with 7-inch quills from
his tail. These quills are like
small poisoned arrows, since they
go in deep, are very hard to get
out, and due to the unsavoury

living conditions of porcupines,
are covered in filth and dirt.
Septicaemia is the mildest result
that can occur out of such an
encounter.

Already an unsuspecting
badger digger, who thought he
found a badger hole and put his
small terrier dog down to ferret
it out, was shocked to find his
dog retreating rapidly out of the
hole with porcupine quills stuck
in its chest. The dog later died
of a pierced lung.

Estimates about the number of
porcupines ranges from two, by
a local naturalist, to 30, by the
Ministry of Agriculture who calculated that at the rate of two to
three litters a year with two to
three young each time they could
have reached this number in
three years.

Apart from creating headaches
for the Forestry Commission, and
dangers for people roaming the
woods, the porcupines have also
been a bit of a shock to local
wildlife. Mrs Ruth Murray, a
Devon naturalist, is worried
about the effects of this foreign
invasion on British born badgers.

"These porcupines have really
upset the ecological balance. I
feel very strongly about it. They
come in and take over the badger
burrows for a short while, and
then move into another burrow.
The badger is up against a species
he cannot possibly compete with.
I mean, nothing is going to get
the best of a porcupine at close
quarters is it? The badgers are
moving out of the area altogether,
they are giving up. Once a porcupine has occupied his burrow no
badger would want to come
back."

Mrs Murray has been asked by
the Universities Federation for
Animal Welfare to try and trap
the porcupines and is at the
moment setting baits for them,
mostly bananas and other fruit.
Her job has been made more
difficult by local publicity about
the porcupines and she hopes
people will keep out of the woods
and let her get on with it.

She also believes more control
should be exercised over wild-life
parks: "Anyone can set up a wild-
life park with lots of exotic
animals, but if they are able to
escape it's not fair to the animal
from the park and it's not fair on
our own wild life. Nature is deli-
cately balanced, and can be easily
upset by escapes of this kind."

We are attempting to get more information on the
state of the situation now - but for the moment
note that the porcupines are still turning up,
as Ministry scientists say they caught one in
"Devon woodland" on 2nd Jan 74. Unfortunately
there is nothing in the report to say which Ministry, or where in Devon. Daily Mirror, 4 Jan 74.
Credit: DJ McAllister.

MAGNETIC ANOMALY IS GROWING.

John De Laurier, an earth-physicist at the Canadian Department of Energy, Mines and Resources,
is continuing his investigations into what is
called Canada's "deepest mystery" - an eccentric
wave in the planetary, magnetic field, "and as far
as I am concerned, its the biggest anomaly in the
world." It seems that this enigma was first noticed in 1957 at the isolated settlement of Alert,
in the Canadian Arctic, and at each successive
yearly charting its size has spread. Something
that could be as much as 18 miles down is causing magnetometers to give higher than normal
readings - and it covers an area about 43 miles
wide on a 450 mile long path beneath Alert and
Eureka -- and De Laurier will attempt to determine
whether it stretches all the way to the western
Arctic regions.

De Laurier said: "There are other such anomaly
features around the world - such as down the
Rocky Mountains in the United States; in fact,
wherever there are recognized earthquake zones.
But ours is enormous and could be larger than
any of them." One theory, he added, was that a
build-up in magnetic forces comes where the
plates upon which the continents are built, rub
together. "But that doesn't explain our anomaly..
Its not on an earthquake zone - the Arctic doesn't
have earthquakes. It's very stable...So far we
can't find an explanation for it. It's a total
mystery."

De Laurier also said that he knew his findings
were being used to "illustrate some pretty odd
ideas,"(as David Quintner reports in the Toronto
(Ontario) Star, 20 March 74. Credit: Mark Hall);
and Brad Steiger has written up De Laurier's
researches in ATLANTIS RISING (which I don't
think we have seen in the UK) in connexion with
theories of the existence of an 'elder race'
existing beneath the earth, and who regularly
interfere with surface life, causing disasters.
Indeed, I'm surprised at no mention of such juicy
'evidence' in Brinsley Le Poer Trench's recent
book on the same subject (see NEWS 7, Reviews)
THE SECRET OF THE AGES.

A SIGN OF THE TIMES.

Without so much as a ripple in the national press
or 'craft' magazines, an event has passed which
may or may not have some significance to someone's
cosmology. This nexus occurred on 15 July 74 -
when the Soviet Union launched another satellite
in the 'Cosmos' series -- its number was 666.
Further details in Novosti Bulletin 15179, 15 July.

PRECESSION OF THE DAMNED.

Anti-Gravity - along with perpetual motion and
squaring the circle has an immortal fascination -
not just for cranks, but for all of us, for the
dream of controlled levitation and the archetype
of a magical, ecstatic flight is a powerful force
in the soul of man. In the last 3-4 months, a
series of demonstrations culminating in a lecture
to the Royal Institution on the night of Friday
8 Nov 74, were given by Professor Eric Laithwaite
of a device hailed by the press as an Antigravity
Machine. He placed the device on a set of kitchen
scales, where it weighed 20lbs, switched it on
and the registered weight dropped to 15 pounds.
Many were impressed; vide Chapman Pincher, who
in the Daily Express next day (9 Nov. Cr: Michael
Start.) wrote of the successful event "which will
reverberate throughout the laboratories and Think
Tanks of the world with a welter of argument
over the coming weeks."

I did not hear of all this till much later. Prof.
Laithwaite had, in fact been on ITV's 'News at
Ten' on the night of the 7th Nov. I searched all
the papers (except the Express, Fort help me!)and
found nothing. I wrote to the Professor on behalf of the NEWS, and a few weeks later, back
came a circular reply (he had had hundreds of
inquiries and could not answer them all personally) saying that the full text of the RI talk
would appear, with maths, in a forthcoming Proceedings of the Royal Institution, and he was
giving the 'Christmas Lectures to Children' on TV
and would cover the principles of the device in a
talk on gyroscopes on the evening of 1 Jan 75.

The New Scientist of 14 Nov 74, had a piece on
the RI demonstration, headed "Eric Laithwaite
Defies Newton." by Robert Walgate, which, if you'
ll forgive the outburst, is classic of snide put-
down. He said that Laithwaite claimed to have
"violated gravity"; simply not true; and
Laithwaite being a sound, cautious and experienced man, as well as that rare thing, a scientist

with some imagination, has denied categorically any such statement or intimation; saying, in the circular, that "A precessing gyroscope does not produce a new force, but rather it produces absence of a force where one might be expected, and that this is thought to be due entirely to the presence of rate of change of acceleration." Nonetheless, the establishment, or at least the professional journals, seem to have closed ranks, as Pincher's 'reverberation' faded into a well-damped squeak. Maybe I haven't looked hard enough.

The children's lectures were conducted with a candour and excited spirit of open curiosity that should be a model to theoretical scientists every where. Laithwaite admitted that his models were still early experiments and that, quite frankly, he didn't understand what was going on in them. That was precisely what interested him as an engineer and scientist. "Newton is not wrong," he said. But these experiments showed that his laws were "restricted to events where there is no change in angular momentum - just as Ohms Law applies only to DC and not AC current."

Some reaction for and against will be found in the New Scientist for 28 Nov; 19 Dec, 74 and 9 Jan 75, in the letter section, and a further item by Walgate in the 9 Jan issue, to which I'll return. I just have to quote an outraged physicist from the University of Bristol (NS.9 Jan) who thought that the RI had 'damaged its reputation as a source of science education for young people. Victorian party tricks involving gyroscopes are certainly entertaining and make good television. But the phenomena must be explained. In this respect the lectures were very bad..." But as I understood it, Laithwaite's point was that with these devices something peculiar was happening that we had no complete explanation for, yet -- so asking him to explain, was to ask him to prejudge the results of experiment. Similarly others have said the gyro has been around for some time, and that cranks always trot it out -- again Laithwaite gave the impression that he had examined even the crank solutions, had discounted many, and was now following up a genuine effect.

For discussions of the technical aspects, please see the items referred to. In context, presentation and attendant questions, I was reminded (as was one of the NS correspondents) of John W Campbell's efforts on behalf of Norman L Dean's 'reactionless' thrust device in 1960. Campbell firstly identified the problem as an emotional one, putting the finger squarely on the main failing of orthodoxy in science. "It is essentially unimportant whether or not Dean's device works. It is important that it was not investigated... The absolute incompetance of our method of detecting important break-through discoveries is thoroughly demonstrated." (1). Let us hope that this sad indictment is not still true 14 years later, and that Professor Laithwaite will continue his voyage of discovery. Ariadne, writing in NS, 28 Nov 74, mentions yet another demonstration of what sounds like a similar device by Professor A di Bella of the University of Gen-

oa, at a symposium on Naval Hydrodynamics in Rome in 1968. It seems strange that the usual response is that if there was 'something in it' the scientists would have investigated it long ago - much the same as the response to a simple invention 'If it is so good, why hasn't anyone done it before?' Indeed they seem to be both sides of a rather negative attitude, and much depends on the expectancy of the question and answer process of inquiry. Laithwaite thinks that people have failed in their analysis of gyros in the past because they were looking for a new force, and he identifies the problem to be an absence of a force.

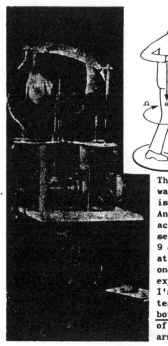

The photo of Laithwaite's device (left) is from NS 14 Nov 74. And the figure above accompanies Walgate's second piece in NS 9 Jan 75, in which he attempts to analyse one of Laithwaite's experiments, though I'm sure that in the test the boy held both hands on the end of the pole with his arms outstretched.

Walgate (and one of the correspondents) championed the inertia of the establishment by criticising Laithwaite for "changing fields too quickly and jumping to conclusions." And again Laithwaite pre-empted the critics by making a nice point that as an engineer he deals primarily with observations of (and with) phenomena that work. . It's as a scientist, not as an engineer, that he expresses his puzzlement over how. But I fear this is too subtle for some -- the fact is that many 'scientists' were annoyed that Laithwaite was planting beans in someone else's patch, and in doing so, exposed an area of embarassment. It seems that even something so apparently simple as motion still has secrets to offer us. (Many thanks to Frank Adey, who pointed out a very interesting paradox of relative mass/motion in Arthur Koestler's 'THE ROOTS OF COINCIDENCE', (p136 et seq.) in the Picador paper edition -- alas we have no room to use it -- but this also questions (indirectly) our concept of gravity.)

But we must admit that Laithwaite did give them some ammunition. OK, so some of his demonstrations did go wrong, but this was so obviously a result of him trying to pack so much in so short a time; jockeying for best camera angle etc etc. I think we can fairly ignore this, because he would not be where he is if he was that bungling a fool as to go 'live' with irrelevant or impractical experiments. No, the big ammunition comes with snide suggestions that he has lost his marbles, especially in his relation of how the device has come about.

It appears he was approached by Edwin Rickman, a man of no scientific training (according to the Daily Express) about 6 months before. Rickman had had a vivid recurring dream in which he had attended a meeting of a learned society and saw a scientist place a small box on a kitchen spring-balance. The pointer registered 15lbs. When the scientist pulled a switch the weight dropped to 10lb. He then opened the box to reveal two electrically driven gyroscopes, each on the end of a rotating arm. He was so impressed by this that he made a drawing, and patented it (No 11353/74 dated 14 March 74). He contacted Laithwaite, because of his reputation as the inventor of the linear electric motor, who with the aid of another amateur inventor, Alex Jones (one of the defenders in the NS correspondence) evolved the form shown at the RI. And like the Dean device, 14 years ago, talk is again of space-drives and silent propulsion of boats. "But it is the consequences for the whole of mechanical and Atomic theory that may be really shattering," said Laithwaite. (Daily Express, 8 Nov 74. Credit: Peter Weston.)

And it is not surprising to find Laithwaite making sure Rickman (and Jones) attended his RI lecture thus completing the circle in a startling example of precognition. Was it good manners only? Add a touch of engineer's attention to detail, & a sensible hedging of bets, methinks. I'm sure, too that this will become a classic in the history of revelatory discoveries, alongside Kekule's Benzene formula, and many others.

@-@   @-@   @-@   @-@   @-@   @-@   @-@

1) "Final Report on the Dean Device." Editorial by John W Campbell. ANALOG Science Fact & Fiction April 61. VolXVII No4.

Dean, an American housing mortgage official, patented his device in 1956 (No 2,886,976.) and also used a gyro-type arrangement of counter-rotating masses. According to Campbell, he had spent a few thousand dollars on various models including a true aerial version to which he beamed power for its motors. Photos, I am told appeared in the American but not the British edition of its first disclosure by Campbell, in ASTOUNDING Science Fact & Fiction, Oct 61. Vol XVI, No8. This also contains an account of Campbell's efforts to get the Office of Naval Research and NASA, both of whom had files on the device from Dean's abortive applications, to conduct practical appraisals of its capabilities.

Campbell never tired of pointing out that the first duty of science was to look into all possibilities, and that if that alone was not enough incentive, what about political advantage? He wrote: "The modern nuclear submarine is, in fact a fully competent space vehicle...lacking only the Dean Drive." (Or equivalent.)

Campbell never lost interest. In 1962, he published a paper, "The Fourth Law of Motion" by Dr William O Davis, in ANALOG,(Aug 62. Vol XVIII No8) which,though a little out of place in the science-fiction magazine, nevertheless gave opportunity to discuss the theoretical Dean effect of a reactionless thrust. It was also an interesting analysis of gyroscopic motion generally.

I also remember a further follow-up, which I can find at the moment, must have been 1963/4, that Westinghouse had bought up, or were otherwise investigating the Dean Device in a secret project. And that Dean came to England and Germany to take out patents there, but was persuaded against it and whisked back to the States. Something like that - perhaps someone can put me right on that? But the whole story was not, is not, yet known - and so relevant in these energy-crisis days.

━━━━━━━━━━━━━━━━━━━━━━━━━━━━━━━━━━

WHIRLWINDS..........Cont:

Mr Morris said: "To our utter amazement, the mass of hay was lifted gradually some two or three hundred feet high, while it was being quickly carried in a straight line and increasing only slightly in height for about a couple of miles, after which it slowly lost height in the next half-mile or so, and finally came to rest on a pasture field at a point slightly higher than the one from which it started its journey. Our attention was riveted to the spectacle; it was only after it was all over that we began to realise our good fortune in not being wrapped up and carried away wholesale, seeing we were so near to the incident at the time." The hay took 15 to 20 minutes to travel and passed over the Bethel and Bwlchyffridd areas of Aberhafesp before landing in the field. The Morris brothers had some difficulty in convincing their neighbour of the stack's curious transporting - since he firmly believed the incident was a prank by local youths.

This latter incident conforms more nearly to the textbook whirlwind - but we underline the detail that interests us as verging on the heretical. The above stories were from issues of the paper mentioned, dated 7th, 14th and 28th July 1974. Credit, as stated, to: Janet Bord.

But what of the earlier incidents? We remember a line from Chapter Four of LO!, where Fort has been discussing the 'snatchings' of clothes-lines into windless skies -- "A suggestion that is not so sensible is that...somebody had learned the secrets of teleportation, and to avoid attracting much attention in any one place was experimenting in places far apart."

REVIEWS

A REVISED COSMOLOGY by Merrill B Taylor. Available from the author at: 1309 Broadway, Little Rock, Arkansas 72202, USA. $3.00. An unexpected and exceedingly curious paper that sets out to rexamine the very fundamental issues of the modern physical cosmologies. Indeed, by stepping back to observe the creation of matter, instead of essentially destruction-derived, Taylor builds interestingly on some of the theories that were pushed aside in the Einstein breakthrough. Einstein himself was constantly reworking his General Theory to compensate for the postulated (and not proved) Riemann Space, in an attempt to answer EA Milne's two questions: "What is it that is curved? And how is it curved?" Instead Taylor postulates Plenum Space to replace Riemann curved space, and finds a whole new world of interesting effects and understandable causes. Plenum Space, as I understand it, is evolved when all the radiating bodies in the universe, all moving relatively to one another, thus fill the whole of space with radiation travelling in all possible directions. And from the constant, and universally consistant events where fractionated radiations meet head on, fundamental particles are brought into being. This process and its effects lead to startlingly different conceptions of gravitation; wave mechanics; faster-than-light theory; the Michaelson-Morley experiment; Einstein's General Theory; strange particles; and Taylor's insistance that compared to today's destruction-orientated physics, his theory should be relatively easier and cheaper to prove and develop ; and, he says, will have a more fundamentally radical effect in terms of spin-off effects, eg a true space-drive. Now this emergence of new ideas on space-drives at this time is interesting (see 'Scientific Curiosities'and our discussion on Laithwaite's and Dean's reactionless thrust devices.) Your editor, who knows nothing about physics, really felt he had learnt something after reading Taylor's paper. I hope it will stimulate further analyses of the idea of Plenum Space, and though I cannot assess its value, I do think it deserves attention, in the interests of science. A point of interest also, is that the author's initial speculation were brought about by his observance of an almost right-angle turn by a UFO, which caused him to work back from the type of forces which would allow such non-G manoeuvers.

EXTRATERRESTRIAL INTERVENTION : THE EVIDENCE. by Jacques Bergier & the Editors of INFO. Henry Regnery Co, Chicago; $7.95; pp164; ISBN:0.8092.-8369.7. First published in France only as LE LIVRE DE L'INEXPLICABLE and recently translated, it suffers from the impression that it was hastily and/or loosely put together. Nevertheless, the book contains its main interest in the many articles drawn from the early issues of the International Fortean Organisation Journal by Ron and Paul Willis, Andrew E Rothovius, Vincent Gaddis, Loren Coleman & Mark Hall, Ivan Sanderson, and a few others. The bulk of this material will be familiar to those who have read the original INFO issues, but to those who haven't, well! after reading this lot you'll wonder why you ever bothered with von Daniken when you could get the real stuff. Ron Willis's "The Burning People"(spontaneous combustion of humans), and "The Acambaro Figurines" (30,000 clay minatures, 3,600 years old, from Mexico); Paul Willis's "The Devil's Hoofmarks" (the infamous Devon event); AT Horak's "The Mysterious Moonshaft" (just that, inside a mountain in Czechoslovakia); and others on anomalous artifacts, UFOs in the New World, "Are there still Dinosaurs?", and Saquatch, etc are all classics of their type, and will no doubt cause a stir when they pass into common record. Bergier, apart from collecting this lot together with a 'slight' preface to each has very little in the book: a summary of the Borley Rectory hauntings; a fall of stones on the Hospital at Arcachon, and an odd electrical/meteoric (?) phenomenon in Rebozer, USSR, both previously unknown to me; and a piece on the poltergeist-girl, Anne-Marie Schneider of Rosenheim, Germany (that used to dominate the pages of the Paralab Journal in 1970.) - which is a small amount of Bergier for your money if you've read the rest. Despite this, I think it will become a useful reference edition, and in the general scarcity of 'true' Fortean books, the most important addition to the available literature in 1974. More than that, it gives me great personal pleasure to see items from the INFO Journal in general print. It should do the business of Fortean studies generally some good.

QUICKSILVER HERITAGE by Paul Screeton. Thorsons Publishers Ltd, Northants; £4.50; pp304; extensive index and bibliography; ISBN:0.7225.0282.6.

"Between the covers of this book is a guide-book, which leads the reader from stylish stone circles, to gaunt standing stones, to crumbling tumuli, to towering pines, by way of lines straight and true. Here too is a manual on the workings of a system of spiritual physics...This is not a book written to entertain or educate. Those who seek within these pages for great truths will be disappointed; those who wish to be titillated by sensationalism will be displeased; those who think that there may be easy answers to the puzzles of prehistory will be disheartened; but those who wish to learn by their own efforts will find guidance."

Thus, Paul Screeton justly sums up his own approach of cramming the book with all kinds of hints, synopses and signposts. There are four main sections: the first deals with the physical attributes of Leys, techniques of Ley hunting, and in passing a history of the interest in the 'mercurial' lines. Secondly we are given a summary of what is known about the megalithic culture from the Ley tradition, and since most of this is at variance with the opinions of the 'Jealous Professors', there are adequate opportunities for hearty swipes at Dr Glyn Daniel and the other Aunt Sallys of archaeology. Thirdly, we are shown the relationships between Leys, Holy sites, etc, and Astronomy, Alchemy and terrestrial Zodiacs, giving many references to sites for the first time outside the pages of THE LEY HUNTER, which Paul edits. Fourthly, the last half of the book ranges over the many esoteric subjects that comprise Ley studies today: Giants, Fairies and Elementals that seem closely bound in tradition and manifestation to the elements of Leys; The Dragon Power and lore; Spiritual physics and metaphysics; and Fortean correlations with gravity anomalies, St Elmo's Fire, disappearances, and cursed stones. The whole book is rounded off with a pretty complete bibliography and a listing of major articles from TLH and elsewhere.

I must mention the striking cover, which looked like a Turner rendition of a Needfire silhouetting a hill, but is in fact a photograph. The whole book is well produced, as it should be for the price. My only quibble - a small one - is that many of the cameos of different aspects of our 'Quicksilver Heritage' stop just as they were getting very interesting indeed. On the one hand this indicates that Ley studies are still in their early days, their great enigmas still a challenge -- and on the other, that the book as a whole does titillate and guide the reader's curiosity rather than satisfy it, and as a Fortean I bow to that acomplishment. 'QH' will undoubtedly become the book to which newcomers to Leys will direct, and thus fills a gap in the literature be that has been felt for some time.

And in paperback:

THE OLD STRAIGHT TRACK by Alfred Watkins. Abacus; £1.25; 256pp; 131 illos & photos; ISBN: 0.349. 13704.8. The book that started the modern interest in Leys & megalithic artifacts. This edition has a splendid photo of a classic 'tump' on the cover, which I don't recall seeing elsewhere.

LETTERS

From: Colin Bord.
'Hollow Earth' Photos, NEWS 7/22,23.

I see in your review of Brinsley Le Poer Trench's recent book SECRET OF THE AGES that you have been more than a little puzzled over the photographs showing the alleged hole at the North Pole. I haven't seen the book yet, but I heard the author talking about it on the radio, and as he said that he had acquired the pictures from an American publisher, and as you mention that they are photographs obtained by the ESSA 7 satellite, they are undoubtedly the same pictures as Mr Ray Palmer of Amherst, Wisconsin, published in his 'Flying Saucers' magazine in June 1970. ((Indeed they are the same ones - Ed.)) This publication was one of the less laudable American ventures of the 1960s (I believe it has since folded,) using unreliable and sensational material, and given to making sensational claims without any substance. The magazine also carried advertising for various books published by Ray Palmer, and often these were of a sensationalist and unsubstantiated nature.

In the June 1970 issue of 'Flying Saucers', the cover carried a picture of the circular Earth with wispy clouds and a large black area in the centre; beneath this photograph is 'First Photos of the Hole at the Pole', 'Satellites ESSA 3 and ESSA 7 Penetrate Cloud Cover', 'Mariners Also Photograph Martian Polar Opening'. (Needless to say, no evidence is given for this last claim; it is simply made again briefly in the editorial.) Although the cover blurb says the satellites 'Penetrate Cloud Cover', the editorial states that there was "a total lack of cloud cover over the North Pole". In a later issue of the magazine when Palmer refuted criticisms of his statements, he wrote that infra-red was used to photograph through the cloud (although there are still plenty of other clouds to be seen in the photo.) In the June 1970 issue editorial he states that the photographs are "official, unretouched photos". Yet in his answer to a reader's letter in September 1970 he writes: "The dark portion of the first photograph of the North Pole (and now I speak as an editor, publisher, printer, photographer, etc) is so 'obviously' retouched it is painful." This sloppy thinking and casual use of words seems to be typical of Palmer. Inside the magazine are three more pictures, two of the South Pole showing it covered in white cloud or ice, and another of the North Pole with a black centre 'hole' that has a soft diffused edge. All these pictures were captioned as being taken in either January 1967 or November 1968.

Three months later, in September 1970, he published about six pages of reader's letters, which now gave the following explanations for the black area:-

1) The pictures as printed were originally composed of a mosaic of photographs of small sect-

ions of the Earth's surface matched together to form an overall view - a common technique in aerial and satellite photography. One reason why this is necessary is because the whole of the planet is not illuminated by the sun at any one time.

2) As the North Pole is tilted away from the Sun during the winter months, it gets very few hours of sunlight during a 24 hour period of revolution. On midwinter's day the sun does not rise above the horizon at all; conversely on midsummer's night it does not set. In Britain we experience this same effect to a lesser extent, hence our long winter nights and short summer nights. The ESSA 7 photographs were taken during November, and so the farthest northern latitudes were too poorly lit to be of use photographically.

3) A grid of longitude and latitude with numerals every 20°, and also the outlines of the continental land masses, has been superimposed on the photographs before being released for publication. These marks are just discernable on the magazine cover reproduction, so it is easy to work out where the edge of the 'hole' comes. It is between 60° and 70° North. If we consult an atlas it shows that a great deal of known land such as Iceland, northern Scandinavia, Greenland, Alaska, etc, must be within the 'hole', which must be somewhere in the region of 3000 miles across. ((The Arctic Circle, that imaginary boundary of the North polar region seems to coincide with the fringe of the dark area at $66^{\circ}32'$ North - Ed.))

Although Palmer used a great deal of space, he made no satisfactory argument against these straightforward points, which sound decidedly more convincing than his ramblings on the subject.

" — " — " — " — " — " — " — " — " — "

From: Roger Randle.
Ghost - Leys - and Phantom Cottage.

Many thanks for NEWS 7 - it gets better with each issue. I heard an interesting little snippet on Radio Solent which may be of interest, concerning Poole (Dorset) Guildhall/Museum. Apparently the spectre of one Henry Jubber makes a fairly regular appearance on a narrow staircase leading to the top floor of the Guildhall, between 0930 and 1000 am. Several of the staff have seen him and report that his presence is accompanied by the usual cold current of air when he passes. Unlike many ghost stories, however, Henry Jubber's name and role are not lost. He was an officer of the council responsible for the operation (and accounts) of Poole Quay during the early 19th century. He was suspected of being party to a revenue fraud just prior to the annual council meeting held to audit the accounts of each department, and was discovered hanging in one of the cells on the top floor (which was used as a 'lock-up' at that time, for the police court held on a lower floor). I tell you this because I haven't seen it recorded elsewhere in any of the standard gazeteers.

I enjoyed Janet Bord's piece even if she did bring home to me that I was (at one stage) guilty of finding literally a spider's web of leys on one 1"OS sheet! However, I cannot agree with her concerning accuracy. Despite what they tell you, 1:50,000 OS maps are notoriously inaccurate - and considering that 1mm is equivalent to 50 metres on the ground, this is hardly surprising. What frequently appear to be dead alignments on the 1:50,000 sheet show a proclivity to definite deviations on larger scale sheets. Ideally, high contrast aerial photographs taken with a lens of high resolution should be the answer, but how many of us have access to such equipment? Anyway, I mustn't quibble over small details.

The mystery of the disappearing cottage on Dartmoor (mentioned in Janet Bord's article) put me in mind of a similar incident reported in "THE RIVER DART" by Ruth Manning Saunders (Westway Books, London, 1951) - a goldmine of Dartmoor lore, legend and fact of this type. I quote: "One day on the moors round Hayford to the 'west of Buckfastleigh, three girls and their father - all strangers to the neighbourhood - went out on a shooting expedition. As so often happens in this haunted region, the party got separated, the girls could not find their father, and making for home in the darkness they lost their way. On and on they walked not knowing where they were going, until to their joy they saw a light ahead, hurried towards it, and found a roadside cottage. Ruddy firelight danced out from an uncurtained window, warming the night with a friendly glow. The three girls looked through the window and saw an old man and woman sitting crouched over the fire. "We never moved from where we stood," declared the girls afterward. But, on a sudden, lo, the fire, the old man and woman, and the entire cottage vanished; and night, like a black bag, fell over the place."

Despite the overdramatisation, the story is true - indeed, the villagers had seen the cottage before - folk memory had preserved some hazy rememberance of a dwelling on the site, long disappeared. Crossing (probably the greatest and most reliable of the Dartmoor antiquarians) had a similar experience in the region of Ugborough Moor, although he put it down to the mist playing tricks with his mind. Dartmoor, of course, is full of such stories, ranging from borderline experiences of the Wish Hounds, or the buccas (the Dartmoor version of the goblin miners legends, ie as in the legend of Chaw Gully) to the rather more tangible and factual experiences of the Hairy Hands, or Devil's Footprints type. One concerning the 'Strange Fire in Wistmans Wood' in 1886 is enclosed. ((Because of lack of space we shall keep this back till we next run our 'Fires' section. Roger also sent us the damndest item we've come across in a long time, which should appear next issue along with some fireballs and odd lights - Ed.)).

did you see.....?

'Unsolved Mysteries of the Great Pyramid' by Ronald Schiller. READER'S DIGEST, Dec 74, pp140-144.

'Growing Cult of the Pyramid' by John Cornwall. OBSERVER MAGAZINE, 15 Dec 74. pp46,47,49,50,52, 54,56, 57,59, 61. Good illos, and an interesting note on the Californian company that markets the razor-blade sharpeners, etc.

'The Ice-Age Cometh' by Nigel Calder. RADIO TIMES, 16/22 Nov 74. pp74 on.

'Never try to coax a ghost' by Innes Gray. TV TIMES, 21 Dec/3 Jan 74/75. For what its worth, ghostly relations from Tommy Steele, and Telly Savalas.

'Deadliest 'Big Foot' Monster of Them All' by Walter Hardiston. MALE magazine, Jan 75, pp14, 15, 74, 75, 76. BF events in Australia.

'Long Delayed Signals may echo from Moon's ghost' by Ian Ridpath. NEW SCIENTIST, 3 Oct 74, p9.

'Apeman on the Loose! Tracking California's Bigfoot' by Paul Ciotti, COAST magazine, Oct 74.

'A case of Stigmata' by LF Early & JE Lifschutz. ARCHIVES OF GENERAL PSYCHIATRY, Feb 74, Vol 30, pp197-200. We shall be carrying a note on this in a future issue.

'The Doctor Fox Lecture: A Paradigm of Educational Seduction' by DH Naftalin, JE Ware jr and FA Donnelly. JOURNAL OF MEDICAL EDUCATION, July 73, Vol 48, pp630-635. You may remember this from NEWS 5 p7.

'Fire-walking Controversy Blazes' MINEAPOLIS TRIBUNE, 6 Oct 74, p13F.

'Universe may be 10 Billion Years Old' by Harry S Pease. MILWAUKEE JOURNAL, 27 Sept 74, p21.

'The Cottingley Fairies' by Nick Witchell. MAYFAIR magazine, Dec 74, Vol 9 No 12, pp40-42,51, 74. Turned out to be little more than a re-write of Edward Gardner's 1945 book published by the Theosophical Society.

'Geller' notes galore in each issue of NEW SCIENTIST between 7 Nov and 12 Dec 74. (Yawn.)

'The Way Home is Blowing in the Wind.' by Jeremy Cherfas. NEW SCIENTIST 28 Nov 74. On bird migration.

'Aerosol Sprays & The Ozone Shield' by Prof. S Rowland...how our misuse of 'Freon' is destroying our protective ozone layer in upper atmosphere. 'The End of The English Landscape.' by Jon Tinker. How and why our land will never be the same again NEW SCIENTIST, 5 Dec 74.

'Mental Maps for Navigation' by Dr K Oatley... human direction finding this time.... 'Psi Story.' by Dr Robert Walgate...on the implications of the first new stable particle discovered in ten years. NEW SCIENTIST, 19 Dec 74.

'Commonsense & Sir William Crookes.' by Eric Deeson...on the relationship between the development of the Radiometer, and his occult investigations. NEW SCIENTIST, 26 Dec 74.

'Lysenko - Beyond the Horizon.' Following the BBC 2 screening of the TV 'Horizon' documentary on the Lysenko affair, further notes on the effects on Russian science since Lysenko was removed from office 10 years ago. NEW SCIENTIST, 9 Jan 75.

'Mystery Gamma Bursts.' SPACEFLIGHT, Jan 75, p24.

'Eyewitness Testimony.' by Robert Buckhout. SCIENTIFIC AMERICAN, Dec 74; Vol 231

'Eyewitness Testimony.' by Robert Buckhout. 'The Search for Black Holes.' by Kip S Thorne. SCIENTIFIC AMERICAN, Dec 74; Vol 231 No 6.

OTHER SCENES: a special double issue on British Folklore, put out by John Wilcock. $1.00, from Dawes Press, 81a Dawes Road, London SW6.

THE LEY HUNTER 60/61, Oct/Nov 74. Contains: 'Two Somerset Sites.'; 'Bristol Cross Sites.'; 'Alignment of Ancient Sites in the Region of the Essex -Suffolk Border.'; 'A Suggestion as to the Possible Origin of Churches that are Dedicated to St Michael and St Andrew.'; 'Power Centres - Whence did they Originate?'; and 'Divining - A Positive Way of Ley Hunting.' TLH is edited by Paul Screeton, 5 Egton Drive, Seaton Carew, Hartlepool, Cleveland TS25 2AT. UK:£150 // USA:$6.00.

LANTERN 8, Winter 74/75. Contains: 'The Haunting of Glasshouse Row' (an astonishing tale of poltergeistery in Great Yarmouth in 1797.); Notes on local curiosities; 'More Mysterious Stones' (on Ley mark-stones in Norfolk.); 'Of Fairy Folk and Will O' The Wisp.'(on some associated Norfolk legends and traditions.); and a UFO report, and news round-up. Published by the Borderline Science Investigation Group (BSIG), edited by I Bunn, 3 Dunwich Way, Oulton Broad, Lowestoft, Suffolk. 65p/year, or single issues at 16p.

++

Compilation Credits: Mark Hall; Phil Ledger, Fran Steve Moore, Nigel Watson.

ADS

a miscellany of Fortean curiosites

FIREBALLS &c .. 10
GHOST LIGHTS .. 14

MYSTERY COASTAL FLARES .. 9

also ---- some antiquities 3 ----
vanishings of animals, fish, and people 5 ----
Stuart Greenwood's pyramid slope hypothesis 12 ----
exotic animals on the loose 15 ----
mystery animals 19

bi-monthly notes
on Fortean
phenomena

april
whole no: 9
volume: 2. 1975

THE NEWS is a non-profitmaking bi-monthly miscellany of Fortean news, notes
and references; and is affiliated to the International Fortean Organisation (INFO)
in continuing the work of **Charles Fort** (1874 — 1932). THE NEWS is edited by
Robert JM Rickard : Post Office Stores, Aldermaston, Berkshire, England.

SUBSCRIPTIONS :   1 year (6 issues) :   UK : £2.10.   USA : $6.00. All
other countries use dollar equivalent. Single issues : 35p / $1.00. Back issues
(if available) : 40p / $1.15. Current INDEX free to subscribers, otherwise 20p/
60¢ each. Cheques, POs, IMOs etc. make payable to **RJM Rickard, not** THE
NEWS. All **overseas subscribers** should <u>add 10%</u> to the total if paying by cheque,
to cover the banking exchange commission and charges.

CONTRIBUTIONS & RIGHTS :   All articles in **THE NEWS** are copyright of the
authors — and the views expressed are not necessarily those of **THE NEWS**, or **INFO**.
Contributions of articles, notes and artwork on related subjects are always welcome and
duly credited.   —   If you encounter any reference or data you think will be of interest,
please make a note of the **source** and **date** (adding your **name,** for the crediting). Please
don't assume our omniscience — there are very few duplications. Remember national
daily newspapers have slightly different regional editions —— and we are especially glad
to see notes from professional sources, local papers, and rare or OP books. All the notes
herein may be quoted freely, though we hope for a credit in return. **All category head
art in this issue by Hunt Emerson.**

RONALD J WILLIS.

Ron Willis, co-founder and Director of INFO, died
on 12th March 75, after a long illness. He is
survived by a wife and daughter, INFO, and brother Paul, editor of the INFO Journal.

—   —   —

'A certain man was believed to have died, and
was being prepared for burial, when he revived.
He sat up, but he was so shocked at the scene
surrounding him that he fainted. He was put in a
coffin, and the funeral party set off for the
cemetery. Just as they arrived at the grave, he
regained consciousness, lifted the coffin lid
and cried for help. "It is not possible that he
has revived," said the mourners, "because he has
been certified dead by competant experts." "But
I am alive!" shouted the man. He appealed to a
well-known and impartial scientist and juris-
prudent who was present. "Just a moment," said
the expert. He then turned to the mourners, cou-
nting them. "Now, we have heard what the alleged
deceased has had to say. You fifty witnesses tell
me what you regard as the truth." "He is dead,"
said the witnesses. "Bury him!" said the expert.
And so he was buried.'
A teaching sermon of the Chishti Order of Sufis.
<u>'The way of the Sufi'</u> by Idries Shah.

—   —   —

I had had only sporadic correspondence with Ron,
and since I have never met him, there is something to look forward to. Goodbye Ron - rest
assured we shall be continuing <u>your</u> work too.

CHANGE OF EDITORIAL ADDRESS.

You may have noticed a new address on the mast-
head above. We anticipate putting out at least
one more issue from the present Birmingham address, and so the new one should become effective
from about July onwards. Adequate forwarding will
be arranged to cover the possible eventualities.

PRICE STATUS.

Paper costs have stabilized to a degree, but will
go up at the end of the year. Postage is now
nearly double due to the recent increase, and
labour costs continue to bugger us about at the
printers &c. We may have to increase THE NEWS
cost at year-end -- we say, may, because our
reluctance to do so is based on the thought that
that way lies pricing ourselves out of existance.
The only practical solution, therefore, rests in
some part with you, dear Readers, by taking every
opportunity you can to bring in new readers. Also
if our USA-readers know of any shops there as
potential NEWS-stockists (we can supply trade
terms) then please write and let us know. It all
helps to garuantee our existance.

WHAT YOU ALWAYS WANTED TO KNOW ABOUT THE STAFFS/ LEICESTERSHIRE BORDER...

Paul Devereaux and Andy York are in the middle of
a gigantic project of collating recent and historical Fortean phenomena and their associated
traditions for a specific geographic region -

in this case the fault area near the Charnwood Forest, Leics. We have been receiving progress reports on this fascinating venture and can unreservedly say that it will ultimately prove to be a very valuable key reference source. We are delighted to report that Paul and Andy will be presenting the more Fortean aspects in THE NEWS, later this year. One curious aspect is that during their investigations, tremors began in the area which focussed their attention on the fault-line (previously of low relevance). We didn't even know of these tremors till Paul told us, because of minimal press coverage. This and the lack of 'expert' attention and comment has so worried the locals that not only have they formed a committee to investigate ((Cr: K Cotton)),

but have persuaded Jack Ashley MP to ask questions in the Commons. Paul added "The 'Sentinel' of Jan 30th reported that Eric Varley, Minister for Energy, had "called for a full report", and there, need I say it, the story comes to a sudden shuddering and complete STOP." For our part, we contacted the professors of the Geology Depts. of the two Universities in the area (sorry, I mean, the Birmingham area), only to find that they were completely ignorant of any tremors in the Stoke, Newcastle-under-Lyme and Leicester regions ((yawn!)). In an attempt at completeness Paul and Andy ask that if any NEWSreaders have any info or cuttings on anything odd in that region, new or old, then please send it to Paul Devereaux at: 64 Cedar Court, Pages Hill, London N10.

HEAVY READING.

An ancient Greek lead scroll has been found on an island at the mouth of the Dnieper river. Now restored and in the Hermitage Museum, Leningrad, it is only the sixth that has ever been found. It is said to be the oldest (2,500yrs), longest and best preserved. ((Bragging, again!)) Novosti Bulletin, 15718, 6 Jan 75.

SHIPWRECKED DOWN A MINE.

Frank Adey sent us a letter containing the following curiosity, which, "falls under the general heading of 'incongruous objects found embedded in rock'. It's the least convincing anecdote of its kind I've ever come across, but it led me to an interesting query. The item comes from The Natural History of Stafford-shire, by Robert Plot, first published in 1686, (Ch II, para 71): '...But the most prodigious story that we have of this kind, is that of Baptista Fulgosus, Ludovicus Moscardus, and Theodorus Moretus, who tell us that, at the village of Bern in Switzerland, An.1460, in a mine 50 fathoms deep, there was dug up a whole ship, with its anchors and broken masts, in which were the carcases of 40 mariners, together with their merchandise: which Fulgosus more particularly tells us, as a thing done in his own time, and seen by many grave and sober men, from whom he received a personal account of it.' Which leads me to ask - why is

it that in all of these kinds of stories, the objects found are contemporary with the finders? Compare the 15th century ship with the nuts and bolts which are allegedly found today (and ascribed to extraterrestrial litterbugs visiting Earth in prehistoric times)." Good question - but I for one would like to know a lot more about this 15th century find. It may have been a ship, or that may have been the nearest applicable concept that occurred to the finders. I mean... what else could have 40 people aboard. Who said UFOs?..Oh hallo! Erich...and goodbye Erich...the answer is NO! Erich...this one is ours. So, any of you diligent NEWSreaders who can scoop the poop on this mystery, please let us know before HE gets hold of it.

ANOTHER REWRITE FOR THE HISTORY BOOKS.

Just how much longer can orthodoxy in archeology resist the growing pressures on in it to change? Good Lord, have they learned nothing from their own views that dinosaurs are extinct because of their refusal to keep up with the times? The evidences are heaping up, that the past was more complex and mysterious than is cozily dreamt of in their philosophy. Professorial opinions these days are as stiff as fossils, pickled in the strata of their establishments. See Sunday Times Magazine, 6 April 75, for a paradox that was too big to ignore - that the conventional history of

early Man in Australia has been completely upset by the discovery of two skeletons; one places
Homo sapiens (modern man) as far back as 30,000
years ago, and the other brings Homo erectus
(Java man, known locally as 'The coffee drinker')
up to as recent as only 9,000 years ago. (Credit:
Steve Moore.)

And now another blow to the academic dream-world
-- with word that a British-backed expedition to
Israel made discoveries near the port of Eilat,
that mean "the entire pre-history of metal technology will have to be re-written." Drs Ronald
Tylecote (Newcastle U) and Beno Rothenburg (London U's Institute of Archeology, & Tel Aviv U)
have been exploring copper mines of great size
and sophistication, but which date from 1400 BC,
making them at least 1000yrs older than any previously known examples of systematic underground
mining. It seems they were operated by Egyptians
using stone hammers and bronze chisels and "displayed remarkable engineering techniques."

"They comprise a network
of 200 shafts and galler-
ies penetrating the white
sandstone for 100s of yds
in all directions and on
several levels. Each shaft
has its own air-channel,
roughly the diameter of a
thumb, which allowed the
miners to breathe freely
several hundred feet be-
neath the surface, and to
work by oil lamps. The
different levels are con-
nected by vertical shafts up to 50ft deep, with
foot and hand holds cut into them. Where shafts
have been sunk to deeper levels, lateral shafts
have been joined up 'blind' (presumably for ventilation) with very few errors."

It seems the expedition also found remains of the
earliest complete smelting plant ever discovered.
The site was first in use around 4000 BC when
the copper-smelter was merely a hole in the gro-
und heated by bellows. "By 1400 BC the miners
had developed clay-lined smelters to produce
small ingots. And analysis of the slag...has
shown that by 1200 BC the smelting method was
every bit as efficient as present-day techniques.
It also seems to have been at Timna that the use
of iron oxide to help seperate out the copper
from the ore was first tried." They also found an
iron ore mine in the valley and suspect that this
is how the Bronze Age gave way to the Iron Age.
Sunday Times, 8 Dec 74. (Credit: Steve Moore.)

UNDER THEIR NOSES ALL THE TIME.

The Director of Greece's National Archeological
Museum, Nicholas Yacouris startled the world by
announcing that "wonderous..archeological pieces
of art..almost priceless," have been found - 15th
century BC stone seals; jewellery; weapons; much
very valuable Mycenean stuff like a compass and
ivory model of a war galleon, and a curious piece
of armour plating for a warrior's heel (as per
Achilles could have done with). And where should
they find this fabulous hoard? - that's right,
in their basement, lying in "layers" of forgotten
crates, unopened since the digs in the 19th C.
Many of the bits and pieces they found were the
missing parts of items already on open exhibition
-- eg, Yacouris mentions a 5th C BC engraved
stone head of a sea-monster that was found to fit
a gap below the goddess Amphitrite on the Parth-
enon's upper western pediment. We can't say we
are really all that surprised at this revelation
of a new archeology -- it stands to reason that
those who live by robbing tombs, should feel now
and then a tugging towards cannibalism. Houston
(Texas) Chronicle, 27 June 74. Credit: Mark Hall.

SPECTRUM : A new bi-monthly occult magazine featuring UFOs, Magic, witchcraft, ESP & psychic
matters, book reviews, readers letters, etc. Illustrated. Send 35p for latest issue, or only
£2.00 for next 6 issues to: Bywood Publications,
62 High Street, Croydon CR9 2UT, Surrey.

THE NEWS is available from the following specialist bookshops, who also keep a wide range of
titles on associated subjects:

TEMPS FUTURS:
3 Rue Perronet, 75007 Paris, France.

COMPENDIUM BOOKS:
240 Camden High St, London NW1.

DARK THEY WERE AND GOLDEN EYED:
10 Berwick St, London W1V 3RG.

It is with some sadness we note the closing of
JAPETUS in Birmingham, which leaves us in even
more of a cultural wilderness than before.
Similarly, NEW DIMENSIONS in Arlington, USA, has
closed - but its service will be continued to
a limited degree by INFO: Box 367, Arlington,
Va 22210, USA.   Incidentally, you'd be doing
us, and yourselves in the long run, a favour if
you could convince your local, or any, bookshop
to take THE NEWS. Trade terms are available.

Cont on page 14.

disappearances

DOG — Do you remember Fort's passage: "Early in the morning of July 26th (1908) a big black dog sauntered past them ((detectives)). 'Good Morning!' said the dog. Re disappeared in a thin, greenish vapor." (Wild Talents, Ch 5.) That incident seems to be pretty unique in the annals of the odd - which was why Fort rejected using it further. We have a tale of a dog that vanished - but one that could not, or was not so polite as to speak. It is a letter to the Eastern Daily Press, 7 Dec 73 :

"I was staying in Norfolk a few days ago when my great friend and companion, a golden retriever, disappeared in what I consider to be a mystifying way. I took the dog out for a walk about midnight on a quiet lane in Cringleford. After a while, a friend and I turned back towards his home, I called the dog, which was nosing around ina field, and as usual he came tearing after us. Then, within half a minute, while we were chatting, the dog simply vanished. He may have chased a rabbit, got onto the scent of a bitch in heat, or even lost his way back to my friend's house. I don't know. Perhaps he was hit by a passing car...perhaps he was stolen and sold to vivisectionists. There are hundreds of possible explanations but I feel disinclined to believe any one of them. Surely a dog cannot vanish without a trace? When we read of Mr Uri Geller and his seemingly paranormal powers, or hear of a wake of misfortune following the arrival of a newcomet ((written at the time of the great expectations from Kohoutek)), it makes me wonder if an enormous hand might have grabbed him and whisked him away into outer space.
      David GL Lacon.
          4 Jopling Way, Hauxton, Cambs."
That suggestion seems no more outrageous than any other to us - especially when there seems to be no evidence towards any normal whisking away.
Credit: RA Hill.

TROUT — We have recorded stories of the disappearance and appearance of fish before, but here is one of a round trip - if that is what it is. Mr CW Foster rears trout in a brick pit at the Marina, Barrow Haven, near Barton-on-Humber, Lincs. There were 8000 fish, all between 10 and 12 inches long, averaging 1lb each — total value £4000. When he came to feed them (which he did

daily) on the afternoon of 1 May 74, they were gone. Police were called, and after much bafflement, announced their theory that "several people" must have been involved, with large nets, between 1pm and 4pm that very day. They don't explain how this could have been done without leaving obvious signs (like water and fish-scales all over the place), or without being seen or heard. And that would be that, if there were not a note in the next day's papers, to the effect that detectives returning to the scene of the 'crime' casually threw some food into the pit, and Lo! the trout were back; all 8000 of them "miraculously reappeared." This was headlined in the paper as "Detectives Trace Trout". Hah! Red faces all round. It is not clear if it was actually established that there were no fish at all in the pit, though it would have been commonsense to have done so, the commonsense of others can rarely be relied upon. The only thing Foster could say was that the fish must have been sleeping when he threw the food in, or ill - both factors that would have normally occurred to anyone who breeds fish. But for them to be sleeping at their routine feeding would itself have been unusual, and "they appear to be alive and well enough now." One would also expect a fish-breeder to tell the difference between a pit-full of $5\frac{1}{2}$ tons of trout from an empty one. In these cases there seems to be a definite reaction to the facts, a deliberate avoiding of the suggestion that fish can vanish (or are vanished) - it's not as though it's never happened before, after all. Story from the Scunthorpe Evening Telegraph, 2 & 3 May 74.
Credit: Nigel Watson.

COWS, SHEEP, CHICKENS & DUCKS — Manchester Evening News, 19 April 74: that 5 crossbred heiffers and 6 sheep were missing from 2 farms in the Rye area early that morning. Rustlers were suspected. (Cr: Peter Pogerson). -- Daily Express, 12 Nov 73: that TV cook Fanny Craddock has lost 11 chickens over the past few days from her Grove Mill Lane home, in Watford, Herts. Police are disinclined to blame a fox since the area was closed off but unlocked. They went a few at a time, nor was any noise heard - but why should a poacher expose himself to repeated risk as the flock dwindled, and leave one dead one? -- Sunday Mirror, 4 Aug 74: that police report that no-one heard the slightest thing when 50 ducklings vanished from a farm at Boulge, near Ipswich. (Cr: Steve Moore.)

FROGS — Last ish we told of the problems caused by "thousands" of frogs returning to spawn in a pond in Hertfordshire (NEWS 8/16-17). John Hillaby ("Bad Times have Fallen on Frogdom" NEW SCIENTIST, 13 Feb 74, p598) bewails the sad de-cline in the UK population of our little leaping friends, by 99% in some areas. Pesticides do not seem to be responsible this time; Hillaby prefers to blame changes in landscape drainage, and believes the southwest and northern parts of the UK have a better survial rate. The following issue of NS (27 Feb) contained a letter which challenges both Hillaby's points, but agreeing on the decline - effectively leaving the whole problem very much a puzzle:

"There is a drainage pond a few acres in extent in part of the Northumberland Coast, with which I have been well acquainted for 20 years or so. (It) lies on the edge of fields and is seperated from the beach by about 100-yds of sand-dunes. For many years the area surrounding the pond was alive with frogs to such an extent that at certain times of the year it was essential to carry a torch after dark to avoid treading on the creatures. About 7yrs ago this population disappeared and since then to see a single individual is quite an event. The pond and surrounding area remain pretty much as they were and it is hard to believe that (this) disappearance has anything to do with changes in drainage. I have always assumed that it coincided with with the introduction of some new chemical on the adjacent fields.
              W Riddell.
              23 Beechcroft, Kenton Rd, Gosforth,
              Newcastle-upon-Tyne NE3 4NB."

VANISHING CHILDREN.

At 2.06pm, 8 April 69, April Fabb, 13, cycled out of Metton village, Norfolk. At 2.15 her bike was found ½mile down the narrow lane to Roughton. She had disappeared in broad daylight, within earshot of picknickers and workers in the fields.

At about 3.00pm, 5 March 70, David McCaig, 13, began to bicycle the ½mile to school in the Wallasey area of Liverpool, for his favourite lesson in French. The next day his bike and cloak were found, and that's all.

At 7.30, 6 June 64, Keith Bennet, 12, waved good-bye to his mother to walk the last few hundred yards to his Granny's house in Longsight, Manchester...and has not been seen or heard of since.

At about 8.00pm, 12 July 63, Pauline Reade, 16, was seen in the distance by a friend, making her way to a dance in Openshaw, less than ½mile from her home in Gorton, near Manchester. She never turned up there, or anywhere else since.

These and other cases, unsolved to this day, were re-opened by Paulette Pratt in 1972 in a big

feature called "The Children who Vanish without a Trace" OBSERVER MAGAZINE, 29 Oct 72, only to find that in all cases the authorities were still baffled - even in one case where tens of thousands of statements were sifted, and over 80,000 posters circulated. Occasionally, papers get this bee in their bonnets and do a feature on missing persons, (MPs). For example, the Sunday Mirror for 18 & 25 Aug 74 also chronicled that lack of progress in these and the cases of Stephen Paul (vanished from outside his home in Fakenham, Norfolk, at 5pm-5.20pm, 2 Sept 69); Christine Markham (last seen at 11.09, 21 May 73 less than 200yds from her Scunthorpe home); and Lucy Partington, 21, (who left a friend's house at 10.15pm to catch the last bus to Cheltenham, on 27 Dec 73, and somehow didn't, though the stop was a short walk away.)

Speaking of such cases, Paulette Pratt wrote: "Not the least baffling aspect of all this is the realisation that no-one knows how many children vanish in this way. A reasonable estimate is that several thousand children are reported missing each year in one circumstance or another, and a significant proportion are never found." And of her efforts to determine just what that 'significant proportion' was, she adds: " Scotland Yard was approached several times during the course of this research, but refused to give even a brief interview, on the grounds that missing persons procedure is being reorganised." But even in the police network, "There is as yet no attempt at the sort of national index for missing persons that there is for example, for stolen cars...in the absence of research, the national pattern is not known. And on a purely practical level, there is no central source to which detectives from any part of the country can refer, when a child vanishes without a trace."

But whatever the administrative hangups, cases continue to mount on a staggering pile. At noon 22 June 74, Alison Chadwick, aged 10, left her home in Old Manor Drive, Isleworth, Middlesex. It was a normal Saturday lunchtime, her favourite bangers and mash was imminent - but she nipped out to fetch her swimming costume from a friend's house in the next street. That was the last time she was seen. Police took 15,000 statements and no clue was too insignificant to follow up - but nothing could be discovered at all. News of the World, 11 Aug 74. Credit: Nigel Watson.

At roughly the same time, Seattle was reeling under a series of vanishings of six young women since Jan 74. Two happened during the same outing to Lake Sammamish State Park, east of Seattle; but they did not know each other. One was last seen agreeing to help a man load his sailboat, and the other left her boyfriend to go to a restroom, and never came back. All were described as "serious and responsible", vanishing in seperate incidents. Perhaps the great hand in the sky is partial to serious young ladies. San Francisco Examiner, 22 July 74. Cr: L Coleman.

Titbits, 12-18 Dec 74 (not particularly known for reports of scientific accuracy), carried an article on 11 children that were "kidnapped or murdered" from the Yugoslavian village of Prilipe in the Slovenia mountains. The horror began in May 72, when 6yr-old Anna Boscovic skipped out of her house to pick lilies in a nearby wood. Subsequent investigations could turn up no sign of her at all, the phrase being "vanished into thin air". Then 5yr-old twins disappeared, to be later found drowned, with no clues about how it happened. And 7yr-old Andreas Militic - gone, and then found later apparently killed by a hit-and-run driver. Then some more clueless vanishings. And, 4yr-old Jirina Kanladic was discovered dead in a meadow, still clutching her doll; no cause for her death could be ascertained. The last was little Bostian Clemencic, who because of the terror that kept the small community in fear, was watched over by his grandmother as he slept. For brief seconds she left him to fetch her knitting - but that was apparantly what was waited for, and long enough for him to have disappeared from their lives. The police, like police everywhere, thought of evil madmen, and conducted their searches accordingly - but there was not much else they could really. By our count, that's 5 dead and 6 vanished in less than two years.

(Cr: BK Bates.)

Daily Mirror, 6 Sept 74: that on 1Sept, Pamela Exall, 21, went for a walk along the beach at Snettisham, Norfolk, never to be seen again. -- The Sun, 6 Nov 74: that late 28 Oct night, 15yr-old Kim Baille was dropped just outside her home in Red Cross Way, Southwark, South London, by the taxi she shared with 3 friends after a dance. Somehow she never made the 50yds to her front door.

A PROTO-STONEHOUSE.

We had quite a juicy file abuilding on the vanishing of John Stonehouse, sometime MP for Walsall North. Just our luck he had to turn up. But to compensate, we found the following story told by Vivian Bird, in the Sunday Mercury, 8 Dec 74. Strictly speaking, Victor Grayson was no longer an MP when he boarded a train at Liverpool in 1920, bound for a speaking engagement in Hull. His bag reached the hotel booked for him, but Grayson never arrived. Bird says: "Some evidence suggests he turned up next day at a hotel in the Strand, London, but disappeared leaving a half-finished drink at the bar." We ponder - perhaps the snatching of Grayson was a mistake, and that later, homing on similar characteristics it was tried again. Grayson may even have been 'returned' (minus memory, naturally) - because in 1927, his mother, who lived in Liverpool, had hired a gumshoe to locate him. Nothing was found except a vague idea that he might be living in Australia. (Hmmm - funny how they always end up there.) The only other information, if you can call it that, was given by Seymour Cocks, Labour MP for Maidstone, who said that a man introduced himself to him as Victor Grayson on 23 Aug 1924, saying that he had been living in New Zealand.

He gave Cocks a Belfast address, which Cocks lost in due course. End of information. An odd story that.

THE GLEN MILLER STORY / Cont.

December 74 also saw the 30th anniversary of the cross-channel flight of the single-engined 'Norseman' that was carrying Glen Miller to Paris for a Christmas broadcast - he never made it. John Edwards spent £100 chartering a light plane and took off on Miller's schedule - 1.55pm, 13 Dec - from the same wartime base, Twinwood, Beds. Add that to the £6800 he has spent so far in his 16-year quest to solve the mystery of Miller's disappearance, and that's a lot of crankpower. At precisely 2.39 (presumably the last known time-check from Miller's craft) Edwards found himself 12 miles out from the Kent coast, in the area where a computer firm, working from weather and flight records, suggests the disappearance took place. Edwards had a salvage tug rendezvousing below, but (again presumably) was not able to dive in the conditions. Last word from Edwards was that he was going to try diving this summer. Daily Mirror, 14 Dec 74.

About two months previously, coverage was given to quite a different story. Medium Carmen Rogers held a seance at the Bedfordshire airfield in October 74, and then declared that Miller was not on board the plane when it crashed. "I can see him walking to the aircraft. He is disturbed and very worried. He does not want to make this trip. He is sick and afraid. I think the pilot decided it would be better if he put down as soon as possible and let Glen Miller get out. He asked for it to land, and it touched down on the Essex side of the Thames estuary. Glen Miller arranged to disappear. I can see him making his way to a pub, where he used the phone for a call to London." Mrs Rogers, an official of the Spiritualist National Union, added: "If they raise the plane they will not find Glen Miller. He had already left it...he died later." Douglas le Vicki, Press Officer of the Glen Miller Soc. attended the seance, and said later: "I find it hard to believe...There have been suggestions before that his disappearance was deliberate, that he was a secret agent, that he was alive but mutilated...None of the evidence points to Glen Miller having landed in England on that flight. I still believe he crashed into the Channel." In view of his own admission of the lack of evidence as to what happened, we wonder how he can be so certain. But that's called being realistic, or scientific, these days. The story is from Sunday People, 20 Oct 74. Credit: Nigel Watson. The only other thing that occurs to our criminally brilliant minds, is that if indeed Glen Miller had stopped the plane intending to disappear from the spotlight, the subsequent crash of the plane was a coincidence of some magnitude. See other sources for stories of those who 'missed' the Titanic etc etc. Only way to solve this thing conventionally is to get that planewreck up - if it exists. But, of course, if those cosmic jokers have done their stuff, it'll be an entirely <u>different</u> plane down there. Kepp (dammit), keep your eyes peeled for developments. (Sorry about the outburst, but I've run out of Tippex.)

MORE MPs (MISSING PERSONS).

Mrs Florence Newitt - snatched away to where the air is thin, by a giant hand from outer space, perhaps - but leaving behind a new £2000 car, a handsome income from rented property, and her washing up half done in her home at Christchurch Dorset. Daily Express, 5 May 74. Cr: P Rogerson.

The shipboard romance of two young teachers ended in mystery. Valerie Young, 22, and Raymond Trait 24, waited in her sister's cabin on the Greek liner 'Ellenis', until 5am, and then went out to watch the Pacific dawn from the decks. They were not seen again. Daily Mirror, 24 June 74. Credit: DJ McAllister.

Tasmanian student Noel Jago was last seen on 20th July, jogging off into the distance on the shore of Lake Burley Griffin, on his way to join the start of a marathon... (Nothing else - just dot dot dot. And we didn't make up either name, either). London Evening News (and the LE Standard), 26 July 74. Cr: Paul Devereaux & S Moore.

Anna Saint,26, drove a taxi, and on the morning of 9 Dec 74, she was on duty as usual outside Newcastle station. Later that day, her blue cab was found abandoned in a quiet street 3 miles from the station. Her handbag containing £28 was on the seat, her coat still in the boot. After extensive investigations, police confessed their mystification. Daily Mirror, 11 Dec 74.

William Nicholson, 71, had just arrived in England to claim his late brothers four-figure bequest. After docking at Southampton, he checked two cases into left-luggage at East Croydon station, and walked out. That was Oct 74, and nothing has been found of his whereabouts etc since. Porters opened his cases after a few weeks, and found his clothes, passport, and a copy of his brother's will. Police revealed that Nicholson's Croydon bank-account had not been touched. And the late bro's executor's confounded the mystery by saying that they did not know he was in the country, not expecting him for a couple of months. Sunday Express, 30 March 75. Credit: Richard Cotton.

UP, UP...AND AWAY...

You may remember the disappearance of the American balloonist, Col Tom Gatch, of whom we have no further news. He was not the first, and to be morbidly practical, we doubt he will be the last. Nigel Watson sent us word that Nature had reprinted an early occurrence in their '100 Years Ago' section (that was back when they were printing more of our kind of rubbish, instead of the present scientific rubbish). We're fairly sure this case is mentioned somewhere in Fort, but cannot put our finger on it just now - so we'll give you this original version: "The Young King of Siam having come of age on October 10 last, great feasts were given to his subjects at Bangkok

the chief town of his dominion. Among other attractions was the ascent of a small mounted balloon, which had been constructed in Paris and had arrived by steam a few days previously. Liberal offers were made to procure an aeronaut, but were of no avail, nobody amongst the Siamese presuming to ascend. Consequently his Majesty ordered a slave, selected from amongst the less heavy of his household, to be sent up in the car. In order to encourage the poor aeronaut, so frightened for his life, he was promised to be rewarded with his enfranchisement. The ascent took place and elicited much enthusiasm from the bystanders, but, unhappily, nothing was heard from the poor fellow or of the craft." NATURE Vol 9 No 350, March 1874. Looks like the 'poor fellow' got his freedom from slavery one way or another.

THERE AND BACK AGAIN.

Some who disappear, it seems, like our Trout hors d'œuvres ((we occasionally like to show our command of the foreign word - we might even learn a new one for next ish)), manage to make the round trip and reappear. Some day we shall go further into the problems of scrambled memories and amnesia in connexion with teleportation, but just know We are having the Devil's own job of remembering what we started out talking about. Ah yes! Reappearances. See if you can accept the following story, told in a letter to the Manchester Evening News, 20 Nov 68. (Credit: Peter Rogerson).

"When my family were young we spent many happy years camping in (the upper reaches of the River Wharfe in Yorkshire). Mr Reay ((an article on that area by him in the MEN, the previous Saturday.)) says that there is a wonderful air of mystery about it all, an air of "farawayness and remoteness", and I too would describe the place as spooky. I will never forget on one occasion, when we had climbed up over the moors. The children played around, while my wife and I rested among the heather, basking in the sunshine. Whether I dozed off or not, I do not know, but suddenly I became aware that my wife was not with us. I called the children and asked them where she had gone, but they could not tell me anything . I got the queerest impression that she had been spirited away by the 'fairies' - there was nowhere on the moors that she could have hidden, and I began to get panicky. This district has that effect on one - the isolation and peace of the place give one the impression that unearthly (sic) things could happen. It is the weirdest place I know.

"We began to get really worried, and even Paddy our dog, who always accompanied us on our outings, started to whimpre ((curses - I still haven't any Tippex)), and appeared very distressed. Suddenly, apparently from nowhere, my wife was with us again, and there was a faraway smile on her face. We questioned her as to where she had been, but she could offer no explanation, and had no recollection of having been away from us at all. There is no doubt in my mind that something very odd had happened - something associated with the "farawayness and remoteness" of the place."

MYSTERY COASTAL FLARES.

We find from time to time stories of flares, or
what are thought to be flares, seen far out to
sea, and which, when investigated, reveal no ship
in distress, and are then thought to be a hoax of
some sort, without much thought as to how or why
a hoaxer would brave the distance and dangers
with minimal prospect of the flares being visible
from ships or people who may or may not be in the
area. We have no idea of whether these events
are what ordinarily passes for "ball lightning"
or "UFOs" because frankly we have no idea in turn
what these latter lights are - but both undoubtedly could give rise to the tales of
mystery flares. Give a thought, though, to the
poor lifeboatmen, who have to turn out regardless
of their doubts.

This type of phenomenon seems to be more prevalent
on the east coast of England. Fort records tales
of the "False Lights of Durham" in 1866 and the
following year ((see Book of the Damned, Ch26.))
and there is no doubt that it is also an ancient
tradition from long before that. And we also
saw a case recorded in Cade & Davis's The Taming
of the Thunderbolts (taken from the Northern
Echo, 22 Nov 1963, originally). On 21 Nov 63,
the coal-ship "Thrift" put into Blyth, Northumberland, 8 hours late. She had come from Aberdeen, when at nearly 6.00pm, 20 Nov, opposite
Girdleness, Kincardine, the captain and 3 crewmen
saw a pulsing red light passing within a mile of
the port side (ie. out to sea) and at a height of
15-30ft above the sea-level. About 3 miles
behind them it disappeared suddenly, and they
then conducted a fruitless search for sign of a
ship, men &c. Please see NEWS 2/18 for reports
of coastal lights off Kent in 1973.

A lifeboat out of Skegness made a 5 hour search
of the Wash on the evening of 30 April 74 and
into the morning of 1 May, after red "distress
flares" were reported in the Lynnwell area. They
found nothing. The coastguard spokesman predictably supposed a flash-bombing exercise by the
RAF on the Wainfleet range. Scunthorpe Evening
Telegraph, 1 May 74. Credit: Nigel Watson.

On 16 July 74, a combined search on part of the
Norfolk coast, by the Gorleston lifeboat at sea
and coastguards and police ashore, was called

off after two hours. Brian Coleman, a coastguard,
had spotted red flares to the north - there were
also calls from other observers. When nothing
turned up it was believed to be a hoax.
Eastern Evening News, 16 July 74. Cr: N Watson.

Four or five days later, a white "flare" was
seen off Souter Point lighthouse, at Marsden,
Northumberland. Lifeboats searched for 2½ hours
on the night of the 20th but found nothing - and
no boats were reported to be in the area. The
Journal (Newcastle), 22 July 74. Cr: P Screeton.

The Western Mail (Cardiff), 13 Jan 75, briefly
mentioned much mystery flare activity around
Anglesey and the mainland of North Wales, bringing in its wake "baffled" coastguards and lifeboatmen. The latest sighting was on the morning
of the 12th, about midway between Great Orme,
Llandudno and Puffin Island, Anglesey. The Beau-
maris lifeboat put out at 1am. and after 4 fruitless hours, gave up. (Credit: FW Holiday.) Our
man on the spot, Phil Ledger, told us: "Phoned
coastguard (lifeboat couldn't be reached by
phone) and they knew exactly the incident I was
referring to, but could not help in any way -
nothing had turned up since - lifeboat just got
report of flares, went to sea, found nothing, and
came in again. Event not covered by our local
paper which never prints anything except WI, and
births, deaths & marriages."

Later we had another card from Phil. "Shortly
after 7.00pm Friday 7th Feb, a motorist passing
Tryfan (that's a mountain 917 meters high and
about 20 kms from the Llandudno flare area)
thought he saw flares at the top. The following
day mountain-rescue went out but found nothing,
and no-one was reported missing. The report was
on the BBC local radio news, Sat. 8th. I phoned
mountain-rescue and they gave me the above details but could give no leads as to the source
of the original report; and got quite up-tight
when I mentioned UFOs. "

And much further down the Welsh coast, flares
are flaring off Llantwit Major in the Tresilian
area. Police, coastguards, fishermen and students of Atlantic College, as well as members of
public have all reported seeing yellowish flares
in 4 or 5 incidents over the past few months.

From the lack of other details we can reasonably assume that the various inevitable searches could turn up no discernable cause for them. Western Mail (Cardiff), 3 Feb 75. Credit: FW Holiday.

FIREBALLS OR WHATEVER THEY ARE.

A case we have not seen recorded elsewhere was sent to us by Steve Moore. It appears that Nature joined in the celebrations of November the Fifth in 1938, when those lucky enough to have lived in central and northwest London saw a very bright object which moved from south-east to north-west. "Its brilliant red drop-shaped head hurtled through the sky followed by a greenish tail which was apparently about six times the width of the moon. As it travelled through space it flared up to great brilliance several times and then, like a rocket, seemed to peter out over Hampstead way." quoted from Modern Wonder, Vol 4, No 79, 19 Nov 1938. Sounds like a fairly typical meteor/thing, but we include in case it isn't and so that we can check for synchronous events if the mood takes us later.

Shifnal, Shropshire - A bright ball of fire, for once not described as a UFO, but as a "mysterious glowing object" (an MGO?) was sighted independently by two waiters of the Park House Hotel, Shifnal. The Headwaiter was at Shifnal station on the evening of 23 June 74 when he saw it. About an hour later another waiter saw the object flying in the direction of Wolverhampton. Spokesman for RAF Shrewsbury said they had no planes in the area at the time. Express & Star, 24 June 74. Credit: Anthony Smith. Curious that 2 waiters from the same hotel should witness a similar (if not the same) enigma at different times.

Bala, Merioneth — 64-year-old George Longworth was driving past Bala lake in North Wales when he saw a light. It was brilliant like a "blinding sun" and as it flashed over his car, it deposited in its wake, an eerie grey powder. "I literally headed for the hills. I drove so hurriedly in fact that it looks as though I've ruined the gears on my car." George, who 'is not given to imagining things" said that the bright light had curious antenna-like protrusions out of each side, and that other motorists were brought to a stop too. "We were all shaken," he said referring to his wife, cousin & granddaughter also in the car, "It was something very odd indeed. I won't stick my neck out and say it was a flying saucer but in my experience at least it was most certainly an unidentified flying object. The shilling-sized white dust blotches it left on the car worried me. I wasn't going to touch them. Thankfully we had a deluge and it was all washed away." This fly-over took place on 4 Oct 74. A Dr Patrick Willmore of the Global Seismology Unit in Edinburgh is quoted: "The description could fit that of a fireball, which is a floating, bright, electrical object - but the odd thing is the grey powder which fell from it. I just don't know about that." Well that's honest enough , but what about those 'antennae'? Incidentally, Bala lake is on the Bala fault-line, and as some of you may remember, about 10 miles up the valley

is Llandrillo of the Jan 74 tremors and lights. Story from Liverpool Echo, 11 Oct 74. Credit: Peter Rogerson.

Ben Nevis, Inverness — is this another mountain fireball, or a return of the phantom tailless helicopter?? Policeman David Dawson was halfway down Ben Nevis, on 13 Oct 74, when he and a friend saw what looked like a "star" travelling slowly along the bottom of the glen about 400ft below. "It was not a meteorite, or any plane or helicopter that we have seen or heard of before. There was an engine and I would have guessed that it was a manned vehicle." Another part of the statement says that it hummed like an electricity generator, which,we suppose, could have given the impression of an engine - though the constable's testimony should be given the benefit of the doubt. He continued: "The light was so bright that it was impossible to make out any shape. We had a torch burning at the time but quickly put it out." We find this interesting in that not only did they feel subjectively that it could have been 'manned', but also felt wary enough about it not to attract its attention, a gesture which in turn suggests the object radiated a feeling of sentience. No other reports were received by authorities and they were said to be baffled - whichmust be pretty near their normal state these days. It was also mentioned that a report of the event was forwarded to the Ministry of Defence under the heading of "Unidentified Flying Object". We have it here for no particular reason except that it seems to be more at home amongst our other stories of lights on or near mountains. Daily Express, 14 Oct 74. Credit: Steve Moore & Roger Randle.

Haverfordwest, Dyfed -- back in South Wales, there was a series of "fireballs" which overlaps with the 'mystery flares' mentioned earlier and in much the same areas,but inland instead of the coastal sea. Cyril Hughes told police he saw a "ball of red fire which also gave off a red glow" falling at "medium speed" towards the river, not far from his home at Hook, near Haverfordwest. He was driving towards Haverfordwest when he saw the object "absolutely clearly. I stopped the car and followed it down until it disappeared behind a bank. I turned the car around and went down to the riverside, but it was dark and there was nothing to be seen. It could have fallen into the wood or into the water. There was not another soul about at the time. I have never seen a flare but it was certainly bigger than any firework I've ever seen. It was certainly no illusion - I saw it for about 10 seconds." No date is given but from the context we would guess 26th or 27th Dec. Police questioned many people in the area but no one else had seen anything - and Hughes remained convinced enough to talk of organising a search in the week to come. The story ends on the cryptic note that the 'fireball' couldn't be tracked on radar screens at RAF Brawdy "because the base was closed for Christmas." Got that? Good Grief! Aliens could be slipping in on public holidays, and we wouldn't know a thing until its too late. Western Mail (Cardiff), 28 Dec 74. Credit: FW Holiday.

However, as it turns out, others did see it. The Western Mail, for 30 Dec 74, mentions two people, also residents of Hook, saw the light for a few seconds. Robert Annesley said: "I would not have thought that it was a flare." And Hughes adds that someone else from Hook had contacted him confirming his sighting - and that a UFO 'expert' was moving in to help with his intended search. All this talk of 'flares', by the way, is a reaction to the concurrent 'mystery flare' events along the coast.

Then a silence - until 2 youths claim to have seen "a strange red ball" in a field "recently" near their home at Clarbeston, and this report was investigated by the 'UFO expert', named as Mr Randall Jones-Pugh, a local BUFORA man. Nothing is said of Hughes's search, so it's our guess he didn't find anything. Also, it is not said, but we presume that the 'red ball' the youths saw, was a ball of red light. Western Mail (Cardiff), 11 Feb 75.

Credit for these Haverfordwest notes to FW Holiday, who also checked the witnesses and the site at Hook - and further, found that both incidents occurred on prominent leys in the area, ((see accompanying diagram)). Mr Holiday also added that: "A most interesting ley crops up which I just haven't got the maps to trace. Cadno in mid-Wales is somehow linked with Carnac in Brittany, and Llantwit Major occurs on one or other of the legs. Hence we get reports like the enclosed of lifeboats turning out after mystery flares." Doubtless, in the continuity of all things, the connexions exist, but hidden to our sensibilities at the present.

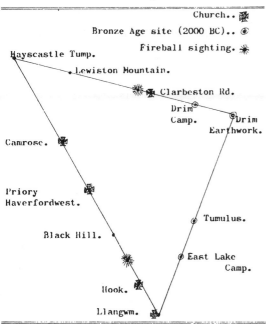

Church.. 🏯
Bronze Age site (2000 BC).. ◉
Fireball sighting. ✳
Hayscastle Tump.
Lewiston Mountain.
Clarbeston Rd.
Drim Camp.
Drim Earthwork.
Camrose.
Priory Haverfordwest.
Black Hill.
Tumulus.
East Lake Camp.
Hook.
Llangwm.

Anglesey — "Astronomers are almost certain that a "mysterious ball of fire" seen over Anglesey, on Saturday night ((19 Jan)) was a meteor." Thats how the report began in the North Wales Chronicle 23 Jan 75 (Credit: Phil Ledger.)((See above somewhere for mystery flares in this area on 12th Jan and 7th Feb.)) Rather than give you the processed press version, here is Phil Ledger's own account of his investigation. "At 00.15 Sunday 20th Jan, Mrs Elizabeth Hughes and her daughter were sat in a room facing SW in their farmhouse at Hendre, Gwalchmai (Map ref: SH 395 765.) when the room became noticeably brightened by a red glow. On looking out of the window, they noticed a red ball of light to the west, apparently moving into their view from behind some nearby trees. The 'ball of fire' was described as brilliant red and throwing off red sparks from all around as associated with a spinning motion (and not as the NW Chronicle reports, from out of the top only). It moved slowly overall but with a rolling or spinning motion (compared by them to a Catherine Wheel). Looking through binoculars Miss Hughes saw that a white smoke was being given off The ball continued to move across in front of the house, but being on a level slightly above the horizon, its true distance was difficult to estimate. After watching for (an estimated) five minutes, during which time the object moved slowly away, apparently to the opposite side of the valley (N 200° - or 20° W of S, if you prefer), Miss Hughes saw the red ball suddenly diminish in size until only a much smaller white ball was left, which itself quickly disappeared. The night was 'quiet' with no rain, little wind and few clouds - and no noise was heard throughout the event. Note: Nearby (5 miles) RAF Valley have no record of this or any other light at relevant times. Only 2 other people were reported as having seen anything and when I spoke to them all they could describe was a vague orange glow. Anglesey is a very flat island and there is a good chance that any high, distant object would have been seen by many more people. This suggests to me that the event occurred close to Hendre, probably in the valley in front of the farm and hence potentially visible to few people."

Llandudno, Gwynedd — if the above account seems more conventionally like ball lightning, Mr Walter Houghton, who witnessed the case that follows is more inclined to think it a UFO. We include it here, again, because of the other activity in the area, and since we are running out of room we shall have to deal with our UFO pile some other time. Mr Houghton's account appeared in the Bangor & North Wales Weekly News, 13 March 75. (Credit: M "The Druid's Wife" Ledger.) Phil Ledger contacted him, and he sent us the following letter, which we have had to shorten because of the lack of space; but none of the relevant details are missing. He began by pleading "to know if any other local people witnessed the passage of a most unusual body in the skies, at the early hour of 4-40am, Wednesday, March 5th. The craft or object was brilliant

Cont on page 14.

pyramid slope & northe

The large pyramids of Egypt are aligned with their base lines close to the four cardinal points of the compass. The largest of all, the Great Pyramid of Cheops at Giza, is aligned to within a few minutes of arc. The Giza group is located at latitude 29 59' N, just one minute short of latitude 30 , or one third of the distance from the Equator to the North Pole. We may infer from this that the early Egyptians had at least an indirect understanding of the fact that the Earth is a globe rotating about an axis.

A continuing puzzle is the question of the choice of angle of slope of each of the larger pyramids. Values taken from Fakhry (1) are given in the attatched table. Fakhry conjectures that the reasons for the choice of angle are probably structural and quotes Lauer (2) who indicates the convenience of selecting an angle such that the vertical rise is a simple multiple of the horizontal distance. Mendelssohn (3) quotes a suggestion of TE Connolly that the horizontal distance was determined by means of a rolling drum (this would explain the supposed early knowledge of the magnitude of 'pi', the ratio of the circumference of a circle to its diameter.)

While such relationships would presumably have facilitated construction, it is of interest to consider further whether there were specific reasons for the choice of any particular angle over any other, equally easy to construct on the simple ratio principle. Mendelssohn has considered the influence of angle of slope in conjunction with the use or otherwise of buttress techniques on the stability of the structures. In particular he considers the outer structure of the pyramid at Meydum to have collapsed, and offers a convincing explanation for this in structural terms.

We here consider the hypothesis that, just as the alignment of the base lines and the location of the large pyramids near latitude 30 N suggests an appreciation of the significance of latitude, so the pyramid slopes corresponded to latitudes of importance to the early Egyptians. Some early centres of religious or other significance to early man in Northern latitudes in the area of Western Europe are indicated in the table, and the latitudes corresponding to some of the angles of slope are superimposed on Figure 1. There are other important centers whose latitudes are not represented by pyramid slopes, so we are open to the criticism that we are being selective.

Ivimy (4) has independently related the slope of the Great Pyramid to the latitude of the Prescelly Mountains, and has suggested that Stonehenge, at latitude 51 10'N, was subsequently selected for the temple as the climate was better and conditions were better for astronomical observations.

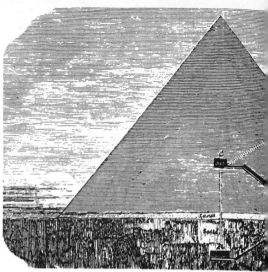

Watkins (5) describes some important alignments of tumuli and other earthworks passing through Stonehenge (Figure 2). __Alignment A__ is the familiar Midsummer sunrise - Midwinter sunset alignment. __Alignment B__ is sometimes considered to be a May sunset or November sunrise alignment, but such an astronomical significance seems weak. A thread stretched on a globe between Stonehenge and Giza coincides with this alignment, suggesting that its true significance may have been to establish ties with Giza. __Alignment C__ puzzled Watkins as it lies 1 North of

Pyramid Group	Pyramid	Slope Angle
	Meydum	51° 53'
Dashur	Southern (Bent)	43° 21' 54° 31'
	Northern	43° 40'
Giza	Cheops (Great Pyramid)	51° 50'
	Chephren	53° 10'
	Mycerinus	51°

ꝓꝺ latitudes
by Stuart W Greenwood.

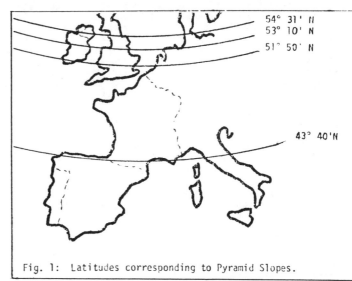

Fig. 1: Latitudes corresponding to Pyramid Slopes.

true East and just fails to qualify for sunrise and sunset alignments at the Equinoxes. However the included angle between Alignments B and C is 30 , the latitude of Giza.

That Egypt and Britain were linked in an important way in early times appears to be a hypothesis deserving further study.

＊ⅲⅲ＊ ＊ⅲⅲ＊ ＊ⅲⅲ＊ ＊ⅲⅲ＊

References:

1) A Fakhry, "The Pyramids", University of Chicago Press, second edition, 1969.
2) JP Lauer, "Sur le Choix de l'Angle de Pente dans les Pyramides d'Egypt", Bulletin de l'Institut d'Egypte, XXXVII, (1956),pp57-66.
3) K Mendelssohn, "The Riddle of the Pyramids", Praeger Publishers, 1974.
4) J Ivimy, "The Sphinx and the Megaliths", Turnstone, 1974.
5) A Watkins, "The Old Straight Track", Garnstone Press, 1970. (Also: Ballantine Books, 1973.)

Stuart W Greenwood : December 1974.

Location	Latitude
Prescelly Mountains	51° 45' -- 51° 55' N
Altamira Armagh	43° 23' N 54° 21' N
Altamira	43° 23' N
Avebury	51° 27' N
Holyhead	53° 19' N
Glastonbury	51° 09' N

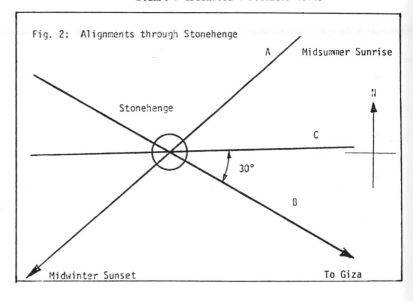

Fig. 2: Alignments through Stonehenge

Midsummer Sunrise

Stonehenge

30°

Midwinter Sunset

To Giza

FIREBALLS / cont:

white, elongated like a cigar shape, which could
easily have been a "saucer" seen edgeways. It
appeared suddenly out of the blackness of the
night sky, having no streaming tail behind it,
being most clearly defined. Its speed was much
faster than an aircraft, yet certainly not so
fast as to be mistaken for a meteorite. Its line
of flight was from south to the north, and was
directly over and parallel with the length of the
Nant-y-Gammar mountain range ((Map ref: SH 802
812)). Its disappearance was as sudden as its
appearance had been, there being no gradual fading out of its light, and no gradual diminution
of size due to distance covered, but a sudden
cutting out of the intense whiteness, just as
if the brilliance had been electrically switched
off. Its flightpath had been perfectly straight
and not arced. It was no optical illusion, my
window being perfectly clear of any condensation,
(and) the sighting was of that crystal clearcut
brilliant white object against a black sky background free of haze or fog." In a PS, Mr Houghton
adds: "Approximate length of object assumed as
30-35ft, according to its distance away from the
viewer. Flight height assumed to be 40-45ft above
the mountain top."

There certainly seems to be a lot going on in
Wales these days.

GHOST LIGHTS, CORPSE CANDLES AND A BIG ?

The Bournemouth Evening Echo, 22 Oct 1969, printed a strange story. Alastair Mackenzie, manager
of the Suncliff Hotel, was drinking coffee with
his wife and daughter when he saw something
fluttering outside. They went out onto a verandah
and saw a shape resembling a jellyfish, apparently 5 inches across and glowing slightly. After
about 15 seconds, the luminous object moved out
to sea gathering speed as it went, at a height of
25-30 ft. We first came across this case in the
Paralab 'Classified Directory' for 1969, and
were intrigued enough to write to Mr Mackenzie,
who replied briefly: The phenomenon I saw was
undoubtedly a UFO type "thing". In trying to
describe it I unfortunately used a jellyfish as
being the only similar earthbound object laymen
could liken it to. It certainly was not a jellyfish. The local press used my phrase to provide
stupid headlines in their newspaper in order to
help sell them to the gullible public." Hmmm -
if it certainly wasn't a jellyfish, it was also
just as certainly jellyfish-like - enough for
Mr Mackenzie to use the analogy in the first
place. Perhaps we are gullible - but   reports
of small glowing spheres of (usually blue) light
are quite common in the records of odd lights,
but more in a minute...

According to a news report in late 1967, a 4-man
expedition with £5000 worth of recording equipment was planning to set off in Jan of 1968 for
the remote south-west corner of Ireland. Led by
a physicist, Dr Wilfred Forbes, they were going
to investigate "one of the strangest, most inexplicable mysteries of all time", known to the
locals as "The Lights of Crusheen." -- "uncanny

flames in the sky" which are said to hover over
the tiny island of Inchicronan and come ashore
at times of death and disaster. Twin flames,
that have been seen "for centuries", are said
to bob along about 6ft from the ground as though
being carried by invisible torchbearers. They
have even been photographed, and Dr Forbes has
interviewed over 20 people, and mentions "hundreds of reliable witnesses." The lights are
like enormous "candle flames" appearing above the
island in the lake, and then at disaster times,
move along a rocky causeway (which is completely
submerged in winter) connecting the island (which
is barren, occupied only by the ruins of Inchicronan Abbey, and Crusheen cemetery), then they
follow the road into Crusheen, floating slowly
up to roof level and remain there, still for
several minutes over the doomed household, before
drifting back the same way, to vanish again over
the island. Even the local priest, the report
adds, believes the appearance of the Lights
heralds a death in the village.

Dr Forbes was hoping to investigate a number of
theories like "marsh gas", and "phosphorescence".
We smile, because these theories themselves are
the pale ghosts of horses that have been dragged
out to be flogged time and again -- see LO! for
the 1904/1905 profusions of luminosities accompanying the last great religious revival crusade
in Wales and other parts of England. And after
all this time our understanding has advanced very
little into the nature of 'corpse-candles' or
'Will-o-the-wisps' or whatever you choose to call
them. Myth and folklore abounds with them - perhaps why scientists steer clear of them, usually.
But Dr Forbes knows where he stands: " Neither
I nor any of my team has much belief in the
supernatural. If there is a rational explanation
I am quite certain we will find it. Certainly
too many people have been frightened for too long
by whatever it is they call the Lights of Crusheen."   And that's the last we heard from him.
So any of you who know, please tell us what
happened to the doctor and his team, and whether
any info exists of their findings subsequently,
or even who Dr Wilfred Forbes is, or was. Perhaps
he got his wish - got to see the light...finally!
Data from Manchester Evening News, 5 Nov 67.
Credit: Peter Rogerson.

Cont on page 20.

ADz / cont:

ASSASSINATION INFORMATION BUREAU. Your Editor
first learned of the AIB in Phil Ledger's car as
we gave an itinerant American a lift to London.
Now, thanks to Loren Coleman, we can stick an
address to that. We in the UK (where such things
can never happen)(says who?) are only dimly
aware of the mysterious hankypanky and Men-in-
Black-type phenomena associated with prominent
assassinations. Tom Miller has organised the AIB
to investigate, promulgate and disseminate the
available info. Get yours on how they got theirs
by writing for details to: AIB, 875 56th, Oakland, California 94608, USA. But watchout for MIB.

Cont on page 24.

OUT OF PLACE

BABOONS.

It hardly seems credible - but it happened none
the less. On the night of Monday 8 July 74,
there was a mass escape of 80 baboons from the
West Midland Safari Park, in the Wyre Forest on
the Worcs./Shrops. border. Tom Mann, general
manager, warned: "When they got out, they were
reasonably harmless, but after four days on the
run in strange surroundings, being frightened
by gunfire and possibly hungry, they could be a
different proposition. We have reluctantly issued
orders to our hunters to shoot to kill if necessary." By the Saturday, all but 4 or 5 were
recaptured, and 3 were dead. It seems that a
gate was accidentally left open, and word soon
got around the baboons. The main story is from
Evening Mail (Birmingham), 13 July 74; and the
succeding days papers contain the inevitable
expressions of official concern, postmortems on
security, etc.

But the saga does not end there. Curiously, the
following month, on the 12th, about 30 calls
were received by police at Chester-le-Street,
Co. Durham, from people claiming to have seen
baboons swinging through trees in the area.
Later officials of Lambton Safari Park admitted
that they had 57 of the critters, but were very
cagey about how many had escaped. "We are trying
to count them," was all one had to say. The next
day, 2 were said to have returned "because they
were hungry." It's not said, but there is an
implication that there were still some on the
loose. The Sun, 13 & 14 Aug 74.

Meanwhile, back at the West Midlands Safari Park,
according to the Sunday Mercury, 18 Aug 74, four
baboons are continuing to evade capture, but we
we are assured they are not dangerous, by Mr
Paolo Sepe, the new general manager. But a committee of local officials was told by Mr Brian
Williams, managing director of a Birmingham
zoological firm, who bought 38 from the park,
that the biggest of them are strong and fierce
and could kill a man - and at official committee
level, statements like that cause as much conster-
nation as shoving a ferret down their trousers.
They radiated panic and concern - but nothing
else happened at all. Presumably they were
waiting till somebody got killed first.

Now it's September and we go back to Chester-le-
Street, where we learn that there has been
another mass escape attempt. This is described
as "organised" in that coaches, bearing incoming
gawpers and litterbugs disguised as visitors,
were waited for, then the crafty monkeys dashed
under the coaches, and rode past the security
checks by clinging to the chassis. Manager of
Lambton, Dick Howard, said: "From observations,
we identified the leaders behind the escape plot
and seven are now being dispersed to other zoos
and parks." It is not said how many got away,
or how many were recaptured, nor this time, if
any more returned out of hunger. Howard said he
had often to deal with brainy baboons. At a zoo
he managed in Holland, he caught some luring an
unsuspecting antelope with a banana to the side
of a compound fence - and then they vaulted up
and over the animal's back to freedom. Daily
Mirror, 3 Sept 74. Credit: Robert Forrest.

But those four stragglers from the escape en
masse are still glimpsed occasionally. The
last note we have is from October 74 when they
were reported seen in Oldington Woods at Foley
Park, Kidderminster, Worcs. A driver on the
Stourport Road said he saw one come out of the
woods, cross the road, then dash back again.
Adjacent to the woods is a British Sugar Corporation factory, and though no-one at the factory
appears to have seen them, 'experts' reckon
they have been attracted by the sweet smell and
pilfering sugarbeet. Sunday Mercury, 27 Oct 74;
Evening Mail (Birmingham), 28 Oct 74. I find
myself hoping they have survived the winter and
get round to breeding - and spring out at passing
naturalists, who, if they had any sense of pro-
priety, would promptly eat (or choke on even)
their UK mammal lists.

BEAR & RACOONS.

Daily Mirror, 22 July 74 -- that the police in
Hongkong were looking for the owner of a black
bear, found lurking on the staircase of a block
of flats on the 21st. Credit: Steve Moore.

Bears sound quite suitably exotic to be wandering
in oriental stairwells - but suppose we were to
supplant Hongkong with Yorkshire. Sounds unlikely,

but you dear reader, have come to expect the unlikely, at least here in the pages of THE NEWS where the public rarely venture, and where we can expose ourselves in relative privacy. But something has intruded elsewhere - the woods on Skipwith Common, near Riccall, Yorks have been the haunt of a creature which has startled many people in the first weeks of Feb this year. The Latest sightings suggest it to be a bear. David Bowlby, who does a 35-mile milk-round each day, had stopped his car by the Common on the Skip-with/ Thorganby road, to write up his sales book. Suddenly, he spotted the animal in woodland about 50 yards from the road. He got out and managed to get within 20 yards of it before it ran into a thicket. "I'm sure it was a bear, not fully grown. It was brown with black foot-pads; standing by a tree. It was about as big as an Alsation dog on all fours; on its hind legs it was about as tall as a 10-year-old child." And he glimpsed it again a few minutes later.

Later that same day, 12 Feb, the dog owned by farmworker Geoffrey Houseman, sniffing on the Common, began to behave oddly. "I couldn't under-stand it. The dog was barking for a full hour. He wouldn't normally bark like that if it was a rabbit. He's never done that before." David Bowlby reckoned there had been at least five previous sightings, and stories about a bear supposed escaped from a travelling circus at Malton, but didn't believe the stories until he had seen for himself. But we wonder...on the map, Malton is over 22 miles away and even the shortest route between there and Skipwith Com-mon would involve crossing a great many roads, some of them busy major ones....and the police state that they had received no reports of any missing bears (and it's fair to assume the circus would have eventually reported such an escape since a bear would be a part of their sources of revenue.)

Then police checked all the zoos and circuses in North Yorkshire, and again no bears were reported missing. But then a spokesman for the Flamingo Park Zoo, near Pickering, came up with the idea that it might be a racoon. Three police-men made a search of the common on 14 Feb but could find no sign of the animal or any tracks. In the next edition of the local paper we learn the reason for the Zoo's odd statement - they reveal that one of their racoons had gone..er.. "missing". However, Inspector Wilf Scott, of Selby police, said "The difference between a bear and a racoon is quite considerable...I'm keeping an open mind about this. There is obv-iously something running about. It may be a bear and it may be a racoon." Referring to the original suggestion of bear, he said "He's no idiot and if he's talking about an animal 5ft 10in. high, I'm not looking for a racoon." The story so far has been reassembled from the Yorkshire Evening Press, 13, 14 & 17 Feb 75. Credit: JW Scaife.

The Evening Standard (London), 19 Feb 75, rep-eated most of the details with the following

differences; a quote from Mr Bowlby: "I mean it sounds so stupid, but when I approached further - gosh -it was a bear. It stood about 4ft 6in., had brown eyes, a darker brown skin (!?!)and big black pads." ; and we learn that 3 racoons had escaped from Flamingo Park Zoo, 2 of which were recovered; and another zoo spokesman, apparently forgetting that the sug-gestion of racoon came from a zoo in the first place, said: "It is incredible to think of anyone mistaking a racoon for a bear - they are only about the size of a fox - a little shorter and fatter though." Then he went on to add that racoons had been known to have become feral in some parts of Britain.(Cr: Paul Devereaux.)

When JW Scaife mailed us the cuttings from the Yorkshire Evening Press, he commented that so far there was no further news, "in spite of snow on the ground to aid in tracking or sight-ing - or it may be the Press is bored with the news, as you well know their methods." So we leave you with the note that a racoon and something else that appears to be a young black bear are both still unaccounted for, and on the loose in our countryside.

"HERE, KITTY KITTY..."

A rare Eastern panther was seen and photographed in the Adirondacks by Alex McKay, a teacher of Huntington, New York, towards the end of April 74. Panthers were considered extinct for many years in the Northeast USA - but in recent decades there have been occasional sightings. The Commercial Appeal (Memphis), 1 May 74. Credit: Mark Hall.

We include two 'Surrey Puma' sightings here, recently sent to us by Janet Bord, and which are not listed in my article on MAs in southern England between 1962 and 1973 (see INFO 13.) though they fall in that period. On the 15th July 71, a policeman spotted a "2ft high, grey cat" at Plaistow Farm, Chiswell Green, Herts, and he thought it was a puma, or at least odd enough to call out his colleagues with tracker dogs. But it escaped them. A local paper a week later confirmed that nothing had been found or sighted during the searches and since; and that no pumas were reported to have escaped from zoos in the region. Evening Echo (Herts), 16 July 71; Herts. Advertiser, 23 July 71. And for the second time in just over a week, a "large catlike animal that can run at speeds up to 35mph" was sighted near Polegate, Sussex. A taxi-driver told police that early on the 14 June 72 he saw the animal, "several times larger than a cat", running along the road between Folkington and Polegate. The earlier report was from a man who saw the animal jump a 5ft fence. Evening News (London), 14 June 72.

A mountain-lion, called Khan, escaped from Miles Madley's garden, in Byton, Herefordshire, on 1 Jan 75, where it was kept as a pet. Squads of police with tracker dogs hunted through remote woods and a forest on the edge of Byton for the

escapee. It was normally gentle and frisky but fear, it was thought, could turn it into a killer -- no prizes for guessing who's putting the fear up it. An impression is given that Khan was tempted out of hiding once, but escaped again. No confirmation of any later capture either, so add one mountain-lion in Herefordshire.
Daily Mirror, 2 Jan 75.

The only catch Fred Lloyd was thinking about on the 5th Jan was a modest pike, as he fished on the banks of the Medway, at East Peckham, out in the wilds of Kent and not far from Tonbridge. But something stirred in the undergrowth, and out leapt a 2ft-long panther cub, all hiss and claws -- its enthusiasm got the better of its prowess and the pretend-tiger came tumbling down the bank towards startled Fred. "I grabbed it by the scruff of its neck, took a look at its claws as it growled away and shoved it straight into my fishing box." He rushed home and transferred his catch to a baby's playpen, and when that looked like being demolished, into a large strong box, putting a beer-crate on the lid. "I phoned all the zoos I could think of to see if they ahd lost a black panther, but they just laughed at me and put the phone down. Fred notes that the cub was quite exhausted, which is why, he reckons, he caught it so easily -- but very interestingly, he adds that it didn't seem to be particularly hungry. "He turned his nose up at all we offered him, eveh raw meat; and when it came to trying to get him to drink, after a few seconds in his mouth, the teat on our sterilised milk-bottle was bitten clean off". It took another 24 hours before an RSPCA Inspector could be convinced into coming to take it away to a home in Godstone, Surrey. "I thought it would probably turn out to be a ferret," he said. The day so-called authorities and experts stop patronizing their public, is the day we pack up and burn our notes. But now the story takes a stranger twist. Over a week later, Colchester Zoo, in Essex, claim the cub as 'Zar', an 8-week-old bundle of fun worth £600, and who had been stolen from them on 4th Jan - the day before he turned up in Kent over 50 miles away; or rather a cub disappears, and the next day, learning that by a stroke of luck a cub has turned up elsewhere, claim it, thinking conventionally that a thief had travelled with it. We wonder, in our perversity, if it was the same cub, since most of us non-'experts' would be hard put to tell one young black panther from another. But to the expert-mind a thief is a less troublesome hypothesis than the one we have suggested ((see NEWS 1/9 for a note on the vanishing of a black swan, and a different one that turned up elsewhere later)). We can only wonder how it was stolen; then why let it go if it was worth a ransom, and after going to that trouble. And as to it escaping and making the journey on its own? - well anything is possible - but the shortest route between Colchester and East Peckham is down a craggy coast, across the Thames estuary and through some well populated parts. For continuity we point out that Fort recorded many cases of things disapp-

earing and other things appearing in their stead, sometimes in a manner that suggests a contrived ending to a mystery - hence The Man's jokes about an Occult Police Force who regularly confound the experts and scramble our brains. The cub could always have teleported ... your guess is as good as ours. Reconstructed from Daily Express, 7 Jan 75 (Cr: Steve Moore.); and Weekly News, 18 Jan 75 (Cr: Nigel Watson.)

They certainly seem to be coming out of the woodwork, this year. Council rat-catcher Bill Crane was asked by his employers to investigate a tip at Langham, Norfolk, for bigger game. A lorrydriver had reported seeing two lion cubs "romping in the rubble" on 15 Jan 75. Crane says: "I haven't found any unusual footprints. I think it's a bit of a tall story - the animals were probably foxes." Ho hum! Practical jokers and liars tend to be conventionalists, as Fort reflected, and not known for their exceptional flights of imagination beyond certain standard patterns of exaggeration. A hoaxer, these days, would get more fun out of a "bomb-warning" - any ordinary liar, we feel, would have blown this incident up into a full grown lion or whatever -- the choice of 'two' and 'cubs' seems to us anyway to be the suggestion of a pretty tame hoaxer at best, and so deserve some token seriousness . We must accept that there have been foxes on tips - perhaps these were - but perhaps not also. The Sun, 16 Jan 75.

The Daily Mirror (22 Jan 75) described Britain raging under a "wild pets storm" - we've noted the odd breezings of bear, scatterings of cats and intermittent outbreaks of baboons, but a 'storm' might be going too far. Except...in the corridors of Westminster, MP, Peter Templemore's cry of: "Sooner or later someone will get kil-' led " brought the usual huffing from red-faced politicians. This was in reaction to an incident in Acton, London, in which an estranged husband dumped his pet puma in the backgarden of his ex-house, with a note saying he had nowhere else to keep it. Police & RSPCA had a 2hour struggle to rescue the wife and terrified kids. In November 74, a man strolled into the Farm House pub, South Harrow, with a puma on a lead. After a while, the uneasy locals asked if he wouldn't mind leaving. He got up to comply, but the puma, with less decorum went berkserk (as it's said round here). Said the landlady, after the cat had demolished the bar, tables, many glasses and the chair-upholstery: "It took the man 15 minutes to get the puma out of the pub and into his car, during which it tore off the man's glove and ripped open his hand." Then as the puma continued to vent its fury on the car's seats, it was clear the man could not get in and drive. The police were called and they towed puma and car away. Later the man was charged with being drunk and incapable. Daily Mirror, 1 Nov 74. And in between the above two events was a running-filler in the press, about an idiot who had a puma in his backgarden for kung-fu practice. We didn't bother to collect that one. The point of this is that there seems to be many private individuals, not just private zoos who are keeping all kinds of wild animals that can escape with relative ease - and no registration or legislation to control it as yet -- not even a census of imported animals is available...and ex-owners,afraid of their neighbour's wrath, or of prosecution for illegal importing (ie. by-passing quarantine requirements)   don't tell of escapes. Fort only knows what's out there in the countryside.

Lastly, we have the latest on the notorious "Surrey Puma" - if indeed it is one animal, or even a puma at all. This latest sighting was hailed by the police as the first "reliable" evidence, being casts of footprints and hairs found on a fence, apparently forgetting all the previous times they have obtained casts of prints and hairs from fences. This newest evidence was generated on the morning of 6 March, at Brooks Green, near Horsham, Sussex, when two girls, out riding in a field, were thrown when a large cat-like animal crossed in front of them, startling the horses. The manager of a nearby caravan site also saw what he described to the police as a puma. Later the same day, police with guns and dogs searched the area, finding the hairs and the prints, which showed "definite cat-like characteristics suggesting a weight of 90 to 120lbs. Two days later (8 March), a woman at Barns Green said she had seen the animal by the M23 at Pease Pottage, the other side of Horsham. And the mystery was compunded (or compounded, even) by a phone-call the the West Sussex County Times received saying the police and RSPCA had caught the puma by Donkey Bridge, a mile north of Brooks Green - this was later denied by both authorities. Again it is also noted that there has been a conspicuous absence of killings or livestock attacks that would be expected from a normal puma. Nothing else is seen or heard - and time soon erodes that earlier certainty into doubts and finally back to good old fashioned disbelief. Two weeks after the initial sighting,a lullaby is printed to smooth our slide into the Land of Nod, about a man who has a 10-month-old puma as a pet on his farm at Southwater, not far from the Greens, Brooks and Barns - but even here there is no suggestion that this one, so conveniently near, was responsible for the incident. So having popped out of nowhere to keep us on our toes - silence... and a perfect mystery capped perfectly. From: The Sun, 7 Mar 75 (Cr: Phil Ledger.); the West Sussex County Times (Horsham), 7, 14 & 21 March 75 (Credit: JDM Start.)

SPRINGS IN THE AIR.

The Sun, 10 July 74. That a wallaby was caught by police on the 9th, after causing chaos in the High Street, Kinson, Hants. We have notes of sightings of wallabies (or kangaroos) in Sussex, (May 1969), and Kent (Aug 73) - and 2 wallabies are known to have escaped from Heathfield Safari Park, Sussex in late Aug 73 ((please see my article in INFO 13 for further details on sources

- sorry to keep bringing that up, but I guess that's what reference articles are for.)) This latest capture might have been one of those two that escaped, but it's plain that there were wallabies in the British countryside before that escape -- for example there is known to be a breeding colony of Tasmanian wallabies established in the Derbyshire Peak District since about 1940, and another is believed to exist in the Ashdown Forest in Sussex, which could account for the sightings in that area. We have the full references to these colonies, but in deference to the request of the authors to minimise publicity, to allow the colonies to flourish in peace, we won't publish the details, and hope you'll agree with the sentiment. But if any of you come across more sightings we shall be pleased to print them since we have a soft spot for marsupial immigrants.

5 Nov 74 and another bounder, a kangaroo this time, gave the good people of the Hampshire/Berkshire border a few coronaries as it leapt over hedges into and out of the small country roads. Many phoned the police who treated it as a joke until Donald Rayfield, the owner of a small private zoo at Baughurst, near Basingstoke, called with the news that 5yr-old Prufrock had gone over the wall. "He will feed on branches and graze, so he'll be all right until we catch up with him," he added. This is from the Sun, 6 Nov 74. I'm not sure, but I think I saw a note in a local paper to the effect that Prufrock had been tied down (Sport), but (blush) I actually forgot to cut it out -- Oh! Abject Shame!

Well, that's got us off to a good start - so see if you can swallow this one. That a 5ft kangaroo was pulled into his boat by an Australian fisherman on 22 Nov 74. He was more than a mile out from the Victoria coast and could not account for what the 'roo was doing out there. Daily Mirror 23 Nov 74 (Cr: Steve Moore.) That fair reminded us of the pig that was found swimming 15 miles out from the beach at Miami, Florida (see INFO 11, p10) -- some folks go to extraordinary lengths to avoid fares.

An extraordinary epic has been playing live at "50 locations in Indiana and Illinois" (New Scientist, 26 Dec 74.) - and the Midwesterners therein experiencing that vertiginous feeling familiar to the wallaby-spotters of Kent and Sussex - nothing wrong with their vertical holds on reality, but the intrusions of a $4\frac{1}{2}$ft, 100lb kangaroo. The first reports are of 2 Chicago policemen who cornered it in an alley on the city's northwest side - but it escaped because the officers were afraid of being bitten and contracting rabies. But they fought, and after giving them some good clouts,with one bound it was free. "Too bad we didn't have our nightsticks there, then we really could have hammered him," gritted one 'roo-ful cop ((sorry about that)) who no doubt enjoys the resisting of arrests bit. The general concensus on the date of this event is 13 Oct, though the New Scientist says 18 Oct. In the days that followed there were at least six more sightings, and a noting that no one had reported any loss of a kangaroo. San Francisco Chronicle, 19 Oct 74. Credit: Loren Coleman.

Ace columnist Dermot Purgavie of the Daily Mail (23 Oct 74) reported: "He was last seen hopping along Mango Avenue heading south," and that the cops, "have this plan to immobilise him by raising his tail off the ground so he loses stability. I'd like to be there to see that." So would we all. (Credit: Steve Moore.)

A hiatus until - A Plano, Illinois, policeman was said to have nearly hit a kangaroo that landed in front of his car in a road in Riverview on the night of 1 November. Then, according to the Chicago Sun Times (9 Nov 74), the magic marsupial pulled off a neat trick. On Saturday night (2 Nov) about 9.00pm, 3 Plano youths said the animal jumped into Shafer Road from a nearby field, sat in the road, then leapt a 5ft fence to vanish into a wood. Onehour later, the kangaroo (or a kangaroo) was seen 40miles away on Chicago's southwest side, where a young couple were walking down New England near 56th when the bounder took an enormous leap in front of them and sproinged off down New England towards Archer ((yes, dear heart, they do talk like that)). Then at 1o'clock early Sunday, 2 friends riding along Montrose, between Cumberland and East River Road, saw it leap from a two-legged stance into Schiller Woods. It was described, for the first time in these reports, incidentally, as "gray in color, with big black legs."(Cr: Richard Crowe.)

Then a trucker, identified only by his radio-code "Lone Wolf", was driving on a rural road near the Fox River, about 40 miles southwest of Chicago, near Millbrook, on the 5th, and radioed a tow-in service-station in Plano that he had spotted what he thought was a kangaroo keeping company with 3 deer. He trailed the deer and the "other animal that definitely is not a deer - its prints in the mud of the field are much different", but lost it as it headed toward the river. Decatur (Illinois) Herald (or Review), 5 Nov 74. (Credit; Loren Coleman.) ((Speaking of codenames, this is the stamping ground of the enigmatic industrial saboteur and pollution-fighter known only as

"The Fox"- about whom we shall have to be more expansive some other time.))

From here on, all restraint is abandoned - this sighting followed by a glimpse elsewhere shortly after (which could be accounted for, according to the Chicago Sun Times, if it bounded from place to place at speeds of over 30mph), has given rise to stories, then beliefs, in several roos on the loose. See Daily Mail, 14 Nov 74.(Credit: Steve Moore.) for a garbled report suggesting one in Chicago, one with the 'herd of deer", and one in Indiana. Indiana? Where did that come from? -- Oh well! Cue for New Scientist, 26 Dec 74 (Credit: JDM Start.) to comment sagely, and no doubt for our own good: "That the affair is a healthy joke made up by the Chicago policemen and continued by a subtle kind of mass hysteria." Ho, healthy ho! but what do they mean by "Mass hysteria" - "People who see some large animal on

the loose tend to assume its a kangaroo because they've heard or read about the animal."

This fatherly concern from on high, we treat with the same disdain that we as children resisted all attempts to civilise us - jumping into puddles and eating worms is much more fun. And who will comfort the anguished Demon Purgavie as he cries with delight: "This has got to stop! There are kangaroos cavorting all over the Midwest, a cow is loose in Brooklyn, and now there's a herd of deer (presumably deaf) that has decided to settle just off the runways at Detroit airport." Daily Mail, 20 Nov 74. Credit: Steve Moore.

We don't know if its the same event - no it can't be really - but a 350lb bull-calf was found romping down a mile of traffic-laden street in the Bronx on 14th Feb 75 -..er..not the same event at all, is it? Do cattle get loose in New York all that often? It seems this one was found near apartment buildings where, last year, an "occult group" decapitated a goat and 54 other animals - so it's assumed that this bull-calf was a survivor of their managerie - but as to how it is supposed to have stayed alive, and without being discovered till this incident is not ventured. Someone else supposes that it could have falled off the back of a lorry. We think he's been listening to scientists. Daily Mail and Daily Express, 15 Feb 75.

MYSTERY ANIMALS.

Now for our stars - though we shouldn't allow ourselves favourites, or if it is illusions we are recording what basis is there for preferring between things that exist only insubstantially?

A "strange striped creature - half cat and half dog, " was seen loping across Western Avenue, Branksome, on the outskirts of Bournemouth, at 3.30am, 7 April 74. It was seen for a moment as the headlights of a car turning into that road from Bury Road swept across it. The driver, Mrs Joan Gilbert, said: "It was the most peculiar animal I have ever seen. It had stripes, a long thin tail, and seemed to be all grey, though it might have had some yellow on it. Its ears were set back like a member of the cat-family, and it was as big as a medium-sized dog. It was thin, and it definitely was not a fox." Checking later through an animal book she found the nearest resemblance to be...a Tasmanian marsupial wolf.

I don't know about you, but several chords were struck in me. A Tasmanian wolf in the UK? Sounds highly unlikely, by ordinary standards. I don't know if any are in captivity at all, and would certainly be so rare that dealing or importing concerns would have notified of any escape immediately - if they had one. It is confined to Tasmania, though remains have been found on mainland Australia, and Heuvelmans writes: "Its existence is no longer in doubt - though it is still not officially recognised." (On the Track of Unknown Animals, Ch 8.) -- the impression given being that no zoo or institution has any specimens, living or dead, and that it is so rarely seen suggests its skill in vanishing whenever Man comes nosing around. Heuvelmans gives the following account from Tasmania, dated 1871 : it was "as big as a native dog; its face was round like that of a cat. It had a long tail, and its body was striped from the ribs under the belly with yellow and black." This description is remarkably concordant with Mrs Gilbert's. Incidentally, of the wolf's relative, the Tasmanian tiger-cat, Heuvelmans says: "Of all the unknown animals dealt with in this book (it is), the one nearest to being officially admitted by science..Although there is neither skeleton nor skin of it in any museum in the world..."

Can it be that an animal barely acknowledged to exist, on only a few eye-witness accounts as evidence, has turned up in southern Britain? Whatever it was that Mrs Gilbert saw, the thought is now in our minds that Tasmanian wolf fits, almost to a tee, the previously puzzling accounts of, for example, the 'Surrey Puma' in that region, particularly the odd and often reported characteristic of both cat- and dog-like attributes; or something cat- dog-and fox-like but that was definitely not a fox. Anyway, we welcome this new flavouring to an old mystery. The story is from the Bournemouth Evening Echo, 7 April 74. Credit: Stefan Mucha.

One has to expect these things, but a couple of days after typing out the above cases, Steve Moore sends us word that the Tasmanian Tiger (or Wolf or Tiger-cat — they seem to imply the same animal) has been seen again, in car headlights, like our Bournemouth supposition. But since the article, from the Sunday Times, 6 April 75, mentions many other items of interest to our subject here, we take the liberty of reproducing it in full. It was written by Celia Haddon, who is becoming a regular goldmine these days...

A CREAMY-COLOURED leopard with startlingly dark spots has been seen and photographed in the hills of Southern Israel. For the past four years Israeli game wardens had put out freshly-killed meat for the animal, which they suspected might be living nearby. Now at last a photograph has given proof of its existence and yet another "extinct" species turns out not to be extinct at all.

The Antipodes seem particularly rich in "extinct" animals. A colony of parma wallabies, once common in Australia then thought to have died out. were rediscovered in an island off New Zealand in 1965. They had flourished undisturbed there since a Victorian animal enthusiast imported them—while in Australia the wallabies were dying out.

In the same way another marsupial, Leadbeater's possum, was rediscovered in Australia in 1961. That year, the noisy scrub bird was detected and in the same area the western bristlebird came to light. Lately there have been tempting reports that the thylacine, a marsupial sometimes known as the Tasmanian tiger, has been spotted in car headlights in Tasmania again.

Smaller animals, of course, quite often just escape human observation. In Cuba and Haiti there is a small mouse-like animal called a solenodon—or at least there probably is. The last living specimen in a European zoo died in Frankfurt two years ago and its death made some people believe the solenodon was extinct. Then a year later a male specimen was caught in Cuba.

But even quite large animals may still exist hidden from men in the wilder parts of the world. In a recent book a Hungarian zoologist reported that a herd of eight wild horses had been spotted in the deserts of Mongolia. These, he claimed, were none other than Przevalsky's horses—a race that have been extinct in the wild for a generation. Or, so most people thought. Like other rarities, Przevalsky's horse may yet turn out not to be so extinct after all.

Celia Haddon

Elsewhere; from the front page of the Runcorn Weekly News of 30 May 74, comes the announcement of "The Thing of Delamere." The shadow of a "strange animal" has been seen several times slinking along backwoods paths in Delamere Forest, near Kingsley, Cheshire. Thomas Merrington, of nearby Norley, first saw it in April. "It was at night and I saw the thing in my headlights, twice." It was about 2ft tall, with a tail like a fox's brush, but in appearance "more like an Alsation dog. It wasn't a fox, I'm certain of that - and yet it had the tail of a fox." His son has also seen it, and locals have spotted it on the shores of Hatchmere lake, and on the main road between Kingsley & Oakmere. (Cr: P Rogerson)

━━━

GHOST LIGHTS &c / cont:

Lastly we have a note on something so odd that it defies all classification into even our arbitrary and somewhat flexible categories. It seems to indicate a cluster of synchronous fortean events - a fall, mystery fires in haystacks, a mobile 'corpse candle', and a mystery smell/illness that affects animals only. Weird. Roger Randle found it and sent us the account verbatim from 'A Description of Caernavonshire (1809 - 1811)', by Edmund Hyde-Hall, and published by the Caernavonshire Historical Society, being No 2 in their series of records :

"In the winter of 1694, we are told (by Pennant*) an extraordinary phenomenon was exhibited to the neighbourhood. A mephites, or pestilential vapour resembling a pale blue flame, arose out of a marshy tract called Morfa Bychan, and traversing the channel, here

8 miles wide, rested upon Harlech and its environs. Sixteen ricks of hay and two barns were consumed by its action, and the village was so poisoned that the cattle and sheep browsing upon it perished in great numbers.

The season of motion with it was night time, and for a second summer it reappeared, but less frequently and with diminished strength. The most curious facts attending it were perhaps the facility with which it was dispelled by any noise, and the impunity with which it could be traversed by human beings. Its cause is attributed, with what correctness I give no opinion, to a fall of locusts near Aberdaron, by the corruption of which the vapour is supposed to have been engendered. " (p241.)

((* Thomas Pennant: "A Tour in Wales" (1784) & "Tours in Wales" (1810).

ICE AND IRON by Wilson Tucker. Victor Gollancz Ltd; £2.50; 181pp; ISBN: 0.575.01908.5. Just as we receive another warning about the imminent Ice Age (only 10,000yrs away - Prof HH Lamb - Sunday Mirror, 13 April 75) we have this latest and long awaited novel from Bob Tucker. Some of you may be familiar with his earlier novels, particularly 'Wild Talents', which was one of the first to treat psychokinesis in a serious fashion, and as the title suggests, drew on Charles Fort's final book. 'Ice and Iron' leans even more heavily on Fortean data. It is set over a fortnight ((a pun could be indicated here)) during which a research station in mid-Canada is abandoned in the face of the advancing ice-wall, only a few hundred years in our own future. Main character Highsmith is determined to puzzle out the strange falls of primative mud-bricks, and charred corpses, found lying on the snow fields about them. This is alternated with scenes set even further in the future on the other side of the Ice Age - and I won't tell you about that, because its disclosure is part of the fun. A colleague believes this is the novel that finally "explains Fort" and I disagree strongly - one possible explanation for a small group of events, still leaves an awful lot of explaining to do. The only other improbability - the station-librarian manages to read the collected books of Charles Fort (well over 1000 pages of close-type) and mentally processes the thousands of jumbled data into usable chunks relevant to the plot, in two or so days, and without loosing any sleep! I should be so talented! Word comes to Highsmith & team that the 17th body has been found - alive...and the book is off to a good start. Don't be fooled by the RL Stevenson quote over the door as you go in: "Ice and Iron cannot be welded." - Tucker has succeeded, and made a damned good tale out of their joining.

GHOSTS - THE ILLUSTRATED HISTORY by Peter Haining. Sidgwick & Jackson Ltd; £3.75; 126pp; ISBN: 0.283.98178.4. I suppose this splendid pictorial volume is what is called a 'Coffee Table' book - being thick on the 'illustrated' and thin on the 'history'. Haining has gone to some trouble to gather as much illustrative material as possible, and this collection is both diverse and fascinating - from early engravings and paintings; stage and drama programme covers; pamphlets, cartoons and satirical commentary from a number of centuries; folklore illustrations; to

spirit photographs, the tools and effects of trickery, and the evidences not so easily explained.

The last and more 'modern' section was particularly intriguing, with many photos I'd never seen before - like the "only known photograph of a poltergeist at work" showing a walking stick hovering over a boy in bed; ghosts in and outside churches; a phantom reclining in an easy-chair. Also included is one that has puzzled me for some time - the ghostly form in a wood near Coroboree Rock, 100 miles from Alice Springs, Australia, yet it's never explained why, of all the imaginable phantoms that could be associated with an initiation site, sacred to the Abos, it should be, apparently, a tall bearded Caucasian in a long white priestly robe, sporting a Flash Gordon-type aviator's helmet. The book is well worth having for its profusion of illustrations - my only niggle being the way some of them straddle the seam in the centre when the book is opened. The text is to the point and informative despite its brevity - altogether a nice balance in content and presentation.

THE BERMUDA TRIANGLE by Charles Berlitz. Souvenir Press; £3.25; 203pp; illustrated; 0.285.62170X
THE BERMUDA TRIANGLE MYSTERY - SOLVED by Lawrence D Kusche. Published in USA by Harper & Row; $9.90. (March 1975)
POSTED MISSING by Alan Villiers. Hodder & Stroughton; £4.25; 336pp; maps & illos. (May 1975).
Britain has been bombarded in recent months by Bermuda Triangle Hysteria - the serialisation of Berlitz's book in Sunday Express (9 Feb onwards), and the double-spread in Daily Mail (7 Jan) being only a part of that exposure...so NEWSreaders will thus, if not already, know of and about this area of mystery. Berlitz begins well but lacks a logical structure - after dealing with his version of the known details, UFOs are brought in, then Atlantis and the suggestion that a giant submerged solar crystal is warping the space about the hapless victims, and then the Great Pyramid, and secret Indian manuscripts- - and as the various solutions to the mystery are compounded upon each other, Berlitz finds himself at a loss for the next step, and ends up hinting darkly at press and government conspiracies. We have not seen Kusche's book, but there is an extensive comparison with Berlitz's in the Sunday Times (Spectrum section), 16 March,

which points out considerable differences in the versions of the evidence, and errors on the part of Berlitz. Kusche, it must be admitted, is attempting a refutation of the "1000 dead and 100 planes missing" statistics - but that can only result in some real discussion of the theories.

John Grimwade

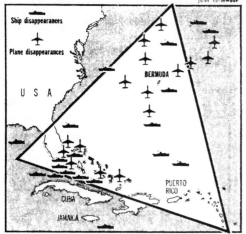

It's the age-old pitch, and the pressure is on you to side with one or another load of pre-digested, packaged opinion. Our only advice in this and similar complexities is to go to the data, and form your own opinion - granted that this is not always practical or possible. So we welcome those with no tub to thump - in this case the decision to up-date and re-issue Villiers' effort, one of the standards on losses at sea over the past century. He is quite matter-of-fact, even when the facts themselves are extra-ordinary (or perhaps because of it), eg. that at least 70 merchantmen have been posted missing in the last decade, despite sophisticated advances in communication & rescue methods. Ships are going down all over the globe - but let's face it, the only thing we can say about the B Triangle is that they are going a bit more than elsewhere.

MYSTERY OF THE ANCIENTS - Early Spacemen and The Maya: by Eric & Craig Umland. Souvenir Press; £3.25; 186pp; illust'd; ISBN: 0.285.62162.9. Scarcely any more credible than Berlitz's theories, this time the Gt Pyramid and B Triangle get hooked into the Mayan mystery. Accept if you will, that 40,000 years ago, aliens came to mine the 5th planet in our system. By bungling on a cosmic scale, they blow the 5th planet into the Asteroid condition, and retreat to their mining ventures on this Earth. Having stranded themselves here, they degenerate, losing all their knowledge, and retire from their gigantic buildings all over the world to sulk in isolation in the steamy jungles of Yucatan to await rescue by the white brother. As a scenario it leaves a lot to be desired, and is undermined further by crass and shallow reasoning, and that all the factual evidence attached thereto is so skimpily identified that in most cases it could have been invented for all we know.

Like Berlitz, the conspiracy theory crops up again, only in reverse: why are the US and USSR racing to the moon and the planets? - obviously because they know that they'll find remnants of that fabulous ole Mayan science out there - yeah! and no doubt they'll put it to the same use and blow our planet to smithereens too. Amongst other patent absurdities is that despite their crucial assertion that an alien species lives alongside us, there is no reference for or against the essential biological proof - tissue-typing, blood grouping, inter-species-breeding, etc - and if these should prove that we are 'no different flesh', what then? Complete silence. The authors believe that these Maya left things like Stonehenge and the Pyramid of Cheops to be later taken over by the locals. Stonehenge, by the way, they say, only makes sence from the air, which is utter rubbish since the computations with the use of back and foresights are clearly ground-observer orientated. The pyramids, we are told, were originally store-houses - which would be fine if the pyramids were hollow. The pyramid shape, they argue, is a Mayan signature - forgetting that until mortar and flying buttresses came along all large buildings had to assume variants of pyramidal structure. Contrary to their belief, the black meteorite in the Kaaba at Mecca, is set in a corner, and is not the cuboid building/block it is set in. We could go on.

The book also has the same fault as the rest of the von Daniken tribe output - and that is the complete disregard, and in a few cases, misinterpretation of the power and the role of spiritual and emotional forces in motivating man's ach- vements. I don't wish to make a case for man being of any significant importance, but to ascribe, as the Ancient God Squad does, all the litter of art and artifacts on earth to the tinkering and untidyness of aliens, not only smacks of the re-emergence of the old 'Deus ex Machina' (to alleviate the guilt, no doubt, now that we have banished the God of our fathers), but also makes irrelevant nonsense of all we know of man's own sentience and sensitivity and creativity.

The Umland Brothers had the chance for once to explore a unified theme (instead of the von D scattergun approach) - they even have some good ideas begging for development - but by indulging in immature sensationalism, they blew it.

STRANGE PLANET - A Sourcebook of Unusual Geological Facts - by William R. Corliss. Vol E1; 283pp; 11 drgs; ISBN: 0.9600712.3.7. $7.95 postpaid from: Sourcebook Project, Box 107, Glen Arm, Maryland 21057, USA. The mixture as before. More extracts and reprintings of the original & in some instances rare, reports of geological oddities: ringing rocks & singing sands; sunken & legendary lands off Ireland and elsewhere; the great dinosaur disaster; fairy stones and rings; geomagnetic reversals; footprints in strata; and strata that appear 'upside-down'; deluge traditions; mystery mounds and earth-heaps; 'when the Mediterranean dried up.'; boulders that wander off on their own; etc etc. My urging of the importance of this series to all researchers etc needs no further emphasis. In many cases these accounts are <u>more</u> interesting and mysterious than the conjectures of the Umland Brothers et al.

Now available inpaperback:

THE OTHER SIDE by Bishop James A Pike. Abacus; £1.10; 292pp; ISBN 0.349.12775.1. Bishop Pike's already famous account of the poltergeist like evidence of events following the suicide of his son. Fascinating as a case history of a bizarre series of synchronistic events.

THE HUMANOIDS by Charles Bowen, ed. Futura; 45p; 256pp; ISBN: 0.8600.7057.3. This now 'classic' <u>ref</u>erence collection of articles by prominent researchers on the physical and psychological aspects of the 'contactee syndrome' - and for only 45p - you lucky people.

did you see ... ?

Further to our gossip last issue about the Japanese nuclear ship, whose reactor had, in mid-voyage, to be patched up with old socks. A note in the Weekly News, 21 Sept 74, added that previously boiled rice was being used to plug the leaks of the radioactive coolant. That's progress.

'The First Observatory' by Igor Bohassian. VERTEX Vol 2, No 4, Oct 74. About the Great Pyramid.

'More things in Heaven & Earth..' WIRELESS WORLD Nov 74, p470. An encounter with and thoughts on psychometry.

'Struggle between Confucian & Legalist Schools & Ancient China's Science & Technology." by Li Chun. PEKING REVIEW No47, 22 Nov 74, pp8-13. Mentions in passing many inventions like the seismograph, and how that "gang of parasites", the Confucians kept a block on invention and scientific advances in order to preserve the status quo, by which they did very nicely thank you. Good stuff sandwiched in propaganda.

NATURE Vol 253, 10 Jan 75, p95: that the earliest record of man's presence in Britain is now pushed back 400,000 to 500,000 BP.

'Faraday and the Psychics' - Science & the Citizen section of SCIENTIFIC AMERICAN Vol 232, No1, Jan 75, pp 52/53.

'One Link that is no longer Missing' by Athene Williams. PREDICTION Feb 75. A study of the extraordinary teenage psychic Matthew Manning, and review of his book "The Link", poltergeist and Geller-effects rampant, including some curious automatic drawings (almost exact copies of Durer engravings?) See also the series on Manning in the Daily Mail, 16 - 18 Sept 74.

'All that Glitters is not God' by Timothy Ferris being a report on the first Ancient Astronaut conference (April 74) in Arlington, fitting in some barbed badinage with von Daniken on the way. ROLLING STONE, 30 Jan 75.

More Geller notes: 'The Pinball Wizard' by Ian Pollock. TIME OUT, 6-12 Dec 74. The words from the Who's opera 'Tommy' seem quite applicable: "There has to be a twist. The Pinball Wizard's got such a supple wrist. How do you think he does it? I don't know. What makes him so good?" What indeed? See also 'The Professor's Dilemma' and 'How Geller Convinced Me' by Prof John Taylor OBSERVER MAGAZINE, 6 April 75, and the following week, being publicity for Taylor's forthcoming book, 'Superminds'(Macmillan) dealing with his tests on Geller and "dozens" of kids who can do the same and more. Taylor needs to put this out himself — his paper was "thrown out" by NATURE, colleagues are getting rattier towards him and in NEW SCIENTIST (Feedback, 13 Feb 75) we learn that the Ministry of Defence was wetting its pants in fussing over a King's College contract, in case Taylor would use it to further his studies of the Geller effect. A MOD scientist was quoted: "It reads as if Taylor was going to study the production of EM radiation <u>by</u> people rather than the effect of EM radiation <u>on</u> people. We didn't want that." Isn't it marvellous! So much for MOD PSIwar conspiracies.

'Why Birds are on the Warpath' WEEKEND 12-18 Feb 75. More tales of aerial attacks.

'To Divine is Human','Kites for Reassembling God' 'Chomsky', & 'Yeats and the Magic of Power' Book reviews with very interesting side discussions of divination, sacred rites, the role of language in perception, and the use of magic ritual as a means of imaginative realisation. An action-packed issue of Times Literary Supplement, 14 Feb.

FATE & FORTUNE: <u>No11</u>: 'Ley Lines - The Magnetic Grid' by Michael Balfour. 'Haunted Versailles' by Andrew Mackenzie on the Moberly/Jourdain psychic time-trip. <u>No12</u>: Geoffrey Ashe on the mystic 'Isle of Avalon'. <u>No13</u>: 'Levitation - Illusion or Reality?' by Andrew Mackenzie. We heard that this excellent general mag will have to fold at No15, leaving quite a gap in the field.

'Is Science a Religion?' by Edward Goldsmith. An ecologist's view of teleology and ontology, and just how far modern science and technology seem to have strayed from the original conception of their usefulness - the original Frankenstein monster. THE ECOLOGIST, Vol 5, No2, Feb 75.

SCIENCE FICTION MONTHLY Vol 2, No3. Walter Gillings writes a short bio/bibliography of Eric Frank Russell, who, as you may be aware, was the mainstay of UK Forteanism in the post-war years -- and Gillings identifies much of Fort's influence in Russell's fiction and non-fiction.

'Arigo -Surgeon of the Rusty Knife' by John Fuller. READERS DIGEST, Mar 75. Gut-wrenching exploits of the famous psychic surgeon.

'Credulity and Coincidence: von Daniken in Perspective' by Jerry Palmer. TIME OUT, 7-13 Feb 75.
von D. had certainly come in for some bashing
lately, but then he just as certainly asked for
it. This being a reaction to "Gold of the Gods"
now in paperback, sh ing clearly how a gullible
public is traded on. One interesting illo shows
a rubbing of the classic Mayan tomb-carving
compared with von D's 'artist's impression', and
how by multiplying tiny differences in emphasis
of detail, he arrives at a "Mayan astronaut"
version that "looks twice as solid and machine-
like" as the original. The business of the
caves in Ecuador and some hoaxes and fallacies
are also of value. Letters from predictably outraged Danikenophiles were printed in the issue
that followed, 21-27 Feb 75.

'LDEs - Not from Alien Spaceprobes'. More info
on the long-delayed echoes that form the basis
of Duncan Lunan's alien probe hypothesis.
Research Notes, WIRELESS WORLD, March 75.

NEW SCIENTIST: 'Do Animals use Radio Telepathy
exploring a microwave basis for extra-sensory
communication in animals. NS, 30 Jan 75. -- 'A
New Medical Psychology' by Drs J Rachman & C.
Philips. A plea for more study on the subjective
& psychosomatic aspects of health & sickness.
NS, 27 Feb 75. -- 'The Quest for Gaia' by Drs
J. Lovelock & S Epton. An intriguing hypothesis
that the atmosphere of the planet behaves like
an organism. See also correspondence on the
subject in subsequent issues. NS, 6 Feb 75. --
'Promises, Promises - Health for Sale' by Dr D
Gould. A review of patent medicines & associated
legislation. NS, 13 Feb 75 -- 'The Genesis of a
Tornado' The account of the idea that driving
on the right-sides of roads can in some cases
help generate tornados. This idea arose during a
University seminar on partly-baked ideas, and a
student set out to refute it, only to end up
convinced by the evidence for it. NS 13 Feb 75.
-- 'The Temporal Dimensions of Consciousness'
The start of a series of extracts on the important & fascinating work by Dr Robert Ornstein on the
different roles of the two halves of the brain.
NS, 27 March 75. -- 'And yet it moves, Again.' by
John Lloyd, on further developments of 'Fluidyne'
derived engines. NS, 3 April 75.

THE LEY HUNTER: No 62/63, Dec74/Jan 75: 'First
Steps in a Mathematical Approach to Ley Proba-
bilities' by Bob Brown. 'Bristol Leys & Solar
Serpent Temple' by Stephen K Jenkins. No64 Feb/
March 75: 'One Man's Quest' by John Wilcock.
'Myth & Cosmos - Towards a Philosophy of Revolu-
tionary History' by Anthony Roberts. 'Belgian
Leys' by Eugene Zimmer. 'Thanet Leys' by Janet
Huitt.

Compilation Credits: Frank Adey, BR Bates, Richard Cotton, Phil Ledger, Steve Moore, JDM Start,
and Nigel Watson. Notes of anything interesting
that you come across, are always welcome, y'hear.

BIGFOOTSES: We also learn from Loren Coleman,
that the tradition of George Haas' Bigfoot Bulletin, and McClarin's Manimals Newsletter is
being continued by Bigfoot News in providing a
wide-ranging coverage of BF activities & info.
Bigfeet, now almost a specialist subject on its
own, is something THE NEWS has yet to deal with,
but all those who are interested are referred to
Peter Byrne's BIGFOOT NEWS: PO Box 632, The
Dalles, Oregon 97058, USA. $5.00 for 12 issues.

VELIKOVSKY: We recently discovered the intent
ion to establish a UK society (no name as yet)
based around "A Rational Approach to Velikovsky
and Catastrophism." Membership £5.50/year, or
£3.50/year to students & those over 65. More
info can be had from Harold Tresman, 18 Fir Tree
Court, Allum Lane, Elstree, Hertfordshire. UK.

UFO NEWSCLIPPING SERVICE sends out a 20 page
(minimum) monthly UFO compilation, plus 2 to 4
pages of Forteana. Worldwide coverage, with
translations into English - extra pages during
flaps at no extra cost. Subscriptions outside
USA are $6.00/month (minimum sub is 3 months.
$18.00/ 3 months, or $65.00 for 1 year. No month
by month payments. UFO Newsclipping Service:
3521 SW 104th, Seattle, Washington 98146, USA.
Rod Dyke, who runs the UFONS, is presently acting
as a clearinghouse for all accounts of the Mid-
west mutilations and the attendant phantom helicopters in preparation for a 'Special Report' -
so those interested should write to him as above.

Ready for take-off—the 30ft. prototype of Britain's flying saucer.

As we go to press, the Sunday
Mirror (13 April 75) features
on front page the disclosure
of Britain's first Identified
FO...but relax! It's a prototype of future 700ft dia,
800 ton, helium-filled air-
ships. The developers, John
West Design Associates, even
have plans for an aerial-hotel
with swimming-pool and port-
holed circumferential verandah.
"Hein! More gas, Wilhelm, und
ve shall ascendink be to ze
stars!" NEXT ISH: we'll have
notes on ghosts & visions;
monsters; and UFOs.

a miscellany of Fortean curiosites

THE BARMOUTH MONSTER ... 18

some recent UFOs...14

UNEXPECTED SPECTRES
& PHANTOM FACES...5

factory and road ghosts 3 ....

Colin Bord on the amazing Fortean menagerie 11

35p:$1·00

ISSN:0306-0764

10

bi-monthly notes
on Fortean
phenomena

whole no: 10
june 1975

THE NEWS is a non-profitmaking bi-monthly miscellany of Fortean news, notes
and references; and is affiliated to the International Fortean Organisation (INFO)
in continuing the work of Charles Fort (1874 – 1932). THE NEWS is edited by
Robert JM Rickard : Post Office Stores, Aldermaston, Berkshire, England.

SUBSCRIPTIONS : 1 year (6 issues) : UK : £2.10. USA : $6.00. All
other countries use dollar equivalent. Single issues : 35p / $1.00. Back issues
(if available) : 40p / $1.15. Current INDEX free to subscribers, otherwise 20p/
60¢ each. Cheques, POs, IMOs etc. make payable to RJM Rickard, not THE
NEWS. All overseas subscribers should add 10% to the total if paying by cheque,
to cover the banking exchange commission and charges.

INFO's 3rd ANNUAL CONVENTION -- FORTFEST 75.

This year held in Chicago, at the Sheraton
Oakbrook Motor Hotel, 1401 West 22nd St, near
O'Hare International airport, over the period
8 to 10 August. The GOH is John Keel, who'll talk
also on the subject of his latest book THE MOTH-
MAN PROPHECIES. Other speakers will include: Dr
Roy Mackal (Univ. Chicago) on the searches for
the denizens of Loch Ness et al; John Carlson
(Univ. Maryland) on Archeoastronomy; Gene Philips with a slideshow on ET visitants; Stuart
Greenwood (Univ. Maryland) on Ancient Astronaut
theme; Jerome Clark on Forteana & Magonia; Joe
Troiani on "Voices on the Tapes", evidence of
the Raudive effect; Christof Friedrich (author of
UFOs: NAZI SECRET WEAPON?); Gordon Melton on Con-
tactees and the origins of their revelations;
Loren Coleman on American monsters and ABSMs;
and quite possibly a whole lot more. There will
also be a chance to experience Richard Crowe's
special nighttime 'Ghost Tour of Chicago'.
Registration: INFO members....$12.00.
Non members.....$ 7.00./day.
Students........$ 5.00./day. + ID.
For more information on the whole bag of worms,
Phone: Richard Crowe (312) 767-4481.
Paul Willis (703) 920-7120.
Or write to INFO, PO Box 367, Arlington, Va22210,
USA. Your Editor, who has had a dramatic con-
version on the road to cynicism and who now be-
lieves in Good Faries, will be travelling to the
States to attend the FEST, and looks forward to
it very much indeed. See you there!

KASPAR HAUSER.

We learned recently that the West German
official entry at the Cannes film festival was
an interpretation of a subject that interests us
very much indeed. Called "EACH FOR HIMSELF & GOD
AGAINST ALL : The Enigma of Kaspar Hauser.", and
directed by Werner Herzog. So you can imagine
our pleasure on learning that it was awarded the
'Special Jury' Prize. No doubt, as with previous
films that distributors like to lable 'Art' films
this will never appear on the commercial circuits
-- but keep an eye on your local cinema clubs, or
if you have an 'Arts Lab' or similar in your area
or indeed any society of your own, pressure them
into hiring it. The only thing we know about it
is that it is centred around the political theories of Hauser's origin, and that he was kept and
reared in the dungeons of Nuremburg Castle before
his puzzling appearance in an equally puzzled
world.

A COMPLETELY REVISED EDITION OF FORT'S WORKS.

Your Editor, and X in Canada, are co-editing
a complete reappraisal of the four books of Charles Fort. A large working index and a complete
bibliography of CF's sources have already been
completed - work is now in progress in checking
out every single reference in the quest for accuracy. Dover (in USA) have recently re-published
the 1941 Fortean Society edition, but sadly they
have ignored or missed the opportunity to correct
all the errors in the text, and to improve the
arbitrary and virtually useless index therein.

Our new revision will not only update the text, but correct many of the minor errors made by Fort; and include as many of the illustrations to which Fort referred as is possible to locate and feasible to print. We may even include some additional material, eg extracts of sources to which CF refers, that are not gone into in the text, etc etc. It is our aim to be as complete and as accurate as possible, making this the definitive sourcebook on Fort - so, we want to throw out an open invitation to any of you who have followed up any of CF's sources and found something that needs correcting. Please write to the Editor at the above address, or X at Box 1598 Kingston, Ontario K7L 5C8, Canada. Thanx to all!

CIRCULATION AND SUBSCRIPTIONS.

Our only way to a healthy existence is too increase our circulation. There is nothing to compare with a personal recommendation to anyone you think might be interested in our work. Other than that, if you know of any local head- or book-shop interested in taking regular supplies of THE NEWS, then put us in touch. We can give the normal trade discounts.

FACTORY GHOSTS.

Beeston, Notts. -- the ghost of a man in a cloth cap and boiler suit is scaring the life out of the girls on the evening shift at the local Plessey Telecommunications factory. They say the phantom worker walks by them and vanishes into thin air. Birmingham Evening Mail, 9 March 1971.

Luton, Beds. -- canteen staff at the Skefco ball bearing factory have asked the management to black the 'White Lady' that haunts their kitchen. Dora Rouget said: "I was standing with my back to the bakery. I sensed something behind me. When I turned round I expected to see one of the girls, but there was this white object. I didn't think about it again until one of the women saw the same thing a few weeks later." Tina Tyrell said: "I was terrified when I saw the ghost. I went white myself and started shaking. I was washing my hands when this figure appeared and walked into the cloakroom. I went across and looked in but there was nothing there." Other workers claim to have seen the ghost and have asked permission to call in a medium. They believe it is the spirit of a former workmate who died nine years ago. London Evening News, 23 Nov 1972.

Soham, Cambs. -- the managing director of Press Moulding Ltd sat in on the night shift after workers complained of frightening appearances of shadowy shapes. Four of the men say they have heard chairs being moved and mysterious voices talking to them, but when they turn round no one is there. They said this had been going on for at least four months. Eastern Daily Press ((precise date unknown)) Dec 1973. Cr: RA Hill.

Dunston, Northumberland — the Raine Engineering Co Ltd of Dunston, near Gateshead, have a haunted toilet, and no one feels the cold flushes more than the early morning cleaner, Elizabeth Liddle, and several grown men are said to be afraid to go to the toilet alone. Mrs Liddle said: "I heard an awful scream like a boy falling to his death. It was so eerie I couldn't sleep for nights." She has also heard toilets flushing by themselves, and the locked doors in reception banging shut. Other workers swear they have heard the name 'Maria' shouted, and thumps and whistling sounds when no one was around. Unlike the previous story though, the management is definitely not amused. The MD, James Morgan, said: "No one has been killed in the factory. One man was injured while the factory was being constructed, but he eventually died in hospital. This is awful - the whole thing is ridiculous. If these people are spiritualists they should do it in their own time, not in the work's time. We have enough problems as it is. Stories like this are in very bad taste." The (Newcastle) Journal, 1 Nov 1974. Credit Paul Screeton.

Ilkeston, Derbys. as gloom mounts and crises threaten from all quarters; and as car-stickers with the slogan "Will the last person to leave the country please switch out the lights." begin to proliferate - have no fear. Santa is not dead. But is he the ghost of a man in rolled up shirt sleeves that has been seen working away furiously in a toyshop in Ilkeston? The Sun, 20 July 74.

SOME FOREIGN GHOSTS.

Caracas, Venezuela. — a ghost of a 'Dancing Cowboy' is making life a misery for the night-watchmen at the Prefect's Office, Eastern Caracas - driving them caracas, you might say, then again you might not. The ghost appears dressed in a pure white 'liqui liqui' ((a typical Venezuelan suit - it says here)) with trousers rolled up peasant-style, roaming through the corridors and grounds of the office. Chief Inspector Jose Rami-rey Noriega said: "One night I saw the man jump from the roof into the patio. A few seconds later he was dancing and laughing. Then he headed for a tree in the garden and...puff, he was gone." Nor-iega, described as a serious-minded detective, has taken much leg-pulling about this. Earlier in October, two plainclothes cops swear they saw a similar figure also performing dances in the Old Colonial building. Noriega's colleague, Detect-ive Roberto Rodriguez, added: "I was standing in the patio the other night when I saw that crazy dancing cowboy wearing the same 'liqui liqui'. He stopped. Suddenly he jumped over and hit me in the chest. Before I could slap back, he ran to the tree and just faded away." Shades of Spring Heel Jack! A local elderly lady remembered an incident many years before about a group of row-dy cowboys who lived near the area. One liked to dance with his trousers rolled up. "But one night they fought with knives and the 'Dancing Cowboy' was one of two men who died," seh said. Hmmmm, why wait all these years, and what happened to the other man/ghost? The last words came from the Prefect, showing that officialdom is much the same the world over: "My men on the night shift seem to have taken some poor quality rum. Otherwise, what they say about the phantom does not make sense." Manchester Evening News, 11 November 1969. Credit: Peter Rogerson.

Empangeni, South Africa. — A series of 'gho-stly' incidents has convinced Mrs Suzette Havenga that the house she moved into in October is haun-ted by a woman who was murdered there only a few months before. Mrs Elsje Mathee was stabbed to death and her youngest son fatally wounded, died in hospital later. Mrs Havenga said: "I was cleaning the house a few days before we were to move in when our servant told me that a woman had been murdered in the lounge and her baby son stabbed. I immediately phoned my husband and told him I wanted another house. He said I was being childish." The first incident happened three weeks (prior to the news reports) while she was sitting in the lounge with her son; her husband in the backyard. She heard light footsteps pass her, and seeing no one, screamed. When her hus-band came running, he said he felt a coldness there. Then followed door bangings, more foot-steps, and mysterious drops of water leading from the fridge up into the passage, in the weeks that followed. Their servant, Emily Mtetwa, said she saw the figure of a white woman enter a room where Mrs Havenga's son was sleeping, and lean over him. Since an exorcism was too expensive at R75 a throw, they were arranging for prayers to be said at a local church, in the hope that

the perturbed spirit be "laid to rest." From the South Africa Daily Mail, 7 Nov 74; & South Africa Sunday Times, 10 Nov 74. Credit: CJ Holt-zhauser.

ROAD GHOSTS.

Chetwynd, Shropshire. — Within minutes of each other, two drivers made seperate midnight calls to local police about a ghost on the part of the A41 near Chetwynd, Newport, Shrops. They said they had seen a ghost dressed in a white sheet walking along the pavement outside the parish church at Chetwynd, cross the road, walk along a path, then turning into the churchyard through an archway, vanishing as mysteriously as it appeared. One of the drivers said: "I've nev-er had such a scare. Anyone with a nervous temp-rament could have had a nasty accident." His wife recalled that a Madam Piggott used to haunt that churchyard after she died in childbirth. It's funny how there always seems to be a con-venient local legend to link to the present. It is rare that you get such continuity established to any satisfaction, and it usually seems that these stories are sorted out, deliberately or other wise, because that's the way tradition has it. Daily Mail, 11 June 1969. Cr: Peter Rogerson.

Sassari, Sicily. — another version of a classic situation: Luigi Torres, driving home one night on his motobike, stops to give a lift to a girl. She is cold, so he gives her his coat, and on dropping her, says he'll call on her the next day. He does so, asking for the return of his coat. The woman who answers the door says her daughter died three years previously. Luigi staggers off, stunned. He drives to the cemetery, where he locates the grave by the photo of the girl that rested on it - the face of the girl he met the previous night. Now, Luigi is said to be slowly recovering from severe shock after seeing his coat draped over the grave. Sunday People, 11 March 73. Credit: Nigel Watson.

A Taxi, Westmorland. — Cabbie Derek Halli-well was driving along the Lonsdale road between Kendal and Kirkby in his empty taxi, when he glanced in the mirror and saw a woman on the back seat. He stopped and looked round, but there was no one there. He hadn't driven another mile be-fore he saw the woman again in his mirror. It's easy for us in our armchairs to be superior - but we've all done silly, inexplicable, even pointless things when we're in a spot. Derek wiped his mirror. My mother speaks several deci-bels louder when she talks to anyone with some kind of infirmity, like a broken arm. Derek wiped his mirror - but the image of the woman in the back seat was still there. "I went cold all over for 10 minutes. I'm convinced there was someone sitting there." Then she vanished again. "I do not believe in ghosts and I think there must be some mechanical explanation. I admit my dogs have refused to travel in the car and some pass-engers have felt cold and uneasy they told me afterwards." The expected groping in memory and history...a woman was killed in the taxi when it hit a milk-tanker in the Lonsdale road; or that's the way they remember it now. Janet Bord's little book GHOSTS has an amazing picture taken by a woman of her husband sitting in a car - and in the backseat can plainly be seen an elderly lady who, the woman claims, is her mother who had died only a week before the shot was taken. We don't know which is the more shocking, haunted cars, or a phantom mother-in-law backseat driver. Sunday People, 14 July 74. Credit: Nigel Watson.

Maidstone, Kent. -- and another ghostly hitch-hiker. Richard Stodholme, lead guitarist with the group 'Chicory Tip' was driving back to London after a night's work and stopped to pick the girl up near the top of Blueberry Hill, 4 miles north of Maidstone. "She asked if I would give her a lift to West Kingsdown. It was on my way, so I agreed." He took the girl's case and put it in the car. "During the journey she said very little, but asked if I would call at her parent's house at Swanley, further along the route to London. She gave me their address, and I dropped her off." The rest is as expected. The girl's father answers the door, saying their daughter was killed in an accident two years earlier, at the spot Richard picked her up. All he could think was that he had been the victim of a cruel hoax. "It wasn't until some months later that I read in a Kent newspaper of other strange happenings at the spot that I began to believe I had driven a ghost in my car. I touched the girl. I

took her bag from her and helped her into the car - there was nothing unusual about it. No peculiar sensations of coldness," he exclaimed. We learn that the mystery hiker has been picked up a number of times at the same spot, and several drivers have called at the address in Swanley with similar stories. "Recently" a driver believed he hit a girl at the top of the Hill, covered her body with a blanket and went for help. When he returned with police, the blanket was on the road with no body to be seen anywhere. Reveille, 9 May 75. Credit: Nigel Watson.

Poundstock, Cornwall. -- not exactly a road ghost, but Richard Stodholme's bafflement at the solidity of his ghostly hiker at the time, prompted us to dig this one out of the files, since we don't think it's had much of an airing. Ivor Potter attended a funeral service at Poundstock parish Church on 2 March 71, when "for about 4 minutes, I saw a priest I assumed was going to take part in the service, standing beside the vicar in the porch. We even wished each other 'Good afternoon'. It was only later I discovered he did not exist." The vicar told him that a priest was murdered at the high altar in 1357. Said Ivor: "I always thought they were supposed to be misty, gossamer creatures. But the ghost was absolutely solid. He answered me back and I walked all round him." Daily Express, 3 March 71.

Cont. on p 10.

One of the great mysteries of Man, if I may venture a humble opinion, is his facility for recognizing pattern and meaning in the incessant welter of signals arriving at the brain. Just how this is done, and the relationship of percepts and concepts, is perhaps the major bone of contention between the opinions of the various schools of learning and child psychology. This problem is particularly relevant to many of our studies, in that it is central to the issue about what constitutes 'Reality'. Our society has evolved a distinctive way of looking at the universe, which achieves its definitive expression in the edifice we call Science. Indeed such is our conditioning that we are often genuinely shocked or surprised to find any evidence or experience that suggests there are other 'Realities' or ways of looking at the world around

us; that Science is not the only world-view, nor a particularly complete one. Our records purport to be accounts of things which conflict (at times) with the general scientific consensus of 'reality', most of them seeming quite real to the percipients at the time. We have no room here to go into the complex arguments, but there is a growing feeling among the more adventurous writers on Fortean mysteries, that 'Reality' is (or can be) conditioned by individual will, and that many of our phenomena (eg Ghosts & UFOs) are subjective manifestations, not of the 'real' world. But this assertion fails to take into account the well-authenticated material evidence at the scenes of the manifestation.

At the other end of the spectrum stands modern Science, leaning its not inconsiderable influence and experience into the scales on the side of the objective nature of phenomena. The subjectivity or objectivity of phenomena is of course an ancient philosophical chestnut, against which better heads than ours have cracked with little gain. In our favouring of the principle of the continuity of all things, we accept that we have continuity of Mind and the objective 'external' universe - but who, even in these days, can tell us what mind is, and where the one ends and the other begins. Experience with 'life' processes in other areas, suggest a two-way relationship of mutual adaption between Mind and Universe - what JC Pearce calls 'mirroring' (see THE CRACK IN THE COSMIC EGG.)

The standard disclaimers that rain down upon those who have experienced a 'different' form of reality from the accepted norm, whether objective (eg a rain of blood & flesh) or subjective (eg precognition) of "You must have been seeing things!", "It's all in the mind!", or "Have another drink and it'll go away!" can no longer be justified, even if they ever were, least of all by anyone calling himself a scientist. There is no getting around the fact that ultimately all information is perceived subjectively. To admit that information between, say, eye and brain can be interfered with, deliberately or otherwise, by forces external to that individual, is to rock the whole scientific boat, beacuse it brings into doubt whether we can ever know that anything is as we perceive it - whether we can be sure of anything at all. Small wonder the whole subject is rarely raised, and even less investigated.

Most of you will have heard of the curious effects that Ted Serios is able to do with film sealed into cameras - somehow imprinting a mental image onto that film in a paranormal way ((see Lyall Watson's SUPERNATURE for a general rundown; and Jule Eisenbud's THE WORLD OF TED SERIOS for the original study)). The stories that follow are of images that have turned up unexpectedly... perhaps they are the product, in some subliminal fashion, of their discoverers, like the Serios effect - perhaps not? Above all they show how fundamental the objective/subjective relationship is to many areas of our Fortean phenomena - and any theory which does not take this into account can be said to be failing to be 'realistic'.

THEIR FACE IS THEIR FORTUNE.

On Sunday 6 Feb 1972, the News of the World printed this photo of a face, or faces, alleged

The ghost face

to have appeared on a stone floor of a cottage in the village of Belmez de la Moraleda, South Spain. ((We have only this small indistinct copy, but it should give you some idea.)) In the reddish-brown stains are said to be the faces of a bearded man, a woman and a child. The same paper the following week (13 Feb) published reader's letters saying what they saw in it:-

"If you turn it upside-down the face of a curly-headed child is seen."; "As each face uses the same mouth, both are evidently trying to be heard."; "I shaded parts in lightly and quite a number of faces appear."; "To the right there is a teddybear. Higher up a man and woman are joined together - the man seems to be wearing a crown."; and.."the cat sitting on the woman's shoulder."; "I see the face of a weasle or a stoat."; "There are six faces in the picture."; and lastly someone who found a significant difference in the distance between the pupil of his wife's eye and the bridge of her nose and the same distance indicated by the photo (?).

This is the sort of story that usually gets scientists grimacing in distaste - and yet a similar process has been a part of the orthodox witchcraft of psychology ever since Hermann Rorschach spilt his lunch over his desk-blotter. In the history of art too this is a time-honoured method for prompting inspiration — perhaps made most famous by Max Ernst, who as a trainee psychiatrist in an asylum was fascinated by spit-stains on a wall, and later refined the technique into rubbings of wood-grain and other textures. It seems to us that there are two issues involved - how the pattern or image originated; and then, its meaningful interpretation by viewers - and both of these get thoroughly mixed into a non-illuminating sensation.

On 27 Feb, the NOW carried a further item. 'Experts' who had been probing the mystery of the face on the floor for about a month, left tape-recorders running one night and picked up strange voices...'macabre sounds of heavy breathing', whimperings of small children and a woman's scream. The voices were said to be in a heated argument, and the following melodrama is related: a woman shouting "Drunkard! I don't want drunkards in here!" and a man's reply "Go in, woman. Go in...I don't want...My God!" It's not said what language the voices are in.

There is a parallel in sound to the imprinting of visual images onto film -- the Raudive effect, as it now seems to be identified, largely centres on the mysterious appearance of 'voices' on magnetic tape in conditions that would preclude normal recording methods. Is it possible for people to imprint verbal and visual messages on matter by some paranormal process? And is that happening here?

These questions are not answered by anything further in this present story. The Sun for 3 April 75 said it has been exposed as a giant hoax put on by the 2,103 villagers and their council. "Father Molina, the parish priest, the Mayor, the police chief, the parish clerk and the local magistrate were all in on the plot to bring prosperity to the village. They used trick photography to superimpose 13 mystery faces on a floor and faked taperecordings." Entry to the cottage was charged at 15p a head, and there was a brisk trade in souvenirs. And that seems to be that.

But we wonder. We see no need to multiply mysteries unnecessarily (to paraphrase Mr Occam), but our Fortean suspicions are always aroused by

neat manoeverings that close the book on a mystery. We have seen such actions before, and have
maintained a keen interest in the way hoaxes run
their courses. Hoaxers, like liars as Fort observed, are often of conservative imagination, preferring often as not to elaborate on some existing mystery, rather than invent a new one, since
there was bound to be some credibility or continuity there to trade upon. We wonder if there
had not been some mysterious happenings already
in the village, and that in exploiting them
things escalated beyond expectations so that
there was discomfort in high places? The Sun
report said that, over Easter, over 5000 visitors
packed the streets every day. For a little, previously inconspicuous village that could be the
size of a panic, and the beginings of yearning
for the peace and quiet of yesterday. We are
told that the experts over a month and with much
expensive equipment were completely baffled
about the nature of the image on the stone floor
and for all our knocking of 'experts' it doesn't
seem likely that the chemicals used in the trick
exposure of the image onto the stone could have
escaped attention for long - scientists being
what they are would have checked the rather obvious idea of trick-photography with some priority. But then again, who can tell? We say
the above in the full knowledge that a cleverly
aged skull with an added ape-jaw and said to be
'Piltdown Man' fooled 'experts' for about 45
years. Clearly we need more investigations.

THE UNEXPECTED SPECTRE OF CHINGLE HALL.

Amateur historian Maurice Fitchett had been
studying the 13th century Chingle Hall, near
Goosnargh, Lancs, for nearly six weeks. Then,
developing a film of interior shots taken the
same day, he saw a whitish patch of light against
the door of the old cross-beamed dining-room.
Naturally he was surprised because he could recall no such illumination when he took the photo.
Tests to determine if it was the glare from his
flashgun were also negative. The whole experience
has changed his mind about the existence of
ghosts, saying that now he definitely believes
in them. He added that he had seen a flashgun go
off by itself, heard mysterious footsteps, and
watched a heavy doorlatch in the dining-room lift
and drop, but ignored them all until he developed
the film. He showed the film to a medium and was
told the white shape was the aura of a guardian
spirit, and that the greenish tinge on some
exteria shots of the Hall could have come from a
healing spirit.

Well, whether or not that is so, we do have
a photo that shows an image where there was none
in the scene photographed (to the naked eye, at
least). Fitchett said that he tried to erase the
white patch through development processes, but it
stubbornly stayed. And when he enlarged it he
could make out a vague body shape. "I made prints
through filters but it wouldn't go. You can see
the outline of two legs and a body." This story
and photo is from the Lancashire Evening Post,
27 July 74 (Credit: DJ McAlister) and it closes

The ghostly outline is pretty
faint and may not be visible
after printing so we take
the liberty of exaggerating
the major differences in tone
in the region of the door, in
the diagram below.

with references to previous sightings of a ghost said to haunt the Hall in the form of a monk. Mrs Margaret Howarth, the present owner, also said that this was not the first time "an inexplicable shape has turned up on a photo of Chingle Hall. Once, an unaccountable 'something' appeared on a photograph taken upstairs. But I must admit I am quite surprised by the photograph taken by Mr Fitchett."

FACES GALORE.

Perhaps there was something in the air, or drinking water towards the end of March this year? Over the same period as the previous story there was a national hunt for ghost faces. The Sunday People, 23 March 75, published a photo of a lane in Devon, taken 8 years ago by Colin Tilney - in fact the hedge that bounds his cottage grounds at Dawlish. He didn't notice any face until he examined the photos nearly a year later, when he saw the image of a young girl in the hedge. About a month ago ((from the time of the SP report)) he learned that a neighbour had seen an apparition in the lane: "The shape of a young girl in the hedge. It frightened the life out of him," said Mr Tilney. She knew nothing about the photo, but said she always had trouble getting her Alsatian past the spot where the girl was seen.

So, either we have another inexplicable image imprinted onto film, or a coincidence that should belong in our synchronicity file. Mr Tilney says he finds the photo inexplicable. "I have examined it minutely and there is no question of the face being caused by a combination of light and shade or leaf formation." A spokesman for Ilford, the makers of the film, said: "Our laboratories have examined the negative and in their opinion it has

LEFT: The photo of Oliver Reed from Sunday People, 27 April 75.
TOP: Mr Tilney's photo of his hedge in Dawlish, Devon. ABOVE: Ringed in black is the face originally seen by Mr Tilney. Nos 1 and 2 were seen by some readers as human faces, No 1 having a black bushy beard. Nos 2 and 3 were seen by others as 'doggy' faces, No 3 being upside-down. (from Sunday People, 6 April 75)

not been tampered with. Nor does it appear to be a fake or copy negative." (Credit: Nigel Watson.)

The same paper on April 27th, declared that many readers had written in to say they had seen clearly another face in another picture in the same issue that carried the above Tilney photo. It was a publicity shot of Oliver Reed, sans pants watering the garden of his mansion in Dorking, Surrey. One even saw a horses head in the undergrowth of the picture. The paper had to plead not to be sent any more news of such shocking discoveries. (Credit: Nigel Watson.)

But back to Mr Tilney's photo. This also brought a flood of letters to the paper, some being printed in the 6 April issue. What astonished the paper was that so many people identified the same images. (Please see the photos, which we hope will turn out recognizably.) This report also mentioned that a Mrs M Farnan of Edgware, Middlesex, sent in a colour picture of herself, husband and daughter, showing in the background something resembling a young Serviceman. She said her son had been killed in 1942 while serving in the Royal Marines. These baffling photos will probably remain mysteries, says the Sunday People. Certainly, if no one bothers to investigate them, say we. Let's hope someone sometime takes up the challenge.

RICHARD III's BACK.

Mr Neville H Davies, of Waltham, played the lead in the Cleethorpes Amateur Dramatic Society presentation of 'Dickon', a play that is said to be free of the Tudor propaganda that blackened the reputation of Richard III. Mr Davies and his friends took the project seriously and spent many weeks in research for the parts they took on. As part of this study, Neville Davies and his wife went to vist Bosworth Field, the scene of the battle in which Richard was defeated and killed. And while there, his wife took a photo of him standing by Richard's well. When the film came back from the processers, the Davieses were surprised to find a larger-than-life figure of a man in medieval clothing "wearing the white rose of York on his breast" standing beside him. This story appears in the Scunthorpe Evening Telegraph, 24 March 75 (Credit: Nigel Watson) which reproduced a black-and-white copy of the original colour-print in which "the 'ghostly' face is a healthy pink, and the jewelled collar round its throat is a bright red."

Mr Davies assures us all that he had put a new roll of film into the camera on the day of the visit, and that this prodigy is on the first frame. "If anyone else had shown me this photo I would immediately say that it was a double-exposure." But he took no such exposure.

On the 27 March, the same paper described the efforts of their photographic staff to unravel the mystery, but they only succeeded in deepening it. "In order to reproduce the colour picture, our darkroom staff took a black-and-white photograph of the colour print. So what you saw in the paper was a reproduction of a reproduction. The 'mystery' face was still visible, however, though obviously much definition was lost." Recall Mr Fitchett's attempts to remove his uninvited patch of light without success. The paper continues: "Thoroughly intrigued, our chief darkroom technician, Colin Partis, borrowed the actual colour negative from Mr Davies. The 'image' in this is clearly visible to the naked eye. Using his most 'contrasty' paper, Colin made a black-and-white print directly from the colour negative. He got a perfectly good picture of King Richard's Well and Mr Davies standing beside it - and not a trace of the 'interloper' to be seen. A

Neville Davies at 'King Richard's Well', Bosworth. Scunthorpe Evening Telegraph, 24 March 75.

Portrait of Richard III.

shaken Colin Partis insists that this is "photographic nonsense". The image ought, logically, to show up, he says, pointing elsewhere in the picture at spots of the same colours which have 'come out' perfectly well."

A final twist came when the photo was shown to members of the 'Richard III Society' who recognized the 'image' as a known portrait of Dick. And again, Mr Davies insists that it was a new film, and not double-exposed on any frame. As the earlier report commented, even if there was a double-exposure, overlooked by the Davieses in some way, "it still is a most odd coincidence." Credit: Nigel Watson.

...A WOMAN SCORNED...

According to the News of the World, 20 April 75, at least three seperate claims had been made that the ghost of a woman, spurned by the man she loved, has returned to haunt the ruins of a monastery in Glendalough, Co Wicklow. The woman, Kathleen, who tried the patience of   Saint Kevin, soon learned to her cost that he had none as far as women where concerned. He is said to have slept on a cliff vowing "Woman shall ne'er found my bed." (or somesuch), and on being pursued by the beautiful Kathleen, whipped her with nettles and pushed her into a lake ((just doesn't have the same finesse as a frog down the front of her dress, does it?)). Anyway, a carpenter, Leslie Armstrong found that pictures of himself and his fiancée Emily Browne, taken at the scenes thereabouts, included the image of a woman wearing a red shawl or dress in one of them. They are certain there was no-one about when they took them. Also mentioned is a Mrs Everette Chisamore of Alberta, Canada, who "claims to have a photo of the legendary woman in red." There are no other details, nor any reproductions of the photos.

Cont from p5:

A COUPLE OF ANIMAL GHOSTS.

Hurst Green, Sussex. — a letter to the Daily Mirror, 28 Jan 74, mentions that the Feetum family acquired a ghost cat when they moved into a 200yr-old cottage. It seems that their own cat ignores it completely, but the humans in the family can see it plainly. No other world-shattering observations. Credit: S Moore; R Forrest.

Motherwell, Lanarkshire. — this one smacks of student prankery, but short of looking into it we can't be sure. It seems that people with houses near the Motherwell Trotting Stadium were frequently disturbed by the sounds of a horse galloping round the track at odd times in the night. Robert Kennedy, who has put in complaints doesn't say to whom) regularly, said: "The first time I heard them, I thought one of the horses had broken out of the stables. But there was no sign of any horse, only the thud of hooves. Since then many people have heard the galloping ghost." It is said that they always stop at a point in the track where a stallion called Lucky Venture died in a track accident almost two years previously. Jim Mann and Tom Robertson, of Strathclyde Univ. somehow managed to get permission to carry out an exorcism on the track with the idea of helping Lucky Venture join those other riders in the sky. Versions of the exorcism conflict. One witness, Duncan Osbourne, said: "I expected the ceremony to be much more spectacular. It could be that they exorcised the wrong horse. Another horse died at the track earlier this year ((1974))." But according to Mann: "It was sensational. Everyone experienced a coldness in the air. The horse stopped about 50 yards from us, jumping up and down, surrounded by a blue-green light. Then I carried out my exorcism and there were no more hoofbeats that night. I think we may have been successful." In a postscript, that the newspaper calls a 'tail piece', it is mentioned that both exorcists claim to have found horse manure on the edge of the exorcism area, and swear that it had not been there when they started.   Sounds like something might be trying to tell them something. News of the World, 4 Aug 74.

THE NEWS is available from the following specialist bookshops, who also keep a wide range of titles on associated subjects:

TEMPS FUTURS:
3 Rue Perronet, 75007 Paris, France.

COMPENDIUM BOOKS:
240 Camden High St, London NW1.

DARK THEY WERE AND GOLDEN EYED:
10 Berwick St, London W1V 3RG.

ANDROMEDA BOOK Co.
57 Summer Row, Birmingham B3 1JJ.

QUEST - a magazine on various aspects of the occult and magic crafts. 35p/issue, from:
  38 Woodfield Avenue, London W5 1PA.

Cont on p24.

AMAZING MENAGERIE

by COLIN BORD

The probability that pumas slink in the
woods of Surrey, Forteans might accept
without question, but are there also to
be found wild boars and lion cubs loose
in Hampshire, kangaroos bounding through
Sussex and Kent, and leopards loping
through outer London? Reports made between 1962 and 1973 suggest that it is so
(1). The list of anomalous animals loose
in the British Isles reads like a work
on zoology. Fort has reports of lynxes
seen and shot in Scotland in 1927 and a
jackal shot in Kent in 1905 (2). The
reports of pumas seen in recent years
seem to provide a link with the widespread folklore of black dog apparitions
known variously as Barguest, Trash hound,
Shriker, Black Shuck or Pooka, depending
on which area of the country the folk
tale originated in.

But animal oddities do not confine themselves to these islands. In 1931 a hairy,
apelike creature was seen several times
in New York county (3 & 13), well away
from the north-west of the continent
where the hairy sasquatch has been seen
regularly since the 1920s (4). Nearer
the centre of the continent, in Missouri,
a very similar beast has been lurking for
many a year. He, she, it or they were
often seen in July and August 1972, when
the locals abbreviated the name of the
Missouri Monster into the more friendly
sound of Momo (5). Although these particular areas have produced many reports,
similar monsters have appeared irregul-
arly in many other localities in the U.S.

Hairy anthropoids appear not only on the
American continent. In 1832 a shaggy biped was seen in Nepal, and one more incident was thus added to the long-standing
legend of the yeti, which was well known
throughout the region. Over the years

many more sightings and some tracks have
provided cumulative evidence for the
existence of this creature (4). Further
to the south-east in Thailand and Cambo-
dia there is an old tradition of the
'Mouth Men' or Tok. The late Ivan Sanderson, in his journal <u>Pursuit</u>, quotes a
report from the area, where, in 1969,
villagers near the Mekong river had seen
two ten-feet-tall monkey men roaming the
jungle (6) A group of hunters were so
frightened that they fled without firing
a shot. Later a farmer saw two creatures
in his fields making sounds like a child
crying. A third sighting was made by a
group of guerillas, and when one of the
creatures hurled a rock at them they ran
for their lives.

From our own native Surrey puma to the
Himalayan yeti and North American sasquatch, the one characteristic that all
these creatures have in common is that
of elusiveness. They are seen briefly
by one or more witnesses, but when the
search parties, trackers and dogs go
out, not a trace can be seen other than
the occasional footprint. In many cases
the question of where such a creature
would find a sufficient food supply
cannot be adequately answered. How could
the Loch Ness monster (or even, as has
been postulated, a herd of such animals)
obtain enough sustenance within the con-
fines of the loch? And if there is a
breeding herd there, why have remains of
a dead monster never been found? These
questions apply not only to Loch Ness
but to other inland lakes in the British
Isles which are of appreciably smaller
area than the Loch and which also have
their legends and reports of monster
life. F.W. Holiday has investigated some
of the lakes in Ireland where sighting

reports and legends have originated, even to the extent of dragging some of the smaller lakes with nets, but with no positive result (7). Wales too has isolated lakes among the mountains where tales of water monsters have long been told, and the same can be said of the U.S.A. and Canada. There is a wealth of sea serpent reports, and some 580 of them dating from the seventeenth century up to 1966, from all the oceans of the world, can be found in Heuvelmans' definitive book, IN THE WAKE OF THE SEA SERPENTS (8).

Strange creatures inhabit our air space, too. Last September, while listening to one of London's new commercial radio stations, I heard a report stating than an unusual bird, later identified as a West African Crowned Crane, had been seen a number of times in the West Drayton area, on the outskirts of London (9). The local paper carried a report which stated that there had been similar sightings over the past two years (10). On the same day, some 150 miles away (as the crane flies), two birds of the same exotic species were seen on the moorlands of mid-Wales (11)* The experts' explanation in both cases was that they must be escapees from private zoos. In neither case was it likely that each expert whose opinion was published in the Press was aware of the other sighting, made at very nearly the same time. I would like to hear their explanation for the giant 15-feet-tall penguin that was seen over several months and left tracks over 13 inches long in Florida in 1948. Similar tracks up to 18 inches long have been found in many parts of the southern hemisphere (12).

In late 1966 the Ohio valley area of West Virginia, U.S.A., became a focal point for reports of an airborne manlike figure that was quickly dubbed by the media as 'Mothman' (13 & 15). The witness descriptions all agreed on a general description which indicated that the figure was usually 6 or 7 feet tall, very broad at the top but without any apparent separate head. Of greyish colour, its striking characteristic was its eyes, described as luminous and bright red, up to 3 inches across and placed near the top of the figure's shoulders. It was sometimes seen on the ground, standing by a roadside or in a witness's yard, but it was more often seen air-

* ((Colin and Janet Bord sent us their news reports on these birds. We have a file a-building on African Crowned Cranes and other exotic alien birds and winged weirdos seen in the British Isles - and we'll disgorge the lot all over our pages about a couple of issues hence - Ed.))

borne on its 10-foot span of wings which did not flap. Then it would often pursue cars up to 70 or 100 m.p.h., to the great terror of the occupants. Although many reports of Mothman exist, there is to my knowledge only one report of the bat lady of Vietnam (14). This creature was seen one night in July or August 1969 by three U.S. soldiers on guard duty. As they studied the night terrain, there floated overhead an all-black female with outstretched arms that had wings growing from them. The whole figure emitted a greenish glow but otherwise appeared to be a normal woman about 5 feet tall.

Many of these reports seem to be linked with an increase of UFO sightings in the area at the same time, notably the sasquatch and mothman reports. These latter very often occur at times of increased aerial activity of the lights-in-the-sky variety (13, 15, 16). In his book, URI, Andrija Puharich reports on the number of times that strange hawk-like birds hovered near him while there was UFO activity in the vicinity (17). Uri Geller's own view was that the birds were one of the forms adopted by the intelligences with which they (Geller and Puharich) were in contact, another such form being that of the spacecraft itself.

All these manifestations are usually considered in isolation. The Loch Ness investigators take no interest in reports of Momo, while those who study reports of sea serpents know nothing of the huge number of folktales and modern reports from all parts of Britain relating to large black dogs. If there were one centralised clearing house to collate and study all such reports, what an amazing web of worldwide paranormal activity might be revealed to us. Could it be that all the above phenomena have the same origin? So that the energy or intelligence that, in the form of an aquatic monster, slowly rises to the surface of a Scottish loch to provide an excited group of watchers with a 'sighting', may on another occasion appear in the woods of western Canada or on the slopes of the Himalayas as a hairy biped, complete with shuffling gait and rancid odour. To try and assign one source to all the phenomena mentioned would probably be an oversimplification. Perhaps some of the more solid and identifiable animals and birds could be accounted for by the little-understood, and even less believable, hypothesis of teleportation. There are a few known cases of this in ufology (18) and in the writings of Fort, though John Keel suggests that the phenomenon may be more widespread than is generally thought (19).

Conceivably, certain magnetic or atmospheric anomalies could occur naturally, and would cause unsuspecting beasts padding about their own business in the jungle to suddenly find themselves transported to the English countryside, where, after an hour or two roaming in the woods and causing a sighting and a search by the authorities, they would equally suddenly find themselves back in their native haunts, when the planetary currents went into reverse switching. This idea need not be confined to our own three-dimensional solidity. The traffic between this world and the unseen dimensions, of which we are becoming increasingly aware, could be of a two-way nature, as is suggested by the strange disappearances in that 'vile vortex' known as the Bermuda Triangle. A two-way ticket is not guaranteed, though the Rip van Winkle tales of fairy lore suggest that the waiting period over there might not be so tedious as it would seem to us, stuck in the 3-D terrestrial world.

The connection between the appearance of UFOs and monsters may be an extremely important one. As suggested by Geller (17), both forms may be a matter of convenience adopted by visiting entities from other realms. To be able to take a form that would keep mankind at a distance while at the same time arrousing his curiosity may very well suit the intentions of these intelligences. What would appear to us as an animal of the 'lower' order could in fact be a carefully monitored organic entity telepathically relaying streams of information up to the waiting UFO. And in the same way that UFOs seem to have the ability to manifest at varying densities, from the most tenuous mist-like forms right through the gamut of solidity to the most solid machines capable of crushing rock lumps as they touch down on the earth's surface, so too may these denizens of the nether regions vary their level of solidity, sometimes being heavy enough to leave tracks on hard earth, while at other times not even leaving a trace on soft mud.

The possibility that some of these phenomena have an earthly origin should not be ignored. With the upsurge of interest in and practice of ritual magic in recent years, we may be considering the results of experiments that have got out of hand. The conjuration of psychic entities and the production of seemingly solid mental phantasms are practices that have long been known to researchers into the occult, and are considered to be a cause of real danger to those without experienced guidance.

The truth, if we ever find it, would probably prove to be more involved than any of the simplistic suggestions above. Whether in our present state we could even attempt to understand it is another matter.

+++ === +++ === +++ === +++

References:

1) INFO Journal, No 13, May 1974 - 'If you go down to the woods today' by RJM Rickard.
2) LO! by Charles Fort.
3) WILD TALENTS by Charles Fort.
4) BIGFOOT by John Napier (Jonathan Cape,1972).
5) Flying Saucer Review, January 1973.
6) Pursuit, July 1969, p.54.
7) THE DRAGON AND THE DISC by FW Holiday (Sidgwick & Jackson, 1973).
8) IN THE WAKE OF THE SERPENTS by Bernard Heuvelmans (Hart-Davis 1968)
9) London Broadcasting Company, 4 September, 1974.
10) Middlesex Advertiser, 5 September 1974.
11) County Times and Express, 28 September, 1974.
12) MORE 'THINGS' by Ivan Sanderson (Pyramid Books, N.Y., 1969).
13) STRANGE CREATURES FROM TIME AND SPACE by John Keel (Fawcett, 1970)
14) Flying Saucer Review, Case Histories 10 June 1972, p.14.
15) Flying Saucer Review, January 1973 'Anthropoids, Monsters and UFOs' by J Clark and L Coleman.
16) Flying Saucer Review, No 1, 1974 - 'Berserk: A UFO-Creature Encounter' by BE Schwarz. Also Flying Saucer Review, No 3, 1974 - 'Anthropoid and UFO in Indiana' by J Clark.
17) URI by Andrija Puharich, Chap. 6.
18) Flying Saucer Review, September 1968 - 'Teleportation from Chascomus to Mexico'.
19) UFOS: OPERATION TROJAN HORSE by John Keel.

"Her unshakeable belief in God would inspire me too, if it weren't for the fact that I know she also has an unshakeable belief in the Loch Ness monster and flying saucers."

It would be impossible for our miniscule set-up to offer any degree of UFO reportage in competition with the established magazines and organisations. Indeed we have no desire to compete -- UFOlogy is such a large subject these days and served well by those mags and orgs. But stories do come our way, and so we print them here to get them recorded somewhere at least. UFOs, in our view, like ghosts, are one of the 'doorway' subjects through which the inquiring mind is brought to a wide range of closely inter-connected unorthodox studies. In our view, UFOs should not be considered without reference to all human knowledge and experience, nor without taking into account the extent of the phenomenon's relationship to the perceptual and conceptual structures of both the individual observer and of our species in general.

The reactions of humans to UFOs is in its way just as interesting as the events themselves. For instance, the Daily Telegraph, which rarely if ever prints news of sightings, did report a curious story under the title 'Martians divide Italian Town.'(18 Feb 74). Two young boys in the town of Marina Franca, near Bari, southern Italy were facing charges of "simulating a crime and spreading reports which could create public anxiety." The boys had told the police that they had seen Martians step out of a spacecraft on the outskirts of the town. A local magistrate with a reputation for unorthodox and lenient sympathies was said to be in danger of losing all his friends because of his attempts to save the two boys. An investigation into the boys' sighting was begun and then dropped, when the magistrate, Francesco di Giorgio, filed countercharges against the Martians "for violating public property by landing on it in a flying saucer." Good Grief! It just goes to show... (Credit: D Sutton.)

12 ALIENS ON ICE IN OHIO?

On Friday 11 Oct 74, a Florida radio station broadcast an interview with a 'UFO expert', Robert Carr, in which he alleged that sometime in 1948, two saucers landed in the Mojave Desert, California, and that, after being tracked on military radar, the bodies of the occupants were recovered intact and being kept frozen at the Wright-Patterson airbase, near Dayton, Ohio. And when this was repeated on other news-stations, it caused quite a stir, as you can imagine. There were immediate denials from the Air Force - and the fact that such denials were expected as part of a general suspicion of a cover-up, only confuses the issue further.

As reporters followed the smell - Carr is revealed as a 65-year-old retired professor of mass communication (State University of Florida), and a "sometime script-writer", and that he was being interviewed as promoting a 'Flying Saucer Symposium' to be held in Tampa the following month. He had kept quiet about this startling story for some time because his job as a teacher forced him to stay "responsible".

Whether this was a planned stunt or not, Carr is suddenly in great demand, as calls jam the switchboards of newspapers and stations in requests for more information. If our two US sources are any indication, that must have been something. Carr said that searchers had found the two crashed UFOs, and discovered 12 bodies inside, "dead as a result of decompression when the windows of their spacecraft cracked." They were 3ft tall, well-muscled, with blue-eyes and military-style cropped blond hair, and fair skin weathered by "the ultraviolet rays they encountered during their space-travel". They were moved to the Wright-Patterson base under tight security in 1950, Carr said, the government keeping quiet for fear of public panic.

All this sounds too good to be true, involving all the standard elements of "nuts and bolts" type stories. By the time it got to the British Sunday papers, there were further details. That a cloak of secrecy hid the comings and goings of experts to the base, all sworn to keep their mouths shut. "A surgeon who conducted a post-mortem was said to have been absolutely stunned by the beings...For little men they certainly had big brains. These were more advanced than the brain of any living human being on Earth." This kind of statement usually gets up our nose. The use of the word 'advanced' can only be justified if you are comparing, say, two stages in a continuous evolution. What they mean perhaps is simply 'different'. The English paper continues: "Reporters at the radio station (?) have already come up with more information. They say the frozen bodies of the 12 spacelings are now in a maximum security base in Alabama. And they claim that psychologists let into the secret are under close guard at another base in New Mexico.

But nobody appears to know what happened to the spaceship." No mention is made of how Carr came by all this highly secret information; no apparent reason why he should be called in on any investigations, except the seed of something... "The government was prepared to let the secret out over a 6-month period after taking advice from social psychologists about the effects of revealing the truth." Who said this? Carr himself!

The perennial argument that the US authorities are supressing information on UFOs has had considerable knocks these days -- and surely most of its credibility should have vanished in the wake of Watergate. We don't doubt that there are cases where info has been sat upon, but to speak of organised conspiracy is to ignore the practicalities in structures that size riddled with inefficiencies, administrative anomalies, and general human error. One newsman, who knew Carr personally, said publicly that Carr was heading "for a rip-off" by promoting interest in his symposium, but this warning was soon forgotten in the raucus hunt for the aliens. A spokesman for station CKLW, Detroit, said: "We believe the story is true and we're not the only ones. The government doesn't want to tell us about it because the alien ships were controlled by anti-gravity power which the US government has been trying to work on for years. Maybe we'll take a little ridicule on this but maybe if several million people start to believe this, then the Air Force will have to tell us more." The last word from Carr: "President Ford is about to embark on a new policy of telling us all about UFOs, and the first revelation will come before Christmas." We didn't hear anything - did you? Compiled from: Arkansas Gazette, 13 Oct 74; Detroit (Michigan) News, 18 Oct 74, (Credit both to Mark Hall); Sunday Mirror, 27 Oct 74 (Credit: Nigel Watson).

Illustration by DON ROBERTS.

As we go to press we notice an item in New Scientist, 29 May 75, that seems calculated to polarise both extreme opposite opinions on UFO cover-ups by governments. It is that J Allen Hynek, director of the brave new Centre for UFO Studies (at Northfield, Illinois) was given five pages of the FBI's 'Law Enforcement Bulletin' to explain the Centre's activities. Some of the points Hynek dealt with were the number of sightings that involved policemen; the establishment

of a "toll-free" hotline so that the various law enforcement agencies could forward news of incidents 24hrs a day, 7 days a week; and the role the policeman can play in protecting the scene of a sighting in the same manner as they preserve the scene of a crime - and also the witnesses, since Hynek observed, "curiosity seekers and souvenir hunters" had wrecked sites and pestered witnesses before investigators arrived, often to the extent that the witnesses became discouraged from reporting their experiences further.

A COUPLE OF ANTIQUES.

Steve Moore came across the following comment in S Baring Gould's CURIOUS MYTHS OF THE MIDDLE AGES, quoting from 'The Thuringian Chronicle': "In 1398, at mid-day, there appeared suddenly three great fires in the air, which presently ran together into one globe of flame, parted again and finally sank into the Hörselberg." Steve notes that the Hörselberg is a mountain in southeast Germany, near Gotha, and is also the site of the Venus and Tannhauser legend.

Anders Liljegren sent us the following translation of a passage from SVENSKA VINGAR (Swedish Wings), issued by Holger Schildts Förlag of Stockholm, 1929, in which the author discribed a strange phenomenon experienced by him and two companions during a baloon trip in 1910: "All three of us caught sight of something at the same time. Something coming down from space. All three were staring. There came a big fireball, ruby red, Grew in size. Course: straight at the balloon! The phenomenon lighted up this foggy world, a giant phenomenon of chaotic, boiling movements; ruby red with black shadows. Seconds of waiting for this glowing ball in a firm orbit towards the balloon felt like a hardening grasp over your throat. The panorama became a vision, overwhelming, straining every nerve and muscle. Then it was gone. In the moment you expected the collision to take place, the light grew weaker and died. There was a deep, black darkess left. A meteor or what? " Make of that what you will.

1973 -- SEDGELEY BEACON & BOURNEMOUTH.

Mrs Bella Hughes, of Kenilworth Cres. Wolverhampton, Staffs, spotted a bright star-like object from her home on the 4th Nov, at about 5.30. pm. "It was hovering just over Sedgeley Beacon. What made me keep looking was that it kept fading then coming back very brightly." This continued for about 15 minutes then it vanished. Express & Star, 6 Nov 73. Credit: A Smith.

The Sun, 13 Feb 73 -- that an unidentified flying object "like a huge luminous wheel" was spotted by Bournemouth coastguards. No further details here anyway, but if you look up Flying Saucer Review, V.19 No4 (July/Aug 74) you'll find letters from one of the coastguards referring to the above 'wheel' seen on the 11th Feb, and a second, not reported to the papers, seen on the 17th Feb, which appeared alongside a fairly conventional UFO complete with portholes.(FSRp30).

PEMBROKE, WALES.

In contrast to the coastguards mentioned above, the Pembroke officers dismissed reports made by camping schoolboys in the early morning, as sparks from a local power-station. Guess it very much depends on what you see with your own eyes - but even then you can't be sure. Anyway, the local police decided to side with the schoolboys. "The coastguards can say what they like, but sparks from the power-station are just an easy way out," said Pc Roger Davies. No date or other information given. Sunday People, 14 April 74. Credit: Nigel Watson.

HANGING HOUGHTON, NORTHAMPTONSHIRE.

David Gwinn and his wife went to their bedroom after watching a late-night TV film one night early in April 73. And from the window of their house in   Hanging Houghton, near Northampton, they watched two strange luminous objects in the sky for more than half an hour, during which time they hovered not 500yds from the house. They were bright orange and appeared to revolve while moving slowly along. They first noticed the lights at about 2.30 am, Mr Gwinn said: "At first there was only one in the sky. Then another appeared about a mile away and started moving until the two were alongside. We watched them for a while then telephoned the police. Eventually the objects began moving away and disappeared behind a hill. It was uncanny and I must admit a little frightening."

At first, the police denied that any such incident had been reported to them -- then an inspector is quoted: "The report of Mr Gwinn's call wasn't passed onto me. But after making inquiries I found there was a record of such an incident." A car crew had been sent to investigate, and the inspector said: "We feel that Mr Gwinn and his wife could have seen the reflections of a barn at Upton which is illuminated at night. There is no other logical explanation." Well, if that's logic, it's a shabby shade of its former self!

Mr Gwinn apparently thinks so too. "I certainly don't accept the explanation. How does one account for them hovering in the sky, appearing one at a time, then slowly disappearing over the horizon? Upton is at least ten miles away from our home. I've never given a thought to UFOs so I wouldn't be prepared to say that this was what we had seen." That last sounds eminently sensible to us. Northamptonshire News, 18 April 74. Credit: BR Bates.

RUNCORN, CHESHIRE.

In the last week of May 74, five boys were walking, late at night, across Runcorn Golf Course when they saw a weird pulsating object flashing in the sky above the Rocksavage Works. It was about 10.40pm and they were making their way from Clifton Rd towards Lambsickle Rd when they encountered the "silver light". It was bigger than a star and moving too quickly for a plane and without any sound. It was very high and disappeared into the clouds. We all thought it was a UFO. We were all scared", said one. A spokesman for Liverpool airport said something about reflection on planes of the sun below the horizon. Runcorn Weekly News, 30 May 74. Credit: Peter Rogerson.

HARBOURNE, BIRMINGHAM.

Reports by the people living near Harbourne Golf Course of glowing objects darting about the local sky were referred to a special "Fling Saucer" department (sic) of the Minisrty ((There you go, crowing over the errors and typoes of others, then tripping over your own fat fingers. I meant, of course:)) Ministry of Defence, after checks by Birmingham University and Birmingham Airport failed to establish any conventional reason. The residents of Bournevale Park estate have had a letter from the MOD, that the reports "are being examined to see if there are any defence implications. A policeman's wife, herself a policewoman in former times, said: "One of the sightings was very frightening. It seemed to hover right overhead then drop suddenly. The objects are quite silent and glow orange turning to white sometimes leaving a red trail. Through binoculars they seem to be a tubular light." She said that more than a dozen people living near her home in Wentworth Way had seen 'UFOs' in the last 3 weeks. Initially they travelled south to north, but after not being seen during a spell of cloudy weather, they reappeared travelling east to west. Birmingham Evening Mail, 8 July 74. Credit: David Sutton.

STOCKTON/HARTLEPOOL, CLEVELAND.

An unidentified man reported seeing a 'UFO' in the sky over Stockton, heading towards Hartlepool at about midnight on the 20th July. The police said they had only the one report. Northern Daily Mail, 22 July 74. Credit: P Screeton.

PLUMSTEAD, LONDON.

On the night of the 8th Sept 74, three people in a flat in Bostall Lane, Plumstead, saw a "brilliant sulphurous light" hovering over the Common and shoot off into the sky at great speed.

Later, three more sightings came to light on that night and into the morning of the 9th. One woman said that something must have roused her from her sleep and when she got up she saw the bright orange light flash across the sky, in the early hours of the morning. Another woman and her husband were having a cup of tea at 11.25pm when they too saw the round blazing light streak past at phenomenal speed. "We just stood on the balcony in awe and we were so amazed we took down the exact time. I saw this with my own two eyes. It was quite an experience." And Mrs Hilda Faulkner of Eltham, said she saw it about mid-morning on the 9th. "I was sitting at home when out of the corner of my eye I saw a fantastically bright glare moving slowly across the sports ground behind our house." MOD said they were looking into it. It seems strange to us that a light of the described intensity over a London suburb during Saturday night into Sunday mid-day, should not have been seen by more people.

Kentish Independant, 12 & 19 Sept 74. Credit: Steve Moore.

BOURNEMOUTH, AGAIN...

The photo below appeared in the News of the World, 3 Nov 74 (Credit: Dave Baldock, BR Bates.) It was said to have been taken at about 8.45pm on the night of 21 Oct 74, by Gregory Marchant, a lorry-driver of Highlands Cres, Kinson, Bournemouth. A fuller report by a member of SCAN, the local UFO group, appeared in Flying Saucer Review V.20 No3, p31 (Dec 74). Through his bedroom window he saw a greeny-blue light zipping through the sky. Grabbing his polaroid camera, he dashed outside. He had forgotten there was a flashcube attatched, and was startled when it went off. When he could see again the light was gone. "It had no particular shape to the naked eye and had the appearance of a fluorescent light, brilliant white, but green and mauve near the top and orange beneath. The upper portion appeared to be rotating, and its size was half to three-quarters of an inch at arms length," says the FSR report, based on a "very strenuous interview" with Marchant.

In the NOW article SCAN's PR man, Ron McClure, said: "This is no fake. There can be no doubt about this one and no 'official' explanation could dismiss this picture. It must be the best ever taken." And regarding its similarity to the Adamski-type craft, he said: "For years some experts thought the famous Adamski pictures were fakes. Until now we've been skeptical, but as a result of this Marchant sighting there's no doubt in our minds that the Adamski craft did exist." The original account appeared in the Bournemouth Evening Echo of 23 Oct, and this contained the information that then, just two days after the sighting, Marchant had been accused of faking it. This he denies, and the FSR report said that his honest and open attitude impressed the investigaters who state that they believe him and discount the idea of a hoax.

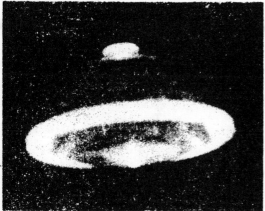

Well - No doubt much to McClure's disgust, the dismissals have not come from 'officials' but from a UFO group based miles away in Northampton. The Northamptonshire News, 9 Jan 75 (Credit: BR

Bates.) The members of MUFORIA claim the photo is a fake. "We have experimented with a Polaroid camera and have found it would be impossible to take such a sharp photograph of an object which it is admitted was moving at speed. It must have been set up either with the use of a bathroom heater or an ultraviolet lamp, " said Robert Birkett, treasurer of MUFORIA. It is not quite clear how they got a copy of the photo, or even the original, but it seems that SCAN may have sent it to them. Birkett wrote to SCAN saying: "This sighting was not only strange but if the facts presented are to be believed, verges on the farcial. Polaroid cameras have a fixed shutter speed of between 1/25th and 1/30th of a second. Yet the photo shows an object totally frozen in flight. Are we to believe that this object, which is said to be moving at a very low altitude, was not seen by more than one individual during its entire flight path across such a highly populated part of the country? This photo is in my opinion and that of other ufologists an unconvincing fake." Stranger things have happened... but in this your guess is as good as ours, probably a darn sight better. See also BUFORA Journal, vol 4 No6, for another SCAN report.

BROCKENHURST, HAMPSHIRE.

We're not sure whether this should be here or in some other section like Mystery Sounds, or something, since it seems to be the sound end of a 'phantom helicopter' story. The Southern Evening Echo, 9 April 75 (Credit: Roger Randle.) tells that Rescue Services rushed to Rhinefield House, near Brockenhurst, where staff reported hearing the engine of a helicopter cut out during a blizzard (itself a rare thing in these parts, says Roger Randle.) Smoke was thought to have been seen over distant woods. Police, fire and ambulance men all joined in the search of dense and boggy woodland in this corner of the New Forest - a chopper from the Royal Navy helped from above. No helicopters have been reported missing in the area. That's the story according to the paper, but in his letter Roger says that a helicopter was seen by a young boy during the blizzard, who said he saw it pass overhead at a low altitude and disappear behind some trees. The only thing that springs to our minds is the search of Hockley Woods near Southend that failed to find any wreckage after someone reported hearing a plane crash in Aug 73 (see NEWS 3/6.) Perhaps we had better break out a new file for 'Phantom Accidents &c'.

HUGE JAPANESE 'SCARE'.

Not of a huge Japanese in a rubber Godzilla suit this time, but a mass sighting of a UFO formation seen over 'half the length of Japan'. There were 15 to 20 of the objects "like a string of pearls" inside a strange cloud, each objects trailing a small grey tail, seen by "hundreds" of people as it sped from north to south Japan "sighted over Japanese cities over 700 miles apart in less than an hour." The first reports came into the police in the city of Asahikawa on

Hokkaido, where the duty-officer said: "All the callers reported seeing a huge cloud passing over the city - they saw the orange objects inside the cloud moving in a straight line." A co-pilot of an All-Nippon plane said he was flying at 6000 ft, prior to landing at Tokyo International when he spotted the mist-shrouded UFOs about 5 miles in front of his aircraft. "15 or 16 luminous objects were flying southward at about 1000 ft above our plane. I could see greyish-blue objects flashing a brighter blue, and as they drew closer, they appeared to line up in two formations. The nearest they came was about a mile. The objects didn't show up on the aircraft's radar. Nor were they reported on the airport's radar." Prof Kitamura saw the dazzling display from the control room of Tokyo's Meteorological Bureau Station near the airport. "I was mystified. Nothing showed up on my radar. I reported my sighting to the airport control tower and they told me nothing showed up on their radar either. A spokesman for Japan's Self Defence Air Force only acknowledged that they had received reports on the evening of 15 Jan, but nothing else is said. The story is taken from Reveille, 25 April 75, headlined 'Silence over UFOs Scare', and we have heard nothing further on this. Credit: Graham Crowley; Nigel Watson.

UNIDENTIFIEDS

It seems ages since we had a gripping monster story from the British coast. There is a periodic flap at Skegness, according to Winston Kime's history of that town "SKEGGY!" (Seashell Books, Skegness, 1969), on page 142 of which he says: "Five or six years ago it was reported that a 'Skeg-ness Monster' had been sighted. A party from Wainfleet, visiting GibraltarPoint, saw this strange object, nine or ten feet long, moving swiftly through the water in the direction of Skegness...The 'monster' has been reported off Skegness several times since, and it always makes a good headline in the local paper." (Cr: Nigel Watson.) Anyone interested might try locating such east coast sightings.

But recently there's been a hue and cry up the Welsh coast, where much of a Fortean nature seems to be happening these days.

THE BARMOUTH MONSTER.

On 2 March 1975, six local schoolgirls, all aged 12, took a Sunday afternoon stroll on Llanaber beach, near the northern end of Barmouth promenade. They stopped in astonishment when they saw something unusual about 200yds ahead of them. "It was like a dinosaur," said two of the girls, Carys Jones and Julie Anderson. "The monster was about 10ft long, with a long tail, long neck and huge green eyes. It walked towards the sea and entered the water." Julie, whose father is one of the local coastguards, added tha the monster had feet like huge saucers, with 3 long pointed protruding nails. "It was horrible," she said. And as they turned to run in fright, the girls said they could see the green eyes above the water until the black monster disappeared into the sea. They rushed straight to the coastguards who later said that the girls were extremely upset by what they saw. Police and the coastguards kept an alert that night but there were no further sightings. As seems to be usual in our experiences with the unknown,the critical evidence of the tracks of the creature soon vanished before the rapidly rising tide. These were the initial details: compiled from The Western Mail (Cr: FW Holiday.); Liverpool Echo (Cr: AF Ashcroft.); Liverpool Daily Post (Cr: R Mowday.) all of 3 March 75; and Merioneth Express, 7 March 75.

The girls, all pupils at Ysgol Ardudwy, Harlech, all agreed on the description. One of their teachers had the idea of compiling a drawing of what they saw, and this was later issued as a postcard. In a letter to Phil & Margie Ledger, who were inquiring on our behalf, the teacher, Colin Palmer,said: "The drawing on the card is one compiled from interviewing each of the six girls seperately. The interesting thing is that respectable, sober citizens, after seeing the drawing, admitted seeing such a creature but either dismissed it as being something else at the time, or convinced themselves quite easily that they had not really seen anything." The card drew quite a lot of media attention and further accounts came forward. some of them, Colin says,are more detailed. We don't have them to hand as we go to press, but we do hope to bring you further details as they emerge, in future issues.

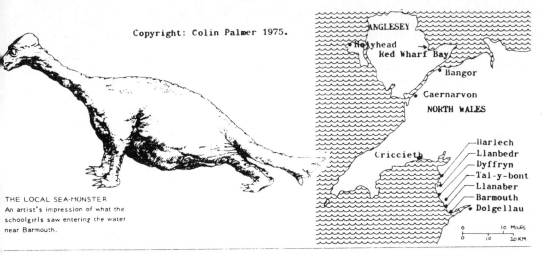

ANGLESEY

Holyhead

Red Wharf Bay

Bangor

Caernarvon

NORTH WALES

Criccieth

Harlech
Llanbedr
Dyffryn
Tal-y-bont
Llanaber
Barmouth
Dolgellau

0   10 MILES
0   10   20 KM

THE LOCAL SEA-MONSTER
An artist's impression of what the
schoolgirls saw entering the water
near Barmouth.

The first we heard of this story was when trusty readers sent us clippings - it seems to have by-passed the national dailies completely. We wrote to a few of the papers that serve the region and were very disappointed by the local coverage, compared to the Liverpool press-reports from much further away. The Merioneth Express told us: "The story lacked authenticity so we only gave it the briefest mention." ((Splutter.')) That shocks us more than stories of monsters on quiet Welsh beaches. The Western Mail, 4 March, (Cr: FW Holiday) trotted out an expert from the University Marine Science Laboratories at Menai Bridge who tried to make out that it was a trick of the light and distance between the girls and an otter, seal or perhaps even an escaped sea-lion. "No known sea creature that could be washed up from tropical waters would fit the girl's description." I think he's trying to tell us it doesn't, or can't exist, bless him.

The North Wales Weekly News, 6 March (Cr: R Mowday) mentioned sightings of a sea-going creature during the previous three weeks on the northern coast of Anglesey. Several people saw it showing only a foot or so of its body, and a "square-cut tail" (similar to the Barmouth sketch) as it moved fast up the main channel of Red Wharf Bay. The NWWN fishing columnist, Tom Evans, mentions three groups of witnesses, including some sea-anglers. The Western Mail, 8 March (Cr: FW Holiday) quoted Philip Wendel, a barman at the Minydon Hotel at the water's edge: "It was too weird and rather frightening to be a basking shark, a dolphin, or even a minature submarine. Five of us saw it going up the channel only 30yds away and two women employed at the hotel also saw it from another viewpoint a few minutes later and they were mystified." He described it as about 12 ft long with a blackish, symmetrical form and a prominent tail. "It resembled a flying-bomb from its tail, and we saw it before hearing about this Barmouth monster," he added.

Tom Evans's fishing column also related that about two years ago a party of anglers from Liverpool fishing off the Black Wall, opposite Ynys y Gorad Goch, were on their way back along the shore in the fading light, when suddenly a large, 10 ft long creature slithered its way across the mud and kelp towards the water. They saw that it had feet, webbed and shaped like saucers with long protruding nails. The Cambrian News, 7 March, mentions a photo owned by Mr Gordon Walters of Tynycoed -- Colin Palmer's postcard, which has a brief history of the Barmouth monster, says that this photo, taken 2 years ago of a "strange water creature" in the Barmouth Estuary, is on display in a shop in Tynycoed. He also says that in 1937, Robert Jones of Harlech, encountered a "weird crocodile-like creature walking along a riverbank near Harlech."

The latest developments increase the mystery. Colin Palmer enclosed an item from the Liverpool Daily Post, 6 May (via Margie Ledger) to the effect that two women staying at a caravan at Talybont found "six young monsters" dead on the beach. They took photos and made a sketch of what they had seen. We will try to obtain copies of these and other evidences. In his letter, Colin says that Granada TV covered the item on one of their news programmes, but mentioned the opinion of a "Marine Biologist" that they were probably badly mutilated Skates. The ladies describe their findings as having longish necks with small heads and two legs at the rear. We await further developments on this item. And yet more sightings are mentioned in this cutting. "A local woman" claimed to have seen four large footprints "as big as elephant's" in the wet sand on an island off Barmouth. And a father and son, "not given to exaggeration" saw turbulence in a calm sea and reached for binoculars and telescope. "They saw a large animal with a head similar to a seal, but with a long neck, playing in the sea between Dyffryn Ardudwy and Llanbedr," said Edmonds Evans, a local businessman who seems to be collecting stories. Some years ago, he said, a woman swimming locally, found herself almost within touching distance of what appeared to be a monster. "She swam for the shore for dear life"

Colin's postcard brings to our attention that Robert Graves, who spent many years at a family home in Harlech, wrote a poem called 'Welsh Incident' in which a Welshman is questioned about 'things' that came out of a sea-cave at Criccieth as the Harlech Silver band played for a hospital collection. These curious things "never seen or heard or written about, very strange, un-Welsh, utterly peculiar things. Oh, solid enough they seemed to touch, had anyone dared it," came out of the sand, "not keeping time to the band." The last one, "The most odd indescribable thing of all," makes a noise before it lumbers for the sea, "A very loud, respectable noise - like groaning to oneself on Sunday morning in Chapel, close before the second psalm." Hmmm - reminds us of Fort's line: "It sang a hymn, and then departed."

SEA-SERPENTS IN THE INDIAN OCEAN?

Helicopters from a Russian whaling ship in the Indian Ocean reported sighting huge 'sea-serpents' basking on 2 Dec 1968. The newsreport said that experts in Moscow were sceptical, suggesting clumps of seaweed, "although the possibility of 'marine animals unknown to man' was not ruled out". It seems to us that men whose living depends on their ability to locate and identify whales etc from the air (or whatever) would know a mass of seaweed from a living animal bulk? Daily Mirror, 3 Dec 1968. (Credit: A Smith.)

A MONSTER IN THE ALPS?

This illo appeared in a general article in the Sunday Times, 4 Aug 74, entitled 'Silly season in the Alps, 1660: yeti claims another victim.' — prompted by the spate of "Yeti killed my herd " stories coming out of Katmandu at the end of July that year. But this illo is certainly of no ABSM. Cany any reader help identify the source, the creature and possibly even the story or incident that gave rise to it?

HAIL NESSIE...AND FAREWELL!

We learn that a group of Hertfordshire firemen are building a giant Loch Ness Monster in a scheme to raise money for a charity. They plan to tow it with a fire-engine from Queensway, near Hemel Hempstead to the Loch, where it will be fitted with propellers and floated in July this year. Lord knows what Nessie herself will make of this - we might be in for the hen-fight of the century. Weekly News, 12 April 75 (Cr: N Watson.)

This comes at more or less the same time as news of the disbanding of the Loch Ness Investigation Bureau that has operated a continuous scientific watch on the Loch since 1962. Inflation, it seems, hits even here, and they could no longer remain a practical proposition. Directorship included Peter Scott, Lord Craigmyle, and Prof Roy P Mackal (who will be addressing the FORTFEST 75 in Chicago — see p.2.), and their full-time secretary, Holly Arnold, the nearest to a Nanny that Nessie ever had, has moved to work for an Inverness lawyer. Daily Mail, 1 April 75 (Credit: Steve Moore.)

A MALAYAN UNIDENTIFIED.

The following quote is from 'Modern Wonder' Vol 5 No106, 27 May 1939, sent by Steve Moore:

"According to newspaper officials in Manila, Philippine Islands, they have seen a type of animal they are convinced cannot exist.

"The animals are the property of a roving photographer who brought the creatures from the Malayan jungles. No zoo in the world has been able to tell to which animal family these weird creatures belong.

"The creatures are four-footed, with heads like racoons, some teeth like those of a cat, others like those of a human, eyes like an owl. The whole weighs about two hundred pounds and is covered with fur like a mole.

"Additionally the creatures have two tongues, eat babanas, and being able to absorb moisture through their skin, never drink."

Whaaaat! The basic situation reminds us of Heuvelmans and Sanderson's investigation of the 'Altura Iceman'. It's not said whether these weirdos were living or dead — but it seems to us like a bit of salesmanship elaborating on some muddled observations. Perhaps one of you Fortean zoologists know more about this — if so, please let us know?

ONE LAST "THING".

Philip Freeman was with his girlfriend on Sunday night, 16 Dec 1967. They stopped outside a deserted mansion in Winterfold, Surrey, and Philip got out to wipe the windscreen. Then he noticed an acrid smell. After getting back in the car he noticed soemthing looking at him from nearby. 'Thing' is the only word that can really be used here — this Thing was about 4ft 6in high with an oblong-shaped luminous head. The waves of the acrid smell seemed to come from its body. "It put an arm on the roof of the car. I said to my girlfriend, 'There's a Thing out there.' But she was too scared to look - although she remembers the smell. We drove off fast." It may be entirely unconnected to the Mystery Animal reports we find emanating from this region in substantial numbers - but we can't help noticing that in many of these too, a powerful acrid smell seems to be part of the phenomenon. This story is from Daily Mirror, 19 Dec 1967.

From: Colin Bord

The Madness of Crowds — THE NEWS 8/9.

"Men, it has been well said, think in herds;
it will be seen that they go mad in herds, while
they only recover their senses slowly, and one by
one " - an observation worthy of the master himself, but this quote does not stem from the pen
of Fort, but from Charles Mackay, who in 1852
produced his epic work EXTRAORDINARY POPULAR
DELUSIONS AND THE MADNESS OF CROWDS. Here he
examined some of the manias that have swept across nations, from the use of tulip bulbs (for
speculation and currency) to the eternal desire
to know the future (listing 52 forms of divination).

It was the request in NEWS 8/9, by our respected Editor, that prompted me to return to the
works of Mackay, for therein lies a report of the
mass poisonings. He says that: "The Italians of
the 16th and 17th centuries poisoned their opp-
onents with as little compunction as an English
man of the present day brings an action at law
against anyone who has done him an injury."

In 1659, Pope Alexander VII was told of the
great number of young women who were admitting
during their confession to having poisoned unwanted lovers or husbands. The poison which was
administered in small doses acted progressively,
was clear, odourless and tasteless. Some of the
poisoners were hanged, and up to 30 at a time
publicly flogged - but this seems to have been no
deterrent to the rest. (One woman by the name of)
Tofania had her potion bottled and sent to all
parts of the country bearing the lable 'Manna of
St Nicholas of Barri'.

In France the mania was in full swing during
1670 to 1680. One noted practioner amongst the
nobility was a Madame de Brinvilliers, who in the
space of a few weeks, poisoned her father and two
brothers. She was beheaded in Paris in 1676.
After this the mania took hold of the popular
mind (and by) 1682 hundreds perished by the fatal
dosage. Only after "upwards of a hundred individuals" had been burnt or swung in the principal
cities of France did the mania finally subside.

A selection from Charles Mackay's book has
been recently re-issued by George Allen & Unwin
at £2.75, (1973), and makes interesting reading
for such as us.

***((Apologies for condensing your letter, Colin,
but I think the gist is there. Our main point
of interest being, of course, that while a mania
like this is in full swing, there must have been
many unfortunates who 'imagined' they had been
poisoned by this stuff they couldn't smell, taste
or detect by colouring. Shades of our 'Phantom
Smells etc'. We note the recent publication of
a paperback on this subject in the Sphere 'Library of the Occult' series: THE AFFAIR OF THE
POISONS by Frances Mossiker; pp320; illos; 70p.
Incidentally I noted two 'coincidences' also on
this theme. Firstly, never having heard of the
'Tulip Bulb Mania' of 1634-37 before, my current
grimoire of Victorian oddities fell open at a
review of this topic - then a few days later
Colin's letter arrives. Secondly, during some
research on 'Spontaneous Combustion' I found a
paper by a famous German scientist of 1851, in
which he compares the arguments of those who
believe that humans can burst into flames with
those who believed in the existance of an undetectable poison called Aqua Tofana - in the former
the evidence is consumed, and in the latter it
was virtually untraceable, therefore both
phenomena, he reasoned (if you can call it reasoning) were clearly superstitious nonsense. - Ed))

 •••   •••   •••   •••

From: Angelo Caparella III

'Tasmanian Wolf' - THE NEWS 9/19-20.

In THE NEWS (9/19-20) several exerpts from
Bernard Heuvelmans's ON THE TRACK OF UNKNOWN AN-
IMALS are erroneously said to concern the Tasmanian wolf (also called the Tasmanian Tiger)
when in actuality they concern the Queensland
marsupial Tiger. There is a great difference between these two creatures.

The Tasmanian Wolf or Tiger has been known
and recognised by science since 1808 and bears
the scientific name Thylacinus cyanocephalus.
Though no living specimens are in captivity (the
last captive Tasmanian Wolf died in the Hobart
Zoo in 1934) there do exist dead specimens. Since
the last Tasmanian Wolf was shot in 1930 there
has been concern that the creature may be extinct,
but regular sightings from Tasmania indicate
some still exist though are seriously endangered.

The Queensland marsupial tiger, to which the
three exerpts from Heuvelmans's refer, is not
officially recognised by science — it remains
an unknown animal never having been collected or
examined by science. Judging from sightings, the
Queensland marsupial tiger appears to be confined
to mainland Australia, while the Tasmanian Wolf
or tiger is, or was, since first known by the
western world, confined to the island of Tasmania.
To see the striking difference between the two
creatures see the illustrations in ON THE TRACK..
(fig 61 of the Tasmanian Wolf, and fig 62 of the
hypothetical Queensland marsupial tiger).

***((Thanks for sorting my own muddle out and
straightening the record. In the UK there is a
Palladin paperback edition of ON THE TRACK... but
this is heavily abridged, and the relevant illos

are figs 38 and 39 respectively. For biblio-
philes, Angelo also sent a copy of a monograph by
Jeremy Griffith, "The Search for the Tasmanian
Tiger" which brings the subject up to date and
includes an extremely rare photo of the critter;
from '<u>Natural History</u>' Vol LXXXI No10, Dec 1972,
published by the American Museum of Natural History. The subject was raised in connexion with
sightings of mystery animals in the UK, some of
which seem to fit the descriptions of Tasmanian
wolf - and it lies there mocking us. We shall go
into this sometime in the future. -- Ed.))

MYSTERIES OF TIME AND SPACE - by Brad Steiger.
    Prentice-Hall (USA); $7.95; 232pp; illos;
    and a good bibliography. Having been out of
touch with Steiger's writing for some time -
being decidedly unimpressed with his earlier UFO
books - this 'rediscovery' has come as a delight-
ful surprise. Steiger has made a statement about
a problem that is central to so many of the areas
that interest us. He has brought his not inconsiderable journalistic skills to bear on the idea
that dogged pursuit of any one subject (eg UFOs)
to the exclusion of developments in other researches is utterly futile unless this exclusionism can be transcended until we can see a common
denominator that takes into account the varieties
of human experience. He believes this common-
denominator to be the way we view 'Reality'.
    You cannot progress into any line of inquiry
very far before encountering the problem of the
ambiguity of phenomena - I mention one aspect
back on p5; in Science,paradoxes abound when you
reach the theoretical limits of any phenomena of
matter, Time & Space - so that how you interpret
phenomena becomes a matter of predisposition
between your views on the Universe as being
structured objectively or subjectively. This
problems faces everybody from the scientists
(who incline to exclude all but finite, objective
events), 'nuts & bolts' UFOlogists, to the spiritualists - indeed any group that bases their
inquiry   on a dogmatic stance. What we know
about the structure of language shows us that the
very act of asking a question means that we are
automatically using a conceptual framework which
dictates what answer we will receive and accept.
Perhaps all knowledge is ultimately so much ton-
nage of red-herring - but as long as we want it
we must be aware of its consequences - and its
ambiguous nature,the bane of all who seek strictly material or linear interpretations.
    The most illumination to be shed on this
stumbling-block in recent times has come from an
unusual source (though historically precedented).
As if in answer to unspoken need there arose the
psychedelic explosion of the late 60s, which more
than any other single event served to focus attention on the nature of consciousness right across the board. Today the phrase "altered states
of consciousness" is to be heard everywhere and
we acknowledge that our everyday-selves slip in
and out of many states of mind each day. Maslow
has shown how some 'high' states ('peak experiences) are central to how we build up a working
model of the world, our personal 'Reality'. Koestler,expanding on Jung, has shown that the relationships between peak experiences and 'coincidences' is a function of 'meaningfulness', which
can only arise from the way in which we relate
events to our personal 'Realities'. And then
JC Pearce came to open our eyes to the states of
mind or being in which the 'Reality-shaping' process can be switched from the passive everyday
adjustment to a changing world, to a dynamic
force capable of being projected into that world
'outside' ourselves to restructure so-called
'objective Reality'; eg Pearce mentions firewalk-
ing, in which the 'normal' concensus of Reality the feet should be badly damaged by the intensity of the heat - yet from the directly observable fact that this has not happened we must
presume that the normal chain of cause and effect
can be restructured or even by-passed.
    And at the other end of the scales we can see
that High Energy Physics in its pathways into the
truly 'occult' states of matter, Time & Space
encounters universe upon universe in which all
our familiar experience is at a loss, the normal
properties of matter/energy being replaced with
bizarre effects that seem both magic and madness.
It is no longer feasible to hold to any simplistic view of how 'Reality' works, or what it is.
    This is Steiger's starting point - data that
confounds doctrinal views on Time & Space. The
first part of the book is given over to discoveries, often by amateurs, that are at varience
with History and Archeology - eg. humanoid footprints in ancient strata (there is a photo that
purports to show a trilobite crushed beneath a
soled foot in rock 500 million years old), an
object like a spark-plug in a rock with fossil-

shells ½million years old, the massive sunken ruins of Bimini; the nails, wires etc in layers of the earth that antedate history as we know it. After reviewing the idea that there may have been civilisations that bloomed and faded before the seeding of modern man, Steiger settles down to his main theme - that the mind by its own power can restructure time and space and matter as an act of will - though it has to be acknowledged that this is largely brought about by accident or conditions as yet beyond our conscious control.

In the middle portion of the work, we move on to evidence from other sources of this amazing mental ability - the image of a hand on a switched-off TV, the film of a man at the Niagara Falls years before he first went there in the flesh, falls of materials from the sky, and apports of things at seances, the 'phantom marksman' that has plagued both UK and USA, etc. Despite the fact that most of these cases appear here for the first time (in a book, that is - some taken from mags such as INFO Journal, PURSUIT, FATE, etc) there seemed to be less consistency in the line of argument here - perhaps too much data to treat it all fairly.

The last section mainly concerns 'entities' and the way they seem to be inextricably twined around the breakaway experiences of a 'different' Reality - Steiger deals at some length with the Men In Black phenomena here. This spills over into consideration of these 'other Realities' and whether people have ever made the transition (voluntary or otherwise) and whether it is possible to learn techniques for manipulating 'Reality'. Several very interesting cases are mentioned, like the man in traction for both broken legs who vanished from his hospital bed leaving behind the traction-pins, an hour later he and the pins were back in place; and the woman walking down a street who found herself suddenly facing a thatshed cottage, a dog barking at her, and a couple in old-fashioned clothes who could not see her, and this melting away to leave her back in the street once more. (Would teleportation work like this - or was it clairvoyance? Then why was the dog barking at her? Fascinating - but this and several other items seem poorly referenced.)

The central concept of a plastic reality is envisaged by Steiger to be like a game, and all of us engaged in its play, willing or not. One of the minor threads through the book is that entities from other dimensions, who, unlike us, know the rules of the game, are deliberately out-classing us, pushing us into situations, like the Gods of old, where we adapt or suffer the consequences. Whilst the concept of a 'Reality Game' is fairly useful, I do think it simplifies somewhat - like Hamlet, after acknowledging that "There is nothing either good or bad, but thinking makes it so," I sense something else that is above and beyond: "I could be bounded in a nutshell and count myself a king of infinite space, were it not that I have bad dreams." There are a good many parts of the jigsaw to come yet - if Steiger has concentrated on a slightly mechanistic reasoning (complete with Deus Ex Machina Men in Black), this is nonetheless a valid app-

roach, and certainly poses many interesting challenges. Though I feel I cannot go along with some of Steiger's conclusions, I have no hesitation in recommending the book for its clear exposition of a very complex idea. This is an important step in the Great Synthesis, extrapolating the work of Pearce, Koestler, Fodor, Max Freedom Long and many others into the realm of Fortean data. The exploration of the actual nature and role of human subjectivity (just one of the 'bad dream' areas yet to be tackled) can wait. If we can reach that through Steiger's work, the future will be exciting indeed. ((Note for UK readers - this book may not be generally available, but most bookshops will order from the States for you. Alternatively you could do it yourself from Other Dimensions Inc, Box 140, 104 Washington St, Decorah, Iowa 52101, USA, payment with order, postage extra. It's bound to be much quicker.))

THE FLYING COW by Guy Lyon Playfair. Souvenir Press; £3.50; 320pp; illustd; bibliography.
The range and wealth of material in this book on psychic phenomena in Brazil is astonishing, not simply because this is one of so few literary explorations of 'psychic Brazil' but because so much seems to happen, or be happening quite openly there, the Spiritist movements being massively supported. The first part of the book deals with four of the most famous mediums. (One has trance-written more than 125 books. Another specialises in materialisations; another healing, etc.) One curious observation is about the strange 'devices' the 'spirit-doctors' bring to healing sessions - eg one "looked like a deep dish of gelatinous substance...pale green in colour and transparent. When placed on the patient's body it proved to be a kind of portable X-ray machine for all present could clearly see through it into the inside of the lady's body."

The second part deals extensively with psychic surgery - with some horrific photos of penknives jabbing into eyes; and shots of fingers probing, thrusting into body cavities, which if they were in a Kung-fu movie would have been removed by a different kind of surgery.

The last section concerns general phenomena from poltergeistery (both disturbances and fires) to reincarnation; and also the work of various individual reaearchers and organisations. Playfair mentions some experimental work on photographing spirits, alluding to a "pre-1945" case of a generating dynamo in a darkened room, over which "a luminous sphere formed itself, in the centre of which there appeared a feminine hand, very delicate and sharply focussed." In fact Steiger mentions a similar incident related by Fay Clark who worked at a power company in Wisconsin in 1931. In this case the image in the cloud over a turbine was of a woman reclining on a couch. Odd.

Many of the photos in FLYING COW are open to criticism: a man levitating (he could have jumped); items burnt by poltergeists (all they show is a scorched area); a landrover against a fence, shoes high on a roof-beam, a chest of drawers at the foot of stairs, all alledgedly thrown or moved by pesky polts. But to judge from the huge amount of data, Playfair's honest approach and intelligence, I'm quite prepared to accept that these photos are what he says they are.

THERE ARE GIANTS IN THE EARTH by Michael Grumley.
Sidgewick & Jackson; £3.50; 154pp; illustd; bibliography. Near the publication date of this book a small note appeared in the Daily Mirror, 26 May 75, announcing that Grumley and Robert Ferro (with whom he wrote ATLANTIS: THE AUTOBIOGRAPHY OF A SEARCH) were in London en route for Loch Ness whose occupant is the subject of their next book. GIANTS mainly concerns the existence or not of giant anthropoids: the Yetis, Momos, Sasquatch, Bigfoot, Mono Grande, ABSMs or whatever name you prefer. Grumley bases himself on the argument that if animals are long thought extinct, then remote, inhospitable regions of this earth, useless to consumer man, may well harbour living remnants from the ancient past. From archeological evidence we know of cases where the "species father outlasted the species son" - and so it's a sobering thought to realise that if these hairy giants have lasted this long, they could well still be here after we're gone - providing of course we don't wipe them out before we go.
Grumley writes very well, if a trifle self-consciously at times - his wry observations having a distinctive style. If like me you know very little about the 'Manimal' scene, this would seem to be a good place to jump in - not too deep and not too shallow. Apart from John Napier's BIGFOOT there aren't any competitors with GIANTS in the UK, and US imports are few and far between - so Grumley has a fairly clear field here.

MYSTERIES OF THE EARTH by Jacques Bergier. 207pp. OUR HAUNTED PLANET by John Keel. 191pp. Both from Futura (paperbacks); 60p; in their 'Mysteries of Time & Space' series. MOTE (published in USA as EXTRA-TERRESTRIAL VISITATIONS FROM PREHISTORIC TIMES TO THE PRESENT) is Bergier's main exposition on his theories of ET visitation — more so that the recent, unfortunately titled EXTRA-TER-RESTRIAL INTERVENTION: THE EVIDENCE (see Reviews, NEWS 8) which in fact contained very little on the subject. MOTE, basicly, is ten general essays on the standard subjects: the lines at Nasca, the maps of the sea-kings, the Tunguska event, the Baalbek terrace, Kaspar Hauser, etc. I enjoy Bergier best on the less well known themes — 'Dr Gurlt's Cube' discusses artifacts found in ancient strata (the cube referred to being found in coal in the 19th C, and which later disappeared from the museum in which it was said to be housed.); the mysterious and prodig-ious geniuses of the Middle Ages (Cardan, Bacon, et al), and their recent counterparts like Sir Henry Cavendish, Boscovitch, Franklin et al, who Bergier maintains, were members of, or received instruction from an 'Invisible College'; and on 'green children' and other visitors from 'else-where'. (Curiously, Bergier does not mention the obvious classic of the 'Green Children of Woolpit (Norfolk, 12th C.) though he does give a Spanish

case of 1887 that parallels most of the details.)
Unfortunately my review copy has pages 81-100 missing — so make sure your copy is complete before you buy yours.
OUR HAUNTED PLANET has of course been around in the USA since 1971, and may be known to some of you already. If not, then this is one of those general rambles that take in the whole gamut of the curious, and rather better than most. Keel says: "Wonder and curiosity have always been an integral part of my life. I am only trying to share that wonder with the reader...I do not pre-tend to know any answers. After a lifetime of study and travel I am still learning the quest-ions." With a guide like Keel you can be garuan-teed a good ride, pertinent observations and a few sensible laughs.

A HISTORY OF MAGIC, WITCHCRAFT & OCCULTISM by WB Crow. Abacus (paperback); 60p; 320pp.
Not strictly a new publication, but worth knowing about - an economic paper edition with a new index - and structured usefully, more like an encyclopedia.
It recently came to our attention that there is an error in the biographical note. It says the author is a Dip Sc. of London University, whoever wrote it being under the mistaken imp-ression that D.Sc. means this diploma. Dr Crow is not only a PhD. as stated but also holds the higher degree of DSc. which means Doctor of Sci-ence. It would be a courtesy if you could corr-ect your copies accordingly. Ta!

ADZ/CONT...
= - = - = - = - = - = - = - = - = - = - = - = - =
THE LEY HUNTER - Ancient Wisdom, Leys, Sacred Sites, Cosmic Energy & UFO related subjects. Now bi-monthly. £1.50/yr. USA: $6.00/yr. Edited by Paul Screeton: 5 Egton Drive, Seaton Carew, Hart-lepool, Cleveland TS25 2AT. Essential reading.
= - = - = - = - = - = - = - = - = - = - = - = - =
SPECTRUM : A new bi-monthly occult magazine featuring UFOs, Magic, witchcraft, ESP & psychic matters, book reviews, reader's letters etc. Illustrated. Send 35p for latest issue, or only £2.00 for next 6 issues to: Bywood Publications, 62 High Street, Croydon CR9 2UT, Surrey.
= - = - = - = - = - = - = - = - = - = - = - = - =
INFINITY NEWSLETTER - a potpouri of news & views in the fields of ESP, metaphysics, paranormal subjects, UFOs, etc. 12 issues $6.00 US & Canada, $12.00 Overseas/airmailed. Infinity Press, Box 140, Decorah, Iowa 52101. Also regularly cont-ains news about Brad Steiger's activities, etc.
= - = - = - = - = - = - = - = - = - = - = - = - =
LANTERN published by the Borderline Science In-vestigation Group, doing sterling work in East Anglia. The Spring 1975 issue contains: Ghosts of the Air; an article on some extraordinary psychic photography produced at a local seance by BSIG's Psychic Research Section; legends of the Ferry Inn, Horning; Suffolk Landscape Geo-metry by Nigel Pennick; and a round-up of local news & curiosities. A quarterly at 70p/year (payable to BSIG). Inquiries to: IAW Bunn, 3 Dunwich Way, Lowestoft, Suffolk NR32 4RZ.
= - = - = - = - = - = - = - = - = - = - = - = - =

a miscellany of Fortean curiosites

THE NEWS

'PORTRAIT OF A FAULT AREA'
part 1 of a Fortean study of Leicestershire
by Paul Devereux & Andrew York...5

A Fortean chocolate-box top! -- Two closely related kittens break legs within hours of each other. Sunday Mirror, 7 April 1974.

some Synchronous aburdities....4

Miracle petrol substitutes 3....
Barmouth Monster continued 22

PLUS FORTEAN FUNNIES

PAGE 11.

35p:$1·00   ISSN:0306-0764

11

THE NEWS

bi-monthly notes
on Fortean
phenomena

THE NEWS is a non-profitmaking bi-monthly miscellany of Fortean news, notes
and references; and is affiliated to the International Fortean Organisation (INFO)
in continuing the work of **Charles Fort** (1874 – 1932). THE NEWS is edited by
Robert JM Rickard : Post Office Stores, Aldermaston, Berkshire, England.

SUBSCRIPTIONS : 1 year (6 issues) : UK : £2.10. USA : $6.00. All
other countries use dollar equivalent. Single issues : 35p / $1.00. Back issues
(if available) : 40p / $1.15. Current INDEX free to subscribers, otherwise 20p/
60¢ each. Cheques, POs, IMOs etc. make payable to **RJM Rickard,** not THE
NEWS. All **overseas subscribers** should add 10% to the total if paying by cheque,
to cover the banking exchange commission and charges.

CONTRIBUTIONS & RIGHTS : All articles in **THE NEWS** are copyright of the
authors – and the views expressed are not necessarily those of **THE NEWS,** or INFO.
Contributions of articles, notes and artwork on related subjects are always welcome and
duly credited. – If you encounter any reference or data you think will be of interest,
please make a note of the **source** and **date** (adding your **name,** for the crediting). Please
don't assume our omniscience – there are very few duplications. Remember national
daily newspapers have slightly different regional editions —— and we are especially glad
to see notes from professional sources, local papers, and rare or OP books. All the notes
herein may be quoted freely, though we hope for a credit in return. **All category head
art in this issue by Hunt Emerson.**

INFO's 3rd ANNUAL CONVENTION – FORTFEST 75.

It's getting very close but this might get
to you in time. Venue is the Sheraton–Oak Brook
Motor Hotel, 1401 West 22nd St, Oak Brook, Ill-
inois 60521. Phone: (312) 325-8555. Dates: 8-10
August. Registration:
INFO Members.....$12.00.
Non-Members......$ 7.00/day.
Students rate....$ 5.00/day with ID.
Full rate inc.
INFO Membership..$18.00.
Contact: Richard Crowe (Chicago area) on (312)
767-4481; and Paul Willis (703) 920-7120.
The event/speaker list has fattened out to
contain: John Keel on The Mothman Prophecies;
Loren Coleman; Dr Roy Mackal (Univ Chicago);
Gene Philips, Ancient Astronaut Society; a tape
from Tim Dinsdale on recent work at Loch Ness;
John Carlson (Univ Maryland) on archaeoastrono-
my; Phil Ledger sends a paper on computer ana-
lysis of Anglesey leys; a Fortean tape from Dr
Berthold Schwarz; 'Paradoxes in UFOlogy' by Dr
Roger Wescott; Sherman Larson, President of the
Centre for UFO Studies; 'We all like a Good Monster', a paper by Dr Bernard Heuvelmans; 'Who
threw that Stone?' a tape on a classic poltergeist case from New Zealand; a paper from FW
Holiday; J Gordon Melton on UFO cults; Joe Troiani with tapes from Europe of the Jurgenson/
Raudive 'voices'; Jerome Clark on what's new in
Magonia; 'Matthew Manning: Study of a Psychic' a
film; Stuart Greenwood (Univ Maryland) on anc-

ient astronaut evidence; Kirlian photography
demonstration by Richard Leshuk; a seminar on
historical ufology; Peter Byrne of BIGFOOT NEWS;
Ray Manners on 'UFO Performance Characteristics'.
Phew! Three INFO packed days – and last but not
least Richard Crowe's nite-time Chicago Ghost
Tour, optional, $5/person, on the Saturday night.

APOLOGIA.

THE NEWS is now fully operational at its
new address. The move went without major disaster. Now if only I could find the things I
want when I want them. Because of certain minor
disruptions, and the roundabout trip to Fortfest
I shall not be back in England until mid-Sept.
So apologies to all who suffer lapses in
communication. Just as we leave, news comes of
another possible rise in postage costs, and this
together with the other problems that affect the
future of THE NEWS will be thunk over and plans
set in motion for our next year's development.

THIS ISSUE – we have part one of Paul Devereux's
and Andrew York's giant study of Leicestershire
phenomena, which takes the greater part of this
issue. Perhps you'll begin to grasp the scope of
this work when we say the the next three issues
of THE LEY HUNTER will carry their more ley-ish
researches under the title of 'The Forgotten
Heart of Albion'. And on pages 11-13 you'll
find a little present to all of you from Hunt
Emerson and myself, to celebrate CF's birthday
(6th August). Meanwhile, everybody holler...

"Happy Birthday Charles Fort"

APRIL FUELS?

An idea advanced by Brad Steiger and John Keel is the linking of the MIB and the mysterious inventors that crop up throughout history. Steiger, citing a case from Mackay's Extraordinary Popular Delusions & the Madness of Crowds, suggests they were up to tricks with the alchemists by flashing a powder that turned lead to gold, and vanishing after an apparently successful demonstration. The modern equivalent seems to be a powder which when mixed with water gives a workable petrol-substitute for ic engines. See Ch 14 of Steiger's Mysteries of Time & Space, and NEWS 5/9 & 7/21, for versions.

Now that it's fashionable to be energy-conscious, not only should we expect more such stories - but some may even be investigated. We have a few for the record.

In 1954, Guido Franch was prosecuted by Du Page County, Illinois, alleging that he had sold more than 100% of his formula for MOTA (atom backwards) fuel to speculators. He was acquitted because all the prosecution witnesses - supposedly the ones who were bilked - all testified that the formula really worked. And after this verdict Franch conducted a spontaneous demonstration on the Du Page couthouse lawn by mixing a green powder with water and running a lawnmower on it. For more than 40 years, Franch has wandered all over Illinois, apparently rejecting all offers from large organisations, in favour of personal private demonstrations using old cars, and disclaiming any interest in possible profits. He says he can make 5000 gallons of 105-octane fuel by processing one ton of coal in chemical vats, for around 4 cents a gallon. He admits he's a dummy, and that he got the formula off an elderly Austrian, Alexander Kraft, who invented it for making cheap rocket fuel - Franch claims to have spent all the money donated to him, in refining the process for suitability for cars etc. The article in the Chicago Tribune, 17 April 74 (Cr: Mark A Hall), asks whether it's all a hoax or not, seems to imply that it is not, then fades out. If Franch's powder really works - and its a good hoax that can survive 40 years - then why the conspicuous silence since?

We had a prosecution on the same subject recently in England - two men, Cummings and Burke, charged with conspiracy to defraud a Canadian company, Sunningdale Oil, of £20 million. They were not the inventors, but having seen Mr Thomas Munson demonstrate his 'Mixture' on TV, approached him after, and made a deal to finance him onto the world market. Cummings even put some in his own car to test it and was thoroughly convinced of the Mixture's effectiveness. Were the con-men themselves conned? - seems unlikely. Munson, who lives in Blaenau Festiniog, North Wales, said he picked up part of the formula in Germany in 1945, and can make a petrol substitute costing only 4p/gallon/216 miles. Results of an analysis (New Scientist, 5 June 75) said the Mixture contained "95.3% distilled water, benzene, methanol, iodine crystals, ignitable oil, borax and Fairy washing-up liquid". The remaining 4.7% included Munson's magic powder "Tracanath". It transpired that Cummings and Burke brought the elderly Mr Munson from the sticks to the big city to do a demonstration. That night they locked Mr Munson in his hotel room (it is not clear whether he had agreed to this) because, they said, he tended to wander when under stress. In the night Mr Munson could not sleep and decided he didn't want to go through with it. If he hadn't known about the locked door, it certainly would have helped him make up his mind. He unscrewed the lock, and was on the first bus back to uncomplicated Wales. Imagine the panic of the two hustlers finding their star vanished on the very morning of the big deal. So they concocted a potion out of what they could remember of its ingredients, and of course lacking Munson's magic powder. They told watching scientists that the Mixture should stand for a few hours, but they had a bottle of ready-made stuff to hand (which later analysis showed to be 97% petrol. The buyers became suspicious and blew the whistle. Cummings and Burke were arrested and charged, but later acquitted because of insufficient evidence . And Munson's Magic Mixture, too, has slipped back into peaceful obscurity. Compiled from Daily Mirror, 15 Jan 75 & Daily Telegraph, 30 Jan 75 (Cr: Bob White.)

In October last year, we heard of a French inventor, Jean Chambrin, of Rouen, who had patented a device enabling ic engines to run on tap water and alcohol - though not strictly a 'magic powder' story, it is of interest. After successful demonstrations on French, Dutch and Italian TVs, the French guvmint have asked their Petroleum Research Institute to follow it up. Chambrin has a 'black box' weighing 33lb fitted between a modified solex carburettor and the engine, and according to Chambrin, it cracks the water into hydrogen and oxygen, and burns the former. The protests of the sceptics center around a belief that it would take at least as much energy to crack the water as could be got from burning the hydrogen, so there would be no net gain in energy. The device, however, appears to work despite objections. In one demo, Chambrin started his car on pure alcohol (from a corner chemist) and

Cont on p19...

...AND, AT THAT SAME MOMENT....

SYNCHRONICITIES

FINDINGS.

Mrs AM Lysons of Walford, Baschurch, Shrewsbury, Salop wrote to the Daily Mirror (7 Jan 75): " Last October I was calving a cow on the farm where I work. After the calving I washed my hands and lost my wedding ring in the bedding of the calving pen. That bedding was spread on a 100 acre field which was later ploughed – the ring obviously lost forever. None of it. A few days ago, the chap who ploughed this field was cleaning off his plough and tractor. Lo and behold, what did he find stuck on a chunk of mud? Yes, you've got it, my wedding ring. This must be the luckiest ring of all time, as it was completely unmarked."

Fort regarded tales of such findings as <u>conventional</u> compared to most of his data – and admitted forsaking them in his pursuit of the "unconventional repeating". He also regarded them as the province of liars, who being conventionally lazy, could only summon enough imagination to copy something only marginally absurd. Well, we don't have Fort's ready-made excuse of the finite dimensions of a book. Besides, in continuity we feel that just as there are incidents in daily life that are nearly fully understood, so there must be a balance of enigmatic trivia. If we were honest we might admit to collecting such stories just for the hell of it – and move on to tell you some more.

A Letter from Mrs S Judges, Chatham, Kent, to the Sun (6 Feb 75): "After I lost my opal ring, I dreamed that it was in our chicken run. As soon as it was light I ran to the run ((ho ho – Ed.)) but could not find my ring. Two days later one of the hens was killed for our dinner, and there in its crop was the lost ring."

Norman Fletcher, a deckhand on a Hartlepool fishing vessel, was helping to pull in the nets, 100 miles out in the North Sea, when a gust of wind blew off his cap. He watched gloomily as the cap sank beneath the waves, and with it his freshly-filled pipe tucked in behind a stud. A month later, he and a mate were again pulling in nets, about 20 miles from where he lost his cap. He could hardly believe his eyes when his mate extracted the lost cap from the net, with pipe in place still. Daily Telegraph, 22 March 75 (CR: John Michell), Weekly News, 12 April 75 (Cr: Nigel Watson.)

Then, for what it's worth – a small shark caught at Nieuport, off the coast of Belgium, was opened by fishmonger Roger Woestyn, who found an English £5note inside, smelly but tenable. ((A rumour that he kept the fish and threw away the money was worth a few guffaws on the Paris stock-exchange – Ed.)) Weekly News, 22 Feb 75 (Cr: N Watson.) Now we're shifting to the even more unlikely subject of finding things inside other things. Example – Knoxville, Tennessee housewife, Norma Pointer, who found a 1 cent piece in her breakfast egg. Los Angeles Times (Cr: Mark Hall) & London Evening News (Cr: Steve Moore) both of 20 March 75.

Iris Fowler, 50, died a fortnight after complaining of a sore throat following her consumption of a pie. An open safety-pin was found lodged in her throat. The Coroner told an Inquest at Chelmsford, Essex: "The inference seems to be that the pin was in the pie." But there is also an inference that it contributed to her death in some unmentioned way. For a story of a girl with a fork in her throat, see NEWS 1/15, but she is known to have put it there. Not so culpable was Jane Vaughan, an 82-yr-old great-grandmother, who had a 6" steel knitting needle removed from her back. Doctors said it had been there a year at least, but all the old lady could say was "I don't know how it got there. I didn't feel a thing" Sun, 4 Oct 74.

We're not sure what we are implying here – they could be perfectly explained by conventional if unusual circumstances. But, phenomenologically speaking, we accept that there could very well have been mysterious transportings of things inside other things – and that if such apportations exist, they are undoubtedly hidden amongst similar, but normally explicable cases – (a mimicking process?). We are thinking of the findings of living frogs in the hearts of stones – or Steiger's suggestion that anomalous artifacts found in ancient strata may have been apported there (see his <u>Mysteries of Time & Space</u>.) Good Lord! there could even be a crab in my mug of tea... ((Many a nip twixt cup 'n' lip – eh?)) Anyway – is this any more preposterous than what is taught kids about flies in amber, fossils in coal-strata, and the unmelted chocolate buttons in Maryland cookies?

Cont on p20...

PORTRAIT OF A FAULT AREA

by Paul Devereux & Andrew York

part one

The material we present here is related to work we have been doing on neglected aspects of Leicestershire lore, in the course of which the fault area to the west of the county became active with accompanying UFO phenomena. The strongest tremor-areas, however, seemed to be along the Trent valley in Staffordshire. As our research was beginning to yield data on the Leics. fault area, as there was current activity, and as fault areas are often associated with anomalous characteristics, we felt that it might prove interesting to undertake a general study of the Leics.-Staffs. fault area. We have approached the landscape in question from several viewpoints, like peeling layers off an onion. We will attempt to indicate that unusual factors can indeed be associated with the area, and we will conclude with some exploratory thoughts that might relate, in a wider sense, to Fortean and Lost Knowledge fields of inquiry.

THE LAY OF THE LAND.

The present writers are mainly concerned with Leics., particularly the west of the county; we feel that a study of a wide range of phenomena and features in a small geographical area is a worthwhile exercise at the present time. Because of the fault/UFO activity, however, our attention was drawn to the E. Staffs area as well. So, for the purposes of this particular study, our region of concern is as indicated on the smaller scale sketch map. The centre of this area is roughly 80 miles NW of the centre of Fort's "London Triangle". As much of our material is concentrated in the west of Leics., we also present a larger scale sketch map of that region.

The two "ends" of the area are dominated by Stoke-on-Trent and Leicester, about

50 miles apart. A thin "wedge" of Derbyshire separates the borders of Staffs. and Leics., except for one mile-long section. Near this spot is a place called Honey Hill, close to where the counties of Warwickshire, Staffs. and Leics. meet.

The region is approximately the geographical heart of England. It is industrial, wealthy and materialistic. Beneath this 20th-Century facade, however, there lies a good deal of poetic, green countryside of exceptional English beauty.

Charnwood Forest lies within the boundaries of Leics., to the NW of the county. It is not a forest of trees, and probably never was a forest in any real sense (1). It was obliquely referred to in Domesday as a "waste". It is a remarkable area. It is high relative to its

surrounding pastoral landscape. Up on the Forest one senses a weird, primeval atmosphere: Charnwood is the overt result of ancient volcanic action. Its landscape is punctuated by sudden, odd outcrops of rock - "the strange spectacle of the strata tilted on end"(1). Everywhere are ancient groupings of trees, often on a tump or hiding a rock outcrop, and often surrounded by old drystone walls.

Charnwood acts like a great obstacle to a major fault system that can be traced from Kent up to the Pennines, and, it is thought by some, may carry on north to Scotland. A major fault within this system occurs actually at Charnwood and is known as the Thringstone Fault. All around the Forest is complex faulting, with many minor fault lines still to be precisely located. Most of Leics., and, indeed, the Midlands plain as a whole, is to some degree affected by this fault complex. To the NW of Charnwood the faulting "goes underground" to some extent, only to reappear in the Trent valley in the vicinity of Stoke. It is believed that part of the fault system goes on into Wales but it has not been traced with any certainty.

THE KEY OF LLYR.

King Lear, son of the magical monarch Bladud, is said to have built Leicester - "Leircestre". Lear is supposed to have been buried in a vault under the River Soar in Leicester. This vault had originally been built in honour of the Roman god Janus. (A temple, thought to be dedicated to Janus, has been discovered in the remains of the Roman forum in Leic-

ester.) Robert Graves (6) links Lear with Janus, and both with the pre-Roman British god Llyr. Janus was two-headed, facing both ways between the Old and New year. Graves demonstrates the link between Llyr and the oak ("Duir" being the oak's Beth-Luis-Nion name). The oak is associated with the thunderbolt and strong connections can be made between Llyr and the thunder-gods - Thor, Zeus and Jupiter. "Duir" has a root meaning "door" in many languages and, of course, oak is the traditional timber for a door. St. John seems to be the Christianisation of Llyr, and St. John's day is June 24th, the mid-point of the Oak Month (June 10th-July 7th). On this day was the sacrifical burning alive of the oak-god (the fuel of the midsummer fires is by tradition oak). A 7-day wake followed this "sacrifice". The second half of the Celtic year began in July. June 24th is the close of the midsummer solstitial period, and happens to be one of the 5 dates in the year that John Keel (8) regards as of major UFO/occult importance.

So Llyr, "king and god", is to be associated with the Druidic oak-cult (if not even earlier activities); with the symbol of the door; with midsummer; with thunderbolts and with the county of Leics. As we have noted, it is in this Land of Llyr that Charnwood Forest is located.

If this door-keeping oak-god, Llyr, was deposed by Christianity and doomed to "languish forgotten in the castle of Arianrhod"(6). we believe he left his key behind for those who would seek it. This "key" is to be found, we think, in the form of Croft Hill, Leics.

Croft Hill stands close by the Roman Fosse Way, 6 miles SW of Leicester and 5 miles NE of Hinckley. It is also 5 miles from High Cross where the Roman Watling Street crosses the Fosse Way. It is a modest eminence of a few hundred feet, with even slopes a grove-like tree grouping on its west flank. Its situation however, is such that its summit, a curiously cracked slab of rock, commands dramatically extensive views over the full circle of the horizon. There are earthworks around the hill, including a ditch and what may be a tumulus. In one spot two curiously stunted trees display remarkable spiral contortions of their trunks, which might indicate geodetic influence (12). The cracks and discolouration of the summit rock might, we speculate, be due to lightning. The hill has long been regarded as an important spot (2) and has had, like Glastonbury Tor, its "human sacrifice", when 44 so-called thieves were tortured and hanged there in

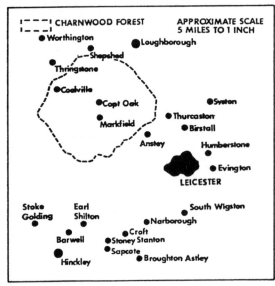

CHARNWOOD FOREST   APPROXIMATE SCALE 5 MILES TO 1 INCH

Worthington
Loughborough
Shepshed
Thringstone
Coalville
Copt Oak
Syston
Markfield
Thurcaston
Birstall
Anstey
Humberstone
Evington
LEICESTER
Stoke Golding
Earl Shilton
South Wigston
Narborough
Croft
Barwell
Stoney Stanton
Sapcote
Hinckley
Broughton Astley

1124.

The ugly village of Croft, at the foot
of the hill, has a few features of interest. Its church is dedicated to the ser-
pent-slaying St. Michael; it has a superb markstone by its main street (one of
two, the other stone has been destroyed),
and a road called "Arbor Road". "Arbor"
has the old meaning of "the central axis
about which a wheel turns, the central
support of any machine" (5).

A view of Croft Hill from the south-east.

The central support of any machine? In
1879, T.L.Walker (13) developed a theory
that Croft Hill was the British Mesomphalos (Central sacred place; navel of
the earth). He pointed out that the Gallic Mesomphalos, said to have been adopted from a British structure, was in
the midst of a plain, surrounded by a
wall and a ditch, and was on the banks
of the Loire. Walker linked the name of
the Soar with Leire, which can be traced
back to "Legra" meaning "Loire". Croft
Hill stands by the River Soar, is earthworked, is situated on a plain and only
4 miles away is a village called Leire.
In addition, the hill stands approximately at the centre of England, and the
claimants to the title "Centre of England" (eg. Leicester Clock Tower; High
Cross; Meriden; Higham-on-the-Hill) fall
within its general vicinity. No one
agrees as to where the actual Mesomphalos was (Lichfield, 35 miles from Croft,
has been put forward by some), but we
feel that Walker's theory is soundly
based. Although his evidence is circum-
stantial, to dismiss it one would have
to seek refuge in coincidence, which we
are not prepared to do.

It is at least symbolic that at this
interesting point in Britain's social
and economic history, the possible Mesomphalos is threatened with destruction
by a quarry company that has not only
eaten away the land on the east side of
the hill, but actually owns the hill as

well! Horrors.

We noted an unusual feature on Croft Hill
consisting of a ledge protruding from the
lower slopes of the hill, resting on a
slightly sloping "wall". A prehistorian
in Leicester, studying our photographs,
decided it was not an archaeological
feature and referred it to his geological
colleagues. They considered it to be "a
natural curiosity" and promised us a
report on it. Croft Hill is an apt location for such a curiosity. Through the
mediation of NEWS-reader Graham Crowley
we have, in fact, been able to secure
our own report (from an authoritative
source) on the feature. This report,
while confirming the geological formation of the ledge and "wall", also gives
us an insight into the nature of the
hill and its vicinity that should be
kept in mind by the reader while studying the totality of the data we present
relating to the region.

The material comprising the feature is
very weathered and its felspars are decomposing towards clay minerals. The rock
is medium-grained volcanic, intrusive or
possibly hyperbyssal. It contains no visible quartz or mica and could therefore
belong to the basic group of igneous
rock, but as the large-grain, acid, high
quartz-content granite is also present
on the hill, the rock is probably of the
intermediate group - probably syenite
(mined by the adjacent quarry company!).
Silicon is present. Rock samples from
the feature were tested for flourescence
with no striking results. The undercut-
ting of the ledge is probably due to
preferential weathering. The age of the
rock is pre-Cambrian which has been fau-
lted and thrusted. The presence of the
ledge could be due to a very large block
moving in relation to another. Our source
has consulted aeromagnetic maps of the
region, but we will have to follow the
matter up with him to pinpoint Croft
Hill in relation to these maps. However,
our source does say: "It is evident that
there are quite a few magnetic anomalies
around Leicester." This is an important
consideration.

It is our experience in compiling data
on the area that Croft Hill seems to
exercise some enigmatic influence, or
attraction, on certain events taking
place in the local sky and landscape. We
will make occasional references to Croft
Hill throughout the text to reinforce
this observation.

We believe, with a few others, that in a
remote time, long before the historical
period, there was a cosmology that defined and supported a geopsychic science.
We think that this early understanding,

more complete than our current mode of thought, was able to contemplate the realisation that physical and psychic reality were one whole package, and would not have differentiated between these facets of existence. It is our feeling that Croft Hill is a sacred hill, a geo-psychic structure left over from antiquity, acting as a sort of multi-dimensional reference point for some of the aerial, terrestrial and psychic events in its vicinity - a beacon in psycho-physical reality. More than that, if Croft Hill is Britain's Mesomphalos, then it may perform a vital function (the arbor) regarding the whole of sacred engineering in the UK.

THE METEOROLOGICAL LANDSCAPE.

Our records for this section begin on June 16th, 1645, when there was a "strange" storm of hail in and around Lough-borough. Gigantic hailstones "did much hurt" in the neighbourhood. In the same year (we have not yet traced the month) the water in Garendon Pool, a mile from Loughborough, turned red "like blood" for 4 days. People came from far and wide to view the phenomenon. Cattle refused to drink the water but fish were unhurt. There used to be an abbey at Garendon. In 1659 Sir George Booth wrote of "The Strange and dreadful Apparition of wonderful Meteors in the Air, at Markfield in Leics., on Thursday September 7th, 1659." Sir George describes how "extraordinary flashes of lightning" broke from angry clouds creating "terrible" claps of thunder. This continued for an hour. There was no rain but "a most black and dreadful storm of hail, and instead of hailstones there fell rattling down from the air halberts, swords and daggers; which...were found to be of the same nature...as were the hailstones; and after a little while both the sight, and the fright the sight brought with it, did melt away at once." The folk of Markfield and its neighbour-hood were not spared for long, however. They heard crackles and bangs as if muskets "in repeated volleys, did discharge their cholerick errands." There were many "prodigious eruptions of fire, which with great violence did fly in the air, and, running lower, did tear in pieces many strong houses and laid great trees on their backs, which in an instant were plucked up by the roots." A lime kiln was destroyed in this part of the storm after which "this part of the fiery tempest, which came so low, was seen by all to take its course up the hill, where it vanished away, and there was heard no more noise of it."(10). We do not know which hill this was, but there is a Snake Hill next to Markfield, which

might indicate ophiolatric references. The 1650s were generally an active time. There was a fierce tempest of wind and thunder in Leicester in 1652, January 16th, which "uncovered 411 baies of houses, and overturned many." In 1658 there was said to have been a remarkable storm that was felt all over Europe. In that year a Leics. church was demolished by a storm. Throsby said of the 1650s that "it is somewhat singular to remark what a number of fires there happened in the county about this time."(11). He records them at, amongst other places, Burton Overy, Cropston, Lutterworth, Hinckley and Desford - all are within 10 miles of Croft Hill, as indeed Markfield is. (The name Markfield relates to an inscribed standing stone that once existed in the centre of a nearby field.) Sir George Booth also tells us: "We have heard and seen of late of many forms of hailstones ...Sometimes they have been taken up and observed for the most part to be flat; as in that dreadful storm of hail; presently after that it rained fire from Heaven: which was beheld by many travellers coming late to London, not far from Epping, about 3 years since..." This dates the event as approximately 1656. On June 2nd 1660, a freak whirlwind was severely felt in Worthington and adjacent villages. It started suddenly, tore a house asunder, ripped apart Spring Wood, blew down chimneys and roofing, "and hurried a man into an orchard". A huge log of wood, no one ever knew from where, smashed against a solitary house. A contemporary wrote: "This whirlwind ran 3 miles in length and the effects of it were seen above 20 yards in breadth. Some say that flames of fire were seen in it."

Fort refers to a 1661 earthquake in the Hereford/Worcester area which was accompanied by "monstrous flaming things" in the sky(4).

The 18th century was literally a phenomenal century, judging by our records. In November 1703 there was what was considered to be the worst storm ever recorded or remembered. Daniel Defoe was an eye-witness of the storm, which seems to have affected most of England. "The air was full of meteors and vaporous fires," Defoe said. Many English towns were devastated and large numbers of mansions were blown down. Hundreds of thousands of trees up and down the country were uprooted. Fleets were cast away at sea. The Eddystone lighthouse was destroyed and its designer killed. There were record high tides in the Severn and Thames. The years 1715-1723 were remarkable ones in Leics., according to the records of a vicar in Shepshed, on Charnwood. He tells us of "unusual lights" that inhabitants of Charnwood Forest saw "in the north part of the heavens, sometimes inclining to the east, but oftener to the west." The lights usually took the form of "spiral streams or columns" that ascended "up to the very zenith". These phenomena sometimes displayed "strong vibrations or dartings". The observers of these aerial sights were at first frightened, but "the frequency of them at length made them less frightful". The vicar says that the experts of the day could not satisfactorily explain away "such prodigious quantity of streams or pillars of light as frequently appeared". The date the first light was seen is given as March 6th, 1715. It appeared a little above the horizon and looked like "a great house on fire at a distance". These lights seem to have appeared at all seasons during their 9-year activity (10). Throsby noted that a meteor was seen over Leicester in 1718. It looked like a ball of fire and seemed to descend to the ground. In the NE of Leics., a little outside our immediate region of concern, is Belvoir Castle. This is an imposing place, built on a mound. Nichols quoted a Mr. Peck who remarked on the number of low mists in the area; so thick were they that "one cannot find one's way home at midday". Mr. Peck also records "a strange appearance" of a herd of deer in the air "all fairly represented in the mist, their shadows running and moving all correspondent with the motions of real deer". Many people had seen this phenomenon and one man claimed he had seen it more than once. Mr. Peck noted these matters in the 1730s. The fellow also referred to "a certain meteor" that was "occasionally observed" at Saltby, not far from Belvoir. Saltby is situated near an earthwork known as "King Lud's

Rents" (Lud is another term for Llyr). Peck records the phenomenon in verse:
  "Oft travellers o'er that wide plain by
                    night,
  Perceive a meteor on themselves and
                    horses light,
  Whose lambent pale flame all about
                    them sticks,
  And frights them strangely with its
                    harmless tricks
  So many fancies it will sometimes shew,
  That even no phosphorus can its tricks
                    outdo."

Our Shepshed vicar recalls that on July 18th, 1727, there was an earthquake. The wind suddenly became calm before the quake, but ten minutes afterwards there blew a "pretty fresh gale" for 15 minutes; then it ceased. On July 31st, 1735, there was a violent electrical storm over Loughborough. It rained for 6 hours causing "knee-deep" torrents of water to course through the streets of the town. On June 17th, 1747, again at Loughborough, there was a freak storm of hail and thunder. Some of the hailstones measured more than $2\frac{1}{2}$" across. In 1755 the church at Husbands Bosworth, about 11 miles SE of Croft was damaged by a fierce storm. Stones in the church walls and pavements were displaced by lightning, the bells were displaced and the spire had a chasm 12 yds long rent in it. Globes of fire were seen in the air and lightning in a "terrible manner ran along the streets". Clouds of smoke with a sulphurous smell issued from the aperture of the spire. Throsby notes than on June 14th of the following year, between the hours of 8 and 10, there was "a remarkable heavy shower of rain, attended with incessant claps of thunder, and very alarming lightning". During this storm a ball of fire was seen "which divided into particles and vanished without

HUSBANDS BOSWORTH.

Lightning striking the spire of the church at Husbands Bosworth, in 1755. An engraving dated 1789 in Nichols's History and Antiquities of Leicestershire.

doing any damage". The steeple of the ancient church of St. Mary de Castro, in Leicester, was struck 3 times by lightning in 1763; twice in one month. The church stands in close proximity to other church spires. 6 years previously, the spire had been damaged by a "remarkable tempest". An inhabitant of Hinckley, 5 miles SW from Croft Hill, observed a fiery meteor in October 1766. It travelled NW to SE, was elliptical, emitted sparks, and made a hissing noise. It appeared after a violent storm of wind and rain. In December 1766, also over Hinckley, "there suddenly appeared a large fiery ball...brisk but unequal in motion" and this also gave off sparks. In October 1769 there was "a remarkable aurora borealis" in the Hinckley skies. A Mr. Robinson stated that "these illuminations began...as soon as the evening twilight would permit, their first appearance being near the horizon. They seemed to proceed from dusky light clouds, as they frequently do, streaming upwards towards the zenith; those from the Westward, after some time, began to be tinged with red, and continued to alternately exhibit great varieties of that colour, which succeeded each other by quick successions, being sometimes of a wan light red, then approaching...a full blood-colour...The illuminations from the other quarters of the heavens had nearly their usual appearance, except from the North East, which were of a remarkable pale bright silver colour for a considerable time; at near seven o'clock they likewise began to be a little tinged with red...it being now half past seven o'clock and the different streams of light arising from most parts of the horizon seemed to be in full strength, directing themselves towards the zenith where they formed a corona, or point,

which appeared and disappeared frequently, and was sometimes partial or broken. This point near the zenith was frequently surrounded by a kind of radii, the points of which at this time were tinged with a light red colour: the strongest appearance was from seven to eight o'clock. It was observable that the corona...was not exactly in the zenith: it appeared and disappeared frequently; but always formed itself a few degrees towards the South; nor was it exactly in the meridian, but inclined a little towards the East." (10). In June 1772 a terrible electrical storm did much damage in Leics. In July 1783 "there was a great storm of thunder and lightning". In Shepshed a man was killed when a bolt of lightning entered his house via the chimney. Another house in Shepshed was struck in the same storm and again the lightning entered by the chimney and cut off one corner of an almanack "with as much regularity as if done by a sharp instrument". The head of an oak tree about a mile from Shepshed was torn from the trunk and thrown a considerable distance. Also in this storm a horse was killed on Charnwood "and near the body were found round holes made deep in the ground by the lightning; but there were no wounds to be seen on the horse. In the said forest several sheep were killed; and, what was very surprising, a rock...was rent and several stones thrown therefrom" (10). A month later, Throsby notes that a ball of fire "with a long train" was seen passing over Leicester in a SW direction. Some people felt the shock of an earthquake too. The spire of Shepshed church was struck in a storm of 1785. On May 29th (Royal Oak Day), 1788, a hailstorm accompanied by thunder and lightning assailed Loughborough and its district. Along with the storm there came a

Lightning striking the steeple of St Mary de Castro, Leicester, in 1763. An engraving dated 1794 in Nichols's History and Antiquities of Leicestershire, showing the old castle mound on the right.

Cont on p14///

great wind that broke windows facing it
and stripped trees of bark and foliage -
the bruising to some trees was percept-
ible years afterwards. A new spire was
erected on Hinckley church in this year
as the old one had "been much injured by
time and lightning".

In 1801 there came on Hinckley "a sudden
and tremendous storm" that destroyed a
windmill. In 1804 the steeple at Sapcote
(2½ miles from Croft) was struck by lightning. In 1850 the spire of St. John the
Baptist at Kings Newton was struck. Pev-
sner considers the church to be "one of
the most remarkable in England" from an
architectural viewpoint. The spire of the
church of St. Michael at Brooksby was
shattered by lightning in 1877. Fort
notes that a luminous object was seen in
the sky to the east of Fair Oaks, Staffs,
in 1852. Fort also records that there was
a peculiar aurora of "rapid flashes" over
Loughborough in August, 1892 (4).

There has been a major event in W Leics.
this century. On Christmas Eve, 1965,
there was a mighty rock-fall known as
the Barwell Meteorite (2), which is the
largest so far recorded in the UK. The
event was preceded by curious hissing
sounds issuing from the earth, and accompanied by a number of fireballs seen
over surrounding counties. Loud acoustic
phenomena also accompanied the fall and
affected hundreds of square miles, causing glass objects to break in certain
areas. December 24th is another of
Keel's 5 key UFO/occult days of the year.
Barwell is 4 miles from Croft Hill. In
the spring of 1971 a meteorite was reported to have landed at Arley, near Nuneaton. In true Fortean manner, some spectators claimed to have seen it land at
7 o'clock in the morning, while others
insisted it came down at night! (A multiple event?) Arley is 10 miles from
Barwell, 14 miles from Croft Hill. Earlier that year, in February, a "bright
green" object was seen to fall to earth
just SW of Leicester; and on another
occasion a "fiery object" was seen to
"suddenly disappear" over Astley, Nuneaton. In December 1971 a bright white
light travelling west to east was seen
in the skies over N Leics. The light was
soundless and seen to disintegrate.
(1971 was an active year UFOlogically in
Leics., but, as we shall argue in our
"THOR FACTOR" essay, we feel it would be
a mistake to class all "fireballs" as
UFOs.) Back to atmospheric electricity:
a Charnwood countryman tells us that an
old wood, Lea Wood, on the Forest seemed
to attract particularly fierce electrical storms, and folk kept well clear of
the place in thundery weather. Apparently, the old trees have now been removed

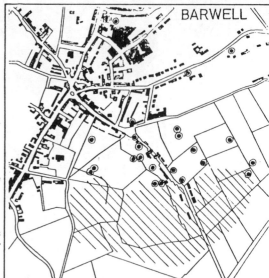

Position of meteoric fragments recovered from
Barwell. Ringed dots indicate single, large
fragments; hatching indicates many small frag-
ments. Diagram from 'The Barwell Meteorite' by
McKellar, Meadows & Sylvester-Bradley. Trans.
Leister Literary & Philosophical Society 1965/6.

and the place no longer possesses its
peculiar attraction for storms. In April
1968 a freak tornado travelled 3 miles
out of Coventry to the hamlet of Barna-
cle, causing much destruction. It so
happens that the Coventry-Barnacle direction is in line with Croft Hill, 10
miles away to the NE.

THE UFOLOGICAL LANDSCAPE.

When we began our study of Leics. we
decided that before considering individual UFO sightings we would assess any
general trends related to UFO reports in
the county. We took the UFO records of
the main local newspaper, the "Leicester
Mercury", as a sample. The records covered a period from 1953-1974. It became
clear that UFOs were sighted predomin-
antly over the west half of the county -
the area most affected by the fault complex. This trend could perhaps be accounted for by the greater population in
this part of the county, though we think
it is debatable. We had already been alerted to the possible significance of
Croft Hill, so, as a test, we drew 2 circles on the map centred on the hill, one
at 10 miles and the other at 5. Well over
50% of the sightings fell within the 10-
mile boundary, and, even more significantly, almost 25% fell within the 5-mile
boundary. Even though the "Mercury" records certainly represent a mere fraction
of UFO activity in the county, and though

the "boundaries" we drew were arbitrary, the "homing-in" of sightings to the Croft area is so strong it is a trend that cannot be ignored.

Another intriguing trend we noted was the lack of UFO sightings in June. So far we have only one sighting recorded as a UFO for the month of June and, as will be seen, even that falls more into a "fireball" category. We wonder if the June "death" of the oak-god might be a mythological recollection of some principle we cannot now grasp. June seems to be quite an active time for natural phenomena such as storms and tremors.

We have a great many UFO sightings on our files and we can do no more than glance at a few examples through the last few decades. Pauline Berger, writing to the "Flying Saucer Review"(3), records an experience she had in the late 1920s near Anstey, Leics., when she was a child. While her father stretched out in a field one sunny afternoon, she read a book. Suddenly looking up, she saw an odd-shaped figure, about 5 feet high, which she at first thought to be a scarecrow. It was black with a large head but no face. Its arms were long and dangling. She looked down at her book but sensed that the thing was looking at her. Glancing up again, she saw what she took to be a "hut" alongside the figure. She woke her father in a panic but the figure and "hut" had disappeared. This "hut" had looked like a large globe on legs, and Mrs. Berger wrote to FSR because an account of a similar figure and sphere sighting was pointed out to her in an earlier issue of the magazine. In December 1954 a Leicester citizen saw a bright strip of light to the SSE. It moved to the West where it appeared like a sickle In August 1958 there were reports of a large aerial object, rounded on top and flat underneath, travelling at "great speed" in the Coventry direction from Hinckley. In August 1959 a Birstall woman saw "a huge double star" moving slowly through the sky. In June 1961 a motorist just north of Leicester saw a coloured ball of flame plummet earthwards. He said it was so bright that it appeared like "a second sun". In November 1965 an object shaped like an "old-fashioned airship" was seen hovering over Humberstone. In September 1966 Leicester citizens reported 3 strange objects in the sky. Two drifted away, but one, "electric blue and round", remained hovering for 20 minutes. In this same month 2 bright objects were seen over Barlestone, Leics., heading toward Leicester. They were making a humming noise. 1966 was, generally, a UFO-active period in the area. Again in September 1966, "a

blue spinning ball" emitting a "strange noise", was seen hovering in the sky over S. Wigston, a village just south of Leicester (and only 5 miles from Croft) where many UFO sightings are reported. On July 3rd 1967, a large silver object was seen approaching Markfield from the Leicester direction. On the 5th July a Leicester man saw a bright object in the sky. "It seemed to line up with a star" he said, "and remained still for a full minute. It came from the Coalville direction and disappeared toward the city centre." This was the fifth object in 4 days reported in the area. In the same month a "cigar-shaped object" was seen over Humberstone. (One of the present writers is particularly interested in the Humberstone sightings because when he was a child living near Thurmaston - a couple of miles from Humberstone - he saw a huge, black, ribbed dirigible in the sky towards the Humberstone direction. While calling someone's attention to it, it disappeared. This must have been in the early 1950s.) Still in July 1967, a Loughborough man heard a "deep noise" and saw a bright light in the sky travelling from Leicester "swerving" and changing colour. Apparently the man had been woken up two months earlier by a noise similar to that emitted by the UFO. A UFO was reported, also in the same July, "travelling in a straight line from Leicester to Markfield". In September 1967 a multiple UFO event was witnessed by spectators standing on Croft Hill. Some of the lights moved slowly around the hill. On October 26th 1967, "T-shaped" and "oblong" UFOs were reported from SW Leicester, and a "flickering kite-shaped object" was seen over Earl Shilton (1½ miles from Barwell; 3 miles from Croft). The object moved off to the west. In November 1967, "a bright fiery ball with 2 distinct black crosses on it" was seen over Leicester during the afternoon. The whole of 1967 was incredibly UFO-active in Leics., as it was throughout the country. An ex-RAF man saw a number of green spheres in a "triangular formation" over Leicester in April 1968. In May of that year a "four-pronged object" was seen over Wigston for half an hour. A silver, stationary aerial object was reported by numerous witnesses in Wigston in August 1968. A "pure white light" was seen travelling north until disappearing "between Hinckley and Earl Shilton" in December 1968. In the same month, a UFO over W Leicester was described as a "very bright light, shrouded in cloud, like a second moon". Hinckley residents reported a similar object that same evening. A UFO was reported over W Leicester in August 1969. The strange light "moved to and fro in a set pattern" for about half an hour. In October 1969 the "Mercury" reported that several Leicester residents had been seeing a UFO hovering over the city every night for several weeks. In March 1970, witnesses reported a white object "like a ball" travelling across the Leicester sky. It was producing a high-pitched noise "like a factory siren". The noise lasted for 5 minutes and a great many people reported hearing it. (This is definitely a scene from the Cosmic Joke Show – though only someone who knows the Leicester population's preoccupation with affluence can savour the full humour of the event!) One May night in 1971, a woman motorist was "buzzed" by a brilliant object "about the size of a double-decker bus" in the vicinity of Croft Hill. The object lit up the countryside and affected electrical equipment in the woman's car. In August 1971 a light described as "red and yellow with a dark rim" was seen circling the SW part of Leicester on 5 successive nights. Another humming UFO was observed south of Leicester in September 1971. There was an upsurge of UFO reports all around the Charnwood/Leicester area in the Autumn of 1971. Windows began breaking inexplicably throughout Leicester. Night after night formations of lights were seen crossing the sky. UFOs emitting trails of sparks were seen; glowing orange discs surrounded by white vapour also made an appearance.

And so the reports go on. The small selection of sightings above all took place within 10 miles of Croft Hill.

A few that caught our eye further afield from the Croft area include a mysterious light "weaving about" viewed from Husband's Bosworth, in August 1971; a glow and "crackling sound" reported in the same month in a field near Syston – the Fire Brigade found nothing when they arrived on the scene; a disc of "enormous size" hovering over Billesdon, in the east of Leics., for 20 minutes, one afternoon in September 1971, and "green flames" seen in the Vale of Belvoir in January 1974. An intriguing case took place just north of the Leics. border, in Clifton, near Nottingham: in July 1967 a silver disc was seen to descend from the sky and police had to be called out to control a crowd of about a hundred people in an "alien landing scare".

A wave of UFO sightings occurred in Leics in January/February 1975 and, as far as we can gather, elsewhere in the country too. On January 5th a woman saw a stationary light "too big and far too bright' for a star, over the outskirts of Leicester. It slowly sank down to tree-top height where she lost sight of it. On

aerial Bow, seen near Mowsley, Sept. 14.1791.

The following article was communicated by the late incomparable draughtsman Mr. Schnebbelie:

" In my last excursion into Leicestershire, I was surprized with a sight of (to me a very) singular phaenomenon. I was going from Mowsley to Knaptoft, on Wednesday morning, the 14th of September, 1791. There was a very thick fog on the ground, which seemed at Mowsley to be dispersing by the Sun, which rose with great warmth ; but, when I got on some high ground about a mile from Mowsley, the fog seemed to increase, and I could see but a very short distance from me, though the Sun was at my back. I was suddenly struck with a most beautiful white arch in the atmosphere, similar to a rainbow, but only of one colour, and that so bright as to dazzle the sight. It lasted only a few seconds, and then disappeared. Having proceeded about a quarter of a mile farther, the ground still rising, another arch appeared, but considerably larger, and more brilliant. This did not disappear so suddenly as the first, but seemed to vanish with the fog. The distance of time between the appearance of the two arches was about twenty minutes, and happened about a quarter before seven in the morning. I have sent you a sketch of the first arch.

From Nichols's History and Antiquities of Leicestershire. ((Alas the incomparable draughtsmanship of Mr Schnebbelie never reckoned on the vagaries of modern Xeroxing. However we have located another engraving of a white 'rainbow' – known as Ulloa's Circle or Ring – which we will show in a future issue – Ed.))

the evening of January 24th 1975 one of the present writers saw red and white lights performing in the sky to the west of Leicester. Other people standing in the street at the time also saw the lights. Suddenly the lights, which seemed to be flickering on an object, gave off 2 bright green flashes and then moved out of sight at a rapid pace. A couple of days later a glowing orange UFO was sighted over Leicester. The local UFO study group, LAPRO (9), have a photograph taken by a Leicester resident of one of the several UFOs sighted during the January/February period. Two separate reports from Narborough described 2 bright objects in the western sky, on February 17th. Some Leicester witnesses had a close-up view of a UFO on February 23rd and gave a superb description of it. It was, they said, circular "but did not appear to be solid; it was composed of twinkling light, the dominant colour being orange mixed with strong white and a dull red. The whole mixture appeared to revolve around itself although the object was stationary". On February 24th a light was seen over Evington, Leicester. It was seen first to be moving very quickly, then it suddenly stopped, drifted to the west and then back to the east, where it became stationary and commenced twinkling like a star.

LAPRO report a good deal of activity in March. "Tawny" and "dull yellow" cigar and saucer-shaped UFOs were reported over Leicester on March 2nd. A "U"-shaped light was seen over Birstall on March 10th. It changed to an "elliptical configuration" and slowly pulsated. UFOs were sighted on March 14th and 16th over Leicester and Thurcaston. On March 18th a police sergeant in Leicester saw a "star-shaped" light moving slowly from west to east. It stopped suddenly and then "shrank" until it disappeared. On March 19th a bright light shot across the sky over the village of Croft. Observers saw the light become stationary and then descend out of sight, as if landing. All the cases we have reported here for 1975 occurred within about 10 miles of Croft Hill.

In mid-January 1975, a saucer-like object was seen gliding across a main road near Leek, Staffs. It landed in a field adjacent to the road. It sat there flashing one red and two white lights until a passing motorist decided to stop and investigate, whereupon it promptly took off. Police were called to investigate the incident. The Stoke "Sentinel" intimated that other UFO reports had been received prior to this event.

THE SEISMOLOGICAL LANDSCAPE.

A few days after the UFO had landed near Leek, earth-tremors were reported in the Trentham/Trent Vale area 12 miles away, just south of Stoke-on-Trent. Residents had been awakened by "thumps and tremors" at 6am. The National Coal Board, which has mines in the general area, claimed that the tremors were "not connected with any mining activities". The Stoke "Sentinel" approached a geologist at Keele University but he was "not available for comment". The tremors continued and residents of the area, convinced that the NCB was the cause of the trouble, sent a petition to Jack Ashley, MP. "Our houses are not made of rubber," one householder said, "and are bound to be affected if these tremors keep going on."

More accusations were levelled at the NCB but a spokesman for the Board insisted that they were not trying to crawl out of their responsibilities and the tremors were not linked with the colliery. He also mentioned that there were geological faults in the area, but nobody seemed to be listening. The "Sentinel" of January 27th reported that Jack Ashley had demanded that the NCB instigate a top-level inquiry. He said that people were becoming "very worried" about the continuing tremors which were imposing a "danger to life and limb". At the end of January the then Minister for Energy, Eric Varley, called for a full NCB report on the tremors. The NCB Area Director said that the nearest workings to the Trentham/Trent Vale area was 500 yards away. "It would be quite abnormal and outside our experience for any measurable subsidence to occur 500 yards in advance of workings 3000 feet deep," he said. He reminded everyone again that there was "severe faulting" in the area. The matter then seemed to be dropped by the press.

We wondered if the tremors had been felt further afield than the Trent valley area between Trent Vale and Stone. Checking on the Charnwood area, we were told by our Charnwood countryman that subterranean rumblings had been heard up on the Forest, which were taken to be a sign of unrest on the part of "the old volcano" (colloquial for the fault). On the 1st February our countryman informant had found that many panes of glass in his greenhouse behind his cottage had been inexplicably broken. The next day he found a drystone wall around a holly bush tumbled down.

The reader will have noticed that concurrent with this tremor activity we have been describing, there was UFO activity in the Leics.-Staffs. region.

At the end of May we visited the Stone - Trent Vale district. We were told that tremors had been reported in Trent Vale only a week before our arrival. One resident told us that he had experienced 2 tremors at the end of January. He pointed out that he hadn't actually _felt_ a tremor in the second incident, but he assumed there must have been one "because all the horse brasses suddenly fell off a shelf" in his house. The local newsagent had felt 6 tremors in the January/February period. We saw the point where a fault crossed Riverside Road in Trent Vale. The houses either side were clearly affected - cracked walls, etc. At this precise point in the road were workings, supposedly by the Gas Board. A resident told us that the tremors were the subject of investigation by geologists from a local university.

The history of tremors in the environs of Charnwood Forest goes back hundreds of years. In 1580 the top of the steeple of the church at Stoke Golding (8 miles from Croft Hill) was shaken down by an earthquake (10). The church was built in the 1200s and today is almost entirely of that period. Hoskins says that it is worth going many miles to see (7). (Just outside the village is Crown Hill, where the crown of Richard III was placed on the head of Henry immediately after the battle of Bosworth.) In July 1738, there was an earthquake. "The weather had been excessively hot for 10 or 12 days; but, for about 24 hours immediately preceding the earthquake, the wind had stood at full North, and the temperature of the air much altered."(10). Our Shepshed vicar reports that he had felt 3 earthquakes during a 10 to 12 year period in the 1700s. "What is remarkable," he noted, "is that they have all happened pretty near the same hour of the day." In September 1750 the severe shock of an earthquake was felt to some degree in counties all around Charnwood. Houses tottered, slates, tiles and "some chimneys" fell. A child at Husbands Bosworth "was shaken out of a chair into the fire and somewhat burnt". At Narborough (3 miles from Croft) "the whole church shook with such violence that the whole congregation ran out with fear and trembling". The shock was attended with a rumbling noise. In 1795 the shock of an earthquake "was perceived" at Sapcote (2½ miles from Croft).

There was an earthquake in 1837, and in 1893 there was another, centred on Charnwood forest. This took place on August 11th immediately after a severe thunderstorm.

On the summer solstice 1904 there were 2 quakes, one of them in the Markfield area. A severe quake in 1931 damaged property in the Charnwood area, caused church bells to clang and people to run into the streets in Coalville. There were other minor quakes in the first part of the 20th century. In 1957 there occurred what was one of the most severe earthquakes ever recorded in the UK (8 on the isoseismal scale of 10). Its epicentre was beneath Charnwood Forest and it affected 11 counties. It took place on February 11th and immediately preceding the tremor curious lights, travelling in straight lines, were seen over Bradgate Park on Charnwood ("tadpole-shaped UFOs" were reported elsewhere). Subterranean rumblings were heard. A great deal of property was damaged and the Hinckley district was severely affected. The steeple of Broughton Astley church (2½ miles from

One of the two twisted trees on Croft Hill.

Croft) was cracked. Another tremor was felt 32 hours after the first. Scientists were interested in members of the public reporting any new sources of water - springs, etc. There was another quake almost exactly a year later, on February 9th, 1958. In June 1965, there was a quake that had its epicentre under Copt Oak on Charnwood. Copt Oak is a high, ancient crossroads and its name recalls a gigantic oak that stood there up until the 19th century. It was a very ancient tree, and had been fashioned into a "Celtic Tau" by the removal of all its branches except two (7). Sapcote was again rocked by a quake in August 1971, with a noise "like thunder". In 1973, on February 11th (again!) and 12th, and in 1974 on February 9th (again!), there were further quakes.

...   .

END OF PART ONE

In the continuation of this work for THE NEWS, we shall chase a couple of Leicestershire Black Dogs and some ghosties through THE SUPERNATURAL LANDSCAPE (while dodging a few poltergeist-type conflagrations); peer briefly into the hidden PSYCHIC LANDSCAPE; take a very quick view over THE ANCIENT LANDSCAPE, and tarry a while at SHUGBOROUGH to consider some of its awesome mysteries. We will conclude with an essay, THE THOR FACTOR, in which we will speculate, we hope constructively, on what we suspect may be the beginning of an understanding of what one of the prime geophysical functions of the megalithic science may have been, and how it could be related to seismological and meteorological factors - and the genesis of UFOs.

...   .

References

1) Dare, MP, <u>Charnwood Forest</u>, 1925, Backus (Leicester)
2) Devereux, Paul & York, Andrew, <u>The Forgotten Heart of Albion</u>, The Ley Hunter, Nos. 66-68.
3) <u>Flying Saucer Review</u>, Jan/Feb 1969, Vol. 15, No 1.
4) Fort, Charles. <u>New Lands</u>, 1923 (Sphere 1974)
5) Goddard, Jimmy. <u>Handbook of Leys and Orthoteny</u>, 1966, private.
6) Graves, Robert. <u>The White Goddess</u>, 1961, Faber & Faber.
7) Hoskins, WG. <u>Shell Guide to Leics</u>, 1970, Faber & Faber.
8) Keel, John A. <u>UFOs: Operation Trojan Horse</u>, 1970 (Abacus, 1973)
9) Leicester Aerial Phenomena Research Organisation, 61 Barclay Street, Leicester.
10) Nichols, J. <u>The History & Antiquities of Leics.</u>, 1795-1815, London.
11) Throsby, John. <u>The History & Antiquities of the Ancient Town of Leicester</u>, 1791.
12) Underwood, Guy. <u>The Pattern of the Past</u>, 1969 (Abacus, 1972)
13) Walker, TL. <u>Leicester Literary & Philosophical Society Transactions</u>, 1879.

APRIL FUELS, cont...

switched over to the 60/40, water/alcohol mixture to get 8 miles to the gallon. He said: "The engine loves whiskey just as well - and starts like a bomb on Normandy Calvados. Red wine too, works at a pinch, though it gums up the plugs." Great! - soon wino-cars will be giving a new look (as well as meaning) to Skid Row. Sunday Times, 13 Oct 74 (Cr: Steve Moore.)

A few weeks later, someone who had seen an account of Chambrin's claim wrote to the Sunday Express, 28 Oct 74 (Cr: CA Worth) telling of a little Portugese-American he met in the early 20s, who possessed a magic powder, which when mixed with water produced a workable substitute for petrol in unmodified engines. "One day we found a motorist stuck on the Aberglaslyn Pass in Wales. Our friend, who had a Mephistophelean appearance, put some powder in his tank, stirred it, flooded the carburretor, pulled the starter and away went the engine. We left its owner too dumbfounded to speak. He must have thought he had met the devil himself in Snowdonia." However, the value of this story is somewhat diminished by an almost identical one told for laffs (substituting Cornwall, and baffled garage-owners) in the New Scientist, 5 June 75. This form of the story now seems to be firmly established in modern rural folklore. Or - God forbid - the MIB can't leave off tricking the locals, even on vacation.

Just recently we learned that a famous Swedish inventor, Prof Baltzar von Platgen, has discovered "the theoretical basis for a perpetual motion machine," involving air, ammonia and salt, and the talk is of efficiently powering aircraft. After examining a 50-page patent specification, Prof Sam Nilsson, of the Royal Academy of Science, said he could find no basic flaw. Swedish scientific circles were said to be very excited - but several non-Swedish scientists remained sceptical, alledging that von Platgen's theory "ran counter to all known laws". Southern Evening News, 9 April 75. Cr: Roger Randle.

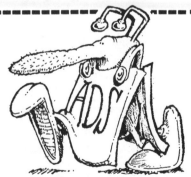

THE NEWS is available from the following specialist bookshops, who also keep a wide range of titles on associated subjects, SF & fantasy.

ANDROMEDA BOOK Co Ltd.
57 Summer Row, Birmingham B3 1JJ.

= - + - = @ = - + = = @ = - + = @ = - + - =
Fans of the artwork of <u>Hunt Emerson</u>, whose krazy headings adorn our pages - and there's a growing crowd of us - may be interested to learn of the latest phase in his direct assault on the grey matters of the world. It is the recent publication of a 20 page lithoed comic about the bizarre 'Dogman'. Just 60p (plus a bit for postage) will insure you a copy of this brain-rotting material, from the Arts Lab Press, Tower Street, Birmingham B19 3UY. Live dangerously.

FINDINGS, cont...

But seriously - whatever we mean by that - we can't help thinking about a little item sent by Steve Moore, gleaned from Modern Wonder, vol4 No 97, 25 March 1939... That "recently" a lady in Ramsgate, Kent, was preparing vegetables for dinner, when there in the middle of a cut turnip she saw the body of a dead sparrow. There was no sign of any way it could have got in there, and the trick seems to have stumped all who examined the evidence.

COACH CRASHES.

During the latter end of May and most of June 47 people were killed in a spate of coach accidents that shocked Britain. Every so often we notice flurries of similar incidents - as though something was in the air, finding a similar expression wherever the conditions were met. Do you remember about 2 years ago, a wave of attacks by guard dogs on children? To our shame, we noticed too late to collect the material. Then we had a rash of people finding bodies which had lain dead and undiscovered for some time - we do have a grim collection of these to be told sometime. And now, coach crashes - though spreading the net to include all public service vehicles (PSVs) we can think of the Moorgate underground disaster, and several British Rail tragedies. Our own tally seems to have become unfindable after our recent move, so we're fortunate in that Colin Bord included his own recollections in a recent letter, on which we draw.

In the UK, it seems to have begun with an unprecedented horror in which 32 were killed when a coach went over the parapet on Devil's Bridge, Yorkshire (end of May); then there were 5 killed in an accident in Ulster (less than 2 weeks before 16 June); and 10 died when a lorry skidded into a coach near Moffat, Dumfriesshire (16 June). We believe a similar series of PSV accidents occured in the USA about 5 years ago. Amazingly, the coach is one of the safest forms of transport if you plot in terms of millions of miles traveled between each death: motorcycle, 3.6; car, 67; air, 185; coach, 500; rail, 770 - statistics from Sunday Times, 22 June 75.

Earlier in May, there were two bridge disasters within hours of each other on the 16th. 13 people were killed and 169 injured when 6 carriages of an express train jumped the rails on a flooded bridge at Vranje, Yugoslavia - and at Leiserhofen, Austria, an Alpine bridge under construction collapsed killing 10 men. Daily Mail, 17 May 75. (Cr: Steve Moore.)

THE MOORGATE UNDERGROUND DISASTER.

Your editor forgot to make a note of the date of this worst underground disaster ever in London, and which resulted in 42 killed and many badly injured when one of the trains rushed past the last station on the line to pile up in the tunnel beyond it. However, as the days went by, we began to notice that the doom visited on all concerned that day was far from ended. The Daily Mirror for the 19th April 75 reports that the guard on that train was fined £5 for stealing two cauliflowers, 5 onions and 3 potatoes from a stall a week after the crash. The previous day, 18th April, he had been criticised for leaving the breaks on the train, just before the crash. — On the 18th April the inquest on the 42 victims closed with a verdict of accidental death - the actual cause of the accident remaining a mystery. The dead driver was that very day cleared of being drunk. Poison pathologist Dr Ann Robinson was reported as saying that blood tests indicated an alcohol-level of 80 milligrams, but Dr Roy Goulding, director of the poisons unit of Guy's Hospital, contradicted this after examination of the same tests: "There are so many anomalies that I would be unable to say conclusively that he had been drinking or not." In fact a top pathologist had warned of this very problem weeks before - a body trapped for 4½ days in the hot wreckage, as Mr Newson's was, would start to generate its own alcohol. Then the coroner, a doctor himself, blamed the barristers for misconstruing Dr Robinson's testimony - the 80mg of alcohol were in Mr Newson's kidney, not in his blood. So the inquest ended, with the driver cleared after much unfortunate misunderstanding, and the actual cause remaining a mystery. — Mike Mills, one of the survivors of Moorgate, faced another horror on the 21 April. He was released from hospital, his foot still in plaster, only a few days previously, and was staying at a hotel in Queensgate, London He and 50 other guests had to flee a blazing fire in the 6-storey hotel, which police thought was started by a firebug. Daily Mirror, 22 April 75. — The Daily Mirror, 1 May 75, in publicising a report on the disaster, drew attention to one fact that would be funny if it wasn't so tragic. A doctor trying to ease the pain of those trapped sent out the message: "I want Entonox" - a form of anaesthetic. By the time the message had been passed down the chain of rescuers to the medical assistants, it had become: "The doctor wants an empty box." — On the 2nd May, Moorgate hero Michael Woods resigned from the St John's Ambulance Brigade after a row over his rescue work. As soon as he heard of the disaster he had paid £6 for a taxi to get to the scene from his home in Slough, and toiled for 7 hours freeing victims from the wreckage. But instead of a pat on the back from the Brigade, he was carpeted for working outside his area. Daily Mirror, 3 May 75. — On the 10th June, Mrs Jane Simpson, 23, finally died in hospital where she had been since the Moorgate crash in February - the 43rd victim. Daily Mirror, 11 June 75.

DOES NATURE SOMETIMES FOLLOW ART?

Back in your editor's college days, one of the design course's dicta was - when in doubt lift a solution from Nature. Thus we were made conscious of the meaning of the fashionable phrase then of 'Art follows Nature'. As the years have gone by, your editor has become fascinated with the idea that Nature sometimes copies art, and that this process seems to indicate a close link between the objective and subjective worlds under certain conditions, and is therefore an aspect of the question of Synchronicity as Jung expressed it. Consider the stories under the next **three** groupings.

The business of a work of fiction preceeding a 'real' event is especially fascinating. In NEWS 7/17, we told of the publication of the book 'The Prime Minister's Yacht is Missing' only five days before Edward Heath's 'Morning Cloud' vanished in a severe storm off the South Coast. So it was with some amusement we noted a brief item in Paul Callan's gossip column in the Daily Mirror, 22 March 75. Lord Ted Willis told him a story about meeting runaway MP John Stonehouse over a drink when both served on a committee of the Inter-Parliamentary Union, last September. Stonehouse asked Willis if he was working on any new books, and Willis answered: "Yes, I've written another political thriller. It's about an MP who disappears the day before an investigation is started into his suspected espionage activities." Says Willis: "Of course no one is saying

" Another question from John Stonehouse — why does bath water drain away in the opposite direction in Australia? "
—by RAUSCH

Stonehouse was a spy, but we now know that at the time he had already collected a fake passport. But he didn't bat an eyelid when I told him about the book. He just remarked: 'How interesting'." — And a recent book 'The Making of Tania Hearst' (New English Library) by David Boulton suggests that the kidnapping of heiress Patricia Hearst was inspired by a hardcore porn novel called 'Black Abductor' published in 1972. In it, an heiress called Patricia is kidnapped, messages are passed to her parents by communiqués printed in the media, is seduced by her captors and joins them. Even if, as Boulton alledges, the kidnapping was copied, they could not have counted on the real Patricia being won over so easily. But it happened nevertheless. Daily Express, 5 June 75 (Cr: S Moore).

In NEWS 8/3, we told of the Canadian Goose that crashed through a window in Derby, as the family were listening to Frankie Laine singing 'The cry of the Wild Goose'. Another two absurdities have come to us. Challenging a long range weather article which claimed that there had been no snow in June in England since 1888, Mrs DB of Telford, Salop, wrote to the Daily Mirror, 6 June 75: "Not true. In the middle 30s there were newspaper pictures captioned 'January in June', and at the time Bing Crosby was singing his highly popular version of 'June in January'. — Mrs Muriel Melkis, of Ridgeway Drive, Dunstable, Beds, and her family were watching the film, on TV, of the sinking of the Titanic, on the evening of 7th July. Mrs Melkis says: "Just as the Titanic was about to hit the iceberg, we heard a terrific crash. We rushed outside and found tiles from our

roof scattered everywhere." A big lump of ice had chosen that moment to fall from the sky smashing a 2ft square hole in their roof. Police, obviously under the assumption that it fell from an aircraft, were said to be trying to contact local aviation authorities. Daily Mail, 8 July 75 (Cr: Steve Moore.) The Titanic, of course, which went down in April 1912, was itself prefigured in a book by Morgan Robertson called 'Futility' (USA, 1898), 14 years earlier. In it, a ship called 'The Titan' strikes an iceberg on her maiden voyage in the very same region of the Atlantic in which the Titanic met her doom. In Arthur Koestler's article on 'The Power of Chance' (Sunday Times, 5 May 74) there is also a letter from a man (born on the day the Titanic sank) who found himself on the bridge at night of a coal-tramp called the 'Titanian' in the exact position of the Titanic sinking, in April 1935. He put out a warning to stop the ship because of a deep feeling of foreboding of peril – and just in time, as a huge iceberg loomed up in the inky darkness. The Titanian was eventually rescued after drifting 9 days with a broken propeller.

On 3rd April, the actress Mary Ure was found dead by her husband, Robert Shaw and their son. Her death came only hours after a triumphant first night in a play called 'The Exorcism' in which she was possessed by the ghost of a woman who starved to death, and made to choke to death on her Christmas dinner. Mary Ure was believed to have suffocated after inhaling vomit. The play had gone well, and in the celebrations that followed Miss Ure was far from depressed or pessimistic – so it was obvious that there would be suggested links between her stage death and actual one. See most national papers on the 4th & 5th April 75. Just for the record, we record a little publicity item that appeared in the Daily Express of 29 March 75 in which the producer of the play expressed his intentions to have the theatre (Comedy Theatre, West End, London) exorcised itself, just in case. After **Miss** Ure's death, he publicly wished he had. What made the whole matter more hysterical in the press was the resumption of the inquest, the day before Miss Ure's death, of Michael Taylor who had, four months previously, killed his wife with his bare hands after an exorcism on him had apparently failed to rid him of his demons (see national papers around 26 March 75, and 2 April 75). — Lastly, we found in our files a note of the death of opera star Marie Collier who was killed when she fell from the balcony, 30ft to the pavement outside her Panton St, London house, on 8 Dec 1971. She had been talking to her financial adviser about a new tour of America, when she opened a window and fell out. Police said foul play was not suspected. She had come to fame when she stood in for Maria Callas in 'Tosca' at Covent Garden, 5 years ago – and 'Tosca' had been the last role before her death, and in fact was being performed again at Covent Garden the very night she died. Your editor, who knows nothing about opera, was astonished to learn that in the last act of 'Tosca' the heroine leaps to her death. Birmingham Evening Mail 8 Dec 1971. One can only reflect on Fort's words about the continuity of truth and fiction, and wonder.

UNIDENTIFIEDS

'THE BARMOUTH MONSTER' CONTINUED...

Colin Palmer, the schoolteacher whose pupils began the current interest with their clear sighting on 2 March, wrote again with further news on the "six young monsters" discovered dead on the beach at Talybont (Liverpool Daily Post, 6 May 75). The earlier thought that these were mutilated rays appears to be confirmed.

"The 'baby' monsters on the beach were Thornback rays, and when these are badly mutilated they appear to have long necks and faces. This was confirmed by the Granada TV expert ((in tow to give his opinion for a news documentary - Ed)) on marine biology, who compared the anatomy of the found specimens with that of a Thorn-back Ray and claimed them to be identical. The two 'legs' at the rear were the highly developed sex-organs of the Ray - perhaps beyond the comprehension of the two, perhaps unmarried, ladies!

"The photograph at Tyn-y-coed is an accident. I have examined the print, using the simple rules of perspective, and arrived at the decision that something crossed the lens, eg. a curl of the camera strap. The person taking the photograph said he saw nothing when he was focusing that looked out of the ordinary - only when the film was developed.

"This does seem to be rather a wet blanket of a letter, but perhaps an encouraging feature of the whole 'monster' episode is the sightings of footprints. Now, if I could only get a plaster-cast of one..."

Colin goes on to mention meeting a fellow yachtsman who claimed to have seen the 'monster' of Loch Ness, very clearly and for about 10 mins. "I showed him my drawing and he was startled because it was so similar - Mainly a large fat body, long neck, small head, and semi-fluked tail, the common features in all descriptions. One new and interesting detail this witness added was that this creature was capable of moving at a speed approaching 30 knots. His first impression was that it was indeed a boat. There were more than a few people with him at the time and they all know that what they saw was was no speedboat, since closer examination through glasses revealed the details of the head and central humps."

...AND CONTINUED...

A few weeks back we were browsing through Charles Gould's MYTHICAL MONSTERS (WH Allen, London 1886) - an amazing book - in particular, chapter 9 on 'The Sea Serpent', when what should we see on page 289 but a tale of a sea serpent in the bay off Llandudno. No date was given for the source, but we have tracked it down to Nature Vol 27, page 293 (1883): being a letter from FT Mott of Leicester, dated 16 Jan 1883:

"About 3pm on Sunday, 3 September 1882, a party of gentlemen and ladies were standing at the northern extremity of Llandudno pier, looking out to sea, when an unusual object was observed in the water near to the Little Orme's Head, travelling rapidly westwards towards the Great Orme. It appeared to be just outside the mouth of the bay, and would therefore be about a mile distant from the observers. It was watched for about two minutes, and in that interval it traversed about half the width of the bay, and then suddenly disappeared. The bay is two miles wide, and therefore the object, whatever it was, must have travelled at the rate of 30mph. It is estimated to have been fully as long as a large steamer, say 200ft; the rapidity of its motion was particularly remarked as being greater than that of any ordinary vessel. The colour appeared to be black, and the motion either cork-screw-like or snake-like, with vertical undulations. Three of the observers have since made sketches from memory, quite independently, of the impression left on their minds, and on comparing these sketches, which slightly varied, they have agreed to sanction the accompanying outline as representing as nearly as possible the object which they saw. The party consisted of W Barfoot, JP of Leicester; FJ Marlow, solicitor of Manchester; Mrs Marlow and several others. They discard the theory of birds or porpoises as not accounting for this particular phenomenon."

What Gould does not mention is that the appearance of this account generated some correspondence on the subject in the same volume of the magazine. On page 315, a Joseph Sidebotham says that he has seen the same phenomenon in Llandudno bay "four or five times" but has "no doubt whatever that it was simply a shoal of porpoises." On page 338, Prof WS Aldis writes that in 1881 in Veulettes, Normandy, he saw many times a sight "almost exactly similar to that of the figure in (FT Mott's) letter" but after much close observation finally resolved into and revealed itself to be nothing but a peculiar flock of birds. On page 366, Dr J Rae confirms his esteemed colleague's observation with the information that the cormorants of the Orkneys, or 'scarps' are known frequently to be seen in this formation. Thus by inference Mott's sighting is 'solved' and rendered respectable.

There was one tiny voice who supported Mr Mott, but his story too was ignored or forgotten. W Barfoot, on page 338, wrote: "Like your correspondent I have frequently seen a shoal of porpoises in Llandudno bay, as well as other places, and on the occasion referred to by Mr Mott (when) the idea of porpoises was at first started but immediately abandoned. I will venture to suggest that no one has seen a shoal of these creatures travel at the rate of from 25 to 30mph ((sic)).
I have seen whales in the ocean, and large flocks of sea-birds, such as those of the eider-duck, skimming its surface; but the strange appearance seen at Llandudno on September 3rd was not to be accounted for by porpoises, whales, birds or breakers, an opinion which was shared by all present."

ENTER THE DRAGON.

The Florida Marine Patrol says that the slant-eyed, scrawny-looking, pink river monster that reared "about three feet" out of the St Johns River near a boat in which Mrs Dorothy Abram and friends were fishing, is probably just a big sturgeon. Mrs Abram, one of five Jacksonville residents who have seen the thing about 5 miles south of the town, disagrees with the FMP. After looking at pictures of the heads of different kinds of sturgeon, none of them matched the "ugly thing" she saw. "It was so ugly looking," said Mrs Brenda Langley, one of the party, "it looked like pictures you see of dragons. I'd like to find out what it was." It was pink "like a boiled shrimp" they said, and had little horns or fins protruding from the back of its long neck. Atlanta (Georgia) Journal & Constitution Sun, 18 May 75. Credit: Mark A Hall.

A MONSTER IN TANZANIA.

A sea monster caught off the coast of Southern Tanzania is said to have two arms sprouting from the chest, two legs (with toes) one eye in the chest, a glowing eye on its side, a toothless mouth, a horn and a beard. The Guardian, 21 May 75. (Cr: Phil Ledger.)

Form: Colin Bord.

Spectres, Aliens & Thing.

With reference to some points in NEWS 10. On page 9, re Richard III picture, the newspaper photoprinter used his 'most contrasty' black & white paper to print the colour negative and the 'ghostly' image did not show up. Kodak make a special paper, Panalure, for using with colour negatives. This comes in one grade only and is not 'contrasty'. Also it is panchromatic, sensitive to all colours in the visible spectrum, and therefore must be handled in darkness before processing, which makes it a nuisance to use – so most darkroom printers do not stock it for the occasional colour neg print, using ordinary bromide paper, which is not sensitive to the yellow/red end of the spectrum, these colours coming out as very dark or black. This is surely what has happened here. The 'pink' face and 'bright red' jewelled collar have merged into the dark background behind them. The original 'ghostly face' is intriguing enough without seeking to compound mysteries where none exist. I have noted a number of occasions in psychic investigations where the results are not readily understood by the photographers – they all too readily adopt an explanation that assumes psychic manifestations rather than acknowledge the limitations of their technical knowledge. (Incidentally, has no one noticed the face of Old Nick himself glowering from the doorway of King Richard's Well, or has this appeared only in my copy of THE NEWS?) ((The marks are in all issues but what you see as Old Nick, may not be what I see as Old Nick, perhaps they're nothing but Old Scratches anyway. You see the problem? → EH.))
Regarding the Spectre of Chingle Hall (p7). I too have had colour shots with greenish tinges to them, but before consulting a medium I complained to the processing laboratory, who admitted their process had been faulty.
Regarding 'Aliens on Ice' (p14), variations of the story have appeared in UFO writings for the last 25 years or more. A report of one well-known version is in Frank Scully's Behind the Flying Saucers, where saucers with bodies were said to have crashed in New Mexico. Elsewhere there are stories of a crashed saucer in Spitzbergen, in the Atlantic Ocean. Either we beli-

eve there is a world-wide hush-up conspiracy involving thousands, or that these reports are part of modern showbiz-type reporting media.

Regarding 'One Last Thing' (p20) – this is reported in greater detail in FSR Jan/Feb 1968, pp15-17. The witnesses were interviewed and the article written by Charles Bowen, and is therefore likely to be more accurate than a Daily Mirror report. I say this because the FSR article gives the incident date as 12/13 Nov 67, not 16 Dec.

DID YOU SEE ..?

FLYING SAUCER REVIEW vol 20 no6 (April 75). 'A Brief Taste of Fairyland' in which Ted Holiday explains further his views on the links between UFO and lake-monster phenomena, and in particular the attempt to exorcise Loch Ness. Also here is his account of his coronary attacks which he associates as a warning from a mysterious man-in-black. 'Believing is Seeing' by Janet Bord - a speculation on the nature of perception bearing in mind UFO, fairy and ghost incidents. 'The Vilvorde Humanoid' by Jean-Luc Vertongen on a most extraordinary encounter with a 'thing'. Part 3 of Schwarz's examination of the images on Stella Lansing's films. Notes on the 'Claw-men' of Pascagoula', and crocodile-skinned entities at Calgary. And 'A UFO with a Taste for Fish' by J Tyrode, hovering over a trout-farm in the French Jura ((remember our own trout-farm incident, NEWS 9/5?)). And lots more goodies. FSR is now 50p a time from: PO Box 25, Barnet, Herts, EN5 2NR, England.

'Archeology Comes Alive' - a collection of articles of the newer techniques and experiments in Archeology, including the work of the Butser Ancient Farm, which attempts to explore theories of ancient life-styles and technology by practical experiment. Glyn Daniel is here too, so any mention of leys is out, natch! Nice pix by Colin 'Mr Ubiquitous' Bord and others, of various landscape features and artifacts. OBSERVER magazine, 18 May 75.

FATE & FORTUNE, No 14: articles on 'Coincidence'; 'Hypnosis' and 'Loch Ness'. No 15: the feats of 'Kung Fu'; 'Modern Ghost Hunting'; 'Sight through Touch alone'; 'Edgar Cayce - Healer & Prophet'; 'Abominable Snowmen; and John Keel on 'The Men in Black'. Alas this mag is no more, kaput - but all back issues are still available at 45p (inc.postage) from Dept T (M/C Ltd) PO Box 80, Slough, SL3 8BN, England. Worth getting the set for the illos alone. No15 has extensive occult and general 'mysteries' bibliography & booklist.

CRIMES & PUNISHMENT, No 7. A general witchcraft crimes issue - but contains a good general article on the murder of Charlie Walton at Lower Quinton on St Valentine's Day, 1945. One of the most interesting of modern cases, apparently of ritual murder, involving the Black Dog haunted Meon Hill. It was never solved (by Fabian of the yard) and even the great Margaret Mead went away baffled. Odd hints too, from a Warwickshire leg-

end that in 1885 a plowboy named Charles Walton encountered the Dog 9 times. For more info see Colin Wilson's THE OCCULT, part 3 section 1.

PURSUIT vol 8 No2 (April 75). An obituary for Hans Stefan Santesson, who died 20 Feb 75. HSS on the Jessup & Allende case; Robert C Wrath on links between UFOs & ABSMs; 'Geomagnetic Storms & Fortean Events', one of the most interesting corelative projects today, by Livingston Gearhart; the first part of Ivan Sanderson's report on his and Heuvelmans's study of the 'Altura Iceman'; and much more. This is the journal of the Society for the Investigation of the Unexplained (SITU), founded by Sanderson. Membership is $10.00/year, to SITU, Columbia, NJ 07832, USA.

' Every Man for Himself' by David L Overbey. A long interview with Werner Herzog, director of the award-winning film of the story of Kaspar Hauser, and some background to the plot, approach and making of the film. SIGHT & SOUND, vol 44 No2.

THE LEY HUNTER No 65. contains articles on the Charlynch Ley (Somerset); the lines from Oldham; the Long Man of Wilmington; East Anglian dragons; and what can only be a jest, on the groundplans, gardens and plumbing of mental institutions. TLH is £1.50/$6.00/year from: Paul Screeton, 5 Egton Drive, Seaton Carew, Hartlepool, Cleveland TS25 2AT.

SPECTRUM a magazine of the Occult, edited by Michael Howard, late of FATE (UK). No 4 contained Paul Screeton on 'The Sacred Alignments of Britain'; MH on 'Shadows of Avalon' discussing Arthur & Glastonbury; and a 'True Psychic Experience'of terrestrial tremors, and a UFO-type thing which drove chickens wild,(alas undated or placed). No 5 has Arthur Shuttlewood on 'The Secrets of the Ancients' - basically Biblical numerology and also a preview of his coming book THE FLYING SORCERERS. SPECTRUM - £2.00/6 issues, from: Bywood Publications, 62 High St, Croydon CR9 2UT, Surrey.

NEW SCIENTIST: 17 April: discoveries of the British Antarctic Survey including the need to correct the true subglacial shoreline by up to 100 miles in places; 'Comets in Perspective' by Dr Keith Hindley. 1 May: 'A Space view of Global Magnetism'; 'Mimicry & Learning in Predator/Prey Interactions'. 15 May: 'Newton's Apple fell Faster' on the measurable decrease in strength of gravitation. 29 May: on an absurd 'Fifth State of Matter Observed' in which an electron orbits a 'hole'. 5June: 'But what about the Children?' in which Joeseph Hanlon, leader of the NS 'Uri Geller' investigation team' on the semi-final of the David Berglas/Daily Express competition for kid metal benders, with a £5000 prize - ½ to the winner & ½ to fund research on him/her. Big surprise of the day was the blatant gall of some of the kids in using all kinds of sleight with some confidence, pathetically fooling only their gullible and doting parents. But there were apparently quite a few who made it through to the finals - which should be quite interesting, following in the wake, of course, of John Taylor's book on SUPERMINDS.

a miscellany of Fortean curiosites

THE NEWS

'PORTRAIT OF A FAULT AREA'
part 2 of a Fortean study of Leicestershire
by Paul Devereux & Andrew York...8

Radio Times Hulton Picture Library

C. CLAPLAN

Quakes & other Geo-oddities, 3 --- Whacky Weather, 5 ---

Washout at Hampstead 7

Polterghosts & Randy Wraiths, 22 --- Coach Accidents, etc, 23.

UK ISSN 0306-0764

bimonthly news & notes
on Fortean phenomena

OCTOBER 1975

THE NEWS is a non-profitmaking bimonthly miscellany of Fortean news, notes and references, affiliated
to the International Fortean Organisation (INFO) in
continuing the work of **Charles Fort** (1874 — 1932).
THE NEWS is edited by Robert JM Rickard:
**Post Office Stores, Aldermaston, Berks RG7 4LJ,
England.**

SUBSCRIPTIONS: 1 year — 6 issues — £3.00 / USA
$7.50. 2 years — 12 issues — £5.40 / USA $13.50
Single issues — 50p / USA $1.25. Back issues (if
available) 50p / USA $1.25. Current annual INDEX
free to subscribers, otherwise 20p. / USA 60¢.
**Special joint subscription to THE NEWS and INFO
JOURNAL** (including regular membership of INFO)
1 year — 12 issues — £5.60 / USA $14.00. All over-
seas subscribers paying by cheque should **add 10%** to
cover banking exchange commission.

CONTRIBUTIONS of articles, notes and artwork on
related subjects are always welcome and duly credited.
You can help us by sending us a copy or clipping of
any reference or data you think will interest us. Please
don't assume our omniscience — there are very few
duplications. We are especially glad to see items from
professional journals, local papers and OP books. But
please don't forget to add the source and date, and your
name for the credit.

NEW PRICE INCREASE.

It is with the greatest regret that we have
to announce that from this issue on our price
will be 50p/USA$1.25. per issue and pro rata —
for the full rates see left.

Our last increase was in Sept 1974, and over
the past year in which all financial hell has
broken loose we have successfully absorbed every
increase in printing and postage costs. The
present increase may seem a lot but is vital to
our survival otherwise we would not even entertain it. Not only do we have to regain the
small security eroded by price rises over the
past nine months, but this month **sees** another
punitive increase in postal charges, and further
increases in paper and printing costs in the
wake of another oil hike. So, please bear with
us. This new price of ours, God willing, will
see us through the next set of crises at least.
All current subscriptions at the old rate will
be honoured. In view of the lack of notice,we'll
accept renewals of subs currently lapsing, at
the old rates, if renewed promptly.

INFO & THE NEWS.

On my recent trip to America, I
had prolonged discussions with Paul Willis,
President of INFO, on how best we can cooperate
in serving the continuance of Fort's work. THE
NEWS has been warmly welcomed into INFO's
family, and our affiliation firmly cemented, and
there has been no compromise on editorial
independence. Several things have emerged from
this destined meeting already. The first is
that the INFO JOURNAL will go onto the same
bimonthly schedule as THE NEWS, and it is hoped
that a slightly thinner and more frequent
JOURNAL will sustain the increasing appetites
of the membership. The second is that we have
worked out a special deal giving a discount on
a joint subscription to both THE NEWS and the
JOURNAL on both regular and contributing levels
of membership to INFO. The basic deal is listed
on the left - but for more information please
write to THE NEWS, or to INFO: Box 367,
Arlington, VA22210, USA. For those who are
already subscribing to either magazine and wish
to take advantage of the Joint Deal — apply as
normal and we'll credit your subscription with
the appropriate mags due to you.

The emphasis in the JOURNAL is towards more
articles and deductive work; THE NEWS leans
more towards reporting current Fortean events —
though neither mag feels particularly bound by
this. Here in THE NEWS your editor would like
to evolve the most up-to-date reporting, and to
do that we need to enlist the help of each
reader, for whom we do this anyway. We need you
to send in material clipped or copied from your
reading, local papers, anywhere. Such is the
pressure on your editor that he can't acknowledge
each clipping - but rest assured. Not only are
they deeply appreciated but will all be used
eventually and credited to you. (Follow the
instructions listed on the left). Sometimes they

are not used immediately, but are kept back for a suitable time (not too long) or a featured compilation. In all cases, the more people we have out scouring the world's media, the better our service to you. It really is a case of the more the merrier - so please spread the word. This goes for both news and data on Fortean events, and any articles on related issues that you think may interest someone somewhere that we can slot into our 'Did You See...?' feature.

FEST & LAST.

For those who have inquired - the proceedings of FORTFEST 75 will eventually be published by INFO. There are considerable technical difficulties that will delay the matter, like finding the time and equipment to transcribe most of

the talks. The Fest was not as well attended as the previous year's, but there were more lectures, and their standard was consistantly high and interesting.

Next year's Fest will be more conveniently located, probably in Washington - and we'll bring you news as it develops.

Last, and by no means least, I'd like to express my sincere thanks to all friends and Forteans in the USA, both those who went out of their way to make me feel very welcome and enjoy my stay there, and those who made it all possible. The best way I can show my appreciation to them all is by endeavouring to continue and improve THE NEWS at every opportunity. With such support dedication is an easy thing. Thank you one and all.

Geophysical Curiosities

As a prelude to several of the items in this issue we have compiled the following list (doubtless incomplete) of quake and volcanic activity over the past few months. You'll find Paul Devereux's and Andy York's discussions of the developments at Stoke in their article on Leicestershire phenomena later on in this issue, and also our own summary of the freakish weather that plagued Britain in your Editor's absence. One thing that occurred to us while assembling this list was the apparent sceneshifting - that each hiatus in the groups of tremors at Stoke was filled by geological activity in some remote region. This may or may not mean anything at all.

MAY: 26 – ocean quake between Azores & Iberian peninsular, felt in Canaries, Madeira, Las Palmas & Lisbon.
30 – minor tremor in Lancashire.
JULY: ? – (early) volcanoes blow in Hawaii & Mount Baker, Washington State, USA.
8 – strong quake in Pagan, Burma.
16 – strong tremors in Stoke in early hours.
19 – strong tremors in Stoke in early hours, & volcano blows in Java.
22 – strong tremors in Stoke in early hours.
23 – minor tremors in Stoke.

? – strong tremor recorded at Fort William, Scotland, about this time.
24 – strong tremor in Stoke.
25 – minor tremors in Stoke.
AUG: 5 – strong tremors in Stoke in evening.
15 – tremor in Kensington, London.
19 – tremor in Stoke.
21 – tremor in Stoke.
24 – tremors in Hereford.
SEPT: 6 – major quake at Lice, Turkey. Estimated 3000 dead, 4000 wounded. 6.8 Richter.
8 – minor tremors in Lice region, Turkey.
10 – tremors in Stoke.
12 – "three tremors in 12 hours." in Stoke.
20 – quake in Hokkaido & Honshu, Japan.

The eruption on Mount Baker, Washington State, sometime in early July was described as "sudden" and experts "baffled and excited" (Daily Mail, 10 July 75. Cr: Steve Moore). Officially listed as the world's 456th active volcano, it has been long dormant. Nevertheless its current throat-clearing is giving authorities some concern, and at least 10,000 acres have been closed off around Mt Baker in anticipation of avalanches, landslides, and the submergence of "tens of miles" under hot mud, ash and lava. Already it has burned its way up through solid rock, melted a 135ft glacier into a lake of 94 degrees F and rising, and produced a runoff of sulphuric acid that has "killed fish miles away". Dr Stephen Malone of Washington University said: "We have nothing in the historical record to compare with it. It is all so unusual we have no way of knowing what will happen."

Interestingly, at a recent meeting of the International Geophysical Union at Grenoble, three US sociologists read a paper on the financial and political effects of predicting quakes 9months to 3 years in advance for populated areas. These ranged from drops in property values, heavy unemployment, permanent closure of businesses, and mass evacuation. Hmmmm - it doesn't seem to be happening much in San Francisco - people seem to have short memories and more immediate problems. (New Scientist, 18 Sept 75.)

Nevertheless, we do have warning about a blow-up that promises to be bigger than that which took out Pompeii. A recent note (Reveille, 2 May 75. Cr Nigel Watson) says that "Washington" scientists expect Mount St Helens, Oregon, about 200 miles from Mt Baker, to erupt in the next 25 years. Mt St Helens, said to be the most powerful volcano on the American mainland, last blew in a serious way in 1500 AD, throwing out nearly a cubic mile of lava and ashes. It erupted again in 1857 and has been rumbling ever since. There is no town in the vicinity - though doubtless one populated by geologists will form when the time comes.

PSI-SMIC ACTIVITY?

One of the standard fobs in the poltergeist game is the blaming of the mysterious activity on undetected tremors or "underground streams". How this latter was supposed to transport objects through the air escapes us, but we do bare in mind the hypothesis favoured by several research-ers of the connexions between Fortean phenomena (including UFOs and Mystery Animals) with water.

The case we are about to mention occurred not long after the tremors in Llandrillo (and else-where) last year (see NEWSes 3,4 & 5.) and raises an interesting question: when things start shaking in one house, is it more reasonable to think of a poltergeist than a tremor, and conversely, when shakes start all over the town, is it more reasonable to think in terms of a tremor than multiple-poltergeists? Perhaps. But suppose all the effects of a tremor occur but nothing seismic is recorded? Ah, what then?

The good people of Stoke and Flash Lane can be forgiven their nerves after going through the things we are recording in the last few months. In that case, pity the poor residents of Bilston, in Midlothian, who have had to put up with eerie noises and vibrations which have remained untraceable for the last 10 years. Over that period, the villagers, who are said to believe hauntings to be the cause of the trouble, have had their fears ignored. But now Councillor Brian Ross plans to call in seismic experts. He said: "These people are not crazy. There is something there and it is most alarming. I have heard it myself."

Villagers claim that plaster has fallen from ceilings and cracks have appeared in window ledges. Mrs Barbara Ketchen, of Caerketton Ave, says she has to take sleeping pills to sleep : "But even then I am often kept awake by the noise. It is really frightening. The whole house seems to shake and sometimes I feel the place is going to fall down." A neighbour, Mrs Isabella Haig, said: "It can be pretty spooky at night when the windows rattle for hours on end."

Councillor Ross favours the idea that surface compressors at Bilston Glen colliery are somehow responsible - but the National Coal Board, who seem to get a lot of stick these days (see p8.) in turn blame it on a geological fault. We'd be interested to know if those seismic fellows found anything interesting - or anything at all. (Scottish) Sunday Mail, 5 May 1974. Cr: L Beer.

SCORCHED EARTH.

The Dorset town of Clavell's Hard, near Kimmeridge, was the scene of some strange effects - smoke rises from cracks in the cliffs, the ground is hot to the touch, and evil-smelling gasses have killed off the grass. Deep down, the ground is actually on fire.

The phenomenon was discovered by Douglas Cole, a young geology research student from South-ampton. He said: "There is a 3'6" layer of oil shale underneath the rock which caught fire. This is an extremely rare occurrence - the last case noted in geological records was in 1826. Immediately under the loose stone the ground is red hot. If you thrust a stick into it, it would burn. I measured temperatures of just over 500 degrees C."

Mr Reginald Leonard, engineer for Wareham Rural Council, said: "We often hear of spontaneous combustion in rubbish tips. But this is the first I have heard of it happening in oil shale." Dail Mail, 13 Dec 73. Cr: Steve Moore.

CURIOUS BOULDERS.

Michael Start sent us an item from one of the Sussex local papers - and we quote verbatim from 'Country Diary' by John T White.

"One large boulder should not have caused me such excitement. But this was a large pink boulder. It was rounded and polished and the place was the Selsey peninsular poking a tentat-ive finger out into the Channel. It looked very much like granite, perhaps from Brittany or the Channel Islands. It was far from home, that was certain. I hunted around the area and found another large boulder of different texture and colour in a village school playground. The head-master told me that it was dug out of the gravels beneath the playground when a new watermain was laid. He directed me along the shore to West Wittering where there were several more boulders resting on the muddy tidal flats. If I had seen them in the North Country I would have been happy to call them glacial erratics, stones dragged far from their origin by the movement of ice. But the conventional view of the Ice Age puts the limit of the ice sheet on a line of the rivers Severn and Thames and leaves the South uncovered. Perhaps icebergs drifted up the Channel and dropped loads of debris as they melted? There have been several indications in recent years that our knowledge of the Ice Age is imperfect."

A GARDEN MENACE IN HAMSTEAD.

This Hamstead is a suburb of Birmingham, and is not to be confused with the one with a 'p' in London with an equally bizarre visitation (see pZ)

Mrs Anne Hodgkins of James Rd, Hamstead, says that her garden and those of her neighbours were constantly under a "sea of black or brown smelly liquid" - and that no one knew what it was. "It is impossible to walk on the lawn because you just sink ankle deep in the liquid. It has been dry now for several days and the problems are just as bad. The gardens have been like this for years and getting steadily worse, and no one knows what is causing it. When it rains, the lawns are completely covered and the garden looks like a lake."

Her neighbour, Mrs Minnie Carr, has been fighting the problem for six years. She said tests had been carried out, but no action taken. Mrs Hodgkins added that the substance had rotted away part of the garden fence and that if her sons got any on their skin they came out in spots.

A spokesman for Sandwell's Technical Services Department said he had no knowledge of the problem but "would have the matter investigated." Birmingham Evening Mail, 29 April 75. Cr: David Sutton.

It happened at least once before - the anniversary of Fort's birthday (Aug 1874, see p9.) appearing to trigger meteorological chaos. You will find a summary of the climatic celebrations of the nativity of 1972 (generally reckoned to have been a vintage year for freak weather) in INFO Journal 9, pp36-38.

From early June this year there were signs that our weather was going mad - on the same day, June 2, there was snow in Edinburgh and London was "hotter than Casablanca". By early August temperatures hit the 90Fs; the hottest in London for 27 years, and the hottest in Paris since records began in 1873. The heat drove people and things crazy: ice-cream vendors fought each other in Bucks, while in Norfolk they were driven off the beaches by swarming flies; there was mass nude sunbathing in (gasp!) Hove, Sussex, while in York people began throwing themselves off bridges, fullyclothed, into the river Ouse; in Guernsey 12,000 trays of tomatoes went soft, while at London docks , 121 lorries became full of melted butter; firemen shipped water to 65,000 parched hens in Cottenham, Cambs, and in Germany farmers feared for the virility of their pigs; and the occupants of an experimental solar-house built by London Polytechnic at Bradville, Bucks, were driven outside by the scorching room-temperatures of 158F. (Daily Mirror, Daily Mail, 8 Aug 75; Sunday Times, Sunday Express, 10 Aug 75. Cr: Steve Moore & Nigel Watson.)

Naturally the meteorologists were loudly berated, and none got more stick than Prof HH Lamb, of the Climatic Research Unit (E Anglia U) who is known to the British press as 'The Ice Man' for his expression (only a month or so prior to this heatwave) that Britain is sliding towards a mini-ice-age. But despite shouting: "No..no..no..no. I'm not going to see anybody." (Daily Mail, 8 Aug 75. Cr: Steve Moore.) he did manage to get quoted in quite a few articles - mostly the sort newsmen like, with experts contradicting each other in succeeding paragraphs. (See Sunday Times & Sunday People, 10 Aug 75, for a cross section.) - and remained with his belief that the very eccentricity of the weather is a symptom of an earth which is growing colder. (For more on this subject see New Scientist, 18 Sept 75, p665.)

At least one honest opinion made the papers - Dr John Green of Imperial College (London) said: "I can tell you the sky is clear because we have an anticyclone. But if you want to know why we have an anticyclone, I have to say that the atmosphere is so infernally and beautifully complicated that I just don't know."

All these events formed the background to

a meeting of the World Meteorological Office at East Anglia University (Observer, 24 Aug 75. Cr: Steve Moore.) on climatic problems. In their pronouncements we find no reference to the influence of the sun on our weather. Yet Nature (v257, p113.) recently published a statistical study that leaves very little doubt about the reality of the theory (that solar flares affect the geomagnetosphere, leading to bright aurorae and troughs of low pressure in high latitudes. And this in virtually the same week that a bunch of 'scientists' attempt to debunk astrology (see item on p23 this issue.) Hah! Anyway, as INFO 9 records, the freak weather in 1972 was preceded by the "most terrific solar storm ever recorded." Indeed it can be pinned down tighter. It seems that ("by a happy coincidence" as New Scientist, 18 Sept 75, says) a Dr JT Horng has published his observation that terrestrial effects are caused by flare groups between 6.7° and 19.9° E of the solar meridian. (Astrophysics & Space Science, v35, p133.) It would be interesting to discover what solar activity preceded our recent freak spell.

HAILSTORMS.

All the hot weather was relieved at intervals by freak storms. We only have cuttings on the following, but we know there were more — one reason for our persistant requests for data.

The year kicked off with a monster hailstone, or what was conveniently labled a hailstone, that hit a block of flats in the Fulham Road, London on Jan 24. Estimates of its weight vary (the London edition of the Daily Mirror says 50lb; the Midlands edition, 65lb). Considerable damage to tiles and bricks was done to the flats (Fulham Court) — and the police were reported to have taken the monster away "as evidence".(?) (Cr: Frank Adey & Steve Moore.)

About May 7, a sudden storm in Mayes County, Oklahoma, precipitated hail about the size of "baseballs". Police dispatcher Movita Turner claimed to have measured one at 7" diameter. (Daily Mail, 8 May 75. Cr: Paul Screeton & Steve Moore. The Weekly News, 17 May 75, Cr: Nigel Watson.)

There was an intense storm on the morning of July 14, that raged for 30 minutes, with violent thunder and lightning, torrents of water, and hailstones up to 3" diameter. Greenhouses were wrecked, as were plastic rooves, cars dented, plants flattened. The sudden volume of water caused back pressure in the sewers, pushing up 3hwt drain covers and flooding the streets with water and debris. A photo of some of the smaller 'stones (this page) with details of the story appeared in the Birmingham Evening Mail, 14 July 75. (Cr: David Sutton.) We can interject a personal note here. The pesky missiles damaged the skylight of the flat so recently vacated by your editor, and much to the chagrin of Hunt Emerson who had just moved in.

FREAK TORNADOES.

What was called a 'freak tornado' "ravaged" the small Quebec town of St Bonaventure on 25th July. In its brief 15 minutes it did considerable damage — estimated at £1½M. About 400 residents were left homeless, at least 45 people injured — and a mother and twins were killed when their caravan was picked up and bowled along the ground. (Daily Mail 26 July 75. Cr: Steve Moore).

On the 5th August, the hot weather in Britain gave way to violent thunderstorms over the whole country — for an itinerary of damage see most papers of the following day. But there were odd things going on elsewhere too — in the Sahara desert, in the first rainfall in 6 years, a man drowned as he plunged into a pool that hadn't been there earlier. (Daily Mirror, 6 Aug 75. Cr: Steve Moore.)

On the night of the 5th, a "freak tornado" ripped through the east side of Coventry, damaging dozens of houses, uprooting trees, and ruining greenhouses and plants with its barrage of hail at it went through Baginton, Ansty, Wood End, Potters Green and Nuneaton. At the Baginton airfield, the airspeed indicator shot from 12mph to its maximum of 100mph, so it's conceivable the wind was even stronger. The height of the fury seems to have been fairly short, and brought with it such a torrent of

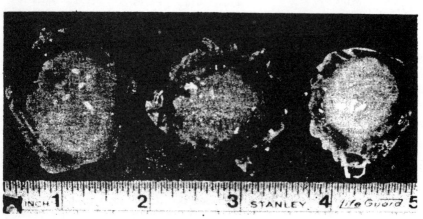

Some of the smaller hailstones that fell in Birmingham, on 14 July.

From: Birmingham Evening Mail, 14 July 75.

hailstones that "We couldn't see a thing out of our windows. It was as if a white sheet had been pulled over them." Another native said: "The storm only lasted for 10 minutes, then it went as suddenly as it had arrived. We were left to stare out in the murky heat at a sheet of ice slowly melting on the lawn. It was most unnatural." Estimates of the hailstones here ran to "at least an inch in diameter." One interesting aspect was the disagreement by some of the victims over the lightning. The news-account says that trees blocked five roads after being struck by lightning, yet a Mr Clark of the same area said: "It was terrifying. There was no thunder or lightning - just hail the size of halfcrowns and a violent wind." For other details - rooves wrenched off, 5ton aircraft blown backwards 20ft, and cows & sheep lifted and carried away - see the lengthy account in Coventry Evening Telegraph, 6 Aug 75. Cr: Ken Ratcliffe.

MORE STORMS.

There was another wave of violent storms a couple of days later, on the evening of the 8th Aug. More houses hit; powerlines down in Cornwall; people missing at sea. At Barrow-in-Furness, a boy was struck by lightning. Lightning striking a house in Great Wakering, Essex, melted polystyrene ceiling tiles onto a mother and her three children who were taken to hospital shocked and burned. Two young boys were trapped in an upstairs room when a house burst into flames in Whitefield, Manchester, during the storm. One was found later cut and burned on an outhouse roof - the other died inside. One curious aspect is that the firebrigade seemed to be in some doubt as to whether the house was struck by lightning or not. A mysterious fire during the height of a violent storm? It's the sort of event that needs looking into. But this is made doubly interesting by a mysterious death during the height of a storm at Huddersfield on the same night (and which we'll keep for our 'Mysterious Deaths' section hopefully next issue) in which a woman was found battered to death in strange circumstances. (Daily Mirror & Daily Express, 9 Aug 75; Sunday Express, 10 Aug 75. Cr: David Sutton & Steve Moore.)

THE DELUGE AT HAMPSTEAD.

Ken Rogers is probably the most dangerous man in Britain. The Aug 15 edition of the Hampstead & Highgate Express & News published a feature about his intentions for an all-night vigil on the heights of Parliament Hill, Hampstead. Accompanying this is a photo of Ken, arm outstretched, jabbing his finger boldly at the sky. Doubtless it was taken a few days previously, but the answer came the previous evening. As the Guardian of the 16th Aug put it. "Darkness fell, the Heavens opened, and with thunder and lightning a Divine Hand reached through the clouds, pointed squarely at Hampstead Heath and hurled down hailstones as big as marbles, flood and disaster."

At 5.25pm on Aug 14 at least 3 million tons of water fell on this small area of North London (apx 4 miles by 2) in three hours. On the Heath, 6.72in of rain were recorded; much more than at any time since records began in 1910; the equivalent of nearly 4 months summer rain (in 3hrs). Needless to say, there was considerable flooding and its attendant damage and problems and you couldn't get a better summary of it than the 5 page special put out by the Hampstead & Highgate Express & News, 22 Aug 75.

Again the meteorologists were brickbatted. The London Weather Centre put the odds on its occurrence at over 1000 to 1. John Hillaby, a regular of the New Scientist and resident in the area, had only praise for the Ham & High's 'Storm Issue', pointing out how lightly the national press treated the matter. For instance, though other parts of London were affected by the storm, Hillaby, marvels at its peculiar localisation over Hampstead - Holborn, not far away recorded only 0.2 inches of rain.

And then there was its unexpectedness. Hillaby, writing in the New Scientist (11 Sept 75) "with the authority of hindsight, I recall plainly how, walking on the Heath early that morning, the hard pan of clay, in places heavily eroded, felt warm to the touch. The sultry breezes raised micro-vortices of swirling dust-devils that scuttled about like crabs. It felt cooler inside the apartment than out... I can't recall a tropical storm that matched the violence of that wet evening. At times there seemed to be no visible lines, no rods of rain as you normally see them. It fell in misty sheets with a noise like boiling fat."

Hundreds were left homeless when they had to hastily evacuate. Damage estimated at "tens of thousands" of pounds, not to mention the great personal losses sustained when sewage was backfired out of the overloaded drains to flood into numberless flats - most of them uninsured. There was utter chaos on the roads, the railways, and many thousands of phones were rendered inoperable. The police, fire and ambulance services mobilized a full-scale disaster alert. One man drowned in his flooded flat; and two people were paralysed and burned when they were blasted by lightning on the heath.

But Hillaby is wrong on one thing. He opens his account by saying that in the preceeding weeks "there had been no rain throughout most of the country..." See above for those on the 5th & 8th of the same month.

Oh yes - the hailstones. These were a modest $\frac{3}{4}$" and were soon lost in the vast quantity of water.

There were a couple of Fortean events, in themselves not out of the ordinary, but happening as they they do in the midst of this chaos are worthy of mention. During the heavy downpour a man in a flat in Onslow Gardens, Kensington, found a West African python on his kitchen window ledge... four storeys up. It was taken away to London Zoo. The other event is of the more esoteric Fortean data. The beginning

cont on p20...

PORTRAIT OF A FAULT AREA

by Paul Devereux & Andrew York

part two

Shortly after NEWS 11 went to the printers a new surge of seismic activity began in the Stoke area, and, later, in Hereford. This study of the Leics. - Staffs. fault area has, figuratively speaking, exploded in our faces. So beset are we by events that we cannot avoid a sneaking suspicion that dear old Charles F. is pulling some strings over there on t'other side of the Great Divide...

SEISMIC LANDSCAPE (& PART 1) REVISITED)

Between midnight on July 15th and 8 a.m. on July 16th tremors were reported affecting an area within a three mile radius of Stoke. At least two distinct, strong tremors were felt. Masonry was affected. One witness said that he heard "a heavy rumble" which he thought was an explosion. He described the tremor as being like "hitting something in a car." Another witness said: "There was a bang and the tremors were terrible, like a gigantic kick. Everyone was terrified." The cause of the tremors was "a mystery" it was stated, but the undercurrent of feeling was still that the National Coal Board was to blame. Another "explanation" that started to become fashionable from these tremors onwards was the idea of old mineworkings collapsing, causing subterranean rumbling and surface disturbance. Trent Vale was again a focus for the tremors, particularly "Flash Lane" to the north of the area.

Between midnight on July 18th and early morning on July 19th there was another set of tremors. Jack Ashley MP angrily demanded an investigation and it was learned that the Dept. of Energy had already ordered an enquiry after the tremors of the 15th/16th. Old mineworkings were again touted as a possible explanation in the press for tremors reported in the Leicester area on the 18th July.

Between midnight (here we go again) on July 21st and early morning on July 22nd there was a third set of tremors. The press slipped in the "collapsing mineworkings" again.

On 23rd July ATV Midlands reported that Stoke had suffered yet another tremor, though it was minor compared to the previous set of quakes.

BBC Radio 2 reported another tremor on Thursday 24th July. It was apparently pretty strong because it "threw furniture around".

Another set of tremors was reported on the night of July 25th. The 'Times' of July 26th reported that a conference to discuss recurring earth tremors at Stoke was to be held on August 5th in Stoke itself. Representatives of the Dept. of Energy, the Global Seismic Unit (Edinburgh) and Keele University were going to attend, along with NCB and local authority officials. The 'Times' piece also reported an incorrect (too few) number of tremors in the Stoke area Was it coincidental that in the same edition the Nature-Times 'Science Report provided news of recently-designed statistical work in geophysics which was yielding evidence of a link between earthquakes, microchanges in the length of the day, variations in the magnetic field of the Earth and the Chandler Wobble (Earth-axis deviation)? The report added that similar work seeking the identification of other geophysical relationships might lead eventually to a more complete understanding of the Earth as an integrated dynamic system.

Newspapers (e.g. Times, Telegraph) reported on August 2nd that the NCB was going to advance cash for homes damaged in the tremors, but the NCB clearly indicated that it did not feel itself to be in any way responsible for the damage. The money was made available as an interest-free loan to whoever would eventually foot the bill.

And so August 5th dawned, and hope of an answer to their torment gleamed bright in the eye of many a Stoke citizen. The conference duly met and ruminated and faced irate residents. What could the tremors be caused by? The results were catalogued by the press on August 6th. Shock headlines: "GEOLOGICAL FAULTS CAUSED TREMORS, EXPERTS BELIEVE" the Times said (notice cute use of past tense). What was this - no collapsing old mines? Indeed, Dr Christopher Browett of the Global Seismic Unit and other experts were confident that the tremors were not caused by old mineworkings collapsing. "It's not going to get into a nasty earthquake," Dr Browett said, to reassure everyone. In addition, seismic monitoring units were to be set up in the area as soon as possible. The Daily Mail became more excited by the issue than the Times and ran a major, tongue-in-cheek article on the tremors and the conference. The article pointed out that "only three quid up the line from Euston" there were series of tremors that were becoming "very scary". A geological expert interviewed on ATV, while trying to minimise the Staffs. tremors, let slip that Fort William in Scotland had had tremors two weeks before "10 times bigger" than the Stoke ones. (WHAAT?) That would date them around July 23rd.

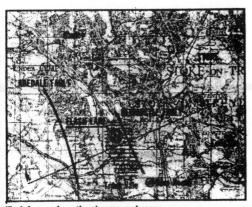

Flash Lane: where the phenomena happen

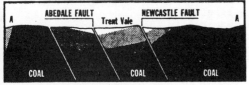

How Trent Vale straddles the geological 'slip'

Diagrams from the Sunday Times, 10 Aug 75.

"Within hours of the conference" the hand of coincidence struck in the form of two severe tremors. The first one came in the evening of August 5th and the second on the morning of the 6th (Happy Birthday Charles Fort).* The Sentinel of August 6th ran huge front-page headlines on the double-tremor. (Ahh, and we have seen the whole story grow from a few teeny-weeny lines in the inner pages in months gone by. Remember you read about it first in the NEWS!) The Sunday Times of August 10th ran a feature on the Stoke tremors, remarking how "decidedly unBritish" the whole affair was. They reported that a Stoke resident was the first person in a particular insurance company's history to claim earthquake damages.

(Up on Charnwood, we heard the old-timers muttering into their beer that the experts could do worse than look in the forest for the cause of the Stoke tremors.)

We have no reports of tremors for the next week or so. On August 14th, ATV reported the setting up of the first of the monitoring stations in the Stoke area. The Times of the 19th August said that the universities of Durham, Edinburgh and Keele were joining forces on the study of the Staffs. seismic phenomena. ATV reported, also on the 19th, that there had been another Stoke tremor - "the 15th in the last 5 weeks."

The tremor-saga took an odd turn on the 15th August. A "mystery tremor" rattled a house in Kensington, W London, and brought a ceiling down. The West London Observer of the 21st August said that the cause of the tremor had not been discovered, although various theories (all rather weak) were put forward.

There was another Stoke tremor on August 21st. Then, on August 24th, a quake shook Hereford (one of Fort's well-chronicled areas)** and people ran out into the streets in their night-clothes. A "double muffled explosion" was heard at the time of the tremor. Experts at Stoke, obviously taken off guard, hurriedly exclaimed that there was "no connection" with the Stoke tremors...

---

* Your editor has always thought August 9th to be Charles Fort's birthdate. Clearly there was some confusion in our minds and we scurried to Damon Knight's biography. He gives August 6th. Elsewhere, in the pages of INFO Journal the 9th is referred to. We'll investigate further — though it seems perfectly in keeping with the subject of our irreverence to establish a movable feast — or better yet, get the flagons out on both days — RJ.

** see NEW LANDS, chapter 29 — RJ.

There are distinctly Fortean aspects of
the Stoke tremors. The Sentinel interviewed a resident who said that the tremors seemed to happen at 10 minutes to
the hour every time. Indeed, the tremors
following the Stoke conference occurred
at 10.50 in the evening of the 5th Aug.
and 10.50 the morning of the 6th (Happy
synchronicity, Charles!). Most of the
tremors seem to have taken place late in
the evening or early morning. It was
this sort of regularity that convinced
many people that the NCB must be involved. One local man also mentioned (in
the Sunday Times) that the tremors were
nearly always preceded by heavy rain.

Certainly, the weather in Britain has
been odd. Like most of N Europe, the UK
has had one of its hottest summers for
years. Yet at Buxton, not far from Leek,
there was snow on the ground on June 2nd.
Within 10 days the temperature was in the
80s at the same place and, later on, in
the 90s. Even by the standards of British weather, that sort of change is ridiculous. Preceding and during the July-
August tremor period, Leics. experienced
some incredibly fierce electrical storms,
particularly on Charnwood Forest. (Some
folk on the Forest told us that they had
also heard the 'old volcano' rumbling).
Between mid-July and mid-August, thunder
was frequently 'in the air' and many
people complained of headaches and nausea. On the 5th August, the day of the
conference in Stoke, there was a fierce
thunderstorm and in the evening, 4 hours
before the Stoke tremor the same day, a
freak whirlwind swept across parts of

the Hinckley area in the Stoke Golding
direction, causing a great deal of damage. One witness said there had been a
very cold wind just before the whirlwind
appeared. The 8th August was the hottest
day in Leicester since the 1880s. Electrical storms affected many parts of
England and Wales during August, and an
incredible flash storm struck London
causing floods and disruption within
minutes. There are no records of anything even approaching such a vicious meteorological event ever having happened
in London before. ***

Around the world, too, there seems to
have been considerable geological/meteo-
rological disturbances. Amongst a whole
procession of natural disasters and freak
events, we note the new volcanoes in the
USSR; tremors in California; the 'extinct' volcano Mount Baker, in Washington
State, unexpectedly reactivating itself;
a freak tornado in Quebec; freak rains
in the Sahara - and so on. All during
the period we are concerned with here.
The recent Turkish earthquake is perhaps
the most tragic example of this worldwide
disturbance. ****

We notice a lunar correlation with regard
to the UK tremors. Quakes in Stoke on the
21st, 23rd, 24th & 25th July (and Fort
William around the 23rd) seem to relate
to the full moon of the 23rd. The next
group of tremors on the 5th & 6th August
preceded the new moon of the 7th. The
next group on the 19th, 21st & 24th (Hereford) August, coincided with the full
moon of the 21st. The Stoke/Leics. tremors of the 15th/16th and 18th July do
not seem to relate to this clear-cut,
full-phase lunar pattern.

We also have more reports of UFO activity in the February - September period -
with an increased number in August coinciding with the key seismic/meteorolog-
ical period in the area. Some of these
sightings are truly remarkable and most
occurred within 10 miles of Croft Hill,
some within 2 or 3 miles. Thus we grow
increasingly confident in our observation that the area to the S and SW of
Leicester, dominated by the probable
Mesomphalos now called Croft Hill, is a
key UFO area (in addition to its affinity for a variety of seismic, meteorological and supernatural events). LAPRO
confirm that this is in accordance with
their findings too. On some occasions
UFOs appeared in the same part of the
sky on 2 or 3 successive evenings. South
Wigston was yet again a frequent UFO-
sighting point.

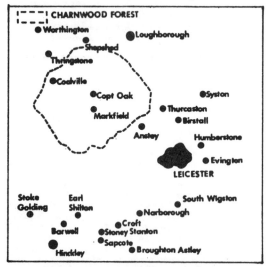

CHARNWOOD FOREST

Worthington • Loughborough •
Shepshed
Thringstone •
• Coalville
Copt Oak • Syston •
Markfield • Thurcaston •
• Birstall
Anstey • Humberstone •
• Evington
LEICESTER
Stoke
Golding • Earl
Shilton • South Wigston •
• Narborough
Barwell • Croft •
Stoney Stanton •
• Sapcote
Hinckley • Broughton Astley •

NB: The above map also appeared in the last
issue. After reduction during printing, the
scale was not, of course, to scale anymore - Ed.

*** see page 7, this issue - Ed.
**** see updated list on page 3, this issue - Ed.

During the summer months,sheep in Leics. have been disappearing in ones and twos and 10 sheep near Melton were "rustled" at the end of July. Police have no leads. As these events link time-wise with the increased UFO-activity, and as we are aware of American UFO-rustling phenomena, LAPRO are conducting an investigation.

Finally, we have just received news of very recent Stoke tremors. There was one on the 10th September, the first for a few weeks. Between the 11th and 12th there were more tremors around Stoke - 3 within 24 hours. During the night of the 11th,an exceptionally violent electrical storm swept across Leics. during which a house in Barwell (of meteorite fame - see NEWS 11/14) was taken apart by a thunder-bolt (ball-lightning). A witness said that it looked like a "3-foot wide ball of fire". The area reeked of sulphur af-ter the incident. The fellow inside the house was in the habit of wearing his cap while watching TV. It got blown off his head on the night of 11th September.

It is evident that meteorological phen-omena and seismic events are somehow interlinked: they may not affect each other directly, but are perhaps expres-sions of some over-riding influence on that part, or the whole, of the planet. Although a few scientists seem to be beginning to think along these lines, most are still not sufficiently object-ive to have even noticed the correlation. It is part of a whole area of consider-ation that we hope to return to at a future date, but for now we must contin-ue with our many-faceted study of the Leics. fault area (with the occasional glance in the Staffs. direction).

THE SUPERNATURAL LANDSCAPE.

A creature called 'Shag Dog' was said to have an abode in a swampy patch of gro-und known as 'Shag Dog Pit' along Black Lane, a track running from Birstall to Belgrave. (A fragment of this lane has survived as a steep suburban road called Kilby Avenue, but the pit has been fil-led in.) "A big, black mastiff kind of dog...wild, with luminous open jaws, like dying coals in a dark room, and eyes wide and staring, and glowing with unearthly light".(9). It was said to be in the habit of following people along Black Lane before disappearing. On one occasion,it is said to have saved a girl from being accosted by appearing and frightening off her would-be attacker. One wonders if Black Lane could have been part of a ley, as the name 'Black' can sometimes be associated with a ley, as Watkins (10) tells us. Both Birstall and Belgrave are linked with the legend of the giant, Bel. He boasted that he could reach Leicester from Mountsorrel

The Hangman's Stone, near "The Oaks" on Charnwood.

in 3 jumps. He mounted his horse at Mou-ntsorrel, took one leap to Wanlip, Bel's horse burst its gall at Birstall, and Bel himself died at Belgrave, just short of Leicester. So we may have here an interesting Black Dog/giantlore/ley connection.

Birstall is about 10 miles from Croft Hill. Another Black Dog encounter took place within 2 or 3 miles of that enig-matic eminence. One fine night in 1806, a man was walking between Stoney Stanton and Sapcote, his mind "anxiously engaged upon a problem in mathematiks"(7). He was about 80 yards from Scholar's Bridge a place noted for its supernatural app-earances, when he heard "a groaning sort of noise" he could not account for, and which alarmed him. He continued a short distance and he had just put his foot on the stone at the base of a stile close to the bridge when an animal, larger than a fox, which the man supposed to be a 'shagged dog', brushed by his right shoulder with "a surprising velocity". He never saw the animal on the ground on either side of the stile, but only in mid-air, after which it was swallowed up in the darkness of the night.

Close to the spot where this encounter took place is Mill Hill, formerly famous for fairy-rings and fairy-dances, about which Nichols noted the local people told many "wonderful, traditionary tales" up to his day.
 "Hand in hand we'll dance around,
  Because this place is fairy-ground."
What qualities, we wonder, does an area have to possess to be considered "fairy-ground"?

Although Leics. is not noted for its ghostlore, we have found a large number of accounts of hauntings and ghostly traditions widely scattered. In this art-icle we can only briefly outline a few of the ones we have gathered together, but we hope this will prove sufficient to indicate that the area is quite rich in the kind of phenomena termed 'ghostly'.

Some Leics. inns seem to have more than merely alcoholic spirits! The 'Woodman's Stroke' in Rothley (where a former temple of the Knights Templars was situated) is reputedly haunted by the ghost of a big fellow, very tall and gaunt. He is known as Gregory and it is a sign of good luck to see him (The Grange at Rothley also has an energetic poltergeist on the premises). A grey lady haunts a pub in Welford. The 'Belper Inn' in Newton Burgoland has an active ghost that moves furniture, half suffocates some male customers but tends to have a grope at the ladies. The 'Moat Hotel' in Humberstone has a similar poltergeist-type ghost. Another noisy spirit haunts the 'Bakers Arms' pub adjoining the village green at Blaby, while at the 'Plough Inn', Birstall, there is a ghost which on occasion heaves barrels all over the place.

Various halls in the county are said to be haunted – among them being the halls at Tilton, Narborough, Bushby (polt) and Bosworth (perpetually damp bloodstain). An extraordinary ghost tradition is attached to Burleigh Hall. A "weird and fearsome ghost" made regular visits to the place, and made the house spin round and round, especially on dark and stormy nights – to the great terror of the residents. One night, during a particularly violent storm, the ghost gave a harsh word of command and the house was transported bodily to its present position from the summit of a neighbouring hill. The ghost has never since returned. This tradition is reminiscent of legends often associated with ancient churches, but in reverse – churches are usually transported to high places.

In 1918 a number of people saw a grey, ghostly figure gliding through Markfield graveyard. In 1965 several people saw a headless figure drifting up the middle of West Street, Leicester. A shapeshifting entity was seen a number of times in 1972 in the 'Freewheeler Club' in Churchgate, Leicester. The club, which was built on an old site, had to be exorcised. The 'Britella' factory in Leicester also had to be exorcised after a fearsome spirit caused trouble with workers.

Asfordby Rectory is haunted by a poltergeist, and a hunch-backed ghost haunts St. Helen's church at Oxenden Magna. The vicar of St. Peter's church in Thornton had to exorcise his own vicarage recently because his wife was disturbed by a ghost. A derelict house near the church

itself was sometimes seen to have ghostly lights in it. The very ancient church of St. Nicholas in Leicester is said to be haunted. The present vicar of Ashby Folville told us that he and his family had recently moved from Coleorton Rectory (near Thringstone) which was haunted by an old woman and a noisy crowd of phantom young girls. The vicar and members of his family had directly experienced aspects of this multiple haunting. His wife had often been surrounded by the ghostly sound of the phantom children's feet; his son had heard his name called while the house was empty; both he and his son watched a housebell being moved inexplicably, and they all felt frequent and sudden drops in temperature. On one occasion the loudspeakers of a disconnected hi-fi began to emit unintelligible mutterings (The hall at Coleorton was a focus for Wordsworth, Scott, Coleridge, Southey, Constable, Wilkie and others in its day)

A headless figure is said to periodically appear on a footpath between Quorn and Barrow. A Dr. Kirkland witnessed a spectral funeral procession on the Ashby road, and the A428 road (about 4 miles south of the Leics. border) is haunted by a phantom lorry. Numerous motorists have reported looking in their rearview mirrors to see a lorry bearing down on them at top speed and then simply pass through their vehicle. Eyewitnesses on the roadside claim to have seen the lorry passing through a whole line of traffic.

Mr C.J.Williams (11) has written about Leics. 'White lady' ghosts. The county has at least three, and possibly more. One is at Grace Dieu Priory (now in ruins), another is at the 'Hermitage' and a third White Lady supposedly haunts the churchyard at Belgrave. We seem to recall the tradition of another one at Bradgate House. Williams links the White

Standing Stone next to Grace Dieu Priory ruins.

lady ghosts with a widely known ghost phenomenon. An example of this type of ghost was named 'Bertha' in Bohemia and Williams speculates that this may refer to an ancient nature goddess 'Berchta', meaning 'the brilliant one'. He also points out that the Leics. White Lady ghosts are associated with ancient sites. The Grace Dieu Priory spectre has been particularly active: buses have stopped for it at the roadside next to the ruins and it has sometimes moved in front of motorists causing them considerable alarm. A standing stone is extant in the field alongside Grace Dieu.

An old man who once lived in Hathern used to walk to his favourite pub in Shepshed almost every night, playing on his pipe. One night he disappeared and was never found again, but people (often strangers) reported hearing the sound of pipes in a nearby wood for years afterwards. Because of the persistence of these reports, the wood became known as 'Pipers Wood' (now destroyed by the M1). A Roman road is suspected to have run through the wood.

In August 1933 the house of a Mr. Long in Bell Lane, Leicester, was plagued by 'spook water'. It poured mysteriously from the ceiling and no rational explanation could be found. Later on, in different incidents, water sprayed from a wall, cascaded down stairs, poured down the living room walls and a jet of water suddenly shot through the wallpaper and splashed onto the fire. Even detectives were called in, but to no avail. A jet of water suddenly emerging from a wall was witnessed by a photographer from the Leicester Evening Mail. The 'spook water' continued its antics for some months but gradually lessened its activities and then ceased altogether.

There is a fascinating tale concerning the appearance of the Devil in Barrow-on-Soar, near Loughborough, "within living memory"(3). The account is tied up with stories of local intrigue, but the essence of the appearance is that early one September morning (a Sunday) "a low trolley with wheels" was seen travelling at an "alarming speed". This trolley had "lights of an astonishing brilliance" fixed to it. The weird vehicle careered off down the village street. A week later, a "dark, sinister figure dressed all in black, riding a white horse" rode up to a farmer and a group of his men. The sinister figure "fixed the labourers with a cold stare" before riding off, laughing. Immediately after the rider there came the brilliantly lit trolley travelling down the street. The Devil? Perhaps - but it sounds to us more like a Man in Black.

On June 30th, 1753, a great fire began at Shepshed (7). 85 bays of buildings were consumed in the flames. The cause of the fire was never determined. Shortly after this fire had begun, another building suddenly erupted in flames, 150 yds from the main conflagration. As people helped their neighbours with the flames, they suddenly discovered that their own property was alight. Several animals were killed in this inexplicable outbreak of conflagrations, but no human lives were lost.

We have located records of the "Cannons of Barisal" type of phenomenon (volleys of inexplicable aerial reports) occurring near Hinckley in 1672 and Buckminster in the 1720s.

Presumed Standing Stone in an Ibstock lane, near the Church.

THE PSYCHIC LANDSCAPE.

The most shadowy and elusive aspects of any landscape are those which relate to the mental lives of its inhabitants. Dreams, prophecies, "otherworld" communications...they slip away, difficult to define and even more difficult to learn about in the first place. We can only record fragments that have come our way - the tip of a psychic iceberg.

During our research, we came across reports of Hinckley-based contactees who were active way back in 1966 (an important UFO-period in Leics. leading up to the incredible nationwide UFO activity of 1967). They employed automatic writing and trance mediums, according to the reports we discovered. The matter reached a climax when the group, accompanied by journalists, visited a site "near Huncote" on the instructions of "extraterrestrials" in order to meet with the alien entities. It proved negative. We set out to trace this group, now dormant for 9 years. We finally located a member of the group who had become custodian of the writings and tape-recordings. We

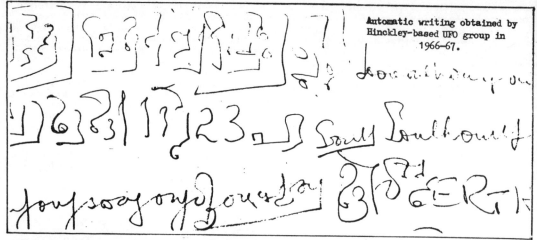

Automatic writing obtained by Hinckley-based UFO group in 1966–67.

were not surprised to find that the site near Huncote (there is a markstone near this village embraced by the trunk of a tree) where the meeting with the extra-terrestrials should have taken place, turned out to be Croft Hill. We saw quite literally thousands of sheets of garbled English and pictographic-type automatic writing and listened to some of the dozens of tapes recorded at sittings with a London medium who was prepared to work with the group. (Other mediums chose not to assist the group which was also shunned by UFO groups: 1965-66 were early days for a psychic approach to UFOs). The ouija, automatic writing and their medium were the only ways the group ever contacted the 'ultraterrestrials', to use John Keel's term. An entity that frequently communicated with the group called himself JIRO - a ludicrous appelation of the sort that seems common to many contactee accounts. The number 23 was communicated repeatedly both in the writings and through the medium, but the members of the group could never understand why. We listened to one tape that consisted of the medium's transformed voice referring constantly to '23' and (phonetically) 'Leer' (Lear, Leire, Llyr?). It may be worth noting that the number 23 is considered a significant day-of-month date by some people, including NEWS-contributor William Porter.***** The entities referred to the concept of a supreme being as KHI - though at other times KHI seemed to be one of the communicating entities. Some of the entities claimed they had lived on Earth millenia ago, and that telepathy had preceded speech. The contactee group could never obtain clear information as to whether these

***** see THE NEWS 5/12 - Ed.

entities were now extraterrestrials or not: it appears to us that though some members of the group were wont to assume that they were, the communications do not altogether support the idea. Typical of much contactee material, the entities warned of nuclear war. One entity claimed it came from LEHRA or LEHAR (Llyr, etc,again?). Sagittarius was also mentioned, and Saturn. On tape, the entities speaking through the medium displayed different characters and voices, all with heavy Asian accents. The communications contain references to the numbers 666 and 33 (sometimes 333) as well as 23. Apart from JIRO, other named entities included characters called MIL, SEPTA SIGS and GILIL.

In general, the prolific communications are difficult to understand and seem by turn cryptic, poetic, symbolic, cliché-ridden and just plain ridiculous. The contactee group were given the occasional small-scale piece of information that could be verified later, but information of a more major kind relating to meetings with the entities or the appearances of UFOs turned out to be hoaxes. Two other sites for meetings were given prior to the Croft Hill occasion. One of these sites was near the village of Wolvey and the other was Groby Pool, the largest sheet of naturally-occurring water in the county. Both these sites are exactly equidistant from Croft.

A member of the group we spoke to admitted that they never really grasped what was going on. Towards the end of 1966 the group split up. "We were going round and round in circles," one of them said, "and becoming overwrought, egged on by promises not fulfilled. We could see, I think, that it would have been dangerous to go on, someone might have gone over the edge". And that seems a sensible point for us to leave it too.

The night before the battle of Bosworth, King Richard camped on the prehistoric earthworks known as 'The Bradshaws'. During the night, Richard had a vision while lying in his tent. "There appeared unto him divers fearful ghosts, running about him, not suffering him to take any rest, still crying revenge, which vision he related to his friends in the morning".(7). We also refer readers to NEWS 10/9.

Late in 1704 there began what became known as the 'Cropston Miracle' (Cropston is on Charnwood). Various local clergymen of the day and other witnesses wrote up an account of the event and this in turn was preserved by Nichols (7). Briefly, the matter involved a young fellow called John Cook. He became inflicted with a strange illness that caused his face and body to become inflamed and swollen, and no part of his body was free from pain. By midsummer 1705, John had been in bed for 6 months and his pain and the contraction of his muscles were worse. He could not move and was expected to die. His father, no doubt with the best of intentions, had someone pull John's legs while he sat on the lad's knees. "Upon complaint of ...pain, they desisted from such afflicting experiments." Early in December, John heard a disembodied voice say:

"John, John, John, arise, for thy limbs are restored unto thee, and walk". John wanted to attempt to rise but his father would not hear of it, and reproved him for his talk of voices. John Cook sank into a deep melancholy, but 12 days later the voice spoke to him again, this time louder than before. "This voice seemed to him as formed about a yard above his head, and was so loud, that he believes it might have been heard into the next room." And John Cook got up, with a crackling of his knees, and walked free, completely cured, to the amazement of relatives and neighbours. Coming right up to the present time we have records of two minor prophecies, a strange dream and more possible 'otherworld' communications.

The Leicester Mercury (July 16th, 1975) reported that a Barwell woman had had a premonition that there was going to be a tragedy involving someone in her family. She communicated her fears to relatives. Shortly afterwards, her daughter-in-law was killed and her son injured in an accident in Majorca.

Stoke's 'Evening Sentinel' reported in August 1975 that there was a prophecy that might relate to the current swarm of tremors. A Mr. Boulton said that his grandfather had prophesied 60 years ago that "the land in this area would shake and tremble, causing cracks to appear on the surface".

The Oaks Hanging Stone.
Quote from Potter (8).

At a very short distance from the spot on which this Quern was found, is the singular stone (see engraving) called Hanging Stone—a name which it has probably borne from very remote times; and I attach considerable importance, in the establishing of my proposition, to the proximity of these two ancient relics to each other.

Many have entertained a belief that the upper of these Hanging Stones was artificially raised upon the platform of the other. The geologist arrives at a different conclusion, and accounts for most of them by means purely natural. But whether the stones were placed in their present extraordinary position by nature or art, they must, in times when superstition held the minds of men under its sway, have been contemplated with extreme veneration. And it should be remembered, that wherever such apparently mysterious formations presented themselves, the Druids, ever alive to what might be auxiliary to their influence over the people, did not fail to turn them to good account. Even in these days, the stranger cannot behold the pile without feelings approaching to awe. No one riding up to the lower side of it, on a spirited horse, can fail to observe the emotion of the animal; and an old forester states, that Mr. Gisborne's Scotch cattle, on their first arrival, always gaze at it with wonder! " I take care," added he, " never to be near it after twilight has begun !"

These stones bear a striking resemblance to those in Wales and Derbyshire, which antiquaries have almost unanimously pronounced Cromlechs. "The word *Crom* signifies *crooked*, or *bending*, and *lech* a *flat stone*. Hence the belief that they were altars, or objects to which the antients bowed."‡ A pile more likely to be selected as an object of idolatrous veneration could not easily be found.†

But to return to the Oaks Hanging Stone.—A spot which is about the centre of a triangle formed by that stone, Kite Hill and the Tin Meadows, was, according to the information of an old Forest Keeper of Lord Hastings', always called " the Grove" before the inclosure. It may, in early times, have been a grove to some temple, or to the Hanging Stone Cromlech.

The woman who reported the close-up view of the UFO mentioned in NEWS 11/17 has subsequently become very upset about the sighting and has suffered dreams. In these she is apparently in a room on a spaceship, unnoticed by, or invisible to, the crew members. The room is filled with control panels. Then one of the crew turns and looks straight at her as if surprised. She feels herself go completely cold and awakes in a heavy sweat. Just her unusual experience playing on her mind - or something more?

Early in 1975, shortly after Leicester's UFO study group, LAPRO, had set up their organisation, they received 3 hoax phone calls, from apparently different callers each time. One caller gave a false number and the other two had LAPRO members going out to false addresses to witness UFOs. Not only were there no UFOs on view, but the phoney addresses were particularly odd. One was once valid but was now a demolished house, while the other was a gap in a row of houses where the house number LAPRO had been given would have existed if the gap had not been there...if you see what we mean. At the time LAPRO members were not aquainted with the Men in Black hoax syndrome outlined by Keel in his books.

We have heard rumours concerning another, current, Leics. contactee group who claim they can lay on telepathic contact with UFOs, causing them to appear. We are following up this information.

Markstone at crossroads near Warren Hills, Charnwood.

THE ANCIENT LANDSCAPE.

We have dealt in some detail with selected aspects of ancient Leics. for TLH (1). Although we will confine ourselves here to an impressionistic portrait of the ancient face of the area, no analysis of the landscape we are dealing with would be complete without some awareness of the work of ancient man. We

are satisfied that it is through a study of ancient man's activities that we will approach a deeper understanding of apparently anomalous phenomena. The ancients appear to have had a greater knowledge than we possess of the interaction between the human psyche and its external environment, as well as the interaction between components of that external world. In fact, the concepts of an 'inner psyche' and an 'external world' are probably false and the cause of our difficulty in seeing what ancient man was up to. But more of this another time.

Leics. has been disgracefully neglected by archaeologists (though, on reflection this may be a blessing in disguise). The county is not noted for its ancient features but this is a false impression engendered by neglect. This situation has, however, made it all too easy for quarries, roadworks, property developments and the like to destroy ancient relics.

There are many earthworks in the county (most of them visually undramatic) but no one knows just how many because there has been no serious, complete survey made. Hoskins has commented (5) that very few known sites have been properly excavated and a considerable number of sites have never been recorded on O.S. maps. This was brought home to us when we were locating the position of two recumbent old stones near Queniborough, not far from Syston. Quite by accident, we stumbled on a large circular earthwork almost hidden from view by a ring of oaks alongside the old church at Queniborough. It had a central mound topped by two very tall Scots Pine trees and ringed by about 7 small yews. This feature, unmarked on the 1" map, had become a dumping ground for dead automobiles. Ah, Leicestershire...

Apart from numerous ancient wells and springs, the county possesses many moat features - we compiled a list of about 40 without any effort. Moats are to fare better than earthworks in the county because Ann Dornier and her Moated Site Research Group are compiling a gazeteer of them. Many Leics. farms and homesteads are old, and quite a large number are, or were, moated. A fair proportion of such places probably occupy ancient sites.

Leics has a number of ancient crosses within its boundaries, including a beautiful Saxon cross at Rothley which is often ignored in the literature. Also, there are old records claiming that Charnwood Forest once had "many crosses" standing on it. The significance of old crosses is that they probably mark points of former importance, in some cases perhaps replacing or using a standing stone. This would seem to be the case, for example, at Ragdale. Nichols described the cross in the churchyard there as a "curious and perfect old cross, the shaft of which is one solid stone". Unusual ancient features were the turf crosses that existed at certain places on Charnwood. These features, formed by cutting or raising the earth, were renewed annually. They are reminiscent of the old turf mazes around the country. A turf cross existed on Nettle Hill near Nanpantan and 3 turf crosses were at the meeting point of the parishes of Shepshed, Markfield and Whitwick.

Leics. is extraordinarily rich in really ancient churches, many of them probably on sites of former, pagan sanctity.

The county contains some earthworked hills, and at least 3 hills specifically named as beacon hills. We suspect Leics. to have supported a tree-lore survival up until fairly recent times.

The county is not particularly rich in old stones but, nevertheless, possesses more than is generally realised. It is frequently assumed that the only standing stone in the county is the Humber Stone, as that alone is marked on the 1" map. This assumption is incorrect, and through persistent research and fieldwork we have located other standing stones and mark stones, or their sites. A sketch map accompanies this text, indicating the distribution of old stones in the county. Obviously, there may be a few more substantial stones to be rediscovered, and there certainly must be many markstones still to be identified. While we continue fieldwork on this, the map can give an idea of the general distribution of stones. The stones numbered on the map are a cross-section of extant and former ones we have selected for the

following summary:

1. St. John's Stone - originally about 7 feet tall, it stood in an "amphitheatre-shaped hollow" not far from Abbey Park in Leicester. Fairy lore was attached to it and children danced around it on June 24th. It is supposed to have shared a midsummer sunrise alignment with the Humber Stone (2) perpetuated in folklore as a tunnel. The stone is no longer extant.

2. Braunstone complex - a flat stone by the church door has a pointed end oriented fractionally north of East. A large markstone is situated on a nearby bridle path. Some other decidedly unusual and distinctive stones are in a copse nearby. Braunstone is now a suburb of Leicester and the church once had a curious hay-strewing ceremony.

3. Humber Stone - originally about 10 feet tall, pentagonal with its north face "exactly oriented". It is said to have been dropped by one of the old gods. Lore attached to it relates to fairies and the supernatural movement of the stone. Only fragments of it now remain, near the village of Humberstone.

4. Moody Bush Stone - pentagonal, with axes precisely related to compass points. 4 feet high, it stands in a field near Syston, 6 miles NE of Leicester. Related to local lore.

5. The Bartholomews - a field from which hay was brought for the hay-strewing ceremony at the church in nearby Ashby Folville. This was discontinued in the 1890s. The hay was taken from a part of the field marked out by 3 stones set in a triangular configuration. We are still researching the current existence of these stones. (The purpose behind hay-strewing ceremonies has never been determined but, as they date from the remotest antiquity, they probably relate to the sites of the churches with which they are connected.)

6. Grimston - a stone stands on the village green next to a large tree. We traced the record of another, larger stone in a nearby field. This stone was said to have fallen off a star. It had been pulled up 20 years ago and thrown into a pond. We were anxious to locate this stone and take a sample for analysis to see if it was meteoric but unfortunately the pond had been filled in and the stone was beyond recall. There is also a mark stone on a road approaching the village green.

7. Star stone - this standing stone existed near the Three Shires Bush where

the counties of Leics., Notts., and Lincs. meet. The Three Shires Bush is now a curiously silent, dying copse and the tree on the actual point where the

Markstone near the village green, Grimston.

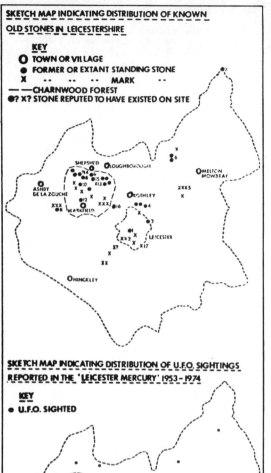

KEY
O TOWN OR VILLAGE
● FORMER OR EXTANT STANDING STONE
X ..   "   ..   "   MARK   ..   "
—— —CHARNWOOD FOREST
●? X? STONE REPUTED TO HAVE EXISTED ON SITE

SKETCH MAP INDICATING DISTRIBUTION OF U.F.O. SIGHTINGS
REPORTED IN THE 'LEICESTER MERCURY' 1953-1974

KEY
● U.F.O. SIGHTED

Note the two trends follow similar distributions.
Closer analysis gives closer correlation. Latest
data also conforms to this pattern. Husbands
Bosworth seems as prone to UFOs as it is to
seismic and meteorological events. We have not
plotted the UFO phenomena seen over Charnwood
during the 1957 earthquake.

counties meet is now an ailing oak tree
planted in the 1960s to replace an earlier oak. Local natives claim that the
stone is no longer extant. The original
existence of the bush and stone quietly
suggests that geomancy may have been
involved in the laying out of the old
county boundaries in England. Nichols
speculated that the Star stone got its
name because of a cross carved on it, a
cross with a rather decorative appearance. We think the star reference might
be more complex than this.
8. The Oaks Hanging Stone - see insert.＊
9. The Hangman's stone - also near the
Oaks, on Charnwood. The standing stone
is situated very close to an oak tree.
10. Forest Rock complex - on Charnwood,
near Colville. The stump of a standing
stone remains near a mump of white quartz. There are other curious (but subtle) features in the vicinity (1). A
mark stone stands on the crossroads beneath Warren Hills where the complex is
situated. Someone of the calibre of Professor Thom ought to visit this site. .
11. Ibstock - 3 mark stones and one standing stone (or uncommonly large mark
stone) are in an old, narrow lane in
this village, near to the church.
12. Markfield - an inscribed standing
stone stood in a field near this village
up until last century. 19th century writers speculated that this stone fell on
the line of a lost Roman road that connected a number of ancient sites. Ley
hunters awake!
13. Stoney stumps - on Charnwood, near
Charley Wood. Nichols drew attention to
the fact that this wood was formerly
known as Chalhenge Wood and he considered the 'henge' ending significant in
view of the fact that certain scholars
of his day believed that a 'Druidical
Temple' existed somewhere near the spot
known as Stoney Stumps and that Chalhenge Wood was a grove belonging to it (It
is our suspicion that some trees and
tree-groupings in Leics. still tell handed down tales of long ago).
14. Strawberry Hill - Potter (8) claimed
that a 'Druidical' stone shaped like an
augural seat existed on this hill on
Charnwood, and was similar to one other
stone in Derbyshire. There are in fact
two Strawberry Hills on Charnwood, quite
close to each other, and we have so far
drawn a blank in trying to locate the
stone.
15. Reynstones - these stones are recorded as having stood on the Shepshed parish boundary between the Conston cross
and the Tin Meadow.
16. Anstey stone - a deliberately leaning stone about 5 ft long. It is a ley
hunter's dream as it visually aligns

* see back to page 15 - Ed.

Anstey Stone. Note the Church and hilltop copse aligned in the background. The hill is "Old John" on Charnwood. (Hope this comes out clear enough — Ed.)

with the old church in Anstey and a hilltop copse. Further work shows that the stone is on an 8-point map alignment. We must also recall Mrs Berger's humanoid sighting near Anstey.

17. South Wigston - a mark stone here gives a good illustration of how the antiquity of such stones could have come about. When a house was put up alongside this stone, many years ago, a niche was formed in the wall by the builders so that the stone could remain undisturbed. The part of the stone that stood proud of the wall was painted black. Even a road sign was erected flush against the stone without affecting it. (We have noticed that the Leics. authorities have a penchant for placing road and telegraph poles against mark stones!) The building has now been demolished to make way for a dual carriageway and the whole stone is revealed surrounded by fragments of masonry. We imagine the stone will also have gone since we photographed it. South Wigston has been a key area for UFO sightings according to our research.

So there we have a brief account of just some of the old stones of Leics. The lore and orientations relating to some of them suggests to us the remains of an astronomical network - at least as one of their functions. We feel it is important that all these stones, or their former positions, need to be identified before all trace of them disappears. Without this data, no serious ley hunting can be done in the county, nor can meaningful correlations be made in other respects.

We have not studied the NE Staffs. region to any great extent with regard to ancient features, but we do notice a couple of interesting items.

The large village of Stone is situated in the Trent valley only a few miles from the heart of the Stoke tremor area. It is said to have got its name from a cairn of stones that once existed locally. Some earthworks are still extant in the vicinity. John Michell has remarked (6) on a circle that can be struck from Whiteleaved Oak in the Malverns with a radius of 504 furlongs so that its circumference passes through Llantwit Major, Glastonbury, Stonehenge and Goring-on-Thames, where an ancient temple once existed. When we continued this circle on the map it passed extremely close to Ibstock and on round through Stone. We note with interest the 'mystery flares' near Llantwit Major earlier this year, reported by F W Holliday in NEWS 9. Holliday links Llantwit Major with a ley: all well and good, but we would also point out its relationship via this Whiteleaved Oak circle with Stone which is near to the areas where seismic and UFO activity was occurring at approximately the same time as the Welsh 'flares' and 'fireballs'. Researchers ignore such correlations at their peril.

Very close to where the UFO landed near Leek (NEWS 11/7) is a somewhat weird range of hills known as the Roaches. Here, on midsummer's evening, is said to occur "a remarkable phenomenon" (4) involving a "double sunset". The sun appears to set only to slide into view again and appear to set once more. Clearly, the precise backsight is necessary to witness this, and our sources did not say where the viewpoint was. On June 21st we arrived at the Roaches, hoping to obtain a sequence of photographs of the event. The sun blazed away all midsummer day (as it has most days this furnace-like summer) and we trusted that local people would give us further information. However, extensive local enquiries failed to reveal anyone who knew anything at all about the phenomenon! Such is the way that knowledge becomes lost.

SHUGBOROUGH.

Shugborough Hall is set in beautiful grounds in the Trent valley, not far from Stone. The research of Henry Lincoln has linked aspects of Shugborough with Rennes-le-Chateau in southern France. The mysteries involved are awesome and far-reaching. We had originally intended to go into this matter at some length in this article but that has proved imposs-

ible as we have had to include the unexpected data on recent tremors and meteorological events in Staffs. and Leics.
We hope it may be possible to remedy
this shortcoming at a future date.

* * *   * * *   * * *   * * *   * * *   * * *

Parts 1 and 2 of this study contain gen-
erous extracts of Leicestershire material that we are compiling for a work
that is currently in progress. We will
be seeking to link this data with observations that we hope will contribute in
a small way to the growing body of understanding concerning the complex inter-
relationships between the cosmos, Earth
and the human mind. We are putting together some speculations in this direction in an essay called THE THOR FACTOR,
which may appear in a future issue of
the NEWS if circumstances allow. If not,
our ideas, correlations and speculations
will be put forward for scrutiny in our
work-in-progress - should it ever see
the light of day!

A number of people have helped us at
various times by providing information,
sharing the fieldwork, and so on. We
take this opportunity to thank them.
They include, in no special order: Harry
Woolman; the Rev. Shepherd and his family; Shirley Torrens; Graham Crowley;
Ann Williams; 'Ned'; Dave Potts; David
Morris; Dennis Fisher; Mr. Warwick, and
Jay. We are also grateful to our editor
for aiding and abetting us.

* * *   * * *   * * *   * * *   * * *   * * *

REFERENCES.

1) Devereux, Paul & York, Andrew, The
   Forgotten Heart of Albion, The Ley
   Hunter, Nos 66-68

2) Dryden, Alice (Ed), Memorials of Old
   Leics., 1911, George Allen.

3) Green, Susan, Further Legends of
   Leics. & Rutland, 1974, Leicester.

4) Hadfield, John (Ed), Shell Guide to
   England, 1973, Michael Joseph.

5) Hoskins, WG, The Heritage of Leics.,
   1972, Leicester.

6) Michell, John, City of Revelation,
   1972, Garnstone Press.

7) Nichols, J, The History and Antiquities of Leics., 1795-1815, London.

8) Potter, TR, The History & Antiquities
   of Charnwood Forest, 1842, Hamilton
   Adams, London.

9) Swift, Eric, Folktales of the East
   Midlands, 1954, Thomas Nelson.

10) Watkins, Alfred, The Old Straight
    Track, 1925, (Garnstone, 1970)

11) Williams, CJ, Leicester Mercury,
    29th October, 1971.

Markstone by a bridle path in Newtown Linford,
Charnwood. Two large stones stand by the walls
of the village pub near here. No one knows
their origin.

DELUGE AT HAMPSTEAD cont...

of August saw the discovery of A0621 minus 0,
"the brightest x-ray star ever observed". In the
days preceeding the Hampstead Washout its
brightness increased from 1,000 units, according
to Prof Kenneth Pounds (Leicester U). "But now
it has reached an astonishing 35,000 units -
and it is still increasing". The Prof broke
this news to the first European Conference on
Astronomy, where else but at Leicester University, and observatories across the world were
immediately mobilized to keep watch on this
"most exciting discovery ever made in the field
of astronomy." (Sunday Times 17 Aug 75.) Fort
would be the first to chuckle at the way nature
keeps pitching these surprises, particularly,
it seems, when experts in that speciality are in
a huddle somewhere.

And then there's this 'coincidence' of the
mystery tremor' that rattled a house in Kensington (surely not the one with the snake) the
day after the Hampstead soaking (15th Aug) as
mentioned by Paul & Andy on page 9 of this issue.

...AND YET MORE RAIN.

As if to make a point, the heavens opened
over southern England once more, exactly a
month later, on Sept 14. Two people died and
three were missing as gales whipped up high
seas all along the south coast. A 'whirlwind'
struck Barnham, a village in Sussex, leaving
an estimated £75,000 worth of damage. The wind
rose to "a roaring" and carried glass from
shattered windows. Southampton recorded its
wettest day this century. (Daily Mirror, 15 Sept
75).

Polter-Ghosts

BIRKDALE, SOUTHPORT, LANCS.

One of the most interesting we knew of but had nothing in the files on, was the activity of a poltergeist during demolition work on the Palace Hotel, Birkdale. Recently, Peter Rogerson sent us his clippings on the case and we record it here.

In April 1969, Jos Smith led his 10-man team of demolishers into the 112-year-old hotel. They had a contract and intended to sleep in the building until the job was done. After about a month they were all sufficiently frightened to move out into lodgings and only work in the daylight. "I don't blame them," said Jos. "Things started to happen soon after we moved in. First of all we were awakened by strange noises in the night. Then the lift would suddenly set off on its own."

About mid April, Jos ordered all the power to the building and the lift to be cut off – but the lift still glided from floor to floor with its gates opening and closing, and its indicator lights flashing. Electricity Board spokesmen were quoted that the building was isolated – not an amp was going into the place. The men removed the emergency winding handle, but still it moved. Workman Fred Wooley said: "Nine of us came back one night and as we entered the foyer the lift doors slammed shut and it shot up to the second floor." The Paralab directory for 1969 has a summary of the case and they mention an "independent witness" a Mrs K Templeton, who had gone into the 1000 room hotel looking for antique mirrors. She said: "While I was talking to the workmen, the lift suddenly began to go up. There wasn't any sound from it – it was very eerie. It just glided up about 7ft almost to the next floor and stopped. I ran all the way up to the winding room with one of the workmen, but there was just no way it could have been moved mechanically. The brake was still on."

A BBC programme ran a report showing a dog that was happy on all floors except the second one – indeed the second floor seems to be the focus of the activity.

The Paralab go on to mention accounts we don't have. That a decision was made to cut the cables, but the lift did not fall. So they cut through the main shafts, to no avail. It was as perverse in its obstinacy as it was in its previous wilful mobility. It did not fall until it had been continually struck with sledge-hammers for 25 minutes, and then it plunged down the shaft to bury itself 4ft into the cellar. This behaviour was naturally found puzzling and "unbelievable" by those present.

There is an epilogue of sorts. In the last week of May 69 the local papers report "hundreds of pounds worth of damage" to the building. Why worry, you ask? Well, for example 200 doors were stacked ready for selling, and during the night they were thrown over a balcony and smashed. Windows were broken, saleable iron balustrades wrecked, and fires started. All this was blamed on vandals "from the Liverpool area" – but there are no reports of the vandalism being witnessed; just discovered next morning.

We are suspicious. On what grounds, we would like to ask in a mood of inquiry that would have had old Fodor beaming with approval, is the distinction made between the vandalism of corporeal and psychic delinquents? Could it be that broken windows and smashed doors are not so 'obviously' unusual as a lift with a mind of its own? A case worthy of further investigation, wethinks. (Daily Mail, Daily Mirror, 7 May 69. Manchester Evening News, 29 May 1969. Cr: Peter Rogerson.)

WOOLTON, LIVERPOOL, LANCS.

A building used as an ambulance training centre in Quarry St, Woolton, has long been reputed to be haunted, mainly by a spectre the previous occupants (before 1967 it belonged to the police) called 'The Sarge'. In the first week of Oct 1974, ambulance trainees complained of breaking windows, phantom footsteps, and doors that unlocked themselves – similar events were reported by the policemen before 1967.

One retired rozzer, Jack Elsworth, 75, who was born in the place, remembered tales told to him by his father, who was station sergeant there near the end of the last century. Jack's dad had helped lay out a dead man under a tarpaulin in a back room, and then locked the door. The next day, the corpse was found lowered to the floor, still completely covered. On another occasion "a horse was uncoupled from the shafts of a cart outside the station, when no human was in sight." And, says Jack, a Union Jack vanished from high on the station flagpole, to be found later in St Helens.

After this news came to light, all night vigils by both the "extrasensory perception class" of the Childwall Institute, and the Merseyside Parapsychotic (?) Society failed to raise even a phantom footfall. (Liverpool Echo, 8 & 23 Oct 74. Cr: Peter Rogerson.)

SEXY GHOSTS.

We seem to have accumulated a few stories of randy wraiths - though none of those that follow are a match for the salacious shade of Sir William Langhorne. In life he is said to so desperately want an heir, that he bedded most of the women for 20 miles around. As good an excuse as any, we suppose. But after his death this obsession was said to still drive him to try any female who spent the night at Charlton House, Greenwich - and doubtless the surprise appearance of buns in ovens was blamed on him too. (Kentish Independent, 27 June 74. Cr: Steve Moore.)

WANDSWORTH, LONDON.

Pamela Purvey, husband and 3 kids moved out of their council flat because they had just had a nightmare year with their polt, in Earlsfield Road. Amongst the usual tricks of flashing the lights on and off, it had pushed her along their passageway, dragged bedclothes from her shoulders "with tremendous force", and trapped her feet in bed in a paralysing grip. While she cooked, it cuddled her waist, and she, thinking her husband was getting affectionate, didn't realise for a while that it was a ghostly groper. The final straw came when she was sitting in the living room and the head and shoulders of an elderly man with a beard appeared out of the wall. A suitcase "a few feet away began to rise in the air and then crashed to the ground just missing me." (News of the World, 29 April 74.)

LEWISHAM, LONDON.

Anyone who spends the night in the guestroom of Graham Smithies in George Lane, Lewisham, is sure of getting a surprise room service. Graham and his wife appear to share the house with a discerning ghost. A "comely guest" sleeping alone, felt, quite distinctly, a kiss planted on her cheeks. A couple in that room were quite far apart, when the girl felt a warm hand clasp hers. When she realised the hand was not her husband's, who had his back to her, she ran from the room screaming. When another couple slept there, the woman had a very comfortable night while the husband felt icily cold. Graham said: "Mainly men complain that they were unable

to get warm in the room, no matter how many covers they put on the bed." (News of the World, 6 May 74.)

LEWES, SUSSEX.

Teresa Dartnell and Gary English stepped into the deserted All Saint's Church Hall for their late-night farewell kiss - it turned into a nightmare. Teresa said: " We heard eerie footsteps. A ghastly cold, clammy feeling came over us and rooted us to the spot as if we were being held down. I grabbed a drum-stand (Gary's band had played there earlier) and used it as a crucifix and we ran out...but Gary went back to switch the lights off. He was thrown out through the swing doors with his feet right off the ground." Gary said: "When we drove off in my van I felt as if I was being strangled." Also mentioned is that Teresa'a watch heated up so that she bore a burn on her wrist. What could it be do you think? Guilt about kissing in a church hall? These two kids certainly seem of a religious turn, talking about sleeping with their crucifixes etc. Certainly all the clichés are here - but their fear was very real. They fled to the nearest police station and convinced 6 policemen to search the place. Needless to say, they found nothing. (Sunday Mirror, 25 Aug 74. Cr: Robert Forrest.)

WORKSOP, NOTTS.

Pretty Beryl Gladwin doesn't get much sleep. Between 4 and 6am, three mornings a week, she is visited by a ghost wearing miner's boots. Her life is made such a misery that her parents are applying for a new home for themselves and their seven children. Beryl, 18, tried sleeping in with her parents, but the amorous spook was not deterred. "First it tugs at the bedclothes and then I feel it get next to me in the bed. It holds my hand and starts kissing me and biting my neck. The haunting began about the end of Feb this year and after a couple of frightening weeks, they called in a clairvoyant, Simon Alexander.

Mr Alexander kept a vigil at one of the regular trysting times, and felt a malevolent presence outside the room. "It tried to make me leave by making me feel ill. I had to fight hard to stay. Then it materialised in the room. It was trying to dodge me and was difficult to get into focus. I could see pit boots clearly, and miner's baggy herringbone trousers held up by a wide belt with a big buckle. It tried to get in with Beryl and kiss her. She was trembling with fear."

He went on: "I believe it's the ghost of a miner called Dexter who used to live in the house. He had 12 children of his own, and I'm certain he will make love to Beryl unless something is done soon." The Gladwins, as seems to be a pattern in council-house hauntings, had only moved into the house six months previously. The Church seems unhurried about who gets laid first. The Vicar of Worksop, conducting his own investigation, said an exorcism might be a possibility.

Sometime after the above story appeared in the nation's Sunday papers, the People carried a little note tucked away where few would see it. It read: " Mr George Dexter, of 31 Windmill Lane Worksop, states that the story we published on March 9 headed 'The Ghost that left Love Bites' was a slur on his dead brother. There was no such intention and we are sorry if the report caused embarassment to the Dexter family." You gotta laugh! (News of the World, Sunday Mirror, Sunday People, 9 Mar 75; Sunday People 11 May 75. Cr: Nigel Watson.)

...AND, AT THAT SAME MOMENT....

SYNCHRONICITIES

ACCIDENT GROUPINGS.

It seems that no sooner had we typed up our notes on the strange series of public coach crashes (page 20 last issue) than more news of a similar nature came in. If this was a vein of the darkest sort of synchronicity, then it was clear it had not yet played out.

A woman was killed at Faversham, Kent, when a coach crashed on 17 July (Sunday Mirror, 17 Aug 75.) ** 40 tourists, some of them British, were injured when a London coach skidded off the autobahn near Bonn on 19 July (Sunday Mirror 20 July 75). ** about the same time, a coach carrying 36 passengers skidded and crashed through a stone parapet, its front wheels coming to rest over a 12ft drop. This happened at the bridge over the Swale in the Yorkshire village of Topcliffe, not far from the similar, but fatal, Hebden Bridge disaster in May (see last issue), (Sunday Mirror, 20 July 75). ** 5 people died and 42 were injured when a coach hit a motorway embankment and overturned on the M6 between Sandbach and Holmes Chapel in Cheshire, while it was trying to avoid a collision between three cars in the torrential rain. (Sunday Mirror, 17 Aug 75). ** one man was killed and several people were injured when at least six coaches and six cars were involved in four seperate accidents in southern England late on Sept 13. (Sunday Mirror, 14 Sept 75). ** on radio news we heard that on the evening of 22 Sept, a coach crashed near Bournemouth, injuring three ladies. There was nothing in the papers the next day.

Some time ago, Robert Forrest, who is something of a coincidence freak, sent us a heap of accidents involving cars plunging off the road into water in Feb & March last year. ** On the 27th Feb the accident in which Ronald Milhench, the man who forged Prime Minister Wilson's signature in a land deal, and his wife were taken into the waters of a lake at Chasewater, Staffs, occurred. Mrs Milhench drowned. (Daily Mirror, 15 Mar 74.) ** On the 3rd March, Ray Everett scrambled out of his Volkswagen as it sank slowly into a canal in Thorne, Yorks. (Daily Mirror, 4 Mar 74.) ** Don Gillanders was trapped in his car after driving into a canal in Ormerod Rd, Burnley, on the 9th. He was rescued eventually. (Sunday Mirror, 10 Mar 74.) ** Bill Shirran, Coventry's ex-director of Parks, was found dead in his car at the bottom of a lake during a police investigation of some council departments. (Daily Mirror, 21 Mar 74.)

About the only thing that has any consistancy here is that something - anything - is repeated. It could be any of the factors involved - but whatever it is, it pops up in mini-serieses of events. We do not completely understand the relationships between single things, let alone the complexities of groups of things. Even Jung was groping (though far ahead of many of us) in his attempts to understand those relationships which seem to hint at some kind of 'organisation' behind things (we use the word here in its biological sense). His thesis on synchronicity was a true scientific gesture, put forward as a tentative hypothesis. Fort too had a feeling for the directions of future studies when he wrote: "I am not so much interested in things, as in the relationships between things." Some people see in strange repetitions the intervention of an external agency. On the other hand Jung has shown that the tendency to, and therefore expressions of, order (archetypes) are as natural to entities as the tendency toward wholeness in , say, cellular division. Fort again: "When it's railroad time, railroads will be invented." And that's not just a clever remark. Any examination of patent records will bear out the fact that there are independent filings all over the world of key in-

ventions at similar times - as if something
were in the air and found expression simultaneously.

It seems awfully flimsy, but sometimes we
have only our suspicions to go upon. As a
species, man is heavily committed to ego - any
suggestion that we are merely puppets working
out an alien will brings out all the classic
phobias. If what we are talking about is the
local expression of a 'Grand Design' (like that
of which an archetype is an expression, an
ultimate unknowable) then we are no further out
of this quagmire of paradoxes, the phenomenal
universe. One sign of hope is the growing
acceptance (or understanding) of a form of God
which is both unspeakably ancient and spanking
new (new in the sense of rediscovered) - a God
that is an ageless organism of totality, not
the 'Deus Ex Machina' who seemed a bad-tempered
old crank. If there is a God, and it is sentient, then it would be of an order of sentience
we could not begin to recognise. Being beyond
(encompassing) all duality, it would have no
need of time. Patterns, like most of our concepts, are inextricably bound up with our ideas
of and need for time, even the absence of time
(vide, synchronicity.) The phenomenal universe
is permeated with causal events, the logical
extension of which is a paradoxical First Cause!
In true fashion, the only alternative is seen
as 'Chance'. And yet - we'd like to ask, are
not both Chance and an (external, causal) God
both ways of sidestepping the most interesting
philosophical issue we'll see in many years -
and that is that there is some aspect of Man
that can directly affect, shape, create the
universe around him. Indeed many recent studies,
not just ours, are hinting that the distinctions
between internal/subjective/mind and external/
objective/universe are in some cases nonexist-
ant. Further - the ontological extension of this
is that 'God' is a state whereby this duality
is perpetually reconciled for every sentient
and nonsentient thing that exists.

All this may be true or not. As long as there
is some element of doubt, let us be content not
saying such a thing is impossible. For our
present purposes, it is simply enough to look
at the data, and say, yes! here is a pattern
which runs through several events - phenomenally
this connects them as much as a leaf, a dress
and a flame, if each were green.

Every pool we look into reflects the same
sun, some more differently than others. What
then is going on in our next tale? On 25 July
this year, Bob Finnegan, crossing the Falls Rd,
in troubled Belfast, became a concrete example
of the indomitable spirit of the ordinary people
there. He bounced off the bonnet of a car. He
got to his feet and another car hurled him to
the opposite pavement. As bystanders gathered
round the bewildered Bob to help him, a van
ploughed through the crowd flattening Bob and
two others. Then behind that came yet another
car and for the fourth time in rapid succession
Bob was flung to the ground. For all that, we
are happy to say that he is recovering well in

hospital. (Daily Mirror, 26 July 75. Cr: Steve
Moore.)

Let us get ghoulish for a moment and consider a few coincidences involving death -
though we'll reserve full fiendishness for next
issue. William Rose was found battered to death
in a house he owned in Willesden, London. Police
called on his wife at another of their houses
about two miles away to inform her of the
tragedy, only to find that she too had been
battered to death, but amidst signs of robbery,
within half an hour of her husband. Faced with
such curious circumstances the police concocted
a story: a thief had threatened Mr Rose to get
a safe combination and killed him when he refused to tell; the killer then went to the other
house, extracted the combination from Mrs Rose,
and killed her after the robbery. Neat, isn't it?
Except that it doesn't really stand up to the
circumstances and in itself leaves too many
questions unanswered. Whatever - Det Super John
Donald said: "I've never seen such injuries.
They must have been done by a maniac." (Sunday
Mirror, 9 June 74.)

On 28 Jan, Charles Davies died at 3am in his
sister's house in Leicester. (This is turning out
to be a real Leics. issue in every way.) The
sister phoned his home in Leeds to inform them,
and she was told in turn that Charles's wife
had also died that day - at 3am. (Leicester
Mercury, 6 Feb 75. Cr: Dave Potts.) And three
of the Basey-Fisher brothers, Frederick, James
and Ronald, all farmers in Norfolk, died within
five days of each other - two within eight hours
on the same day. (Eastern Daily Mail, 11 April
75. Cr: RTA Hill.)

What does it matter that some of our stories
are full of the commonplace? The truly universal mysteries are all the more mysterious for
their universal presence in all things. Isn't
that what thousands of years of mysticism has
been telling whoever will listen? In this
sense, THE NEWS is a journal of everyday
cosmology. Perhaps we are moved, with or without
our conscious will or knowledge, moved like the
trees to flower at a certain time. And who is
there to say that these dances do not well up,
even in part, from those areas of the mind we
know least about?

There can be few stories as enigmatic as the
following. Erskine Lawrence Ebbin was knocked
off his moped by a taxi and killed in Hamilton,
Bermuda. It was the same taxi with the same
driver, carrying the same passenger, that killed
his brother Neville in July the previous year.
Both brothers were 17 when they died, and had
been riding the same moped in the same street.
Ah! but history never quite repeats itself -
the time of both accidents differed by (only) 50
minutes. (Liverpool Echo, Scunthorpe Evening
Telegraph, 21 July 75. Cr: Ann Williams & Nigel
Watson. Buenos Aires Herald, 22 July 75. Cr:
Jean Bastide.)

SAVING FACE.

In January this year, Teresa Haro, working
in a shop in Los Angeles, had a lucky escape.

A gunman fired a shot in her face from close range. The bullet hit Mrs Haro above the nose, bounced off her skull, skidded under her skin and emerged above her forehead. Detective Joe Beiro said he'd never seen anything like it. (The Sun, 20 Jan 75.)

We oughtn't to be surprised that in this violent age such a feak occurrence should be repeated. We already had in our files a more extreme version. Frankie Lane, a young British soldier serving in Belfast, was hit by a sniper's bullet. It went up his nose, round his skull (presumably via the bony ridge below the eye), and out of his ear. (The Sun, 15 Oct 74.)

And we picked up a less bizarre story during our recent USA sojourn. Patrolman Ted Carlton (see photo, this page) was chasing two escaped convicts in Oklahoma City, Okla., when a bullet smashed through his car windscreen, loosing enough energy so that it could be finally stopped by the thin metal frames of his specs – his only injury a gashed cheek. (National Enquirer, 26 Aug 75. Cr: Ruth Barrowcliff.)

FALLING BABIES.

Among other trends for July, we have three stories of falling babies – one was injured on 16th in Cavendish St, Ramsgate (London Evening News, 17 July 75) – one fell unharmed on 25th at Breedon-on-the-Hill, near Derby (Daily Mirror, 26 July 75) – one was killed on 28th in Eastern Rd, Brighton (London Evening News, 28 July 75). Cr the lot to Steve Moore.

For want of somewhere to put it, here is a tale of two climbers. Ian Cochrane, savouring the heights of the Cairngorms, fell 300ft down during an avalanche and survived with minor injuries. (Daily Mirror, 24 Dec 73.) Less than a month later, David Morris, an experienced Alpine climber, died at Little Bispham, Lancs, after falling only 10ft – down stairs. (Daily Mirror, 19 Jan 74.) Cr both to Robert Forrest. One man's fall is another man's fatality.

* * * * * * * * * * * * * * * * * * * *

BUFORA announce their London lecture programme for 1975/76, held at Kensington Central Library, London W8.
* UFOLOGY AS FRINGE SCIENCE – Dr Ivor Grattan-Guinness. Sat 4 Oct 75, 7pm.
* UFO SCENE IN BELGIUM & THE EEC – Ruby de Groote (Belgium). Sat 1 Nov 75, 7pm.
* BUFORA AGM, FILM & LECTURE: UFO ACTIVITY IN SCOTLAND – Stuart Campbell. Sat 6 Dec 75, 7pm.
* UFOs AND THE PRESS – Richard Beet. Sat 3 Jan 1976 , 7pm.
* RESEARCH EVENING, short papers. Sat 7 Feb 76 7pm.
* MINISTRY OF DEFENCE, PARLIAMENT & UFOs – Lionel Beer. Sat 6 March 76, 7pm.
* EXTRATERRESTRIAL PROBABILITIES – Anthony R Martin. Sat 3 April 76, 7pm.

For further details write: The Hon Sec, BUFORA. 6 Cairn Ave, London W5. For details of BUFORA enclose a 9 x 4½" SAE.

Subscribers to THE NEWS will note that we are trying an experiment in addressing our envelopes which, it is hoped, will make us more efficient (joke) and in the long run SAVE MONEY. By combining the label with an acknowledgement slip and renewal form in this way, it will save us much time and effort previously spent with several bits of paper. Many people pointed out that they had thrown their envelopes away before realising the label told them when their sub expired. This way, you'll have a record and can return it with your renewal. Ed.

THE UNIDENTIFIED by Jerome Clark & Loren Coleman. Warner Paperback Library; $1.50.; 272pp; bibliog & index; ISBN 0.446.78735.3.

Every so often, a book comes along that impresses me so much that I urge my friends to buy, or at least read it. This is such a one. It deals with a very complicated problem, not in depth, but across its spectrum, being one of those valuable resumés of current research thought that re-examines how we reached the present position. The book's subtitle is 'Notes toward solving the UFO mystery' and in it we find a restating of the central issues of the mystery, working them through to the present with unusual and new material, often from the authors's own investigations.

They begin by listening to a source that provided much embarassment to the UFO 'Nuts & Bolts' cause. This was the tendancy of Contactees (those who believed themselves contacted by other intelligences) to deliver surprising accounts of that contact, involving ambiguous evidence; baffling behaviour of the 'aliens', often childish or with sexual overtones; anti-materialistic philosophies couched in quasi-religious or simplistic terms; and sometimes patently absurd details, like the names of the entities and their home-planet. This 'Contactee Syndrome' extended to their subsequent behaviour - forming cultish groups, etc. Indeed this is such a strong pattern of behaviour that one wonders why it was never examined before. Perhaps because it fitted in quite explicitly to the known varieties of mystical and shamanistic experience, in its morphology. The authors note, for example the upsurge in paranormal phenomena that often occurs around a contactee or close witness of UFO events, and show cases which are indistinguishable from spiritualist sittings and religious visions.

Taking as a datum the visionary nature of a meeting with an 'entity', Clark & Coleman draw parallels from fairy mythology of all cultures with convincing effect. But they don't stop there - devils, angels, demons, elementals, spirits and poltergeists - the parallels with contactee-UFOlogy are there in astonishing profusion. (EG: The Cottingly fairy photographs, by all accounts genuine, raise the same physical and philosophical problems as the genuine UFO photos, and the effects of people like Stella Lansing and Ted Serios who seem to be able to imprint (mentally?) images directly onto film.)

One fact emerges, constantly and consistently - the subjective experience itself. Driven by a powerful subconscious desire for psychic unity, the body becomes immobile, oblivious to its surroundings, while the conscious mind is shown archetypal material (from the collective unconscious) of such intensity that it passes for a 'real-time' experience. This in no way belittles the religious content of the experience - but in an age that has forsaken its deep-rooted need for religious experience, the old symbols hold little conviction. It was Jung's discovery that the UFO was a new symbol of psychic unity - the gesture originating as an expression of the anima, the circle being the sign of integration and wholeness.

Symbolic journeys are an ancient archetype (eg the mainstay of shamanism) - being taken to another planet, often Paradise-like, or simply travelling in or entering the saucer is its comtemporary clothing. The different forms of this experience are gone into at length, and even give rise to an interesting theory of the origin of MIB phenomena, which in this context has much in common with poltergeistery. It is dangerous to dismiss as being "all in the mind". The authors examine the idea that these states of mind are accompanied by great releases of psychic energy, capable of manifesting phenomena that transcend normal concepts of space and time, and are directly responsible for the more ephemeral items in the contactee repertoire - teleportation of the body; psychosomatic wounds (stigmata); audio and visual phenomena; interference with machines by PK; etc. Emergence from this state also brings well-known symptoms - incoherance, paralysis, amnesia; or in a more positive form, healing, rejuvenation and personality changes. There is necessary discussion of this strange state of mind but it is not obtrusive, the authors preferring to ignore the basically unanswerable questions (eg Why just some people, and what triggers them off - there is no data or depth study of these aspects available as yet); they concentrate on the effects and symptoms of that state that relate to the UFO mystery.

This is an important book - a worthy successor to Vallee's 'Passport to Magonia' - and an informal exploration (for newcomer and old-hand alike) of Jung's conviction that aerial phenomena, especially lights in the sky, were portents of "long-lasting transformations of the collective psyche." We are being warned, as the contactees are told time and again, that our runaway materialist attitudes are destroying nature's balances. If Clark & Coleman are right, we are in considerable danger.

MAGIC AND THE MILLENIUM by Bryan Wilson. Paladin (pb); £2.50; 547pp; bibliog & 2 indexes; ISBN 586.08208.5.
One of those mammoth sociological studies - but this concentrates on religion in dire times, when men turn to magic and a belief in a millennium, and what happens to those beliefs when the Great Day doesn't turn up, or the magic fails. It contains many insights that help us understand the sociology of dogmatic cults & magic as background to much of interest to us.

THE NATURAL HISTORY OF VAMPIRES by Anthony Masters. Mayflower (pb); 60p; 259pp; bibliog & index; illust.; ISBN 583.122132.2.
For 60p, you can't go wrong. A handy encyclopedia of vampire lore and legend from all over the world. It's very well researched and I'd say a useful reference work for your library.

NB: Those readers in Britain who are trying to locate American books might try those shops listed in our Ad section (p25). They often carry many otherwise unobtainable imported books

PAPERBACKS.

'Our Haunted Planet'- John A Keel; Futura; 60p.
'The Rosicrucian Enlightenment'- Frances A Yates; Paladin; £1.50.
'Haunted Britain'- A Hippisley Coxe; Sept 75; Pan; £1.50; (illustrated gazeteer).
'The Bermuda Triangle'- Charles Berlitz; Panther; 60p.
'UFOs from behind the Iron Curtain' - J Weverbergh & I Hobana; June 75; Bantam; $1.95.
'Handbook of Psycic Discoveries'- S Ostrander & L Schroeder; July 75; Berkeley; $1.75.
'Sasquatch'- R Dahinden & D Hunter; Signet;$1.25.
'Hidden Worlds: Fresh Clues to the Past'- Vander Veer & Moerman; Bantam; $1.50.

HARDBACKS.

'Miracles of the Gods'- E Von Daniken; Oct 75; Souvenir Press; £4.00.
'The Magic of Findhorn'- Paul Hawken; Oct 75; Souvenir Press; £3.50.
'Parapsychology & the Nature of Life'- John Randall; Oct 75; Souvenir Press; £3.50.
'Apparitions'- Celia Green & Charles McCreery; June 75; Hamish Hamilton; £3.75.
'The Mothman Prophecies'- John A Keel; Mar 75; Saturday Review Press; $7.95.
'Other Worlds, Other Universes: Playing the Reality Game'- Brad Steiger & John White, eds; June 75; Doubleday; $7.95.
'Phantom Soldiers'- Raymond F Brown; June 75; Drake; $9.95.
'PK: Mind over Matter'- Jose Feola; May 75; Dillon; $6.95.
'Life after Death?'- MQ Sibley; Sept 75; Dillon; $6.95.

'Living Aura: Radiation Field Photography & The Kirlian Effect'- Kendall Johnson; June 75; Hawthorn; $15.00.
'The Probability of the Impossible'- Thelma Moss; JP Tarcher; $10.00.
'The Bermuda Triangle Mystery: Solved'- Lawrence D Kuche; Mar 75; Harper & Row; $10.00.
'UFOs: Interplanetary Visitors'- Raymond E Fowler; Exposition Press; $8.50.

DID YOU SEE ..?

'Americans hope for Proof of Noah's Ark'- Dudley Lynch. CHRISTIAN SCIENCE MONITOR, 31 March 75.

'Stanford Workshop on Extraterrestrial Civilisations: Opening a new Scientific Dialog'- JB Carlson & PA Sturrock. ASTRONAUTICS & AERONAUTICS, June 75.

'Hi, Columbus! Like the Trip?'- pre-Columbian contacts summarized by Peter Gwynne. Also, a report on the 2nd world conference of the Ancient Astronauts. NEWSWEEK, 9 June 75.

POPULAR SCIENCE, June 75. Jack Bowers (Stanford U.) sends out very low frequency radio signals from Siple Station, Antarctica, to antennae at Roberval, Canada, as part of some magnetosphere experiments. They leave Siple at 100kW, but some mysterious process boosts them to an extraordinary degree. At Roberval they appear to represent a broadcasting power of 100,000kW.

NATURE, 10 July 75 - Prof Thomas Gold's (Cornell U.) work on relativity and ageing.

'Our Victor'- by Mervyn Jones. SUNDAY TIMES MAGAZINE, 13 July 75. a preview/precis of a new biography of Victor Grayson, the Welsh MP whose mystery vanishing has remained unsolved for 55 years. ('The Strange Case of Victor Grayson' by Reg Groves; Pluto Press; £2.00.)

'New Clues to the Stonehenge Masterminds'- Ronald Schiller. READERS DIGEST, Sept 75.

Two items on the 'Zeta Reticuli' starmap. The map is hotly debated in the July & August issues of ASTRONOMY. Universal Studios have completed a dramatized documentary based on the famous Betty and Barney Hill UFO kidnap case, scripted from John G Fuller's 'Interrupted Journey' and with advice from many of the principals in the case, including Mrs Hill. The map and other details of the case, reconstructed under hypnotic regression are featured in the film, scheduled to be shown on NBC-TV (USA) sometime in Sept or Oct. Lets hope the UK can eventually get a peek too. Photos of the film-making in NATIONAL ENQUIRER, 12 Aug 75.

NEW SCIENTIST. 3 July: p7, mention of a debate at the Royal Society on Lunar Transient Phenomena (LTPs) with the suggestion that these lights in the lunar landscape (which Fort collected notes on) may have some connexion with moonquakes. This theory could be verified with existing records both of the heap of earthbound

observations, and data from the   litter
left by recent visitors to the moon. It would
also provide a useful comparison with the aerial
lights observed (and usually ignored) during
terrestrial quakings (see Fort again.) - -
11 Sept: 'Scientists Attack Astrology' Martin
Sherwood looks at the recent vaporings of many
scientists. 168 of them signed a public statement, supported by two critical articles (see
THE HUMANIST for Sept 75) deploring the popular
interest in such obvious rubbish. Yawn! - -
18 Sept: after yelling at us gullible plebs, the
scientists had their own fevered
rampage of speculation following the announcement of the discovery of a magnetic monopole,
which as far as I can understand it, is like
finding one end of a stick! (see NS v67 p412 for
a good summary). Now the wet blankets are out,
and the profession is indulging in a little
intellectual self-flagellation.

'A Leap in the Dark' - a four part TV series
(BBC2, Fridays, 19 &26 Sept, 3 & 10 Oct) on the
paranormal, introduced by Colin Wilson. The
first dealt with the Anne-Marie Schneider poltergeist from Rosenheim, Germany. The second,
about psychic detective Gerard Croiset. The
third will be about the multiple personalities
of 'Miss Beacham'. The 4th is unknown as we go
to press. The format seems to be a filmed case,
then studio discussion with Prof John Taylor,
Anita Gregory, and that professional spoilsport
Dr Chris Evans. A note in The Sun (12 Sept 75.
Cr: Ann Williams) disclosed that as the first
film was being edited a poltergeist interfered
with sound equipment and lights in the cutting
room. A likely story!

The INFO JOURNAL No15 - Ron Willis's last
article, on the most haunted mountain in Scotland, Ben MacDhui — Richard Hall on aerial
anomalies at sea — 'New Light on Mayan Origins'
by Wally Kennicutt (an important step backward)
— Stuart Greenwood on 'Underwater Bases in the
Bermuda Triangle' — Paul A Roales on a meteorological puzzle, bands of red light — X and
Richard Hall with more on 'Flight 19' — Jacob
Ornstein & WW Gage on the Exo-linguistics of ET
communication — a critique of Costello's 'In
Search of Lake Monsters' by Loren Coleman —
and more historical notes located by Ronald
Dobbins & 'Frater Ignoramus'. This issue
should be on its way (by sea) to the subscribers outside the USA by now. From No16 INFOJO
goes thinner and bi-monthly in an effort to
achieve regular and frequent publication. More
details of INFO can be had from the editor of
THE NEWS, or write to INFO, Box 367, Arlington
Va 22210, USA.

LANTERN, the journal of the Borderline Science
Investigation Group (BSIG) No10, Summer 75 -
'Signs from Heaven', notes on East Anglian
aerial visions — Ivan Bunn on 'Norfolk's
Phantom Coaches' — 'The Castle Acre Diamond'
another 'ley' pattern?, by RCA Hill — plus
other notes. Annual sub. only 70p from BSIG,
3 Dunwich Way, Lowestoft, NR32 4RZ, E Anglia.

FLYING SAUCER REVIEW, June 75, v21 n1. - reports
on landing cases from Burbank, California, and
Stelling Minnis, near Canterbury, England —
Gordon Creighton on 'Underwater Base off
Venezuela' — part 4 of the Stella Lansing saga
in which apparent paranormal imposition of
images occurs on the films she uses, an investigation by Dr Berthold Schwarz. — Charles
Bowen reports a remarkable teleportation of a
car in South Africa — Jerome Clark on a curious
encounter between a 'Frightened Creature' and a
farmer in a country road in Wisconsin —
A Schneider & E Berger on UFOs in the Bavarian

Alps — part 3 of the 'Mysterious "UMMO" affair
— and Jerry Clark again with a critique of John
Keel's 'The Mothman Prophecies'.

THE LEY HUNTER No66 - Paul Screeton relates two
encounters with two "earth gnomes", "curiously
disproportionate to our senses." — Paul Devereux & Andy York with curious stones in 'The Forgotten Heart of Albion — two discussions of
ley theories & metaphysics — and an account
of a weekend at Carnac before 1930, thoroughly
curious. A very interesting issue. Edited by
Paul Screeton: 5 Egton Drive, Seaton Carew,
Hartlepool, Cleveland TS25 2AT. 1yr:£1.50/$6.00.

INFINITY NEWSLETTER - 'A search for Truth from
many Sources' news & views on ESP, Metaphysics,
Paranormal subjects, UFOs & related subjects.
from Other Dimensions Inc: Box 140, Decorah,
Iowa 52101, USA. 1yr: $3.50, USA & Canada;$7.00,
all other countries (airmailed).

QUEST - a quarterly magazine of esoteric &
practical magic. 1yr: £1.20. from BCM-SCL QUEST,
London WC1V 6XX.

SPECTRUM - a magazine of the Occult, edited by
Michael Howard. No6 has a review of a German
study of alchemy not yet available in English
translation — more on little known episodes in
the life of Crowley — articles on magical
principles, and reincarnation. No7 includes an
article by Dion Fortune — RM White on the
identity of the 'horned Gods' of pagan Britain
— Mike Howard on 'Holy Places of America' —
plus articles on magical principles, groups, and
the 'Luna Ritual'. 1yr: £2.00. from Bywood
Publications Ltd, 62 High St, Croydon, Surrey.

NEARA JOURNAL - a quarterly collection of
articles from the New England Antiquities
Research Association. $4.00/yr. from NEARA:
4 Smith St, Milford, New Hampshire 03055, USA.
■■
As a postscript to this disaster issue of
Summer 75, we can end on a dramatic note. As
your editor s in the final stages of nailing
this issue together over the weekend 27/28 Sept,
there are gales of 70mph being recorded; rooves
of houses in Cheshire being ripped off; people
lost at sea; the coldest Sept recorded in the
Cairngorms for many a year; and it's very wet.
And in many parts of the country, especially
here in Aldermaston for the last 24hrs, the
power cables are down and we're working by
candlelight. Real pioneer stuff!

a miscellany of Fortean curiosites

THE NEWS

MYSTERY DEATHS and
PHANTOM ATTACKS 14

Killer Bees, 2 ... Recent UFOs, 3 ... UFO Kidnap, 5 ...

STUART GREENWOOD on the Slope of Silbury Hill ... 6

Falls of Frogs and Ice ... 7

ROBERT FORREST on Leys, UFOs and Chance ... 12

50p: $1·25

UK ISSN 0306-0764

the news

bimonthly news & notes
on Fortean phenomena

DECEMBER 1975

THE NEWS is a non-profitmaking bimonthly miscellany of Fortean news, notes and references, affiliated
to the International Fortean Organisation (INFO) in
continuing the work of **Charles Fort** (1874 — 1932).
THE NEWS is edited by Robert JM Rickard:
**Post Office Stores, Aldermaston, Berks RG7 4LJ,
England.**

SUBSCRIPTIONS: 1 year — 6 issues — £3.00 / USA
$ 7.50. 2 years — 12 issues — £5.40 / USA $13.50
Single issues — 50p / USA $1.25. Back issues (if
available) 50p / USA $1.25. Current annual INDEX
free to subscribers, otherwise 20p. / USA 60¢.
**Special joint subscription to THE NEWS and INFO
JOURNAL** (including regular membership of INFO)
1 year — 12 issues — £5.60 / USA $14.00. All over-
seas subscribers paying by cheque should **add 10%** to
cover banking exchange commission.

CONTRIBUTIONS of articles, notes and artwork on
related subjects are always welcome and duly credited.
You can help us by sending us a copy or clipping of
any reference or data you think will interest us. Please
don't assume our omniscience — there are very few
duplications. We are especially glad to see items from
professional journals, local papers and OP books. But
please don't forget to add the source and date, and your
name for the credit.

RIGHTS. All articles and artwork in THE NEWS is
copyright of the authors and artists — and the views
expressed not necessarily those of THE NEWS or INFO.
All the notes herein may be freely quoted — all we ask
in return is an acknowledgement of the source. All
loony heading artwork in this issue is by Hunt Emerson.

A MILLION MAD BEES ON THE ATTACK.

Mrs Judith Reed was clearing away after
lunch, about 2.30, when there was a loud
buzzing, and her home in Rensselaer County,
Indiana, was plunged into a dark "gloom".
Calling to her children to stay indoors, she
found bees crawling thickly on her kitchen
window. "There were thousands of them...the
brilliant sunshine was blocked out. Their
buzzing seemed to fill the inside of the
house." They had pets in the garden and
managed to catch glimpses of huge "fighting-
mad" clouds of bees "dive-bombing the geese
and chickens, and there was nothing we could
do but watch them die in agony." Her husband was at work, so she called the police -
but when a car pulled into her drive, the
two officers were as trapped as she was. In
fact the bees swarmed so thickly around the
car that they dared not back out - they were
stuck there for at least 2½ to 3 hours. One
officer said that the bees actually seemed
to be deliberately attacking them.

Then as suddenly as they came, they flew
off. "The silence was electrifying, and the
sense of relief undescribable," said Mrs
Reed. A local pest exterminator blamed the
curious behaviour on the stifling heat. On
searching the Reed's attic, he found a hive
an astonishing 18ft long, which must have
contained, he reckoned, over a million bees.
"It took five gallons of insecticide to wipe
them out." The temperature outside was 97°F,
but neared 120°F inside the hive. Sunday
Express, 21 Sept 75. Cr: S Moore & R Randle.

...AND SOME ON THE WAY...

Curiously the above incident has nothing
to do with vast swarms of killer African
Bees that are threatening to invade the USA.
In 1956, professor of genetics Warrick Kerr
was working on crossbreeding with the local
bees to improve honey production in São Paulo.
Then 26 African queens (and their swarms)
escaped -- and as usual in escapes of imported animals, they bred prolifically,
virtually wiping out the local bees and
spreading at the rate of 200 miles a year,
much to the chagrin of US observers, north-
wards from Brazil. Daily Express, 19 June 75,

reported that the National Academy of Sciences in Washington were already debating ideas like traps across Central Mexico, aerial spray and poison networks, or dumping millions of non-aggressive bees in their path in the hope they'd make love not war.

Human deaths have varied in accounts from "dozens" to "300" (Daily Mail, 15 April 75). The first ones were in Brazil in 1966; the next year a man died in Rio de Janeiro from "1000 stings" (Scunthorpe Evening Telegraph, 21 May 75). Since then, they have been on a rampage of death, with animal victims numbered in the thousands. Already Bolivia, Paraguay, Peru and Venezuela have felt their sting. The US government is obviously taking the threat that the killer bees will reach them by 1980 very seriously -- $125,000 has been allocated by the US Agricultural Department for a study of the bees, and a call has gone out to Mexico, Canada and Central American countries to cooperate in quelling the hazard. (Compiled from contributions by Steve Moore & Nigel Watson.)

...MEANWHILE, DOWN IN KENT...

A letter to Sunday Times, 3 Aug 75:
"Sir - I have not seen a single bee in our area of Kent this year. I don't know whether this is just local, but if it is general it could become very serious ecologically with a disastrous effect on the food chain.
FMD Robertson, Sundridge, Kent."

A COUPLE OF OLDIES...

...which we don't recall recording at the time. A bright bluish-green light, which may or may not have been a fireball (whatever they are) was seen "on numerous occasions" as it passed over Abernyte, Pitlochry, Longforgan, and Madderly, all in Perthshire, about 9pm, 27 Dec 73. One witness said: "A bright burning object like a huge firework descended from the sky. Streamers of fire licked from it, and it was brighter than my car headlights. It filtered itself out and appeared to drop over the Crieff Road area of Perth." Perthshire Advertiser, 29 Dec 73.

In the week or so prior to this, there seems to have been a mini-flap in the Epping area of Essex, as we learn from the Epping & Ongar West Essex Gazette, 4 Jan 74. Caroline Ebborn, a designer, was visiting her sister in Abridge when she saw a "mysterious array of lights" pass high over her head. There was a plane in the sky and the two were completely dissimilar. "It started off as a red pulsating ball near the moon, then started to rise. It became paler, then turned towards me at remarkable speed." She described it as diamond-shaped with bright yellow lights on two opposite points, and "neon-red lines" at the back. Later, it turned a pale fluorescent green. That evening, two persons saw something similar over Epping. Several days later, an object with "incredibly blue lights whirling around a red one" moved fast, silently and smoothly over Buckhurst Hill in the direction of the forest. Unfortunately, we have no precise dates, but these should be accessible to a little poking around. (Cr: UFORC.)

A ROUND-UP OF RECENT SIGHTINGS.

Night-duty officers at the Heston fire station, Middlesex, claim to have seen flying saucer-like objects. Daily Mirror, 11 June 75.
Mystery lights over Aughton, Lancs, 16th June, mystified lunchtime visitors to the Tower Restaurant on Liverpool's St John's Beacon. They flashed as they periodically "descended to the ground" and were visible for several minutes around 1.45pm. A housewife in Wirral, Cheshire, that evening said she saw a rapidly moving bright object cross the sky in the direction of Warrington. Liverpool Echo, 17 & 18 June 75. Cr: AF Ashcroft.
Arthur Wherrett of Lown Hill, Acomb, Yorks, saw a disc-shaped object giving off a bright light as it headed north, noiselessly, about 11.30pm, 10th Aug. Through his binoculars he saw that it was travelling slowly and jerkily at about 2000 ft. The night before, a man at Gower Walk, Hartlepool, Cleveland, reported a bright light outside his bedroom window at about 2.30am. A policeman also reported a bright light in the sky that night.

Two schoolboys in Middlesborough, Yorks, said they saw lights; and the Cleveland UFO Research Group said they had reports of sightings along the coast from Saltburn to Redcar. Yorkshire Evening Press, 11 Aug 75. Cr: JW Scaife.

The photo below, taken by professional photographer Chris Waller, was the highlight (literally!) of a skywatch held at Cradle and Starr Hills, Warminster, Wilts, over the weekend 29/30 August. It was one of nine lights seen by many observers at Starr Hill in the space of an hour. They were orange or reddish and bobbed "elegantly" above the treeline for several seconds. Southern Evening Echo, 2 Sept 75. Cr: Roger Randle.

No, it's not a hole in the paper—it's what the photo-grapher saw at Starr Hill, Warminster.

KEN ROGERS - SCAREMONGER EXTRAORDINARY!

Fresh from provoking the soggy vengence of Hampstead's rain-god (see NEWS 12/7), Ken has been poking his finger at the Hampshire skies.

On the 12th Sept, 5 boys fishing at Burgh-field Bridge, Holybrook, Berks, saw a white light that descended to the ground, then rose up in a red flash. Suddenly there were six or seven of them. Earlier that evening, Mrs Carol Ward of Island Farm Road, Ufton Nervet, saw eight lights in the sky, from Earley, Reading, like "a train in the dis-tance"; they remained stationary for a time then moved off in the direction of Winnersh. (Reading) Evening Post, 15 Sept 75.

Two days later, the (Reading) Evening Post revealed that Ken's British UFO Society had taken an interest in the activity around Reading. Other sightings alluded to (ie. no details given) were: 2 schoolboys seeing a light over Caversham, and a Wokingham woman seeing a "bell-shaped" object hovering over Winnersh, both toward the end of August; a Reading boy spotted a "ball of fire" over the town, and a Wokingham couple saw a "glowing orange ball" a few days later over Twyford, both about mid Sept.

On October 31st, the Basingstoke Gazette gave a full page to the British UFO Society, the subject in general, and in particular Ken's prediction that more UFOs will be seen in the Basingstoke area. Why? Because it's in the middle of a UFO flight path that takes in the Thames Estuary and Warminster, not forgetting Stonehenge. The article also revealed that a lady in Little Basing saw a light in the sky that did antics, "recently"; and that there was another sighting over Reading the week before (the article). Whether it's deliberate or not, Ken's getting some amazing publicity for the BUFOS. Probe behind the reports of most sightings, it seems, and there is Ken beaming all over his face.

It is an experiment (deliberate or not) that would have met with Fort's approval. Point to an area - any area - and predict UFOs, or unicorns, anything, as long as it is publicised - and see what transpires (though I guess many people in Hampstead are begining to think Ken pushed things a little too far.)

The same paper a week later, reveals that a Miss Ruth Rees, of Contact, saw a ball of orange light over Stratfield Turgis, two weeks before, and near the Duke of Welling-ton's estate of Stratfield Saye, between Reading and Basingstoke, and of which Miss Rees is the park manager. One unfortunate quote from Miss Rees is: "I believe in the facts. I'm anxious to get the subject away from the nasty psychic image that it has."

Further letters on the subject, including a sighting by two brothers on the evening of the 27th Oct, over Basingstoke, appear in the Basingstoke Gazette, 14 Nov 75. That is all to our press date - but we will be keeping an eye on the area.

THE RIDDLE OF THE VANISHING WOODSMAN.

As we go to press, an astonishing UFO-kidnap story has broken. We use the descrip-tion lightly, bearing in mind all the para-doxes involved in the questionable existence of solid craft from other star-systems.

Most papers around 10 & 11 th Nov carried the story that forestry worker Travis Walton and five workmates were driving back from trimming trees in the Sitgreave-Apache Nat-ional Forest, near Snowflake, Arizona, when the crew-boss, Mike Rogers, braked the truck. Hovering 15ft above the trees was a flying saucer. Despite shouted warnings, Walton jumped out and ran towards it. Suddenly, there was a brilliant blue and white flash and Walton crumpled to the ground. The others panicked and drove off -- when they returned for Walton, both he and the object were gone. This happened on the night of 5th Nov, and in the following five days a massive hunt scoured the countryside for any sign of him. On the fifth day, Travis Walton turned up, gaunt, hungry, 10lbs lighter and talking of capture by an alien race.

We take our details from the Daily Express, 15 Nov 75 (Cr: Steve Moore & Mike Rickard.)-- doubtless investigations are at present under way, and we look forward to the reports in the UFO media. The Daily Express item con-tains several interesting statements: there is the description of the zapping of Walton by Mike Rogers, who says the flash was greenish-blue and had affected their eyes when they later stopped a quarter of a mile away to look back; and there is the statement from Marlin Gillespie, the Navajo County Sheriff who says Walton's workmates all made apparently true statements under his lie-detector. But, most interesting of all is a lengthy interview with Walton himself, and which for lack of space we condense here:

"We all saw the saucer that night. I knew what it was right away. When Duane (his brother) was a kid he was followed by a saucer and we promised each other that if it happened again I would not be afraid...I just jumped out and ran towards the glow. I felt no fear. I got close and something hit me...like an electric blow to my jaw...I fell backwards and everything went black...When I woke there was a strong light...I had problems focussing and pains in my chest and head...I was on a table...I saw three weird figures...not human ...they looked like well-developed foetuses, about 5ft tall, in tan-brown robes, tight-fitting. Their skins were mushroom-white, with no clear features. They made no sound. They had no hair, their foreheads were domed and their eyes very large...I panicked...jumped up knocking over a plastic tray...I wanted to attack them but they scampered away...a man appeared a few feet away...human, in helmet and tight-fitting blue uniform...he smiled at me and led me through a corridor into another big, bright room...a planetarium. Outside it was dark but I recognised some galaxies... (then Walton fiddles with some buttons on the arm of a chair, and gets frightened he might destroy the craft when the scene 'outside' changes as he fiddles)... the man in blue re-appeared...led me down a ramp, suddenly I was in bright sunlight...some kind of hangar. I saw some small space saucers nearby. Then I saw 3 other people (in helmets). They were human, one a woman, all dressed in blue...

They took me to a table and eased me on it. They put a mack on my face...then things went black again... When I woke up I was shaky... on the highway. The trees were lit up because their saucer was just a few feet away. I saw nobody...I ran until I came to a phone booth. I recognised I was in Heber (a few miles from Snowflake)...I phoned my sister, and they came to get me."

Many elements of this story fit the pattern of contactee experiences generally and I can only refer interested readers to Jerry Clark and Loren Coleman's excellent discussion of this pattern in their recent US paperback The Unidentified (see review last issue). Those who have already read it will recognise some of those elements: the alternating periods of bright light and darkness that might be an analogue of the passage of time elapsed in the 'kidnapping'; the entry into and exit from the experience via unconsciousness; the 1+3 and 1+1 motifs (the symbols 2 and 4 of the square-symbol of psychic-integration); the transformation of the 3 foetuses into 3 humans (with the feminine anima component); the vision of the cosmos and the fear that tampering with the equipment could destroy it (Faust and the modern dilemma in a nutshell); his psychic immaturity showing up as impotence in the experience ("I guess I was angry most of the time. I just wasn't able to communicate with them. If only they'd answered my questions "); the fact that he went voluntarily into the experience minimised his resistance to the force of the dissociation, so that he was able to emerge without burns, wounds, paralysis or any other subjective confirmation of his inability to integrate the elements of his psyche; and lastly, probably of critical importance to the shape of his experience, the fact that he had some background in the folklore of the subject (ie the UFO as passed into popular vocabulary) and some expectation (his promise to his brother) of the experience.

Doubtless there are some readers who will agree with Miss Rees' statement (p 4) about getting the subject of UFOs away from all this "nasty psychic" stuff. To be fair, there are theories and theories, but sheer logical sensibility demands greater credence to the theory that 'includes' (not necessarily explains) the greatest variety of phenomena. We must bear in mind Fort's dictum about substituting 'acceptance' for 'belief' -- and thus only accept a theory until a better (ie more complete or inclusive) comes along. Only one obstacle to our subjective experience theory -- and that is, just where was Travis Walton during the five-day search... on a saucer, teleported elsewhere for the duration, jumped 'up the line' in time, or maybe somnambulating around that (large) forest while his conscious mind, divorced from its more artificial functions, was locked in deep communion with the symbolic processes that are all we can ever know of the collective unconscious? Who knows?

On The Slope Of Silbury Hill

Stuart W Greenwood

Silbury Hill is the largest man-made mound in Europe. Located close to the A4 roadway between Bristol and London, the present writer observed it from the road perhaps a hundred times in his early life with no more than passing curiosity. But now it takes on fresh and stimulating significance.

In an earlier article (1) it was suggested that Egypt and Britain were linked in an important way in early times, part of the stimulus for this argument being suggested by the correspondence of the slopes of some of the larger Egyptian pyramids with the latitudes of Britain, and part being the indications of some alignments of tumuli and other earthworks centred on Stonehenge.

Ivimy (2) independently developed similar and additional arguments; his studies including references to Silbury Hill.

The contours of Silbury Hill are a little irregular, but essentially it is a circular mound with a flat top and having sides sloping at a mean angle of 30 degrees (3). Ivimy refers to radiocarbon dating of Silbury Hill at 2145 BC ± 95 years and to the more recent adjustments based on bristlecone pine studies that would modify this to a central date of 2745 BC. As pointed out by Ivimy, such dating is subject to further adjustment,

but it may be reasonable to consider Silbury Hill to be roughly contemporary with, if not slightly earlier than, the early pyramid builders of Egypt.

We now put our treatment of the significance of pyramid slope into operation once more and apply it to Silbury Hill. If a slope of 30 degrees were to indicate an important site in the Northern Hemisphere, where would we expect to find it? The answer, of course, is at latitude 30 degrees, and the site, by reciprocal application of our earlier arguments, would be in Egypt. The solution is simple: Giza.

For good measure, the sarsen stones at Stonehenge were taken from the region of Avebury, adjacent to Silbury Hill, and itself the site of a major stone ring. Any questions?

+++   +++   +++   +++   +++   +++

References:

1) Stuart W. Greenwood, 'Pyramid Slope and Northern Latitudes', NEWS 9/12.
2) John Ivimy, 'The Sphinx and the Megaliths', Turnstone, 1974.
3) Andrew Davidson, 'Silbury Hill', contribution to 'Britain: A Study in Patterns', a publication of the Research into Lost Knowledge Organisation, 1971.

Stuart W. Greenwood: August 1975.

Silbury Hill as surveyed by JW Brooke, Marlborough District Surveyor (from 3). Reproduced by kind permission of the Research into Lost Knowledge Trust

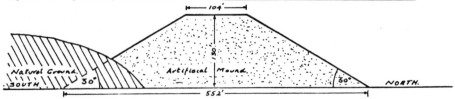

Figure 1. SILBURY HILL
Meridian Section South-North, with measurements as given to Mr. Cottsworth by Mr. J. W. Brooke, Surveyor.
Scale — 1:1250.   Redrawn Feb. '70. ©

SHOWERS OF FROGS?

The following article appeared in the Eastern Daily Press, 11 July 75, by their regular contributor, EA Ellis.

"Following heavy rain yesterday (11th July) a friend living at Brundall reported the appearance of hundreds of young frogs or toads all over his lawn (he described them as dark brown so they were probably toadlets). This was on high ground, some distance from the nearest pond. It was tempting to assume that these young creatures had arrived in a shower from the sky, but the explanation, at least in most cases of sudden swarming after rain, is that the young amphibians, having migrated from the water where they developed as tadpoles, tend to remain under the cover of grass and other herbage by day and move only at night, but are tempted out of cover at any time by a heavy shower.

"Nowadays I find that most authorities on the amphibia tend to avoid references to showers of frogs and toads, but the subject has often been debated fiercely by naturalists in the past. I think it very unlikely that the alleged phenomena occurs at all frequently, but having myself seen a variety of objects sucked up in waterspouts and whirlwinds on several occasions, and having also been at the receiving end of the material showered down afterwards, I see no reason to discredit every tale of froglets descending from the air. The most convincing incident of this brought to my notice by two friends whom I fully believed, concerned a shower of frogs which descended on top of a loaded hay wagon nearby, at the same time, during a cloudburst." -- EAE.

This attracted the attention of two of our readers, Nigel Watson, and RTA Hill. The article brought a few letters in succeeding issues, and Nigel secured us permission to reproduce them here. Ron Hill wrote a letter to the paper putting frog-falls in the general picture of Fortean records of all manner of animals that have dropped from skies all over the world. He attempted, too, to counter the ideas that frog-falls were rare, and attributable to whirlwinds.

To the efforts of these gentlemen, and the helpfulness of PJ Roberts, Editor of the EDP, we are indebted for the opportunity to record these East Anglia frog-falls.

EDP: 15 July 75.

"Sir - When a girl at school during the summer holidays, I used to help cart the corn from the field to the stackyard. On one occasion I had just arrived at the field with my empty waggon, when a storm broke. The men and I ran for shelter. When we returned to the waggon the bottom was covered with tiny frogs. The men scooped them up on a sack and carried them to the verge of the field. - -
Yours faithfully , RE Spinks (Mrs. Aged 82.)
Bean Vista, Kimberley Green."

EDP: 19 July 75.

"Sir - Mrs RE Spinks' letter in today's EDP is quite remarkable; the more so as it is not without precedent. In a letter dated 24th October 1683, John Collinges wrote to Sir Henry Hobart as follows:
'The other (piece of news) is more strange, brought by one Gargrave, a good sober fellow that collects the hearth money. Being last week at Acle, the innkeeper told him the night before, most of their houses were filled with greate toads so as he gathered them up with shovels and threw them into the fire for the stench he could hardly abide in the house, the rest he threw into a yard. Next morning they were all gone. They talk how that they came down in a shower.' From the Historical Manuscripts Commission report re. the Marquess of Lothian MSS, preserved at Blickling Hall.

The only explanation that occurs to me is that of another local phenomenon known as a 'water-spout' where, in rare climatic conditions, water was seen to be sucked up into the atmosphere. Of this there are several recorded eye-witness accounts.
Yours faithfully, RC Fiske.
26 Yarmouth Rd, North Walsham."

Whaaat! A water-spout breaking inside a house? The way I read it is that these non-paying ~~ghosts~~ pests somehow appeared <u>inside</u> the houses - if so this is the first such case to my knowledge, and is quite remarkable. Can anyone help follow this up? - Ed.

EDP: 19 JULY 75.

"Sir - It was with interest that I read Mrs RE Spinks' letter, as I experienced the same thing in the 1940s. We were farming at the time, carting and stacking the wheat, when a thunderstorm broke out. We hastily covered the stack (about 10ft high) with the stack-cloth and ran for shelter. When the storm was over and the sun came out again, we took the cloth off the stack and it was covered with little frogs.
     Yours faithfully, D Slack (Mrs).
     Great Plumstead, Norwich."
     Its not quite clear here whether the frogs were on the cloth, or on the stack <u>under</u> the cloth - Ed.

EDP: 26 July 75.

"Sir - I was interested in the letters about the showers of frogs. Many years ago a friend of mine, Mr Loft Durrant of Reedham, told me he was helping with the hay on the marshes near Reedham Ferry, when suddenly a storm came up and they went to shelter. When they came back the ground was covered with frogs and natterjack toads.
     Yours faithfully, HJ Walpole.
     30 St Mary's Close, Hemsby."

     At this point the Editor of the EDP tried to close the correspondence- saying that "at times East Anglia must have been thickly carpeted with these amphibians from the sky!" The last letters to appear on the subject were the following, and Ron Hill's defence.

EDP: 30 JULY 75.

"Sir - Reading your footnote to Mr Walpole's letter on Saturday, I feel you are a little sceptical and think perhaps that my late old friend, Mr Loff ((sic)) Durrant was stretching it a little. At this time (1920) I was employed on Reedham swing-bridge, and an old resident, Mr Dan Prettyman, now dead, told me the marsh between the bridge and the ferry was covered with frogs. 'There were hundreds and thousands,' said Dan. I did not see them myself, but the noise they made after dark could be heard all over the village and beyond. The mist rising from the marshes and the eerie experience remains with me to this day.
     Yours faithfully, WS Rouse.
     36 Bradfield Road, North Walsham."
     This to me seems to offer some evidence for the fall theory. A gathering of frogs that large would take several days to accumulate, and there would have been many witnesses to the migration. Besides, if the huge number of frogs were merely "under the cover of grass and other herbage" as mentioned by EAE, they would have sounded off on previous nights too. Perhaps, since it

seems that despite many witnesses after the event, no one saw them actually <u>fall</u>, we can only honestly say that in this case large numbers of frogs appeared during a storm. This suggests an affinity with poltergeist apports - and may render the appearance of frogs inside a house more of a probability. This, of course, explains nothing.

CARDAN'S THEORY OF FROG-FALLS.

     In our very first issue, we published a letter from Mrs Sylvia Mowday, recounting her experience of a frog-<u>fall</u> (they fell quite visibly in her vicinity) in Sutton Park, Birmingham, on 12 June 1954 (see NEWS 1/8). Later she wrote again, saying that she had discovered a reference in Izaak Walton's <u>The Compleat Angler</u>, Ch 8 (see NEWS 3/10), saying that some frogs breed by eggs; " and others...by the slime and dust of the earth, and that in winter they turn to slime again, and that next summer that very slime returns to be a living creature; this is the opinion of Pliny; and Cardanus undertakes to give a reason for the raining of frogs..." What, Mrs Mowday asked, was Cardan's reason for the raining of frogs?
     We attempted to trace this reference to the 19th Book of Jerome Cardan's <u>De Subtilitate</u>, but it was unavailable, even in Birmingham's excellent reference library. However, not long ago we were browsing in an old encyclopedia, bought in a secondhand bookshop for the illustrations, and it actually fell open at a passage that discussed Cardan's theory. It is as follows:
     "As far back as the epoch of the Renaissance, a celebrated physician, Cardan, who brought out so many strange hypotheses, nevertheless hit upon the truth in respect to this phenomenon ((frog-falls - Ed.)) He supposed that the showers of frogs were to be attributed to water-spouts which carried these animals off from the mountains, and let them fall at some distance, when they burst."
     So there you have it -- Cardan, writing in about 1549, was the originator of the modern scientist's get-out theory. For our part we admit that some frogs have fallen by whirlwinds - others have been seen falling with no whirlwind about.

SOME USA FROG-FALLS.

     While we're about it, we have a clipping sent by Lucius Farish, of a 'Dear Abby' column, from the <u>Camden (Ark.) News</u>, 2 Jan 1973, which contains the following letters:
     "In the summer of 1926, I caddied at a local golf course. There had been a long drought that summer and the fairways were brown and dried up. One afternoon, a sudden storm came up and a terrific thundershower followed. Rain came down in torrents, and with it, a shower of tiny frogs about the size of nickels. They were alive and jumping - thousands of them. The golfers and I

couldn't believe our eyes as we watched thousands of frogs come right down with the rain from the sky. - WA Walker, Evansville, Indiana."

"I was raised on a farm in Minnesota, and as a boy I remember a storm coming up. It looked serious, so we ran to the cellar. In 40 minutes it was over. Afterwards we went outside and saw our chickens going wild - eating tiny frogs and fishes. - FJ McManus, Laguna Beach, California."

"I personally drove through a 'rainstorm' of tadpoles in western Missouri, 14 years ago. - (?) Dodge City, Kansas."

"About 35 years ago while I was driving through a thunderstorm near Hershey, Pa., dozens of tiny frogs came down and pelted the hood of my automobile. - DE Carner, Baltimore, Maryland."

...AND...

Hundreds of frogs rained into the streets of Istanbul, on 17 June 1969. A 'freak wind' was blamed as picking them out of a nearby lake. Daily Mirror, 18 June 69. Cr: A Smith.

MANCHESTER - ICE BLOCK.

Early in 1973, if Charles Fort had been around, he would have been scrabbling for his scissors, or a scrap of paper to note on, and perhaps scooting his chair over to a fresh edge of carpet to prize out a tack to pin the two together. A strolling meteorologist nearly got clobbered by a chunk of ice falling from the sky. As chunks go, it was modest - an estimated 1 to 2 kilograms (apx 3½lbs). Fort notes a monster of over 20ft diameter (between ½ to 1 ton) that fell at Ord, in Scotland, in 1849 - Book of the Damned, Ch13. But there is no doubt that this latest fall is among the best of all corroborated cases.

The story in essence is this: on Monday 2 April 1973, RF Griffiths was at the junction of Buttesford Aveenue and Burton Road, Manchester (N.Grid.Ref: SJ839922) when "a large object struck the road, about 3 metres to my left front. The object fell fast enough to be shattered into many pieces on impact. The time was 2003GMT." Griffiths picked up the largest of the many pieces (weighing 612gms, and 14cm on its longest axis.) On holding it up to a street-light, he saw a clearly defined layered structure (see photo) and anxious to

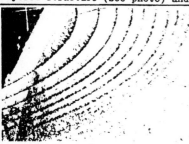

51 "rings of clear ice alternating with rings of bubbles trapped in the structure."
Photo from N Sci. 2 Oct 75.

preserve it ran off into the night with his booty. Less than 10 minutes later it was safe in the freezer of his house, and later taken to a laboratory in Manchester University.

As regards the conditions at the time, Griffiths says that there were "unusual meteorological conditions" over the whole country that day - gales and heavy rains, high winds and poor visibility over the Mersey area. Manchester had some snow that morning, but things cleared up later (3/8 cumulus at a base of 600m, at 1900GMT). At the time of the fall there was no rain, but it was followed by sleet in a light breeze (too slight to fix a direction), with an air temperature of 3°C.

From the two aircraft that were anywhere near the area at approximately the fall-time, there were no reports of icing or its effects, and the structure of the ice-layers, which would have been considerably elongated by the airstream if it had formed on a plane, suggested a hailstone shaped like a rugby-ball. Griffiths concludes: "The ice sample displays a puzzling collection of features. Whilst it is clearly composed of cloud water, there is no conclusive evidence enabling one to decide precisely how it grew...In some respects it is very much like a hailstone, in others it is not." The possibility that it was formed on an aircraft, the usual scapegoat-theory, is not bourne out by the available flight records, nor for that matter by the physical examination of the two planes. For the full details of the examination of the ice, the weather records, and flight details, see the write-up by Griffiths in the Meteorological Magazine, Sept 75, p253ff - from which we extract our notes, including Griffiths' own account of his near extinction. (Cr: Phil Ledger.) The story also appeared in the New Scientist, 2 Oct 75; and the Guardian 29 Sept 75 (Cr: Graham Crowley, John Michell & Ann Williams.) which roared "Mystery meteor ...defies the laws of cloud physics and dynamics." However, they got the year wrong (at 1975) which no doubt caused some confusion.

Griffiths could give no conclusions, other than it was formed out of cloud water, and that it had not formed in a container (!). It is estimated that an updraft of at least 200mph would be needed to keep a 6" hailstone in the air (see INFO Journal No3, p12ff in which Ron Willis analyses the standard theories of ice-falls). Griffiths gives figures of wind-shear for the nearest vertical sounding station, but the deeper mysteries of metric-conversion are beyond your editor's capabilities. We do know, though, that over at Whitby, on the Yorkshire coast, there were winds of about 110mph -but that's miles away. Griffiths does say that the wind-shear figures are "comparable with those recorded during the storm of 1 July 1968, near Cardiff, in which giant hailstones fell," - but gives no dimensions.

Although the New Scientist lauds Griffiths for "leaving the matter open", it strikes us Forteans that despite his use of the term hydrometeor to describe the object, there is nothing in his report suggestive of a meteoric origin. Quite the opposite - it was "clearly composed of cloud water."

There is another interesting aspect of this incident. 9 minutes before the fall, Griffiths was walking along Burton Road. Suddenly there was "a single flash of lightning which extended over a very wide area of Manchester. This was noted by many people because of its severity, and because there were no further flashes." The professional Griffiths made a note of the time and nature of the flash, and the weather conditions. In his subsequent efforts to check out the possibility that the ice dropped from a plane, he was able to establish accurately the position of the most likely of the two, because it was actually struck by that single blast - 12km NW of the fall. Indeed because its position is accurat-known, Griffiths estimated the bolt length at anything up to 25km long - and it was more than likely the presence of the plane actually precipitated the discharge.

If there is no connexion between the vivid single flash of lightning (an interesting enough event in itself), and the fall of the largish chunk of ice 9 minutes later, then we have an extraordinary meteorological coincidence. But the datum that would have really had Fort leaning forward was the presence at the scene of both events of a professional meteorologist, who was also, at that time, employed as a lightning observer for the Electrical Research Association.

CASHEL, EIRE - ICE BLOCK.

A block of ice, estimated to have weighed about 2 lbs, fell, burying 1½ inches into the lawn at the entrance gate of St Patrick's Hospital, Cashel, Co Tipperary. The ice narrowly missed two of the maintenance staff working nearby. One, Thomas Furlong, said: "It sounded like a shot." This is very interesting in that some kind of aerial sound or detonation is one of the most con-sistent elements common to fall-stories. In the Manchester fall (above), the flash was followed about 3 seconds later by thunder, which was in turn followed by the fall - though here, of course, the 8min 57sec gap between the last two events may be too long to establish any useful causal connexion.

A spokesman for the meteorological office at Cashel could only imagine the ice fell from a plane - both witnesses said there was no plane around at the time. However, they did say that there was a large black cloud overhead. A contradiction creeps in here, as the spokesman proclaimed the clouds "not high enough" to produce such a piece of ice.

Alas, we have no accurate date for this, and we can only ask that any Irish readers so inclined, follow it up. The story was cut from an Irish paper about June 20th, 1974, by John Michell. We wrote to the Cork Evening Echo, many months ago, but no reply to date.

It is worth noting here that Fort recorded an earlier fall for Cashel, toward the end of Ch 8, Book of the Damned. On 2 Aug 1865 (darn nearly 100 years earlier) a "worked" pyramidal stone wedge fell from the sky. A Dr Haughton commented on a singular feature - the rounded edges bore regular lines marked in the black crust "as perfect as if made by a ruler."

ROUEN, FRANCE - ICE BLOCK.

We found another old ice-fall in the file not recorded in our earlier round-up (see NEWSs 3/8; and 6/10.)

Jean Preypys was working in his garden in Rouen when he heard a whistling sound. He looked up just in time to see a 2 lb block of ice plummet into his flower bed. Birmingham Evening Mail, 26 June 71.

VENUS UNVEILED.

On 21 Oct, the Russian probe Venera 9 fell to the surface of Venus and sent back a dramatic panoramic photograph. On the 25th, Venera 10 did the same from a spot about 1400 miles away. Several startling points were immediately apparent. Not only was the atmos-phere more transparent than predicted (the horizon in the photo is 200-300m away), there were rocks scattered as far as visiblity allowed you to see, and some of these bore the sharp-edged fractures of recently formed rocks. Boris Nepoklonov, chief Venusian topographer of the Central Institute of Geodesy, said: "On the first picture we saw a scattering of large rocks, a typically young mountainscape; the second station showed us a landscape typical of old mountain formations."

Venus, it seems, as dead as theory has up to now led most scientists to believe -- these indications of tectonic and volcanic activity suggest the planet is "alive" and still in the process of formation -- although the Russians are careful to other factors as well. Dmitry Grigoryev, chairman of the International Commission on Space Minerology said it was difficult to believe these rocks were destroyed in situ. "It looks more likely that some unknown force has scattered these rocks over the surface. Perhaps they fell or slipped down from surrounding rocks. It could also be that these are the outbursts of giant meteoric craters." Though, as New Scientist, 30 Oct 75, comments, "There is no evidence from this particular picture of any of the craters which have been mapped by radar." More detailed and technical information on the results of the two probes can be found in the Novosti Bulletin Nos 26488 (24 Oct 75), 26491 (27 Oct 75) & 26520 (4 Nov 75), from which we have taken most of our details.

There is one person to whom these revelations have not come as a surprise: Dr Immanuel Velikovsky, whose catastrophic theory of the formation of the solar system, particularly the peregrinations of Venus which, says Velikovsky, came from outside and brushed near the Earth on its way to its present position, had driven most orthodox cosmologists speechless with fury. The 82-year-old psychoanalyst who derived this theory from the analysis of mythical history, has, since the publication of Worlds in Collision 25

years ago, been highly gratified at what he considers confirmation of his theories. There is no denying that he is substantially correct in his predictions that Venus is "young" (ie still geologically active), just as previous Venus-probes confirmed his idea of the high temperature, atmospheric pressure and atmospheric constituents. See Sunday Express 2 Nov 75, for a fuller comment. Cr: S Moore.

THE NUMBER IS UP.

In the weeks at the end of October and the begining of November, TV viewers were confronted with a strange downward ripple (on all channels) - a compulsive twiddler's delight. It seems that many sets in England were also picking up programmes from Sweden, Germany and Switzerland. The met.men blame it on "strange weather conditions" - something like a reversal in the temperatures of layers of air -- an inadequate explanation if you ask us. One IBA spokesman said that normal TV transmissions range up to 50 miles, but the weather conditions were permitting signal distances of up to 500 miles.

What astonishes us is that in the wake of all the highly unusual meteorological and geological events so far this year, not to mention the flaring of a couple of new stars (see last issue), no one has correlated this with the current freak TV reception conditions. What is going on? But, like Alfred Bester's Pi-man, we believe in balance, and will now correct the omission with an amazing correlation of our own. On 29th Oct, the Russians launched another satellite. The full significance of its name and number will not escape those with a numerological bent. It was Cosmos 777. Although we have mentioned it before, for the benefit of those who missed it earlier, Cosmos 666 went into orbit 15 July 74. Between these two nexuses (?) everything has gone haywire. Novosti Bulletin No 26504 (30 Oct 75).

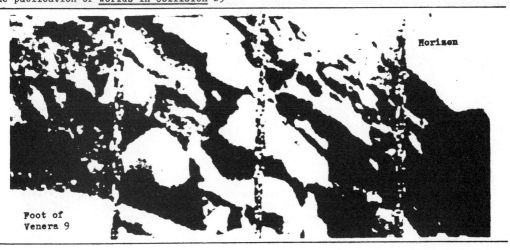

Horizon

Foot of
Venera 9

Leys, UFOs & Chance

Robert Forrest

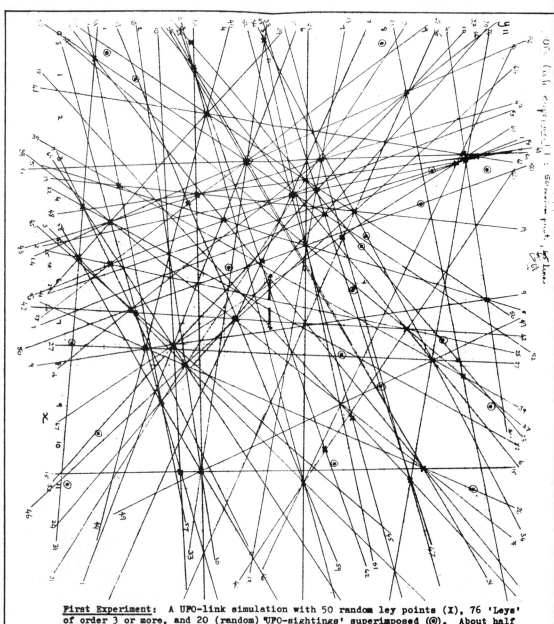

First Experiment: A UFO-link simulation with 50 random ley points (X), 76 'Leys' of order 3 or more, and 20 (random) 'UFO-sightings' superimposed (◎). About half the UFOs fall on or near a 'ley'. Both UFOs and Ley points were generated from random number tables.

Having studied the 'chance hypothesis vs. ley lines' problem over the past few months, I have at length concluded that the mathematical evidence for the existence of ley lines is poor. I hope shortly to publish a booklet outlining the methods by which I came to this conclusion, but for the present article I restrict myself to one particular problem - the alleged link between UFOs and ley lines.

If ley lines do not exist, if they are merely a chance effect, then such statements as "90% of UFO sightings occur on or close to leys" must be a predicted outcome of the chance hypothesis. I have found this to be the case, and will outline three experiments - all backed up by theoretical considerations - which point the way to this conclusion.

The first experiment is a small scale simulation of what goes on. Using random number tables (to avoid 'personal bias') I drafted 50 random points onto a sheet of graph paper (the graph paper was 17.5 cm square, and each ley point a small disc 0.5 mm in diameter). These were to represent ley points on a map. Next I inserted all connecting lines between the points which were of order 3 or more (ie. lines going through 3 points or more). These were to represent ley lines. (about 70 such lines were obtained on this scale). Finally, I drafted 20 more points onto the map (the 'points' being the same size as the ley points, and determined by random number tables) and used these to represent UFO sightings. The result was that, on this scale, about half the UFOs appeared on or close to a 'ley'.

The second experiment was designed to show what an average map would look like if all leys of order at least 4 were inserted.

Fifty random points were again drafted onto a sheet of paper and each point joined to every other, the connecting line being produced to the edges of the paper. About 1100 distinct lines were thus obtained which cut the paper into a vast number of, on the whole, tiny regions. (it can be shown that this number of lines slices the paper into about 300,000 such regions!). If we were to draft UFOs onto this sheet of paper as we did in the first experiment, there would be precious little room for them to fall without actually landing on or near some line or other.

Now it can be shown that on a 1:50,000

O/S map, containing about 330 ley points, we can expect about 1100 ley lines each of order at least 4, and each aligned to within 35 yards. So that, if all these ley lines were to be actually inserted on the map, the result would look rather like the piece of paper above. That is, scarred beyond recognition in many places by criss-crossing pencil lines.

From personal experience on a smaller scale, I very much doubt if any ley hunter has ever actually inserted all the possible ley lines on a map containing this number of points. Such a task would be unbelievably tedious, and I suspect that most ley hunters stop before they have got anywhere near their full quota. But the leys will be there, if they should need them - and this point raised an interesting third experiment.

Suppose the ley hunter drafts UFOs onto his map and then looks for the leys on which the UFOs might lie.

I therefore took an old 1" O/S map (sheet 159) of the Chilterns and ringed all the churches, ancient sites, etc. There were 560 odd of them, many of which were probably non-valid as ley-points (eg. modern churches), but nevertheless I went ahead to see what would happen. I then drafted 6 spurious UFO sightings onto the map using random number tables. Each UFO sighting was a disc about 0.1" in diameter, corresponding to a possible error in fixing the UFO position from the UFO sighting of 200 yards.

Each UFO was found to lie not on just one ley, but at the intersection of a minimum of 3 leys, each ley of order at least 4. Two of the UFOs actually fell on the same ley of order 7 (Here again, leys were aligned to within 35 yards).

Now it is possible to predict the average number of leys of order at least 4 which we can expect to intersect at a UFO sighting. For the above case it works out at about 5, so the results actually obtained were well in accord with the chance hypothesis.

Even if we reject 200 or so of the 560 points as non-valid, we are still left, remember, with a map which, if all the leys were inserted, would be chopped into some 300,000 pieces.

That 90% of UFO sightings occur in the vicinity of leys, I, for one, am not surprised.

+***+   +***+   +***+   +***+   +***+

R Forrest. June 1975.

THE MYSTERY OF MERRY'S WOUNDS.

The strange case of 35-year-old Frederick Merry began quietly with an announcement in the Daily Mail, 13 June 75, that a "streaker" was critically ill in Mile End Hospital, with brain damage, after being arrested by police dancing naked in Victoria Park, Bethnal Green, London, early on the morning of the 12th. He had waded across an ornamental lake to a wooded island where he was running about bumping into trees.

Next day, the papers said he had died in the night - doctors did not know why and tests were being carried out. There was much play made of the tidbit that Merry had, only ten days before, joined a nature sect called The Emin, or "Faithful One", and that they encouraged talking to plants, etc. Senior sect member, John Edge, protested that nothing they taught him could have led him to act this way.

As usual with these cases, one feels that all the public statements conceal more than they reveal. Indeed, three weeks later, Time Out, 4-10 July 75, reveals an altogether sinister version of the events. Relatives of the "Mystic Streaker", as the media tagged Merry, said he had obviously taken a terrible beating, and called for an inquiry into his death. When he emerged from the woods on the island with 2 policemen, a woman officer and two park-keepers, he was "still naked, badly injured, handcuffed, and chained around the legs." By the time he arrived at hospital, he was "virtually dead." Attempts were made to get him breathing, but they failed. An anonymous caller from the hospital told the local paper that he had never seen such shocking injuries on a person who had just been arrested. His brother David spoke of "appalling injuries", marks and bruises all over his body. Merry's mouth was reportedly clogged with earth. Later at the inquest it was said that his body was covered with earth and twigs; and his chains (like those for securing gates) had to be struck off by hospital workers.

Now, you might be thinking, even if (stress if) this was a case of bizarre police brutality - of what interest to us Forteans could

it be? Well, your editor has bizarre afflictions of his own - perhaps (stress perhaps) there might be some affinity in the case with other of our tales of wounds mysteriously appearing on people, whether from an attack by an invisible; a psychosomatic projection (eg stigmata) or (wow!) the teleporting of wounds from an unguessable somewhere to appear instantaneously on the victim. In the absence of evidence to the contrary, we maintain that all hypotheses should be borne in mind. And just in case, we do have adequate records of wounds that have appeared, and just as mysteriously disappeared -- at least they seem like records.

The inquest on Merry was closed as soon as it opened, and much to the disgust of Time Out (ever vigilant on behalf of defenceless hippies against the machinations of the police-state), with no date set for resumption. However, with the prospect of a full-scale police-atrocity scandal hanging over their heads, Scotland Yard's A10 branch did their own investigation and sent a report to the Director of Public Prosecutions.

The inquest, when it resumed, contained no evidence of murder or manslaughter. Merry's father said that his stepson had been agitated for some days previously, and on the morning of the 12th, at 1am, began to spread his arms, crosslike, standing naked, murmuring and staring at the sky - then he drove off in his van to the park. It would seem that a crowd had gathered watching Merry on the island, used as a bird sanctuary. When he saw the keepers coming, he began screaming and shouting. He resisted "with the strength of ten", butting one on the chin. Then the police turned up and overpowered him while he was bumping around in the trees. Somehow we think of a headless chicken running in circles, oblivious to obstacles - perhaps all Merry could think of was the avoiding of things that had intruded into and debased his meditations. Perhaps he was not even human. The park-keepers said Merry was in a fairly good condition when he left the park - yet when he arrived at the hospital later he had bruising to nearly every part of his body. A family friend said he looked like "a young man who had been beaten to death."

A forensic expert testified that no drugs or alcohol were involved - and that a "severe continuous pressure to the side of the neck" had resulted in brain damage and heart failure. But since some of Merry's actions in the park were attributed to this "brain damage" - the whole matter of when the "continuous pressure" was applied is in question.

A barrister for the family questioned the differences between the testimonies of the park-keepers and the police, and the condition in which Merry arrived in hospital. Before this could be answered, the Coroner adjourned the court (with no date for resumption, again) on the grounds that witnesses might be about to incriminate themselves, and that the question was a thinly disguised allegation of perjury. Nevertheless - if the keepers said he was OK when he left the park, and the police imply they didn't touch him but that he injured himself in the park - perhaps someone is lying. To press-date no more has been heard of this case. But our minds tick over - there is a condition that would satisfy the testimony of both parties. We think of the unfortunate recipients of unexpected wounds - wounds that materialise on their bodies often during a profound mystical experience, or an equivalent communion with forces we know little about -- and how inexplicable and embarrassing this could be if it happened during police custody! We do not say this happened, but following the admirable lead of Stuart Greenwood in tossing out hypotheses to be tested, we toss out this one. After testing it we may even throw it out. (above details from Daily Mail and Daily Express, 24 Oct 75; Time Out, 31 Oct - 6 Nov 75. Credit for all items: Steve Moore). Let us consider some other stories on this theme - they may throw some light on our hypothesis, and each other.

CAUSE OF DEATH...UNKNOWN!

Three boys, aged between 16 and 20, were found dead in the living-room of a house in Calverton Road, Arnold, Notts, in early Feb 1972. They had been playing guitars - which for the record, were acoustic - no electrical equipment around. One was the son of the woman who owned the house - the other two, identities unknown at the time of the clipping, had been put up for the night. When the woman came back from shopping she found one boy slumped in a chair, guitar on lap, the others on the floor. A Det. Inspector said: "The cause of death at this moment is a complete mystery." One faint wisp of a clue - - the lady said the house was noticably warm. Sun, 9 Feb 72.

A couple and their baby were found dead in a caravan at Alnesbourn Priory, near Ipswich. The only theory (which does not seem to be substantiated) is that they were gassed by fumes from a heater. Guardian, 25 Feb 74.

George Hicks, 38, serving 6 months for motoring offences, was found dead in his Pentonville cell, 14th March. Cause of death was given at the inquest, as unknown - no other info available. Daily Telegraph 15 March 75.

ATTACKS BY INVISIBLES?

In the late summer of this year, a "hammer fiend" stalked the Beechwood estate, Sunbury Cross, London. In at least three attacks, he crept up silently "like a ghost" and felled the three girls with one blow, then just stared at them before running off into the night. There is a thin discription of a man the police are looking for, so this is no phantom, as such. Sunday Mirror, 24 Aug 75.

What interests us here is that the history of polterghost hauntings are replete with ghostly pushes, pokes in the ribs, slaps and pinches and punches. Besides, we feel that across a century, that arch-mystery-attacker, who breathed flames into the faces of unsuspecting girls and fled into the night - Spring-heeled Jack, a classic man-in-black - is still laughing at us.

Just to confuse the issue, we'll relate here the blow that knocked out Mrs Santuzza Campbell, 55, who was alone on a clifftop at Bridlington, Yorks, in Sept 1954. Nothing could be found on the site that could account for the lump on her head that put her into hospital. One theory was that something had fallen from a plane - if so, she would not have been alive. Daily Express, 8 Sept 54. Cr: Harold SW Chibbett.

On 10th Oct 1968, cuts and scratches were found on seven babies, aged between 5 and 6 days, in Nether Edge Hospital, Sheffield. One was cut on the foot, which was, of course, under the bed-covers, which rather foundered the belief that an animal somehow got in. This maternity ward was on the 3rd floor and three staff were on duty in the ward during the night - and security is fairly tight. It was thought that finger-nails could not account for the injuries,(all the babies were well after treatment), and since animals and other intruders could be discounted, the actual cause of the injuries was unknown, said the hospital secretary Frank Turner. Daily Mirror 11 Oct 68. Cr: Anthony Smith.

11-year-old Ian Salt was startled by something as he set out from his home in Solihull, Warks, to go plane-spotting at Birmingham Airport, in March 1974. He was found drowned in a hidden pool well away from his normal route. Forensic experts, studying his tracks across a field, believe that he was being chased, and had crashed through a hedge into the pool, in panic. Nothing is said about any other sets of tracks in the ploughed field - and nothing more was ever said about the case. Daily Mirror, 5 March 74.

Similarly, the police are baffled over the strange drowning of Garnett Oliver, a retired

farmer of 85. He was found in 4ft of water
in a well at Field Farm, Partney, Lincs,
where he lived, only an hour after chatting
cheerily with a friend. A heavy concrete slab
had been removed from the well-top. The
Spilsby District Coroner, Mr Ian Mitchell,
said there were no marks on the body such as
would indicate a fall into the narrow well;
no suggestion of a coronary collapse; and no
evidence of interferance by another person.
The death remained unexplained. Scunthorpe
Evening Telegraph, 24 April 75. Cr: N Watson.

The photo below (from the Sunday People,
22 June 75) shows the bruises on the throat
of Mrs Gladys Worthington. She says that
her house in Salvin St, Croxdale, Co Durham,
gives both her and her husband the shivers.
Recently, things have been moving about on
their own, and once saw a ghostly white
figure. They have asked the council to rehouse them after this latest experience.

She was lying in bed when she felt a hand
on her throat - it was 2am, her husband was
on night-shift and her four dogs sleeping
downstairs. "I woke with a start. In the
darkness I could see nothing. But I felt a
tingling sensation running up my body from
my toes. I tried to scream, but I couldn't.
As quickly as it came, the sensation went.
Then, seconds later, it happened again. I lay
awake for the rest of the night. I got up
thinking I'd been dreaming. Then I went to
the mirror to make up my face, and got a
terrible shock. There were five bruises like
pressure marks from a thumb and four fingers."
The doctor she went to agreed that the marks
were made by a deep pressure ("apparently a
hand") on her throat - but he won't believe
her story about being strangled by a ghost.
He may be wiser than he thinks. Perhaps it
wasn't a ghost - look at the date! It's only
about 9 days after Frederick Merry died from
the effects of "a severe continuous pressure
to the side of the neck." Perhaps a phantom
strangler stalked London that month!

INSTANT GRIEVOUS BODILY HARM.

Now we're getting frighteningly heavy - and
our tales are far from entertaining. Barry
Lacy, 26, kissed his wife and children and
set off at 8 o'clock to begin his morning's
work at a nearby farm, Summer 1969. He did
not turn up for lunch. Later he was found in
a field he had been ploughing - 200 yards
from his tractor, which was still upright,
motor running. He had serious head injuries
and beneath his body, his flask of coffee was
crushed. He was rushed to Battle Hospital,
Reading, Berks, with a fractured skull and
his left side paralysed. Now, more than two
years later he is completely paralysed and
can remember nothing of the circumstances of
his accident. The case was investigated by
the police, solicitors, farm machinery
experts, and insurance claim investigators,
Lacy's workmates and the farm owner — and
all remain baffled. Sunday Express, 28 Nov 71.

On the 7th July 73, a man was found
unconscious near Port Angeles, Washington -
with a broken shoulder and knee. He was about
40, did not know his own name, address or
even face, and had never heard of Port Angeles. He was thought to have fallen to the foot
of a bluff, where he was found, but there
seems to be an element of uncertainty in the
statement, as though the most obvious explanation was grasped at in the absence of any
confirming evidence. Washington Star News,
20 July 73.

What was said to be a "riddle of a murder
without a motive" was reported in the Sun, 27
Sept 74. Aubrey Packham, 60, was found battered to death in a coach firm's office in
Southall, Middlesex, that day. Nothing was
stolen from the firm or the man, and there
was no sign of a break-in. Police say there
was no evidence of a fight and no murder
weapon has been found.

On the 27th Dec, a young man, identity
unknown, was found dead in a room of the
Excelsior Hotel, Glasgow airport. His name,
passport number and Glasgow address were all

alse. A curious detail -- despite a "6 inch
urgical wound" in his chest ((shades of
aspar Hauser, et al.)) a post-mortem failed
o reveal the cause of death. Guardian, 30
ec 74. Credit: JDM Start.

  Another tractor driver! Edward Russell,66,
ied in hospital on 22nd Feb this year, after
eing found unconscious beside his tractor -
earing only his shoes and socks - on Broad-
eed Farm, Rowlands Castle, Hants. It was
hought that the "power take-off gear" had
tripped him of his clothes.(!!!?). News of
he World, 23 Feb 75. Cr: RE Cotton.

  The little village of Nayland, Suffolk,
elebrated the Bank Holiday of 26th May with
ts usual dance at the church social - and
ts three pubs were crowded. Shortly before
1pm, vetinary surgeon Sebastian Salaman and
widow Mrs Alice Hawes left - he giving her
 lift to her remote cottage. Next morning
rs Hawes, 79, was found with a broken leg in
er living room, and Mr Salaman,69, was
ying outside in the road with fractured
kull, broken ribs and pelvis. He died in
ospital, 24 hours later, without regaining
onsciousness. Detectives thought he was
he victim of a hit and run accident, but the
nly cars that use the single-track lane
elong to the residents and they were cleared
ithin the week - now they think it might be
urder. But Det.Super. Jack Sharman of
uffolk CID says later: "This is a most un-
sual inquiry in that we still cannot say
ith certainty that a crime has been commit-
ed." Mrs Hawes, recovering in hospital,
ays she can only remember falling down in
he cottage shortly after Salaman left. Tony
sborne and his son were leaving their house
pposite Mrs Hawes' at 6·45am when he saw
alaman lying half in the road, five yards
rom his car. There was blood on the rockery,
he garden fence and Mr Salaman's car, and
he cottage door was open. Everyone is said
o be dazed and baffled in the village - not
he least, Mrs Hawes' neighbours at Campion
ill, who heard nothing at all that night,
s something savagely battered Mr Salaman.
f you postulate two coincident accidents,
ou are still left with Mr Salaman's myster-
ous wounding. Sunday Express, 8 June 75.

  78-year-old Mrs Sarah Davies died of
"extensive injuries". She was found lying in
he yard of her daughter's home at Cilcennin,
ear Aberaeron, Dyfed, Wales, on 14th May,
emi-conscious and with fractures in pelvis
nd skull. A consultant pathologist to the
ronglais General Hospital, Aberystwyth,said
hat the injuries were concurrent with "some
onsiderable fall" — yet Det.Chief Inspector
ohn Owen-Evans said that she could not have
ownstairs, or from a window, or been in a
oad accident. Foul play was not suspected -
nd the only idea he could come up with was
hat she fell once in the house, and then
gain outside. The Western Mail, 5 July 75.
r: FW Holiday.

  During the height of the storm that

battered England on 8th Aug (see NEWS 12/7)
Mrs Alice Mellor, 75, was found battered to
death in a field at Pond Farm, South Crosland,
near Huddersfield. She had gone out looking
for one of her Friesian cows who was due to
calve, and one theory was that lightning
spooked the cows into trampling over her. But
the police were not happy with the theory and
  there were suspicious and contradictory
elements involved in the evidence. Assuming
something worse, house-to-house inquiries
were made, and there was a search for any
murder-weapon - but to no avail. Despite
being battered "beyond recognition" (according to the People), the post-mortem could
not establish the cause of her death. Sunday
People & Sunday Express, 10 Aug 75. Cr:
Steve Moore & Nigel Watson.

MASS CARDIAC ARRESTS?

  The Veterans Administration Hospital, Ann
Arbor, Michigan, was embarrassed - over the
first three weeks of August an extraordinary
number of patients have died. The exact figure has not been given but hospital spokesmen have been quoted at 23, 34 and as high as
41, dying of heart failure and respiratory
collapse. Dr Laurence Foye, Deputy Chief Med.
Director, said an investigation centred on 15
patients whose doctors had not expected them
to have gone into this condition, had failed
to explain what had happened, or why.
  Many of these patients were in a post-
surgery intensive care ward - but another
doctor said that collapses had happened on
other floors and wards. Tests were made of the
patients' bile, blood and fluids, but the
results were "inconclusive" because some of
the testing equipment "malfunctioned". Intravenous drip units were examined for contam-
ination, and searches were made for mislabled
bottles and medicines. Nothing!
  It would seem that the symptoms of this
collapse were similar to those suggestive of
muscle relaxants like Curare, Pancuron, and
Succinylcholine chlorine - all used at the
hospital. So another search was made, and
despite Dr Foyes careful statement that he
would not confirm these collapses were
"induced", speculations began to mount about
a maniac poisoner. Dr Ronald Bishop, Chief of
Medicine,said that traces of a muscle relaxant were found on an IV drip in use. ((Even
though we naturally root for the outré theory
- please bear in mind that as Fort showed
ad nauseum, anybody who sets out to find or
prove something, usually can, if he's halfway
competant.)) Dr Duane Freier, Hospital Chief
of Staff, believed the drug was the relaxant
Tavulom. "If this is true," he said, "It is
likely to be intentional." Security was tight-
ened and,as if to confirm the poisoner theory,
there were no more occurrences.
  That would seem to be that - but for the
suspicious lack of developments. Reading
between the lines, the identity of the fiend
could not be established and no source found

for the drug - despite the involvement of the FBI. If the patients were in intensive care, there would be records and monitorings, yet the fiend slipped in and out of many wards and floors slipping nasty stuff into people's intravenous drip bottles, and hung about to see them suffer (for that is the only conceivable motive). All this without arrousing suspicion, in a hospital on edge as the collapses increased. Now, in true MIB-panic tradition, a patient speaks out - he woke one night (presumably _after_ the scare was over) to find someone trying to inject something into his arm — we wonder if this was simply a response to the panic, or indeed the incredibly elusive poisoner?

Fort wrote about many kinds of panics — the jabbers and stabbers, the rippers and clippers, the snatchers and snipers, the 'kissing bug' and Typhoid Mary — they all politely fit a pattern. They are masters of etiquette, appearing to conform to the most acceptable theories of the day, until a closer examination reveals certain crude but fundamental disagreements. They respond with all the fawning grace of those desiring social respectability - relaxants are postulated - and by the minutest trace they are found with malfunctioning equipment. This is a veneer - beneath it lurks the MO of the 'attack'. "All would be well, all would be heavenly" - if only the victims would keep their mouths shut. (Story from New York Times, 21 Aug 75. Cr: Bill Grimstad.) The line between fiction and what people call truth is impossible to draw, except by resorting to fictional absolutes, or points which are only relative to other relative points. The trouble comes thickest in our kind of data. You will have to decide for yourself, find your own way through this hall-of-mirrors of shifting and ambiguous data. About the only thing we can say that makes any sense is: please tread carefully.

PHANTOM SNIPERS.

A man enjoying a rifle-range at 'Playland' Amusement Arcade, Coventry St, London, on the 20th June 71, collapsed with a bullet in his shoulder. There were witnesses, but no clue to the origin of the shot. As if to confound what was already a mystery, it was revealed that six weeks previously a Greek died on the same spot after shooting himself with one of the rifles, and within the year a third man was wounded there. Daily Mirror, 21 June 71. Cr: A Smith.

Police were hunting a gunman after three people were injured in south-west London on the night of 2 April this year. Not much information is given in the report, except that a woman in Twickenham, a man in Richmond and another in Wimbledon were all wounded by what looked like pellets from an airgun. No mention is made of witnesses - but how conventional to think of a gunman — we know better don't we? The Sun, 3 April 75.

But then to think of phantom snipers is our own conventionality - that just won't do. It's when we're lazy or tired, that we're at our most conventional, as Fort noted, and then it's only too easy to think of gunmen when bullets are found, phantom or otherwise. Consider this — Miner Tom Coxon driving with his wife and two daughters in the car, on 8 Oct, near the aptly named No-Man's Heath, Ashby-de-la-Zouche, in Leicestershire. Suddenly he cries out, and blood begins to spurt from a hole in his head. He managed to drive to a service station, where someone took him to hospital. He was then transferred to the neuro-surgical unit of North Staffs General Hospital, where he now lies paralysed down one half of his body, with three pieces of metal lodged near his brain. Daily Express 9 Oct 75. Two days later the police hunt down and arrest two brothers who were driving a van that was passing at the time Tom got 'hit' — their assumption is that they fired an airgun at Tom. If so, they must be the most remarkable marksmen ever, to have a man through a car window (it is not said whether it was open or not!) three times as the two cars pass, and to get all three pellets into the same hole in the man's head. It is worth noting here that the three pieces of metal must have arrived simultaneously, on the same trajectory, because Tom cried out once and put his hand up to his head, which then would have been hit by numbers 2 & 3. Secondly, and I'm open to correction here, I wouldn't have thought an airgun would have the power to penetrate a skull. Since the two brothers were remanded (Daily Express, 11 Oct 75) we have heard nothing, not even what the pieces of metal were. As the hunt began for the passing van, Superintendant Thomas Bush did not sound too convinced: "We are completely snookered. This is one of the most baffling mysteries I have ever known." I suppose they had to be seen to be doing something, at least. It's my guess the case against the two brothers was dropped for lack of evidence. (Cr: Steve Moore.)

POST SCRIPT.

Having typed up the above notes days ago, I came across a passage in Father Thurston's Ghosts and Poltergeists (Burns Oates 1953 p21) - quoted from a study of an astonishing case, published in 1800 - and we give it as a postscript to the 'strangling' on p16. Two girls were the center of many attacks. Of one, the investigator, Henry Durbin, said: "I saw the flesh at the side of her throat pushed in, whitish as if done with fingers, though I saw none. Her face grew red and blackish presently, as if she were strangled, but without any convulsion or contraction of the muscles. We went to her and I touched her head. It went off in a moment and she was well, which could not have taken place had it been the effect of a natural disorder." The case happened in Bristol, December 1761.

MIRACLES OF THE GODS by Erich von Daniken.
   Souvenir Press; £3.75; pp237; illos, refs &
   bibliog (though most of it's in German);
ISBN 0 285 62174 2.
   It took courage to read this book!
   Von Daniken explains its context - "When I
was following the trail of my astronaut gods
through the five continents, I made a point of
visiting every accessible visionary shrine."
On this evidence, I'd say he hasn't been cured
yet. "Riding a bold steeplechase through
history," he opens with a summary of the most
famous visions, and some less well-known ones.
The book ends with a useful (though admittedly
incomplete) chronology of visions, from 5000BC
to the face on the chalice-cloth last year at
Castelnaud-en-Guers, France (see NEWS 7/11).
   Who are the people who see visions? vonD
askes himself. "Are visions simply psychological phenomena caused by mass autosuggestion,
as the materialists often conclude?", though
this begs the question (a familiar vonD technique). Visions in the broad context are far
from simple, and 'mass autosuggestion' explains
nothing, least of all to materialists. He then
reviews the standard theories: hysteria, probably heightened by asceticism and shaped by
dogma; bio-feedback techniques, and other
methods of self-induced 'ecstasy'; or actual
messages from Gods; etc; taking in associated
material like water-divining (vision-sites
are often by wells and springs); theories of
space-time(some of the phenomena seems to
transcend these categories); and healing. The
book is subtitled 'a Hard Look at the Supernatural" but he restricts himself largely to
visions.
   Many of the classical visions have been
accompanied by strange aerial phenomena, not
visible to all present, but a good many -- eg.
the visions of the Blessed Virgin Mary (BVM)
at Fatima (1917) and Cairo (1968) are often
quoted in UFO literature, and it is here that
vonD returns to his magnum opus. His conclusion is that visions are induced by intervention from space. He never really defines
what he means by a 'vision', and so he appears
to be constantly contradicting himself by
including the gamut from an individually witnessed event where we have to take the person's
word, to group visions of obviously religious
characters, to group witnessing of solar and
other curious aerial and astronomical phenom-

ena, to visionary dreams, to images and faces
that appear on surfaces, and weeping statues
etc. One example of this difficulty is that,
contrary to his previous books, the angels
that abound in the Old Testament (used as non-
Christian evidence) now become 'visions' in
place of visiting extraterrestrials (ETs).
   After a most interesting dissertation on the
past evils and exploitation (of visions) by
the Church, he finally goes off the deep end.
His reasoning (some will jibe at that) is
simple. Animal man has latent paranormal (he
calls them parapsychological) faculties, and
these can be stimulated when the ETs shoot
their beams into our brains. The resultant
imagery is the product of our conditioning.
Children figure prominently as recipients
because they are "ideally prepared for the
supernatural by their intensive religious
upbringing" - a highly contentious point, both
on biographical data, and from his own chronology where children account for probably a
third of the visions, and then only from
about 1835 - a comparatively recent phenomenon. Anyway, vonD maintains that children are
frightened by these flashes in their heads,
and being predisposed religiously, seek some
security in projecting a mother-image. "In
fact, faster than light communications produced oscillations in the sub- or supracon-
sciousness and communication with extraterrestrial beings was established." Whaaaat!?
Another curious line of reasoning ignores his
previous comments on our innate dowsing talents -- only the ETs could have revealed the
hiding place of the Mormon tablets to Joseph
Smith, because only they could have placed
them on Earth thousands of years previously.
The Angel Moroni? - oh! he's dismissed as a
projection of the "fairy-tale factory", an
unfortunate byproduct of the ET contact. The
"solar miracles" (which as far as I remember
were only sun-like and nothing to do with Sol)
are in fact visions of the aliens spacecrafts,
shown to the masses in order to reveal their
hand behind all this. (Why not reveal the
same to the scientists, whom vonD maintains
are the true interpreters of the ET effort,
instead of fooling around in such a field and
in such a manner as to arouse the scientists'
deepest suspicions, is not even asked!). And
when the founders of "all" the world's religions have proclaimed that it was not them-

selves speaking, "but that which is in me", what they really mean, says vonD, is this ET intervention. And so on.

His logic is not all that bad - it's his premises that are pure crank; a) that because electricity is involved in processes in the brain, para-electrical processes must also be involved in thought, and are capable of being projected from afar to control the processes in the brain; and b) the ETs are doing this from space. Apart from anything else, there is a whopping assumption about the one-to-one correlation of mind and brain. In criticising the Church for the corners it backs itself into by strict adherance to high dogma, he doesn't seem to realise that his own devotion to "my astronaut gods" creates the same sort of idiotic paradoxes as the Church's invocation of the Holy Spirit - the existence of both being virtually impossible to prove to non-believers.

VonD's climax is the last chapter, where he gaily explains away every achievement in Art, Science, Technology and Religion as the product of "extraterrestrial impulse fields". Apparently Man has never had an original thought in his entire existence! In some people, this intervention cannot be turned to its 'proper' use, and visions (with spontaneous psychic phenomena) occur which are basically useless to our alien puppeteers. According to vonD, this is no error on the ETs' part - they can't help who stumbles into their 'impulse fields'. But when it goes according to plan - ah!, then we get practical visionaries like Einstein and da Vinci, to name but two (though there is quite a list of those scientific breakthroughs attributable to some kind of mystical experience.) When we talk of geniuses, says vonD, we are talking of a "chosen few, those ripe for contact, who are able to convert extraterrestrial impulses into thought molecules."

I was discussing this idea with an old acquaintance, Brother Bufo, a servitor at the crypt of St Ranunculus, when my thought molecules went into a tizzy. "Suppose one of their beams went wrong at a critical stage?" He observed me strangely, then rummaging in the heaps of shrine records, finally thrust this photo into my hands - conclusive evidence he said solemnly, that the Pogs..Bods..They were still perfecting their miracle molecule magnetizers. We laughed well into the night!

GODS OF AIR AND DARKNESS by Richard E Mooney. Souvenir Press; £3.50; pp203; ISBN 0 285 62175 9.

ON THE SHORES OF ENDLESS WORLDS by Andrew Tomas. Sphere paperback; 50p; pp175; index & bibliography; ISBN 0 7221 8545 6.

It seems strange how many Russian emigrés turn up in the Ancient God Squad - Tomas is probably the best writer among them and I enjoy his speculations immensely. When he casually tosses in tidbits, such as knowing the explorer Nicholas Roerich during his stay in China, I begin to realise some of the depth of experience in his writing. The atmosphere is that of a fireside or after dinner chat with a scholar, compared to Mooney's at times lecturing tone.

Shores is divided into two parts: the first explores the chemical, genetic and animal-social bonds that tie man to this planet; the second roams among the stars and our conviction that there is also life out there. Mooney is more pedestrian, dwelling on the theme begun in his previous book Colony:Earth —that our pre-historic beginings are founded in the ashes of the colony begun by aliens on this planet and which ended in nuclear warfare. If Mooney tends to regurgitate the same old facts at least he devotes some time to supplementing and discussing them.

There is a war brewing between Mooney, von Daniken & Kolosimo, of what I call the 'factoid' school, versus Charroux and Tomas (at least) of the more spiritually orientated mythographers. Some shots are fired in Mooney 's book, mainly the allegation that Charroux's (et al) fondness for the unsubstantiated works of Madame Blavatsky bring the whole subject into disrepute — Tomas, aiming a broadside at "those who, sitting in their comfortable soft armchairs, pass judgment on a subject totally unfamiliar to them," goes on to cite a formidable list of explorers who ventured into Tibet and made "definite statements confirming the existence of hidden treasures of the stellar civilisers," - Cacella, Csoma de Koros, Przhevalsky, Kosloff, Grunwedel, Francke, Blavatsky, David-Neel, Ossendowski, and of course Roerich. If the basic issue is over establishing authorities, then I think Mooney and school ought to be very careful - their own works leave much to be desired.

Besides other differences, their themes reflect, I think, their basic approaches -- Mooney prodding laboriously for evidence of a nuclear disaster in our past; Tomas waxing expansively about our glorious future among the stars if only we would live in harmony with the living planetary entity first. Looks like a war could be brewing, and as our batrachian brother would say, Pog knows we need one!

THE LINK - THE EXTRAORDINARY GIFTS OF A TEEN-AGE PSYCHIC by Matthew Manning. Corgi pb; 65p; pp176; illos, index & appendices; ISBN 0 522 99955 5. -- One of the Fortfest events was to have been a film on Matthew Manning made by the New Horizons Research Foundation, Toronto. Matthew, of Cambridge, has been manifesting many forms of psychic phenomena since he was 11: poltergeists, automatic writing & drawing, even out bending Geller. This book is his personal account of being the centre of manifestations that would frighten the life out of most of us, and is well illustrated with astonishinly recognizable spirit-drawings in the styles of Picasso, Durer, Klee, and Beardsley. There are two valuable appendices, one by Peter Bander on the messages via Matthew from a Greek Orthodox saint, Nektarios (d.1920) who wants a monastery built in England. Interestingly, the site is to be indicated by a vision of the BVM. The other is a personal statement by Dr ARG Owen, director of New Horizons and author of Can We Explain the Poltergeist?, of how he came to be involved in the testing of Matthew. Altogether, they make a valuable record of a case of genuinely inexplicable activity - the saga of which has not yet reached its conclusion.

THE MAGIC OF FINDHORN by Paul Hawken. Souvenir Press; £3.50; pp216; ISBN 0 285 62175 0.
  Most people known the name 'Findhorn' even if the connexion is as vague as "something to do with fairies - isn't it?" The Findhorn community was founded by Peter Caddy when he retired to this caravan site on the bleak Moray coast in Scotland, to practice Rudolf Steiner's 'Bio-dynamic' theory of plant growth - and where, much to the astonishment of interested observers and sceptics alike, horticultural miracles bloomed and fruited in the poor sand, within feet of their neighbour's stringy plants. The secret, they said, was in living in harmony and working in close co-operation with the etheric and elemental forces of nature (the Landscape Angel, the Spinach Deva, etc). As word of this New Age community spread through the alternative grapevine, the rootless searchers of two generations made pilgrimages to work there. Somehow, the gardens became the symbolic crucible for their own spiritual regeneration. Paul Hawken spent one year among them and tells his and some of their stories - if you can put up with his rather self-conscious imitation of Tom Wolfe's 'New Journalism'. If I tell you that here are accounts of romping with fauns in a park, or walking down Edinburgh's Prince's St beside the god Pan, and so on - I hope you won't judge too hastily. It is ultimately a matter for personal judgment - but read it first - it's a fascinating account of a true enigma.

STRANGE POWERS by Colin Wilson. Abacus pb; pp126; 65p; ISBN 0 349 13733 1.
  Since completing his monumental study The Occult, Wilson says that he met at least three people who deserved inclusion -- Robert Leftwich,a retired businessman who dowses and claims to demonstrably 'Astral Project'; Mrs Eunice Beattie, a retired hospital sister who

has produced hundreds of pages of automatic writing, with prophetic elements; and Dr Arthur Guirdham, one of the central figures in a reincarnated group of Cathars from 13th century France, a case which is either "a carefully planned deception, or an important breakthrough in our knowledge of the universe" -- each an example of what Wilson has called 'Faculty X'.
  Wilson regards this fairly short book as a postscript to The Occult. I too share his interest in the way people think, and their motivations in going 'against the herd', and so I find Wilson's own personal anecdotes of his inevitable and growing involvement with the literature, personalities and philosophies of the occult as interesting as any of the material here.

THE HERO WITH A THOUSAND FACES by Joseph Campbell. Abacus; £1.70; illos & index; pp350; ISBN 0 349 10480 8. -- Campbell has been instrumental in the propagation of the Jungian thesis in the field of comparative religion. I find him eminantly readable (compared to Eliade) and his clear identification of the critical elements in myth and mystical experience has illuminated many an obscure corner of the human mind for me. There are two major cycles of myths here: the masculine hero of the monomyth, and the feminine hero, or 'mother' of the cosmogonic cycle - and the stages of each are examined in depth. Perhaps the most interesting chapter is the last, which can shed some light on the millenarianism of "nuts and bolts" ufology, with its promise of salvation from the skies. The modern manifestations of fundamental myths or archetypal patterns is something we should never lose sight of in our studies.

UFOs FROM BEHIND THE IRON CURTAIN by Ion Hobana & Julien Weverbergh. Corgi pb; 65p; Illos & Bibliog; pp307; ISBN 0 522 10023 4. There are so few studies of Communist UFOlogy that it is impossible to judge this work by comparisons. Naturally, the political and official scientific views are gone into, and the role of the mass media in this context is particularly interesting. I suspect that most of the interest in this book will lie in the valuable compilations of sightings for Bulgaria, Hungary, Jugoslavia, Poland, Czechoslovakia, Rumania and Russia. There are also very useful chapters on the Tungus event, and the strange occurrence at Robozero in 1663, when "from the clearest of skies a great fire descended."

STRANGE UNIVERSE - A Sourcebook of Curious Astronomical Observations. Volume A1.
  Compiled and published by William Corliss; pp279; $7.95; ISBN 0 9600712 7 X. -- being the latest in the laudable Sourcebook Project and indispensible to anyone seriously interested in Fortean matters, or the history of ideas and discoveries. This volume establishes categories ranging through the planets, to

astronomical bodies of all kinds, including comets, meteors, 'Planet X', and the enigmatic objects seen floating around solar space (and which we call 'Vulcans' after Fort). Other aspects of astronomy-based controversy are also given their own sections: meteorite biology, myths and legends that seem to indicate real events, cosmic rays, gravity and relativity experiments, and the early (almost unbelievable) discussions of Bode's Law that appears to govern the distribution of the planets. The Sourcebooks are building nicely. I cannot over-estimate their value, especially in the future, when many of these critical sources will become generally unavailable in libraries.

I believe the second volume in the Strange Phenomena series, G2, has been published, and a new series Strange Life (biology) will be launched with its first vol. very soon, in turn to be followed by G3 and M2, the second in the Strange Artifacts series. Such endeavours are worthy of your support. Sourcebooks and further info are available from Corliss: Sourcebook Project, Glen Arm, MD21057, USA.

VIOLENT UNIVERSE by Nigel Calder. Omega pb; 90p; illos; 160pp; ISBN 0 8600 7720 9.
First published by the BBC in 1969, this review of modern cosmology has been brought up to date with additional material.

THE MAGIC OF URI GELLER by James Randi.
Ballantine Books pb; pp320; 65p. Randi has a feud on with Geller, and here discloses clever sleight-of-hand methods for achieving 'Geller effects' - which of course does not prove that Geller uses the same method.

▪▪▪▪▪▪▪▪▪▪▪▪▪▪▪▪▪▪▪▪▪▪▪▪▪▪▪▪▪▪▪▪▪▪
STOP PRESS: as we put this ish together, the papers are full of the news that a team from Boston Academy have substantial proof of the monsters in Loch Ness. A symposium will be held in Edinburgh in December when all will be revealed. We'll cover it in the next issue.
▪▪▪▪▪▪▪▪▪▪▪▪▪▪▪▪▪▪▪▪▪▪▪▪▪▪▪▪▪▪▪▪▪▪

Did You See...?

Reader's Digest, Oct 75 — 'Science Bends its mind to Uri Geller' by John Fuller; 'In Search of Noah's Ark' by Gordon Gaskill; 'Francis - A Saint for Today' by Ernest Hauser.

'Stone Axe Boom in the Bronze Age' an educated guess at ancient economics. Duetscher Forschungsdienst, Vol xiv (1975), p12.

'Plant "Primary Perception" - Electro -physiological unresponsiveness to Brine Shrimp Killing' by KA Horowitz, DC Lewis & EL Gasteiger. Fairly self-explanatory, if you followed that ruckus about whether a girl was being cruel to shrimps. An extension of Backster's experiments - measuring plant responses to killing shrimps. Science vol 189 (1975).

"Did Chinese Cosmology anticipate Relativity?" by John Gribbin. Nature vol 256, Aug 1975.

"Radiation Field Photographs" by Robin Frost. A general guide to DIY Kirlian photography. Amateur Photographer, 1 Oct 75, pp108-110.

"The Glozel Affair" by ET Hall — a summary of the controversy surrounding the thermoluminescence method of dating archeological plunder. Nature, vol 257, 2 Oct 75.

"A Megalithic Observatory on Dartmoor" by JE Wood & A Penny. Nature, vol 257, 18 Sept 75.

"The Year of the Shark" by Paul Betts — stories & photos of killer sharks and their victims (some of whom survived); including a summary of the enigmatic 'Shark Arm Murder' which rocked Sydney, Australia, when the only clue to an underworld murder was a tattooed arm found whole in a shark's belly. Yukk! Observer magazine, ? Aug 75.

"There were Fairies at the bottom of the Garden" — an interview by Walter Clapham with Elsie Wright & Frances Griffiths (now elderly ladies) who were the central figures in the controversy over the 'Cottingley Photos' which to this date (they were taken in 1917) have not been proved fakes, and purport to show 'real' fairies that the girls met in a local glen. This is a valuable reference because it sheds additional light on the background and motivation of the girls at the time. Woman, 25 Oct 75.

"Fabulous Animals" — a David Attenborough TV series on BBC 1 (Fridays 5pm) on mermaids, unicorns, yetis and dragons. An article on the programme, "Man, Myth & Monsters" by Adrian Bailey, appears in Radio Times 8 Nov 75.

"Riddle of the Pampa" — excellent photos of the Nazca lines, Peru (by Loren MacIntyre) accompany an article and interview (by Bruce Chatwin) with Maria Reiche, who has worked nearly 40 years on charting and preserving the lines. As we go to press, the Sunday Times, 16 Nov 75, relates tnat a Britisher, Julian Knott, is to take part in a balloon ascent to probe the theory that this is how the pre-Incas carried out these fantastic designs. News has reached us, too, of an exhibition of Maria Reiche's photos - we shall keep you informed. Chatwin & MacIntyre's exposition can be found in Sunday Times Magazine, 26 Oct 75.

New Scientist: 2 Oct - 'New Evidence for the Flood'confirms Plato's date of 11,600 years ago, not from the Med area but from drilling core samples in the Mexican Gulf,which show that a glacial surge about then raised the sea levels dramatically; the 'Flurocarbon File' reviews the study and effects of the gasses that threaten with cancer-risks and depletion of the Ozone-layer vital to our survival *** 16 Oct -'Bent Metal - or Children' news on the latest kids tested on bending metal sealed into tubes, and how the kids can cheat..but do they really? *** 23 Oct - 'Is Monoceros X-1 a Black Hole?'; and John Gribbin asks 'White

Holes - A Coming Fashion?' *** 4 Nov - Studies reveal that rainfall in South Africa comes in cycles of 3-4, 10-12, & 16-20 years. Even more interesting is the statement that different geographical areas have different periodicities (which confounds the obvious theories.) *** 13 Nov - 'In Search of the Biological Clock', something that regulates all the rhythms of growing things; Dr Roger Levin reports on an International convention on the present state of our knowledge and search.

LANTERN, the journal of the Borderline Science Investigation Group (BSIG), No11 Autumn 1975. Contains a special report on UFOs over Aldeby, East Anglia -- part 3 of MW Burgess' study of 'Mysterious Stones'-- Ron Hill on 'Bio-rhythms' -- another spook from the 19th century -- and roundup of latest UFOs & ghosts. Price 12p, annual sub is 70p. BSIG have also published a booklet, "Haunted Lowestoft", available for 40p. Write to the Editor, Ivan Bunn, 3 Dunwich Way, Lowestoft, Suffolk NR32 4RZ.

SPECTRUM, a quarterly journal of the Occult. No 8 contains a review of the 'arts' that comprise 'The Occult' - editor Mike Howard exploding some myths of Black Magic warfare - articles on the Runic Tradition, the modern occult movement, divination, and a report on the annual conference of the Astrological Association. Single issues 35p - annual sub £1.40. Cheques/POs payable to M.A. Howard: 18A Church Hill, Purley, Surrey CR2 3QN. NB: new address, prices and schedule.

After a noticeable absence due to a marketing dispute, FATE is back on the British newsstands - in a large format UK-edition with major articles from the US-edition. The First issue (Nov 75) deals with the Bermuda Triangle Hoax theory (of Larry Kuche), Avebury (James Dyer), the reality of UFOs as machines (Frank B Salisbury), and a 'Prehistoric Alphabet' (George Wagner). One sad omission is Curtis Fuller's rambling Fortean news column, which for me was one good reason for buying FATE. 25p per copy, from most newsagents.

* * * * * * * * * * * *

Compilation credits: Phil Ledger, Steve Moore, and Mum. Please send us a note of anything interesting that you come across.

Dr WB Crow, author of A History of Magic, Witchcraft & Occultism (amongst other works) is offering special tuition to a limited number of students in the following subjects: Kabalah; Tarot; Depth Psychology; Crown and Chivalric Symbolism; Church Symbolism; The Holy Grail; Astrological Symbolism; Oriental Religions (Brahminism, Buddhism, Taoism, Ancient Egyptian); Druidism; Atlantis and other lost civilisations.

Dr Crow was not only intimately acquainted with Dr CG Jung, but was analysed for some years by Jung's English assistant Dr Baynes, and was also privileged to write the reports of Dr Jung's Summer Schools in England and circulated to those attending (see p44 of Contact With Jung, edited by Michael Fordham.) Dr Crow gives tuition in the above subjects, especially Depth Psychology, including Jung's so-called Zurich School, more precisely known as Analytical Psychology.

If you're interested, please write to:
Secretary for Tuition.
78 Broadmead Road, Woodford Green, Essex.

or phone 01 504 9953.

◊ -- ◊ -- ◊ -- ◊ -- ◊ -- ◊ -- ◊ -- ◊ -- ◊ --

CONTACT-UK are holding their Annual General Meeting and London Lectures on Dec 6th, 2.30 to 10.00pm, at Caxton Hall, Caxton St, London. Although the Meeting is for members only, the public are invited to attend the lectures at 30p per head, commencing at 5.30pm. The speakers will include the Hon. Brinsley Le Poer Trench, and Prof John Taylor (who'll have films and slides).

" - ◊ - " - ◊ - " - ◊ - " - ◊ - " - ◊ - " -

We heard from Brad Steiger who is compiling a book on experiences of fairies and other so-called elementals. "I have never forgotten that night in my childhood when I lay in bed and watched out of the window in fascination as a small man in a conical hat stood on his tip-toes to another window and watched my parents move about in the kitchen of our Iowa farmhouse. After several moments the little man must have felt a sensation of someone watching him, for he turned to peer at me over his shoulder. I was able to get a good look at his tiny, pinched features in the light from the kitchen window. He smiled and shook his head. I'm not certain what happened next, but it seemed that his face came closer to my own. And then he simply disappeared.

"I am able to discuss this experience quite intellectually and "explain" it in approved psychological terms. I am prepared to regard the episode as the single most vivid dream of my childhood. At the time, though, I was convinced that I had seen a brownie or an elf - and I guess, regardless of my façade of sophistication toward the matter, I still believe that is precisely what I saw.

"I have since met many adult men and women who have privately admitted that they have seen "little people". Perhaps we comprise a rather unique secretive society, but I suspect that there are thousands of people who are "closet believers" in fairies, elves, and other nature spirits.

"I am gathering data and case histories of men and women who have seen the wee folk and/ or who have interacted with them on various levels of consciousness. If you, or your readers, have had such an experience and would like to share it for publication, please contact me at your earliest convenience."

Well - your editor's experience is singularly devoid of having little men peer at him -- but those of you with tales to tell can write to Brad , care of <u>Other Dimensions Inc</u>, 104½ Washington St, Decorah, Iowa 52101, USA .

_/= _/= _/= _/= _/= _/= _/= _/= _/=

<u>WARK</u> -- a magazine that reviews the Fantasy fanzines, and key reading if that's your bag. Copies can be had for 25p (20p to British Fantasy Society members), or free in return for usable letters or contributions. Rosemary Pardoe is your capable editrix, and can be contacted at 24 Othello Close, Hartford, Huntingdon PE18 7SU.

" * " * " * " * " * " * " * " * " * " * "

<u>L'ETA' DELL' ACQUARIO</u> a magazine devoted to the spiritual philosophies of the 'New Age' put out by Bernardino del Boca and edited by Edoardo Bresci. Unfortunately, it's all in Italian, but I can say it is distinctly Theosophical. Signor Boca is compiling the second edition of an <u>INTERNATIONAL GUIDE TO THE AGE OF AQUARIUS</u> which will list magazines and other publications, groups and movements, study groups and university courses, organisations, personalities -- a general cultural guide to the study, experimentation, research and implementation of spiritual philosophy in the New Age. All interested should write to Bernardino del Boca: Viale Monza 40, 20127 Milano, Italy. He is also keen, he tells me, to find an agent for the <u>Guide</u> in England.

@ * @ * @ * @ * @ * @ * @ * @ * @ * @ *

* * * * * * * * * * * * * * * * * * * *

"Most of the orthodox theories of the cosmos are collapsing. I would suggest that the universe is like a pair of trousers, in which we, and all the visible stars are in one leg, and the unknown parts, into which matter can collapse through a black hole, are in the other."
- Prof Yuval Ne'eman, Tel Aviv University. Quoted in 'Weekend', 14-20 Oct 1970.

* *   * *

Liu Ling (221-300AD), one of the seven Taoist 'Sages of the Bamboo Grove' famed for their perpetual inebriation, was in the habit of going about his house naked. Once, his perambulations were interrupted by some stuffy Confucians, come to consult him. They expressed surprise at his lack of trousers. Liu replied: "The whole universe is my house and this room is my trousers. <u>What are you doing here inside my trousers?</u>"

* *   * *

"Come unto me, and I shall make you fashionable. I conceive of nothing, in religion, science or philosophy, that is more than the proper thing to wear, for a while."
- Charles Fort.

a miscellany of Fortean curiosites

THE NEWS

SPECIAL 'MONSTER' ISSUE!!!
'SURREY PUMA' and other mystery animals...3

PLESIOSAURS?.... IN LOCH NESS?
PLESIOSELF!--THE RINES-SCOTT EVIDENCE ON NESSIE ------11

FW HOLIDAY on leys & UFOs ------9

STEEV MOORE on Greenwich phenomena ----18

UK ISSN 0306-0764

bimonthly news & notes
on Fortean phenomena

JANUARY 1976

THE NEWS is a non-profitmaking bimonthly miscellany of Fortean news, notes and references, affiliated
to the International Fortean Organisation (INFO) in
continuing the work of **Charles Fort** (1874 – 1932).
THE NEWS is edited by Robert JM Rickard:
**Post Office Stores, Aldermaston, Berks RG7 4LJ,
England.**

SUBSCRIPTIONS: 1 year – 6 issues – £3.00 / USA
$6.00. 2 years – 12 issues – £5.40 / USA $10.80
Single issues – 50p / USA $1.00. Back issues (if
available) 50p / USA $1.00. Current annual INDEX
free to subscribers, otherwise 30p. / USA 60¢.
Special joint subscription to **THE NEWS** and INFO
JOURNAL (including regular membership of INFO)
1 year – 12 issues – £6.40 / USA $12.80. All over-
seas subscribers paying by cheque should **add 10%** to
cover banking exchange commission.

CONTRIBUTIONS of articles, notes and artwork on
related subjects are always welcome and duly credited.
You can help us by sending us a copy or clipping of
any reference or data you think will interest us. Please
don't assume our omniscience – there are very few
duplications. We are especially glad to see items from
professional journals, local papers and OP books. But
please don't forget to add the source and date, and your
name for the credit.

SUBSCRIBE - OR DIE!

The old death-rattle of IT has passed,
like the Black Spot, to us. We need more
subscribers or we die! Here are the facts:
mid-75 we had a circulation of 200 plus –
which dropped to about 140 at year-end. This
was due to some (necessary) free issues, but
mainly lapsed subscriptions that have not
been renewed. Some of this may be a reaction
to our regrettable but very necessary price-
rise late last year, but I think this is more
probably the effect of the depression. Either
way it is a sad blow — thankfully, it's not
too late to do something about it. We only
need 200 people at the present rate - not many,
considering the number of Forteans there must
be.

Some people suggest we advertise more - I
wish we could. Subscriptions are staggered
over the year, so that not all the 140 plus
have paid the £3/$6.60, and the kitty total
fluctuates alarmingly - so that several times
I've only had a few pounds left after paying
for printing and postage, then over the inter-
issue period enough subs come in for the next
issue, and so on. It's not healthy - for me
or the mag - but there's no money for ads.
I have a plan — we must have a small fund
of working capital to level out the valleys
and peaks in revenue. Since there is no
other way, and since the NEWS is also its
readers (without whom it'd be vanity on my
part) - I appeal to you, the readers and
contributors who have supported us thus far,
for donations towards a working fund. With
that we can advertise more. With more readers,
we can look toward better printing, more
pages, and more reader services. For example:
the binders we mention below - if we had the
capital, we could go ahead immediately, but as
we are, we have to wait until we can muster
enough interested parties so we do not sustain a loss on the venture.

My future dreams for THE NEWS, apart from
building it up to the consistent quality and
standing of FSR, and the broad news and
article coverage of, say, a New Scientist, is
to get to the stage of a positive attack on
Fortean events, funding projects and research,
and with INFO, generate our own publishing
of reference works. I'd also like to see us
make use of the GPO Freepost scheme, issuing
our readers with postpaid cards, so that keeping us informed of events is not so much of a
direct burden on them. I'd also like to
increase our scope of coverage by subscriptions to news-clipping agencies, and to the
Centre for Short-lived Phenomena.

The alternative to failing to get more
readers one way or another, is to alter our
format. The way we are now is the lowest
equitable balance between low-cost and the
advantages of litho printing. Our small size
is very economical (2 pages on one side of
paper), but we pay the cost by being limited
...cont/ back page:

"It is not necessary that a gamekeeper should kill a luminous owl, and so
put an end to a mystery. A story that he did will serve just as well."
                                        Charles Fort. The Books, p627.

The 'Surrey Puma' & Friends: More Mystery Animals.

by RJM Rickard.

THE SURREY PUMA - REVISITED.

The list below is comprised of reported
sightings of 'Mystery Animals' (MAs) since,
or not included in,the list I published in
the INFO Journal 13 (1974)(pp3-18) which also
reviewed some 'wild' correlations with the
somewhat similar modus operandi of UFOs and
ghosts. As I mentioned at the time,some information was gleaned from the file on the
phenomenon at the Zoological Society of London
(hereinafter ZSL), being mainly correspondence
on the 62-64 flap, the 'Munstead Monster' and
sightings mentioned by ZSL members, addressed
to the Public Relations Officer, JA Dale, and
his predecessor, Miss Joan Crammond. I'd like
to express my sincere thanks here to Mr Dale
for his patience with my questions over a
couple of years, and his agreement to my
quoting from a few items in this file (designated in the list below, ZSL). By some
oversight, I omitted to credit the photo of
the Munstead pawprint (INFO 13 p16) to the
ZSL, and hope this rectifies that.

This present compilation of notes that have
accumulated since then is intended to supplement and extend the INFO article - and if
it seems I'm chucking you in the deep end,
please bear with me (or better still buy a
back copy of INFO Journal.)

IT'S RAINING FERAL CATS AND DOGS.

You'll find many references to tracks and
hair being found, but nothing conclusive has
been deduced from them so far. Even the famous
Munstead Monster prints (case 8 & photos in
INFO 13) succeeded in a public difference of
opinion between Dr Maurice Burton (who thought
they were bloodhound) and the ZSL who initially
thought it to be puma. Later, the ZSL changed
their mind - but even if Dr Burton was having
doubts himself he never voiced them. In the
face of conflicting evidence he grudgingly
admitted to the Daily Telegraph, 28 Aug 66
that there were tracks and sightings not
entirely explained by his theory. He said: "I
would not rule out the possibility that there
is something out of the ordinary in the area."
If I may be permitted to be harsh for a moment
this element of doubt is soon forgotten; this
"something out of the ordinary" is ignored
for the more provable theories and comfortable
evidence of "feral cats and dogs" (see Dr
Burton's statements in the Daily Telegraph,
23 Nov 66, and his writings listed in my
INFO article). What is sadder, is that we all
know this 'selective amnesia' (as JC Pearce
would call it) is only too typical of the
modern scientific orthodoxy. Thus the golden
moments,when it seemed as though we (all of us)
might be getting somewhere, slip away, and we
are left as much, if not more, in the dark as
we were - only this time with another muddle
to confuse the already hopelessly confused
issue. As an example of the rosy-glow time
puts on our memories, we attach part of a
letter to your editor from Dr Burton, dated
27 Oct 75. (I had asked Dr Burton if he was as
confirmed in his opinion now as he was then. By
reply he kindly summarized his position.)

"I was sceptical about the puma from the
very start, despite Miss Gompertz' observation
((one of the conflicting evidences I referred
to above; see also INFO 13 p9 col2 - Ed.)) and
after a long investigation I think I settled
the matter. To begin with,there was a large
feral domestic cat, ginger in colour, that was
highly aggressive, in the Farnham district.
This gave rise to the stories of a mystery
animal. Then came the discovery of the large
pawmark on the Munstead track of which the
police took a plastercast. This was pronounced
'puma' by the then Scientific Director of the
London Zoo. It proved to be beyond doubt the
pawmark of a large dog bloodhound although he
had said 'puma'. All the eye-witness accounts
that I was able to investigate at first-hand
proved to be either otter, badger, fox, deer,
or feral cats and dogs. Finally, two couples
of police patrol officers reported an unusual
animal near the Hog's Back Hotel ((on A31

between Farnham & Guildford - Ed.)) where the puma had been reported more frequently than anywhere else. After having had the opportunity to interrogate them, I came to the conclusion that we were dealing with a feral dog and within days of reaching this conclusion I learned that a greyhound had been feral in that area for two years and that it had an injured left paw which gave it a most unusual bouncing run, and that this animal had been shot on the order of the landowner because people were going onto his land allegedly to look for the puma, but probably also looking for his pheasants.

I wrote a long letter to the local news paper setting forth all my findings and after that the puma died a natural death except for occasional sporadic letters published in that paper's columns about a strange animal having been seen, each of which seemed beyond question to be merely a fox running across the road in the headlights of a car. During the two years that the hunt for the Surrey puma was on, there were reported throughout the southern half of England about a dozen large members of the Felidae, including lioness, cheetah and panther. All proved beyond doubt to be feral dogs or cats. There can be no doubt that the hysteria engendered by stories of a puma loose in the Surrey countryside spread well beyond the boundaries of that County and played on the imaginations of people far and wide.

(Signed) Dr Maurice Burton."

THE FORTEAN POSITION.

Clearly there is a division of opinion here and I'll declare where we Forteans stand. It should matter little to us whether there is a puma out there or not - since we accept that adherance to one theory at the expense of any other automatically conditions the sort of evidence you will find 'acceptible'. The point that interests us is that "there is something out of the ordinary in the area", to use Dr Burton's own words.

The Surrey Puma controversy is a microcosm of worldwide evidence for MAs of different kinds. The investigators of cases (eg Dr Burton & the ZSL) are clearly arguing on the basis of a 'real' puma being involved, and this has shown up anomalies in the evidence (as Dr Burton has several times written about) eg. the varieties of descriptions; the stories of 'puma' being seen in different places and it being 'impossible' to traverse the distance between in the time; the lack of depredations and other evidence, like carcases, lairs etc. These same problems of paradoxical evidence are met in nearly every area of investigation into the unknown, particularly UFOs and ghosts. They are generated by the limits of logic in extrapolating towards a complex phenomenon from single physical instances, even assuming this is done from rigorously established facts. On this level, we can applaud when a particular

case proves to Dr Burton's satisfaction (and anybody else's) to have involved a feral dog, but to extend that judgment to all cases, ipso facto, is sheer folly. Our opinion here is based on the stories below (and INFO 13), most of which were close observations, and the details in some cases do not suggest feral cats or dogs at all. Another reason for our attitude is that (as noted in the list below) we simply do not know what is running around out there. Just in the data to hand, there is an escaped mountain-lion (case 77); at least 4 baboons in Worcs (case 71) and an unknown number of baboons in Co Durham (cases 74 & 75); a racoon in Yorkshire (case 80)...not to mention the sudden appearance of at least four wild boars (see INFO article) in Hampshire, and the wild wallaby colonies in Derbyshire and Kent. Analytically too, the morphology of evidence in (some) of the listed cases presents correspondences with MA sightings from all over the world.

Just how complex the MA problem is, we are perhaps just begining to realise. If Jung can write of lights in the sky as symptoms of "long-lasting transformations of the collect-ive psyche" (Flying Saucers, Introduction), it could be suggested on the basis of Jung's own theories of transformation symbolism that these "changes in the constellation of psychic dominants" extend to unconscious shamanistic experiences involving animal phantoms, especially shape-changing ones. This argument includes whatever it is that happens to people at Loch Ness. Further, we have the problem of whether the mind can influence our 'Reality', and Ted Holiday's article (this issue) goes into that to some degree.

Nor should we neglect to mention the con-tinuity with ancient folk tradition and lore. Just as, for example, the medieval legends of phantom ships in the sky can be shown to be comprable and continuous with modern UFOs (see 'The Phantom Ship & The UFO' by Peter Rogerson MUFOB, new series 1), so the MA phenomenon has its avatars; in our case, with 'Fairy Dog & Cats', the Black Dog, and other phantom beasts.

But lest we be hoist with the same petard, let us say that undoubtedly there have been cases of feral dogs and cats; and people mistaking badgers and otters for something else - but, by and large, the witnesses are those who live in the country, who have lived with country sounds and sights, and when they say it was not a fox, I'm inclined to believe them. Too often in the past, in this and other subjects (like meteorites), scientists have too easily dismissed evidence because the witnesses were only countryfolk, less educated than themselves, their sense of superiority blinding them to their duty to impartial scientific investigation. Hoaxers in this subject are extremely rare and usually readily apparent. Our data is mainly from reported firsthand experiences, and I think deserves to be considered seriously.

Supplementary list of Mystery Animal Phenomena in England. (Extension from INFO Journal 13.)
NB: These cases have been subnumbered for correct insertion into chronological sequence.

9.2	1? Sept 64.	Wyphurst, Hants?	Deer carcase devoured. (Mentioned in ZSL correspondence to Miss J Crammond, PRO. 1 Nov 66.)
12.	25 Sept 64.	Dunsfold, Surrey.	Add info: ginger-colour; 5-6ft long; 3ft high. Daily Mirror, 26 Sept 64.
12.2	25 Sept 65.	nr Godalming, Surrey.	Big cat seen crossing road during hunt for it. "but when the alarm was raised, police & zoo officials who were hunting it, were all at lunch." Daily Express, 26 Sept 64.
13.2	2 Oct 64.	? (Hants/Surrey.)	Animal seen leaping 10-12ft into undergrowth. (Source: as 9.2 above.)
13.3	Early Oct 64.	Robins Garth Kennels, West Sussex.	Lady walking dogs in woods, although couldn't see its head, was "In no doubt.." it was the "Puma". 6ft long; 3ft high; fawn gold colour. Dogs chased it into woods whence came "spitting & scree-ching sounds". Paw marks found near farm showing clear claw impressions. Midhurst & Petworth Observer, 13 Oct 64.
14.2	Late Oct 64.	Farley Mount, nr Winchester, Hants.	Police search following reports of wounded "puma". Gamekeeper shot at "black slit-eyed animal". (London) Evening News, 24 Oct 64.
14.3	Late Oct 64.	Kings Sumbourne, nr Winchester, Hants.	Gamekeeper saw "puma" twice.
		Crondall area, Hants/Surrey border.	"Puma" reported several times. (London) Evening News, 28 Oct 64.
23.2	4 Feb 65.	Woodlands, nr Southampton.	Woman phones paper, "Puma" is on her lawn.
		Newforest, (both in) Hants.	Girl in village (4 miles from above) says she has seen an animal resembling puma. (London) Evening Standard, 4 Feb 65.
28.2	4 May 66.	Newton Valance, Hants.	Lady write to ZSL of "strange animal" that left footprints. Correspondence to JA Dale, PRO ZSL, 4 May 66.
30.2	1 Sept 66.	Chiddingfold, Hants.	Lady farmer stopped Landrover ("for unknown reason") and walked through thistle patch - step-ped on tail of "puma". It reared, attacking with both paws, scratching her cheek. She hit it with stick - it ran, climbed tree. She went for assist-ance, but it had gone during absence. A Ministry of Agriculture & Fisheries official found no tracks, only some hair. Internal ZSL memo, 2 Sept 66.
40.2	? Dec 70.	Buckland Housing Estate, Dover, Kent.	7 reports of "puma" over 3 weeks. 4 sheep killed. "large animal believed to be a puma." (London) Evening Standard, 21 Dec 70. Cr:N Watson.
45.2	15 July 71.	Chiswell Green, nr St Albans, Herts.	2ft high grey cat-like (but bigger) animal seen at derelict Plaistow Farm by policeman who thought it was "puma". Search later-nothing-no escapes. (Herts) Evening Echo, 16 July 71; Herts Advertiser, 23 July 71. Cr: Janet Bord. NEWS 9/16.
45.3	Mid-July 71.	Nutley, Ashdown Forest, Sussex.	2 policemen saw puma-like animal; black & tan with streaks of yellow; pointed ears. It attacked a dog at Outback Farm. We wrote - but no reply to date. The Times, 23 July 71. Cr: Nigel Watson.

47.2	Mid-June 72.	Polegate to Folkington road, Sussex.	Large cat-like animal running at 35mph. Larger than cat. Seen week before jumping 5ft fence. (London) Evening News, 14 June 72. Cr: Janet Bord. NEWS 9/16.
48.2	? June 72. 3.30am.	Stone St (Roman road) between Lympne and Canterbury, Kent.	Large "definitely cat-like" animal ran in front of car. Broad, bushy, black-banded tail. Folkstone Herald, 27 Jan 73. Cr: L Coleman.
58.2	4 Jan 73.	Capel-le-Ferne to Alkham road, Kent.	7ft long; short brown hair; sleek & graceful; ran in front of car. Tracks found - pads, big as "man's hand." No reports of lambs killed. Folkstone Herald, 10 Jan 73. Cr: L Coleman.
58.3	Early Jan 73.	Sway, Hants.	Ref to "puma" seen. (Source: see 58.4 below.)
58.4	Late Jan 73	A35. Christchurch to Lyndhurst - by turning to Bank, Hants.	"Largest cat I've seen in my life"; "not a badger". Large, black, low-slung, cat-like body; longer than, but not high as, Labrador; short head. Ran in front of car - car hit tail. Southern Evening Echo, 29 Jan 73. Cr: Coleman.
59.2	Feb (73?).	Winsor, near Southampton, Hants.	Animal seen "larger tnan Alsatian." Deep claw marks in clay ditch. (Source: see 64 below.)
64	Late 73.(?)	Woodlands, near Southampton, Hants.	3 children & dog on Lower Bartley Rd see cat-like animal, larger than their Alsatian, creeping along in grass; big head; stick-up cat-like ears; fierce eyes; tawny brown. It bounded away at a noise. Boy later identifies 'Puma' from an animal book. Southern Evening Echo, late 73. Cr: L Coleman.
65	3 Nov 73.	Rake to Harting Combe road, Hants.	Large black cat-like animal; tufted fur on back; lighter flanks; long black tail; bigger than Alsatian. Ran in front of car. The (?) News, 5 Nov 73. Cr: Loren Coleman.
66	28 Nov 73.	Winchester by-pass, Hants.	Woman Pc saw "jaguar" cross in front of car. None missing from zoos. Southern Evening Echo, 28 Nov 73. Cr: Coleman.
67	Early 74.	Ayrshire.	Anonymous caller to RSPCA asks them to pull the teeth on his "growling cat". Nothing more known. NEWS 7/2. Sunday Mirror, 23 June 74. Cr: Robert Forrest.
68	7 April 74. 3.30am.	Junction of Western Ave. and Bury Rd, Boscombe, Bournemouth, Hants.	Big as a medium-sized dog; "half cat, half dog"; "not a fox". Thin striped body; long thin tail; grey with some yellow; ears set back like cat. Identified 'Tasmanian pouched wolf' from book. "loping" across road in car headlights. Bournemouth Evening Echo, 7 April 74. Cr: Mucha. NEWS 9/19-20.
69	? May 74. (over several weeks.	Delamere Forest, nr Kingsley; Hatchmere Lake; & Kingsley to Oakmere road, Cheshire.	Dog-like animal with a tail like a fox. "Certain it wasn't a fox". 2ft high. Runcorn Weekly News, 30 May 74. Cr: Peter Rogerson. NEWS 9/20.
70	14 June 74. (apx). 7am.	Barrmill to Beith road, North Ayrshire.	"like some kind of lion"; "not a dog"; bounded across road into fields. 2½-3ft high; heavy legs; large paws; long curled-up tail.
	12pm.		Second incident. Driver forced to stop few feet away from animal sitting in road, in full beam headlignts. After 5mins, he attempts to drive around it; bumps it; it growls.
			Police search - nothing "unusual" found. No eascapes from zoos. Conjectured that animal in case 67 (above) had been let loose. NEWS 7/2.

			Sunday Express, 16 June 74. Cr: P Rogerson. Big cat, believed to weigh "40lbs". Sunday Mirror, 23 June 74. Cr: R Forrest.
71	8 July 74.	Wyre Forest, Worcs/Shrops border.	80 baboons escape from West Midlands Safari Park. (Birmingham) Evening Mail, 13 July 74. NEWS 9/15.
72	9 July 74.	Kinson, Hants.	Wallaby caught in High St. The Sun, 10 July 74. NEWS 9/18.
73	13 July 74.	Wyre Forest, Worcs/Shrops border.	Case 71 cont. All but 4 baboons recaptured. (Source: see Case 71 above.)
74	12 Aug 74. (apx).	Chester-le-Street, Co Durham.	Unstated number of baboons escape from Lambton Safari Park. Some returned - some still loose. The Sun, 13 & 14 Aug 74. NEWS 9/15.
75	? Sept 74.	Chester-le-Street, Co Durham.	Another "mass escape" of baboons from Lambton Safari Park. Some recaptured - some still loose. Daily Mirror, 3 Sept. Cr: Forrest. NEWS 9/15.
76	? Oct 74.	Oldington Woods, Kidderminster, Worcs.	Case 71 cont. Baboons seen crossing road near sugar factory. Sunday Mercury, 27 Oct 74. NEWS 9/15.
77	1 Jan 75.	Byton, Herefordshire.	Mountain-lion escapes. Caught during search. Escapes again - still free. Daily Mirror, 2 Jan 75. NEWS 9/16-17.
78	4 Jan 75.	Colchester Zoo, Essex.	8 week-old panther cub vanishes from zoo. Presumed stolen.
	5 Jan 75.	East Peckham, Kent.	2ft long panther cub found by fisherman on banks of river Medway. NEWS 9/17. Daily Express, 7 Jan 75. Cr: Steev Moore. Weekly News, 18 Jan 75. Cr: Nigel Watson.
79	15 Jan 75.	Langham, Norfolk.	2 'lion'cubs seen romping on council rubbish tip. Council ratcatcher failed to find them. The Sun, 16 Jan 75. NEWS 9/17.
80	12 Feb 75.	Skipwith to Thurganby road, Skipwith Common, nr Riccal, Yorks.	Man sees "bear"; "I'm sure it was a bear." Not fully grown; brown/black footpads; apx 5ft high; big as Alsation on all fours; dark brown skin (sic). Police check on zoos - no bears missing. Ref. to 3 racoons escaping from Flamingo Park Zoo, near Pickering, Yorks - 2 recaptured; 1 still loose. Cr: JW Scaife. NEWS 9/16. Yorks. Evening Press, 13,14 & 17 Feb 75.
81	6 March 75.	Brooks Green, near Horsham, Sussex.	"Large cat-like animal" made two horses shy, throwing their girl riders. It crossed fields towards Barns Green. Also seen in area by man. Police search find tracks & hair on fence. RSPCA say "90-120lbs animal; no claw-marks, so not dog." Police say "First reliable evidence of its ('Puma's') existence." West Sussex County Times, 7 March 75. Cr:Start. The Sun, 7 March 75. Cr: Phil Ledger. NEWS 9/18.
82	9 March 75.	M23. Pease Pottage, Sussex.	Thought to be cont. of Case 81. "Puma" seen sitting by the motorway. NEWS 9/18. West Sussex County Times, 14 March 75. Cr:Start.

The NEWS reference refers to a fuller account published in our pages.

ADDITIONAL DATA - ATTACKS & ESCAPES.

We include some material in the above list which is not strictly "Surrey Puma" stuff, but which seems directly related to the question of MAs generally, at the time. For instance: the anonymous caller in case 67, seems related to the appearance a cat-like animal later that year (Case 70); 80 baboons escape in the Wyre Forest, the next day a wallaby turns up in Hampshire, and shortly after that there are two mass escapes of baboons in Co Durham

(Cases 71 - 76). One cannot help but dwell on whether synchronicity is involved in these events. Consider case 78: a panther cub 'vanishes' from a zoo - next day a fisherman 40 miles away finds a panther cub. It was claimed to be the same cub - but was it? Why would someone steal it (and how?) just to let loose in the wilds? (There's no accounting for the freaks of human endeavour!) Or again, during the bear-scare in Yorkshire (case 80) it becomes known that there is also a racoon on the loose in the area - please turn to NEWS 9/16, where the witness & searchers say they can positively distinguish between the two.

We have too much material to fit it all in here, but some issues this year will have more on attacks on animals, escapes, and attacks by animals. But having just mentioned a noticable element of synchronicity in some recent cases, I must mention that on 5 Nov 75 4 lions escaped from Robert's Circus at Gainsborough, Lincs. One of the lionesses mauled a 10-yr-old boy who died later. On the same day (and apparently about the same time) a park warden at Windsor Safari Park, Berks, was stalked and killed by a tiger. Details can be found in most national papers 6,7 & 21 Nov 75. Cr: Steev Moore, Robert Forrest.

Though many stories turn out to be of no great significance to us here, I must mention my favourite non-story in all this mish-mash. In May 1969, A Mr & Mrs Faulder of Purley, Surrey, phoned the police in terror, saying that a strange small monster with a white head was tapping at their door. PCs rushed to the scene and found the beast in some nearby bushes. It was a hedgehog with a yoghurt carton jammed over its head. Reveille, 19 Dec 70. Cr: Nigel Watson. Somehow it could be an object lesson to the human race.

The old "kill the mystery" gambit continues to be played for all its worthlessness. Harking back to the INFO listing: a feral tomcat was shot in Feb 66 (case 27) and the end of the 'mystery' was proclaimed. Same again when the strange bear-like prints (case 41, photos in INFO 13) were identified by Chessington Zoo as "seagull" prints. And again when, during a series of sightings by Fleet station (case 55), someone saw a Siamese cat in the area. To this we can add that at Avening, Gloucestershire, a stray cat which had attacked 9 children over a period was trapped and shot, in mid Sept75. Sunday Express, 21 Sept 7" Laughably, we have had no "puma" reports since then.

★ ★ ★ ★ ★

In our reading we have come across three interesting stories of historical MAs that relate to our study.

THE WILD BEAST OF GEVAUDAN - 1764/5.

Something similar to the "Surrey Puma" scare occurred in the Languedoc area of France in the winter of 1764/5 - but a good deal more sinister. We have seen allusions to the case in various places, and thought it'd be nice to put the material on a more modern record - especially since it has definite affinities with the problems of reporting strange animals that we dwell on in this issue, and is an important case in its own right in the chronology of MA history.

The earliest account is found in the Paris Gazette, late 1764; that a strange beast had already devoured 20 persons, mainly young girls, in the region of Langagne and the forest of Mercoire, and terrified the woodcutters. It is described as "much higher than a wolf, low before, and his feet are armed with talons. His hair is reddish, his head large, and the muzzle of it is shaped like that of a greyhound; his ears are small and straight; his breast is wide and grey; his back streaked with black; his large mouth is provided with sharp teeth that have taken off several heads as clean as a razor." It attacked swiftly, crouching low, springing for the neck and throat. "He is afraid of oxen, which he runs away from."

The 'Wild Beast of Gevaudan' (as it came to be called), continued to elude many hunts for it. At Meude, a letter dated 21 Dec 1764 says, a detatchment of dragoons had been after it for 6 weeks; yet "The day before yesterday he devoured a little girl who looked after cattle." Not surprisingly, the province offered a bounty of 1000 crowns.

On 12 Jan 1765, it attacked seven children near Montpellier. A letter (presumably to the Paris Gazette) said: "The beast flew at one of the boys; but the three eldest, by beating him with stakes, the ends of which were iron, obliged him to retire, after having bitten off part of the boy's cheek, which he ate before them. He then seized another child; but they pursued him to a marsh close by, where he sank up to his belly. By continually beating him they rescued their companion. A man at last coming up, put the creature to flight. He afterwards devoured a boy at Mazel, and on the 21st ((Jan - the letter is dated 8 Feb.)) flew on a girl, who, however, escaped with dangerous wounds. The next day he attacked a woman and bit off her head. Captain Duhamel of the dragoons has caused several of his men to dress in women's apparel and to accompany the children that keep the cattle." Louis XV, on hearing of the boys beating off the beast awarded them 700 livres.

In England these reports were treated with no less incredulity than elsewhere in Europe. Lloyds Evening Post quoting from Dutch papers said: "The accounts of the wild beast of the Gevaudan are of such a nature that it is hardly possible to give any credit thereto, and

Cont on p17//.

We had scheduled for this issue an article by Ted Holiday on the Rines' photos - he was up at the Loch when the photos were taken - but a hasty note asked us to hold it back because something quite important had happened that related to his theories of The Great Orm of Ness and other lochs. We'll bring you news as it unfolds - meanwhile we present Mr Holiday's reply to Robert Forrest's article, 'Leys, UFOs & Chance' in the last issue.

Leys and those Whatsits.

by FW Holiday.

I see that Robert Forrest has put his critique of leys, UFOs and the chance factor into print in your journal. My own approach is pragmatic rather than theoretical.

In 1966 I had a splendid view of a UFO at a range of about half a mile through 10x50 binoculars. The oval object looked like a beautiful golden easter-egg which I judged was about 25 feet long on its axis. It was cruising through the night sky almost level with my position on a hillside over a landscape I knew well. It was moving about the speed of a fast car on a road. It seemed to be translucent and was lit from within. There were no visible features such as wings, windows or engines; it was soundless.

At that time I doubt if I had even heard of ley-lines. It was only when I started plotting the   lines connecting megalithic sites in South Wales that I noticed the object had in fact been travelling up a line 24 miles long connecting the following:
* a tumulus near Pendine (the origin);
* summit of a 600ft hill;
* site of ancient church at Church Farm;
* Whitland Abbey ruins;
* tumulus at Cross Hands;
* Hebron Church;
* hill-top cairn on Foel Dyrch;
* cairn on Crugiau Dwy;
* Crug-yr-Hwch burial chamber;
* ancient church at Plas Lawrence; and the
* ancient burial chambers at Pant-Y-Croes (terminates).

Early last year, two UFOs were reported close to the ground near Haverfordwest on dates a week apart.((see NEWS 9/11-12 - Ed.)) Together with a friend - Randall Jones-Pugh, MRCVS - who reports these sightings to BUFORA, we interviewed the witnesses. I also took maps. One sighting was of a strange light which descended into a wood: the other was of a smallish oval object hovering at ground level, much to the fright of two witnesses who encountered it on a tractor, when it at once flew away. These objects came down on or very near the lines of the ley triangulation shown in this diagram.

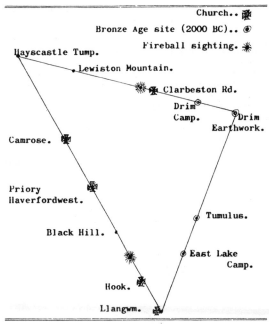

Church.. 🕱
Bronze Age site (2000 BC).. ◉
Fireball sighting. ☀

Hayscastle Tump.
Lewiston Mountain.
Clarbeston Rd.
Drim Camp.
Drim Earthwork.
Camrose.
Priory Haverfordwest.
Tumulus.
Black Hill.
East Lake Camp.
Hook.
Llangwm.

One swallow (or even three) doesn't make a summer, nor do these three observations prove a theory. When monks found that wounds often healed when you slapped a slice of cheese on them, that proved nothing much either. It was some 400 years before we found that this does work and why. Today we call it penecillin. I think that UFOs and leys are like a slice of cheese.

In my opinion ley-lines stand or fall in correlation with megalithic artefacts such as tumuli, cromlechs, together with religious buildings which were often built on these sites. We should remember, however, that many sites have been almost completely obliterated, such as the megalithic village which existed on the Prescelly Hills near where the Stonehenge bluestones were collected. This village can be clearly seen from the air using infrared photography. Few archeologists have even heard about this site.

In correspondence, Mr Forrest queried my insistence that a megalithic ley-line triangulation I had given him was in fact in the proportions 8:15:17. Professor Thom, however, says that megalithic man knew at least three Pythagorean triangles, including the largest, 12:35:17.

Mr Forrest asked me if this example was integral in megalithic yards. Since we are dealing with a triangle with a hypotenuse of some 11 & 5/16 miles, and a base of some 7 & 15/16 miles, such precise measurements are not known. Ordinary surveying is accurate to about 1:1000. To obtain an accuracy of 1:100,000 you would need ground markers, a helicopter and two lasers.

There are three options with leys. You can argue that they do not exist - in which case the critics have an awful lot of aligned tumuli to get rid of. You can argue that the lines are a product of prehistoric surveying for purposes unknown. Or you can take the attitude that the lines are places where some sort of linear force exists which can be detected by dowsing. I take the latter view - and my dowsing rods agree.

Mr Forrest is a professional mathematician whereas my humble talent sank without trace in the bogs of calculus, so I cannot comment on his diagram. I simply have a gut reaction

that leys and the flying whatsits are just a big slice of smelly Roquefort ((Nice to see you fitting Fort in somehow - Ed.)) waiting for a latterday Fleming to come along and slap a label on them. But, as with cheese, the time may not be ripe.

Some very good mathematical minds have applied themselves to the UFO-ley-line mystery and Mr Forrest is in the good company of Aimé Michel and Jaques Vallée in failing to discover a meaningful pattern. It is nobody's fault. There is almost certainly a paranormal block in action over this, just as there is in most psychical research. The ancients certainly believed this when they wrote in Ecclesiasticus:

"For at the first she will walk with him by crooked ways, and bring fear and dread upon him, and torment him with her discipline until she may trust his soul, and try him by her laws. Then she will return the straight way unto him and comfort him, and show him her secrets."

The brilliant psychologist Sir Cyril Burt believed there are such blocks and so does Dr Lyall Watson. So do I.

I suggest that Mr Forrest explains the meaning of the 8:15:17 Pembrokeshire triangle instead of arguing why UFOs would not appear on it.

FW Holiday, 1976.

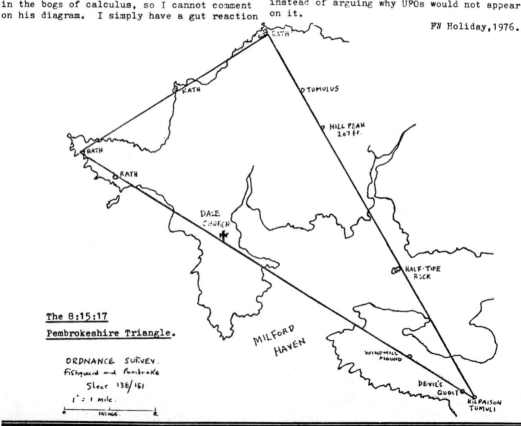

The 8:15:17
Pembrokeshire Triangle.

ORDNANCE SURVEY.
Fishguard and Pembroke
Sheet 138/151
1" : 1 mile.

"Then the Emperor walked along in the procession under the gorgeous
canopy, and everybody in the streets and at the windows exclaimed:
"How beautiful the Emperor's new clothes are!"...Nobody would let it
appear that he could see nothing, for then he would not be fit for
his post, or else he was a fool." Hans Christian Anderson.

The Emperor's New Monster

by RJM Rickard.

I have before me a vast heap of clippings
on the recent Nessie business. For a subject
that annually attracts the ridicule of the
mass-media, the reporters certainly got some
milage out of their pencils this time. We'll
ignore most of the pap and concentrate on
the central issues as they were reported, and
leave the rest to tne next issue, including
a salutory assemblage of all the different
versions of what plesiosaurs are supposed to
look like.

The much-heralded meeting at which all
would be revealed, to be held in Edinburgh
on 9 Dec, under the aegis of the Royal Society
of Edinburgh, and the Universities of Heriot-
Watt, and Edinburgh, was cancelled 8 days in
advance, because, it was said, the principal
parties had all stated their positions in
public, and loudly, and that "useful or
impartial discussion would no longer be
possible." (1). Tim Dinsdale was reported as
saying: "It's like the calm of a battlefield
before the crunch. A few star shells have
gone up showing where everybody is. Soon the
gunfire will start." (2). Yes folks! It's the
Science-in-Action show!

Nevertheless, Sir Peter Scott and Dr
Robert Rines went ahead with their public un-
veiling, timing a press-conference held in the
House of Commons on the 10th Dec, with the
publication next day of their article in
Nature, to be shortly followed by Nicholas
Witchell's history of the phenomenon and the
Loch Ness Investigation Bureau, The Loch Ness
Story, in paperback by Penguin.

THE PHOTOS.

The photographic evidence was shown to a
number of experts all over the world, who, as
Dr John Sheals, keeper of zoology at the
British Museum, said, were sworn by "a solemn
vow of secrecy." (3). Surprisingly, it seems
Rines was the first to break this pledge, as
various newspapers reported on the 5th Dec, by
flashing the pictures at a law school lecture
at Concord, New Hampshire.

I wasn't at the Commons press-conference,
I hazard a guess there were no gasps of surprise when the photos were unveiled - more

probably the creak of straining neck-muscles,
and the whirr of mentally riffing through
repertoires of glib questions and pat comments.

The presentation and press exposure has
been geared to notions of a 'monster' in Loch
Ness, something the British Museum team, dubbed
the 'Kensington Five' by the Observer (4), could
not agree with. It may seem to Rines et al
the the Five were being deliberately pig-headed
in ignoring their "convincing" proof, but
hair-splitting, especially in Taxonomy (the
naming and identification of things), is their
daily business.

A 4-page document was handed out at the
Commons conference, setting out the endorse-
ments of the experts who had examined the
photos, including Alan Gillespie of the Jet
Propulsion Laboratory, Caltech, in charge of
the image enhancement process used for
clarifying images on foggy film, who wrote:
"One picture showed a body with a long neck
and two stubby appendages..The second frame
appeared to show a neck and head, with the
head closer to the camera than the body..The
neck was reticulated. The head supported
projections..I see no evidence that they are
pictures of a model, toy..or whatever. I
emphasize: I detect no evidence of fraud.
These objects are not patterns of algae,
sediment or gas bubbles." (5). The other 7
endorsees were also at pains to point out
Rine's earlier (1972) photograph which appeared
to show a flipper-like appendage, and concurred that the current photos show an object
"most reasonably interpreted as the upper
third of the body of an animal.." in the
words of Prof Roy Mackal, Chicago University.
(5). Dr Zug, curator of reptiles & amphibians
at the Smithsonian, was more specific: "I
believe these data indicate the presence of
large animals in Loch Ness, but are insufficient to identify them." (5)

Sir Frank Claringbull, Director of the
British Museum, said to the press: "Five of
our experts have seen the pictures of the so-
called monster and they don't believe it's an
animal. It's a piece of tree." (6). This must
have had Rines groaning aloud - but the actual
statement issued by the Kensington Five makes

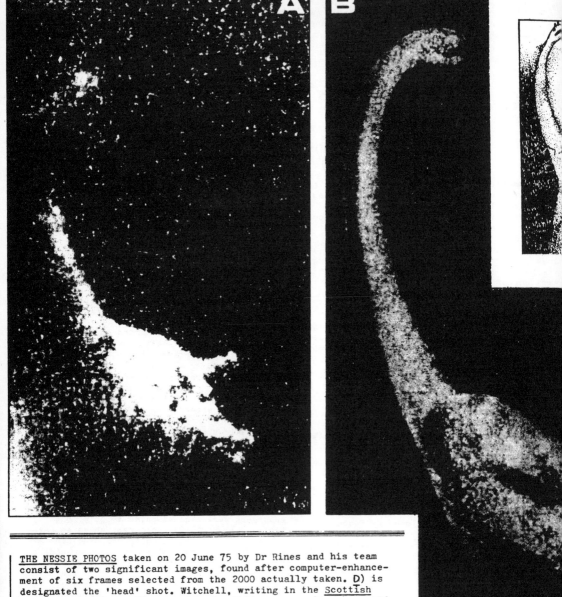

THE NESSIE PHOTOS taken on 20 June 75 by Dr Rines and his team consist of two significant images, found after computer-enhancement of six frames selected from the 2000 actually taken. D) is designated the 'head' shot. Witchell, writing in the Scottish Sunday Mail, 23 Nov 75, visualised a "hideous, angular, bony and revolting" face, with a prominent bony ridge running down the face into a thick, hard-looking upper lip, below two nostrils. There were "two tubes or stalks protruding from the top of its head," and its skin was "rough and mottled" and coloured "red-brown". E) is a visualisation by Daily Mirror artist Terry Dickie, 11 Dec. A) the photo claimed by a string of experts to show a body, long neck and head, taken by the Edgerton equipment at 35ft down in 80ft of water. Nature (1) says the body is 20-25ft from the camera, which is pointing 30° up from horizontal. The head & neck are estimated to be 7-12ft in length. The adjacent frames (1 min before and after) show nothing. B) how the Daily Mail artist Kevin Crowley interpreted it, and C) the Daily Mirror's version (both of 11 Dec). Note one shows the back & the other a side view. Sir Peter Sc (5) said he thought it was front view. The result, s

no reference to a tree. They are "entirely satisfied with the integrity and sincerity of the investigating team and the authenticity of the photographs," but the photos did not constitute "acceptable evidence of the existence of a large living animal."(7). My underlining is to emphasize that the BM did not suggest the photos were a hoax. But this is where the hairsplitting begins -- Rines & Scott say the two photos, plus the flipper ones of 72 and the verified sonar traces,all suggest a large living creature, even a family of them, in the Loch. The detractors say Rines has not proved they are photos of (even) the same animal, and that,when considered individually,were wholly inconclusive, and to conjecture a family of monsters from apparently unconnected evidence is verging on fantasy. To be fair, the sonar records are synchronous with the 72 photos. And despite the fact that the JPL expert in charge of image-enhancement, Alan Gillespie, spoke of control experiments, Rines could not satisfy the BM that test photos were taken in situ to judge visibility, resolution, perspective, etc, in the peaty murk of the Loch. Drifting trees were suggested, and I have no record of Rines refuting that either. But Gillespie said he was quite happy that there was a solid body in the water suggestive of a large animal.

THE EVIDENCE.

The photos, then, show up something, with insufficient clues to it being a tree or a monster, or to link it to the flipper-photos. It is suggestive - but so is a Rorschach blot. Technically I think the BM is right in this detail, but to say that only bones or a carcase will convince them immediately assumes the physicality of the monster phenomenon, and they become as guilty as Rines of prejudging the issue. Such unproductiveness is the result of a slavish automatic application of an inflexible scientific procedure. There is nothing wrong with the 'scientific method' per se - like everything else it responds best to intelligent application. Fort was writing the scenarios for these types of confrontation nearly 50 years ago. Deliberately or not,there are also historic processes at work. The BM and other establishment detractors have negated or discredited single pieces of evidence every time they arise, often in an unjust and bigoted way. But the evidence has, nevertheless,accumulated - but instead of examining the total case anew, they adopt an ancient position atop their heap of precedents. By God! gentlemen, you're capable of better than that! The trouble is that such a re-examination would take time and money, and an untrammelled spirit of inquiry - and in this era of 9-to-5 scientists, governments watching their money, and establishments their vaunted reputations,the odds on all three elements coming together grow daily more improbable.

In an article in Field, a few months before this storm broke, David James MP spoke hotly of zoologists being impervious to the accumulated evidence, the

e Mail, is remkably like a esiosaur, ast seen ound the earth me 40 million ars ago." Ch ah? By whom ..?

difficulties of fraud as gadgetry gets more complex, and of the arrogant writing-off of all the solid eye-witness accounts.(8).

Dr Maurice Burton, whom we have met earlier in these pages, adopts the same technique with Nessie as he does with the MAs in the south of England. In 1961, he wrote: "My final conclusion is that the phenomenon known as the Loch Ness Monster is a mixture of gas filled vegetable mats, turbulences caused by gas escaping from faults in the bed of the Loch, commonplace objects including boats and birds seen at a distance and sometimes distorted by mirage effects, waves due to convection currents and to winds, slicks, windrows, otters and deer, and doubtless other things besides."(20).

Pomposity and obstinacy among scientists is as hard to budge as that of sheer crankery - not because of any inherant virtue, but because of the cumulation over decades of refusing to look dispassionately, so that prejudice snowballs - and refutation becomes a task that involves volumes of historical material, which in turn scares each side off. It was left to the able TC Lethbridge to call Dr Burton's bluff: "I do not believe that Highlanders could have been deceived by the explanations he suggests. It is altogether too much to expect one to believe that a Grant of Invermoriston, beside the loch, could be mistaken by a mat of rotting vegetation, a swimming deer, or a string of bubbles, into thinking that he was witnessing some very unusual occurrence. (Many of the observers) were obviously not the kind of people who could make the astonishing mistakes in observation ascribed to them."(9).

A rather jocular piece of sniping using some of Dr Burton's type of 'explanations', by New Scientist, before the photos were published, failed to come off, when they published a letter from Peter (In Search of Lake Monsters) Costello pointing out all their inaccuracies. For example, NS alleged that "one of the most famous" of the Nessie photos had been printed upside down "ever since it was first published in 1934." Costello answers: "It is nonsense to suggest that the Wilson photo of a long neck has been printed upside down since 1934. True, the Hugh Grey 1933 photo was once printed upside down by an Oslo paper in 1933 - but nowhere else." (21).

As a track record, the establishment can only point to a string of feeble attempts at discrediting. We have to agree with Lethbridge that, "we seem to find that the zoologists have not made out an acceptable case against the monsters. They must do far better if they are to refute the observations of a great number of intelligent people. Here and there they are probably right and can account for some of the things that have been observed. As a whole, however, they have not produced a good explanation."(9).

Just to drive the point home, Holiday, in his Dragon and the Disc, mentions a BBC TV debate on this subject, in late July 1968, with himself and Prof Mackal for, and Dr Burton against, with 30 members of the Law Society as jury. "The opposition..mustered the same stale arguments I had heard so often before. None of these critics had done a field-study, checked the many witnesses, or tried to see the phenomena for themselves. They merely presented an unscientific chunk of indigestible prejudice. The Law Society took note of this and we won our case." (10).

Paul Willis, President of INFO, quoted an apt passage from a story by Arthur Machen in his letter to the Washington Star, 12 Dec 75: "'The paleontologist might see monstrous, significant marks in the slime of a river bank, but he would never draw the conclusions that his own peculiar science would seem to suggest to him: he would choose any explanation rather than the obvious, since the obvious would also be the outrageous - according to our established habit of thought, which we deem final.'"

Thus an exasperated Rines was heard to moan: "Jeeeesus...why do they all keep talking about a goddam object? Why don't they call it an animal?"(4). He has our sympathy.

I have heard of references to people's theories that Rines was hoaxed by a third party, but I haven't the sources - besides it gets incredibly complicated and too far fetched. A monster-hunter called Roy Muir suggests the evidence might be caused by a fake Nessie lost in the 1960's during the making of a film (16). Somebody else had already suggested the shifting hulk of a real Viking ship, way back in June (18). Even the British Society of Underwater Photographers jumped in with the proposal that Rines' photos were of a decomposing cow's head, overdeveloped by 30% and enlarged 100 times. (19). This contradicts much of the technical info given by Rines et al, and virtually accuses him of complicity in a hoax, because Geoff Harwood, chairman of this society and author of the letter, suggests the film was overdeveloped to increase film speed. Dr G Corbet, another of the Kensington Five, deputy keeper of zoology, is quoted in one paper as suggesting that because there was no evidence of a hoax, and no evidence that rules out a hoax, it would have been easy for a third party to "drop something in the loch and tow it in front of the camera." Why, I wonder, do solid scientists go overboard in conjuring up elaborate hoaxes (they would have had to have secrecy, the equipment, the time, the knowledge of where the cameras were, etc) - would it not be simpler to believe that the camera merely took a picture of something? The British Museum still lives in trembling memory of the Piltdown hoax, so everything tends to be damned in the same swipe.

I am, myself, in considerable doubt about the physicality of any denizen in Loch Ness.

The question is complex, otherwise it would
have been settled quickly, easily and def-
initively by now. I see it relating closely
to the questions of the physicality of UFOs
and Mystery Animal phenomena (see back to
our opening pages), in that the significant
factor in common is that paradoxical evidence has been accumulating for centuries. As
Lethbridge concludes: "..I believe the observation must be right. If there are no real
animals in the lochs, then the observers
were seeing ghosts."(9).

THE PROBLEM.

Once physicality is debated, without reference to the vast accumulation of human
experience, the paradoxes creep in. In retro-
spect, it is impossible to say who first began
to interpret the Loch Ness Monster (LNM) as a
plesiosaur, but, doubtless to much paleontol-
ogical disgust, this is what the newspapers
did.

Having marshalled the experts who saw in
the photos something of an animal, the next
question for Rines & Scott is, what is it, and
how did it get there? We don't have the space
to argue the various hypothetical beasts
proposed over the years, in answer to the
first question - you'll find endless pros and
cons in the literature. In the immediate
instance, we find drawings of plesiosaurs
begining to crop up in the media about 22 & 23
Nov. Sir Peter Scott & Rines say nothing
about identifying the 'animal' in their
Nature article (1), but in the press blurb,
Sir Peter says the body, neck, head photo
"recalls the shape of certain fossil specimens
from pre-history." (5). Not explicit; but to
the press, who are child-like in these matters,
virtually an admission of 'plesiosaur'.

David James (Scott's colleague from the
Loch Ness Investigation Bureau, which, incidentally is not mentioned to be defunct in the
Commons handout, or even re-formed) in his
Field article, suggested the old tectonic-
movement-in-the-last-ice-age theory, which
says that during the end of the ice-age, about
8-12000 years ago, the land rose up..."Had,
therefore, any hypothetical species been
present in force at the headwaters, they
would have been cut off overnight, and if
large, shy and living deep, with no natural
enemies, it would have been a matter of surprise if they had died out." (8). I'd hardly
call 8-12000 years 'overnight' - however, when
the press took the idea up they published an
amusing range of dates for this land-locking:
from "3000"(11) to "5000 to 7000"(12) years
ago.

Most authorities obviously thought the idea
of plesiosaurs in the Loch too contemptible
to refute - but Dr Beverly Halstead, reader in
zoology and geology at Reading University, did
expand on the subject, and as the author of
The Evolution and Ecology of the Dinosaurs, he,
if anyone in the business, ought to be well
acquainted with the problem.(17) Plesiosaurs

survived right through the Mesozoic era to
vanish suddenly like most of the other dinosaurs at the begining of the Tertiary period,
about 60-70 million years ago. If there are
plesiosaurs or any of their descendants in the
Loch, where had they been hiding between then
and the time the land rose at the Great Glen
(say, just under 69 million years)? QED.

The other paradoxes are more subtle - if
not a plesiosaur then, but a plesiosaur-like
animal, what does it live on, how has it bred
since the land-locking period to the present
(say, 12000 years at the most)? Adrian
Desmond, of Harvard and author of a recent
book claiming that the dinosaurs were in fact
hot-blooded creatures, wrote a critical article in the Times asking "How can one describe
a beast that leaves no dead to be described?
Why do corpses never rise to the surface, as
they do in other animals? (If there is a
viable breeding population) why do we not see
one on the surface gulping air every few minutes? Why do we not encounter them at sea?"
and ends with a statement that must have
Machen laughing his socks off, wherever he is:
"As a paleontologist I need bones, something
to grapple with; not sonar traces."(13) God help
us all!

I think these points are sufficiently
answered by Sir Peter Scott (14) and Sir
Robert McEwen (15) considering the physicality
question to be in doubt anyway. They point
out many reptiles that can stay underwater
for long periods; that corpses stay down if
they are below a certain depth; that the
animals may even be cannibals. Sir Robert
mentions the caverns under the sides of the
loch; and Sir Peter the notion of gastroliths
(stones eaten, even by dinosaurs, to aid in
digestion). Both mention a number of animals
that have survived with astonishingly low
populations. Perhaps the most puzzling
feature is, as Desmond acknowledges, that the
bio-mass of the loch can support (theoretic-
ally) 17tons worth of 'monsters',(David James
suggests 300 30ft carnivores (8), and Rines
& Scott speak obliquely of a "population of
large animals"(1)). If so, then why haven't
the fishery authorities responsible for that
area, who keep a track of the salmon migrations and other fishes, been able to report
depredation on such a significant scale? This
smacks too much of the argument (Dr Burton
and others) for there being no 'Surrey Puma';
no lairs, no corpses, no significant depredation of flocks or heards, etc, not even the
expected remains of kills in the wilds. Some
investigators clearly cannot see past the
appelations of 'Puma' or 'Monster', which
began as a convenient handle and have ended
up hamstringing the research - even the pro-
monster school, as I have tried to suggest,
are preconceiving the results in this way.

HANDLE - WITH CARE!

The main reasoning in Rines & Scott's

splash in _Nature_ concerned giving Nessie the scientific name of <u>Nessiteras rhombopteryx</u>.(1). They had to do this from conservationist principles,they said; and from photographic evidence, because any hunt for a live specimen might considerably endanger the survival of their small community. Under Schedule 1 of an Act of Parliament passed last year for the conservation of wild beasts and plants, the LNM would require a scientific name before it would qualify, "even though the creature's relationship with known species, and even the taxonomic class to which it belongs, remain in doubt.".(1). Naturally,this upset the British Museum who take many years over the intricacies of naming new species, and, as Pearson Phillips wrote: "When they see amateurs inventing new animals after a few summers spent dipping cameras into water, they get upset." (4). This is facile,I know - Dr H Greenwood, one of the Kensington Five, senior principal scientific officer of the Fish Section of the BM) said: "My conclusion (from spending 7hrs with Rines & Scott) is that they have no proof at all of the existence of any unidentified creature. They have not identified a new species and I do not believe they have the right to coin a new name."(7). Rines and Scott quote as precedents the naming of sea-serpents by Rafinesque (1817), Oudemans (1892) and Heuvelmans (1958). Desmond, after referring to the naming battles between the paleontologists Cope & Marsh during the American wars againsts the Indians, writes sarcastically of this current fuss: "Paleontologists are now restrained by law from taking potshots at one another from rival quarries, but near riots still ensue from heated debates over the correct naming of a thimbleful of miniscule teeth attributable to mammals thriving 200 million years ago."(13).

But this naming has backfired on Rines & Scott in a most unexpected way, much to the amusement of everybody else. On the 13th (of all days) Dec. most national papers gleefully pointed out that their scientific name for the LNM is in fact an anagram of <u>Monster Hoax by Sir Peter S</u>. Sir Peter had coined the name with a friend, a Dumfriesshire schoolteacher, Alan Wilkins,who was stunned by this "amazing coincidence." To us Forteans, who are more interested in the wider implications of all mysterious phenomena, this has been a development our own studies ought to have lead us to expect, and to my mind confirms that we are witnessing something more fundamental being played out than rather superficial questions of whether there be plesiosaurs in Loch Ness. Oh! that Jung and Fort could see this - perhaps they have, and both are thumping the table in some celestial tavern, helpless with mirth. Perhaps the gales that swept Britain and Europe at the beginning of January was the laughter of the heavens themselves. All-in-all a classic of synchronicity!

Robert JM Rickard -- Jan 1976.

REFERENCES:

1) 'Naming the Loch Ness Monster' by Sir Peter Scott & Robert Rines. <u>Nature</u> 11 Dec.
2) <u>Observer</u>, 30 Nov 75.
3) <u>Sunday Times</u>, 23 Nov 75.
4) <u>Observer</u>, 14 Dec 75.
5) 'Summary statements of scientists who have presently studied the 1972-1975 underwater sonar & photographic results at Loch Ness of the American Academy of Applied Science, and the Loch Ness Investigation Bureau -- Presentation of Loch Ness evidence to all members of both Houses of Parliament, scientists, and press in the Grand Committee Room, House of Commons on Dec 10,75.'
6) <u>Daily Mirror</u>, 25 Nov 75.
7) <u>Daily Mail</u>, 11 Dec 75.
8) 'Life in the deep in Loch Ness' by David James MP. <u>Field</u>, 23 Oct 75.
9) <u>Ghost & Divining Rod</u> by TC Lethbridge. Routledge & Kegan Paul; London 1963. Ch8.
10) <u>The Dragon & the Disc</u> by FW Holiday. Sidgwick & Jackson; London 1973 - also Futura paperback, 1974.
11) <u>Daily Mirror</u>, 26 Nov 75.
12) <u>Boston Globe</u> (Massachusetts), 22 Nov 75. Cr: Mark A Hall.
13) 'Why Nessiteras rhombopteryx is such an unlikely Monster' by Adrian J Desmond. <u>The Times</u>, 27 Dec 75.
14) 'Letters to the Editor' <u>Times</u>,31 Dec 75.
15) 'Letters to the Editor' <u>Times</u>, 2 Jan 76.
16) (London) <u>Evening News</u>, 13 Dec 75.
17) (Reading) <u>Evening Post</u>, 27 Nov 75.
18) <u>Sunday People</u>, 8 June 75. Cr: N Watson.
19) A lette to <u>Nature</u> which I've not read, but which is extracted in (London) <u>Evening News</u>, 30 Dec 75.
20) <u>The Elusive Monster</u> by Dr M Burton. Rupert Hart-Davis; London 1961.
21) <u>New Scientist</u>, 27 Nov 75; 'This Week' -- & 11 Dec 75; 'Letters'.

My thanks go to Steev Moore, and especially to Ken Rogers, who collected most of the bulging file on Nessie 75 between them; and again to Ken for sending me all the stuff from the House of Commons conference.

* * *   * * *   * * *

"But there are no such things as waterbabies."

"How do you know that? Have you been there to see? And if you had been there to see, and had seen none, that would not prove there were none -- no one has a right to say that no waterbabies exist, till they have seen no waterbabies existing, which is quite a different thing from not seeing waterbabies." CHARLES KINGSLEY.

'Gevaudan' cont...

yet most of them have appeared in the Paris
Gazette, a paper whose authors, known to be
men of letters, are too judicious to be suspected of credulity..." etc.

The St James's Chronicle, 6 June 1765 gave
a woodcut (see illo), thought to be based on
a discription sent, in April 1765, to the
Intendant of Alençon. It accompanied a summary
of the story which ran thus:

> "For the *St. James's Chronicle.*
> "Of this beast, which has already devoured upwards of
> seventy Persons and spread Terrour and Desolation throughout
> the whole Gévaudan, the Sieur de la Chaumette, who lately
> wounded it, has given us the following Description. It is larger
> than a Calf of a year old, strongly made before, and turned like a
> Grayhound behind. His Nose is long and pointed, his Ears
> upright and erect; his Mouth of a most
> enormous size, and always wide open; a Streak of Black runs
> from his Shoulders to the Beginning of his Tail. His Paws are
> very large and strong; the Hair on his Back and Mane thick,
> bristly, and erect; his Tail long and terminating in a Bush,
> like that of a Lion; his Eyes small, fierce, and fiery. From
> this description it appears that he is neither a Wolf, Tiger, nor
> Hyena, but probably a Mongrel, generated between the two
> last, and forming, as it were, a new Species. All the accounts
> lately received agree in assuring that there are several of them."

On 20 Sept 1765 the beast had the great
misfortune to run into a Monsieur Beautermé,
a gentleman hunter, in a wood at Pommieres.
Intrigued by the stories, he thought to test
his skills by tracking it down. He shot it in
the eye, but it still had the fury to rush at
him, and was finished off by a gamekeeper
named Reinhard. Later, several people who had
survived its attacks identified it. Beautermé
accompanied the carcase to Versailles to
present it to Louis.

A court surgeon dissected it. It was 32ins
high; 5ft 7½ins long , inc. tail. The surgeon
said the animal was more like a hyena than a
wolf; its teeth being 40 against a wolf's 26
((it says here. Can anyone confirm this? - Ed.))
It had strong neck muscles; a large, broad,
thick tail that bristled with black hair; feet
with strong claws; and "its eyes sparkled so
with fire that it was hardly possible to bear
its look." It was thought in Paris that it was
a cross between a tiger and a lioness, and
brought to France to be shown as a curiosity.

STRANGE WILD BEAST SEEN IN FRANCE.
From the "St. James's Chronicle," 1765.

The author of 'A Sketch of the Rise and
Progress of Pictorial Journalism' in the
Illustrated London News, 14 June 1879, from
which I have all these facts, adds his opinion
that it was, in all probability, a hyena that
escaped from a travelling show, distorted into
a horrific beast by the terrors of the people.

SOUTHAMPTON 'WOLF' SCARE - 1876.

As evidence of the opinion just mentioned
above the author (simply referred to as "MJ")
goes on to illustrate with the following story
from Jan 1876, of:

"Captain Sir Allen Young's pet Esquimaux
dog, which was either stolen or wandered from
the Arctic ship 'Pandora' as she lay in
Southampton harbour after returning from the
polar regions. Quite a panic arose in that
part of Hampshire where this most valuable and
harmless animal was wandering about, and every
sort of story was circulated of the ravages
and dangers the country was subject to. The
people began to think their sheep, pigs and
children were in danger. Some said it was a
gigantic black fox, others that it was a
Canadian wolf. Expeditions were organised to
attack it, and after being chased for some
miles by people on horseback, it was ultimately
shot and exhibited at sixpence a head in
Winchester market-place. There could be no
doubt about the dog's identity, for Sir Allen
Young afterwards got back his skin."
Illustrated London News, 14 June 1879, p566.

MAs IN ASIA MINOR - 8th CENTURY.

Returning to the theme of historical MAs, we
remember a passage in Strange Mysteries of
Time and Space by Harold T Wilkins (Ace, NY,
1958), one of the better post-Fort writers. On
pp194/5, he quotes from the Chronicon of
Denys de Tell-Mahre, who was born in Mesopot-
amia (now Iraq) near the end of the 8th C.

"Before the reign of the (Byzantine-Greek)
Emperor Leo IV (ie prior to 774 AD), there
raged a plague, followed by the appearance of a
frightening and terrible animal who feared
nothing and no man. They fled from no man, and
indeed, killed many. Very little they were
like wolves, but their muzzle was small and
long, and they had great ears like those of
horses. The skin on their dorsal spine resembled the bristles of pigs, and stuck
straight up. These mysterious animals commit-
ed great ravages to the people in the Abdin
Rock region, near Hoh. In certain villages,
they devoured more than 100 people, and in
many others from 20 and 40 to 50. Nothing
could be done against them for they were fearless of man. If, by chance, men pursued them,
in no wise did the monsters become scared or
flee, but turned on the men. If men loosed
their weapons on a monster, it leapt on the
men and tore them in pieces. These monsters
entered houses and yards and seized and
carried off children. They climbed in the

cont on back page///

NOTES ON GREENWICH PHENOMENA

Part 1 of a Fortean interpretation of Taoist phenomenology by Steev Moore.

This collection of data is preparatory to a couple of articles (which will be published in subsequent issues of the <u>NEWS</u>) attempting a tentative interpretation of various Fortean phenomena in terms of Chinese Taoist and Yin-Yang philosophies. As certain features of the physical landscape are relevant to this interpretation, I intend to concentrate on an area of South East London well known to me, as a 'laboratory'. So, before coming to the main theories, a summary of phenomena in the Greenwich area is presented.

The area under consideration is small, perhaps too small, but this factor is out-weighed by the easy availability of information, and personal local knowledge. It is aproximately 4¼ miles by 3¼; bounded on the west by the River Ravensbourne, north by the Thames, east by the Kent border, and on the south by a rather arbitrary line 3¼ miles south of the Thames. Further geographical considerations will be discussed in the subsequent articles.

THE SHOOTERS HILL 'CHEETAH'.

(The following material is drawn from <u>Kentish Mercury</u>, 19 & 26 July, 1963. See also <u>Kentish Independent</u>, same dates)

1. 1 am, 18th July, 1963. Lorry-driver David Back, driving up the west side of Shooters Hill, stopped to assist what he thought was an injured dog. As he approached, it got up and ran off into the woods. Whatever it was, it was not a dog, and had long legs and a long, pointed tail that curled up. It appeared to have a mouth full of food. Mr Back's report to the local police station sparked off a hunt which eventually included extra police from other stations, troops and sixth formers from the local grammar school.

A patrol car went into the woods and disturbed the animal, which 'jumped clean over the bonnet of the car'. The 'cheetah' was reported several times that night and early morning, but there are no further details. The '<u>Daily Mirror</u>' of the 19th reported the animal to be golden in colour. The 'Evening News' of the same date states that there had been previous sightings, but we have been unable to locate any. All large animals in the area were accounted for.

On the south-eastern side of Shooters Hill, near Welling Way, the searchers found claw marks on a tree and, in the mud of a dried up stream,'a number of prints several inches across with the marks of claws clearly visible'.

2. ¾ of an hour before dawn, 23rd July, 1963. Johnson & Phillip's sports ground, Kidbrooke. Head groundsman Jim Green was awoken by loud snarling noises, starting near Kidbrooke Park Road, and moving along the course of the River Quaggy, a stream running behind bushes and trees along one side of the sports ground. A security sergeant from the nearby RAF

station also heard the snarls, and investigated with a constable. As dawn broke, they saw 'a big dark animal, between 18 and 24 inches high, silhouetted against a white cricket screen'. It walked off into the bushes. Five carloads of police arrived, by which time, naturally, the beast had disappeared.
Incidentally, streams leading to the Quaggy rise on the west side of Shooters Hill, where the animal was first seen.

UFOs.

We have been able to trace only one UFO report for this area, details of which may be found in NEWS 10/16. Briefly:

3. 8th Sept 74: a bright, sulphurous light seen over Plumstead Common at 11.25pm. It hovered, then shot off at great speed.

4. 9th Sept 74, mid-morning. The same, or a similar object was seen at Eltham, a fantastically bright glare, moving slowly.

GHOSTS

5. George Lane, Lewisham, SE13
(See NEWS 12/22) An invisible presence pays court to the ladies, while making the room uncomfortably cold for male guests.

6. Blackwall Tunnel, SE10.
The ghost of a young motorcyclist, who fell off his bike in the tunnel, in 1972 and was killed, has been seen on the Greenwich approach to the tunnel, complete with black leather gear, goggles and crash-helmet. (Kentish Times, 18 Dec 75).

7. Hare & Billet Rd, Blackheath, SE10.
A shadowy figure of a woman, dressed in dark Victorian clothes, has been seen on autumn eveinings in the mist. She is thought to be a married woman looking for her lover, who had arranged to meet and take her away. When he didn't show, she hung herself on one of the trees. Last seen in November 1971 (Andrew Green: Our Haunted Kingdom, Wolfe, 1973)
We note that, until the early years of this century, a convent stood near this site, the nuns being known locally as the 'Grey Ladies'...though whether this is relevant, we have no idea...

8. Catherine House, Blackheath Rd, SE10.
A woman, dressed in dark brown and carrying some keys, glides silently downstairs and into the butler's pantry (Greenwich Borough Council Local History Centre (LHC))

9. (?), Blackheath, SE3.
A woman at Blackheath saw a vision of her mongrel dog, at the same time as it died in Bath, according to Elliott

O'Donnell:(Casebook of Ghosts, Foulsham, 1969) No date, no further details.

10. Blackheath Library, St John's Park, SE3.
The vicarage of nearby St John's church was converted into the library in 1956, since when library staff have reported feeling something invisible pushing past them, and lights go on after the library has shut. The ghost is believed to be that of Elsie Marshall, who was raised in the vicarage. In 1892, she went to China as a missionary, and on 1 Aug 1895 was murdered, with others, by a local secret society, the 'Vegetarians' (Chai-chiao), near Foochow, Fukien. Her ghost is now supposed to have returned to her birthplace. (LHC).

11. Greenwich Park, SE10.
O'Donnell (ibid.) records seeing, 24 Jul 1898, what he describes as a 'nature spirit' here. Sitting on a bench beneath a giant, diseased elm, he saw fall from the tree 'a figure half-human and half-animal – stunted, bloated, pulpy and yellow. Crawling sideways like a crab, it made for a bush opposite, into which it disappeared'. Terrified, he fled. Like so many of O'Donnell's tales, it is of course impossible to confirm this story.

12. Queen's House, National Maritime Museum, Greenwich, SE10.
Here the Rev. R N Hardy took his famous photograph in 1966, showing a shrouded figure on the Tulip staircase. A figure, hooded and robed in monkish fashion, ascends the stairs, left hand on the bannister. Another hand clutches the rail a short distance ahead, but this also appears to be a left hand, and is too far ahead to be connected with the first figure, so it is assumed that the 'monk' is chasing someone. The second figure is obscured by the glare of an electric lamp on the wall nearby. No figures were visible to the naked eye. Full details of the photograph (lens-settings, etc) may be found in Peter Underwood: Haunted London,(Harrap, 1973) as well as the following: An investigation party spending the night there heard footsteps, but found no other evidence. A former warder found the doorway to the Tulip staircase 'uncomfortable and disturbing', and also saw an unexplained figure which vanished in the tunnel which runs beneath the collonade immediately outside the Queen's House. No historical legend attaches to this ghost.

13. Staff College, Royal Naval College, Greenwich, SE10.
(Underwood, ibid.). Queen Anne block, 1 Jan 1962. Edward C Hull and a colleague were working when a door-handle jig-

gled, and was then violently thrown open. The door was closed again, and the event repeated a few seconds later. They then heard faint footsteps, followed by sounds resembling grit dropping, or very light taps. On discussion, they found they had both previously seen filmy figures, and also a shrouded figure in one room, which faded out when greeted. The ghost is thought to be Admiral Byng, who was imprisoned in the college prior to his execution for treason in 1757.

Both this and the above building lie on the site of the medieval Greenwich Palace.

14. Charlton House, Charlton Village, SE7.

See (NEWS 12/22) for the standard version of this story, according to which the ghost of Sir William Langhorne attempts to rape female visitors in hope of getting an heir. The LHC records a more detailed but less romantic set of events: 'An old lady, still living in the village' says that when the house was being used as a military hospital in WW1, the then owner, Lady Wilson, warned nurses not to put injured men in what had been her bedroom. The warning was ignored, and some soldiers reported seeing a ghost. Both Mr Barker, the warden, and his predesessor, Mr Jenkins, have had reports from overnight guests of a presence in their bedroom. Mr Jenkins' dog was obviously disturbed whenever it passed a certain spot on the first landing of the staircase, and Mr Barker frequently felt a chill at the same spot.

Sir William Langhorne died, aged 85, in 1714, without issue, having married twice. There is no evidence that he was particularly perturbed at being the last of his line. One letter in the LHC file asserts that this tradition is less than five years old, and was constructed on the basis of the above events (and, we suspect, from the name Langhorne!). Another letter states, however, that it is a strong local tradition.

15. No 33 Woolwich Common, SE18.

This house has since been demolished. In 1971, the owner personally reported to the LHC that she had seen the ghost of a Victorian nurse or nursemaid bending over her young daughter.

16. Academy Road, Woolwich Common, SE18.

We are told that a letter to the Kentish Independent, probably some time in the early 1970s, mentioned a troop of soldiers in WW1 uniform seen marching along the road, which leads from the Royal Artillery barracks, at about that date. With

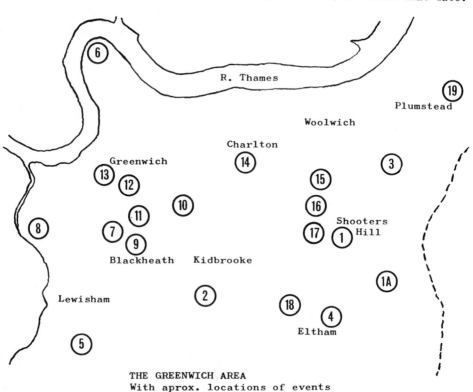

THE GREENWICH AREA
With aprox. locations of events

such a vague reference, it has been impractical to track down the original letter so far.

17. Shooters Hill Rd / Well Hall Rd, SE18
This crossroads at the foot of Shooters Hill is reputed to be haunted by a 'White Lady'. According to Eric Maple, quoted in (Kentish Independent, 27 June, 74), the ghost is probably the spirit of a suicide case, who would traditionally have been buried at a crossroad with an iron stake through her heart. However, we have found the original newspaper report (unreferenced) to the discovery of the body, and there is no evidence of suicide or an iron stake. The body was some 30 yards from the crossroads, and was treated as an unidentified murder victim. O'Donnell (ibid.) gives the story, apart from getting the date wrong by a mere 6 months...June 10th, 1844, a labourer unearthed the skeleton of a woman with the back of her skull badly fractured, indicating foul play. Much long, golden hair was still attached to the skull, indicating that the body was not too old. Prior to this, in the 1830s, it seems that people passing by had heard unaccountable noises and seen the phantom of a woman in a white dress gliding along. The remains were interred in a nearby churchyard, and her identity never discovered. Apparently the ghost appeared a number of times later in the 19th century, usually preceded by a cry of terror and despair. We have found no 20th century cases.

18. Kidbrooke Lane, Well Hall, SE9.
O'Donnell (ibid) gives a curious parallel case, about a mile distant from the above. On 25 April, 1871, Jane Maria Clousen was murdered here, struck on the head with a hammer. The man accused of the murder, Edmund Pook, produced an alibi, and the case remained unsolved. After the murder it was claimed that the lane was haunted nightly by cries and groans, and the apparition of the murdered girl. The place got such a bad reputation that it was shunned after dark. The LHC crime file contains no record of the murder, nor have we found any evidence to corroborate O'Donnell's story.

19. Barnfield Gardens, Plumstead, SE18.
(NEWS 2/8) for details. A pre-war council flat was haunted by a white-haired old man with a goatee beard. Lights were switched off and on, and something cold brushed past the occupants.

20. Tavy Bridge, Thamesmead, SE28.
Strictly, this case falls a mile or two outside our area, but we include it as it has only recently come to our attention.

The story, according to the Kentish Ind-

ependent, 11 Dec 75, is that when excavations for the 'new town' of Thamesmead were being carried out, a complete WW2 fighter plane was discovered buried in the marshes, but with no pilot. He, in sergeant pilot's uniform, and nicknamed Joseph, is said to haunt several premises near Tavy Bridge, especially the butcher's shop which stands over the site of the plane's grave. The former owner claimed to have seen and spoken with the ghost, the current owner only claims to have felt a presence late at night and to have heard footsteps. The ubiquitous Eric Maple is quoted as saying that local residents have told him that, ever since the plane came down, there have been sounds of a phantom aircraft, with engine trouble.
The Kentish Times, 18 Dec 75, has a different story. First, the pilot was found strapped in the aircraft, and is seen outside the shops. Their reporter then did some research, consulting the GLC. No plane had ever been found, but the council's spokesman had heard a story of a WW1 plane crashing there. The Ministry of defence could throw no light on the matter, suggesting searches of the Imperial War Museum and the Public Records office...but both institutions said it would take two days research to check out. The reporter gave up...looking back at the whole mess, he has our sympathy...

THE GREAT 'ICE-STORM'.

Drawn from Kentish Mercury & Kentish Independent, both 24 July, 1925.
21. 22nd July, 1925. This storm appears to have covered most of the eastern half of our area, including Eltham, Shooters Hill, Woolwich and Plumstead, before moving away eastwards into Kent, dying out around Bexleyheath and Erith.
The afternoon was the hottest for 2 years, reaching 90 degrees, though it was sultry with no strong sunshine. Thunder started rumbling about 5.00pm, and at 6.00 the storm broke. There was considerable flooding, with water running in torrents through the streets, and buses and fire engines grinding to a halt when they ran into deep water. Lightning struck trees and set off fire-alarms. But worst of all was the ice...
The hailstones started quite small, but soon reached the size of eggs, then, among the smooth round ones, jagged fragments started to fall, and some 4 or 5 inches long were picked up. Some had sharp, jagged edges. Lawns were turned white. There was terror in upper Plumstead, as a 'tornado-like wind' hurled down showers of ice for up to ten minutes. 'For several minutes, there was one long succession of crashing glass, windows were driven in, and huge pellets

carried far into rooms.' Birds on Plumstead common, knocked out of their trees,
were killed and injured. Cows and horses
ran about in panic in the fields. People
running for cover were cut by flying ice
and some even had their clothing cut 'as
by jagged knives'.

A hailstone picked up at Abbey Wood weighed 10¼ oz. At Woolwich, a fragment
weighed over a pound. Ice weighing up
to 8 oz was picked up at Eltham, and
Belvedere, where it made a hole in the
roof of the Conservative Club, and another made a six-inch hole in the roof of
the Salvation Army hall. Although these
are the exceptionally large falls, ice

seems to have showered over the entire
area in ungodly large lumps...
After this short and exceedingly fierce
display, the storm subsided, but returned later and continued until nearly
midnight...but this time without ice.

　　　　***********

I would like, briefly, to pay tribute to
the charming ladies at the G.B.C. Local
History Centre, who smilingly put up
with my idiotic impositions while preparing this uncouth offering. Their assistance has provided many more items than
those actually credited to them. Thank
you and goodnight.

Steev Moore -- Jan 1976

The formation of the Institute of Geomantic Research recently, to co-ordinate and
publish original research on landscape geometry; leys and figures, etc; terrestrial
zodiacs; geodesic studies (dowsing, etc);
sacred geometry and ancient metrology; and
legendary geometry; was announced quietly.
Membership costs £2.50 annually, including a
journal and occasional papers, the first of
which,'Landscape Geometry of Southern Britain'
by Michael Behrend, costs 35p plus p&p (free
to members). More details from and applications
to: IGR, 142 Pheasant Rise, Bar Hill,
Cambridge CB3 8SD, England.

Chile says an emphatic 'No!' to suggested
Rolling Stones retirement concert on Easter
Island -- Sunday Times, 14 Dec 75.

The Arts Council exhibition of 'Peruvian
Ground Drawings', featuring the tireless work
and photos of Maria Reich on the Nazca plateau,
will be at the ICA gallery, London, from
9 April - 2 May; after which it will travel
around England (we'll publish the itinerary
next ish). A catalogue will be available at
£4 - an essential reference volume on these
ancient boggling patterns.

We learn from Anthony Roberts that Dr Glyn
Daniel will address a meeting on the "lighter"
side of archeology, held at Cambridge University under the auspices of the Philosophical
Society, and promises to "deal" with cranks,
forgers and the lunatic fringe in the subject.
As Tony writes: "Being one of the most pompous

of the orthodox cranks he is well qualified
to pontificate on such subjects. His infamous
eating tours of France with a little tepid
archeology on the side were a great joke
amongst his more bright students. The IGR (se
above item) will be bringing out a leaflet fo
the meeting pointing out some of his own
amusing cock-ups, like Piltdown Man, the
Glozel Carvings and the ley-line fiasco in th
Ley Hunter (TLH 14 and earlier). We hope that
members who can will attend in force and give
Dr Daniel the sort of reception he so richly
deserves." This meeting, entitled "Fable,
Fraud, Forgeries & Archeologists", will be
held at 5pm on the 9th Feb. All Forteans are
invited to add their raspberries to this
deserving cause.

We also heard that a lecture series called
'In search of Ancient Astronomies' will be
hosted by the University of California at Los
Angeles (Dept. Bio & Physical Sciences).
Among the many topics of Archeoastronomy,
which begin on 15th Jan, we see that EC Krupp
will deal with much the same sort of subjects
as Dr Daniel, on 4th March, in a talk entitle
'Observatories of the Gods & other Astronomical Fantasies'. I wonder how they will compare?

REVIEWS:REVIEWS:REVIEWS:REWIEVS:REIWVSE:REVIE
This issue has become a bit short on space
and we shall have to carry over the stack of
booknews, reviews and mentions to next issue.

Did You See...?

'The Fleet-footed Dinosaurs' Bryan Silcock waxing warms on Adrian J Desmond's book The Hot-blooded Dinosaurs (Blond & Briggs, £5.95) Good pictures of cute monsters "gettin' it on". Sunday Times Magazine, 30 Nov 75. In the same paper for 9 Dec 75, Dr Beverley Halstead challenges Desmond's views. (We met both gents in this issue locking horns over Nessie).

The Ghost Hunters, an extremely shallow documentary by Hugh Burnett on BBC 1 (TV), 4 Dec 75, in which (it is admitted) he gives people enough rope to hang themselves. Sets scepticism back a 100 years. Contrary to expectations, Dr Chris Evans'two documentaries Into the Unknown, ITV 2 & 9 Dec 75, were models of restraint: the first being a quick resume of a number of areas of paranormal experience; the second a look at current research. Evans surprised me by admitting that the "scientific approach has failed to deliver the goods". It is not a phenomenon that can be quantified on demand, and therefore sad to see thousands of dollars propping up wholly materialistic gadget-orientated approaches.

New Scientist: 20 Nov: 'The 7 Elementary Catastrophies' by Dr Ian Stewart on the revolutionary mathematical theories of Rene Thom -- 4 Dec: 'Science detects the Forgeries' by Dr Stuart Fleming; 'Metals that can be like glass' by Dick Taylor -- 27 Nov: 'What's so special about Man's Brain?' by Dr R Passingham; 'Did the Anaerobes defeat the Dinosaurs?' suggestive evidence on the old mystery of why the dinosaurs disappeared 64 million years ago -- 11 Dec: Another blow to the claims for gravity waves as an experiment at Reading U., Berks., fails to detect any -- 18 Dec: 'What happened to the Universe before the Big Bang?' ; 'Time & Lysenko's unsung Critic' by Daniil Granin; and Dr P Chadwick investigating why geologists are only just begining to report certain strata-patterns, when they were there all the time, is it a psychological problem? -- 1 Jan 76: 'The Brain's own Opiate'Dr R.Lewin -- 8 Jan:'Black Holes are hot' in which Dr G Gibbons finds BHs radiating heat; 'Ice Age is writ in the Canadian Snows' asks why we are not already 200yrs into the next Ice Age?

Psychic Eye No1, Dec 75; 35p -- a rather gushy new mag with a panting approach to the whole range of media-occult subjects. Only items worth mentioning are: an extract of Colin Wilson's forthcoming sequel to his best-selling 'The Occult', being a chapter on the 'Ghosts, ghouls & pendulums of Tom Lethbridge' (also met in this issue); and an uncredited article 'UFOs from Atlantis' which doesn't tell you anything you don't already know if you've been keeping up with your reading.

Fate, Dec 75: Curtis Fuller on some pix from Ted Serios of Patricia Hearst before her recent capture; 'Thunder of the Mackimoodus': HV Brooke on the strange aerial detonations of the East Haddam area of Connecticut, also mentioned by Fort. Jan 76: 'The Merveilleux Veilleux' in which Jule Eisenbud finds two brothers able to think images onto sealed film; David Henry looks at Wegener's theory of continental drift and concludes 'No Room for Atlantis'.

Flying Saucer Review, V21 Nos 3&4 (double issue). Amongst the usual interesting material are: Dr Leo Sprinkle with a preliminary report on the Colorado UFO kidnap of Carl Higdon; Dr Berthold Schwarz on yet another thoughtographist (see Fate above), this time a lady who experienced a UFO landing; Wido Hovill on a UFO EM-effect that stopped Army manoeuvres in Wales; Poher & Vallée on 'Basic Patterns in UFO Observations'; Gordon Creighton on a UFO that shone a light,turning a car transparent; 3 cases involving 'humanoids' and lots more. After a long delay, I hope FSR gets back on schedule again.

MUFOB, New Series No1 — We heartily welcome the return of MUFOB, which consistently prints sound and original UFO-oriented papers. This issue contains Peter Rogerson on the historical continuity of 'The Phantom Ship & The UFO'. More details from John Rimmer (Ed): 11 Beverley Rd, New Malden, Surrey KT3 4AW.

The Ley Hunter, 67.— 'It ain't no coincidence', Robin Holtom on synchronicity; Pt2 of 'Forgotten Heart of Albion' by P Devereux & A York; 'Survey of Saxon Church at Bradford -on-Avon & Alignments' by Janet Roberts -- 68: Jimmy Goddard on 'Ley Hunting in Wales'; Andrew Larman on John Cooper Powys, Britain & the Golden Age'; Pt 3 of the Devereux & York 'Forgotten Heart of Albion'. TLH: 5 Egton Drive, Seaton Carew, Hartlepool, Cleveland TS25 2AT.

Lantern, Winter 75 — Nigel Pennick on 'The Puddingstones at Coton'; Ron Hill concluding his study of 'Bio-rhythms & Psi'; a 'Mystery Aeroplane' case of Aug 75; investigations into 'Ghosts at Westwood House'; a Lowestoft UFO case of 3 Dec 62; and the 'Mummified Cats' of Sudbury, Suffolk; plus a review of BSIG's first 5 years (Congratulations). BSIG: 3 Dunwich Way, Lowestoft, Suffolk NR32 4RZ.

Pursuit, Oct 75 -- Report on the 'Strange World' exhibit at 'Man & His World' (formerly Expo 67) Montreal; Tim Church on 'The Flathead Lake Monster'; Robert E Jones on an unusual ape, and 'Bigfoot in New Jersey'; Ron Dobbins explains the '"Fishfalls" of Yoro, Honduras'; 'Octopus Giganteus Verrill' the paper that Gary Mangiacopra was scheduled to give at Fortfest 75 and prevented by misfortune; 'The Dodecated Globe' by William H Whammond, being an exploration of Sanderson's idea of 'Vile Vortices'. Pursuit is the Journal of the Society for the Investigation of the Unexplained, SITU: Columbia, New Jersey 07832.

'Did You See'is compiled from notes sent in by readers. We need someone who regularly reads Nature, Science, Scientific American, Proceedings of the Royal Society, etc (not necessarily all the same person) who drop us a line every 2 months on anything interesting. Any volunteers please contact the editor. Thanks.

night onto the terraces, abducted children from their beds and went off before any could oppose them." The story continues in this vein; the countryside becoming bare of cattle and men afraid to travel, even in groups of 2 or 3. Eventually, "...These monsters passed into Arzanene (Armenia's southern border with Assyria) and badly ravaged every village, as well as the country of Maipherk, and on Mount Cahai, and they caused damage at Amida (Upper Tigris)."
                                      Robert JM Rickard -- Jan 1976.

EDITORIAL cont...

in the quality of photo reproduction. We simply cannot afford to screen our photos for good repro. The next cheapest format would be a judicious combination of stencil-duplicated pages with a few litho ones for illos. The price would be heavy in terms of extra editorial time in preparation, not to mention the added burden of manual collation and stapling. We'd also have to change to the larger A4 format. Personally, I'd be very reluctant to change our format, unless it was for the better - ie typesetting, or more pages. But this is as much your mag as it is mine - after all, you pay for it - and so I'd like your help and advice in this difficult time. Please let me know how you feel.

I want us to grow - and you can help. We need money. I'm not sure even, God help me, how we stand in law about this. But we need money, for sure, either from more subs, the kindness and support of donations, or (indefinite) loans against our future. So if you've been waiting for the call to arms -- HEEEEELLLPPP!!!!

NEW PRICES

Due to the disgraceful slide of the pound, it has become necessary to re-evaluate the rates of INFO and THE NEWS at the internationally more equitable rate of $2 to £1. This means that all overseas prices become slightly more expensive to us in England - and English prices cheaper to foreigners. These new prices can be found in our colophon and on the address sheet, and will be valid from 1st Jan 76 onward. All current subscriptions will be honoured. If you feel you've lost out, sorry, but it really has hurt us since it hurt you - better take it up with your governments, since they got us into this mess.

BACK ISSUES

Due to lack of capital, we can't print a huge stock of NEWSs; Nos 1-4 are gone, and, as is sensible with a dwindling resource in our state of poverty, we must ask 50p for each back copy in print (ie Nos 5 to date). We have a price of 60p/$1.20 per copy for a Xerox facsimile of Nos 1-4. Since this is a

bulk price,we need to make up batches of ten. So please write if you want them.

Backnumbers of INFO Journal are also available, and at a reduced price, to create some free space outside Paul Willis' bathroom. Nos 1,2 & 8 are OP. Nos 3,5-7,9 &10 will cost 75¢/38p. Nos 4 (in short supply), 11-13 will cost $1/50p. No14 (inshort supply) will cost $1.50/75p. UK orders to THE NEWS -- USA & overseas orders to INFO: Box 367, Arlington, VA 22210, USA.

GET ON THE FORTIBUS

INFO now has a large stock of The Complete Books of Charles Fort, recently reprinted by Dover, keeping the same pagination as the 1940 Holt/Fortean Society edition. It consists of the four books (Book of the Damned; New Lands; Lo!; Wild Talents) in 1125 pages, with the old (but limited) index. Costing $15.00/£7.50, postage included, from the INFO address above.

A SPECIAL 'NEWS' BINDER

We've looked at the idea of a special binder for THE NEWS. How'd you like a good-looking black 3-ring cover, with a silver NEWS design? At £2.00/$4.00 at time (inc. postage) we can have one that holds 2yrs copies of the NEWS & indexes. To save punching holes in your copies, it will come with the right number of strong stick-on strips, punched to fit the 3-ring binder. Once again, because of lack of capital,we have to get your orders first, since the minimum quantity we can order is 100. The price, which includes VAT paid, is not bad for keeping 2yrs issues in good condition.

INDEX 1975 & SOME GOOD NEWS

The 1975 index will be delayed till later this year because of pressure of urgent work. You know, I still get letters thinking I have a staff to do all this, but I don't. Most regrettably, I have to use some time and energy in the business of staying alive. However, one of the most pleasant projects under way is a book on Fortean phenomena, commissioned by Thames & Hudson from your editor and John Michell. We'll keep you posted.

a miscellany of Fortean curiosites

THE NEWS

OH NO! NOT ANOTHER ONE!

More monsters on land, in lakes, rivers and the sea:

Giant lizards in Italy ___ __9.   Barmouth Monster returns ___ __12.

a dragon off Cornwall ____ l3

visions: BVMs ___ __3, and a Celtic werewolf ___ __4   Mutant pony ___ __6

STUART GREENWOOD on Giza and Stonehenge ___ 14   Falls ___ __17

STEVE MOORE on Greenwich phenomena ___ ___18

50p : $1·00.

UK ISSN 0306-0764

bimonthly news & notes
on Fortean phenomena

THE NEWS is a non-profitmaking bimonthly miscellany of Fortean news, notes and references, affiliated
to the International Fortean Organisation (INFO) in
continuing the work of Charles Fort (1874 – 1932).
THE NEWS is edited by Robert JM Rickard:
Post Office Stores, Aldermaston, Berks RG7 4LJ,
England.

SUBSCRIPTIONS: 1 year – 6 issues – £3.00 / USA
$6.60. 2 years – 12 issues – £5.40 / USA $10.80
Single issues – 50p / USA $1.00. Back issues (if
available) 50p / USA $1.00. Current annual INDEX
free to subscribers, otherwise 30p. / USA 60¢.
Special joint subscription to THE NEWS and INFO
JOURNAL (including regular membership of INFO)
1 year – 12 issues – £7.00 / USA $14.00. All over-
seas subscribers paying by cheque should add 10% to
cover banking exchange commission.

CONTRIBUTIONS of articles, notes and artwork on
related subjects are always welcome and duly credited.
You can help us by sending us a copy or clipping of
any reference or data you think will interest us. Please
don't assume our omniscience – there are very few
duplications. We are especially glad to see items from
professional journals, local papers and OP books. But
please don't forget to add the source and date, and your
name for the credit.

RIGHTS. All articles and artwork in THE NEWS is
copyright of the authors and artists – and the views
expressed not necessarily those of THE NEWS or INFO.
All the notes herein may be freely quoted – all we ask
in return is an acknowledgement of the source. All
loony heading artwork in this issue is by Hunt Emerson.

*** A CHANGE OF NAME ***

In the past I have been rather obstinate
in ignoring criticism of our name THE NEWS,
and stuck by the various justifications given
in our first two issues. I now bow to the
opinion that if we are to appeal to more people, our title will have to be a little more
descriptive of our contents. From the next
issue we will be known as FORTEAN TIMES, with
a subtitle of "Portents and Prodigies". To
use the event to advantage, we have commissioned a 3-colour silk-screened poster from Hunt
Emerson, to be displayed in shops, and even to
be sold to readers. More on this next issue.

DONATIONS, PLANS & SUGGESTIONS.

Life has been exceedingly hectic since
the last (which, as a few spotted, was wrongly
dated January, instead of February). Our plea
for donations towards a working capital fund
had a small but encouraging response, in that
those who were kind enough to express their
support in this most practical way, did so
with generosity beyond expectation. For their
gifts, I'd like to express my thanks, on behalf of all NEWSreaders, to: Alice Ashton;
Janet & Colin Bord; Nick Cohn; Robert Forrest;
Judith Gee; John Harvey; RTA Hill; Mrs V
Martin; Steev Moore; SN Morgan; Roger Sandell;
Leslie Shepard; A Smith; & Nigel Watson.

Although this helps us immediately, we
need to sustain it so that our aim of a position of security can consolidate itself. We
are not out of danger - yet! And with further
aid from more readers, we can avoid it entirely. So please help us with donations if you
can. It's against our principles to twist
anyone's arm. It's my sincere view that there
is no limit to how good we can become in
quality, value, coverage and reader-services.
If you think we're doing good work, please
help us get over this rough patch, to survive
and do even better work.

Some of the money we have received has been
spent on adverts in a wide variety of magazines
- but to date this has resulted in only one
inquiry. This poor return has given the edge to
the thought that we should concentrate more on
improving our quality. But these things take,
and must be allowed, a reasonable time. We are
still convinced, though, that there must be several thousand potential readers 'out there' --
and would dearly like to be better known and
more widely read in America. In the meantime,
personal recommendation to friends is a proven
method of growth, and I'd like to renew my
plea that as many of you who can, introduce a
friend. If you want some blurbs, please write.

APOLOGY.

David James, MP., has asked us to point out
that last issue's cover was based on a painting
bt Sir Peter Scott, now owned by Mr James, and
on view at Torosay Castle, Craignure, Mull.

cont on back page..

Ghosts and Visions

THE BLOB WITH RED EYES.

This story was told by Mrs Marie Browne of Huntington Beach, California, about the last and most horrible in a series of incidents that drove her and her family from their house in Chatsworth, California in 1971. It was reported in the <u>National Enquirer</u> sometime towards the end of 1973. (Cr: Cheryl Hardin.)

"I woke up in the darkness of my bedroom gasping for air. As my eyes adjusted to the dark, I saw a dim form above me that turned my blood to ice. I'll never forget the terror that swept through me when I realised that a huge shapeless black blob was squatting on my chest. Its massive quivering arms embracing me like a vise. From out of that horrible blackness, two blood-red eyes glared at me with such hatred that I was speechless with terror. The thing was making terrible hissing noises like laboured breathing. With the tiny bit of air left in my tortured lungs, I screamed.. The thing slid from my bed as Art (my husband) awoke. He isn't a man who scares easily - but when he saw the monster undulating between our beds, he cried out in fright.

He lunged for the bedside lamp, knocking it over in his panic. The evil-looking thing sat glaring at me, changing shape as it pulsated, while Art groped for the lamp. When he finally flicked it on, and light flooded the room, the blob recoiled and slithered across the room to our clothes closet. In an instant it had vanished - going right through the clothes and back-wall of the closet. We stared after it in astonishment, gasping for breath, trying to slow our pounding hearts. finally Art said: "My God! In the name of God, what was that?" We compared what we had seen and made the chilling discovery; they were the same. The thing had been real!"

Blimey! Pardon me while I go look for my old nightlight.

FOREBODINGS IN TRANQUILITY.

Tranquility, Ohio, is a small, sincerely religious community with a population of 48.

In mid-January 1974, one of them, Mrs Edna Combess, 30, mother of three, had a vision: "I wasn't asleep. I had just finished praying like I do every night when this vision came. And then I saw this beautiful person and I believe with all my heart it was Jesus. He had the prettiest white robe on, like real soft mohair I guess you'd call it, and all around it and Him was the prettiest blue you ever saw, just like the brightest blue in the sky. he was telling his children, and some others I didn't know, it was time to get ready and come home. He welcomed them and held their hands. It only lasted a few seconds and disappeared as I lay there and had this wonderful feeling of seeing Him. Some people laugh when I tell them, but most of us here consider it a sign, and believe the time is near."

Another lady, Mrs Gertrude Hughes, who lives at Seaman nearby, but attends the same (and only) church in Tranquility as Mrs Combess, also claims a dream-vision. "I was standing on a little piece of ground and the clear water was coming up all around me, but God told me not to be afraid, but to help other people live good lives and not perish when the end comes. I think it was a warning that the end is near." Rev. Cox, of the Tranquility Church, to whom both women related their dreams, also believe they were a warning but not so imminent. He said he had a dream in mid-December 73 in which he saw the fields in the coming Spring flooded with water.

It seems to me that things have got a bit mixed in their minds. If they were that virtuous why should the Lord smite them - but I could be being impertinant there. Also, about the turn of the year, the account says a tornado touched down in the area, missing Tranquility completely. I'd say that if anybody, it was <u>they</u> who had little to worry about, having friends in high places. <u>Cleveland Press</u>, 21 Jan 74. Cr: Mark Hall.

THE VIRGIN OF 56th AVENUE.

We are told that every Sunday, just after lunch, the Blessed Virgin Mary (BVM) appears suspended above 56th Avenue in the New York suburb of Bayside Hills, Queens. According to the Sunday Times, 6 April 75 (Cr: Nigel Watson) the local residents, despite being 60% Catholic, have had it up to here, the crowds, coaches and chanting making their lives a misery and even at times, prisoners in their own homes. The crunch came when 20 buses brought over 1000 people from all over the USA that Easter. Mrs Vernoica Luekens conducts her services opposite a church there, on the spot where she first had her vision. Mrs Luekens is the only one to see the BVM regularly and the leaders of the Catholic community and Church strongly disapprove of her actions. Residents are pressing the police Commissioner to get her to have her visions elsewhere -- so much for the land of religious freedom! .

We dug around and found a note sent some time ago by Mark Hall, from the Atlanta Constitution, 5 Sept 1974, which even then described the "carnival atmosphere" of these Sunday soirees, with Mrs Luekens passing on messages from the Virgin and the saints that accompanied her. The Brooklyn diocese investigated and announced the visions spurious and forbade their members from attending the vigils, saying they were simply the product of a "fertile imagination". There were said to be photos (which we haven't seen) and experts have been found to pronounce them the products of double-exposures "or more sophisticated tampering, suggesting the involvement of experts seeking to exploit the affair for monetary gain." Hard words indeed! Mrs Luekens was warned by her bishop to desist, but it seems she has persisted in her claims for the visions since about 1970. The Daily Express, 4 June 75 (Cr: Steev Moore) is the last we have on the matter; and the hostility between pilgrims and residents has escalated into open exchanges of blows, abuse and writs.

Personally, I doubt that dishonest motives alone could sustain this kind of fervour for so long -- I could accept there being, at the very least, some initial vision, that would give Mrs Luekens conviction and impetus. As for the rest, who can say? I'd welcome any light our American readers can shed on the matter. It is worth noting however the last and cynical word we have, that "Mrs Luekens has had a vision which told her to move her vigils from the streets into the parks." That kind of convenient solution only heightens the ambiguity. If it's a con-game, it is remarkable: it's being worked out in the open, before and involving thousands, and is preposterously blatant. Intriguing.

LOVE ALL.
Margaret Court, 3 times singles champion at Wimbledon, has abandoned her tennis for higher things. An interview in the Daily Express, 16 March 76 (Cr: Steev Moore) said that it began about 5 months ago when she embarked on a personal spiritual quest. At the end of week in which she attended some Pentecostal lectures in Perth, Australia, she began to ha visions. "I was up in the children's room and I looked above the door and saw Our Lady. I said to myself: 'Margaret, you're seeing things,' but it was there. I knelt down to pray. Something made me put my hands to my face and I saw a gate. The Lord told me to go through that gate. Later, in my hands, I saw a vision as if I was looking through a big window and I saw a cross on top of a hill wit a big crowd of people. It was as if light was coming through my fingers. What does it feel like? How can I be so different, suddenly? The Lord says look at the sky and you look at me. Look at the earth and you look at me. Loo at the flowers and the trees and you look at me. I've never seen them before. When He touches you, everything changes." Amen!

Before we leave BVMs, I'd like to appeal for help in identifying one we have only the briefest note of. An image of the BVM appear ed regularly each evening (about 7.45pm) on a wall in Latimer St, Denver, Colorado, lasting till sunrise. It appeared first on Mother's Day 1973. Anyone have any more info on this?

A CELTIC WEREWOLF?
On BBC's evening current affairs programme, 'Nationwide', 20 Feb 76, an astonishing story was told about a werewolf figure associated with two Celtic stone heads, found near Hadrian's Wall along the Scottish-English border country. Fortunately for us, Steev Moore kindly transcribed the interesting bits for us. (We've taken the liberty of editing out some of the reporter's journalistic waffle, and summarise it thus):

To the Celts, the head was as powerful a symbol as the cross is to Christianity. "It represented all the great, deep, dark and dreadful things of man's nature. It was an avenging, insatiable god-figure, in which good and evil were mixed up. All destiny was there. This ghastly deity wasn't just a head; it was a severed head. The Romans were no great believers in having a dog and barking yourself, so they employed Celtic mercenaries to man the fortifications and discourage the Scottish drift south. These Celts brought their religions with them. They varied from tribe to tribe, but had in common, the head. Prisoners taken in battle were disembowelled in front of the many shrines; and the severed heads of the bravest and wisest were kept as a gruesome talisman. The gods themselves were heads of stone, and if there's any truth in the old stone-tape theory, what more likely receptacle could there be to store up the awesome memory of those savage times? Those cold impassive eyes must have soaked up death like blotting paper."

At this point, the reporter, Luke Casey, speculates about the possibility that people with psychic sensitivity can somehow activate the stone-tapes and revive those frozen fears and agonies. This is conjecture, of course, because there is no apparent reason why his theory should be connected with the specific manifestion of a werewolf-type demon. So, while we let Casey take up the story, we suggest it would make more sense (or rather less nonsense) if you forgot the sensational stuff about beheadings and disembowellings, and simply focused on the fact that the houses into which these heads were taken became the scene of a weird manifestation.

Casey: "The action replay? Well just recently something very strange happened in this most unmagical-looking council house, at Hexham, Northumberland. Two stone heads were dug up in the garden, in what may very well have been an ancient Celtic shrine. Understandably they caused a bit of curiosity, and Mrs Jenny Robson showed them to people around the estate including the lady next door."

Mrs Robson: "Well, it was a few nights later, there was such an awful crash next door - the screams..it was terrible..we were all awake. Next morning I asked her what had happened, and she said..this horrible thing had come into her bedroom. One of the children was ill with toothache and she's been in the bedroom with her, and this thing came in the bedroom. It was half-man, half beast. Of course we laughed, but..it sounded so horrible y'know..something like a werewolf..and her husband came running in to see what it was, but this thing had gone padding down the stairs, and she could hear it, y'know..padding down the stairs..as if..on its hind legs..and when he went downstairs the frontdoor was open ..so evidently it had gone out of the front door."

Casey: "A werewolf? Padding around a Geordie council estate? It sounds ridiculous. So, who, or what, was it? Mrs Robson hasn't a clue, and it must be said that neither she nor her neighbour knew anything about Celtic mythology, or the horrible things associated with those ritual heads. They were sent off to be examined, and eventually arrived in the home of Dr Anne Ross, in Southampton. Dr Ross is one of the country's leading experts in Celtic studies - she's written three definitive books on the Celts and their culture. So it's reasonable to assume she's a level-headed lady, not given to wild flights of fancy. And yet she too claims to have had strange experiences after coming into contact with the heads."

Anne Ross: "I didn't connect it with the heads then, but two or three days afterwards ((receiving the heads)) I woke up in the middle of the night. We always keep the hall light on and the doors open, because our small son is a bit frightened of the dark - so there's always a certain amount of light coming into our room - and I woke up, and felt extremely frightened ..in fact, panic-stricken, and terribly, terr-

ibly cold. There was a sort of dreadful atmosphere of icy coldness all round me..and something made me look towards the door, and as I looked, I saw this..thing..going out of it. It was about 6ft high, slightly stooping, and it was black, against the white door..and it was half-animal and half-man..the upper part, I would have said, was a wolf, and the lower part was human, and, I would have again said, that it was covered with a kind of black, very dark fur. It went out and I just saw it clearly, and then it disappeared, and something made me run after it..a thing I wouldn't normally have done, but I felt compelled to run after it. I got out of bed, and I ran, and I could hear it going down the stairs, then it disappeared toward the back of the house. When I got to the bottom of the stairs I was terrified."

Casey: "Did you see this thing again?"

Anne Ross: "A few days after I saw it, we had to go up to London, and our teenage daughter had the key and came home from school about 4pm, and we got back from London about 6pm. When we opened the door, she came to it and looked extremely pale and terribly shaken. Finally I got it out of her what had happened. She had opened the front door ((when she came home from school)) and as she opened it, a black thing, which she described as being as near a werewolf as anything, jumped over the bannister and landed with a kind of plop, you know, like padded, heavy animal feet, and it rushed toward the back of the house, and she felt compelled to follow it, It disappeared in the music room, right at the end of the corridor, and when she got there it had gone, and suddenly she realised she was terrified. The day the heads were removed from the house everybody, including my husband, said it's as if a cloud had lifted; and since then there hasn't been, really, a trace of it."

Casey: "With something less than enthusiasm, we tried to trace the two heads that were being blamed for all the aggro. We didn't find them. It seems the various people who had them were only too happy to see the back of them, and they wern't terribly worried about where they went."

The Goro/Forli Beast... (cont from p10.)

We found another cutting, from the Sunday Express 26 July 1970, in which Samorini describes the "multi-legged" beast as a "huge scaly thing at least 15ft long. It walked on thick legs and its breath was searing hot. I ran for my life and it followed me for a couple of hundred yards." Police were reported as being sceptical until they were shown footprints in a glade in woods near Forli. Police Chief Dr Pedoni said: "We are convinced some sort of creature of colossal size is hiding in the woods. Three other people have seen it."(NB: some confusion on dates.)

ꭲHE MALTON MUTANT.

When your editor returned from his visit
to the United States in August last year, he
found a letter from Paul Screeton, editor of
The Ley Hunter, enclosing the following item
from the Darlington & Stockton Times, 9 Aug
1975, by a country columnist:

"REMARKABLE FOAL -- I have records of
foals born without tails, with five legs and
without eyes but never of one like that born
recently at Miss Jacqueline Maw's Battenburg
Pony Stud at Malton (Yorks.) Miss Maw told
me this week that she had bought a Shetland
mare in foal at Aberdeen to obtain an out-
cross for her own stallions. Five vets have
seen the foal and say they have never seen
its like. The mare showed no signs of foaling
and was not due for three weeks. When discovered, the dam was guarding him in a hedge-
bottom as the other mares and a stallion were
most agressive. Miss Maw says: 'The colt
foal was about ten inches high, his legs
about the thickness of a pencil and he was
crawling about on his knees. He had no ears
and getting him and his dam to safety from
attack was a nightmare. I half carried the
tiny foal and led his dam to a loose box. The
stallion attacked the foal, knocking it to
the ground, and biting the dam. It was remarkable to see how the mare propped up the foal
until it could walk. He had several other
oddities, among them his two voices. One is
like that of a guineapig, and the other is
like the bleat of a sheep. He has odd shaped
hooves, a sheep-shaped head, tiny nostrils
and mouth. He is now growing little stubs
for ears, much further back than usual. He
crosses his legs as he walks, and walks
almost on his hocks behind. He was born with
a very curly black and silver tail (carried
to one side), and a mass of curly black mane."

Well, this was most interesting; since we
are always on the lookout for mutations of
any kind, we wrote to Miss Maw for further
details. She very kindly wrote back several
times in response to our inquiries, and even

** The photos on this & the facing page are
the copyright of Miss Jaqueline Maw. **

sent along photos of the little wonder, which we have her permission to reproduce here. I've taken the liberty of editing Miss Maw's letters (written during Dec 75) into one statement.

"I purchased his mum, Glide of Marshwood, at the 1974 Aberdeen Shetland pony sales in October. She came from Orkney already in foal by several months. Therefore I did not actually breed the Shony.((Shony is Miss Maw's name for the foal - explained below.)) The last owner of Glide had put her out on the scaterlands (areas of common land) with the stallion, Scapa Surf. In the Shetland Islands, each crofter is allowed to turn out a certain number of animals on the scaterlands. No one actually supervises the ponies or arranges the times to put mares in foal, the idea being to leave it completely in the hands of mother Nature.

"When the Shony was born, I informed the breeder in Orkney, and I was assured he was a pure-bred Shetland. The breeder had signed the form for the Shony to be registered - presumably the only registered pedigree Shetland mutation in the world!

"The foal was born on Thursday, 8 May 1975 - Ascension Day. As mentioned in the article ((above)) the mare showed no signs at all of being about to foal. This is very unusual, as mares always as a rule show ample signs from about 24 hours before the birth. The other ponies being so agressive to Glide and her foal was also much against the rule of nature; the usual action being for all other mares to form a protective semi-circle around the new-born foal. Presumably, the strange reaction to the foal was because of nature's rejection of the abnormal or the weak. At first the creature could only crawl around, but has now become healthy and active. He is still <u>very</u> small and his legs are very thin up to the knee joints, becoming much thicker above the knee. His back is still in a curve and his hindquarters are set very low.

"The foal's hooves are very odd, as the photos show. Now he has become much stronger and able to move about without his mum for support, he can also canter at top speed. This canter is most peculiar, very similar to the action of a deer or a fawn. Nothing like the way a pony moves! His tail is carried to one side; the dock (tail-joint) being bent. On the day of his birth, the foal had an absolute mass of thick black <u>curly</u> mane. Foals are usually born with only a few short hairs along the top of their necks, looking somewhat like a toothbrush. I have never seen a foal with such a mass of mane, even when several months old. His mane has continued to grow in length and thickness.

"The Shony was named by the Yorkshire TV film crew when he and his mum appeared on their news programme, Calendar. They made the name from 'Sh' for a sheep or a Shetland, and 'ony' for a pony; their idea being that the foal was half sheep because of its sheepy looks and its sheep-like noises. The name stuck and he is now registered in the Shetland Pony Stud Book as 'Jacob Shony of Battenburg'. He has been examined by five vets and, as I have been assured he is in no pain or suffering, I have not put him to sleep. The Shony is very quick-witted and <u>most</u> intelligent. I feel I can safely say he is the most quick-witted foal I have ever known, handled or owned.

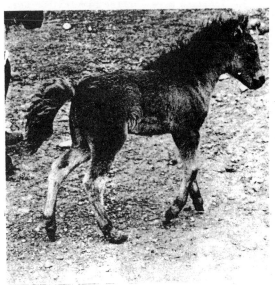

"I have had many letters from people all over the country wanting to know about the Shony. Many people have suggested that his father might be other than a pony. The popular idea is that he is a cross between pony and sheep, or deer! The vet on Yorkshire TV said in his opinion the foal was a mutation, and that he had never seen such a strange creature, and that Shony's survival was most remarkable. 'Look North' of Newcastle BBC TV also came to see the Shony and they recorded some of his very strange sounds. Everyone who sees him is absolutely fascinated by him, especially when he decides to make his noises. When the blacksmith came to trim his hooves, Shony lay down on his side like a dog. The blacksmith had to crouch down on the ground and hold one hoof up at a time. The Shony was perfectly happy to lie in this way to have his hooves trimmed. He appeared to accept it as the normal thing to happen.

"As he gets older, he certainly becomes even more odd. As mentioned, he has not grown very much in size or weight since his birth, certainly not making the normal growth rate for a foal. He carries and holds

his head at a very odd angle for a pony. His
appearance around the head and neck is
becoming much stranger than when the photos
were taken. The mouth and nostrils have
remained the same size as at birth.

"Another strange fact about the Shony is
that he now has two 'mums'. Mares are very
funny about foals other than their own
coming up to them. As all the other brood-
mares were so nasty with Glide and the Shony,
I did not dare to risk them out again for
fear of further attacks. I own a 16-year-old
barren Shetland mare called Harviestoun Sari
and turned her out with Glide and the Shony.
Sari took to Shony immediately and looks
after him now as well as his own mum. Sari
does everything possible for him, apart from
feeding him milk of course. She becomes most
upset if the Shony moves out of her sight,
and calls to him just as his mum does. He
spends a lot of time standing close to Sari
as though she were his mum, and she shares
her food with him; so he now has two mums.
The three make a strange but charming
picture.

"Shony is now weaned and no longer takes
milk from his mother, so they have not been
parted; besides, both mums and Shony get very
upset if they are parted. (Glide is believed
to be in foal for 1976). The three live
together in a large loose box, and go out in
the paddock for daytime exercise. Shony's
most favoured food is 'Gillmans Glucose Lick'
a large bucket filled with a solid mass of
glucose and vitamins. He spends ages licking
it; he also eats up all of his hay each day.

"I would never part with him as I would be
most afraid that he would fall into the
wrong hands. He is a most intelligent little
animal, and will always have a good home at
my stud. If anything has fought for life he
has and I love him dearly and could never
part with him."

We asked if Miss Maw had contacted any
geneticists for their opinion, but she replied
that she had only begun thinking about it.
We assured her that we'd be interested in the
results of any such testing, and indeed in
the Shony's development generally. Glide, it
seems, according to another write-up in the
Farmers Guardian, 17 Oct 1975, had had three
previous foals of show quality, being a show
quality pony herself; so we will be interested too in Glide's latest foaling.

Well, it is gratifying to hear the Shony
will have security and love in his life. Without such love, curiosity can be callous and
cruel. May he live long, and happily, Miss
Maw; and to you our thanks for sharing your
information with us.

POST SCRIPT.
Fort, of course, had a word to say on the
subject of the supposed inability of different
species to interbreed, which we append here
for the edification of those who think the
notion of the Shony's father being a ram or
a deer is utterly preposterous:

"I could quote many authorities against
the occurrence of bizarre hybrids, leaving
hard to explain, in terms of terrestrial
origin, strange creatures that have appeared
upon this earth. There are no biologists who
will not admit fertility between creatures so
much alike as hares and rabbits. Nevertheless,
I think that there have been strange hybrids.
"A cow that gave birth to two lambs and a
calf.

"I don't know how that will strike all
minds, but to the mind of a standardized
biologist I'd not be much more preposterous,
if I should tell of an elephant that had produced two bicycles and a baby elephant.

"Toronto Globe, May 25, 1889 - The reporter went to the farm of Mr John H Carter, at
South Simcoe, and wrote that he had seen two
lambs, which were larger and coarser than
ordinary, less romantically derived lambs...
Other newspapers published statements by
well-known stockbreeders who had examined the
lambs, and were compelled to accept the story
of their origin." --
-- Charles Fort - Lo!, ch9; The Books, p611.

STRANGE HORSES.
This might be as good a place as any for
a few historical notes we have lying around,
and vaguely relevant to the Shony, though we
have many more contemporary notes on animal
curiosities which will have to wait.

The Oracle, a long defunct London magazine, in its November 1789 issue tells that:
"There is at present a fine horse in the
menage of the Earl of Pembroke, at Wilton
House, which when worked, sweats exceedingly
on one side, whilst on the other he is perfectly dry and cool; and this extraordinary
operation of nature is so exact, that it
describes a palpably regular line from the
top of the nose up the middle of the face,
between the ears and along the back to the
tail."

The Times, 16 Sept 1836, reported a horse
in Brussels, that was carnivorous. A few days
before, it had burst from its stall and
devoured two breasts of mutton hanging in a
butcher's shop.

Under the heading 'Singular Taste of an
Ass', a tale is told of a 50-year-old ass,
called Billy, owned by a farmer at Great
Lever, near Bolton, Lancs, who had a fondness
for tobacco and snuff. As the Monthly Review
vol 22, p156, tells it: "When he had finished
the tobacco, a pinch of strong rapee was
administered, which Billy snuffed without the
least demur, and curling up his olfactory
organ delivered one of those charming solos
so peculiar to his species."

UNIDENTIFIEDS

When Louis XIV got bored with lamb and beef, he is said to have cried out: "Oh, God! send me a new animal." If he was around this last year he would've probably regretted his outburst, because since last Spring strange things have been popping up all over. Since June 75, Nessie hogged the limelight, but in tiny paragraphs and provincial papers there has been a monstrous cavalcade of such proportions that even that 19th C naturalist-gourmet Frank Buckland would have stopped in his tracks. He boasted, disgustingly, that he'd try anything - and once even invited a friend to share with him the heart of the above mentioned monarch, plundered from the royal tomb during the French Revolution. What irony! Anyway -- let's join the procession...

ON LAND ..

JAKARTA, INDONESIA.

Draw ye near, and prepare to boggle. An animal was caught in the jungle near Kalimanan, that a local news agency has labelled a 'Tigelboat'. It was said to have the claws of a rooster, the legs of a goat, a tiger's body and an elephant-like trunk -- Rand Daily Mail Nov 75. Cr: CJ Holtzhausen.

GORO, NORTHERN ITALY.

Our Italian correspondent, Edoardo Russo, sent us two notices from La Stampa on the Goro Monster', a lizard-like creature, described as "a large snake with legs, 3 metres long and as big as a dog," seen several times in mid-June last year in the Po delta, near Ferrara. Following a close-range sighting by a Goro farmer, Maurizio Trombini, the Carabineri, and the Ente Protezione Animali (a Soc. for Prevention of Cruelty to Animals) were both involved in searches to allay the fears of people in the area. A few years earlier, there were similar sightings in the same area, which led to speculation of a crocodile (or something like one) having escaped from a zoo or circus and living wild. Whatever it was, it left clear prints and tracks ((but apparently these have proved no help in identification of the beast - Ed)) We will quote the main item from La Stampa, 29 June 75, by their reporter Francesco Santini:

"Like every sultry Italian summer, this too has its viscid, black, cylindrical and howling venusian monster. Two days ago, it was walking in a tomato-field, almost on the Ferrara-Rovigo border, and the man who saw it panicked, dropping his hoe to raise the alarm. Among the 5000 inhabitants of the Ferrarese town, divided from Venetia by an arm of the Po, they call it the 'Goro Monster' and remember ancient and unusual stories of terrible "Austrian (sic), suspicious, insidious, animals". To see the track, a little faded in the sand of the sunny fields, you leave the Romea Road between Mestre and Ravenna, just past the Pomposa Abbey, and through the Mesola woods. Here, near a well-preserved 17th century tower, is Scola Farm, assigned to Maurizio Trombini by the Ente Delta Reclamation in the 60s. Trombini is a vigorous and careful man; marked by 40 years as a fisherman on the Po and the Adriatic Sea.

"Perhaps the Goro Monster, like a snake, "but with so many, many little legs, and an ugly and mean dangling tongue" won't become a home monster ((?)), but in this town Maurizio Trombini has a reputation for seriousness... and the first person who took his account seriously was Sergeant Starchielli, at the local police station, who immediately reported to Ferrara. In the little Goro barracks, the officer keeps a copy of the telegram in a scrupulous yellow folder. The animal is described as: "Black colour; 3 metres in length; 20 centimetres in diameter, and howling like a wolf. On-the-spot investigation by army troopers revealed a track left by the above-mentioned reptile, 20 centimetres large ((?)) and well-visible." Among Maurizio Trombini's tomatoes, next to the canal by the Mesola Woods the tracks are still visible.

"He has only one worry: nobody can classify his monster. The Mesola Woods forester suggested a crocodile had escaped from a zoo or circus and has been able to acclimatize among the scores of canals crossing each other in the Goro country. Trombini doesn't like the crocodile hypothesis. "I'd have identified it if it was," he says convincingly. "Besides, don't crocodiles live in the heat. Here in winter and the fog it's freezing cold. It's a gigantic lizard. I couldn't have been mistaken." The Goro lads have invented a new sport. In the morning they dive into the Po arm touching the town; in the afternoon they make for the Mesola Woods on their mopeds on safari. They find no monster-tracks, of course, but now and then there is a report that someone has sighted the animal. Sr Trombini sighs with relief: "I'd prefer not to be alone in this story," but he investigates and finds the news is groundless.

"It grows dark and the old ones in the Goro taverns around the harbour recall adventures of monsters, sea-horses, luminous and flying fish. Someone is telling an ancient time-honoured tale of a terrible animal, crossing the border by night. It came from Venetia, which they still call 'Austria' here. "We were at war, and the Austrians sent wild howling beasts." Trombini listens to them hopefully, then sets out for the harbour. "When you're at sea you listen to a lot of tales. When I'm old, I too will be able to report how my monster was very long and black, with its tongue hanging out." A rustic monster which a lot of people hope to see."

Edoardo Russo adds that the reporting is distinctly sarcastic; and that no further developments have been heard of.

Interestingly, we have an old note on file from Reveille, 19 Dec 1970; that a "15 foot reptile, like a dinosaur" attacked a man named Antonio Samorani, in July 1969. The scene of the attack was Forli, near Ravenna, and about 50 miles SSE of Ferrara. (cont. in footnote on p.5.)

BERRI, SOUTH AUSTRALIA.
Reader FE Cater sent us a note that is worth recording, taken from Michael Hervey's UFOs Over the Southern Hemisphere (Robert Hale 1975) p157:

"Residents in Berri, near Adelaide, were frightened on January 2, 1953, by a ghastly looking animal described as over 6 feet long, with a peculiar head and eyes, and a long scaly body. It hissed at them from the top of a tree. Someone went to fetch a gun, but the animal,'which looked as if it had come from another world' according to one of the witnesses, leapt out of sight and vanished before a shot could be taken at it."

SAN ANTONIO, TEXAS.
We have quite a few clippings on the "automobile-sized" Big Bird sighted in Southern Texas, throughout January this year. According to reports,it has a 15-ft wingspan, stands 4ft tall, and has a bald head with a bat-like face. We'll present the reports in more detail in our forthcoming 'Bird' issue.

Sounds like Keel's Garuda is coming home to roost!

ANDES, CHILE.
News has just arrived of mystery footprints, photographed by English mountaineer Steven Read. He was on the South Patagonia Ice-cap Expedition, climbing in the Paine region of the Andes on the Chilean border. He says, in the (London) Evening Standard, 15 March 1976: "We climbed seven new peaks, and it was right on the summit of one, near a rock ridge, that we saw the tracks in the snow. They started from the rocks and stretched about 200-300 yards across the snow before vanishing again over a rock ridge."

"It was an even track of some two-footed animal, evenly spaced and certainly not human. There were no other climbers within 20 or 30 miles of us. There is no explanation of what the animal could be. The only large animal there is the puma, which is four-footed and would not go as high as that. The ridge, although not very high as mountains go, was about 6000 ft, and had been quite a climb up the south face. The tracks were about 6 inches long by 4 or 5 inches wide and had no toe marks. We did not think they were a large bird as there were no wing marks in the snow." ((!!!)) Cr: Paul Devereux. It is not explained who or what this expedition was, but it would seem from this statement that they had no zoologist along. Despite Read's insistance to the contrary, the Evening Standard headlined the story as 'Yeti'. From Read's photo the tracks appear to your editor to be cat-like, but then the nearest I've been to this sort of sight is the snow in our garden.

While we're on the subject of ABSMs, permit me a sarcastic sigh as I report that Major John Blashford-Snell, "the nation's leading explorer" and known in the Mess as Blashers, has solved the riddle of the Abominable Snowman. Most national papers here for 12 Jan 1976, reported in the silliest manner possible, that Blashers, returning from a trip to Nepal, spotted footprints in mud near the village of Meghauli, 100 miles from Everest. Villagers explained that they were those of a holyman with congenitally deformed feet who ran off into the jungle. The story ought to be good for free drinks for a while.

ORINOCO, VENEZUELA.
In the Andes story above, Read asked around among the locals back at their camp, but could get no hint about the origin of his tracks; a similar questioning of locals was not only enlightning to another British climber, David Nott, but gave his discovery extra mystery. Nott and another Englishman, Steven Platt, and two Venezuelans, Wilmer Perez and Carlet Reves, investigated "what geologists say is the oldest cave in the world, 400ft from the top of a 4500ft rock tower on the El Autana mountain, deep in the Orinoco jungle of Venezuela. The cave pierces the mountain, like an eye in a rock needle, and to the Piaroa Indians it is the home of a centuries-old giant, in vaguely human form, who descends on stormy nights to devour people from their tribe. The intrepid climbers had to negotiate four rivers and 15 miles of jungle to reach the mountain; it took 3 days to climb and they spent 3 days in the caves.
In the Toronto Sun (Ontario) 1 March 1976, Nott said: "Inside, it is as big as a cathedral with a perfectly sculpted dome. Tunnels and galleries run from the main chambers with smoothly vaulted roofs and level floors, in rock coloured white to rose-red. It is breath-taking, but we don't understand it." They did not find any monster or bones, but did see some charred wood, like an old campfire. He told reporters that he discovered four more openings, and that as soon as he had collected new equipment and worked out a plan, he was heading back there to look into them. (Cr:MX). Not perhaps an Unidentified Monster story but interesting nevertheless. We'll keep our ears open for developments.

BELLINGHAM, WASHINGTON.
On 23 October 1975, police sergeant Ken Cooper investigated a report in Bellingham that a plastic storm door had been ripped from its hinges at a home. He switched on his patrol-car spotlight and saw a 7½ft tall hairy creature standing in the bushes. "It appeared to have no neck. Just a head on shoulders, very big and muscular, with very short blackish hair. The face had a leathery wrinkled look, like a woman's black purse. It had steam coming off the body as if it had been wet and running." He aimed his shotgun at it, then thought that discretion was the better part of valour and retreated. Later he found several sets of large tracks and thinks there are three of the things in the area. Daily Mail, 15 Nov 1975. Cr: Steev Moore.

IN LAKES & RIVERS ..

MUSKRAT LAKE, ONTARIO.
There have been several "recent" sight-ings (unfortunately undated) of the legendary denizen of this 10-mile lake, about 75 miles west of Ottawa. In 1941, a man reported seeing "an object as large as the average horse" while he was fishing. In 1968, Don Humphries, paddling his canoe on a clear Spring night, saw the monster "out of the water, scratching in the cat-tails with its snout, apparently eating them." But he had startled it, and it slid back into the water "without a splash." Other sightings describe an "alligator head" and "grasshopper-like legs" and a body about 20ft long. It is old too, for Indians described a similar creature to the explorer Champlain at least 350 years ago. Saskatoon Star Phoenix (Saskatchewan) 4 Feb 1976. Cr: MX.

SOMEWHERE UP THE AMAZON.
This is a curious little story, and told by a Swiss businessman who met, whilst on holiday in the region, a 75-year-old guide, called Sebastian Bastos. Bastos told the un-named Swiss that he had lived among the Indians in remote parts of the rain-forest for 13 years, could speak many of their languages, and had seen sights no white man had ever clapped eyes on before. The Indians, he said, know that many prehistoric animals still live in the deep waterholes in the jungle, occasionally emerging at night. He himself recalled a trip up the Amazon some years earlier to a

pre-arranged rendezvous with an Indian on a beach in the heart of the rain-forest. That year the water level was exceptionally low. He had just beached his boat and walked up to his friend when he heard a tremendous noise behind him. Turning round he saw an enormous "prehistoric animal" rising from the water, gripping his canoe and smashing it. The attack was in broad daylight, and both men ran for cover and watched the animal dive into the water. The Indians, he said, told of other such beasts, about 18ft long, and the few Indians who approached them were killed. The Swiss gentleman says that he had no reason to believe Bastos lied, and that he had been frightened as he recalled the incident. This curious story ends there - there is no pitch for a monster-hunt, or any other sign that anyone is trying to make any money out of it. Wherefore art thou, Professor Challenger? Liverpool Daily Post, 3 Jan 76. Cr: P Ledger.

LOCH NESS, INVERNESS.
We have decided to shelve our plans for a Nessie-chronology of the Rines-Scott affair. Salvos are still being sporadically fired in the letter-columns of the national dailies and thanks to the efforts of many readers, particularly Ken Rogers, we have these on file here. However, they don't add much one way or the other to the situation, and since space is limited we thought it was more important to devote it to more urgent news.

There was a sighting of Nessie just before the storm broke, last year. On 18 July, Alan Wilkins, of Annan, Dumfriesshire, and his family, spent 14 hours at the loch, during which he saw the monster, or at least "something strange", four times. His statement to the Loch Ness Investigation Bureau, reads: "At 0720, a long dark line appeared in mid-loch off the western point. It sank slowly, only to reappear soon afterwards. It sank and rose two or three times. On the final appearance, I took two still photos. I guessed the object must have been at least 20ft long, but perhaps not more than 2ft high. I looked through the binoculars in time to see a large black shape. After a further appearance as a long line, it was suddenly gone. At 1015, a long dark line appeared in the water (in the same area). I passed the binoculars to Margery. By the time I had refocused the binoculars, the object had become three well-spaced triangular humps." A man nearby also looking through binoculars confirmed there were three humps. Mr Wilkins later describe two more incidents in which humps "emerged majestically from the water."

The film was sent to the LNIB and developed in two separate laboratories, and David James MP called them "far and away the best over a period of 34 years." Poor light and range has spoiled all but a few of the photos and these will be examined by experts, and even sent to NASA for computer-enhancement. The Sunday Express, 5 Oct 75, (Cr: BR Bates) from whom we take our details, also printed the photo we show here.

IN THE SEA ..

BARMOUTH, GWYNEDD.
While the centre-stage was being hogged by the Nessie debate (see last issue), the beast that has been haunting Cardigan Bay has come and gone a few times - but not it seems entirely unnoticed. Our correspondent in the area, Colin Palmer, has been following the phenomenon and keeping us informed. Since the original sightings made by his six girl pupils on 2 March 1975 (see reports in NEWS 10/18f), there has been a trickle of further information. (By 'original', I mean, of course, the key sighting that brought the matter to our attention. The Barmouth Monster sightings go back farther than that, as the next datum testifies). Following an appearance on a Granada TV news programme, Mrs R Griffith, of Colwyn Bay, Clwyd, wrote to Colin (dated 9th July 75):

"I thought it would be of some interest for you to know that a relative and myself have also seen very large foot tracks along the beach at Llanaber. We were walking along the beach between the end of the promenade and the footbridge, about 3 to 4 years ago, when we came across these very big footprints not very far from the water. They were about 12" to 18" in diameter. We both felt rather apprehensive on seeing them, but quickly came to a decision that there was no animal with feet as big as those, and that someone must have been fooling about with something - though they did look very real. I really do regret now that we did not study them closer, or maybe it was just as well we did not follow those tracks! I really am convinced now that those girls did see a very large creature."

Sometime in November or December (we shamefacedly admit to not having the date) the Cambrian News reported that more footprints had been discovered on beaches further up the coast. Colin received a letter from a Mr Holmes, of Dolgellau, dated 16 Dec, who saw the prints at Penmaenpool toll-bridge:

"The Cambrian News gave a version of what happened, and the footprints were a little larger than a good-sized dinner plate and you got the impression they were webbed. They were very deep in the soft sand, and when whatever it was went back in the water, its feet slithered along. Since (I saw them 7 days ago) the tide has been in several times a day, and you can still see the impressions."

That would fix Mr Holmes's sighting as 10th Dec. The CN is published on Fridays, so perhaps the item appeared in its issue for 12 Dec 75?

Colin himself writes: "Since your last coverage of the Cardigan Bay 'monster', I have been given two fully authenticated accounts, one of clear footprints in wet sand, and the other at sea of the creature at close quarters. Neither of these accounts has been passed on to anyone else, because the news of 'Nessie' hit the headlines and I thought - well, people will have to believe it now, because if Peter Scott said so, then it must be true, therefore no further need for my small attempts at convincing the community. The first sighting is that of Mr Holmes (above). Colin relates the second:

"A fishing boat making its way to Pwllheli was off Bardsey Sound in calm water when its skipper saw a most strange creature break surface only yards from the boat. He called to his crew and both men had a clear view of a large fat body mostly in the water, but with a long extended neck and a large head. The creature viewed the boat and then submerged with a speed that was difficult to believe. Within an hour the creature had surfaced three more times, again close to the boat - and once, narrowly avoided being rammed. This was no quick flash-and-away observation - these fishermen are very experienced in these waters, and being professionals, not given to exaggeration. When they saw my drawing ((NEWS 10/19)) there was instant recognition. To me, this was all the confirmation I needed of the existance of a creature that had been innocently described to me by the five schoolgirls last Easter. The Pwllheli fishermen have not, and I doubt if they ever would, put pen to paper - they are content in the telling of it."

KILWA, TANZANIA.
About mid-May last year, the Tanzanian Press reported that a fisherman in this southern part of the country had landed in his nets a fish-like creature the like of which had never been seen before. Reports reaching Dar-es-Salaam said the man, Mohamed Sefu, found the strange fish had arms and legs. "It had two legs with ten toes on each. The arms protruded from its chest, where there was also one eye. On its right-side there was another eye which glowed brightly at night. It also had a small horn, like that of a cow, one ear and a hump. A large toothless mouth and a beard under its chin completed the description." No measurements were given but it was said the creature remained alive for some time after it was caught. Biologists were said to be puzzled and unable to classify it - and Tanzanain officials promised to preserve it in the national museum. (South African) Rand Daily Mail, 23 May 75. Cr: CJ Holtzhausen. We notified our contact in the Fish section of the British Museum (Nat. Hist.), to find they didn't know of this prodigy. However one of their men would be in that part of the world shortly and would make inquiries. We'll keep you informed of any developments.

VERA CRUZ, MEXICO.
We discovered something equally monstrous that we have somehow missed in earlier issues. Fisherfolk in the Gulf of Mexico were convinced the strange creature, caught off Vera Cruz in April 1973, was "a marine monster from another world." It had one enormous sinister eye, and a giant mouth with triple rows of razor-sharp teeth. Local 'experts' had preserved the thing in alcohol for identification, but this is the last we ever heard of it. Sunday People, 15 April 1973. Further 'Bug-eyes-of-the-Deeps' can be found in the pages of the INFO Journal, particularly No8, p20ff.

THE DURGAN DRAGON.
Even as we started work on this issue, we were sent news of a series of 'sea serpent' sightings that has caused much excitement down in Devon, who are calling it the 'Durgan Dragon'. Tony 'Doc' Shiels, the Wizard of the West, was kind enough to write to us with some background info. In a recent letter he says: "I suppose I should mention that there were a few odd sightings of UFOs, around Falmouth, late last year. The most spectacular, a group of 3, being seen by Mr R Good, of Budock, near Falmouth. I don't know if this should be tied in with the monster sightings or not (though it has become fashionable of late to make connections between dragons and discs). The monster was first seen, I believe, by a fisherman, around Christmastime. I'm told that at least two of the mackerel fishermen who have seen the monster, now refuse to put to sea, until it's been captured, killed or driven away from

...cont on p16.

We were scheduled to feature Robert Forrest's reply to FW Holiday's
riposte to Robert Forrest's article on 'Leys, UFOs & Chance, but we
ran out of room. We apologise to him, and will definitely have it in
the next issue. Meanwhile...another hypothesis from Stuart Greenwood:

Stuart W Greenwood

The Giza ~ Stonehenge Connection

In pursuit of a guess that alignment B
through Stonehenge in Watkins' book (1) might
point to Giza in Egypt, I stretched a thread
on a globe between Stonehenge and Giza and
found that it did indeed do so within the
limits of accuracy of my measurements (2).
The thread still graces my globe, and in an
idle moment recently I checked the angle
made by the thread with the parallel of
latitude through Giza. As far as I could
determine, the angle as measured with a
simple protractor was 52 degrees.

Now that gives one pause, as it happens
to correspond with the typical angle of slope
of the pyramids at Giza; just as the
measurement of 29 degrees for the corresponding angle in the Stonehenge region corres-
ponds fairly closely with the 30 degree
slope of Silbury Hill near Avebury (3).

I was fortunate in securing the cooperation of Captain William W Bull of the
Department of Aerospace Studies here in
Maryland, in a check on the quoted figures
using a Global Navigational & Planning Chart.
(His results are appended). It appears that,
in addition to the links between Stonehenge
and Giza (and Giza and Silbury Hill) already
suggested in (2) and (3), there may be a
further relationship indicated by the
relative positions of the sites on their
respective parallels of latitude. Of course,
we may just be looking at a series of
coincidences. And then again, perhaps not!

References:

1) A Watkins, The Old Straight Track, Garnstone Press, 1970. (Also Ballantine Books,
   1973).

2) Stuart W Greenwood, "Pyramid Slope and
   Northern Latitudes", THE NEWS, 9/12.

3) Stuart W Greenwood, "On the Slope of
   Silbury Hill", THE NEWS, 13/6.

Stuart W Greenwood, December 1975.

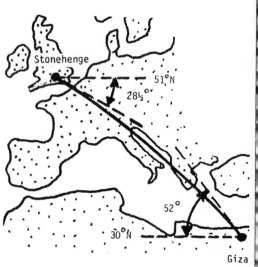

Great Circle Route between Giza and Stonehenge

DEPARTMENT OF THE AIR FORCE

DETACHMENT 330, AFROTC (AU)
UNIVERSITY OF MARYLAND
COLLEGE PARK, MARYLAND 20742

6 November 1975

At the request of Mr. Stuart Greenwood, Department of Aerospace Engineering, University of Maryland, I have measured certain geographic relationships which he believes exist between Stonehenge and Avebury, England, and Giza, Egypt. The coordinates are:

Stonehenge	51 10'N	001 50'W
Avebury	51 25'N	001 52'W
Giza	29 59'N	031 09'E

These coordinates were laid out on a Global Navigation and Planning Chart (GNC). The GNC 4N Chart, eighth edition, was used. This chart is constructed to a scale of 1:5,000,000. The chart is constructed mathematically using a Lambert Conformal Conic Projection. This method employs a secant cone intersecting the spheroid at two parallels of latitude called the standard parallels; in this case, they are 37 00'N and 65 00'N. These points are normally located at the one-sixth and five-sixth points of the projection. This particular chart covers Europe, part of North Africa, and part of the Middle East.

On any Lambert Conformal Chart, a great circle route is approximated by a straight line. The actual form of the great circle is concave toward the mid-parallel. But the distortion between the straight line and great circle is negligible.

Straight lines were constructed between Stonehenge, Avebury, and Giza. Where these lines intersected the parallels of latitude, measurements were made using a standard Air Force navigational plotter. We find that the measured angle at Avebury is 29° and at Stonehenge is $28\frac{1}{2}^\circ$. When we measure the angles at Giza, we obtain angles of $52\frac{1}{2}^\circ$ and 52°. Since Giza lies beyond the 37 parallel, it lies in the realm of greatest distortion; therefore, these readings are subject to a potential error of up to $1\frac{1}{4}^\circ$. Since the Stonehenge and Avebury areas are within the standard parallels, their potential error is less than $\frac{1}{2}^\circ$.

WILLIAM W. BULL, Captain, USAF
Assistant Professor of Aerospace Studies

WWB:eef

these parts. I've also heard that the monster
has been blamed for a run of bad luck and odd
accidents (not to mention unusually bad weat-
er) suffered by some fishermen lately."

The first of our collection of notes from
the Falmouth Packet records a carcase and
bones found washed up on Durgan Beach earlier
this year. The skeleton was described as about
10ft long, and a 13-year-old naturalist, Toby
Benham, told the paper he was fairly sure it
was a whale. It's skull, showing "blow-holes"
now graces his collection of bones. It seems
too small to be a whale to us, but doubtless
it is one of the many dolphins and porpoises
washed ashore all year round ((A handy ref. on
the subject is A Guide for the Identification
& Reporting of Stranded Whales, Dolphins &
Porpoises on British Coasts -- British Museum
(Natural History) publication No: 549; by FC
Fraser.))

The Packet for 5 March 76 printed two
photographs of the monster, looking remarkably
like Nessie on a good day, sent in by 'Mary F'
of Falmouth. We reproduce them here with the
kind permission of the Packet, with Mary F's
account of the incident, dated 29th February:

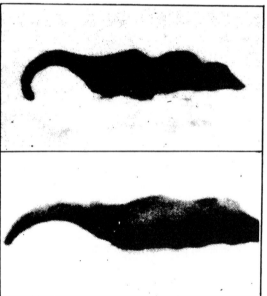

Mary F took her photos very early in February, saying the animal was only visible for
a few seconds and that the light was shining
into the camera. "I'd say it was 15 to 18ft
long (I mean the part showing above the water)
It looked like an elephant waving its trunk,
but the trunk was a long neck with a small
head on the end, like a snake's head. It had
humps on the back which moved in a funny way.
The colour was black or very dark brown, and

the skin seemed to be like a sealion's. I'm
glad to know other people have seen the great
Cornish sea serpent. As a matter of fact the
animal frightened me. I would not like to see
it any closer. I do not like the way it moved
when swimming."

The photos brought forward several more
sightings, in letters printed in the Packet
for 12 March. Mr S Bennett of Seworgan wrote
"I have myself, during the last Christmas
holidays, witnessed the sighting of a similar
creature, although until now I have remained
reticent about it. It was off the shore at
Durgan, Helford, about 4pm, near dusk. When I
first spotted it, I thought it was a dead
whale, but as I drew nearer, it started to move
away smoothly and I could see it was not a
whale, nor like any other creature seen
around here. I judged that the part of it I
could see above water was about 12ft in lengt
with an elongated neck, similar to the one in
your photographs...I would like to add that
some of your readers may remember the old
Dolphin - a pub, alas, no more. Over the fire
place, there hung a replica sea-serpent which
as the story goes, was frequently seen in
Falmouth bay in the days of sail."

Mr Dunvan Viner, of Truro, wrote: "I now
have the courage to admit, however disquiet-
ing it may be, to having seen a creature not
unlike that in the photographs, a few hundred
yards off Rosemullion Head. My first impression was that I had seen a whale, as only a
dark hump was visible. But as I watched, it
started to rise in the water, and a long neck
similar to that described by Mary F, appeared
It seemed to look around and then sank back
under the surface. It is difficult to say how
large the creature was because of the distanc
but it must have been about 30 or 40ft in
length, the major part of it being the neck."

The Packet for 19 March said that Tony
Shaw, a writer and member of the Folklore
Society, remembered hearing of similar report
about five years ago, and that there had also
been monster sightings off the Irish coast
"recently" -- we'll be looking into both of
these further, since we have nothing on our
files. There was also a letter from Amelia
Johnson, now living in London, who recently
stayed with her sister near Falmouth. "One
afternoon we decided to take a walk..in the
direction of Rosemullion...Looking out to sea
I saw a strange form suddenly emerge from the
water in Falmouth Bay. It was just like the
sort of description one hears of the Loch
Ness monster; a sort of prehistoric dinosaur
thing, with a neck the length of a lamppost.
I raced back to my sister and told her what
I'd seen. She told me she thought I must be
"batty" and when we went back to see if we
could see it again, it was no longer there."
Miss Johnson goes on to say that she allowed
her sister to convince her she must have
imagined it - which she accepted - until her

sister sent her the clipping from the Packet with Mary F's photos. "The only point on which I disagree with Mary F is in the collouring. I should say it was more of a dark grey; but then, like her, I didn't stay around too long."

'Doc' Shiels, a writer and entertainer, announced several weeks ago his intentions to organise a hunt for the Dragon, and if he fails here, he'll switch to the Irish coast. His plan is to raise the monster by making psychic contact with it. Some of the plans are in operation and we'll bring you news of any developments. 'Doc' also told us that he was contacted by someone else who claimed to be able to call the beast psychically -- she is an attractive young witch called 'Psyche'

who plans to swin in the bay, naked, sometime in April -- so we'll be keeping an eye on this too (yes indeed!)

Even as we work on the layouts for this issue, more cuttings arrive from Doc Shiels. He has a letter in the Packet for 26 March, announcing his plans to make psychic contact with the thing...and the front page of the same paper says that a Prof Mike McCormick was sailing from New York to join the hunt. (A prof. of what we don't know, but if it's any help, he does a fire-eating act and has a collection of 'specimens' (("a young basilisk" etc)) from his world-wide 'monster-hunts.) Doc tells us that the Prof, Tony Shaw (above) and himself will probably cooperate closely in a combined hunt.

IT'S RAINING SHITSICLES!
That, believe it or not, headlined an item in Esquire for Jan 76 (Cr: John Carlson.) Mr & Mrs James McBride of Denver, Colorado, had a 60lb ice mass came through their kitchen ceiling. They thought it was a bomb and called the police, who later said the stuff was "frozen human waste leaked from the sanitary system of a jet flying overhead." However that may be, some stuff, described as the contents of an airliner's toilet, came down from the sky at Bason Bridge, near Bridgewater, Somerset, much to the disgust of Mr Leslie Skuse, who said: "It was all over the washing, and my cabbages. I can laugh at it, but it's not very nice." A spokesman for Lulsgate Airport (the nearest) doubted it was an aircraft: "They have chemical toilets which are sealed." Interestingly, there is no mention of the goop being frozen. Perhaps someone up there is trying to tell us something -- or we send them spacecraft, so they send back their rubbish too! Daily Mirror, 22 March 76. Cr: Anne Williams, S Moore.

THE SILVER CASE FROM NOWHERE.
Sometime in December last year, Mrs Lynn Connolly was hanging out her washing when she felt a sudden sharp tap on the top of her head. A neighbour heard her cry, and when they both searched the grass, they found a

small silver notecase, about 1½" by 2½", hinged, and containing a half used notepad. It was marked with the initials 'TB'(or 'JB') and the word 'Klaipeda', which was the name of an old Lithuanian seaport, now behind the Iron Curtain. Mrs Connolly heard no plane overhead ((if it dropped from a plane it'd have given her more than a tap!)). No one claimed it at the police station, so it was given back to Mrs Connolly - and there the mystery of the case that fell out of the sky and into the garden at The Quadrant, Hull, remains. It seems like it fell only a short distance onto Mrs Connolly's head -- but from where...? Sunday Express, 21 Dec 75. Cr: Steve Moore, Richard Cotton.

BANGERS IN THE SKY.
In a letter to the Sunday Express, 12 Oct 75, Mrs JP Adams, of Belmont Crescent, Swindon, Wilts, says she looked out of her sitting-room window to watch the storm which was fiercely thrashing the trees together outside. Then she noticed, high up in one tree, a string of four uncooked sausages. It was not windy enough for them to be blown there -- did a bird drop them, she wondered? We, as you know by now, incline toward the view that they were dropped by a celestial butcher's boy who once worked for the Worcester Fishmonger. Can you suggest anything better?

Journals cont from p27.

wheedling info out of institutions. INFO:
Box 367, Arlington , VA 22210, USA. 1yr: £5.00
/$10.00. See our colophon for apecial joint
rate for both NEWS & INFO Journal. All UK
subscribers who haven't yet received INFO 15
(they got lost in the mail) should receive
replacements with No16. We don't know until
you tell us - so please write if after a reasonable while nothing turns up.

The Christian Parapsychologist -- a small new
quarterly journal which explores a specifically
Christian interpretation of paranormal phenomena. Much of its contents are highly pertinent and of interest to Forteans, and some of
it deals with Forteana. For a sample, send
stamps to cover postage to: Leslie Price, Ed.,
CP: 1 Devonshire Gardens, London W4 3TW.

Kexue Tongbao, No10 1975 -- valuable reference
article on ancient Chinese records of astronomical events.

New Scientist -- 5 Feb: "Courage, Fearlessness
& Fear" by Dr J Rachman; Jon Darius on new
approaches to testing Relativity theory --
12 Feb: "When do Earthquakes Occur?" by Dr J
Brander; "New Nessie Sonar Tracks are Fake" on
the laughable attempt by Videomaster to drum
up publicity during the Brighton Toyfair;
David Bohm commemorating "Heisenberg's Contribution to Physics" (he died on 1 Feb) --
26 Feb: more on the row about whether Astrology has any 'scientific value'; "Ball Lightning Photographed" (but still unexplained) --
4 Mar: "Rise & Fall of an X-ray Star" by Ken
Pounds (it peaked during the meteorological
chaos last August (see NEWS 12/7) -- 11 March
'15 Months of New Particles' Dr R Walgate
reviews the latest lepton and Hadron discoveries -- 25 March: 'When did we first
migrate to the New World?'; 'Components of
the Solid State' a review of the basic ideas
of solid state physics by Sir Nevill Mott --
1 April: Eric S Binns on mites that hitch-
hike on flies direct to a safe food supply;
'Deus est Machina?' You've got to read this
to believe it! George Sassoon and Rodney Dale
have worked out from three cabbalistic texts
(13th & 16th century) a giant machine for
making single-cell protein. The machine, called 'Ancient of Days' looks like a cross
between an alcholics vision of a super-still
and the classic mad scientist's giant brain,
and brought to Earth on the spaceships 3000
years ago. In New Scientist? The papers the
next day claimed it was a hoax, but Reading
Evening Post, for Fool's Day, quoted Rodney
Dale as denying the hoax. Just a good bit of
free speculation on old texts, he said. Move
over, Ezekiel! The manna-machine cometh!

Thanks to: D Baxter, S Moore, Wilfried Pardon, Ken Rogers, Roger Sandell, Phil Ledger.

NOTES ON GREENWICH PHENOMENA

Part2 of a
Taoist interpretation of
Fortean phenomenology
by Steve Moore.

In the previous issue of the NEWS, I
presented a collection of data which I
intend to tentatively interpret in Taoist terms. However, before reaching this
stage (in the next issue) it is necessary to look at some basic theoretical
considerations. I apologise to those
readers for whom I am going over old
ground...but on the other hand it seems
to me that one of Fort's basic notions
(and to me one of his most important),
that of the Continuous Universe, has
been sadly neglected. Perhaps a restate-
ment would not be out of place after all.

The variety of Fortean phenomena being
almost infinite, a composite approach

using various modes of thinking may well promise greater success than a single system. The scientific explanation of a comet, for instance, takes no account of the psychic response of the percipient who sees it as a portent...and if all things are continuous, who is to say which of the two is most important?

As a beginning, then, I intend to compare Fort's Continuous Universe with some classical Chinese concepts, before moving on to interpret the phenomena in terms of the latter. Hopefully, by comparing these two differing points of view (and, perhaps, others may be tempted to continue the process with other philosophies), some new insights, if only symbolic, may emerge...

FORT'S CONTINUOUS UNIVERSE

The western scientific mode of thought has very great uses, whether we consider it covers a wide enough field or not (some of the attacks currently against science disturb me, especially those against archaeology, as they betray exactly the same narrow-mindedness as they profess to attack...). But it does also have its limitations. Primary amongst these is its methodology...the practise of studying a single event in isolation, picking it out from its surroundings and largely disregarding the latter. Fort argued against this with considerable ferocity, pointing out that all things are related to one another: that the universe is continuous.

Basic to Fort's notion is that 'everything merges away into everything else': that it is impossible to look at an event in isolation without taking into account all its surrounding circumstances. Taken to its logical extreme, this means that it is impossible to examine one object without examining the entire universe. From this, it is a simple step to posit a connection, no matter how tenuous, between everything in the universe ...although in practical terms it is not necessary to carry this connection too far. But knowing where to draw the line, and which threads of connection to include in the examination, is the heart of the problem. The simple answer of science is to draw the line very close, and to rigidly regulate the lines of connection. By so doing, there is a possibility that entire lines of connection remain unknown...connections which, because they cannot be regulated and, possibly more important, used, are neglected or, more probably, ridiculed. It is those very outlawed lines of connection that should interest us.

Using this notion of continuity, Fort went on to develop his concept of the Organic Universe. His example that most readily springs to mind is that of the period in 19th century England when, after several insectless months, vast swarms of the critters appeared, seemingly from nowhere. Insects were needed: they suddenly appeared although, as it turned out, in vast excess. From this and other examples, Fort evolved an idea that would verge on the religious, were it not for the fact that he saw it as an automatic process. He saw the universe in terms of a vast organism, with some form of proto-consciousness, able to compensate its own deficiencies (and yet still capable of error). It is interesting to note that when a similar hypothesis, that of 'Gaia', was put forward by two scientists (1) it met with indifference or hostility from the scientific establishment. Fort, however, having got this far, went no further. I am groping toward, if not an explanation of the mechanics of the process, at least a framework within which the process could occur.

Jung, with his concept of synchronicity, also acknowledged the possibility of lines of connection ignored by science, going beyond usual connection of cause-and-effect to examine simultaneous links between the psychic and material world (2). He adduced considerable evidence, both from his own experience and from a statistical analysis of certain aspects of astrology, to demonstrate the existence of this connecting principle, which simply is to do with the 'meaningful coincidence'...a strong psychic state finds some reflection in a happening in the material world, although the connection may be tenuous, or even 'mistaken'. This is an interesting parallel with the case of the insects mentioned by Fort. Here, though, we seem to have 'communal synchronicity': the psychic state (disturbance at the unnatural lack of insects) would be felt by large segments of the population, which may relate in some way to the massiveness of the response.

If all things are continuous, then man's physical being and his thought are connected. This may seem simplistically obvious, but according to this reasoning, there is a connection between the objective and the subjective, the world of matter and of thought, and, come to that, of the unconscious as well. By extension, we can also conceive of a 'mass-psyche', the sum-total of the psyches of the continuous human race, operating as a single unit. If many Fortean phenomena are synchronistic, this may explain why t' phenomena seem to have no correlation with the psyche of the single percipient ...they are rather reflections of the state of the mass-psyche.

We might then be moving toward a structure in which some Fortean events could be fitted (although it should be remembered that the concept of synchronicity only posits that there is such a thing as an acausal connection; it does not explain how such things happen). But this only takes us as far as events concerning physical objects, such as insects. With phenomena such as UFOs, the very nature of which is uncertain, the problem becomes more difficult. Jung himself (3) drew back from explaining them as materialised psychisms. To the Chinese, as we shall see, such a concept presented no problems...

THE CHINESE UNIVERSE

Firstly, it is not my intention to examine the entire system of Chinese philosophy. Over 3000 years or more, a conglomerate has formed: various schools of thought, with widely divergent origins, have become fused together, sometimes none too comfortably, and later ages have incorporated or rejected earlier ideas into their own systems. I intend, therefore, to stick to basics as much as possible, except where some other development might cast light on the subject.

First then, let us see how the intuitive all-encompassing Chinese point of view contrasts with, and compliments, western rationalism...

Western science is, I believe, a product of urbanisation. The trend of western man to live together in small areas is connected with his approach to life. The tendency is inwards, toward the centre, and, as a result, the mode of thought also turns inward, to examine one thing at a time, to make it the centre of attention and cut off its broader connections.

The Chinese, however, have always been, and continue to be, an agricultural nation, and although they have large cities, Chairman Mao's 'resettlement campaigns' are but another example of the tendency to look outwards, away from the centre. The tendency is to look at the universe as a whole, and the relations between things, rather than just the things themselves.

Having established this polarity of attitudes in opposite halves of the world, we are led toward the Chinese theory of dualistic monism, a union of opposing principles that make up one universe. The traditional Taoist/yin-yang theory goes like this:

The basis, and the most difficult to define because of its abstractness, is the Tao. Beyond form or name (Tao is merely a convenience name), it is the underlying principle of the universe, containing both existence and non-existence. Before the universe was formed, there was the Tao, and it is diffused throughout the universe. It is that which gives things their form, their very essence, and yet it is incapable of apprehension by rational means. 'When looked for, it is not there'...and yet it is there, in all things. It is only knowable by intuitive means. It is the mother of all things.

The Tao 'gave birth' to the One, the universe in its unity, and the One gave birth to the Two, the polar opposites. And yet there is no idea of progression here, nor, really, of the 'past tense'. It is the way things are. These polar opposites are called the yin and the yang. We are still talking in terms of universal principles here, rather than opposites such as strong and weak: everything can be defined in terms of yin and yang. From the yin and yang and their interaction, all things are 'given birth to'. The total interaction of the yin and yang, their workings throughout the universe, is known as the T'ai Chi, the 'Supreme Ultimate'. It is usually demonstrated diagramatically as in Fig.1

Fig. 1.

The two principles, yin:dark, yang:light, interact to form the great circle. And yet it is also important to note that the yin contains, within itself, the 'seed' of the yang, and vice versa. The major attributes of the yin and yang are as follows:

"Yang, the positive principle, is assoc-

iated with all that is bright, benific-
ent, active and masculine: symbolised by
Heaven and the Sun. Yin, the negative
principle, with darkness, passivity, the
feminine in nature: symbolised by the
Earth and water.

"The Yang is said to transform, the Yin
to unite. By these processes they brought into being the five essences (elements), water, fire, wood, metal, and earth.

"The interaction of Yang and Yin, in due
season and right proportion, produce,
and continue forever the normal phenomena of nature; sunshine and rain, growth
and decay, life and death. Man, especially his mental part, is built up of the
finer portions of the five essences, but
mind and matter have a common origin, in
the operations of the First Principle
through the Yang and the Yin." (4)

The Tao, though, is not merely a passive
underlying principle. One of its mean-
ings is a 'path' or 'way'. So it is also
the active principle, and at the same
time the method or pathway followed by
activity. If all this seems confusing, I
can only crave indulgence, but in attempting to describe the Absolute all labels are inadequate.

The T'ai Chi can be taken as synonymous
with the One. It is also inseparable
from the yin and the yang, for they together make up the T'ai Chi, and the T'ai
Chi is no more than the yin and yang.
Guiding and underlying the T'ai Chi is
the Tao, and yet the Tao, being in all
things, is also part of the T'ai Chi.

How does all this fit in with the Continuous Universe? Many Fortean phenomena
seem to fall into a border area between
material and psychic states; as the yin
and yang are posited to be the principles which constitute the universe in
all its varying states, their operation
in this particular area may be especially applicable. In terms of yin and yang,
interaction between the material and non-
material is therefore quite feasible.
The materialised psychisms that Jung
drew back from are acceptable when both
matter and psyche are seen as differing
forms of the same principle.

The Continuous Universe can be seen as
analogous with the T'ai Chi. That organising principle which Fort added to make
the Organic Universe, I see as analogous
to the Tao. The framework within which
the organising principle works, I shall
attempt, in the final part of this article, to interpret in terms of yin and
yang. If the Organic Universe seeks balance, I hope to show that it does so by

uniting the two great opposing principles
harmoniously. Applying a Chinese (Yin)
viewpoint to phenomena that have previously been studied by a Western (Yang)
method, I hope to obtain a similar balanced view.

GEOGRAPHICAL CONNOTATIONS.

Returning a little closer to the everyday,
the world as we know it, in geographical
terms, is also interpretable in terms of
yin and yang. Heaven (seen more as the
sky than the theological Heaven, for
the yin-yang concept works adequately
without any religious connotations) is
Yang, while the Earth is Yin. Although
these are seen as opposites, the yin and
yang, in all their manifestations, should be looked on as complimentary opposites, rather than working against one
another.

The geographical features of the landscape can also be seen in yin-yang terms.
Valleys and low-lying areas are yin,
hills and plateaux are yang. The higher,
sheerer, more 'pointed' a hill is, the
more yang it is: similarly, a deep, sheer gorge has great yin.

Just as others are attempting to find
some connection between ley-lines and
Fortean phenomena, so I will attempt to
find similar connections with a yin-yang
interpretation of nature. Indeed, many
speculations will rely heavily on these
geographical connotations, which is unfortunate, as collections of Fortean data
tend rather to concentrate on the events
than their surroundings. If the speculations contained in the final part of
this article are seen to have any value
at all, in order to correlate them, we
are going to have to compile considerably greater geographical detail about
each event. Whatever system of interpretation is chosen, leys, yin-yang or other, this geographical data is bound to
be of immense importance. Events must be
looked at in context, rather than isolation.

*** *** *** *** *** *** ***

REFERENCES:

1) Drs J Lovelock & S Epton: The Quest
   for Gaia. New Scientist, 6 Feb 75.

2) C G Jung: Synchronicity. Collected
   Works, Vol 8. Routledge.

3) C G Jung: Flying Saucers. Collected
   Works, Vol 10. Routledge.

4) G Willoughby-Meade: Chinese Ghouls &
   Goblins. Constable, 1928.
                    ****
Steve Moore. MARCH 1976.

News

Keith Rawlings, a C-of-E lay-reader and teacher at Winton Boy's School, Bournemouth, Hants, came under concerted attack by local church leaders who were "horrified" about his discussions with pupils. What has the vicars in a twist is that Mr Rawlings uses von Daniken's Chariots of the Gods as a basis for discussion. Mr Rawlings protested that they'd got things out of proportion: "In another lesson I use another book The Gospel According to Science-fiction which shows that some of von Daniken's facts are wrong." Exit apoplectic clergy. London Evening News, 18 Dec 75. Cr: Steev Moore.

Early next year, ATV will screen a late night horror/SF series called Beasts, written by Nigel Kneale, the man who brought you Quatermass, 'The Stone Tape', and 'The year of the Sex Olympics' and other great plays.

Tomsk University, Siberia,will mount a "cosmo-chemical" survey this summer on the site of the Tungus 'meteorite', according to Novosti Bulletin 36762. Also mentioned herein that I've not seen elsewhere, is the info that: "the natural rate of change in the heredity of plants in this region (is) speeded up about 12 times."

The Church of Scientology's patent on the E-meter (BP 943012) will expire on 27 July, and there has been no attempt by L Ron Hubbard to renew it. N.Sci, 12 Feb 76.

Peruvian Ground Drawings: the exhibition of photos and Maria Reiche's work on the lines at Nazca, mounted by the Arts Council, has the following schedule:
ICA Gallery,London: 9 April - 2 May.
Hereford, Museum: 8 May - 30 May.
Folkstone, Arts Centre: 5 June - 27 June.
This exhibition is well worth seeing; and I believe catalogues with many high quality reproductions of the exhibits, will be on sale during the showing times, and at the ICA Gallery, or from the Arts Council (who will also be producing a smaller illustrated leaflet), costing about £4.

The computing gallery is now open in the Science Museum, London. For some time though there was a terminal (linked to the Imperial College computer) on display, and kids would delight in typing up "rude words" and seeing them displayed on the video screen. A list of forbidden words was programmed in to veto the electronic grafitti...until, recently, some spotty young genius, to the joy of his mates and horror of passers by, conjured out of the computerised depths a complete visual display of the forbidden vocabulary.

Further to our story on the mysterious shooting of Tom Coxon (NEWS 13/18),the Daily Mirror 21 Feb 76, reported that the two brothers were jailed for 4 yrs after admitting to wounding Coxon, at Leicester Crown Court. Far from ending the mystery, it is not explained how there could be 3 pieces of metal in the victim's head, if the shot was fired as the two cars passed. There is no doubt the brothers were that day driving around firing their gun at targets — could it be that some gigantic coincidence caused them to pass Coxon as he became mysteriously wounded?

After the hilarious failure of Comet Kohoutek, the media seems to have gone to the opposite extreme over Comet West, which by all accounts, has been more spectacular than predicted, (5 times brighter, N.Sci 4 March). It can be seen by naked eye in the eastern sky, in the region of the constellation Delphinus. A note from our Asian correspondent Ion Will says that its three tails are clearly visible from Hongkong, where it has been a dramatic portent for the beginning of the Year of the Dragon.

Hardbacks

The Tao of Physics by Fritjof Capra. (Wildwood House; £6.95; pp352; index, bib, notes, illos; ISBN 0.7045.0142.2.)
Number and Time by Marie-Louise von Franz. (Rider; £3.75; pp332; index, bib, notes, illos; ISBN 0.09.121020.8.) -- The nature of physics has changed considerably since Fort attacked its myopic exclusionism in the 1920s.

For one thing, Neils Bohr and Werner Heisenberg did not formulate their (still widely held) model of quantum mechanics until the late 1920s; in turn followed by Heisenberg's own principle of 'Uncertainty' in particle interactions. Then, for the first time in several centuries, physicists began issuing public statements that were virtually indistinguishable from those of the mystics. Some profound change had entered the temple of high materialism. Since then, Einstein has consolidated this new position by giving dramatic expression to another ancient mystical concept - relativity and the effects of the observer on the very events he wishes to observe.

Capra became interested in mysticism, partly because of the obvious role it played in the thought of some of his heroes (Heisenberg, Oppenheimer, et al), and partly as a result of some mystical experiences of the unity of nature himself. (In one vision he saw the underlying ceaseless motion of the sub-atomic world as the 'Dance of Shiva'.) In his own quest for an understanding, he discovered that his own chosen path (theoretical physics), in the meaning of another of his mentors, Castaneda, "had a heart". It may come as a surprise to the reader to see dissertations on basic physics side-by-side with eastern mysticism, but the real surprise is that they dovetail together so beautifully, and to Capra's great delight, illuminate each others dark corners so well.

The main body of this book explores the nearly identical conclusions that can be drawn from what these two polar disciplines tell us about the nature of phenomena: the difficulties of expressing and communicating knowledge when you have to "put it into words"; the duality of phenomena (light as a wave and a particle is a classic example); the reflexive nature of phenomena which automatically adjusts to the observer (including his moral notions); the realisation that change, not permanence, is the true constant; and that beyond the 'appearances'(phenomena) lies the formless boundless ground of being in which all things have their origin, called Tao, Brahman or Dharmakaya (for convenience) likened by the Taoists to the 'Uncarved Block' wherein lies an infinite potential of form. In this book, Fort's vision is validated and his implications confirmed. If there could be such a thing as a spontaneous arizing of Zen from the scientific materialism of the West, then Fort would be a neat expression of it (see Steve Moore's article, this issue).

Capra has a natural facility (reminiscent of the late Alan Watts) to express the ineffable, and his summaries of Hinduism, Buddhism, Tao and Zen are among the best I've seen; the elements of modern particle physics come across similarly, with ease and understanding. In this respect The Tao of Physics prepares the way for Number and Time, essentially an extension of Jung's thesis of 'Synchronicity' by his student and colleague, Dr von Franz, who adds to the mystical/physical unified world model the important dimension of the human psyche. In calling this latter book one of the most important in my life, I am still aware that I have not yet plumbed its depths, for I believe it signposts the way to a radical new understanding of how 'mind' connects and interacts with 'matter' on the most fundamental level. Please allow me to digress...

We Forteans come together because we are interested in non-ordinary phenomena, which we accept as part of a continuous spectrum of the manifesting universe. We cannot say we know what 'Reality' is, so we cannot say that Fortean events are exceptions or special cases. For most people, 'Reality' is that which is agreed by general consensus; a semantic construction designed to filter the vast unpredictable Unknown into a secure, predictable, ordered, controllable and altogether more sociable world. This consensus is inculcated into us all at birth; growing up for most of us is an aquiescence to its dominance; and it remains with us, conditioning our responses, perceptions, behaviour and expectations. Freeing ourselves of its power is not so much dependant on our strength of character, individuality or will (the 'mind-over-matter' school are in error here) as it is a function of bypassing this semantic universe to establish direct communion with the Unknown, of which it is an imperfect and artificial image.

The semantic universe, the world that is known and labelled, is not the only possible one - a fact most of us are aware of, but usually seen as a function of madness or mysticism (ie "not-Real" to most of us) - and the process which brought about this consensus is of paramount interest to us, because since it determines the nature of our 'Reality', it could (given other constituents) produce other 'Realities'. Heisenberg echoes a similar phrasing of Jung, when he wrote: "What we observe is not nature itself, but nature exposed to our method of questioning." Our answers are determined by our questions and the true "nature itself" (the Tao, etc) can never be expressed or experienced within the semantic universe. But because of the reflexive nature of the Unknown, all our interactions with it are 'mirrored'. Just as our questions invoke a semantic-response, the 'reflected question' invokes archetypal imagery in our pre-conscious minds.

Of all the archetypes, Dr von Franz argues, the concepts of numbers are the most fundamental and universal: they seem to be innate throughout the natural world, and in man, are less susceptible to mythological variations. Even in inorganic nature, number is the basis of form, structure, rhythm, symmetry and sequential growth. Dr von Franz explores the parallels between the pre-conscious "numerical field" and the Tao or Unknown or 'ground of Being' that underlies the physical universe. These parallels have been dealt with by others in many different ways, but rarely so deeply or importantly as here. Although this book discusses only the first four numbers, it is enough of a peg on which to hang the theoretical context, and is rich in illustrations, both graphic and textural. Number and Time (ie numerical progression or series) constitute the main connection between 'mind' and 'matter' since both are thereby ordered in similar ways. A mandala, for example, can serve at once as a representation of divinity or divine order (the 'New Jerusalem'), the physical universe (the cardinal points) and the self, by the harmonic interplays (the 'numerical field') of the four, the two and the one. It is impossible here to give an idea of the full scope of the discussion which draws its examples from the complete range of human experience and knowledge. The number archtypes are rarely directly expressed, but enter into the mythological archetypes and order them. Dr von Franz writes: "Since, generally speaking, contents of the collective unconscious which have not yet reached the threshold of consciousness tend to engender parapsychological syndromes, especially when they are constellated contents (in an 'excited state' as the physicists would say) these contents appear in conjunction with the pre-conscious aspects of the number archetype." Some excellent examples of this can be found in Clark and Coleman's <u>The Unidentified</u>, in which they discuss the 3 plus 1 symbolism of the UFO contactee syndrome (see also Jung's <u>Flying Saucers</u>.) On these foundations too, she maintains, rests the concept and process of divination by numerical combinations – and, since it unifies the internal and external worlds with numerical (and temporal) portents applicable to both, it can be found structuring phenomena, synchronistically.

This is a difficult book, not because of any fault of Dr von Franz (to the contrary her narrative is concise and gripping) but because the thesis is so strange to our habitual views that one is even a little afraid, for truly you are in the presence of awesome and far-reaching powers and their implications. The full effect of this book will not be felt immediately, I think, but it will be a source of inspiration to thinkers in the decades ahead, as they grapple with the problems of the nature of phenomena and 'Reality'.

<u>The Eighth Tower</u> by John A Keel. (Saturday Review Press/EP Dutton; $8.95; pp218; ISBN 0.8415.0403.2.)
<u>The Invisible College</u> by Jacques Vallée. (EP Dutton; $8.95; pp216; index, bib; ISBN 0.525.13470.0.)
Two new works here by respected authors in the field, at almost the same time, about much the same subject (UFOs and related phenomena as a control system), but written with differing approaches, and reaching slightly different conclusions.

Keel's book is divided into three parts. In the first, he proposes his theory of the "super-spectrum", a range of energy fields operating on a higher series of frequencies than the electromagnetic spectrum, and which we are unable to perceive. Thus UFOs, for example, which according to him are basically masses of energy, manifest themselves by 'sliding down the frequency scale'. In the second part, he attempts to relate monsters, Men in Black and similar oddities to the super-spectrum, and in the third presents some speculations about just what is using the phenomena as a control system for human behaviour.

Keel's style is journalistic and highly colourful: speculations and odd ideas abound as he swashbuckles along...amusing, thought-provoking, but, perhaps, dangerous...the reader is invited to walk a tight-rope, and there's always the peril of falling, either into believing blindly everything he says, or rejecting the book in its entirety. Accepting that most of Keel's other work is written in the same style, I still find myself wishing, personally, for a slightly more inhibited approach.

As far as the mechanics of paranormal phenomena go, Keel sticks fairly solidly by his super-spectrum. I find myself stumbling over his assertion that science <u>will</u> soon discover more about it, when at its introduction its only a theory, but perhaps that's a minor quibble. As to <u>what</u> is using the super-spectrum to control human behaviour, he seems unable to make up his mind, offering various ideas, all of which seem highly speculative. But he does seem convinced that the human race are just puppets, puppet-master unknown...with the implication that he, she or it, is decidedly unfriendly.

Vallée's approach is more cautious. He too reaches the conclusion that UFOs constitute some kind of control system, but he draws back from the question of what has set up the system and why... which is perhaps the safest thing to do.

He covers a wider field than Keel, and in a more restrained fashion. He spends perhaps too long complaining of human bungling and government cover-ups, but then concentrates mainly on contact cases in many forms: religious manifestations, UMMO, Geller and SPECTRA, and, of course, more 'normal' man/UFO contacts, attempting to demonstrate an underlying connection between them all. His conclu-

sion is that UFOs and the contact syndrome are causing a change in mankind's
mythological structure, causing us to
learn a new kind of 'cosmic behaviour'.
The questions begged are, of course,
'why?' and 'to what?'...and while it's
admirable of Vallée not to attempt answers when he doesn't know, by so doing he
leaves the book rather like a body without a head.

The book's title refers to 'an international network of UFO scientists', and
one could get the impression that he
thinks UFO studies should be the private
domain of enlightened scientists--all
others keep out. I hope that isn't the
case...for we certainly don't need that.

It's good to see the psychological
aspects of the UFO problem continuing
to get coverage, though both authors
tend to make these subservient to the
physical aspects, unlike Clark and Coleman's recent work along Jungian lines.
Despite their disclaimers, both Vallée
and Keel seem to be suffering from resi-
dual traces of the Extraterrestrial Hypothesis: for both of them, UFOs are from
'out there', somehow alien to mankind
and his world. Whether that is so, or
whether they are phenomena not as yet
understood, dependant on man and his
psyche, is naturally a highly controversial question. I can't, in all honesty,
say that either author has convinced me
of their point of view...but at least
they have given us something to argue
about.

Steve Moore.

Mazes & Labyrinths of the World by Janet
Bord. (Latimer; £7.50; pp181; index,bib;
ISBN: 901539.35.X.) If you can get beyond
the price barrier this is a useful visual
reference indeed. The main body of the book is
an exciting compendium of photos and illustrations, and after a brief introduction to the
use of the labyrinth symbol, you are plunged
into its graphic and three-dimensional applications from all cultures and times. Janet
does admit the collection is not exhaustive
apart from a brief reference and 2 illustrations there is little from China, and the
Islamic culture with its fine sense of pattern
geometry is omitted entirely) however, what is
here is a feast without calling for more.

Here are mazes from India, Africa, America
and Australia, and of course Europe; carved
spirals on the stones of an Irish passage
grave; tile-patterns on cathedral floors;
mazes cut into turf, or marked out by hedges,
walls, trenches or stones; in literature and
architecture and art; maze games and dances;
mazes in allegory, and mazes as symbols of
spiritual pathways (mandalas etc); labyrinth

patterns as decoration (some excellent designs
using words or knots) and displays of graphic
virtuosity like the Celtic patterns of complex
interweaving; and so on.

I found the material on the (known) English
turf mazes most interesting, for as Janet
writes (TLH 69) "A turf maze is soon lost in
an English summer of rain and fast growth, and
needs frequent and careful maintenance." It is
at once astonishing and gratifying to realise
that they have survived as long as they have
(certainly pre-Christian). Doubtless many have
been lost, but hopefully books like this one
will open more eyes to the ancient treasures
of our landscape, making that survival a
little less precarious.

Strange Life: vol B1 ($7.95; pp287.)
Strange Phenomena: vol G2 ($7.95; pp264).
Both compiled and published by William R
Corliss: Sourcebook Project, Glen Arm, Maryland 21057, USA. Two more volumes in the impressive, valuable, indispensible and highly
recommended Sourcebook series. S.Life begins a
new series on biological and organic curiosities. Contents include: myths & legends of
extinct animals; evidence of life in meteorites?; lifeforms that resemble artifacts; intelligence, fascination and unusual behaviour
in animals; data that challenges Darwinian
evolution theory; freaks and mutants; unusual
capabilities (strength, speed, etc); unrecognised species; artificial creation of life?;
effects of magnetism; etc. S.Phenomena supp-
lements vol G1 with data on mirages & other
transmission phenomena; falls of webs, chemicals, fish, insects, gelatin, leaves & thunder-
stones; auroras, ball-lightning & light wheels;
volcanic, meteoric, magnetic & quake anomalies;
strange noises; strange clouds & rains, winds
& waterspouts, dark days & deluges; etc.

Paperbacks

Did Spacemen Colonise the Earth? by Robin
Collyns. (Mayflower; 75p; pp256;bib,photos.)
Hidden Worlds: Fresh Clues to the Past by
MHJTh van de Veer & P Moerman.
(Corgi; 60p; pp206; index.)
In Search of Ancient Gods by E von Daniken.
(Corgi; 75p; pp218; bib, photos.) 75p is
about all I'm prepared to pay for vonD's
effort - in fact hardbacks are dear enough
these days, without finding that you've just
bought a bucket of tripe - I must be one of
many who decided to wait for the paperback.
Collyns, for reasons best known to himself,
seems to be a disciple of vonD in both subject
approach and style, asking leading questions
and half answering them with conjecture. What
can you say about an author who confronts you
with a forest of exclamation marks, & clumps
of threatening question marks? What can you
say about headings like:"Is this the fossil-

ised brain of a Spaceman who landed in Russia in the Carboniferous Period?", "Did Elijah call down Atomic fire on Mt Carmel?", "Was the Cabbage artificially developed?" (I kid you not!). What else is there to say about an author who still insists a "Giant Spaceship abducted a British Regiment in 1915!" except that he seems to be pretty good at artificially developing his own cabbages. The two Dutchmen, alas despite the bold promises on the jacket, merely pose the same old questions. Their answers are somewhat different to vonD's in that they try to find terrestrial solutions to the classic enigmas of the past. Hidden Worlds makes no significant contribution to the subject, but at least there are no ET plots to foist cabbages on the yokels in our end of the galactic arm.

Secret of the Ages by B le Poer Trench. (Panther; 60p; pp206; index, refs, photos.) Passport to Magonia by Jacques Vallée. (Tandem, 45p; pp169.) Extraterrestrial Intervention by Jacques Bergier & the Editors of INFO Journal. (Signet; $1.25; pp143; photos.) — Vallée's book is now generally recognised as one of the classics of UFOlogy, tracing the phenomenon back to medieval accounts of demons and fairies. At 45p, it is superb value; doubly so, in view of the higher-priced rubbish available. BLPT's book is a classic of another sort, and should stand as an example to anyone who takes as gospel the writings of Ray Palmer. The Secret here is that UFOs come from inside a hollow earth. The book is full of slightly cranky ideas that can be interesting if you don't take them too seriously; also contains the notorious satellite pictures of an alleged hole at the North Pole (via Palmer's Flying Saucers) and similar sized holes can be found in poor BLPT's arguments. The Bergier book would win a prize if they gave one for a title that had nothing to do with the contents. But don't let that put you off: here are a collection of some of the best articles from the early issues of INFO Journal, and destined, when they pass into general circulation, to become classic references on a host of Fortean subjects. Most articles have refs appended.

In Search of Lake Monsters by Peter Costello (Panther; £1.25; pp400; index, bib, photos.) Another classic reference now in paperback and again super value considering its important contribution to the serious study of 'Unidentified Animals' and allied phenomena. Though he concentrates mainly on Lake Monsters, it is the best book since Heuvelmans's In the Wake of the Sea-Serpents, which it compliments with new material from Canada, USA, Australia, Asia and other key sighting areas (many hardly known), patiently collected and verified as far as possible, intelligently discussed and clearly written up. In addition to the comprehensive bibliography on the subject, there

are useful analyses of UK sighting evidence. Highly & rightly acclaimed & recommended.

Destiny Mars by MW Saunders. (Downs Books Caterham, Surrey; £1; pp64; index, refs.) Not a crank book, but an intelligent and thought-provoking exploration of data relationships between terrestrial pyramids and the various planetary satellites, and which, if true, are of incalculable importance. Recentl' Downs Books were offering a grant of £300 to the first person to get a research project on the subject accepted by a university (N.Sci, 8 Jan 76).

The Devil's Triangle 2 by Richard Winer. (Corgi; 50p; pp158; index, bib, photos.) No Earthly Explanation by John W Spencer. (Corgi; 60p; pp178; photos.) Part of the bombardment by 'Bermuda Triangle' material, which, as a BBC TV Horizon documentary showe' recently, contains such distortions of factua' evidence that most of us will never know for sure one way or the other. Writers have some responsibility to their public, and we are unfortunate indeed to be afflicted with many who think more of having a sensational bestseller, than of the veracity of their materi' You'll have to make up your own mind about these books, written in a goshwow! style (at times Spencer verges on the hysterical) that does not inspire me with much confidence. Students of Atlantis and UFOs will know, of course, that they are heavily invoked herein

Other useful paperback releases: Sphinx & the Megaliths by John Ivimy. (Abacus; £1.20; pp192.) Secret Life of Plants by P Tompkins & C Bird. (Penguin; 75p; pp340; index, bib.) The Loch Ness Story by Nicholas Twitchell (Penguin; 70p.) The Alchemists by F Sherwood Taylor. (Paladin; £1.25; pp191; index, illos.) An excellent survey of the chemical side of alchemy, with a review of symbolic and orienta' alchemy, by ex-director of the Science Museu' Other Lives by Brad Steiger. (Award Books; $1.50.) The Jupiter Effect by JR Gribbin & SH Plagemann. (Vintage Books; $1.95; pp17'

It is very gratifying to realise that the age of pamphleteering is not dead, and that many of today's pioneer researchers have not been daunted by the orthodox scientific pres' steadfast ignorance and hostility towards th' studies that challenge the very tenets of their institutions, but have taken to producing their own tracts. Two of these small presses, Zodiac House, and Fenris-Wolf, spec'ialise in different aspects of the field becoming known as 'Earth Mysteries'. We'll list here some of their publications, but please write to them for details and to be p' on their mailing list, etc:

Zodiac House:
'Principles of Prehistoric Geography' by
  J Heinsch, trans. by Michael Behrend.
'Atlantean Traditions in Ancient Britain: pt1,
  Visions of Albion' by Anthony Roberts.
'Songs of Mu & Atlantis' poems by R Holder.
  ZH: 7 Hugon Rd, Fulham, London SW6.

Fenris-Wolf:
'Runic' by Nigel Pennick (guide to Runes).
'Madagascar Divination' by Nigel Pennick.
'Dene-holes & Subterranea' by Ann Pennick.
'The Swastika' by Nigel Pennick (study of the
  universal use of the symbol).
'Ancient Hill Figures of England' by Nigel
  Pennick (being the Institute of Geomantic
  Research (IGR)'s Occasional Paper No2.
  FW/IGR: 142 Pheasant Rise, Bar Hill,
  Cambridge CB3 8SD.

** ** As you can see, there have been quite a
few new books, and we have not been able to
fit all our reviews in, and have kept back the
following for next issue: 'Guide to Occult
Britain' (J Wilcock); 'The Sirius Mystery' (R
Temple); 'The Mystery of Atlantis' (C Berlitz);
'Brigantia' (GR Phillips); and others. ** **

Journals

Gnostica: 37 — "Ghosts, Ghouls & Pendulums",
Colin Wilson on the genius of Tom Lethbridge,
being a first chapter preview of the sequel
to The Occult.

Startling Detective, March 76 — "Manhunt for
a Supernatural Suspect" by Duane Bostick; a
lengthy account of the Jan 1974 'Bigfoot'
scare in South Florida.

Sunday Times, 29 Feb 76 — 'Was it Suicide?" by
Laurence Marks & Penny Hallowes; a review of
the Moorgate tube disaster (last year - & see
NEWS 11/20) which still remains a mystery.

Street Life 29 Nov 75 — "People just catch
Fire..." by Idris Walters; a glib and facile
look at spontaneous human combustion.

Sunday People 18 Jan 76 — "The Amazing Man
who leaves his Body"; an interview with Blue
Harary, star turn at the Psychical Research
Foundation, N Carolina.

Wildlife March 76 — Nigel Sitwell on the
"Loch Ness Monster Evidence" plus Sir Peter
Scott on "Why I believe in the Loch Ness Monster"; good diagrams of Rines's photo-setup,
and high quality prints of the photos, in
colour too.

Journal of Meteorology, Jan 76 — GT Meaden
giving "A Meteorological explanation for some
of the Mysterious Sightings on Loch Ness &
other Lakes & Rivers"; Feb 76 — "The Great

Gale of 2-3 Jan 76"; a new small journal that
often contains historical information and
correlations of interest to Forteans. Inquiries to, J. Met: Cockhill House, Trowbridge,
BA14 9BG, England.

MUFOB, ns 2 — congratulations to ed. John
Rimmer for a neat switch to a NEWS-size format.
Main contents: "Experimental UFO Hoaxing" by
DI Simpson; and again congratulations for
having the courage to tackle the fundamental
question of the reliability of UFO reporting.
The results of the controlled hoax herein
described show up rampant gullibility throughout the field's media, but no suggestions are
made as to what can be done about it. MUFOB:
11 Beverley Rd, New Malden, Surrey KT3 4AW.

Flying Saucer Review, 21:5 — Charles Bowen on
the Travis Walton abduction from Snowflake,
Arizona; Peter Johns on some East Anglian UFOs;
Jacques Vallée on Geller; Pierre Guerin on
"The Profound Unity of all Paranormal Phenomena"; FW Holiday on a similar theme but different tack; sightings & news. FSR has a new
address: FSR Publications Ltd, West Malling,
Maidstone, Kent.

SOBEPS, the Belgian UFO association, whose
quality journal has been inaccessible to those
who cannot read French, have taken the laudable step of publishing an English-language
abstract, with additional material, called
SOBEPS News, to accompany Inforespace, and is
ably edited by Alice Ashton. This venture is
highly commendable and we urge you all to
support it. SOBEPS: Boulevard Aristide
Briande 26, 1070 Brussels, Belgium.

The Ley Hunter: 69 — letters; PS Hannah on
the "Hemlockstone Line" (Notts-Leics); Anthony
Roberts on the lost land of "Lyonesse"...etc.
TLH: 5 Egton Drv, Seaton Carew, Hartlepool,
Cleveland TS25 2AT. 1yr: £1.50/$7.00.

Fate, March 76 — articles on "Windigo - The
Cannibal Demon"; "UFO over Chicago"; 250 mil-
lion-yr-old "Footprints of Adam" in Kentucky
Rock; April 76 — lunar periodicities in
crime waves; Ozark ghosts; "Spirit healing in
Brazil"; and an amazing case of an apported
figuring.

Kadath — a glossy and well produced Belgian
journal devoted to 'lost civilisations'. (In
French). The Jan/Feb 76 issue deals with the
Nazca lines & Maria Reiche. Kadath: 6 Boulevard St-Michel, 1150 Brussels, Belgium.

INFO Journal: 16 — FW Holiday on "Water Monsters: The Land Sighting Paradox."; Stuart W
Greenwood on an interpretation of "Quetzal-
coatl"; Robert B Gair on "The Secret of the
Anorthosites" (are they evidence of a near
collision with the moon 1.3 million yrs ago?);
plus material on ball-lightning, lunar periodicities of earthquakes & the problems of

cont on p18...

INFO-NEWS JOINT SUB RATES.
We have recently discovered that your ham-headed editor made a mistake when he was working out the Joint sub-rate, and compounded the error with another mistake when he was typing out a list of the prices. In full, they should be as follows:
INFO Journal - 6 issues - $10.00/£5.00.
INFO & NEWS: 1yr - 12 issues - $14.00/£7.00.
INFO & NEWS: 2yr - 24 issues - $24.50/£12.25.
THE NEWS - 6 issues - $6.00/£3.00.
THE NEWS - 2yrs - 12 issues - $10.80/£5.40.
Because of time delays and the rapid fall of the pound, we have attempted to correct various advertised prices, which, by the time they appeared in print, were invalid. However for the foreseeable future both INFO and NEWS - or rather Fortean Times - will be keeping to the above prices, and an exchange rate of £1:$2.

INFO'S 4th ANNUAL CONVENTION
Fortfest 76 will be held this year in Washington, at the Hospitality House Motor Inn, in Arlington, Virginia, over August 6-8. Those interested in attending, or wishing to receive the bulletin mailing, please write to Fortfest, INFO, Box 367, Arlington, VA22210.

OTHER INFO NEWS...
INFO 16 has just been mailed from the USA. All UK subscribers who have not received INFO 15 yet...do not dispair. I've been assured that there will be another attempt to send replacements to these shores...and this

thim they might not be snatched...Back issues of INFO, Nos 1 to 14 (expept Nos 1,2,4 & 8 which are OP) will henceforth be $1/50p; and from No15 on, $1.50/75p. -- INFO Journal will soon be indexed; a project underway by Larry Bryant -- The Complete Books of Charles Fort This invaluable tome, we should have explained, can be ordered from the INFO address (above): INFO members - $12.50/£6.25; non-members - $15.00/£7.50. Considering that one NY firm is charging over $30 for what amounts to hardback versions of the unindexed and badly typeset Ace paper editions, the above omnibus is superb value, (includes postage). Sterling may be paid to the NEWS address for UK convenience & orders will be forwarded.

BINDERS.
Many thanks to those of you who have paid in advance for binders. We were on the point of ordering from the manufacturer when we heard from Paul Willis, President of INFO, that they were looking into what sounded like a more attractive system and price. So we have held off until the details can be compared. We hope you can bear with the delay.

*** *** *** NEXT ISSUE *** *** ***

Our debut as Fortean Times will include your ed. on Scottish Coastal Monsters, Steev Moore concluding his interpretation of Taoist phenomenology, Robert Forrest's reply to FW Holiday on 'Leys, UFOs & Chance', and notes on Miracles and Strange Fires. *** *** ***

FINIS.